onouring the
graduation of
*Julie Anne
Shea*

Class of

1992

University of
St. Jerome's College

BLOOMSBURY
DICTIONARY OF
PHRASE *&*
ALLUSION

BLOOMSBURY
DICTIONARY OF
PHRASE *&*
ALLUSION

NIGEL REES

BLOOMSBURY

First published
by Bloomsbury Publishing Limited, 2 Soho Square, London
W1V 5DE

Copyright © 1991 by Nigel Rees
The moral right of the author has been asserted.

British Library Cataloguing in Publication Data

A CIP record for this book is available from
the British Library

ISBN 0 7475 0789 9

Designed by Geoff Green
Typeset by Florencetype Ltd, Kewstoke, Avon
Printed by Butler and Tanner Ltd, London and Frome

Contents

INTRODUCTION

This *Dictionary of Phrase & Allusion* is what at one time would have been termed a 'dictionary of phrase and fable'. I always felt that 'fable' was mentioned primarily for alliterative effect. It sets out, however, to cover much the same field: to explore the origins and meanings of words, names, and phrases, to show how they are used, and to provide a mine of information about the language we speak and write.

At its broadest, this dictionary's aim is to examine words and phrases which require a measure of explanation to understand why they are used in literature, the Bible, politics, historical writing, and the popular arts. Indeed, this book lays special emphasis on allusions based in popular entertainment, hence the entries on DRAGON LADY, THE KILLING FIELDS, STEEL MAGNOLIAS, and WICKED WITCH OF THE WEST, and on the names of pop groups like THE DOORS, SOFT MACHINE, THEY MIGHT BE GIANTS and THE BEE GEES. It is more aware of recent phraseology than some of its predecessors – CABBAGE PATCH KIDS, RAMBOESQUE, TRIVIAL PURSUIT – but it also contains the classical allusions the reader would expect, here presented in special sections designed to provide a quick and easy approach to the main characteristics of GREEK NAMES, ROMAN NAMES, SAINTS' NAMES, and so on. Other special sections are devoted to ACRONYMS, COLLECTIVE NOUNS, INITIALS, NICKNAMES, and PSEUDONYMS.

The *Dictionary of Phrase & Allusion* aims to be the reader's dictionary of first resort when seeking information on phraseology – and especially on allusions, those glancing references that tend to go unexplained. We use words and phrases allusively because we choose to suppress their sources or because we simply do not know what these are. In addition, much popular phraseology – TO GET DOWN TO BRASS TACKS, TO BE HOIST WITH ONE'S OWN PETARD, TO BE SOLD DOWN THE RIVER – is a form of unconscious allusion, although in some cases it is impossible to say quite why we make use of certain sayings at all.

We use some other phrases, vaguely knowing that they are quotations but without stopping to think about it. A major concern of this dictionary is the way titles of books, plays and films are often allusive. How many of us stop to think where such titles as GONE WITH THE WIND, SPEED-THE-PLOW and DAYS OF WINE AND ROSES come from? Or, even if we know, do we ever realize what relevance they have to the books, plays and films in question?

There are some 2000 main entries in the *Dictionary of Phrase & Allusion*, involving a total of almost 5000 words, names, and phrases. Cross-references are made in SMALL CAPITALS. The swung dash symbol ~ is used in cross referencing to indicate the headword. This work has been conceived as a companion volume to my *Dictionary of Popular Phrases* (Bloomsbury, 1990) which generally has fuller entries on the more recent phrases.

For help with many individual pieces of information, I should like to thank, among others: Richard Brooks, the *Observer*; David Barlow, Instant Sunshine; John Culme, Sotheby's; John Hawkesworth; Donald Hickling; Armando Iannucci, producer, and many listeners to the BBC Radio programme *Quote . . . Unquote*; John B. Meade, producer, and many viewers of the Yorkshire Television/Channel 4 programme *Countdown*; Adrian Room; William Shawcross; Horst Vey; Kevin Thurlow; the BBC Radio Research Library, London; the British Library Newspaper Library, Colindale; the London Library.

NIGEL REES
London 1991

ABBREVIATIONS

Bartlett: *Bartlett's Familiar Quotations* (15th ed.), 1980

Benham: *Benham's Book of Quotations*, 1948 (1960 revision)

Bible: The Authorized Version, 1611 (except where stated otherwise)

Brewer: *Brewer's Dictionary of Phrase and Fable* (14th ed.), 1989

Burnam: Tom Burnam, *The Dictionary of Misinformation*, 1975

Burnam (2): Tom Burnam, *More Misinformation*, 1980

CODP: *The Concise Oxford Dictionary of Proverbs*, 1982

DOAS: Wentworth & Flexner, *Dictionary of American Slang*, 1960 (1975 revision)

DPP: Nigel Rees, *Dictionary of Popular Phrases*, 1990

Flexner: Stuart Berg Flexner, *I Hear America Talking*, 1976

Flexner (2): Stuart Berg Flexner, *Listening to America*, 1982

Halliwell: Leslie Halliwell, *Halliwell's Film Guide* (6th ed.), 1987

Mencken: *H.L. Mencken's Dictionary of Quotations*, 1942

Morris: William and Mary Morris, *Morris Dictionary of Word and Phrase Origins*, 1977

ODCIE: *The Oxford Dictionary of Current Idiomatic English* (2 vols.), 1985

ODP: *The Oxford Dictionary of Proverbs* (3rd ed.), 1970

ODQ: *The Oxford Dictionary of Quotations* (3rd ed.), 1979

OED2: *The Oxford English Dictionary* (2nd ed.), 1989

Partridge/*Catch Phrases*: Eric Partridge, *A Dictionary of Catch Phrases* (2nd ed., edited by Paul Beale), 1985

Partridge/*Slang*: Eric Partridge, *A Dictionary of Slang and Unconventional English* (8th ed., edited by Paul Beale), 1984

Prayer Book: *The Book of Common Prayer*, 1662

Radford: Edwin Radford, *To Coin a Phrase* (edited and revised by Alan Smith), 1974

Safire: William Safire, *Safire's Political Dictionary*, 1978

Shakespeare: *The Arden Shakespeare* (in the most recent editions available in 1990)

A*A*

The headwords are listed in alphabetical order of letters within the whole sentence and not just the first word. Cross references to other entries are made in SMALL CAPITALS.

abandon hope all ye who enter here! A popular translation of the words written over the entrance to Hell in Dante's *Divina Commedia* (*c* 1320). 'All hope abandon, ye who enter here!' would be a more accurate translation of the Italian '*Lasciate ogni speranza voi ch'entrate!*'

Abba. (1) An alternative name for God the Father, as in Mark 14:36 and Romans 8:15. (2) The name of a Swedish pop quartet of the 1970s, derived from the initials of its members: *A*gnetha Faltskog, *B*enny Andersson, *B*jörn Ulvaeus, and *A*nni-Frid Lyngstad.

à Becket. See BECKET.

abilities. See FROM EACH ACCORDING TO . . .

Abominable Snowman, the. An unidentified creature of the Himalayas, which derives its name from the Tibetan *meetoh kangmi* [abominable snowmen] or *yeti*. It is said to raid mountain villages and to be tall, powerful and bearlike, with a near-human face. The name became known to European mountaineers attempting to climb Mount Everest in the 1920s and was popularized by climbing expeditions in the 1950s. In 1960 Sir Edmund Hillary found footprints which seemed to be those of an animal such as a bear. The mystery surrounding this creature gave rise to the detective novel *The Case of the Abominable Snowman* (1941) by Nicholas Blake. There was also a separate film on the subject, *The Abominable Snowman* (UK 1957).

The phrase may now be used to describe anyone or anything indescribable and unpleasant. In 1953, David Eccles, Minister of Works responsible for the Coronation decorations in London, became known as 'the Abominable Showman'. General de Gaulle, having obstructed British entry to the European Common Market in the 1960s by saying '*Non!*', was dubbed 'the Abominable No-man'.

Abraham's bosom. The place where the dead sleep contentedly. From Luke 16:23: 'And it came to pass, that the beggar died, and was carried by the angels into Abraham's bosom.' It alludes to Abraham, the first of the Hebrew patriarchs.

Compare ARTHUR'S BOSOM.

1

Absent in the Spring. The title of a novel (1944) by Agatha CHRISTIE (under the name 'Mary Westmacott'). Taken from Shakespeare, Sonnet 98: 'From you I have been absent in the spring'.

absit omen. See GESUNDHEIT!

A C A S. See ACRONYMS.

accidents will occur in the best-regulated families. A proverbial expression best remembered in the form spoken by Mr Micawber in *David Copperfield* (Chap. 28, 1850). Charles Dickens had earlier used the saying in *Pickwick Papers* (1836–7) and *Dombey and Son* (1844–6), but it is not original to him.

according to Hoyle. See HOYLE.

accountancy/accounting.
See CREATIVE ~.

accuse. See J'ACCUSE.

ace in the hole. A hidden advantage or secret source of power. The title of a Cole Porter song in *Let's Face It* (1941), and a Billy Wilder film (US 1951), the phrase came originally from the game of stud poker. A 'hole' card is one that is not revealed until the betting has taken place. If it is an ace, so much the better.
   DOAS dates the use of the expression, in a poker context, to the 1920s, *OED2* to 1915. In British English the nearest equivalent would be to talk of having an 'ace up one's sleeve'.

Achates. See ROMAN NAMES.

Achilles. See GREEK NAMES.

Acis. See GREEK NAMES.

Across the River and into the Trees. The title of a novel (1950) by Ernest Hemingway, alluding to the dying words of Stonewall Jackson, Confederate General in the American Civil War. Having been shot in error by his own troops in May 1863, he said: 'Let us cross over the river, and rest under [the shade of] the trees.' E.B. White's noted parody of Hemingway's style (collected 1954) was called 'Across the Street and Into the Grill'.

Actaeon. See GREEK NAMES.

action. See INDUSTRIAL ~.

Action Man. A person who is given more to action than to thought, named after a boy's doll which could be dressed in various military-type costumes with appropriate accoutrements. Prior to his marriage in 1981, Charles, Prince of Wales, was noted for his enthusiastic sporting activities in many fields. Coupled with his active service in the Royal Navy, such expenditure of energy caused him to be given the nickname.
   An *Independent* report of a General Medical Council disciplinary inquiry (29 March 1990) states: 'He told the hearing: "Mr Bewick is an Action Man, not a philosopher. Action Man's advantage is that at the drop of a hat, he can go anywhere and do anything".'

Action This Day. Sub-titled 'Working with Churchill', this was a collection of reminiscences of those who had been closely associated with Winston Churchill during the Second World War (published 1968). 'ACTION THIS DAY', 'REPORT IN THREE DAYS' and 'REPORT PROGRESS IN ONE WEEK' were printed tags Churchill started using to glue on to memos at the Admiralty in February 1940.

actor laddie. Often used to describe the booming voice or manner of Victorian actor-managers, this expression presumably derived from their habit of adding

ACRONYMS are words made up of the initial letters of other words. Sets of INITIALS like 'BBC' do not qualify because they cannot be pronounced as one word. These examples have been chosen because it may come as a surprise that they *are* acronyms. Those marked with an asterisk show alternative words for the initials.

ACAS: Advisory, Conciliation and Arbitration Service

ANZAC: Australian and New Zealand Army Corps

AWOL: Absent WithOut Leave

BOBO: Burnt Out But Opulent

BURMA: Be Upstairs/Undressed Ready My Angel

CREEP (originally CRP): Committee for the RE-Election of the President

DERV: Diesel-Engined Road Vehicle

DINKIE: See under YUPPIE

ERNIE: Electronic Random Number Indicator Equipment

ENSA: Entertainments National Service Association; *Every Night Something Awful/Atrocious; *Even NAAFI Stands Aghast

GULAG: *Glavnoye Upravleniye ispravitelno-trudovykh LAGerei* [main administration of correctional labour camps]

ITALY: I Treasure/Trust And Love You

LASER: Light Amplification by Stimulated Emission of Radiation

MASH: Mobile Army Surgical Hospital

NAAFI: Navy Army and Air Force Institutes

NATSOPA: NATional Society for Operative Printers and Assistants

NIBMAR: No Independence Before MAjority (African) Rule

NIMBY: Not In My Back Yard

NORWICH: (K)Nickers Off Ready When I Come Home

ODEON: *Oscar Deutsch Entertains Our Nation (see also ODEON)

QANTAS: Queensland And Northern Territories Air Services; *Queer And Nasty Try Another Service; *Queers And Nancies Together As Stewards/Train All Staff

RADAR: RADio And Ranging

SABENA: *Société Anonyme Belge d'Exploitation de la Navigation Aérienne*; *Such A Bloody Experience, Never Again: *Sodomy And Buggery Endanger Natural Appetites

SALT: Strategic Arms Limitation Talks

SCUBA: Self-Contained Underwater Breathing Apparatus

SITCOM: See under YUPPIE

SMERSH: SMERt SHpionam (a section of the KGB, from the Russian for 'death to spies')

SNAFU: Situation Normal All Fouled/Fucked Up

SWALK: Sealed With A Loving Kiss

TARDIS: Time And Relative Dimension In Space

TINA: See THERE IS NO ALTERNATIVE

TISWAS: *Today Is Saturday, Wear A Smile (see also TISWAS)

UNCLE: United Network Command for Law and Enforcement (see MAN FROM UNCLE)

VERDI: Vittorio Emmanuelle Re D'Italia

WASP: White Anglo-Saxon Protestant (see WASP)

WOOPIE: See under YUPPIE

YUMPIE/YUPPIE: See YUPPIE

ZIP: *Zone Improvement Plan

See also ABBA; BOMFOG.

the somewhat patronizing endearment 'laddie' when talking to the junior members of their companies.

actress. See AS THE BISHOP SAID TO THE ~.

Adams, Fanny. See SWEET ~.

Adam's Rib. The title of a film (US 1949) about husband and wife lawyers opposing each other in court (also of a 1923 Cecil B. de Mille marital film with biblical flashbacks). It alludes to Genesis 2:21-2 which states that God made woman from one of Adam's ribs. Compare SPARE RIB.

Admirable Crichton, The. The title of J.M. Barrie's play (1902; films UK 1918, 1957) about a butler who succours his shipwrecked aristocratic employer on a desert island, and used to describe any resourceful servant. The name had earlier been applied to James Crichton (d 1585), the Scottish traveller, and – broadly – to anyone of intellectual accomplishment.

Adonis. See GREEK NAMES.

advertise. See IT PAYS TO ~.

A E I O U. See INITIALS.

Aeneas. See ROMAN NAMES.

Aeolus. See GREEK NAMES.

aerobics. The name of a physical fitness programme created by Dr Kenneth Cooper, a former USAF flight surgeon, who coined the phrase for a book called *Aerobics* (1968). The adjective 'aerobic' means living on free oxygen and comes from the Greek words for 'air' and 'life'.

Aeschylus. See GREEK NAMES.

Aesculapius. See GREEK NAMES.

Affluent Society, The. The title of a book (1958) by the economist John Kenneth Galbraith about the effects of high living standards on economic theories which had been created to deal with scarcity and poverty. The resulting 'private affluence and public squalor' stemmed from an imbalance between private and public sector output. For example, there might be more cars and TV sets but not enough police to prevent them from being stolen. Revd Dr Martin Luther King Jr, in a 1963 letter from gaol, used the phrase thus: 'When you see the vast majority of your twenty million Negro brothers smouldering in an airtight cage of poverty in the midst of an affluent society ... then you will understand why we find it difficult to wait.' The notion was not new to the mid-twentieth century, however. Tacitus, in his *Annals* (c AD 115) noted that 'many, amid great affluence, are utterly miserable' and Cato the Younger (95–46 BC), when denouncing the contemporary state of Rome said: '*Habemus publice egestatem, privatim opulentiam*' [Public want, private wealth]. The punning tag of 'effluent society', a commonplace by the 1980s, had appeared in Stan Gooch's poem 'Never So Good' in 1964, and before that.

afford. See IF YOU HAVE TO ASK THE PRICE ...

afoot. See GAME'S ~.

Africa. See DARK CONTINENT.

Africans. See ENGLISH HAD THE LAND ...

After Many a Summer. The title of a novel (1939) by Aldous HUXLEY, taken from Tennyson's 'Tithonus':

> The woods decay, the woods decay and fall,

The vapours weep their burthen to the
ground,
Man comes and tills the field and lies
beneath,
And after many a summer dies the swan.

against. See HE WHO IS NOT WITH US
. . .

Agamemnon. See GREEK NAMES.

Agatha, St. See SAINTS' NAMES.

age. See DANGEROUS ~; GOLDEN ~.

Aglaos. See GREEK NAMES.

Agnes, St. See SAINTS' NAMES.

agnus dei. See MASS PHRASES.

Agonistes. Denoting a champion con-
testant, the word comes from the Greek
– as in *Samson Agonistes*, Milton's poem
(1671) and *Sweeney Agonistes*, T.S.
Eliot's poetic drama (1932).

agonizing reappraisal. A political
term for the process of reconsideration,
possibly before a decision is made to
take a U-TURN. The modern use stems
from a speech that John Foster Dulles,
US Secretary of State, made to the
National Press Club, Washington, in
December 1953: 'When I was in Paris
last week, I said that . . . the United
States would have to undertake an agonizing reappraisal of basic foreign policy
in relation to Europe.'

agony aunt. One who answers questions about personal problems from
readers of a newspaper or magazine.
Hence the term **agony column**, originally
a 'personal column' in newspapers containing messages for missing relatives (by
the 1860s), but from the 1930s the name

given to the space in which 'advice' journalism appears. Neither phrase was in
wide use until the 1970s.

agreement. See GENTLEMAN'S ~.

Aidos. See GREEK NAMES.

ain't. See IF IT ~ BROKE(N) . . .

aisle, to go up the. Sir Thomas Bazley
fired off a letter to *The Times* in July
1986: 'Sir, You report that Miss Sarah
Ferguson will go up the aisle to the
strains of Elgar's "Imperial March".
Hitherto, brides have always gone up the
nave. Yours faithfully . . . ' Indeed, the
nave is the main route from the west
door of a church to the chancel and
altar; the aisles are the parallel routes at
the side of the building, usually separated from the nave by pillars.

Ajax. See GREEK NAMES.

alarm. See SPREAD ~ AND DESPOND-
ENCY.

Alcestis. See GREEK NAMES.

Alcmena. See GREEK NAMES.

Alethia. See GREEK NAMES.

Alexis. See SAINTS' NAMES.

Alfred E. Newman. The name of a
cheerfully ignorant character in the US
magazine *Mad* (founded 1952).

Alice-blue Gown. Celebrated in song,
the colour of this garment, a light
greenish-blue, takes its name from a particular Alice – the daughter of President
Theodore Roosevelt. The song 'Alice-
blue Gown' was written for her by
Joseph McCarthy and Harry Tierney in
1900, when she was sixteen, though
apparently not published until 1919. In

Alice in Wonderland Quoted almost as extensively as Shakespeare and the Bible, *Alice's Adventures in Wonderland* (1865) and *Through the Looking Glass and What Alice Found There* (1872) by Lewis Carroll are alluded to for their particular characters and incidents and as a whole, to denote a mad, fantastic world.

See also *ANGLO-SAXON ATTITUDES*; *ARE YOU OLD – FATHER WILLIAM?*; *CABBAGES AND KINGS*; *CHANGE LOBSTERS AND DANCE*; *DECISIONS DECISIONS!*; *HOW DOTH THE LITTLE CROCODILE*; *MAD AS A HATTER*; *MALICE IN WONDERLAND*; *'TIS LOVE 'TIS LOVE THAT MAKES THE WORLD GO ROUND*; *TWINKLE TWINKLE LITTLE BAT*; *WE ARE THE MASTERS NOW*; *WHITE RABBIT*.

the late 1930s, there was another (British) song, called 'The Girl in the Alice-blue Gown'.

alienation effect. Bertolt Brecht's name (in German '*Verfremdungseffekt*') for his theory of drama, first promoted in 1937, in which the audience has to be reminded that the play it is watching *is* a play and not real. The effect is to distance the watchers from the players, to prevent too much emotional involvement.

alive and well (and living in —). In the preface to *His Last Bow* (1917) Conan Doyle wrote: 'The Friends of Mr Sherlock Holmes will be glad to learn that he is still alive and well . . .' The extended form was popularized when the Belgian-born songwriter and singer Jacques Brel (1929–78) was made the subject of an off-Broadway musical show entitled *Jacques Brel is Alive and Well and Living in Paris* (1968). A film in 1975 was entitled *Sheila Devine is Dead and Living in New York*.

'All Along the Watchtower'. The title of a song (1968) by Bob Dylan which begins: 'All along the watchtower, princes kept the view'. It is probably after Isaiah 21:5, prophesying the fall of Babylon: 'Prepare the table, watch in the watchtower, eat, drink: arise ye princes, and anoint the shield.' (*The Watchtower*, magazine of Jehovah's Witnesses, presumably takes its name from the same source.)

all animals are equal but some are more equal than others. A fictional slogan from George Orwell's novel *Animal Farm* (1945), a commentary on the totalitarian excesses of communism. The saying alludes to Thomas Jefferson's 'All men are created equal and independent', from the Preamble to the American Declaration of Independence (1776).

Only the second half of the phrase need actually be spoken, the first half being understood: 'You-Know-Who [Mrs Thatcher] is against the idea [televising parliament]. There aren't card votes at Westminster, but some votes are more equal than others' (*Guardian*, 15 February 1989).

all dressed up and nowhere to go. From the song popularized by the US comedian Raymond Hitchcock in *The Beauty Shop* (New York, 1914) and *Mr Manhattan* (London, 1915):

> When you're all dressed up and no place to go,
> Life seems dreary, weary and slow.

The words gained further emphasis when they were used by William Allen White to describe the Progressive Party following Theodore Roosevelt's decision to retire from presidential competition in 1916. He said it was: 'All dressed up with nowhere to go.'

all for one and one for all. [French: *tous pour un, un pour tous*]. The motto of the Three Musketeers in the novel (1844–5) by Alexandre Dumas. As 'one for all, or all for one', it had appeared earlier in Shakespeare's *Lucrece* (lines 141–4).

All Gas and Gaiters. The title of a BBC TV comedy series about the clergy (1966–70), taken from Charles Dickens, *Nicholas Nickleby* (Chap. 49, 1838–9): 'All is gas and gaiters' – gaiters (leg coverings below the knee) being traditionally associated with bishops.

all good things must come to an end. A proverbial expression meaning 'pleasure cannot go on for ever'. There are versions going back to 1440 and as 'Everything has an end', the idea appears in Chaucer's *Troilus and Criseyde* (1385). The Prayer Book version of

Psalm 119:96 has: 'I see that all things come to an end.'

all hell broke loose. This popular descriptive phrase comes from Milton's *Paradise Lost* (Bk. 4, line 917, 1667), when the Archangel Gabriel speaks to Satan:

> Wherefore with thee
> Came not all hell broke loose.

As an idiomatic phrase it was already established by 1738 when Swift compiled his *Polite Conversation*. When there is 'A great Noise below', Lady Smart exclaims: 'Hey, what a clattering is there; one would think Hell was broke loose.'

all human life is there. A slogan for the *News of the World* in 1958–9, from Henry James's 'Madonna of the Future' (1879): 'Cats and monkeys, monkeys and cats – all human life is there'. (See also *DPP*.)

'All our yesterdays' speech. Almost every phrase from Macbeth's speech in Shakespeare's *Macbeth* (V.v.22) seems to have been used as title material:

> To-morrow, and to-morrow, and to-morrow,
> Creeps in this petty pace from day to day,
> To the last syllable of recorded time;
> And all our yesterdays have lighted fools
> The way to dusty death. Out, out, brief candle!
> Life's but a walking shadow; a poor player,
> That struts and frets his hour upon the stage,

> And then is heard no more: it is a tale
> Told by an idiot, full of sound and fury,
> Signifying nothing.

A slight exaggeration, but *All Our Yesterdays* was the title of Granada TV's 1960–73 programme devoted to old newsreels; 'full of sound and fury' is echoed in the title of William Faulkner's novel *The Sound and the Fury* (1929); *Told By an Idiot* was a novel by Rose Macaulay (1923); *Tomorrow and Tomorrow* was a film in 1932; *The Way to Dusty Death* was the title of a novel by Alastair Maclean (1973); and 'strutting and fretting' and the other phrases are frequently alluded to. See also *BRIEF CANDLES*.

all my eye and Betty Martin.
Meaning 'nonsense', *O E D 2* finds a letter written in 1781 by one S. Crispe stating: 'Physic, to old, crazy Frames like ours, is all my eye and Betty Martin – (a sea phrase that Admiral Jemm frequently makes use of)'. The shorter expressions 'all my eye' or 'my eye' predate this. As to how it originated, Radford repeats the suggestion that it was a British sailor's garbled version of words heard in an Italian church: '*O, mihi, beate Martine*' [Oh, grant me, blessed St Martin . . .], but this sounds too ingenious. Probably there *was* a Betty Martin of renown in the eighteenth century (Partridge/*Catch Phrases* finds mention of an actress with the name whose favourite expression is supposed to have been 'My eye!') and that her name was co-opted for popular use.

Compare GORDON BENNETT.

All Quiet on the Western Front. The title of the English translation of the novel *Im Westen Nichts Neues* [Nothing New in the West] (1929, film U S, 1930) by the German writer, Erich Maria Remarque.

'All Quiet on the Western Front' had been a familiar phrase of the Allies in the First World War, used in military communiqués and newspaper reports and also taken up jocularly by men in the trenches to describe peaceful inactivity. Partridge/*Catch Phrases* hears in it echoes of 'All quiet on the Shipka Pass' – cartoons of the 1877–8 Russo–Turkish War which Partridge says had a vogue in 1915–16, though he never heard the allusion made himself. For no very good reason, Partridge rules out any connection with the US song 'All Quiet Along the Potomac'. This, in turn, came from a poem called 'The Picket Guard' (1861) by Ethel Lynn Beers – a sarcastic commentary on Gen Brinton McClellan's policy of delay at the start of the Civil War. The phrase (alluding to the Potomac River which runs through Washington DC) had been used in reports from McClellan's Union headquarters and put in Northern newspaper headlines.

all Sir Garnet. Meaning 'all right, correct', the phrase alludes to Sir Garnet Wolseley (1833–1913), a noted soldier who led several successful military expeditions from 1852–85 and helped improve the lot of the Other Ranks. *Sir Garnet* was the name of a boat in *Coot Club*, the novel (1934) by Arthur Ransome.

All's Well That Ends Well. Revd Francis Kilvert's diary entry for 1 January 1878 has: 'The hind axle broke and they thought they would have to spend the night on the road . . . All's well that ends well and they arrived safe and sound.' Is the allusion to the title of Shakespeare's play (*c* 1603) or to something else? It was a proverbial expression before Shakespeare. *C O D P* finds, 'If the ende be wele, than is alle wele' in 1381, and points to the earlier form, 'Wel is him that wel ende mai.' See also *WAR AND PEACE*.

all the news that's fit to print. This slogan was devised by Adolph S. Ochs when he bought the *New York Times* and it has been used in every edition since – at first on the editorial page, on 25 October 1896, and from the following February on the front page near the masthead. It became the paper's war cry in the 1890s' battle against formidable competition from the *World*, the *Herald* and the *Journal*. It has been parodied by Howard Dietz as 'All the news *that fits* we print' – which, at worst, sounds like a slogan for the suppression of news. However, no newspaper prints everything.

All the President's Men. Carl Bernstein and Bob Woodward gave this title to their first book on WATERGATE

(1974, film US 1976). It might seem to allude to the lines from the nursery rhyme 'Humpty Dumpty' (first recorded in 1803):

> All the king's horses
> And all the king's men,
> Couldn't put Humpty together again.

There was also a Robert Penn Warren novel (and film, US 1949) based on the life of Southern demagogue Huey 'Kingfish' Long called *All the King's Men*. More directly, the Watergate book took its title from a saying of Henry Kissinger's at the time of the 1970 Cambodia invasion: 'We are all the President's men and we must behave accordingly' (quoted in Kalb and Kalb, *Kissinger*, 1974).

all the world and his wife. Everybody – though a phrase in decline now after the rise of feminism. Christopher Anstey in *The New Bath Guide* (1766) has:

> How he welcomes at once all the world
>   and his wife,
> And how civil to folk he ne'er saw in his
>   life.

Swift included it in *Polite Conversation* (1738): 'Who were the Company? – Why; there was all the World and his Wife.' There is an equivalent French expression: 'All the world and his father.' From F. Scott Fitzgerald, *The Great Gatsby* (Chap. 4, 1926): 'On Sunday morning while church bells rang in the villages alongshore, the world and its mistress returned to Gatsby's house and twinkled hilariously on his lawn.'

'All Things Bright and Beautiful'. The popular hymn (1848) by Mrs Cecil Frances Alexander is notorious for the line about the RICH MAN IN HIS CASTLE. It also provided the author James Herriot with new titles for his volumes about life as a vet – books originally called *It Shouldn't Happen To a Vet*, *Let Sleeping Vets Lie*, *Vets Might Fly*, etc. When these titles were coupled together in three omnibus editions especially for the US market, Mrs Alexander's hymn was plundered for titles and they became *All Things Bright and Beautiful*, *All Creatures Great and Small*, and *All Things Wise and Wonderful*. *The Lord God Made Them All* was given to a further original volume.

All This and Heaven Too. The title of a novel (1939, film US, 1940) by Rachel Field. As acknowledged in the book, Matthew Henry, the English Bible commentator (*d* 1714), attributed the saying to his minister father in his *Life of Philip Henry*. Compare the film title *All This and World War II* (US, 1976).

Alms for Oblivion. The novel sequence (1964–84) by Simon Raven takes its overall title from Shakespeare's *Troilus and Cressida* (III.iii.145):

> Time hath, my lord, a wallet at his back,
> Wherein he puts alms for oblivion.

Alpheus. See GREEK NAMES.

Altered States. The title of a film (US 1980), from a novel by Paddy Chayevsky, about a 'psychophysiologist who hallucinates himself back into primitive states of human evolution, in which guise he emerges to kill' (Halliwell). This might have something to do with what Dr Albert Hofmann observed of his discovery, the psychedelic drug LSD. He noted in his diary for 1943: 'An intense stimulation of the imagination and *an altered state of awareness of the world*'.

alternative. See THERE IS NO ~.

'Always True to You in My Fashion'. The song by Cole Porter from *Kiss Me Kate* (1948) echoes, consciously or unconsciously, the line 'I have been faithful to thee, Cynara! in my fashion' from 'NON SUM QUALIS ERAM' (1896) by Ernest Dowson.

Amaryllis. See ROMAN NAMES.

Amazons. See GREEK NAMES.

amber nectar. Nectar was the (sweet) drink of the gods, in classical mythology. 'Amber fluid' and 'amber liquid' are both Australianisms (acknowledged by the *Macquarie Dictionary*, 1981) for beer (particularly amber-coloured lager). Put all this together and you have the term 'amber nectar' used by Paul Hogan in 1980s' TV commercials in Britain for Foster's lager.

Ambrosia. See GREEK NAMES.

Amen Corner. (1) A place near St Paul's Cathedral, London, where monks would conclude saying the Pater Noster as they processed on Corpus Christi Day. Hence the other place names: Paternoster Row, Ave Maria Lane, Creed Lane. (2) (in US use by 1860) The name given to the part of a church or meeting-house where people sat who used to assist the preacher by calling out the responses, especially 'Amen'. (3) The name of a British pop group of the late 1960s.

America. See MIDDLE ~.

American Dream, The. The title of a play (1961) by Edward Albee. A novel by Norman Mailer had the title *An American Dream* (1965). It comes from the expression used to describe the ideals of democracy and standards of living that inspired the founding of the United States, and which was probably coined by J.T. Adams in *The Epic of America* (1931). Before that, in 'America the Beautiful' (1893), Katharine Lee Bates

had written of a 'patriot dream that sees beyond the years'.

Amphitrite. See GREEK NAMES.

Amphitryon. See GREEK NAMES.

amused. See WE ARE NOT ~.

anatomy of —, the. A title format, the first notable one was *The Anatomy of Melancholy* (1621) by Robert Burton. That book used the word 'anatomy' in an appropriate manner, its subject being a medical condition (*anatome* is the Greek word for dissection).

The modern vogue for 'anatomies' of this and that began with the film *Anatomy of a Murder* (US, 1959) and was followed by Anthony Sampson's *Anatomy of Britain*, first published in 1962 and revised a number of times thereafter.

Ancestral Vices/Voices. *Ancestral Vices* is the title of a novel (1980) by Tom Sharpe; *Ancestral Voices* is the title of the first volume of diaries (1975) of the architectural historian, James Lees-Milne. Both derive from the poem 'Kubla Khan' (1798) by Samuel Taylor Coleridge, which contains the lines:

> And 'mid this tumult Kubla heard from far
> Ancestral voices prophesying war!

Lees-Milne went to the same source for his three subsequent diary volumes, *Prophesying Peace* (1977), *Caves of Ice* (1983) and *Midway on the Waves* (1985), viz:

> The shadow of the dome of pleasure
> Floated midway on the waves . . .
> It was a miracle of rare device,
> A sunny pleasure-dome with caves of ice!

See also XANADU.

Anchises. According to Greek mythology, Anchises and Aphrodite had a son, and so we say farewell . . .

Aeneas. The story of Aeneas rescuing his father is told in Virgil's *Aeneid*. In Shakespeare's *Julius Caesar* (I.ii.111) we have Cassius describing how he once rescued Caesar from drowning:

> I, as Aeneas, our great ancestor,
> Did from the flames of Troy upon his
>   shoulder
> The old Anchises bear, so from the
>   waves of Tiber
> Did I the tired Caesar.

Shakespeare also alludes to this incident in *King Henry VI, Part 2* (V.ii.63). In his diary for 15 October 1940, Harold Nicolson is describing what happened when a bomb fell on the Carlton Club in London: 'They saw through the fog the figure of Quintin Hogg escorting old Hailsham [his father, Lord H.] from the ruins, like Aeneas and Anchises.' (*Harold Nicolson: Diaries and Letters*, Vols. 1–3, ed. Nigel Nicolson, 1966–8.)

'And Death Shall Have No Dominion'. The title of the notable poem (1936) on immortality by Dylan Thomas. A straightforward allusion to Romans 6:9: 'Christ being raised from the dead dieth no more: death hath no more dominion over him.'

And Justice for All. The title of a film (1979) about the US legal system. The phrase come from the Pledge of Allegiance to the Flag (put into its final form by Francis Bellamy in 1892): 'I pledge allegiance to the flag of the United States of America and to the republic for which it stands, one nation under God, indivisible, with liberty and justice for all.' The idea of 'justice for all' is, however, one that goes back to the Greeks. It also gave rise to the remark by Lord Justice Sir James Mathew (*d* 1908): 'In England, justice is open to all, like the Ritz Hotel.'

And Now For Something Completely Different . . . The title of the

first cinema feature (1971) from the TV comedy team *Monty Python's Flying Circus*. At first a catch phrase, it was usually delivered by John Cleese as a dinner-jacketed BBC announcer, seated before a microphone on a desk in some unlikely setting. Taken from the linking material at one time much-loved by magazine-programme presenters on radio.

Andrew, St. See SAINTS' NAMES.

Androcles. See ROMAN NAMES.

Andromache. See GREEK NAMES.

Andromeda. See GREEK NAMES.

And shall Trelawny die? The refrain 'Here's twenty thousand Cornish men will know the reason why' from 'Song of the Western Men' (1825) by Revd Robert S. Hawker refers to Bishop Trelawny of Bristol. In 1688, Trelawny was sent to the Tower with six other bishops by James II on charges of seditious libel. They were acquitted. Hawker obtained the whole refrain from an old Cornish ballad.

And So To Bed. The title of a play (1926) by J.B. Fagan, which was then turned into a musical (by Vivian Ellis, 1951). It comes from Samuel Pepys's famous signing-off line for his diary entries, occurring first on 15 January 1660. However, on that particular occasion, they are not quite his last words. He writes: 'I went to supper, and after that to make an end of this week's notes in this book, and so to bed.' Then he adds: 'It being a cold day and a great snow, my physic did not work so well as it should have done.'

and so we say farewell . . . Travelogues made by James A. Fitzpatrick were a supporting feature of cinema programmes from 1925 onwards. With the advent of sound, the commentaries to 'Fitzpatrick Travel-talks' became noted for their closing words: 'And it's from this paradise of the Canadian Rockies that we reluctantly say farewell to Beautiful Banff ... '; 'And as the midnight sun lingers on the skyline of the city, we most reluctantly say farewell to Stockholm, Venice of the North ...'; 'With its picturesque impressions indelibly fixed in our memory, it is time to conclude our visit and reluctantly say farewell to Hong Kong, the hub of the Orient ...'

and that ain't hay! The title of the 1943 Abbot and Costello film which is said to have popularized this (almost exclusively US) exclamation was *It Ain't Hay*. But in the same year Mickey Rooney exclaimed, 'And that ain't hay!' as he went into the big 'I Got Rhythm' number (choreographed by Busby Berkeley) in the film *Girl Crazy* (the scene being set, appropriately, in an agricultural college). It means 'and that's not to be sniffed at/not negligible', usually with reference to money.

and thereby hangs a tale. As a story-telling device, this is still very much in use to indicate that some tasty tit-bit is about to be revealed. It occurs a number of times in Shakespeare. In *As You Like It* (II.vii.28) Jaques, reporting the words of a motley fool (Touchstone), says:

> And so from hour to hour, we ripe and
>   ripe,
> And then, from hour to hour, we rot and
>   rot:
> And thereby hangs a tale.

and they all lived happily ever after. The traditional ending to 'fairy' tales is not quite so frequently used as ONCE UPON A TIME, but it is (more or less) present in five of *The Classic Fairy Tales* gathered in their earliest known

English forms by Iona and Peter Opie (1974). 'Jack and the Giants' (*c* 1760) ends: 'He and his Lady lived the Residue of their Days in great Joy and Happiness.' 'Jack and the Bean-Stalk' (1807) ends: 'His mother and he lived together a great many years, and continued always to be very happy.' (See also *DPP*.)

and this too shall pass away. Chuck Berry 'spoke' a song (1979) called 'Pass Away' which told of a Persian king who had the words 'Even this shall pass away' carved up. George Harrison had called his first (mostly solo) record album 'All Things Must Pass' in 1970. These musicians were by no means the first people to be drawn to this saying. As Abraham Lincoln explained in an address to the Wisconsin State Agricultural Society (1859): 'An Eastern monarch once charged his wise men to invent him a sentence to be ever in view, and which should be true and appropriate in all times and situations. They presented him with the words, "And this, too, shall pass away". How much it expresses! How chastening in the hour of pride! How consoling in the depths of affliction!'

But who was the oriental monarch? *Benham's Book of Quotations* (1948) says the phrase was an inscription on a ring (according to an oriental tale) and the phrase was given by Solomon to a Sultan who 'desired that the words should be appropriate at all time'. The next year, 1860, Nathaniel Hawthorne wrote in *The Marble Faun* of the 'greatest mortal consolation, which we derive from the transitoriness of all things – from the right of saying, in every conjuncture, "This, too, will pass away".'

'And When Did You Last See Your Father?' The title of a painting (1878) by William Frederick Yeames R A. First exhibited at the Royal Academy, the original is now in the Walker Art

Gallery, Liverpool. In Roy Strong's book *And When Did You Last See Your Father? – The Victorian Painter and British History* (1978), he notes: 'The child . . . stands on a footstool about to answer an inquiry made by the Puritan who leans across the table towards him . . . To the left the ladies of the house . . . cling to each other in tearful emotion. They, it is clear, have not answered the dreaded question.'

The title of the painting became a kind of joke catch phrase, sometimes used nudgingly, and often allusively – as in the title of Christopher Hampton's 1964 play *When Did You Last See My Mother?* and the 1986 farce by Ray Galton and John Antrobus, *When Did You Last See Your . . . Trousers?*

angel. An investor or backer of theatrical productions, in the US, originally – a fairly obvious extension of 'guardian angel'. Perhaps the most far-fetched version of the phrase's origin is that one Luis de Santangel was the man who put up the money for Christopher Columbus's voyage to America. The use of the word 'angel' in this sort of context seems not to date from much before the 1920s, however.

Angel of Death. A nickname bestowed in the Second World War upon Dr Joseph Mengele, the German concentration camp doctor who experimented on inmates – 'for his power to pick who would live and die in Auschwitz by the wave of his hand' (*Time*, 17 June 1985). 'Angel of death' is not a biblical phrase and appears to have arisen in the nineteenth century.

Angels One Five. The title of a film (UK, 1952) about RAF fighter pilots. It comes from air force jargon: 'angels' for height measured in units of a thousand feet; 'one five' stood for fifteen; so '20 MEs at Angels One Five' meant 'Twenty Messerschmitts at 15,000 feet'.

Anglo-Saxon Attitudes. The title of Angus Wilson's novel (1956) about a historian investigating a possible archaeological forgery. It originates from Lewis Carroll's *Through the Looking Glass* (Chap. 7, 1872). Alice observes the Messenger 'skipping up and down, and wriggling like an eel, as he came along'. When she expresses surprise, the King explains: 'He's an Anglo-Saxon Messenger – and those are Anglo-Saxon attitudes.' Harry Morgan Ayres in *Carroll's Alice* suggests that the author may have been spoofing the Anglo-Saxon scholarship of his day.

angry young man. Any writer from the mid-1950s who showed a social awareness and expressed dissatisfaction with conventional values and with the ESTABLISHMENT – John Osborne, Kingsley Amis and Colin Wilson among them – was likely to be so labelled.

Leslie Paul, a social philosopher, had called his autobiography *Angry Young Man* in 1951, but the popular use of the phrase stems from *Look Back in Anger*, the 1956 play by John Osborne which featured an anti-hero called Jimmy Porter. The phrase did not occur in the play but was applied to the playwright by George Fearon in publicity material from the Royal Court Theatre, London. Fearon later told the *Daily Telegraph* (2 October 1957): 'I ventured to prophesy that this generation would praise his play while mine would, in general, dislike it . . . "If this happens," I told [Osborne], "you would become known as the Angry Young Man." In fact, we decided then and there that henceforth he was to be known as that.'

animals. See ALL ~ ARE EQUAL . . . ; NEVER WORK WITH CHILDREN AND ~.

animal vegetable or mineral. A way of describing three types of matter, though not necessarily in that order. In

W.S. Gilbert's lyrics for *The Pirates of Penzance* (1879), Major-General Stanley sings:

> But still in matters vegetable, animal, and
>   mineral,
> I am the very model of a modern
>   Major-General.

For British television viewers in the 1950s, the order was clearly stated in the title of the long-running archaeological quiz *Animal, Vegetable and Mineral* in which eminent university dons had to identify ancient artefacts just by looking at them. The trio of words was also invoked in the long-running US radio and TV game *Twenty Questions* (on BBC Radio from 1947 to 1976) in which panellists had to guess an object by asking not more than a score of questions. This was based on the old parlour game of 'Animal, Vegetable or Mineral' which seems to have been known on both sides of the Atlantic in the nineteenth century. Charles Dickens also refers to it by the name of 'Yes and No'. 'Twenty Questions' is referred to as such in a letter from Hannah Moore as early as 1786. (See also *DPP*.)

Anne. See QUEEN ~'S DEAD.

Annie. See LITTLE ORPHAN ~.

Another Country. The title of a play (1981, film UK, 1984) by Julian Mitchell, showing how the seeds of defection to Soviet Russia were sown in a group of boys at an English public school. Not, as might at first be thought, from the celebrated line in Christopher Marlowe's *The Jew of Malta* (c 1592):

> Fornication: but that was in another
>   country;
> And besides the WENCH IS DEAD.

Rather, as the playwright has confirmed to me, from the second verse of Sir Cecil Spring Rice's patriotic 'Last Poem' (1918), which begins 'I vow to thee, my country' and continues:

> And there's another country, I've heard
>   of long ago
> Most dear to them that love her, most
>   great to them that know.

In the original context, the 'other country' is Heaven, rather than the Soviet Union, of course. *Another Country* had earlier been used as the title of a novel (1962) by James Baldwin.

another day – another dollar! What one says to oneself at the conclusion of toil. Now as well known in the UK where there does not appear to be an equivalent expression using 'pound' instead of 'dollar'. Partridge/*Catch Phrases* dates it from the 1940s in the UK and from *c* 1910 in the US.

Another Heart and Other Pulses. The title of Michael Foot's account (1984) of his unsuccessful leadership of the British Labour Party during the 1983 General Election. From a Keats sonnet 'Addressed to the Same' (Benjamin Robert Haydon):

> And other spirits there are standing apart
> Upon the forehead of the age to come:
> These, these will give the world another
>   heart,
> And other pulses.

'Another Little Drink Wouldn't Do Us Any Harm'. The title of a song written by Clifford Grey and Nat D. Ayer, sung by George Robey in *The Bing Boys Are Here* (1916). It includes a reference to the well-known fact that Prime Minister Asquith was at times the worse for drink when on the Treasury Bench:

> Mr Asquith says in a manner sweet and
>   calm:
> And another little drink wouldn't do us
>   any harm.

The title-phrase has since become a boozer's jocular justification for another snifter.

Another Part of the Wood. The title of the first volume of autobiography (1974) by Kenneth (Lord) Clark, the art historian, taken from the stage direction to Act III Scene 2 of Shakespeare, *A Midsummer Night's Dream*: 'Another Part of the Wood'. Locations such as this were mostly not of Shakespeare's own devising but were added by later editors. Clark said he wished also to allude to the opening of Dante's *Inferno*: 'I found myself in a dark wood where the straight way was lost.' Lillian Hellman had entitled one of her plays, *Another Part of the Forest* (1946).

Anthony Eden. A black felt hat – also known as a Homburg, after the German health spa – popularized in the 1930s by Anthony Eden (later Lord Avon) when he was Foreign Secretary and one of the best-dressed members of the House of Commons.

Anthony the Great, St. See SAINTS' NAMES.

Antic Hay. The title of a novel (1923) by Aldous HUXLEY, taken from Christopher Marlowe's *Edward II* (1593):

> My men, like satyrs grazing on the
> lawns,
> Shall with their goat feet dance an antic
> hay

[An antic hay is a grotesque country dance].

Antigone. See GREEK NAMES.

antimacassar. A name given to coverings thrown over chairs and sofas from Victorian times onwards to protect them from hair-oil stains. The impressive-sounding name reflects that 'Macassar'

was the proprietory name of a hair oil and so the coverings acted 'anti' [against] it. They really did exist, which is more than can be said for the legendary coverings said to have been put over too-shocking piano legs in Victorian times.

any colour so long as it's black. An expression to convey that there is no choice, this originated with Henry Ford who is supposed to have said it about the Model T Ford which came out in 1909. Hill and Nevins in *Ford: Expansion and Challenge* (1957) have him saying: 'People can have it any colour – so long as it's black.' However, in 1925, the company had to bow to the inevitable and offer a choice of colours.

anyone for tennis? A phrase expressive of the 'teacup' theatre of the 1920s and 1930s (as also in the forms **who's for tennis?** and **tennis, anyone?**). A clear example of its being used has proved elusive, however, although there is any number of near misses. The opening lines of Part II of Strindberg's *Dance of Death* (1901) are (in translation): 'Why don't you come and play tennis?' A *very* near miss occurs in the first act of Shaw's *Misalliance* (1910) in which a character asks: 'Anybody on for a game of tennis?' Teddie in Somerset Maugham's *The Circle* (1921) always seems on the verge of saying it, but only manages: 'I say, what about this tennis?' One is told that Gladys Cooper definitely said it in the musical *The Dollar Princess* (1909) but tangible evidence is lacking. Unfortunately, a terrible wild-goose chase was launched by people claiming it had been Humphrey Bogart's sole first line in his first stage appearance, but he denied it.

In the form 'Anyone for Tennis?' the phrase was used by J.B. Priestley as the title of a 1968 television play, and in 1981 it was converted into *Anyone for Denis?* by John Wells as the title of a farce guying Margaret Thatcher's husband. (See also *D P P*).

anything you say may be taken down and used in evidence against you. The police 'caution' to a person who may be charged with a crime does not have a fixed form in the UK. The version you might expect from reading fiction would go something like: 'You are not obliged to say anything unless you wish to do so but, I must warn you, whatever you do say will be taken down and may be given in evidence *against you*.' But this does not conform with modern practice. British police are advised that care should be taken to avoid any suggestion that evidence might only be used *against* a person, as this could prevent an innocent person making a statement which might help clear him of a charge.

Old habits die hard, however. The phrase is etched on the national consciousness – and it must have been said at one time. Charles Dickens in *Our Mutual Friend* (1864–5) has 'Mr Inspector' (an early example of a police officer in fiction) give 'the caution' (which he refers to as such) in these words: 'It's my duty to inform you that whatever you say, will be used against you' (Bk. 4, Chap. 12). Examples of the 'against you' caution also appear in Sherlock Holmes short stories by Conan Doyle (1905 and 1917). In the US, the phrase may still be found. In *Will* (1980), G. Gordon Liddy describes what he said during a raid on Dr Timothy Leary's house in connection with drugs charges (in March 1966): 'I want you to understand that you don't have to make any statement, and any statement you do make may be used against you in a court of law.'

Any Woman's Blues. The title of a novel (1990) by Erica Jong. From the title of a song by Bessie Smith (*c* 1929).

ANZAC. See ACRONYMS.

a-okay. Another way of saying 'OK' or 'All systems working'. From NASA engineers in the early days of the US space programme 'who used to say it during radio transmission tests because the sharper sound of A cut through the static better than O' (Tom Wolfe, THE RIGHT STUFF, 1979). Now largely redundant, it seems never to have been used by astronauts themselves. President Reagan, emerging from a day of medical tests at a naval hospital in June 1986, pronounced himself 'A - O K'. Another derivation is a melding of 'A 1' and 'O K'.

Aphrodite. See GREEK NAMES.

Apollo. See GREEK NAMES.

appeal. See LAST ~ TO REASON.

appeasement. A name given to the policy of conciliation and concession towards Nazi Germany, around 1938. The word had been used in this context since the end of the First World War. On 14 February 1920, Winston Churchill was saying in a speech: 'I am, and have always been since the firing stopped on November 11, 1918, for a policy of peace, real peace and appeasement'. The word may have become fixed following a letter to *The Times* (4 May 1934) from the 11th Marquess of Lothian: 'The only lasting solution is that Europe should gradually find its way to an internal equilibrium and a limitation of armaments by political appeasement.'

See also CLIVEDEN SET.

apple. See BIG ~.

apple of one's eye. This phrase describes what one cherishes most. The pupil of the eye has long been known as the 'apple' because of its supposed round, solid shape. To be deprived of the apple is to be blinded and lose something extremely valuable. The Bible has: 'He kept him as the apple of his eye' (Deuteronomy 32:10).

apple-pie order, in. Meaning 'with everything in place; smart', the expression possibly derives from the French *cap-à-pied*, wearing armour 'from head to foot'. Another suggested French origin is from *nappe pliée*, a folded table cloth or sheet (though this seems a more likely source for the term **apple-pie bed** – for one made so that you can't get into it). On the other hand, a folded cloth or napkin does convey the idea of crispness and smartness.

après nous le déluge [after us, the flood]. The Marquise de Pompadour's celebrated remark to Louis XV was made on 5 November 1757 after Frederick the Great had defeated the French and Austrian armies at the Battle of Rossbach. It carries with it the suggestion that nothing matters once you are dead and has also been interpreted as a premonition of the French Revolution. Bartlett notes that this 'reputed reply' by the king's mistress was recorded by three authorities, though a fourth gives it to the king himself. Bartlett then claims the saying was not original anyway, but 'an old French proverb'. However, the *ODP* has as an English proverb, 'After us the deluge', deriving from Mme de Pompadour. Its only citation is Burnaby's 1876 *Ride to Khiva*: 'Our rulers did not trouble their heads much about the matter. "India will last my time . . . and after me the Deluge".' Metternich, the Austrian diplomat and chancellor, may later have said '*après moi le déluge*', meaning that everything would grind to a halt when he stopped controlling it. The deluge alluded to in both cases may be a dire event like the Great Flood or 'universal deluge' of Noah's time.

Arabs. See FOLD ONE'S TENT LIKE THE ~.

Arachne. See GREEK NAMES.

Arcadia ego, et in. This inscription means either that, in death, the speaker is in Arcadia, or that he was formerly there. '*Et in Arcadia ego vixi*' [I lived] or '*Et in Arcadia fui pastor*' [I was a shepherd] are variants. Or it is Death speaking – 'Even in Arcadia, I, Death, cannot be avoided.' Arcadia is the Greek name for a place of rural peace and calm taken from an actual area in the Peloponnese but used generally since classical times. '*Et in Arcadia ego*' is a phrase associated with tombs, skulls and Arcadian shepherds in classical paintings, but not before the seventeenth century. Most notably the phrase occurs in two paintings by the French artist Nicolas Poussin, both of which depict shepherds reading the words carved on a tomb.

Ares. See GREEK NAMES.

are there any more at home like you? Partridge/*Catch Phrases* traces this chat-up line to the musical comedy *Floradora* (1899) which contains the song (written by Leslie Stuart), 'Tell Me, Pretty Maiden (Are There Any More at Home Like You?)'

Arethusa. See GREEK NAMES.

Are You Now or Have You Ever Been? The title of a radio/stage play (1978) by Eric Bentley. From the stock phrase of McCarthyism, the pursuit and public ostracism of suspected US communist sympathizers at the time of the war with Korea in the early 1950s. Senator Joseph McCarthy was the instigator of the 'witch hunts' which led to the blacklisting of people in various walks of life, notably the film business. Those appearing at hearings of the House of Representatives Committee on UnAmerican Activities (1947–*c* 1957) were customarily challenged with the question: 'Are you now or have you ever been a member of the Communist Party?'

are you old – father William? The nonsense poem from ALICE IN WONDERLAND begins:

> 'You are old, father William,' the young man said,
> 'And your hair has become very white;
> And yet you incessantly stand on your head –
> Do you think, at your age, it is right?'

This is a parody of a much more sober piece, 'The Old Man's Comforts and How He Gained Them' (1799) by Robert Southey:

> 'You are old, father William,' the young man cried,
> 'The few locks which are left you are grey;
> You are a hale, father William, a hearty old man;
> Now tell me the reason, I pray . . . '

are you sitting comfortably? Then I'll/we'll begin. The customary way of beginning a story on BBC Radio's daily programme for small children, *Listen with Mother*, used from the programme's inception in 1950 until its demise in 1982. (See also *DPP*.)

Argo. See GREEK NAMES.

Argos. See GREEK NAMES.

Argus. See GREEK NAMES.

Ariadne. See GREEK NAMES.

Arion. See GREEK NAMES.

ark. See OUT OF THE ~.

Arms and the Man. The title of a play (1894) by George Bernard Shaw, later turned into a musical called *The Chocolate Soldier* (New York, 1909 – from the German *Der Tapfere Soldat* [*Brave Soldier*], 1908). From the first line of Vergil's *Aeneid*: '*Arma virumque cano*' [Of arms and the man, I sing] or perhaps from Dryden's translation of the same: 'Arms, and the man I sing'. See also I SING.

ars gratia artis. The motto of the Metro-Goldwyn-Mayer film company since *c* 1916. Howard Dietz, director of publicity and advertising with the original Goldwyn Pictures company, had left Columbia University not long before. When asked to design a trademark, he based it on the university's lion and added the Latin words meaning 'art for art's sake' underneath. The trademark and motto were carried over when Samuel Goldwyn retired to make way for the merger of Metropolitan with the interests of Louis B. Mayer in what has become known since as Metro-Goldwyn-Mayer.

Artemis. See GREEK NAMES.

Arthur's bosom. The former Mistress Quickly's malapropism for ABRAHAM'S BOSOM from Shakespeare's *King Henry V* (II.iii.9). She says of the dead Falstaff: 'Nay, sure, he's not in hell: he's in Arthur's bosom, if ever man went to Arthur's bosom.'

artichoke. See JERUSALEM ~.

Artist Descending a Staircase. The title of a radio play (1972) by Tom Stoppard, involving three avant-garde artists, after the titles of Cubo-Futurist or Dadaist paintings by Marcel Duchamp: 'Nude Descending a Staircase 1 & 2' (1911, 1912).

Art of the Possible, The. The title of the memoirs (1971) of R.A. (Lord) Butler, the British Conservative politician. In the preface to the paperback edition, he noted that this definition of politics appears first to have been used in modern times by Bismarck in 1866. Others who had touched on the idea included Cavour, Salvador de Madriaga, Pindar, and Camus.

Asclepius. See GREEK NAMES.

As Dorothy Parker Once Said . . .

The title of a stage show (*c* 1975) performed by Libby Morris, and devoted to the wit of Dorothy Parker. The phrase is testimony to the fact that of women in this century, she is undoubtedly the most quoted. (George Bernard Shaw is probably the most quoted man – though his remarks are usually prefaced with 'I think it was Bernard Shaw who once said . . .') It is probably an allusion to the verse in Cole Porter's song 'Just One of Those Things' (1935), which begins: 'As Dorothy Parker once said to her boy friend, "Fare thee well" . . .'

as every schoolboy knows. A phrase used to introduce an obvious piece of information. Bishop Jeremy Taylor (*d* 1667) used the form 'every schoolboy knows it'. In the next century, Jonathan Swift had 'To tell what every schoolboy knows'. But the most noted user of this rather patronizing phrase was Lord Macaulay, the historian, who would say things like: 'Every schoolboy knows who imprisoned Montezuma, and who strangled Atahualpa' (essay, 'Lord Clive', January 1840).

Ashes, The. The 'trophy' played for in Test cricket matches between England and Australia. Whichever side wins is said to have 'retained' or 'regained the Ashes', although the trophy itself never leaves the pavilion at Lord's cricket ground in London. However, it was allowed to be taken to Australia during the bicentennial celebrations in 1988. The name dates from 1882 when an Australian team won for the first time in England – by seven runs in an exciting game. A group of supporters of the English team inserted the following mock death notice in the *Sporting Times*:

> IN AFFECTIONATE
> REMEMBRANCE
> of
> ENGLISH CRICKET
> Which died at the Oval,
> on
> 29th August, 1882.
> Deeply lamented by a large circle
> of sorrowing friends and acquaintances.
> R.I.P.
> N.B. – The body will be cremated, and the
> ashes taken to Australia.

The following winter, when England defeated Australia and retrieved its honour, a group of ladies in Melbourne burned straw and placed the ashes in a small urn. They then presented this – saying it contained the ashes of the stumps and bails – to the English captain who duly carried it back to Lord's.

as I was saying before I was so rudely interrupted . . . A humorous phrase used when resuming an activity after interruption. In September 1946, 'Cassandra' (William O'Connor) resumed his column in the *Daily Mirror* after the Second World War, with: 'As I was saying when I was interrupted, it is a powerful hard thing to please all the people all the time'. In June of the same year, announcer Leslie Mitchell is also reported to have begun BBC TV's resumed transmissions with: 'As I was saying before I was so rudely interrupted'. The phrase sounds as if it might have originated in music-hall routines of the I DON'T WISH TO KNOW THAT, KINDLY LEAVE THE STAGE type. Compare A.A. Milne, *Winnie-the-Pooh* (1926): ' "AS – I – WAS SAYING," said Eeyore loudly and sternly, "as I was saying when I was interrupted by various Loud Sounds, I feel that – ".'

ask not what your country can do for you '. . . ask what you can do for your country.' The idea behind the most ringing sentence from President John F. Kennedy's inaugural speech (20 January

1961) had been used three times earlier by him during the election campaign. In a TV address during September 1960, Kennedy had said: 'We do not campaign stressing what our country is going to do for us as a people. We stress what we can do for our country, all of us.'

Arthur M. Schlesinger, a Kennedy aide, in his book *A Thousand Days* (1965), traced Kennedy's interest in the 'ask not . . .' theme to a notebook of the President's dating from 1945 which included the Rousseau quotation: 'As soon as any man says of the affairs of state, What does it matter to me? – the state may be given as lost.' Other antecedents cited include Warren G. Harding at the Republican National Convention in Chicago, 1916: 'We must have a citizenship less concerned about what the government can do for it and more anxious about what it can do for the nation'; the Mayor of Haverhill at the funeral of John Greenleaf Whittier in 1892: 'Here may we be reminded that man is most honoured, not by that which a city may do for him, but by that which he has done for the city'; Oliver Wendell Holmes's Memorial Day Address (1884) contains the words: 'It is now the moment when by common consent we pause to become conscious of our national life and to rejoice in it, to recall what our country has done for each of us, and to ask ourselves what we can do for our country in return.' It was Kennedy's inverted use of 'Ask not', however, that made what was obviously not a new concept eminently memorable.

as pleased as Punch. The earliest citation for this phrase in *OED2*, meaning 'obviously and extremely pleased' is in a letter from Thomas Moore to Lady Donegal in 1813: 'I was (as the poet says) as pleased as Punch'. This alludes to the appearance of Mr Punch, a character known in England from the time of the Restoration. As his face is carved on wood, it never changes expression and is always beaming. Even earlier than this, it appears, there was the expression **as proud as Punch**. A description of a visit by George III and his Queen to Wilton House in 1778 is contained in a letter from a Dr Eyre to Lord Herbert, dated 1 January 1779. He says: 'The Blue Closet within was for her Majesty's private purposes, where there was a red new velvet Close Stool, and a very handsome China Jordan, which I had the honour to produce from an old collection, & you may be sure, I am proud as Punch, that her Majesty condescended to piss in it.' This version – 'as proud as Punch' – would now seem to have died out of general use, although Christy Brown, *Down All the Days* (Chap. 17, 1970) has: 'Every man-jack of them sitting there proud as punch with their sons . . .'

assassination. See DESPOTISM.

assemblage, nouns of. See COLLECTIVE NOUNS.

Assisi. See FRANCIS OF ~.

Asterius. See GREEK NAMES.

as the Bishop said to the actress! A device for turning a perfectly innocent remark into a *double entendre* (e.g. 'I've never seen a female "Bottom" . . . as the Bishop said to the actress').

Aston Martin. Fast, smart sports cars have been made with this name by the Aston Martin Lagonda company since 1921. According to Adrian Room, *Dictionary of Trade Name Origins* (1982), the company was founded by

Lionel *Martin* who used to race cars near *Aston* Clinton in Buckinghamshire.

Astoria. See under ODEON.

Astraea. See GREEK NAMES.

Atalanta. See GREEK NAMES.

Ate. See GREEK NAMES.

Athena. See GREEK NAMES.

Athens of the North. A nickname for Edinburgh, presumably earned by the city as a seat of learning, with many long-established educational institutions and a university founded in 1583. When the 'New Town' was constructed in the early 1800s, the city took on a fine classical aspect. As such it might remind spectators of the Greek capital with its ancient reputation for scholastic and artistic achievement.

Calling the Scottish capital either 'Athens of the North' or 'Modern Athens' seems always to have occasioned some slight unease. James Hannay writing 'On Edinburgh' (*c* 1860), said:

> Pompous the boast, and yet a truth it
>   speaks:
> A Modern Athens – fit for modern
>   Greeks.

Belfast has been called the 'Athens of Ireland'; Boston, Mass. the 'Athens of the New World'; and Cordoba, Spain, the 'Athens of the West'.

Atlas. See GREEK NAMES.

At the Drop of a Hat. The title of a revue (1957) featuring Michael Flanders and Donald Swann – who followed it up with *At the Drop of Another Hat* (1963). From the (originally US) expression meaning 'at a given signal', when the dropping of a hat was the signal to start a fight or race. The phrase has come to mean something more like

'without needing encouragement, without delay': 'He'll sit down and write a witty song for you at the drop of a hat.'

Atticus. See ROMAN NAMES.

Audrey, St. See under TAWDRY.

Augean/Augeas. See GREEK NAMES.

August for the People. The title of a play (1961) by Nigel Dennis. From W.H. Auden's 'Birthday Poem' (sometimes also known as 'August for the People') (1935): 'August for the people and their favourite islands . . .'

Augustine of Canterbury, St. See SAINTS' NAMES.

auld lang syne. [Old long since]. Meaning 'long ago.' 'Syne' should be pronounced with an 's' sound and not as 'zyne'. In 1788, Robert Burns adapted 'Auld Lang Syne' from 'an old man's singing'. The title, first line and refrain had all appeared before as the work of other poets. Nevertheless, what Burns put together is what people should sing on New Year's Eve. Here is the first verse and the chorus:

> Should auld acquaintance be forgot,
> And never brought to min[d]?
> Should auld acquaintance be forgot,
> And days of o' lang syne.
> (*Chorus*) For auld lang syne, my dear
> For auld syne,
> We'll take a cup o' kindness yet
> For auld lang syne.

'For *the sake of* auld lang syne' should *not* be substituted at the end of verse and chorus.

aunt. See AGONY ~.

Aunt Edna. During the revolution in English drama of the 1950s, this term was called into play by the new wave of ANGRY YOUNG MAN dramatists and their supporters to describe the more conservative theatre-goer – the type who preferred comfortable three-act plays of the Shaftesbury Avenue kind.

Ironically, the term had been coined in self-defence by Terence Rattigan, one of the generation of dramatists they sought to replace. In the preface to Vol. II of his *Collected Plays* (1953) he had written of: 'A nice, respectable, middle-class, middle-aged maiden lady, with time on her hands and the money to help her pass it . . . Let us call her Aunt Edna . . . Now Aunt Edna does not appreciate Kafka . . . She is, in short, a hopeless lowbrow . . . Aunt Edna is universal, and to those who may feel that all the problems of the modern theatre might be solved by her liquidation, let me add that . . . she is also immortal.'

Auntie/Aunty BBC (*or simply* **Auntie/Aunty**). The BBC was mocked in this way by newspaper columnists, TV critics, and her own employees, most noticeably from about 1955 at the start of commercial television – the BBC supposedly being staid, over-cautious, prim and unambitious by comparison. A BBC spokesman countered with: 'An Auntie is often a much-loved member of the family.' The corporation assimilated the nickname to such effect that when arrangements were made to supply wine to BBC clubs in London direct from vineyards in Burgundy, it was bottled under the name *Tantine*.

In 1979, Arthur Askey suggested to me that he had originated the term during the *Band Waggon* programme in the late 1930s. While quite probable, the widespread use of the nickname is more likely to have occurred at the time suggested above. Wallace Reyburn in his book *Gilbert Harding – A Candid Portrayal* (1978) ascribed the phrase to the 1950s' radio and TV personality, while the politician Iain Macleod used it when editing the *Spectator* in the 1960s. Jack de Manio, the broadcaster, entitled

his memoirs *To Auntie With Love* (1967) and the comedian Ben Elton, a BBC TV show *The Man from Auntie* (1990).

Aurae. See ROMAN NAMES.

Aurora. See ROMAN NAMES.

Autolycus. See GREEK NAMES.

Averni/Avernus. See *FACILIS DESCENSUS ~*.

Awfully Big Adventure, An. The title of a novel (1989) by Beryl Bainbridge. From the line in J.M. Barrie's play *Peter Pan* (1904), 'To die will be an awfully big adventure.' The last words of Charles Frohman, the US theatrical producer, before going down in the *Lusitania* in 1915 were: 'Why fear death? It is the most beautiful adventure in life.' He had produced *Peter Pan*.

awkward squad, one of the. Sloppy in *Our Mutual Friend* (1864–5) is described by Charles Dickens as 'Full-Private Number One in the Awkward Squad of the rank and file of life'. Of military origin and used to denote a difficult, uncooperative person, the phrase originally referred to a squad which consisted of raw recruits and older hands who were put in it for punishment, but seems to have been used in other contexts for quite some time. The dying words of Robert Burns in 1796 are said to have been, 'John, don't let the awkward squad fire over me' – presumably referring to his fear that literary opponents might metaphorically fire a volley of respect, as soldiers sometimes do over a new grave.

AWOL. See ACRONYMS.

axe to grind, to have an. The expression meaning 'to have an ulterior motive, a private end to serve', would appear to come from an anecdote related in Benjamin Franklin's essay 'Too Much for Your Whistle'. A man showed interest in young Franklin's grindstone and asked how it worked. In the process of explaining, Franklin – using much energy – sharpened up the visitor's axe for him. This was clearly what the visitor had had in mind all along. Subsequently, Franklin (d 1790) had to ask himself whether people he encountered had 'another axe to grind'.

Axis Sally. See LORD HAW-HAW.

babbled of green fields. Revd Francis Kilvert in his diary entry for 15 May 1875 notes: 'At the house where I lodge there is a poor captive thrush who fills the street with his singing as he "babbles of green fields".' Conan Doyle in 'The Three Students' (*The Return of Sherlock Holmes*, 1905) has: 'The landlady babbled of green peas at seven-thirty'. These allude to Shakespeare's *King Henry V* (II.iii.17), where the Hostess is relating the death of Falstaff: 'A' parted ev'n just between twelve and one . . . I knew there was but one way; for his nose was as sharp as a pen, and a' babbled of green fields.'

But what appears as one of the most pleasing touches to be found in all Shakespeare may not have been his. The 1623 Folio renders the last phrase 'and a Table of green fields', which makes no sense. The generally accepted version was inserted by Lewis Theobald in his 1733 edition. As the 1954 Arden edition comments: ' "Babbled of green fields" is surely more in character with the Falstaff who quoted the Scriptures . . . and who lost his voice hallooing of anthems. Now he is in the valley of the shadow, the "green pasture" of Psalm 23 might well be on his lips.' Shakespeare may well have handwritten 'babld' and the printer read this as 'table'.

Babe, The. The nickname given to George Herman Ruth (*d* 1948), the US professional baseball player. He also became known as the **Sultan of Swat** in about 1920 because of the way he slugged at the ball. There had been a real Sultan (or more properly, Akhoond) of Swat, now part of Pakistan, in the 1870s whose death had given rise to doggerel by Edward Lear. The most popular baseball player in the history of the game was so famous that a battle cry of Japanese soldiers first heard in the Pacific in 1942 was: 'Go to hell, Babe Ruth – American, you die.'

baby boomer. A person born just after the Second World War during the 'baby boom'. This US term was hardly known in Britain until a 'Baby Boomer' edition of the TRIVIAL PURSUIT board game arrived in 1986. It was intended to appeal to those who had reached maturity during the 1960s. For a while, British journalists took to using the phrase 'baby boom' and even 'baby boomers' in preference to the **bulge** or **post-war bulge** which had been used hitherto (and which was a much better way, surely, to describe a pregnancy-related phenomenon). In fact, both 'baby boom' and 'bulge' had been used to describe the rise in births after the *First* World War and, specifically, the effect this had when those children became of school age. The Japanese also have a phrase for the phenomenon: *dankai no sedai* [the cluster generation].

Baby Ruth. The name of the popular US candy bar does *not* derive from the foregoing BABE Ruth, though one story has it that the manufacturers had wanted to call the bar a 'Babe Ruth'. They offered him $20,000 but he held out for $50,000. They settled instead for an approximation and did not have to pay a nickel.

The bar is also said to have taken its name from President Grover Cleveland's daughter, who was born in the White House. However, that event took place in 1891 and the bar did not make its first appearance until the 1920s. More probably, it was thus dubbed by Mrs George Williamson, whose husband was president of the Williamson Candy Company which originally made the bar. As Burnam 2 suggests, she named it after a granddaughter. Babe Ruth had to content himself with giving his name to a home run in baseball.

Bacchus. See ROMAN NAMES.

backroom boys. A nickname given to scientists and BOFFINS – and specifically to those relied on to produce inventions and new gadgets for weaponry and navigation in the Second World War. Compare the title of the novel (1943) by Nigel Balchin, *The Small Back Room*.

The phrase was originated, in this sense, by Lord Beaverbrook as Minister of Aircraft Production when he paid tribute to his research department in a broadcast on 19 March 1941: 'Let me say that the credit belongs to the boys in the backrooms [*sic*]. It isn't the man who sits in the limelight who should have the praise. It is not the men who sit in prominent places. It is the men in the backrooms.' In the US, the phrase 'backroom boys' can be traced at least to the 1870s, but Beaverbrook can be credited with the modern application to scientific and technical boffins. His inspiration quite obviously was his favourite film *Destry Rides Again* (1939) in which

Marlene Dietrich jumped on the bar of the Last Chance saloon and sang the Frank Loesser song 'See What the Boys in the Back Room Will Have'. Beaverbrook said that Dietrich singing this song was 'a greater work of art than the Mona Lisa'.

backs to the wall, with our. This expression, meaning 'up against it', dates back to 1535 at least, but was memorably used when the Germans launched their last great offensive of the First World War. On 12 April 1918, Sir Douglas Haig, the British Commander-in-Chief on the Western Front, issued an order for his troops to stand firm: 'Every position must be held to the last man: there must be no retirement. With our backs to the wall, and believing in the justice of our cause, each one of us must fight on to the end.' A.J.P. Taylor in his *English History 1914–45* (1966) commented: 'In England this sentence was ranked with Nelson's last message. At the front, the prospect of staff officers fighting with their backs to the walls of their luxurious chateaux had less effect.'

back to normalcy. Together with 'Return to normalcy with Harding', this was a slogan effectively used by President Warren G. Harding. Both were based on a word extracted from a speech he had made in Boston during May 1920: 'America's present need is not heroics but healing, not nostrums but normalcy, not revolution but restoration, not agitation but adjustment, not surgery but serenity, not the dramatic but the dispassionate, not experiment but equipoise, not submergence in internationality but sustainment in triumphant nationality.' Out of such an alliterative bog stuck the word 'normalcy' – a perfectly good Americanism, though it has been suggested that Harding was actually mispronouncing the word 'normality'. He himself claimed that 'normalcy' was what he had meant to say, having come across it in a dictionary.

back to square one. Used to mean, 'back to the beginning', this phrase appears to have gained currency in the 1930s through its use by British radio football commentators. *Radio Times* used to print a map of the football field divided into numbered squares, to which commentators would refer. Partridge/ *Catch Phrases* prefers, however, an earlier origin in the children's game of hopscotch or in the board game Snakes and Ladders. The commentators may have done no more than build on this use.

back to the drawing board! Meaning 'we've got to start again from scratch', this is usually said after an original plan has ended in failure. It is just possible that this began life in the caption to a cartoon by Peter Arno which appeared in the *New Yorker* during the early 1940s. An official, with a rolled-up engineering plan under his arm, is walking away from a recently-crashed plane, and saying: 'Well, back to the old drawing board.'

back to the jungle. A return to primitive conditions, nearly always used figuratively (like 'a return to the Dark Ages'). Winston Churchill, in a speech about post-Revolution Russia on 3 January 1920, referred to a recent visitor to that country: 'Colonel John Ward . . . has seen these things for many months with his own eyes . . . [and] has summed all up in one biting, blasting phrase – "Back to the jungle".'

back to the land! A slogan first heard at the end of the nineteenth century when it was realized that the Industrial Revolution and the transfer of the population towards non-agricultural work had starved farming of labour. *OED2*

cites *The Times* (25 October 1894): 'All present were interested in the common practice that it was desirable, if possible, to bring the people back to the land.' By 23 December 1905, the *Spectator* was saying: ' "Back-to-the-land" is a cry full not only of pathos, but of cogency.' In the 1980s, an ITV comedy series was called *Backs to the Land*, playing on the phrase to provide an innuendo about its heroines – 'Land Girls', members of the Women's Land Army conscripted to work on the land during the Second World War. (See also *DPP*.)

bacon. See BRING HOME THE ∼.

badger. See BALD AS A ∼.

bag. See GLADSTONE; LET THE CAT OUT OF THE ∼.

Baisers Volés [Stolen Kisses]. The title of a film (France, 1968) by François Truffaut is taken from a phrase in the song, '*Que Reste-t-il de Nos Amours*' (1943), written and performed by Charles Trenet (and which is featured in the film). This film title may suggest that fleeting moments of happiness are all that can be snatched. In English, there was a song 'A Stolen Kiss' (1923) by R. Penso; also a ballad, undated, by F. Buckley, 'Stolen Kisses are the Sweetest'.

baker's daughter. 'They say the owl was a baker's daughter' Ophelia says mystifyingly in Shakespeare's *Hamlet* (IV.v.43). The reference is to an old English legend about Christ going into a baker's shop and asking for something to eat. A piece of cake is put in the oven for Him, but the baker's daughter says it is too large and cuts it in half. The dough swells up to an enormous size, she exclaims 'Woo! Woo!' and is turned into an owl.

baker's dozen. In use by the sixteenth century, this phrase to denote the number thirteen may date from the medieval baker's habit of giving away an extra loaf with every twelve to avoid being fined for providing underweight produce. The surplus was known as 'inbread' and the thirteenth loaf, the 'vantage loaf'. A **devil's dozen** is also thirteen – the number of witches who would gather when summoned by the devil.

Baker's Wife, The. The title of the Stein/Schwartz musical (Los Angeles, 1976) based on Marcel Pagnol's film *La Femme du Boulanger* (France, 1938) about village infidelity. Also in France, Louis XVI had been known as 'The Baker' and thus his Queen, 'The Baker's Wife', because of their action in giving bread to starving Parisians at Versailles in October 1789.

bald. See FIGHT BETWEEN TWO ~ MEN . . .

bald as a badger/bandicoot/coot. A phrase used to mean 'completely bald'. The aquatic coot has the appearance of being bald. The Australian marsupial, the bandicoot, is not bald but presumably is evoked purely for alliteration and because the coot expression is being alluded to. As for badger, the full expression is 'bald as a badger's bum'. There was once a belief that bristles for shaving brushes were plucked from this area.

baldheaded, to go at something. Meaning 'to act without regard for the consequences, to go at something full tilt' – e.g. from J.R. Lowell, *The Biglow Papers* (1848):

> I scent what pays the best, an' then
> Go into it baldheaded.

This is an American expression, dating from the nineteenth century. The suggestion is that of a man tackling a problem as though he had just rushed out of the house without putting on his wig, or without wearing a hat.

Earlier sources have been suggested – notably that the Marquis of Granby, a colonel of the Blues, led a cavalry charge at the Battle of Warburg (1760) despite his hat and wig falling off. He was an enormously popular figure (hence the number of British pubs named after him), but it is unlikely that his fame was sufficient to have led to the expression being used in the US.

Baldock. The Hertfordshire town takes its name from the city of Baghdad which became the capital of Iraq. The Knights Templars who once held the local manor named it in honour of the Levantine city which was known as *Baldac* in Old French.

Balfour Declaration. See *DEAR LORD ROTHSCHILD.*

Balfour's poodle, Mr. A reference to the House of Lords. David Lloyd George spoke in the House of Commons on 26 June 1907 in the controversy over the power of the upper house. He questioned the Lords' role as a 'watchdog' of the constitution and suggested that A.J. Balfour, the Conservative leader, was using the party's majority in the upper chamber to block legislation by the Liberal government (in which Lloyd George was president of the Board of Trade). He said: '[The House of Lords] is the leal and trusty mastiff which is to watch over our interests, but which runs away at the first snarl of the trade unions. A mastiff? It is the Right Honourable Gentleman's poodle. It fetches and carries for him. It bites anybody that he sets it on to.'

ball(s). See COLD ENOUGH TO FREEZE THE ~; HITLER HAS ONLY GOT ONE ~

balloon's gone up, the. Current by 1924 and meaning 'the action or excitement has commenced, particularly in military activities', this expression derives from the barrage balloons introduced during the First World War to protect targets from air raids. The fact that these balloons – or observation ones – had 'gone up' would signal that some form of action was imminent.

banality of evil. 'The fearsome word-and-thought defying *banality of evil*' was how the German-born philosopher Hannah Arendt described her reaction to what emerged from the trial of Adolf Eichmann, the Nazi official, who was executed as a war criminal in 1962. Her book *Eichmann in Jerusalem* (1963) was sub-titled 'A Report on the Banality of Evil'.

bang. See BIG ~; NOT WITH A ~ . . .

bang goes/went sixpence! A lightly joking remark about one's own or another person's unwillingness to spend money. The origins of this lie in a *Punch* cartoon of 1868. A Scotsman who has just been on a visit to London says: 'Mun, a had na' been the-rre abune two hours when – bang – went saxpence!' The saying was repopularized by Sir Harry Lauder, the professional stage Scotsman.

bang to rights. As in 'You've got me bang to rights!' said by a criminal to an arresting policeman, this is an alternative to 'It's a fair cop!' [You are quite right to have caught me, constable!]. There is also an element of 'You've caught me red-handed'. Partridge/*Slang* dates this from the 1930s, but *OED2* finds a US

example in 1904. Compare the somewhat rare Americanism 'bang' for a criminal charge or arrest, as in 'It's a bum bang', perhaps having some connection with the banging of a cell door.

banjaxed. An Irishism used to mean 'banged about; smashed', introduced into popular British speech by the broadcaster Terry Wogan in the early 1970s. Possibly from Dublin slang of the 1920s. When he wrote a book called *Banjaxed* (1979), Wogan supplied this definition of 'to banjax': 'To hornswoggle, corpse, knacker, rasher, caramelize, malfooster, malavogue, powfagg, keelhaul, macerate, decimate, pulverize, make rawmeish of. Hence *banjaxed*, reduced to the condition of a pig's breakfast, and *banjaxing*, tearing a plaster from a hairy leg.'

bank. See CRY ALL THE WAY TO THE ~.

Barabbas. See NOW BARABBAS.

Barbara, St. See SAINTS' NAMES.

Barbarella. A sexy, blonde astronaut who made her debut as the heroine of a comic strip in the French *V* magazine in 1962, and who was celebrated in the French/Italian film *Barbarella* (1967) with Jane Fonda in the title role. Like the British 'Jane' during the Second World War, she was always falling out of her clothes.

Bard of Avon. One of several sobriquets for William SHAKESPEARE, alluding to the river running through his birthplace at Stratford in Warwickshire. 'Pen introduced [Shakespeare because he] professed an uncommon respect for the bard of Avon' said William Thackeray in *Pendennis* (Chap. 6, 1848–50). Ben Jonson called Shakespeare 'Sweet Swan of Avon' (in a verse prefacing the First Folio of plays, 1623) and David Garrick, who excelled in

Shakespearean parts at the Drury Lane Theatre, London, felt intimate enough to nickname him 'Avonian Willy'. **The Bard** on its own is also, unfortunately, common, though anything is better than the assumed familiarity, chiefly among actors, of 'Will' or 'Bill' Shakespeare.

bark. See DOGS ~ BUT THE CARA-VAN ...

bark up the wrong tree, to. This phrase meaning 'to follow a false scent' is of US origin (by 1832) and appears to come from racoon hunting. As this is done at night (racoons being nocturnal animals) and as, if chased, racoons run up trees, it would be quite possible for a dog to mistakenly bark under the wrong tree in the dark.

barnstorm, to. (1) (Of actors) to perform unsubtly. (2) (Of US politicians) to give speeches drumming up votes in rural areas.

The word originated in the US in the early nineteenth century when actors did indeed go bustling around the country-side performing in barns and similar informal venues. Their style was akin to that found in melodrama. On the other hand, perhaps it was more the make-shift, improvised nature of the touring which has led to the word being used about politicians who stump about seeking votes, although now the term has largely been superseded by WHISTLE-STOP tours.

baron. See RED ~.

barrel. See LOCK STOCK AND ~.

Basingstoke. In the Gilbert and Sullivan opera *Ruddigore* (1887), the character Mad Margaret says: 'When I am lying awake at night, and the pale moonlight streams through the latticed casement, strange fancies crowd upon my poor mad brain, and I sometimes think that if we could hit upon some word for you to use whenever I am about to relapse – some word that teems with hidden meaning – like "Bas-ingstoke" – it might recall me to my saner self.' Ian Bradley in his *Annotated Gilbert and Sullivan: 2* (1984) dismisses a suggestion that Basingstoke was chosen because it had a well-known mental hospital – on the grounds that this had not been built in 1887.

bats in the belfry, to have (*or* bats/ batty, to be). Meaning 'to be mentally deficient, harmlessly insane, or mad', these expressions convey the idea that a person behaves in a wildly disturbed manner. As for 'batty', in particular, attempts have been made to bring in William Battie (*d* 1776), author of a *Treatise on Madness*, but he was the psychiatrist and not the patient. On the other hand, there was one Fitzherbert Batty, a barrister of Spanish Town, Jamaica, who made news when he was certified insane in London in 1839. 'Batty' surely derived from 'bats in the belfry', but there do not seem to be any examples of either expression in use before 1900.

battle. See LOSE A ~ ...

Battle of Britain. The urge to give names to battles – even before they are fought and won – is well exemplified by Winston Churchill's coinage of 18 June 1940: 'What General Weygand called the Battle of France is over. I expect that the Battle of Britain is about to begin.' It duly became the name by which the decisive overthrowing of German invasion plans by the FEW is known. The order of the day, read aloud to every pilot on 10 July, contained the words: 'The Battle of Britain is about to begin. Members of the Royal Air Force, the fate of generations is in your hands.' Another Churchill coinage – 'The Battle of Egypt' (speech,

10 November 1942) – caught on less well.

Battle of Waterloo was won on the playing fields of Eton, the. This opinion was first ascribed to the 1st Duke of Wellington in Count Charles de Montalembert's *De L'Avenir Politique de l'Angleterre* (1856). The Frenchman stated that the Duke returned to Eton in his old age and, recalling the delights of his youth, exclaimed: 'It is here that the battle of Waterloo was won' (i.e. he made no mention of playing fields). Burnam 2 suggests that Sir Edward Creasy built on this in *Memoirs of Eminent Etonians* (though this was published in 1850), by describing the Iron Duke passing the playing fields in old age and saying: 'There grows the stuff that won Waterloo.' Then in 1889, a third writer, Sir William Fraser, in *Words on Wellington* put together Montalembert's remark with Creasy's playing fields to produce the popularly known version. The 7th Duke (*d* 1972) tried to pour cold water on the matter in letters to *The Times*: 'Wellington's career at Eton was short and inglorious and, unlike his elder brother, he had no particular affection for the place.' The nearest the 1st Duke came to any sort of compliment to the influence his old school had on him was: 'I really believe I owe my spirit of enterprise to the tricks I used to play in the garden' [of his Eton boarding-house] – quoted in Vol.1 of Elizabeth Longford's biography (1969).

battle royal, to wage a. Meaning 'to take part in a keenly-fought contest; a general free-for-all', this term originated in cockfighting, or at least has been specifically used in that sport. In the first round, sixteen birds would be put into a pit to fight each other, until only half the number was left. The knock-out competition would then continue until there was only one survivor. *O E D*2 finds the phrase in 1672, general use; 1860 for cockfighting.

batty. See BATS IN THE BELFRY.

BBC. See AUNTIE; INITIALS.

beans. See HOW MANY ~.

bear. See EXIT PURSUED BY A ~.

Beast of — . Used as a nickname formula. (1) The 'Beast of Belsen' was Josef Kramer, German commandant of the Belsen concentration camp during the worst period of its history from December 1944 to the end of the Second World War. He was executed for his crimes in 1945. (2) The 'Beast of Bolsover' is Dennis Skinner (*b* 1932), the aggressive and outspoken left-wing MP for Bolsover in Derbyshire (since 1970). Noted for interrupting speeches and making loud comments. (3) The 'Beast of Jersey' was E.J.L. (Ted) Paisnel, who was convicted of thirteen sex offences against children and sentenced to thirty years' imprisonment in 1971. The name was applied to him during the eleven years he evaded arrest on the island.

beat. See IF YOU CAN'T ~ 'EM . . .

beat a path to someone's door, to. 'If a man write a better book, preach a better sermon, or make a better mousetrap than his neighbour, 'tho he build his house in the woods, the world will make a beaten path to his door.' Sarah Yule claimed (1889) that she had heard Ralph Waldo Emerson say this in a lecture. Elbert Hubbard also claimed authorship. Either way, this is a remark alluded to when people talk of 'beating a path to someone's door' or a **better mousetrap**. In his journal for February 1855, Emerson had certainly entertained the thought: 'If a man . . . can make better chairs or knives . . . than anybody else, you will find a broad hard-beaten road to his house, though it be in the woods.'

Beat Generation. 'Beatniks' were young people who opted out of normal society in the 1950s (first of all in the U S) because they were unable or unwilling to conform to conventional standards. Careless of appearance, critical of the ESTABLISHMENT, they were less intellectual than the average ANGRY YOUNG MAN, but rebellious like Teddy Boys who preceded them (in the UK) and the Hippies who followed.

The name with its Yiddish or Russian suffix (compare the Russian sputnik satellite orbiting the earth in 1957) derived from the phrase 'Beat Generation' which was probably coined by Jack Kerouac, although in his book *The Origins of the Beat Generation*, he admitted to borrowing the phrase from a drug addict called Herbert Huncke. In Randy Nelson's *The Almanac of American Letters* (1981), there is a description of the moment of coinage. Kerouac is quoted as saying: 'John Clellon Holmes . . . and I were sitting around trying to think up the meaning of the LOST GENERATION and the subsequent existentialism and I said: "You know, this is really a beat generation" and he leapt up and said: "That's it, that's right".' Holmes himself attributed the phrase directly to Kerouac in the *New York Times* magazine of 16 November 1952.

beating. See WHEN DID YOU STOP ~ YOUR WIFE?

Beatle(s). See FIFTH ~; POP GROUP NAMES.

beautiful. See ALL THINGS BRIGHT AND ~.

beautiful people, the. Coinage of this term for glamorous, trendy people is credited in *Current Biography* (1978) to the US fashion journalist, Diana Vreeland (*d* 1989). Whether she deserves this or not is open to question (although she does seem to have helped launch the associated term SWINGING LONDON).

The earliest *OED2* citation with capital letters for each word is from 1966. The *OED2* makes it refer primarily to ' "flower people", hippies' though I would prefer the less narrow 'fashionable social set of wealthy, well-groomed, usually young people' (*Macquarie Dictionary*, 1981). The Lennon and McCartney song 'Baby You're a Rich Man' (released in July 1967) contains the line 'How does it feel to be one of the beautiful people?' William Saroyan's play *The Beautiful People* had been performed long before all this, in 1941, and Oscar Wilde in a letter to Harold Boulton (December 1879), wrote: 'I could have introduced you to some very beautiful people. Mrs Langtry and Lady Lonsdale and a lot of clever beings who were at tea with me.' Compare GETAWAY PEOPLE.

beaver! The cry identifying a man with a beard appears to have been common among children in the 1910s and 20s, though now redundant. But why *beaver*? Flexner notes the use of the animal's name to describe a high, sheared-fur hat in the US. The beaver's thick dark-brown fur, he says, also refers 'to a well-haired pudendum or a picture showing it, which in pornography is called a "beaver shot".' Beaver for beard may derive rather from the Middle Ages when the 'beaver' was the part of a soldier's helmet which lay around the chin as a face-guard (the 'visor' was the bit brought down from the forehead). In Shakespeare's *Hamlet* (I.ii.228), the Prince asks: 'Then saw you not his face?' (that of his father's ghost). Horatio replies: 'O yes, my lord, he wore his beaver up.'

because it is there. A flippant justification for doing anything and chiefly associated with the mountaineer, George Leigh Mallory, who disappeared on his last attempt to scale Mount Everest in 1924. The previous year, during a lecture tour in the US, he had frequently been asked why he wanted to achieve his goal. He replied: 'Because it is there.' The saying has become a catch phrase in situations where the speaker wishes to dismiss an impossible question about motives and also to express acceptance of a challenge that is in some way daunting or foolish. There have been many variations (and misattributions). Sir Edmund Hillary repeated it regarding his own successful attempt on Everest in 1953.

Becket, to do a Thomas à. This phrase is used to suggest a course of action in a general way, which is then interpreted more positively by others than might have been the speaker's intention. King Henry II's rhetorical question regarding Thomas à Becket, 'Will no man rid me of this turbulent priest?' (which was acted upon by the Archbishop's murderers in 1170) is ascribed to 'Oral tradition' by O D Q in the form: 'Will no one revenge me of the injuries I have sustained from one turbulent priest?' The young king, who was in Normandy, had received reports that the Archbishop was ready 'to tear the crown from' his head. 'What a pack of fools and cowards I have nourished in my house,' he cried, according to another version, 'that not one of them will avenge me of this turbulent priest!' Yet another version has, 'of this upstart clerk'.

An example of the phrase used allusively in conversation was played at the conspiracy-to-murder trial involving Jeremy Thorpe M P in 1979. In a tape-recording, Andrew Newton, speaking of the alleged plot, said: 'They feel a Thomas à Becket was done, you know, with Thorpe sort of raving, "Would nobody rid me of this man?".'

beef. See WHERE'S THE ∼?

Bee Gees, The. The name of a British pop group, popular in the 1960s and 70s, derived from 'the BGs' – 'the Brothers Gibb' – which they were.

beeline. See MAKE A ∼ FOR.

bee's knees, to be the. Used to mean 'the very best around; absolutely top hole'. There has always been a fascination with bees' knees. In the eighteenth century there was the expression, 'as big as a bee's knee' and, in the nineteenth, 'as weak as a bee's knee'. But the bee whose knees became celebrated in US slang by 1923 was probably only there because of the rhyme. At about the same time, we find 'the kipper's knickers', 'the cat's whiskers' (perhaps because of the importance of these in tuning wireless crystal sets in the 1920s), 'the cat's pyjamas' (still new enough to be daring), 'the cat's miaow / eyebrows / ankles / tonsils / adenoids / galoshes / cufflinks/roller skates'. Not to mention 'the snake's hips', 'the clam's garter', 'the eel's ankle', 'the elephant's instep', 'the tiger's spots', 'the flea's eyebrows', 'the canary's tusks', 'the leopard's stripes', 'the sardine's whiskers', 'the pig's wings' – 'and just about any combination of animal, fish, or fowl with a part of the body or clothing that was inappropriate for it' (Flexner).

before/as quick as one can say 'Jack Robinson'. This expression meaning 'immediately; straight away', appears to have been employed by Richard Brinsley Sheridan in the House of Commons (some time after 1780) to avoid using a fellow member's name (as was, and is partly still, the custom). Having made a derogatory reference to the Secretary to the Treasury, John Robinson, and been asked by members shouting: 'Name, name!' to disclose the person he was referring to, Sheridan said: 'You know I cannot name him, but I could as soon as I can say Jack Robinson.' Clearly, Sheridan was alluding to an already established expression.

Neil Ewart in *Everyday Phrases* (1983) cites the theory that it 'refers to an erratic [eighteenth-century] gentleman of that name who rushed around to visit his neighbours, rang the front-door bell, and then changed his mind and dashed off before the servant had time to announce his name'. Eric Partridge in his *Name Into Word* (1949) suggests it was a made-up name using very common first and last elements. Fanny Burney has 'I'll do it as soon as say Jack Robinson' in her novel *Evelina* (1778), so that pushes back the date somewhat. A promising explanation is that the phrase may have something to do with Sir John Robinson who was Officer Commanding the Tower of London from 1660–79. In that case, the original reference might have been to the speed of beheading with an axe. (See also *D P P*.)

Beginning. The title of the youthful autobiography (1989) by the actor Kenneth Branagh might not appear to be a quotation at first glance, but it is, and is suitably modest. From Shakespeare's *As You Like It*: 'I will tell you the beginning, and if it please your ladyships, you may see the end, for the best is yet to do' (I.ii.104).

beginning of the end, not the. In a speech on the progress of the war on 10 November 1942, Winston Churchill said: 'Now this [success in the Battle of Egypt] is not the end. It is not even the beginning of the end. But it is, perhaps, the end of the beginning.'

behind. See GET THEE ~ ME SATAN.

behind every — man stands a — woman. A much-used format: 'Behind every successful man you'll find a woman who has nothing to wear' (James Stewart or L. Grant Glickman); 'We in the industry know that behind every successful screenwriter stands a woman. And behind her stands his wife' (Groucho Marx); 'As usual there's a great woman behind every idiot' (John Lennon); 'Behind every successful man stands a surprised mother-in-law' (Hubert Humphrey, 1964); 'Behind every successful man there stands an amazed woman' (Anon., by 1977); 'Behind every good man is a good woman – I mean an exhausted one' (Duchess of York, 1987). What all these quips allude to is an untraced core saying, almost proverbial, to the effect that 'Behind every good/successful man there stands a woman'.

Behold a Pale Horse. The title given to a film (UK, 1964) about a survivor from the Spanish Civil War. As with the 1939 novel *Pale Horse, Pale Rider* by Katherine Anne Porter and the 1961 Agatha CHRISTIE novel *Pale Horse*, the allusion is to Revelation 6:8: 'And I looked, and behold a pale horse: and his name that sat on him was death'. Oddly, the 1964 film was based on Emeric Pressburger's rather differently titled novel *Killing a Mouse on Sunday*.

'Being for the Benefit of Mr Kite'. The title of a track on the Beatles' *Sgt Pepper* album (1967), from a standard nineteenth-century phrase used in advertising 'testimonial' performances. The title of Chapter 48 of *Nicholas Nickleby* (1838–9) by Charles Dickens is: 'Being for the benefit of Mr Vincent Crummles, and Positively his last Appearance on this Stage'. As for the lyrics, largely written by John Lennon though credited jointly to him and Paul McCartney, they derive almost word for word, as Lennon acknowledged, from the wording of a Victorian circus poster he bought in an antique shop. Or that was the story until Derek Taylor revealed in *It Was Twenty Years Ago Today* (1987) that the poster was 'liberated' from a café during filming of promotional clips for the 'Penny Lane/Strawberry Fields Forever' record. Headed 'Pablo Fanque's Circus Royal' in the Town Meadows, Rochdale, the poster announces:

> Grandest Night of the Season!
> And Positively the
> Last Night But Three!
> Being for the Benefit of Mr. Kite,
> (late of Wells's Circus) and
> Mr. J. Henderson,
> the Celebrated Somerset Thrower!
> Wire Dancer, Vaulter, Rider, &c.
> On Tuesday Evening,
> February 14th, 1843.

['Somerset' is an old word for somersault.]

belfry. See BATS IN THE ~.

believe it or not! This exclamation was used as the title of a long-running syndicated newspaper feature, and radio and TV series, in the US. Robert Leroy Ripley (1893–1949) created and illustrated a comic strip, *Ripley's Believe It or Not* (c 1923), but citations before this are lacking.

Belisha beacon. An orange glass globe atop a pole which is painted in black and white bands and situated on both sides of a pedestrian crossing as a warning to motorists, the beacon was introduced in 1934 when Leslie Hore-Belisha (created Baron, 1954) was Minister of Transport. On 27 January 1935, Chips Channon noted in his diary: 'Belisha Beacons, unheard of a few weeks ago, are now

world famous', and on 31 January: 'He is the most advertised man in England today.'

Bell Book and Candle. The title of John Van Druten's play (1950; film US, 1958) about a publisher who discovers his girlfriend is a witch. It refers to a solemn form of excommunication from the Roman Catholic Church. Bartlett says the ceremony has been current since the eighth century AD. There is a version dating from 1200 AD which goes: 'Do to the book [meaning close it], quench the candle, ring the bell'. These actions symbolize the spiritual darkness the person is condemned to when denied further participation in the sacraments of the Church. Sir Thomas Malory in *Le Morte d'Arthur* (1485) has: 'I shall curse you with book and bell and candle.' Shakespeare has the modern configuration in *King John* (III.ii.22): 'Bell, book and candle shall not drive me back.'

Bellerophon. See GREEK NAMES.

Bellman and True. The title of a film (UK 1988) based on a novel by Desmond Lowden. It alludes to the hunting song 'D'ye Ken John Peel' where in the list of hounds there are the names Ruby, Ranter, Ringwood, Bellman, and True. The book and the film are about a 'bellman' in the criminal sense: the man who interferes with alarm systems so that robberies can take place.

belt and braces. The name applied to a system with its own back-up, suggesting that if one falls down, the other may stay up. An engineer's expression, used for example by a BBC sound engineer to describe the two microphones placed side-by-side when broadcasting the sovereign's Christmas message. In the days when this was broadcast live, it ensured transmission. Belt and Braces was also the name of a British theatre group of the 1970s.

Be My Guest. The title of a book (1957) by the hotelier, Conrad Hilton. What is not obvious is when the phrase originated. *American Speech* in 1955 had 'be my guest' as a way of saying 'go right ahead; do as you wish', and Hilton hotels may also have used 'be my guest' as a slogan at some time.

Ben. See BIG ~.

Bendor. The nickname for the 2nd Duke of Westminster (*d* 1953), commemorating a defeat in heraldic law for his ancestor, Sir Robert Grosvenor, over the coat of arms he could bear. In 1389 the Court of Chivalry ruled in favour of Sir Richard le Scrope in his action over the right to arms 'Azure, a bend or' [a blue shield with a diagonal gold bar]. Grosvenor refused to accept this and appealed to Richard II. The monarch also ruled against him and Grosvenor was forced to bear the costs of the action. He ended up using 'Azure, a garb or' [a blue shield with a golden sheaf of corn].

Robert Lacey in *Aristocrats* (1983) suggests, however, that the nicknaming was not direct and that the 2nd Duke was called after the colt that won the Derby for his grandfather, Hugh Lupus, in 1880. 'According to family legend, some similarity of colour was discerned between the chestnutty animal and the reddish fluff on the head of the baby born within a few months of the horse's first successes on the turf.'

benedictus. See MASS PHRASES.

benefit. See BEING FOR THE ~ OF MR KITE.

Bennies. The inhabitants of the Falkland Islands were so named by British forces stationed there following the 1982 conflict with Argentina. The uncomplimentary reference is to a not-very-bright character in the ITV soap opera *Crossroads*. When reprimanded for the coinage, troops resorted to calling the islanders 'Stills' (for 'Still Bennies'). An even later variant by sections of the occupying forces for some of the islanders, was 'Bubs' [Bloody Ungrateful Bastards]. The islanders responded by calling the soldiers 'Whennies' – from their constant references to past exploits: 'When I was in Belize, when I was in Cyprus . . .'

be prepared. The motto of the Boy Scout movement (founded 1908), which shares its initials with the movement's founder, Sir Robert Baden-Powell. With permission, the words were subsequently used as an advertising slogan for Pears' soap.

berk. Morris cites Dudley Moore as saying of Peter Cook (in a magazine interview): 'It is hard to distinguish sometimes whether Peter is being playful or merely a berk.' Morris then goes on, coyly, to say '*berk* is British slang – originally a bit of Cockney rhyming slang – meaning "fool" ' – and leaves it at that. In fact, 'berk' is short for 'Berkeley/Berkshire Hunt' ('cunt'). Spelling the word 'birk' or 'burk(e)' helps obscure the origin. Theoretically, if it comes from this source, the word should be pronounced 'bark'. The use probably does not date from before 1900.

Berkeley Square. See NIGHTINGALE SANG IN ~.

Berliner. See ICH BIN EIN ~.

Bernadette, St. See SAINTS' NAMES.

Bernard of Menthon, St. See SAINTS' NAMES.

Bertha. See BIG ~.

Bertie. See BURLINGTON ~.

best, why not the. See under JIMMY WHO?

best foot forward, to put one's. Meaning 'to walk as fast as possible; to make a good impression', this probably derives from an earlier form: 'to put one's best foot/leg foremost'. In Shakespeare's *King John* we find: 'Nay, but make haste; the better foot before' (IV.ii.170). The *right* foot has from ancient times been regarded as the best foot, right being associated with rationality, the left with emotion. To put your right foot forward is thus to guard against ill-luck.

best of order. See GIVE ORDER.

best Prime Minister we have (*or* never had). R.A. (later Lord) Butler (*d* 1982) has sometimes been known as 'the best Prime Minister we never had' (as have others, like Denis Healey, for example), and it is to Butler we probably owe both formats. In December 1955, having (not for the last time) been passed over for the Conservative leadership, he was confronted by a Press Association reporter just as he was about to board an aircraft at London airport. As criticism was growing over the performance of Anthony Eden, the Prime Minister, the reporter asked: 'Mr Butler, would you say that this [Eden] is the best Prime Minister we have?' Butler assented to this 'well-meant but meaningless proposition . . . indeed it was fathered upon me. I don't think it did Anthony any good. It did not do me any good either' (*The Art of the Possible*, 1973).

best-regulated. See ACCIDENTS WILL OCCUR . . .

best thing. See GREATEST THING SINCE . . .

better. See EVERY DAY AND IN EVERY WAY . . .; IT IS A FAR FAR ~ THING . . .

better mousetrap, a. See BEAT A PATH TO ONE'S DOOR, TO.

better red than dead. A slogan used by some (mainly British) nuclear disarmers. Bertrand Russell wrote in 1958: 'If no alternative remains except communist domination or the extinction of the human race, the former alternative is the lesser of two evils.' The counter cry: 'Better dead than red' may also have had some currency. (In the film *Love With a Proper Stranger* (US, 1964) Steve McQueen proposed to Natalie Wood with a picket sign stating 'Better Wed Than Dead'.)

Betty Martin. See ALL MY EYE AND ~.

Beulah – peel me a grape! A catch phrase expressing dismissive unconcern, which was first uttered by Mae West to a black maid in the film *I'm No Angel* (1933) after a male admirer had stormed out on her. It has had some wider currency since then but is nearly always used as a quotation.

Beyond the Fringe. The title of a revue presented in the West End in 1961 and then on Broadway. It had first been shown, however, at the 1960 Edinburgh Festival as part of the main programme of events, and had thus been 'beyond' the unofficial series of theatrical manifestations at Edinburgh known as the 'Fringe'. Note also an allusion to BEYOND THE PALE.

Beyond the Mexique Bay. The title of a travel book (1934) by Aldous HUXLEY. From Andrew Marvell's 'Bermudas':

O let our voice his praise exalt,
Till it arrive at Heaven's vault:

Which thence (perhaps) rebounding,
    may
Echo beyond the Mexique Bay.

beyond the pale. Meaning, 'outside the bounds of acceptable behaviour'. The Pale was the area of English settlement around Dublin in Ireland, dating from the fourteenth century, in which English law had to be obeyed, but there have also been areas known as pales in Scotland, around Calais, and in Russia. The derivation is from Latin *palus*, meaning 'a stake'. Anyone who lived beyond this fence was thought to be beyond the bounds of civilization. The allusive use does not appear to date from earlier than the nineteenth century.

Bible. See ENGLISH HAD THE LAND . . .

Bic. See FLICK YOUR ~.

b/Big. See BOOTS, TO BE TOO ~ FOR ONE'S; MR ~.

Big Apple, the. As a nickname for New York City, this expression seems to have arisen in the 1930s. There are various possible explanations: the Spanish word for a block of houses between two streets is *manzana* which is also the word for apple; in the mid-1930s there was a Harlem night club called 'The Big Apple', a mecca for jazz musicians; there was also a jitterbugging dance from the swing era (*c* 1936) which took its name from the nightclub; 'big apple' was racetrack argot and New York City had a good reputation in this field. *O E D2* has 'Big Apple' for New York City in 1928 *before* the dance explanation, but Safire plumps for the jazz version, recalling a 1944 jive 'handbook' defining 'apple' as: 'the earth, the universe, this planet. Any place that's large. A big Northern city.' Hence, you called New York City the Big Apple if you considered it to be the centre of the universe. (In the eighteenth century, Horace Walpole had called London 'The Strawberry' because of its freshness and cleanliness in comparison with foreign cities.)

Big Bang, the. The so-called 'Big Bang' theory of the beginning of the universe was being discussed during 1950 by Fred Hoyle in his book *The Nature of the Universe*. But, on 27 October 1986, the London Stock Exchange deregulated the British securities market, to which this light-hearted appellation was applied by those hoping for a 'boom' and fearing a 'bust' (which duly followed a year later). The system of fixed commissions on stock trading was eliminated in favour of negotiated rates. At the same time, the practice of separating brokers (who take orders and execute trades on behalf of investors) from jobbers (who buy and sell stock on their own account in order to make a market in that stock) was abolished. The previous March, banks and brokerages, domestic and foreign, were allowed to become members of the exchange in a move dubbed 'Little Bang'.

Big Ben. Although used to refer to the whole of the clock tower of the Houses of Parliament, London, the nickname is more correctly applied to just the bell. Weighing thirteen and a half tons, it was named after Sir Benjamin Hall, Commissioner of Works when it was hung in 1856.

Big Bertha. A soldiers' nickname for a German long-range gun in the First World War. It was used to shell Paris in 1918. Bertha, the only child of Friedrich Alfred Krupp, who had inherited the great engineering and armaments undertaking, married in 1906 and her husband became head of the firm.

Big Brother is watching you. This fictional slogan comes from George

37

Orwell's novel *Nineteen Eighty-Four* (1948). In a dictatorial state, every citizen is regimented and observed by a spying TV set in the home. The line became a popular catch phrase following the sensational BBC TV dramatization of the novel (1954). Aspects of the Ministry of Truth in the novel were derived not only from Orwell's knowledge of the BBC (where he worked) but also from his first wife Eileen's work at the Ministry of Food, preparing 'Kitchen Front' broadcasts during the Second World War (*c* 1942–4). One campaign used the slogan 'Potatoes Are Good for You' and was so successful that it had to be followed by 'Potatoes Are Fattening'.

big butter and egg man. As a description of small-town businessman trying to prove himself a big shot in the city, the phrase was much used by Texas Guinan, the US nightclub hostess (*d* 1933). Cyril Connolly in his *Journals* (1983) characterized the man in question as a small-town success, often a farmer who produced such commodities, and who attempts to pass for a sophisticate in the big city. Finding it first in the 1920s, *OED2* emphasizes that the man in question – 'wealthy, unsophisticated' – spends his money freely.

Big Chill generation, the. Alluding to those who grew up in the 1960s, and taken from the title of a film *The Big Chill* (US, 1983) 'the story of eight old friends searching for something they lost, and finding that all they needed was each other' (Halliwell).

big one, the. This boast, beloved – in particular – of a certain type of advertiser, almost certainly dates back to 1907 when Ringling Brothers Circus bought up its rival, Barnum and Bailey. The two together were understandably billed as 'The Big One'. When the circus closed in 1956, the *New York Post* had the headline, 'THE BIG ONE IS NO MORE!' *DOAS* points out that a 'big one' is also a thousand dollar bill (from gambling) and a nursery euphemism for a bowel movement. Partridge/*Slang* has 'big one' or 'big 'un' for 'a notable person' and dates it to 1800–50.

Big Sleep, The. The title of a novel (1939; films US, 1946 and 1977) by Raymond Chandler and a synonym for death.

bike. See ON YOUR ~.

bikini. Bikini was originally the name of an atoll in the Pacific Marshall Islands. In July 1946 it was chosen as the site for US atomic bomb tests and the following summer, in France, the word 'bikini' was taken to apply to the skimpy two-piece women's bathing costume which had become all the rage. An unlikely pairing, but it is a word with an interesting sound and, just possibly, Louis Réard, the French motor engineer who designed the garment, was not too worried when what *he* called *le minimum* was replaced by a name which expressed the explosive effect of the new fashion. According to the *Guardian* (20 December 1988), Mrs Annie Castel, who took over the Réard company, thought that not only had Mr Réard himself re-christened the garment but he had been thinking of the minute size of Bikini atoll rather than its explosive connotations.

Bill. See BUFFALO ~; BUNGALOW ~; OLD ~.

billion/trillion. Britons and Americans use these words differently. So:

1 billion (US) = a thousand millions
1 billion (UK) = a million millions
1 trillion (US) = a million millions
1 trillion (UK) = a billion millions.

In other words, the British amounts are *bigger* in each case, though the US values are beginning to predominate.

bimbo. In 1987–8, there was an explosion in the use of this word in the British press to describe a type of empty-headed but sexually attractive young woman. In fact, coinciding as it did with another explosion in the use of the verb BONK, the world seemed suddenly full of allusions to 'bonking bimbos'.

In Italian, like *bambino*, *bimbo* is the word for a baby or infant. From this, probably, we get the US slang use of the word for a foolish man ('poor bimbo') or whores ('blonde bimbos'). *OED2* finds both these senses current around 1920. There was also a song in 1954 by Rodney Morris which went: 'Bimbo, Bimbo, does your Mummy knowio/ You're going down the road to see a little girlio'.

The resurgence in the use of the term occurred in 1987 when US girls Donna Rice and Jessica Hahn, who had had much-publicized flings with a presidential candidate and TV evangelist respectively, both felt it necessary to declare that they were not 'bimbos in bathing-suits'. By this time, the roots of the word, whatever they might be, had long been obscured. Simon Carr in the *Independent* (23 July 1988) mused that the word was right because it had a 'certain pneumatic promise . . . a pleasant combination of bulge and bubble-headedness'.

Bingo. In 1919, at a carnival near Jacksonville, Florida, Edwin Lowe saw people playing what they called 'beano' – putting beans on a numbered card. This game of chance was already established elsewhere under the names 'Keno', 'Loo', and 'Housey-Housey'. Lowe developed the idea and launched a craze which netted him a fortune. One of his friends stuttered, 'B . . . b . . . bingo!' on winning, and that is how the game is said to have got its name. The word had already been applied to brandy in the seventeenth century, but – as a result of this development from 'bean-o' – it turned not only into an exclamation on

winning Lowe's game but also into a generalized exclamation on achieving anything, like 'Eureka'.

Binkie. For many years in British theatrical circles, this nickname meant only Hugh Beaumont, managing director of H.M. Tennent, the play production company. He was the most influential force in West End theatre from the 1940s to the 70s, and was always known thus within the profession, as he disliked his given name. There is an echo of 'Dandie Dinmont', the terrier named after a character in one of Sir Walter Scott's novels, but according to Richard Huggett's biography (1989), he became 'Binkie' as a baby when two women from the seamy side of Cardiff gazed into his pram and said: 'Oh, he's a proper little binkie, isn't he?' The word was local slang for black, Negro, dirty or unwashed, and the remark was heavy with sarcasm, because the baby was never anything but blonde, pink and immaculate.

Birch. See JOHN ~ SOCIETY.

bird, to get the. Originally the expression was 'to get the big bird'. Used as such since the nineteenth century, it means 'to be rejected by an audience'. What do audiences do when they do not like something? They boo or they hiss, sounding something like a flock of geese, perhaps.

birds. See STRICTLY FOR THE ~.

Birds Eye. It may come as a surprise to consumers of the frozen foods sold under this brand name that the allusion is to one Clarence Birdseye (*d* 1956). An American, he thought up the freezing process while fur-trapping in Labrador. In 1923, he launched Birdseye Seafoods

Inc in New York. Eventually the company was absorbed by General Foods Corporation. The two-word form of the name may be appropriate as family tradition holds that it was given to an English ancestor, a royal page at court, who once shot a hawk through the eye.

Birds of the Air, The. The title of a novel (1980) by Alice Thomas Ellis. This is essentially a biblical phrase: e.g. Matthew 8:20 ('the foxes have holes, and the birds of the air have nests'). However, it makes a later notable appearance in the rhyme 'Who Killed Cock Robin?' (first recorded in the eighteenth century): 'All the birds of the air/Fell a-sighing and a-sobbing,/When they heard the bell toll/For poor Cock Robin.'

A variant is 'fowl(s) of the air' (Genesis 1:26), though much more commonly one finds 'fowls of the heavens' in (mostly) the Old Testament. The 'fish(es) of the sea' occurs at least three times in the Old Testament (e.g. Genesis 1:26). 'All the beasts of the forest' is biblical too (Psalms 104:20), though more frequent is 'beasts of the field' (e.g. Psalms 8:7).

biro. There was actually a Mr Biro – László Biró (*d* 1985), a Hungarian by birth, who settled in Argentina before the Second World War. In 1943, he patented the capillary attraction system – a method of writing with quick-drying ink, using a ballpoint rather than a conventional nib, which is the basis of all ballpoint pens today. The success of the pen was helped by its being offered to US and UK forces in the Second World War. It would not leak at high altitudes and could even be used to write under water. The word 'biro' – which is also a brand name – is now often applied indiscriminately to all types of ballpoint and is pronounced to rhyme with 'giro' rather than the original 'hero'.

bishop. See AS THE ~ SAID TO THE ACTRESS.

bites. See IF A DOG ~ A MAN . . .

bitter end. Meaning 'the last extremity; the absolute limit', bitterness doesn't really enter into it. The nautical 'bitt' is a bollard on the deck of a ship on to which cables and ropes are wound. The end of the cable that is wrapped round or otherwise secured to the bollard is the 'bitter end'. On the other hand, ends have – for possibly longer – been described as bitter in other senses. Proverbs 5:4 has: 'But her end is bitter as wormwood, sharp as a two-edged sword'.

black. See ANY COLOUR SO LONG AS IT'S ~; ~ BOMBER under BROWN BOMBER; LITTLE ~ DRESS; YOUNG GIFTED AND ~.

Black and Tans. These were members of a special armed force (made up of ex-servicemen) sent to Ireland in 1920 by the British government. Their purpose was to put down Republican rebels which they attempted to do with much bloodshed. The name was derived from the colour of their mixed uniforms – army khaki combined with the black belts and dark green caps of the Royal Irish Constabulary – but also from the name of a pack of hounds in County Tipperary. Earlier, during the Reconstruction period after the American Civil War, the name had been given to Republicans unwilling to abandon the Negro as a basis of the party's power in Alabama; also to a type of terrier dog and to a drink of porter and ale.

black as Newgate knocker, as. This comparison meaning 'extremely black' alludes to Newgate gaol, the notorious prison for the City of London until 1880. It must have had a very formidable and notable knocker because not only do we have this expression but a

'Newgate knocker' was the name given to a lock of hair twisted to look like a knocker.

Blackboard Jungle, The. The title of a novel (1954; film US, 1955) by Evan Hunter. It is one of several phrases which suggest that there are urban areas where the 'law of the jungle' may apply – in this case, the educational system. Earlier, there had been W.R. Burnett's novel *The Asphalt Jungle* (1949), though *O E D2* finds that phrase in use in 1920. A little after, in 1969, come references to 'the concrete jungle'.

black box. After a plane crash there is usually a scramble to retrieve the aircraft's 'black box' – or, more properly, its 'Flight Data Recorder'. This contains detailed recordings of the aircraft's performance prior to the crash amd can be of value in determining what went wrong. The name has been used since the Second World War. Originally it was R A F slang for a box containing intricate navigational equipment. Flight recorders are in fact *orange* so as to be more easily seen. The popular name arose probably because black is a more mysterious colour, appropriate for a box containing 'secret' equipment – (Pye produced a record player with the name in the 1950s) – and because of the alliteration.

black-coated workers. Referring to prunes as laxatives, this term, of earlier origin, was popularized from 1941 onwards in an early-morning BBC programme *The Kitchen Front* by the 'Radio Doctor', Charles (later Lord) Hill, who noted in his autobiography *Both Sides of the Hill* (1964): 'I remember calling on the Principal Medical Officer of the Board of Education . . . At the end of the interview this shy and solemn man diffidently suggested that the prune was a black-coated worker and that this phrase might be useful to me. It was.' Earlier, Chips Channon (8 April 1937) was using the phrase in a literal sense when he wrote: 'The subject was "Widows and Orphans" the Old Age Pensions Bill, a measure which affects Southend and its black-coated workers.' (*Chips: The Diaries of Sir Henry Channon*, ed. Robert Rhodes James, 1967)

black dog. Used notably by Winston Churchill to describe the fits of depression to which he was sometimes subjected, this is an old phrase. It was known by the early nineteenth century, as in the country/nursery saying about a sullen child: 'The black dog is on his back'. Brewer has the alternative, 'a black dog has walked over him'. The reference here is to the devil, as in J.B. Priestley's *The Good Companions* (1929): 'He [Jess Oakroyd] was troubled by a vague foreboding. It was just as if a demoniac black dog went trotting everywhere at his heels.'

Black Friday. Originally this was a description of Good Friday, when clergymen wore dark vestments. However, there have been any number of specific 'Black Fridays', so designated. In Britain, on one such day (15 April 1921), certain trade unions withdrew support from the hard-pressed miners, a general strike was cancelled, and this is recalled in the Labour movement as a day of betrayal. In the US, the 'first' Black Friday was on 24 September 1929 when panic broke out on the stock market. During the Wall Street crash there were similarly a **Black Wednesday**, a **Black Thursday** – the actual day of the crash – and a **Black Tuesday**. In 1988, on stock markets round the world, there was a **Black Monday** (October 19) and another Black Thursday (October 22).

black hole. A term in astronomy for what is left when a star collapses gravitationally, thus leaving a field from which neither matter nor radiation can escape.

The term was in use by 1968, and is sometimes used figuratively to describe the place into which a person is presumed to have disappeared.

Black Hole of Calcutta. In 1756, 146 Europeans were condemned by the Nawab of Bengal to spend a night in the 'Black-Hole' prison of Fort William, Calcutta, after it had been captured. Only 23, including the one woman, survived till morning. Subsequently the phrase has been applied to any place of confinement or any airless, dark place. From Francis Kilvert's diary entry for 27 October 1874 (about a Church Missionary Society meeting): 'The weather was close, warm and muggy, the room crowded to suffocation and frightfully hot, like the Black Hole of Calcutta, though the doors and all the windows were wide open.' (*Kilvert's Diary*, Vols.1–3, ed. William Plomer, 1961)

black is beautiful. Revd Dr Martin Luther King Jr launched a poster campaign based on this slogan in 1967 but Stokely Carmichael had used the phrase at a Memphis civil rights rally in 1966. It may have its origins in the Song of Solomon 1:5: 'I am black, but comely.'

Black Maria. A US explanation for this name used for a police van is that a brawny Negress called Maria Lee kept a lodging house in Boston and helped bundle arrested people into the police van. The term was known in the US by 1847 and in the UK by 1869.

Black Power. A slogan encompassing just about anything that people want it to mean, from simple pride in the black race to a threat of violence. Adam Clayton Powell Jr, the Harlem congressman, said in a baccalaureate address at Howard University in May 1966: 'To demand these God-given rights is to seek black power – what I call audacious power – the power to build black institutions of splendid achievement.' On 6 June the same year, James Meredith, the first Black to integrate the University of Mississippi (in 1962), was shot and wounded during a civil rights march. Stokely Carmichael, heading the Student Non-violent Coordinating Committee, continued the march, during which his contingent first used the phrase as a shout. Carmichael used it in a speech at Greenwood, Mississippi, the same month. It was also adopted as a slogan by the Congress for Racial Equality. However, the notion was not new in the 1960s. Langston Hughes had written in *Simple Takes a Wife* (1953): 'Negro blood is so powerful – because just *one* drop of black blood makes a coloured man – *one* drop – you are a Negro! . . . Black is powerful.'

Black September. The name of a Palestinian terrorist group, established after the P L O's eviction from its strongholds in Jordan in September 1970. The name was known by the autumn of 1972.

black velvet. A drink made up of equal parts champagne and stout (especially Guinness) and which derives from its appearance and taste. Also used to describe the sexual attributes of a black woman, according to Partridge/*Slang*. Compare BLUE VELVET; LITTLE GENTLEMAN IN ~.

Blade on the Feather. The title of a T V play (1980) by Dennis Potter, whose main character was an Old Etonian author and spy. Taken from the 'Eton Boating Song' by William Cory Johnston:

> Jolly boating weather,
> And a hay-harvest breeze,
> Blade on the feather,
> Shade off the trees;
> Swing, swing together,

With your bodies between your knees.

'On the feather' is a rowing term for when the oar's blade is returned horizontally at the end of a stroke, and out of the water.

blah-blah-blah. 'Blah' or 'blah-blah', signifying 'empty talk; airy mouthings', are phrases that have been around (originally in the US) since the end of the First World War. More recently the tripartite version has become marginally more frequent to denote words omitted or as another way of saying 'and so on'. Ira and George Gershwin wrote a song called 'Blah, Blah, Blah' for a film called *Delicious* (1931) which contains such lines as 'Blah, blah, blah, blah moon . . . Blah, blah, blah, blah croon'.

Other examples of the phrase's use are as follows: '*Burt* [a journalist]: 'You wouldn't object to that angle for the piece? Here's what he says: The Family bla-bla-bla, here's how he lives . . .' (Peter Nichols, *Chez Nous*, 1974); 'Saul Kelner, 19, . . . was the first person in line to see the president. He arrived at the White House . . . $11^1/_2$ hours before the open house was to begin. "We didn't sleep," he said. "What we did, we circulated a list to ensure our places on line. 'WE THE PEOPLE, blah, blah, blah,' and we all signed it" ' (*Washington Post*, 22 January 1989); 'Bush referred to the diplomatic language [after a NATO summit conference in Bonn] in casual slang as "blah, blah" ' (*Washington Post*, 31 May 1989). The latter caused foreign journalists problems: 'After all, how do you translate "blah, blah" into Italian?'

blarney. Kissing the Blarney Stone at Blarney Castle near Cork in Ireland is supposed to bestow the gift of the gab on the kisser, but the custom is of relatively recent origin, having not been mentioned in print until the late eighteenth century. The word 'blarney' seems, however, to have entered the language a little while

before. The origin traditionally given is that in 1602, during the reign of Queen Elizabeth I, one Cormac Macarthy or Dermot McCarthy was required to surrender the castle as proof of his loyalty. He prevaricated and came up with so many excuses that (it is said) the Queen herself exclaimed: 'Odds bodikins, more Blarney talk'.

blessing in disguise. Meaning 'a misfortune which turns out to be beneficial', this phrase has been in existence since the early eighteenth century. A perfect example is provided by the noted exchange between Winston Churchill and his wife, Clementine. She attempted to console him after his defeat in the 1945 General Election, saying: 'It may well be a blessing in disguise.' To which he replied: 'At the moment, it seems quite effectively disguised.' Despite this comment, Churchill seems to have come round to something like his wife's point of view. On 5 September 1945, he wrote to her from an Italian holiday: 'This is the first time for very many years that I have been completely out of the world . . . Others having to face the hideous problems of the aftermath . . . It may all indeed be "a blessing in disguise".'

blimp. When used to describe a type of stupid, reactionary, elderly gentleman this name derives from the cartoon character 'Colonel Blimp', created between the wars by David Low, and who reached a kind of apotheosis in the film *The Life and Death of Colonel Blimp* (1943). The character, in turn, took his name from an experimental airship/balloon developed during the First World War. Without frames, these were described as 'limp'. There was an 'A-limp' and a 'B-limp'. The aviator Horace Short may have been the man who dubbed them 'blimps'.

Another suggestion is that the name is onomatopoeic. In 1915, a Lt Cunningham of the Royal Navy Air service is said to have flicked his thumb against the surface of one of the airships and imitated the odd noise thus produced. Alternatively, J.R.R. Tolkien, writing in 1926, hazarded a guess that the name derived from a mixture of 'blister' and 'lump', both of which the balloons resembled.

blind, in the country of the '. . . the one-eyed man is king'. A phrase often ascribed to H.G. Wells because of its use by him in the story 'The Country of the Blind' (1904) – though he quite clearly labels it an old proverb. As indeed it is, and in many languages. An early appearance is in a book of *Adages* by Erasmus (*d* 1536): '*In regione caecorum rex est luscus.*'

blind leading the blind. This phrase, alluding to ineffectual leadership, comes from the Bible: 'They be blind leaders of the blind. And if the blind lead the blind, both shall fall into the ditch' (Matthew 15:4). This famous observation from the gospels seems to cry out to be tampered with. In 1958, Kenneth Tynan wrote: 'They say the *New Yorker* is the bland leading the bland. I don't know if I'm bland enough.'

Blithe Spirit. The title of Noël Coward's comedy (1941; film, U K 1945) about a spiritualist, and taken from Shelley's poem 'To a Skylark' (1819):

> Hail to thee, blithe spirit!
> Bird thou never wert.

block. See CHIP OF(F) THE OLD/ SAME ~.

blonde bombshell. This phrase is used to describe any blonde woman of dynamic personality, usually a film star, show business figure, or model. The original was Jean Harlow who appeared in the 1933 film *Bombshell*. In Britain –

presumably so as not to suggest that it was a war film – the title was changed to *Blonde Bombshell*.

blood. See RIVERS OF ~.

blood libel. This was the name given to accusations by medieval anti-Semites that Jews had crucified Christian children and drunk their blood at Passover. In September 1982, following allegations that Israeli forces in Lebanon had allowed massacres to take place in refugee camps, the Israeli government invoked the phrase in a statement headed: 'BLOOD LIBEL. On the New Year (Rosh Hashana), a blood libel was leveled against the Jewish state, its government and the Israel Defense Forces . . .'

blood sweat and tears. In his classic speech to the House of Commons on 13 May 1940 upon becoming Prime Minister, Winston Churchill said: 'I would say to the House, as I said to those who have joined this Government: I have nothing to offer but blood, toil, tears and sweat.' Ever since, people have had difficulty getting the order of his words right. The natural inclination is to put 'blood', 'sweat' then 'tears' together – as did Byron in 1823 with 'blood, sweat and tear-wrung millions' and as did the Canadian/US rock group Blood Sweat and Tears in the late 1960s and 70s.

Much earlier, however, there had been yet another combination of the words in John Donne's *An Anatomy of the World* (1611): ' 'Tis in vain to do so or to mollify it with thy tears, or sweat, or blood.' Churchill seemed consciously to avoid these configurations. In 1931, he had written of the Tsarist armies: 'Their sweat, their tears, their blood bedewed the endless plain.' Having launched his version of the phrase in 1940, he referred to it five more times during the course of the war, but from the very beginning people confused the order: Joan Wyndham in *Love Lessons – A Wartime Diary* (1985) concludes her entry for 13 May 1940: 'Later we listened to a very stirring speech by Churchill about "blood, toil, sweat and tears".' Suspicion is cast on this entry, however, because the speech was not actually broadcast (although Joan Wyndham would not be alone in claiming to have 'heard' the speech). Sometimes Churchill *did* repeat his House of Commons speeches later in the day on the wireless, but not on this occasion. He also recorded the speech for gramophone records, but not until after the war.

Bloody Sunday. As with BLACK FRIDAY, there has been a number of these. On 13 November 1887, two men died during a baton charge on a prohibited socialist demonstration in Trafalgar Square, London. On 22 January 1905, hundreds of unarmed peasants were mown down when they marched to petition the Tsar in St Petersburg. In Irish history, there was a Bloody Sunday on 21 November 1920 when, among other incidents, fourteen undercover British intelligence agents in Dublin were shot by Sinn Fein. More recently, the name was applied to Sunday 30 January 1972 when British troops killed thirteen Catholics after a protest rally in Londonderry, Northern Ireland. Perhaps the epithet sprang to mind readily on this occasion because of the film *Sunday Bloody Sunday* (1971).

Later (1973) the UK/US group Black Sabbath had a record album with the title *Sabbath Bloody Sabbath*.

bloom. See MAKE THE DESERT ~.

bloomers. Originally, the name given to a female costume consisting of a close-fitting jacket and a skirt reaching to just below the knees, under which were worn wide trousers gathered at the ankles. The fashion was introduced in New York – though not invented – by Mrs Amelia Jenks Bloomer around 1851. It was soon adopted in England where it had a vogue for a time and delighted cartoonists. The trousers were especially suitable for younger ladies taking up bicycling and the word became a nickname for these undergarments.

Bloomsbury. The tag 'Bloomsbury Group' or 'Set' was applied to a group of mildly-Bohemian writers, artists and thinkers who either lived or met in the Bloomsbury district of London in the early decades of the twentieth century. They included Leonard and Virginia Woolf, Duncan Grant, J.M. Keynes and David Garnett. Their well-documented personal relationships gave rise to a torrent of biographies in the second half of the century. Keynes was using the phrase 'Bloomsbury Set' by 1914. Harold Nicolson (who was loosely connected with the circle through his wife, V. Sackville-West) noted in his diary for 2 September 1940: 'Vita says that our mistake was that we remained Edwardian for too long, and that if in 1916 we had got in touch with Bloomsbury, we should have profited more than we did by carrying on with . . . the Edwardian relics. We are amused to confess that we had never even heard of Bloomsbury in 1916.'

blow hot and cold, to. Meaning 'to vacillate between enthusiasm and apathy', this expression comes from one of Aesop's *Fables*. On a cold day, a satyr comes across a man blowing his fingers to make them warm. He takes the man home and gives him a bowl of hot soup. The man blows on the soup, to cool it. At this, the satyr throws him out, exclaiming that he wants nothing to do with a man who can 'blow hot and cold from the same mouth'.

blow one's own trumpet, to. Meaning 'to boast of one's own achievements', this is sometimes said to have originated with the statue of 'Fame' on the parapet of Wilton House, near Salisbury. The figure – positioned after a fire in 1647 – originally held a trumpet in each hand. Brewer, more reasonably, states that the 'allusion is to heralds, who used to announce with a flourish of trumpets the knights who entered a list'. (See also *D P P*.)

blow the gaff, to. An earlier (eighteenth-century) form was 'to blow the gab' meaning 'to blab about something; to let the secret out; give the game away' and, conceivably, 'gaff' could have developed from that. 'Gaff' may here mean 'mouth' (like gab/gob) and, coupled with 'blow', this gives the idea of expelling air through it and letting things out.

blow the whistle on, to. Alluding to the police use of whistles, this phrase means 'to call a halt to something by exposing it'. *O E D2* finds a 1934 use in P.G. Wodehouse. More recently, the *Listener* of 3 January 1980 reported: 'English as she is murdered on radio became an issue once more. Alvar Lidell stamped his foot and blew the whistle in the *Listener*.' Sir Robert Armstrong was quoted as saying: 'I do not think there could be a duty on a civil servant to blow the whistle on his Minister.' (*Observer*, 2 March 1986)

BLT. See INITIALS.

blue. See ENOUGH ~ TO MAKE A . . .; ONCE IN A ~ MOON.

blue-blooded. This phrase is used to mean 'aristocratic; socially superior'. Human blood is red, but during the fifteenth century many Spanish aristocrats had fair complexions which made their veins appear bluer than those of darker-skinned Moorish people. Thus they were said to have blue blood.

Blue Meany. In the Beatles' animated film *Yellow Submarine* (1968), the music-hating baddies are called Blue Meanies. There may have been limited use of this pejorative thereafter, perhaps aimed in a general sense at anyone not liked, but particularly the **boys in blue** (the police).

blue pencil, to. In the B B C wartime radio series *Garrison Theatre* (first broadcast 1939), Jack Warner as 'Private Warner' helped further popularize this well-established synonym for censorship (O E D2's first citation is a US one from 1888). In reading out blue-pencilled letters from his brother at the Front he would subdue expletives in the form 'not blue pencil likely'!

Blue Remembered Hills. The title of a T V play (1979) by Dennis Potter about childhood, in which the children were played by adults. From A.E. Housman's 'A Shropshire Lad':

> Into my heart an air that kills
> From yon far country blows;
> What are those blue remembered hills,
> What spires, what farms are those?

bluestocking. Denoting 'a literary or studious woman', this word derived from the gatherings of cultivated females and a few eminent men at the home of Elizabeth Montagu in London around 1750. Boswell in his *Life of Johnson* explains that a certain Benjamin Stillingfleet was a popular guest, soberly dressed but wearing blue stockings: 'Such was the excellence of his conversation, that his absence was felt as so great a loss, that it used to be said, "We can do nothing without the blue stockings", and thus by degrees the title was established.'

Blue Velvet. The title of a film (US, 1986) about drugs and menace. This alludes firstly to the song 'Blue Velvet' (1951) written by Wayne and Morris, which is sung by the night-club singer heroine in the film, and secondly – as *DOAS* describes – to the name for 'a mixture of paregoric, which contains opium and . . . an antihistamine, to be injected', which is also relevant to the film.

blundered. See SOMEONE HAD ~.

blurb. This word refers to the promotional notes on the cover of a book, describing its contents and merits in encouraging tones. In 1907, Gelett Burgess, the US novelist, is said to have produced a comic book-jacket featuring an alluring female called 'Miss B[e]linda Blurb'. Presumably she was intended to attract readers in the way that a publisher's written, descriptive notes are now meant to do. Seven years later, Burgess defined the word he had invented as 'to make a sound like a publisher'.

See also BROMIDE.

B O A C. See INITIALS.

B O B O. See ACRONYMS.

Bob's your uncle! This is an almost meaningless expression of the type that takes hold from time to time, as another way of saying 'there you are; there you have it; simple as that'. It was current by the 1880s but doesn't appear to be of any hard and fast origin. It is basically a British expression – and somewhat baffling to Americans. There is the story of one such who went into a London shop, had it said to him, and exclaimed: 'But how did you know – I do have an Uncle Bob!?' In 1886, Arthur Balfour was appointed Chief Secretary for Ireland by his uncle, *Robert* Arthur Talbot

Gascoyne-Cecil, 3rd Marquis of Salisbury, the Prime Minister. Could this be a possible source?

body odour (*or* BO). This worrying concept was used to promote Lifebuoy soap, initially in the US, and was current by 1933. In early radio jingles, the initials ' B O' were sung *basso profundo*, emphasizing the horror of the offence. In the U K, T V ads showed pairs of male or female friends out on a spree, intending to attract partners. When one of the pair was seen to have a problem, the other whispered helpfully, 'B O'.

boffin. Alluding to a scientist and inventor, this term was probably of RAF origin in the Second World War but was adopted by the other services. Such men produced navigational aids, bomb-aiming and gunnery gadgetry. There was an eccentric gentleman called Mr Boffin in Charles Dickens, *Our Mutual Friend* (1864–5).

bogey. See COLONEL ~.

Bognor. See BUGGER ~.

Bohemia coast. 'Our ship hath touch'd upon/The deserts of Bohemia' – *The Winter's Tale* (III.iii.1). A supposed geographical error on Shakespeare's part. Bohemia (now part of Czecho-slovakia) does not have a coast. However, at certain points in history it *did* have an outlet on the Adriatic.

Boldness Be My Friend. The title of a book (1953) by Richard Pape about his exploits in the Second World War, and taken from what Iachimo says when he sets off to pursue Imogen in Shakespeare's *Cymbeline*: 'Boldness be my friend!/Arm me, Audacity, from head to foot' (I.vii.18). In 1977, Richard Boston wrote a book called *Baldness Be My Friend*, partly about his own lack of hair.

b/Bolshoi. The Russian word for 'big' – as in the name of Moscow's principal theatre for opera and ballet, and especially the world-famous Bolshoi Ballet. The building was opened in 1856.

bomber. See BROWN ~.

bombshell. See BLONDE ~.

BOMFOG. An acronym for a pompous, meaningless generality. When Governor Nelson Rockefeller was competing against Barry Goldwater for the Republican nomination in 1964, reporters latched on to a favourite saying of the candidate – 'the brotherhood of man under the fatherhood of God' – and rendered it with the acronym BOMFOG. In fact, according to Safire, they had been beaten to it by Hy Sheffer, a stenotypist on the Governor's staff who had found the abbreviation convenient for the previous five or six years. The words come from a much-quoted saying of John D. Rockefeller: 'These are the principles upon which alone a new world recognizing the brotherhood of man and the fatherhood of God can be established . . .' Later, BOMFOG was used by feminists to denote use of language that demeaned women by reflecting patrician attitudes. The individual phrases 'brotherhood of man' and 'fatherhood of God' do not appear before the nineteenth century.

Bona Dea. See ROMAN NAMES.

bond. See MY WORD IS MY ~.

Boneless Wonder, the. A spineless character named after a fairground freak, notably evoked by Winston Churchill in an attack on Ramsay MacDonald (28 January 1931). During a debate on the Trades Disputes Act, Churchill referred to recent efforts by the Prime Minister to conciliate Roman Catholic opinion regarding education reform (including the lowering of the school-leaving age to fifteen): 'I remember when I was a child, being taken to the celebrated Barnum's Circus which contained an exhibition of freaks and monstrosities, but the exhibit on the programme which I most desired to see was the one described as the Boneless Wonder. My parents judged that the spectacle would be too revolting and demoralizing for my youthful eyes, and I have waited fifty years to see the Boneless Wonder sitting on the Treasury bench.'

bonk, to. A hugely-popular euphemism for sexual intercourse in Britain around the summer of 1987, though McConville and Shearlaw had it in *The Slanguage of Sex* (1984) and *OED2* finds it in a magazine in 1975. Like 'bang', used in a similar way, the notion seems to be one of sex as a brutal, bashing matter. 'To bonk' used to mean, simply, 'to hit'. Perhaps the appeal of the word had something to do with its resemblance to 'conk' (nose – as in the expression: 'big conk, big cock') and 'bunk' (as in the verb meaning 'to sleep'). Nicholas Fairbairn MP listed his hobbies in the 1977 edition of *Who's Who* as 'bunking and debunking', which undoubtedly conveyed this sense. Another theory is that 'bonk' is back-slang for 'knob', a well-established name for 'penis'.

book. See ~ YOU WOULD WISH YOUR WIFE TO READ under LADY CHATTERLEY; LITTLE RED ~.

Booker T. and the MGs. The name of a US pop group of the 1960s and 70s. If it had been 'Model T and the MGs' one might have thought there was a motoring theme afoot: the US 'Model T Ford' (1909) coupled with the UK 'MG' (1922) from 'Morris Garages'. Booker T. Washington (*d* 1915) was a former slave who became a leading black educationalist in the US. 'M Gs' are Machine Guns or Gunners. In fact, the keyboard player was Booker T. Jones and the 'M G' stood for 'Memphis Group'.

Books Do Furnish a Room. The title of the tenth volume (1971) in Anthony Powell's novel sequence, A DANCE TO THE MUSIC OF TIME. According to the BLURB on the dust-jacket of the first edition: 'The book's title is taken to some extent from the nickname of one of the characters, Books-do-furnish-a-room Bagshaw, all-purpose journalist and amateur of revolutionary theory, but the phrase also suggests an aspect of the rather bleak post-war period – London's literary world finding its feet again.'

The notion of books being looked upon as furniture – and the consequent taunt to people who regard them as such – is an old one, however. Lady Holland in her *Memoir* (1855) quotes the Revd Sidney Smith as joking: 'No furniture so charming as books.' And Edward Young in *Love of Fame: The Universal Passion* (Satire II, 1725–8) has: 'Thy books are furniture.'

boom boom! These words are used by comedians as a verbal underlining to the punchline of a gag. Ernie Wise suggested (1979) that it was like the drum-thud or trumpet-sting used, particularly by US entertainers, to point a joke. Music-hall star Billy Bennett (d 1942) may have been the first to use this device, in the UK to emphasize his comic couplets. Morecambe and Wise, Basil Brush, and many others, took it up later.

boondocks/boonies. During the Second World War, US GIs stationed in the Philippines were sometimes sent to the mountain regions. *Bundok* means 'mountain' in Tagalog, the official language of the Philippines. Hence, 'boondocks' or 'boonies' arose as words for somewhere obscure, out of the way and 'in the sticks'.

bootleg. Originally applied to the illegal selling of liquor, in more recent times this term has been applied to such things as records and cassettes to mean 'counterfeit'. The word arose in the American Far West during the mid-nineteenth century when illegal liquor sales were made to Indians on reservations. The thin bottles of alcohol are said to have been concealed in the vendor's long boots.

boots. See LIE TRAVELS ROUND THE WORLD BEFORE . . .

boots, to be too big for one's. Meaning 'to be conceited'. An example: in 1948, reports of a speech by Harold Wilson, then president of the Board of Trade, wrongly suggested he had claimed that when he was at school some of his classmates had gone barefoot. Ivor Bulmer-Thomas consequently remarked at the 1949 Conservative Party Conference: 'If ever he went to school without any boots it was because he was too big for them.' This remark is often wrongly attributed to Harold Macmillan.

booze. One derivation for this word for 'alcoholic drink' is from the name of E.C. (or E.S. or E.G.) Booz, a Philadelphia whisky distiller (c 1840), but the word was current in the fourteenth century. Middle English *bousen* meant 'to drink deeply'. Mr Booz merely helped popularize the word.

Born Yesterday. The title of a play (1946, film US, 1951) by Garson Kanin, about an ignorant girl who wins out in the end. O E D2 has 'I wasn't born yesterday', meaning 'I'm not as innocent as you take me for', as an established saying by 1757.

B/bosie. (1) The nickname of Lord Alfred Douglas (d 1945), poet, friend of

Oscar Wilde and ultimate cause of that writer's downfall. He was known as 'Bosie', a corruption of 'Boysie', the name given to him by his indulgent mother. (2) An Australian cricketing nickname (also spelt **bosey**) from the 1900s for the googly, a method of bowling a ball, named after its inventor, the Middlesex and England player, Bernard Bosanquet.

bosom. See ABRAHAM'S ~; ARTHUR'S ~.

bottle. Used in the sense of 'courage; guts' since the late 1940s at least, 'bottle' may have acquired the meaning through rhyming slang: either 'bottle and glass' [class] (said to date from the 1920s); 'bottle and glass' [arse]; or, 'bottle of beer' [fear]. But the reason for the leap from 'class/arse' to 'courage', and from 'fear' to 'guts', is not obvious. Though it has been explained that 'arse' is what you would void your bowels through in an alarming situation, and 'class' is what a boxer has – if he loses it, he has 'lost his bottle'. Much earlier, *Swell's Night Guide* (1846) has: 'She thought it would be no bottle [no good] 'cos her rival could go in a buster.' In a play by Frank Norman (1958), there occurs the line: 'What's the matter, Frank? Your bottle fallen out?' There is an old-established brewers, Courage Ltd, whose products can, of course, be had in bottles.

Bottle in the Smoke, A. The title of a novel (1990) by A.N. Wilson, derived from Psalm 119:81: 'My soul fainteth for thy salvation . . . for I am become like a bottle in the smoke.'

bottle-washer. See CHIEF COOK AND ~.

bottomless pit, the. A description of Hell from Revelation 20:1: 'And I saw an angel come down from heaven, having the key of the bottomless pit'; also in Milton's *Paradise Lost* (Bk. 6, line 864):

> Headlong themselves they threw
> Down from the verge of Heaven, eternal wrath
> Burnt after them to the bottomless pit.

William Pitt the Younger, British Prime Minister (1783–1801, 1804–6) was nicknamed the **Bottomless Pitt,** on account of his thinness. A caricature attributed to Gillray with this title shows Pitt as Chancellor of the Exchequer introducing his 1792 budget. His bottom is non-existent.

bound. See WITH ONE ~ . . .

bountiful. See LADY ~.

bowdlerize, to. Meaning 'to expurgate', this verb derives from Thomas Bowdler who published (1818) *The Family Shakespeare*, a ten-volume edition of the dramatist's works with all the dirty bits left out (or, as he put it, those words 'which cannot be read aloud in a family'). 'Out damn'd spot' became 'Out crimson spot', and so on. Dr Bowdler, in consequence, has given his name to any form of literary expurgation. Possibly the word 'bowdlerize' caught on because of its resemblance to 'disembowel'. It was already current by 1836.

box, the. A slightly passé term for a TV set (having earlier been applied to wirelesses and gramophones), and one of several derogatory epithets which were applied during the medium's rise to mass popularity in the 1940s and 50s. Groucho Marx used the expression in a letter (1950). Maurice Richardson, sometime TV critic of the *Observer*, apparently coined the epithet **idiot's lantern** prior to 1957. See also BLACK BOX.

boy(s). See BACKROOM ~; GOLDEN ~ ; ~ IN BLUE under BLUE MEANY.

boycott, to. Capt Charles Boycott was an ex-British soldier who acted as an agent for absentee landlords in Co Mayo, Ireland, during the late nineteenth century. He was extremely hard on the poor tenants and dispossessed them if they fell behind with their rents. By way of retaliation, the tenants isolated him and refused to have any dealings with him or his family. They were encouraged in this by Charles Parnell of the Irish Land League who said that those who grabbed land from the people evicted for non-payment of rent should be treated like 'the leper of old'. Eventually, the tenants brought about Boycott's downfall by leaving his harvest to rot and he fled back to England where he died in 1897. Note that the verb 'to boycott' (which became current soon after the above incidents took place in 1880) describes what was done *to* him rather than what was done *by* him.

bra. See BURN ONE'S ~.

Brains Trust, The. The title of a BBC Radio discussion programme, from 1941 onwards, originating in term for a group of people who give advice or who comment on current issues. In the 1930s, President Franklin D. Roosevelt set up a circle of advisers which became known as his '*brain* trust'. In Britain, the term was borrowed and turned into '*brains* trust'.

brand new. This expression for 'very new' comes from the old word meaning 'to burn' (just as a 'brand' is a form of torch). A metal that was brand (*or* bran) new had just been taken out of the flames, having just been forged. Shakespeare has the variation 'fire-new', which points more directly to the phrase's origin.

Brandy for the Parson. The title of a film comedy (UK, 1951) about smuggling, from 'A Smuggler's Song' by Rudyard KIPLING: 'Brandy for the Parson,/'Baccy for the Clerk;/Laces for a lady, letters for a spy,/Watch the wall, my darling, while the gentlemen go by!'

brass. See COLD ENOUGH TO FREEZE . . .

brass tacks, to get down to. Probably of US origin, this phrase means 'to get down to essentials'. There are various theories as to why we say it, including: (1) In old stores, brass tacks were positioned a yard apart for measuring. When a customer 'got down to brass tacks', it meant he or she was serious about making a purchase. (2) Brass tacks were a fundamental element in nineteenth-century upholstery, hence this expression meant to deal with a fault in the furniture by getting down to basics. (3) 'Brass tacks' is rhyming slang for 'facts'.

Brave New World. The title of a novel (1932) by Aldous HUXLEY, from Miranda's exclamation in Shakespeare's *The Tempest* (V.i.183): 'O brave new world,/That has such people in't!'

Bray. See VICAR OF ~.

breach. See CUSTOM MORE HONOUR'D IN THE ~ . . .

bread. See GREATEST THING SINCE SLICED ~.

bread never falls but on its buttered side. See IF ANYTHING CAN GO WRONG – IT WILL.

break a butterfly upon a wheel, to. See WHO BREAKS A BUTTERFLY UPON A WHEEL?

break a leg! This traditional theatrical greeting is said before a performance, especially a first night, because it is considered bad luck to wish anyone 'good luck' directly. Partridge/*Slang* has 'to break a leg' as 'to give birth to a bastard', dating from the seventeenth century, but that is probably unconnected. As also is the fact that John Wilkes Booth, an actor, broke his leg after assassinating President Lincoln in a theatre. Morris has it based on a German good luck expression, *Hals und Beinbruch* [May you break your neck and your leg]. Perhaps this entered theatrical speech (like several other expressions) via Yiddish.

Breakfast of Champions. The title of a novel by Kurt Vonnegut (1973), from a slogan used to promote Wheaties breakfast cereal in the US, since 1950 at least.

break the mould, to. This phrase means 'to start afresh from fundamentals'. When the Social Democratic Party was established in 1981, there was much talk of it 'breaking the mould of British politics' i.e. doing away with the traditional system of a government and one chief opposition party. This was by no means a new way of describing political change and getting rid of an old system for good, in a way that prevents it being reconstituted. In *What Matters Now* (1972), Roy Jenkins, one of the new party's founders, had quoted Andrew Marvell's 'Horatian Ode Upon Cromwell's Return from Ireland' (1650):

> And cast the kingdoms old,
> Into another mould.

A.J.P. Taylor in his *English History 1914–1945* (1965), had written: 'Lloyd George needed a new crisis to break the mould of political and economic habit'. The image evoked, as in the days of the Luddites, is of breaking the mould from

which iron machinery is cast – so completely that the machinery has to be recast from scratch.

Br'er fox – he lay low. An expression used to suggest that doing or saying nothing for the moment is the best course, it comes from the 'Tar-Baby Story' in *Uncle Remus: Legends of the Old Plantation* (1881) by Joel Chandler Harris: 'Tar-Baby ain't sayin' nuthin', en Brer Fox, he lay low.'

brewery. See COULDN'T RUN A PISS-UP IN A ~.

Bride/Brigid, St. See SAINTS' NAMES.

bridegroom on the wedding cake. A memorable insult, this is usually attributed to Alice Roosevelt Longworth (1884–1980). She said that Thomas Dewey, who was challenging Harry S. Truman for the US presidency in 1948, looked like the 'bridegroom' or just 'the man' 'on the wedding cake'. Dewey did indeed have a wooden, dark appearance, and a black moustache.

bridesmaid. See OFTEN A ~ BUT NEVER A BRIDE.

Bridge Too Far, A. The title of Cornelius Ryan's book (1974; film UK/US, 1977) about the 1944 airborne landings in Holland. These were designed to capture eleven bridges needed for the Allied invasion of Germany – an attempt which came to grief at Arnhem, the Allies suffering more casualties than in the invasion of Normandy. In advance of the action, Lt-Gen Sir Frederick Browning protested to Field-Marshal Montgomery, whose brainchild the scheme was: 'But, sir, we may be going a bridge too far.'

The phrase is sometimes used allusively when warning of an unwise move, e.g. 'A BRIDGE TOO NEAR. A public inquiry opened yesterday into plans to re-span the Ironbridge Gorge in Shropshire' (*The Times*, 20 June 1990); 'Ratners: A bid too far?' (*Observer*, 8 July 1990).

Brief Candles. The title of a novel (1930) by Aldous HUXLEY. See 'ALL OUR YESTERDAYS' SPEECH.

bright. See ALL THINGS ~ AND BEAUTIFUL.

bring home the bacon, to. Meaning 'to be successful in a venture', this probably has to do with the Dunmow Flitch, a tradition established in 1111 at Dunmow in Essex. Married couples who could prove they had lived for a year and a day without quarrelling or wishing to be unmarried could claim a gammon of bacon. Also, country fairs used to have competitions which involved catching a greased pig. If you 'brought home the bacon', you won.

brinkmanship. Referring to political policies which bring a country to the brink of war. The term was popularized by Adlai Stevenson during the 1956 US presidential campaign with reference to the Secretary of State, John Foster Dulles. Dulles had said: 'If you are scared to go to the brink, you are lost.'

brioche. See LET THEM EAT CAKE.

Bristols. Rhyming slang provides the origin for this word meaning 'breasts', which otherwise is far from obvious. The rhyme is 'Bristol Cities' [titties] – a use more or less restricted to the UK. As Paul Beale suggests in his revision of Partridge/*Slang*, the football team Bristol City probably only gets invoked because of the initial similarity of the words 'Bristol' and 'breasts'.

Britannia. See RULE ~.

broad sunlit uplands. In Winston Churchill's long speaking career, there was one thematic device he frequently resorted to for his perorations. It appears in many forms but may be summarized as the 'broad, sunlit uplands' approach. In his collected speeches, there are some thirteen occasions when he made use of this construction. 'The level plain . . . a land of peace and plenty . . . the sunshine of a more gentle and a more generous age' (1906); 'I earnestly trust . . . that by your efforts our country may emerge from this period of darkness and peril once more in the sunlight of a peaceful time' (at the end of a speech on 19 September 1915 when Churchill's own position was precarious following the failure of the Gallipoli campaign); in his 'finest hour' speech, Churchill hoped that, 'The life of the world may move forward into broad, sunlit uplands' (1940); 'it is an uphill road we have to tread, but if we reject the cramping, narrowing path of socialist restrictions, we shall surely find a way – and a wise and tolerant government – to those broad uplands where plenty, peace and justice reign' (1951, prior to the General Election).

See also LET US GO FORWARD TOGETHER.

broke(n). See IF IT AIN'T ~ . . .; NIGHT OF ~ GLASS.

bromide. Gelett Burgess, the US novelist, invented this word in 1906 to describe someone addicted to clichés. The word later came to mean a trite remark or platitude.

See also BLURB.

Bronx cheer. A noise of derisive disapproval. *DOAS* suggests that this form of criticism originated at the National Theater in the Bronx, New York City, although the Yankee baseball stadium is also in the same area. The UK equivalent is 'to blow a **raspberry**', from rhyming slang, 'raspberry tart' [fart].

brother. See BIG ~.

Brown. See CAPABILITY ~.

Brown Bomber. A nickname which denotes colour and power, the original holder of this 'title' was Joe Louis, world heavyweight boxing champion from 1937 until his retirement in 1949. He was noted for his large number of knockouts. The nickname was also applied to a Burmese cat at stud in West London in 1983.

A **black bomber** is an amphetamine drug, first called this in the 1960s.

browned off. See CHEESED OFF.

Brown Eminence. See under GREY EMINENCE.

brownie points, to earn/win. Originating in US business and meaning 'to gain credit', this may have nothing to do with the Brownies, the junior branch of the Girl Guides/Scouts, and the points they might or might not gain for doing their 'good deed for the day' (though that is the explanation offered in *DOAS*'s 1975 revision). The origin may be scatological, not unconnected with brown-nosing, brown-tonguing, arse-licking, and other unsavoury methods of sucking up to someone important. Note also the US term 'Brownie', an award for doing something *wrong*. According to *DOAS*, 'I got a pair of Brownies for that one' (1942) refers to a system of disciplinary demerits on the railroads. The word was derived from the inventor of the system.

Bruno, St. See SAINTS' NAMES.

brush. See DAFT AS A ~.

brush, to live/get married over the (or jump over the broomstick). Meaning 'to live together as though married', this expression possibly derives from some form of informal ceremony which involved the couple jumping over a stick.

brush-off. Meaning 'a rebuff', this noun is said to derive from a habit of Pullman porters in the US who, if they thought you were a poor tipper, gave you a quick brush over the shoulders and passed on to the next customer. However, perhaps the mere action of brushing unwanted dirt off clothing is sufficient reason for the expression.

Brutus. See ET TU BRUTE.

bucket. See KICK THE ~.

buck stops here, the. President Truman had a sign on his desk bearing these words, indicating that the Oval Office was where the passing of the buck had to cease. It appears to have been a saying of his own invention. Compare PASS THE BUCK.

buff. (1) An enthusiast, e.g. 'film-buff', 'opera-buff', etc. This use came from people who liked to watch fires being extinguished or who helped extinguish them in an amateur capacity. They were called 'buffs' either because of their buffalo uniforms or because the heavy buffalo robes they wore to keep them warm in winter (before the fires were started, presumably) somewhat hindered their usefulness. In which case, the term was used as a mild form of rebuke by the real fire-fighters. (2) Naked, e.g. 'in the buff'. This seems to derive from the buff-coloured leather shorts down to which people in the services were sometimes stripped. Although strictly-speaking they were not naked, the term was extended to apply to those who were completely so. An English regiment has been known as 'The Buffs' for over three hundred years – not because it goes naked but because of the colour of its uniform.

Buffalo Bill. This was the nickname applied to William Frederick Cody, the showman, in 1869 by his friend Ned Buntline who made Cody the hero of a series of dime novels. It alludes to his early days as a buffalo hunter. Cody organized his first 'wild west show' in 1883, with cowboys and Indians, and brought it to England in 1887 with spectacular success.

bugger Bognor! It is popularly supposed that, at some stage in his final illness in 1936, King George V was assured that he would soon be fit enough to visit his favourite watering place at Bognor. 'Bugger Bognor!' he is supposed to have replied. Some mistakenly believe they were his dying words. Kenneth Rose in his biography of the King (1983) suggests, however, that the remark probably dates back to George V's recuperative visit to Bognor after his serious illness in the winter of 1929: 'A deputation of leading citizens came to ask that their salubrious town should henceforth be known as Bognor Regis. They were received by Stamfordham, the King's private secretary, who, having heard their petition, invited them to wait while he consulted the King in another room. The sovereign responded with the celebrated obscenity, which Stamfordham deftly translated for the benefit of the delegation. His Majesty, they were told, would be graciously pleased to grant their request.'

Buggins's turn. This is the explanation given of an appointment made because it is somebody's turn for a job rather than because the person is especially well-qualified. The name Buggins is used because it sounds suitably dull and humdrum ('Joe Buggins' and 'Joe Muggins' were both expressions current before the

earliest recorded use of this phrase by Admiral Fisher, later First Sea Lord, in a letter of 1901).

Bulge, the. See BABY BOOMER.

bull. See LIKE A RED RAG TO A ~.

bulldog breed. In 1857, Charles Kingsley wrote of: 'The original British bulldog breed, which, once stroked against the hair, shows his teeth at you for ever afterwards.' In 1897, the British had been called 'boys of the bulldog breed' in a music-hall song, 'Sons of the Sea, All British Born' by Felix McGlennon.

John Bull as a British symbol (sometimes shown accompanied by a bulldog) dates from before John Arbuthnot's *The History of John Bull* (1712). At the outbreak of the First World War in 1914, Winston Churchill spoke at a 'Call to Arms' meeting at the London Opera House. 'Mr Churchill has made a speech of tremendous voltage and carrying power,' the *Manchester Guardian* reported. 'His comparison of the British navy to a bulldog – "the nose of the bulldog has been turned backwards so that he can breathe without letting go" – will live. At the moment of delivery, with extraordinary appositeness, it was particularly vivid, as the speaker was able by some histrionic gift to suggest quite the bulldog as he spoke.' Indeed, during the Second World War, small model bulldogs were manufactured bearing Churchill's facial pout and wearing a tin helmet.

Bunbury. An imaginary person whose name one invokes in order to furnish oneself with an excuse not to do something, from Oscar Wilde's *The Importance of Being Earnest* (1899): 'I have invented an invaluable permanent invalid called Bunbury, in order that I may be able to go down into the country whenever I choose.' Bunbury is the name of an actual village in Cheshire.

Bungalow Bill. This was the nickname applied to a man called Bill Wiggins who achieved a certain amount of media fame in 1987–8 simply by being an amour of the actress Joan Collins. 'The Continuing Story of Bungalow Bill' (a joke upon BUFFALO BILL, of course) was the title of a Lennon and McCartney song (1968). However, it was also alleged that Mr Wiggins got his nickname because he did not have 'much up top'.

bunk(um). In 1820, Felix Walker, a Congressman from Buncombe County, North Carolina, made a totally worthless speech in the House of Representatives. He justified himself by saying he was not speaking to the House, 'but to Buncombe', and the name has come to mean 'worthless rubbish' ever since, though the spelling was simplified and shortened.

Hence, also, **to debunk**, meaning 'to draw attention to nonsense' or 'to deflate a reputation'. This was the creation of William E. Woodward in his book *Bunk* (*c* 1920), an exposé of Henry Ford (famous for saying: 'HISTORY IS more or less BUNK').

Burlington Bertie, a. A swell gentleman, after the one with the 'Hyde Park drawl and the Bond Street crawl' commemorated in a song with words and music by Harry B. Norris (first published 1900) and performed by Vesta Tilley. He is not to be confused with 'Burlington Bertie from Bow', a parody written in 1915 by William Hargreaves for his wife, Ella Shields, the male impersonator. In this song, now the better remembered of the two, Bertie is a more down-at-heel character.

BURMA. See ACRONYMS.

burn one's bra, to. Demonstrating solidarity with the feminist cause, this expression comes from a US slogan (*c* 1970) encouraging women to destroy an item of apparel quite clearly designed by a male chauvinist and likely to make a woman more of a sex object. It followed the burning of draft-cards as a protest against the Vietnam War.

burns. See FIDDLE WHILE ROME ~.

burnsides. See SIDEBURNS.

Burton. See GONE FOR A ~.

Bury My Heart at Wounded Knee. The title of a book (1970) by Dee Brown, it was a historical survey of the West and alludes to Stephen Vincent Benét's poem (1927) celebrating 'American Names': 'I shall not rest quiet at Montparnasse . . . Bury my heart at Wounded Knee'.

business as usual. This is the standard declaration posted when a shop has suffered some misfortune like a fire or is undergoing alterations. However, in the First World War the phrase was adopted in a more general sense. H.E. Morgan, an advertising man, promoted this slogan which had quite a vogue until it was proved to be manifestly untrue. In a Guildhall speech on 9 November 1914, Winston Churchill said: 'The maxim of the British people is "Business as usual".'

Butch Cassidy and the Sundance Kid. The title of a film (US 1969) using the nicknames of Robert LeRoy Parker and Harry Longbaugh, American outlaws who both died in 1909. Parker/Cassidy was called 'Butch' because he had once been a butcher (not because he was manly, in the later sense of the term, though this is how that term probably arose) and Longbaugh had once carried out a daring bank raid in the town of Sundance, Arizona.

Butcher of Lyons, the. This nickname was given to Klaus Barbie (*b* 1913), head of the German Gestapo in Lyons from 1942 to 1944, who was so called because of his alleged cruelty, torture, and murder of French Resistance fighters and others. Twice tried *in absentia*, Barbie was brought back to Lyons from exile in Bolivia in 1983 and tried again in 1987. Patrick Marnham in the *Independent* (18 March 1987) protested that Barbie had never been known thus in Lyons and that his nickname was '*Le Bourreau*' [the executioner]. Other 'Butchers' include: Ulysses S. Grant, for his alleged carelessness with the lives of his men; Alexander Woollcott, drama critic – 'The Butcher of Broadway'; the Duke of Cumberland, second son of George II – 'The Butcher of Culloden'; and General Gholam Ali Ovessi (*d* 1984), 'the Butcher of Tehran' under the Shah of Iran's rule.

butler did it!, the. An explanation of a mystery, originally the suggested solution to detective stories of the 1920s and 30s, its source is obscure. The earliest citation to hand is from the film *My Man Godfrey* (1957 – not the 1936 original) which is not even a whodunnit: 'The butler did it! He made every lady in the house, oh, so very happy!' (See also *DPP*.)

butter. See BIG ~ AND EGG MAN.

buttered side. See IF ANYTHING CAN GO WRONG . . .

butterfly. See WHO BREAKS A ~ UPON A WHEEL.

buttonhole, to. In the sense, 'to detain a reluctant listener', this verb does not derive from 'buttonhole', the hole through which a button passes, nor from the flower, so called, worn in the slit on a coat-lapel. The verb is really 'to button-hold', to stop persons going away by holding on to one of their buttons.

Buzz, Buzz! The title of a collection of reviews (1918) by James Agate, the drama critic, it comes from what Hamlet says (II.ii.389) when told by Polonius: 'The actors are come hither, my lord.' One commentator has described the phrase as 'a contemptuous exclamation dismissing something as idle gossip or (as here) stale news'.

— by Christmas. Initially, it was not thought that the First World War would last very long. Having started in August 1914, it would be 'over by Christmas', hence the anti-German slogan 'Berlin by Christmas'. The fact that this promise was not fulfilled did not prevent Henry Ford from saying, as he tried to stop the war a year later: 'We're going to try to get the boys out of the trenches before Christmas. I've chartered a ship, and some of us are going to Europe.' He was not referring to American boys because the United States had not joined the war at this stage. The *New York Tribune* announced: 'GREAT WAR ENDS CHRISTMAS DAY. FORD TO STOP IT.'

In her *Autobiography* (1977), Agatha Christie remembered that the South African War would 'all be over in a few weeks'. She went on: 'In 1914 we heard the same phrase. "All over by Christmas". In 1940, "Not much point in storing the carpets with mothballs" – this when the Admiralty took over my house – "It won't last over the winter".'

In *Tribune* (28 April 1944), George Orwell recalled a young man 'on the night in 1940 when the big ack-ack barrage was fired over London for the first time' insisting, 'I tell you, it'll all be over by Christmas.' In his diary for 28 November 1950, Harold Nicolson wrote, 'Only a few days ago [General] MacArthur was saying, "Home by

Christmas", and now he is saying, "This is a new war" [Korea].' As Flexner comments in *I Hear America Talking*: '*The war will be over by Christmas* was a popular 1861 expression [in the American Civil War]. Since then several generals and politicians have used the phrase or variations of it, in World War I, World War II, and the Korean war – and none of the wars was over by Christmas.'

by hook or by crook. *OED2*, while finding a couple of references in the works of John Wycliffe around 1380, states firmly that while there are 'many theories', there is no firm evidence for the origin of this phrase which means 'by some means or another'. In fact, the only real theory is the one about peasants in feudal times being allowed to take for firewood only those tree branches which they could pull down 'by hook or by crook' – 'crook' here meaning the hooked staff carried by shepherds (and also, symbolically, by bishops). (See *DPP*.)

by Jingo! Now a mild and meaningless oath, this phrase derived its popularity from G.W. Hunt's notable anti-Russian music-hall song 'We Don't Want to Fight (but by jingo if we do . . .)' (1877). The song gave the words 'jingo' and 'jingoism' their modern meaning, but the oath had existed long before. Motteux in his translation of Rabelais in 1694 put 'by jingo' for '*par dieu*' and there is some evidence to show that 'jingo' was conjuror's gibberish dating from a decade or two before. It is impossible to say whether there is any connection with Jingo, the legendary Empress of Japan who invaded Korea victoriously in the second century.

BYOB. See INITIALS.

By the Pricking of My Thumbs. A thriller (1968) by Agatha CHRISTIE, it takes its title from Shakespeare's *Macbeth*. The Second Witch says (as Macbeth approaches, IV.i.44):

> By the pricking of my thumbs,
> Something wicked this way comes.

It was an old superstition that sudden pains in the body were signs that something was about to happen. Compare *SOMETHING WICKED THIS WAY COMES*.

By the Sword Divided. The title of a BBC TV historical drama series (1983–5) set in the English Civil War, it was created by John Hawkesworth who commented (1991): 'When I first wrote down the idea for a story about the Civil War I called it 'The Laceys of Arnescote' . . . [but] I decided the title didn't convey the sort of Hentyish swashbuckling style that we were aiming at, so I thought again. The title "By the Sword Divided" came to me as I was walking along a beach in Wales.'

In dealing with the Civil War period, Macaulay in his *History of England* (Chaps.1–2, 1848) had earlier written: 'Thirteen years followed during which England was . . . really governed by the sword'; 'the whole nation was sick of government by the sword'; 'anomalies and abuses . . . which had been destroyed by the sword'.

C & A. A joke explanation of this clothing store's name in Britain, usually put in the mouth of a London bus conductor, is that the initials stand for 'Coats and 'Ats'. In full, 'C&A Modes', the name comes from the first names of Clemens and August Brenninkmeyer, the Dutch brothers who founded the business in 1841.

cabal. This word for a group of plotters is from the Hebrew *qabbalah* meaning 'accepted by tradition', used in connection with a Jewish mystical system of theology and metaphysics. It is *not* true to say that it gained its modern meaning from the initial letters of Clifford, Ashley, Buckingham, Arlington and Lauderdale, ministers in the reign of Charles II who signed the Treaty of Alliance with France in 1672. Their initials merely conformed to a word already in existence.

Cabbage Patch Kids. Millions of soft, ugly dolls with this name were sold in 1983–4. Created by an American called Xavier Roberts they became a craze around the world. People did not purchase them but, tweely, 'adopted' them. Whereas, in Britain, babies that are not delivered 'by the stork' are found 'under a gooseberry bush', in the US, they are found in 'cabbage patches'. Compare *Mrs Wiggs of the Cabbage Patch* (1901), the title of a US children's novel by Alice Hegan Rice.

Cabbages and Kings. This has been the title of more than one T V series, including the I T V version (1979–82) of the radio quiz *Quote . . . Unquote*. It derives from Lewis Carroll's 'Walrus and the Carpenter' episode in *Through the Looking Glass and What Alice Found There* (Chap.4, 1871):

> 'The time has come,' the Walrus said,
> 'To talk of many things:
> Of shoes – and ships – and sealing-
>   wax –
> Of cabbages and kings . . .'

The US writer O. Henry also took it for his first collection of short stories published in 1904, and there is a book *Of Kennedys and Kings: Making Sense of the Sixties* by Harris Wofford (1980). However, the conjunction of 'cabbages' and 'kings' pre-dates Carroll. In Hesketh Pearson's *Smith of Smiths*, a biography of Revd Sydney Smith (*d* 1845), he quotes Smith as saying about a certain Mrs George Groce: 'She had innumerable hobbies, among them horticulture and democracy, defined by Sydney as "the most approved methods of growing cabbages and destroying kings".'

cabin. See LOG ~ TO WHITE HOUSE.

Caesar's wife must be above suspicion. It was Julius Caesar himself who said this of his wife Pompeia when he divorced her in 62 BC. In North's translation of Plutarch's *Lives* – which is how the saying came into English in 1570 – Caesar is quoted thus: 'I will not, sayd he, that my wife be so much as suspected.' Pompeia was Caesar's second wife and according to Suetonius, in 61 BC she took part in the women-only rites of the Feast of the Great Goddess. But it was rumoured that a profligate called Publius Clodius attended wearing women's clothes and that he committed adultery with Pompeia. Caesar divorced Pompeia and at the subsequent inquiry into the desecration was asked why he had done so. 'Caesar's wife must be above suspicion,' he replied. He later married Calpurnia. An example of the phrase in use occurs in Lord Chesterfield's letters (c 1740): 'Your moral character must be not only pure, but, like Caesar's wife, unsuspected.'

Cain. See RAISE ~.

cake. See LET THEM EAT ~.

Cakes and Ale. The title of a novel (1930) by W. Somerset Maugham, comes from Sir Toby Belch's remark to Malvolio in Shakespeare's *Twelfth Night*: 'Does thou think, because thou art virtuous, there shall be no more cakes and ale?' (II.iii.114). The Arden edition comments that cakes and ale were 'traditionally associated with festivity, and disliked by Puritans both on this account and because of their association with weddings, saints' days, and holy days'. In due course, 'cakes and ale' became a synonym for enjoyment, as in the expression 'Life isn't all cakes and ale' (or 'beer and skittles', for that matter). On 4 May 1876, Francis Kilvert wrote in his diary: 'The clerk's wife brought out some cakes and ale and pressed me to eat and drink. I was to have returned to Llysdinam to luncheon ... but as I wanted to see more of the country and the people I decided to let the train go by, accept the hospitality of my hostess

and the cakes and ale which life offered, and walk home quietly in the course of the afternoon' – a neat demonstration of the literal and metaphorical uses of the phrase.

Calais lying on my heart. Queen Mary I ('Bloody Mary', 'Mary Tudor', who ruled 1553–8) reputedly said: 'When I am dead and opened, you shall find Calais lying on my heart.' She was referring to the re-capture by the French of Calais in 1558, a notable defeat for the English, as the town had been an English possession for more than two hundred years and was its last territory in France. In the cod history book *1066 and All That* by Sellar amd Yeatman (1930), we find: 'The cruel Queen, Broody Mary, died and a post-mortem examination revealed the word "CALLOUS" engraved on her heart.'

Calamity Jane. This nickname for a female prophet of doom derives from Martha Jane Canary (d 1903) of Deadwood, South Dakota. She behaved like a cowboy but was generally unlucky in nefarious activities and brought catastrophe on her associates. Eleven of her twelve husbands died untimely deaths. She dressed, swore, and shot like a man, eventually went into show business, and threatened 'calamity' to any man who offended her.

Calcutta. See BLACK HOLE OF ~ ; OH! ~!

Calliope. See GREEK NAMES.

Callisto. See GREEK NAMES.

Call Me Madam. This was the title of Irving Berlin's musical, first performed on Broadway in 1950, starring Ethel Merman as a woman ambassador appointed to represent the US in a tiny European state. It was inspired by the case of Pearl Mesta, the society hostess, whom Harry Truman had appointed as ambassador to Luxembourg, and the title arose from a misquotation. When Frances Perkins was appointed Secretary of Labor by President Roosevelt in 1933, she became the first US woman to hold Cabinet rank. It was held that when she had been asked *in Cabinet* how she wished to be addressed, she had replied: 'Call me Madam.' She denied that she had done this, however. It was *after* her first Cabinet meeting that reporters asked how they should address her. The Speaker-elect of the House of Representatives, Henry T. Rainey, answered for her: 'When the Secretary of Labor is a lady, she should be addressed with the same general formalities as the Secretary of Labor who is a gentleman. You call him "Mr Secretary". You will call her "Madam Secretary". You gentlemen know that when a lady is presiding over a meeting, she is referred to as "Madam Chairman" when you rise to address the chair' (quoted in George Martin, *Madam Secretary – Frances Perkins*, 1976). Some of the reporters put this ruling into Perkins's own mouth and that presumably is how the misquotation occurred.

camel. See EASIER FOR A ~ TO . . .

Camelot. (1) The legendary location of King Arthur's court. (2) The nickname for President Kennedy's 'court'. In January 1961, the inauguration of a stylish young US President, with a glamorous wife at his side, aroused hopes of better things to come, following the sober Eisenhower years. But this in itself was not enough for people to apply the epithet to members (and hangers-on) of John F. Kennedy's administration. What triggered it was the fact that the Lerner-Loewe musical *Camelot* (about King Arthur and Queen Guinevere) had opened on Broadway in December 1960. See also ONE BRIEF SHINING MOMENT.

camp. A word used to refer to anyone, male or female, who ostentatiously, exaggeratedly, self-consciously, somewhat vulgarly and theatrically flaunts himself or herself, without necessarily being homosexual. It is probably derived from the word used of prostitutes (male and female) who used to trail along behind the military and were thus 'camp followers'. It entered popular speech in the 1960s, although its origin is older.

can. See CARRY THE ~.

can a (bloody) duck swim! (*sometimes* **does/will a fish swim!)** This is said by way of meaning 'You bet!', 'Of course, I will'. *O D P* has 'Will a duck swim?' in 1842. Winston Churchill claimed he said the 'can' version to Stanley Baldwin when Baldwin asked if he would accept the post of Chancellor of the Exchequer in the 1924 government. Lady Violet Bonham-Carter used the phrase *to* Churchill when he asked her to serve as a Governor of the BBC in 1941. Thence he proceeded to refer to her as his 'Bloody Duck' and she had to sign her letters to him, 'Your BD'.

can I do you now sir? This was said by 'Mrs Mopp' (Dorothy Summers), the hoarse-voiced charlady or 'Corporation Cleanser', when entering the office of Tommy Handley, as the Mayor, in BBC Radio's 1940s comedy series *ITMA*. (See also *DPP*.)

Can't Pay Won't Pay. The English title of the play *Non Si Paga! Non Si Paga!* (1974) by Dario Fo, it was adopted as a slogan by those objecting to the British government's Community Charge or 'poll tax' in 1990 and by other similar protest groups.

Canute. The name of King Knute (*or* Cnut *or* Knut) (*d* 1035), the Danish King of England, Norway and Denmark, is often evoked in a mistaken fashion. The tale is told of his having his throne carried down to the water's edge, his instructing the waves to go away from him, and his failure thereat. The image is evoked when one wants to portray pointless resistance to an idea, of the clinging on to an untenable position. However, it is wrong to paint Canute as being a fool. After all, the whole point of the story is that Canute carried out the demonstration in order to show his courtiers that there were limits to his power. The original anecdote, pointing the correct moral, first appears in Henry of Huntingdon's *Historia Anglorum*, a twelfth-century manuscript.

cap. See FEATHER IN ONE'S OWN ~.

Capability Brown. Lancelot Brown (*d* 1783) was an architect and landscape gardener, noted for planning a naturalistic type of garden for the great houses of England, with vistas of trees, lakes, and flower-beds. His usual comment after carrying out a survey was: 'It's capable' or 'It has capabilities.'

Captains and the Kings. The title of a novel (1972) by Taylor Caldwell, about an immigrant orphan boy who founds a US political dynasty (based on the Kennedy family), it comes from Rudyard KIPLING's 'Recessional':

> The tumult and the shouting dies;
> The Captains and the Kings depart.

caravan. See DOGS BARK BUT THE ~ . . .

carbuncle. See MONSTROUS ~.

careful. See IF YOU CAN'T BE GOOD BE ~.

carry the can, to. Meaning 'to bear responsibility; take the blame; become a scapegoat', this is possibly a military term, referring to the duties of the man chosen to get beer for a group. He would have to carry a container of beer to the group and then carry it back when it was empty.

cart, to be in the. Meaning 'to be in trouble', this expression may come from the fact that prisoners used to be taken in a cart to punishment or execution, or from when a was horse was put in a cart (because it was ill or dead), the owner being left in a spot.

cash. See under IN GOD WE TRUST.

cash/throw in one's chips/checks, to. Meaning 'to stop gambling', also 'to die', and then, as *DOAS* has it: 'To terminate a business transaction, sell one's share of, or stock in, a business, or the like, in order to realize one's cash profits'. It may also mean 'to make a final gesture' – Tom Mangold wrote concerning the US arms race in space: 'Under malign command, a technological guarantee of invulnerability could induce the holder to cash his chips and go for a pre-emptive first strike' (*Listener*, 8 September 1983).

Cassandra. See GREEK NAMES.

Cassiopeia. See GREEK NAMES.

Castor. See GREEK NAMES.

cat. See LET THE ~ OUT OF THE BAG.

catch. See FIRST ~ YOUR HARE.

'Catch a Falling Star'. The title of a 1958 song, popularized by Perry Como:

> Catch a falling star
> And put it in your pocket,
> Never let it fade away.

Since at least 1563, a 'falling star' has been another name for a meteor or shooting star. John Donne's 'Song' has a somewhat different message:

Go, and catch a falling star
Get with child a mandrake root,
Tell me, where all past years are.
Or who cleft the Devil's foot.

Here it is clearly just one of four impossible tasks. Compare 'Hitch Your Wagon to a Star' – R.W. Emerson, *Society and Solitude* (1870).

Catch My Soul. The title of a rock musical (1970), based on Shakespeare's *Othello*. The title comes from Othello's words about Desdemona (III.iii.91):

Excellent wretch! Perdition catch my
    soul,
But I do love thee, and when I love thee
    not,
Chaos is come again.

When Shakespeare plays have been adapted for stage and screen, especially as musicals, the tendency has been to use a quotation from the original as the new title of the piece. Thus, *The Taming of the Shrew* became the musical KISS ME KATE; a production of *Othello* featured in the 1936 film *Men Are Not Gods*; a 1959 German film of *Hamlet* was called *The Rest is Silence*; *Hamlet* was featured in the two films called TO BE OR NOT TO BE (1942, 1983); a compression of both parts of *King Henry I V* became the 1966 film *Chimes at Midnight*. On the other hand, *The Comedy of Errors* became *The Boys from Syracuse* and *Romeo and Juliet* became *West Side Story*.

Catch-22. This was the title of Joseph Heller's novel (1961, film US, 1970) about a group of US fliers in the Second World War. 'It was a Catch-22 situation,' people will say, as if resorting to a quasi-proverbial expression like 'Heads you win, tails I lose' or 'Damned if you do, damned if you don't.' Heller gave a name to the popular view that 'there's always a catch' – some underlying law

which defeats people by its brutal, ubiquitous logic, though, oddly, Heller had originally numbered it 18. In the book, the idea is explored several times. Captain Yossarian, a US Air Force bombardier, does not wish to fly any more missions. He goes to see the group's MO, Doc Daneeka, about getting grounded on the pretext that he is crazy:

Daneeka: There's a rule saying I have to ground anyone who's crazy.
Yossarian: Then why can't you ground me? I'm crazy.
Daneeka: Anyone who wants to get out of combat duty isn't really crazy.

This is the catch – Catch-22.

catgut. Sheep, horse, ass, but *not* cat intestines are used in the making of strings for musical instruments. Shakespeare got it right in *Much Ado About Nothing*: 'Is it not strange, that sheeps' guts should hale souls out of men's bodies?' (II.iii.59). Cats' intestines are never used – though they are for tennis racquets. Possibly the word was introduced as a pejorative way of describing the sound made by badly played violin strings, whatever their actual source.

Catherine of Alexandria, St. See SAINTS' NAMES.

cathouse. In *Catwatching* (1986), Desmond Morris traces this term for a brothel (mostly US use) from the fact that prostitutes have been called 'cats' since the fifteenth century, 'for the simple reason that the urban female cat attracts many toms when it is on heat and mates with them one after the other'. As early as 1401, men were warned, Morris says, of the risk of chasing 'cat's tail' – women. Hence the slang word **tail** to denote the female genitals (compare 'pussy').

cat in hell's chance, not to have a. Meaning 'to have no chance whatsoever', the full expression makes the expression clear: 'No more chance than a cat in hell *without claws*.'

Cat on a Hot Tin Roof. The title of a play (1955; film US, 1958) by Tennessee Williams, in which the 'cat' is Maggie, Brick's wife, 'whose frayed vivacity', wrote Kenneth Tynan, 'derives from the fact that she is sexually ignored by her husband'. From the (mostly US) expression 'as nervous as a cat on a hot tin roof', which derives from the common English expression 'like a cat on hot bricks', meaning 'ill-at-ease, jumpy'. John Ray in his *Collection of English Proverbs* (1670–8) has: 'to go like a cat upon a hot bake stone'.

cats. See RAINING ~ AND DOGS.

cat's paw. Meaning 'someone used as a tool by another', this term was known in Britain by 1657, but chiefly derived from one of La Fontaine's fables (1668–94), 'The Monkey and the Cat' in which a monkey persuades a cat to pick up chestnuts off a hot stove. 'The Cat's Paw' is the title of a painting (1824) by Sir Edwin Landseer, illustrating the story.

cat that walks alone, the. 'I am the cat that walks alone' was a favourite expression of Lord Beaverbrook, alluding to 'The Cat That Walked by Himself' in *The Just-So Stories* (1902) by Rudyard KIPLING.

Caudle lecture. See CURTAIN LECTURE.

caviare to the general. A famously misunderstood phrase meaning 'of no interest to common folk', this has nothing to do with giving expensive presents of caviare to unappreciative military gentlemen. In Shakespeare's *Hamlet* (II.ii.434), the Prince refers to a play which, he recalls: 'pleased not the million, 'twas caviare to the general' (the general public, in other words). The Arden edition notes that in *c* 1600, when the play was written, caviare was a novel delicacy. It was probably inedible to those who had not yet acquired a taste for it.

Cecilia, St. See SAINTS' NAMES.

Celtic fringe (*or* edge). The area occupied by the Celtic peoples of Ireland, Scotland, Wales and Cornwall, seen – usually derogatively – as being on the fringes of the British Isles (compare LUNATIC FRINGE). The phrase arose in the late nineteenth century.

Celtic Twilight, The. The title of a collection of stories on Celtic themes (1893) by W.B. Yeats. The phrase came to be used (by others) to describe the atmosphere and preoccupations of Celtic Britain – particularly in the sense that they were on the way out (compare TWILIGHT OF EMPIRE).

Centaurs. See GREEK NAMES.

centre cannot hold. See THINGS FALL APART.

Cerberus. See ROMAN NAMES.

Ceres. See ROMAN NAMES.

certain substances. This police euphemism for drugs is used chiefly in the UK where restrictions are placed on the reporting of criminal activity before a charge has been made. Starting in the 1960s, newspapers would report raids on pop stars' houses and conclude: 'Certain substances were taken away for analysis.' From the episode of TV's *Monty Python's Flying Circus* broadcast on 16 November 1969: *Policeman:* 'I must warn you, sir, that outside I have police dog Josephine, who is not only armed, and trained to sniff out certain substances, but is also a junkie.'

Chad, the (*or* Mr Chad). The little figure peering over a wall and drawn to accompany the message KILROY WAS HERE is known in the US as 'Chad', 'Mr Chad', or 'the Chad'. In the UK, the figure is more associated with the slogan 'Wot no —?' than with Kilroy. Various suggestions have been advanced as to how the little figure took the form it did, most probably in the early part of the Second World War. But why was he called 'Chad', particularly when in other parts of the world (notably Canada and Australia) he acquired the names Flywheel, Clem, Private Snoops, the Jeep, or Phoo? A correspondent suggests that the Women's Auxiliary Air Force (WAAFs) had links with a building called Chadwick House in Bolton. Brewer says the name comes from 'Chat' the cartoonist (George Edward Chatterton) who also created the figure in 1938. Or possibly the name comes from the film *Chad Hanna* which was released in Britain in June 1941 just as the craze was taking off.

chalk. See LONG ~.

Cham. See GREAT ~.

Chamberlain, Neville. See UMBRELLA.

chance. See CAT IN HELL'S ~.

Change and Fortune. The title of the memoirs (1980) of the former Labour Cabinet Minister, Douglas Jay (later Lord Jay), comes from one of A.E. Housman's *Last Poems*:

> When summer's end is nighing
> And skies at evening cloud,
> I muse on change and fortune
> And all the feats I vowed
> When I was young and proud.

Change Lobsters and Dance. The English title of the autobiography *Dicke Lilli, gutes Kind* (1974) of the film actress Lilli Palmer, it alludes to the 'Lobster Quadrille' passage in ALICE IN WONDERLAND, perhaps referring to her numerous screen partners. These precise words do not appear in *Alice*, though the instruction 'change lobsters' does.

Chapter of Accidents, A. The title of the autobiography (1972) of Goronwy Rees, comes from the phrase meaning 'a series of unforeseen happenings or misfortunes'. The 4th Earl of Chesterfield used it in a letter to his son in 1753; in 1837, John Wilkes was quoted by Southey as saying: 'The chapter of accidents is the longest chapter in the book.'

Chariots of Fire. This title was given to the film (UK, 1981) about the inner drives of two athletes (one a future missionary) in the 1924 Olympics. Appropriately for a film whose basic themes include Englishness, Christianity and Judaism, the title comes from William Blake's 'JERUSALEM' which is sung in Parry's setting at the climax of the film:

> Bring me my bow of burning gold,
> Bring me my arrow of desire
> Bring me my spear! Oh, clouds unfold
> Bring me my chariot of fire.

Note the singular. 'Chariots of fire' in the plural occurs in 2 Kings 6:17: 'And the Lord opened the eyes of the young man; and he saw: and, behold, the mountain was full of horses and chariots of fire round about Elisha.'

Charley/Charlie. See CLAP HANDS – HERE COMES ~; PROPER ~.

charm offensive. A happy coinage (along the lines of 'peace offensive') for the the newly-warm, gregarious, open tactics towards the West of the Soviet leader, Mikhail Gorbachev, around 1986. These tactics contrasted greatly with the frosty style of his predecessors.

Charon. See GREEK NAMES.

Charybdis. See GREEK NAMES.

Chase. See CHEVY ~.

chattering classes. This description is applied to newspaper journalists and broadcasters who are paid to discuss topics of current interest, to the opinion-formers, but also to those who simply likely to dissect current events. Coinage has been ascribed to the journalist Frank Johnson in the early 1980s. In the *Observer* (4 August 1985), Alan Watkins wrote: 'At the beginning of the week the *Daily Mail* published, over several days, a *mélange* of popular attitudes towards Mrs Thatcher. Even though it contained little that was surprising or new, it was much discussed among the chattering classes.'

Chatterley. See LADY ~.

chauffeur. The first motor cars ran on a steam-operated principle, so the drivers had to heat up (French *chauffer*) the vehicles before they would start. 'Chauffeur', the name for these warmer-uppers (also used in French to describe the firemen on steam engines) has since been applied in English to the person paid to drive a vehicle for an employer.

chauvinist. See MALE ~ PIG.

Checkmate. See END GAME.

checks. See CASH ONE'S ~.

cheers. See CUP THAT ~.

cheesed/browned off. This expression means 'fed up'. 'Cheese' and 'off-ness' rather go together, so one might think of cheese as having an undesirable quality. Also, when cheese is subjected to heat, it goes brown, or gets 'browned off'. On the other hand, it could derive from 'cheese off', an expression like 'fuck off', designed to make a person go away. 'Cheesed off' may just be a state of rejection, like 'pissed off'.

cherry tree. See WASHINGTON.

che sera sera. In 1956, Doris Day had a hit with the song 'Whatever Will Be Will Be' which made use of this foreign phrase. She had sung it in the re-make of Alfred Hitchcock's *The Man Who Knew Too Much* in that year. Ten years later, Geno Washington and the Ram Jam Band had a hit with a song entitled '*Que Sera Sera*'.

So is it *che* or *que*? There is no such phrase as *che sera sera* in modern Spanish or Italian, though *che* is an Italian word and *sera* is a Spanish one. *¿Que sera? ¿sera?* in Spanish translates as 'What will be? will be?' – which is not quite right; *lo que sera, sera* makes sense but is not the wording of the song. However, in Christopher Marlowe's *Dr Faustus* (published 1604) Faustus's first soliloquy has:

> What doctrine call you this?
> Che sera, sera,
> What will be, shall be.

This is an old spelling of what would be, in modern Italian *che sara, sara*. In *Faustus*, however, it is probably Old French.

The *idea* behind the proverbial saying is simpler to trace. 'What must be, must be' can be found as far back as Chaucer's 'Knight's Tale' (*c* 1390): 'When a thyng is shapen, it shal be.' However, *che sera sera* is the form in which the Duke of Bedford's motto has always been written and so presumably that, too, is Old French or Old Italian.

Chevy Chase. This was the assumed name of the US comedy actor who came to the fore in the 1970s. He appeared on *Saturday Night Live* on TV and in films such as *Foul Play*. He was born Cornelius Crane Chase in 1943, so why did he adopt the name 'Chevy' – except to get away from Cornelius? Could it be that he wanted to allude to Chevy as in the abbreviated form of **Chevrolet**, the US motor car which derives its name from Louis Chevrolet, a Swiss engineer? Or could he have wanted to allude to the fifteenth-century ballad 'Chevy Chase' which describes an old dispute between the Percy and Douglas families on the Scottish border, arising from a hunting accident? ('Chevy' or 'chivvy' is a huntsman's call meaning 'chase or harass the fox'.) More likely it comes from the suburb of Washington DC known as Chevy Chase, though this was probably named after the fifteenth-century ballad by colonists who settled there.

chewed every mouthful ... See GLADSTONE.

chew the cud, to. See CUD, TO CHEW THE.

chew the rag, to. This expression means 'to chew something over; to grouse or grumble over something at length, to discuss matters with a degree of thoroughness' (compare 'to chew the fat'). As in the expression 'to chew something over', the word 'chew' here means simply 'to say' – that is, it is something that is carried on in the mouth like eating. The 'rag' part relates to an old meaning of the word, in the sense 'to scold' or 'reprove severely'. 'Rag' was also once a slang word for 'the tongue' (from 'red rag', probably). Compare 'TO CHEW THE CUD'.

chief cook and bottle-washer. This phrase is used to refer to 'a person put in charge of running something (sometimes head cook ...); a factotum'. What may be an early form of the phrase occurs in Schikaneder's text for Mozart's *Die Zauberflöte* (1791). Papageno says: 'Here's to the head cook and the head butler' [*Der Herr Koch und der Herr Kellermeister sollen leben!*] (II.xix).

child. See GIVE US A ~ ...

'Childe Roland to the Dark Tower Came'. This is the title of Robert Browning's poem (1855) which concludes with the lines:

Dauntless the slug-horn to my lips I set,
And blew. 'Childe Roland to the Dark Tower came.'

Earlier, Edgar in Shakespeare's *King Lear*, mouthing snatches of verse in his assumed madness, says (III.iv.179):

Child Rowland to the dark tower came,
His word was still 'Fie, foh, and fum,
I smell the blood of a British man'.

Shakespeare, in turn, was quoting a line from an older ballad (a 'child' was a candidate for knighthood). In certain Scottish ballads of uncertain date, Childe Roland is the son of King Arthur who rescues his sister from a castle to which she has been abducted by fairies. In the *Chanson de Roland* (French, twelfth century) and other tellings of the legend, he is the nephew of Charlemagne. Shakespeare probably combined material from two completely different sources – the first line from a ballad about Roland, the second two from the old story of Jack the Giant-killer.

children. See NEVER WORK WITH ~ AND ANIMALS; WOMEN AND ~ FIRST.

Children of a Lesser God. The title of Marc Medoff's play (1979, film US, 1986), about the relationship between a deaf girl and her speech therapist, it comes from Tennyson's 'The Passing of

Arthur', lines 13-15 in *Idylls of the King* (1859-85):

> For why is all around us here
> As if some lesser god had made the world,
> But had not force to shape it as he would.

Medoff's suggestion, presumably, is that people with a disability like deafness could be said to be the work of a 'lesser god'.

children should be seen and not heard.

This proverbial expression was, according to *CODP*, originally applied to (young) women. 'A mayde schuld be seen, but not herd' was described as an 'old' saying in *c* 1400. It was not until the nineteenth century that a general application to children of both sexes became common, though Thackeray in *Roundabout Papers* (1860–3) still has: 'Little boys should not loll on chairs . . . Little girls should be seen and not heard.'

chill. See BIG ~ GENERATION.

Chinese whispers.

This phrase, used for gossip inaccurately passed on, derives from the name of a children's party game. Seated in a circle, the children whisper a message to each other until it arrives back at the person who started, usually changed out of all recognition. An alternative name for the game is 'Russian Scandal', which *OED2* finds in 1873, (or 'Russian Gossip' or 'Russian Rumour(s)'). Presumably, Russian and Chinese are mentioned because of their exotic nineteenth-century connotations, the difficulty of both languages, and because the process of whispering might sound reminiscent of the languages when spoken.

chip of(f) the old/same block.

Referring to a child having the same qualities as its parent, the use of this expression was established by the 1620s.

Edmund Burke said of the first speech in the House of Commons by William Pitt the Younger (1781): 'Not merely a chip of the old "block", but the old block itself' (referring to Pitt the Elder, 1st Earl of Chatham).

chip on one's shoulder, to have a.

Meaning 'to bear a grudge in a defensive manner', the expression originated in the US where it was known by the early nineteenth century. A boy or man would, or would seem, to carry a chip (of wood) on his shoulder daring others to dislodge it, looking for a fight.

c/Chips. See CASH ONE'S ~; MR ~.

chips are down, when the.

Meaning 'a crucial stage in a situation', the phrase alludes to the chips used in betting games. The bets are placed when they are down but the outcome is still unknown.

Chips With Everything.

The title of Arnold Wesker's play (1962) about class attitudes in the RAF during National Service, derived from the belief that the working classes tended to have (potato) chips as the accompaniment to almost any dish. Indeed, the play contains the line: 'You breed babies and you eat chips with everything.' Partridge/*Catch Phrases* dates the phrase *c* 1960 and says it has 'been applied to that sort of British tourist abroad which remains hopelessly insular'. 'Declaration', written earlier, in 1957, by the film director Lindsay Anderson, states: 'Coming back to Britain is always something of an ordeal. It ought not to be, but it is. And you don't have to be a snob to feel it. It isn't just the food, the sauce bottles on the cafe tables, and the *chips with everything* [my italics]. It isn't just saying goodbye to wine, goodbye to sunshine . . . We can come home. But the price we pay is high.'

Chloe. See GREEK NAMES.

Chloris. See GREEK NAMES.

CHRISTIE (Agatha). A prolific writer of detective novels and plays (1890–1976), she more often than not used quotations as the titles of her books – with a marked preference for phrases from nursery rhymes. See *ABSENT IN THE SPRING; BY THE PRICKING OF MY THUMBS; EVIL UNDER THE SUN; HICKORY DICKORY DOCK; IN A GLASS DARKLY; THE MIRROR CRACK'D FROM SIDE TO SIDE; MOUSE-TRAP; MOVING FINGER; MUR-DER MOST FOUL; N OR M?; ONE TWO BUCKLE MY SHOE; PALE HORSES; POCKETFUL OF RYE; SAD CYPRESS; TAKEN AT THE FLOOD; TEN LITTLE NIGGERS.*

Christmas. See — BY ~.

Christopher, St. See SAINTS' NAMES.

Chronicles of Wasted Time. The title of Malcolm Muggeridge's two volumes of autobiography (1972–3) is taken from Shakespeare's Sonnet 106:

> When in the chronicles of wasted time
> I see descriptions of the fairest wights
> . . .

chuck it —! Meaning 'abandon that line of reasoning, that posturing'. An example from the BBC's *World at One* radio programme in May 1983 during the run-up to a General Election: Roy Hattersley complained that he was only being questioned on the ten per cent of the Labour Party manifesto with which

he disagreed. Robin Day, the inter-viewer, replied: 'Chuck it, Hattersley!' This format was used earlier and notably by G.K. Chesterton. In his 'Antichrist, or the Reunion of Christendom' (1912), he satirized the pontificating of F.E. Smith (later 1st Earl of Birkenhead) on the Welsh Disestablishment Bill:

> Talk about the pews and steeples
> And the cash that goes therewith!
> But the souls of Christian peoples . . .
> Chuck it, Smith!

chuffed. (1) Pleased. (2) Fed up. This is a JANUS word because it has two opposite meanings. The first meaning of 'pleased' possibly predominates. When Paul McCartney of the Beatles returned to Liverpool to receive the Freedom of the City in November 1984, he declared that he was 'well chuffed'. Paul Beale in Partridge/*Slang* suggests a development (in military circles) from the word 'chow' (meaning food in general). This might account for the pleased or well-sated meaning. The opposite meaning of 'fed up' may derive from a dialect use of 'chuff' (dating from 1832) meaning 'churlish, gruff, morose'.

chunder, to. This Australian word of uncertain origin, according to the *Macquarie Dictionary* (1981), means 'to be sick'. However, the *Dictionary of Australian Quotations* (1984), has: 'Barry Humphries states that, to the best of his knowledge, he introduced the words "chunder" and "chundrous" to the Australian language [by 1964 at least]. Previously "chunder" was known to him only as a piece of Geelong Grammar School slang.'

The usual derivation concerns people about to be sick overboard shouting to those on lower decks: 'Watch under!' Partridge/*Slang* has that it is rhyming slang for Chunder Loo ('spew'), from Chunder Loo of Akin Foo, 'a cartoon figure in a long-running series of advertisements for Cobra boot polish in the *Bulletin* [Australia] from 8 April 1909'.

CIBP. See INITIALS.

Cinderella. Describing a young woman (usually) who is neglected or whose merit or beauty goes unrecognized, the name derives from the heroine of Perrault's famous fairytale from *Histoires ou Contes du Temps Passé* (Paris, 1697). In it, a 'cinder-girl' is able to go to a ball through the intervention of a fairy godmother provided she returns before midnight. Her eventual marriage to a prince concludes the archetypal RAGS-TO-RICHES story.

Cinema names. See under ODEON.

Cincinnatus. See ROMAN NAMES.

Circe. GREEK NAMES.

circle. See MAGIC ~.

circus. See IF YOU CAN'T RIDE TWO HORSES . . .

Citizen of the World, The. This was the title of a collection of letters by Oliver Goldsmith purporting to be those of Lien Chi Altangi, a philosophic Chinaman living in London and commenting on English life and characters. They were first published as 'Chinese Letters' in the *Public Ledger* (1760–1), and then again under this title in 1762. Earlier, OED2 finds the phrase in Caxton (1474) and, 'If a man be gracious and courteous to strangers, it shows he is a citizen of the world' in Francis Bacon's 'Goodness, and Goodness of Nature' (1625). Even earlier, 'I am citizen, not of Athens or Greece, but of the world' is ascribed to Socrates, and Cicero has '*civem totius mundi*', meaning 'one who is cosmopolitan, at home

anywhere'. James Boswell, not unexpectedly, in his *Journal of a Tour to the Hebrides* (1786) reflects: 'I am, I flatter myself, completely a citizen of the world . . . In my travels through Holland, Germany, Switzerland, Italy, Corsica, France, I never felt myself from home; and I sincerely love "every kindred and tongue and people and nation".'

city. See SHINING ~ ON A HILL.

civilization. See END OF ~ AS WE KNOW IT.

clanger. See DROP A ~.

Clapham. See MAN ON THE ~ OMNIBUS.

clap hands – here comes Charley. This apparently nonsensical catch phrase, popular at one time in Britain, derived its popularity from its use in the signature tune of the pianist Charlie Kunz, well known on British radio in the 1930s and 40s. The song went: 'Clap hands, here comes Charley . . . here comes Charley now'. With lyrics by Billy Rose and Ballard MacDonald, and music by Joseph Meyer, it had been recorded in the US in 1925. According to *The Book of Sex Lists*, the song was written 'in honour of a local chorine, first-named Charline, who had given many of the music publishers' contact men (song pluggers) cases of gonorrhoea – a venereal disease commonly known as "the clap" '. According to Partridge/ *Slang*, 'to do a clap hands Charlie' was 1940s RAF slang for flying an aircraft in such a way as to make the wings seem to meet overhead.

clapometer. See SWINGOMETER.

Clare of Assisi, St. See SAINTS' NAMES.

classes. See CHATTERING ~.

clattering train. Lord Beaverbrook (*d* 1964), was a newspaper proprietor notorious for interfering with the running of his papers. His favourite enquiry as his mighty media machine rumbled on was: 'Who is in charge of the clattering train?' Ominously, this quotation was based on a remembering of the anonymous poem 'Death and His Brother Sleep', which includes the lines:

> *Who* is in charge of the clattering train?
> The axles creak, and the couplings strain
> . . .
> For the pace is hot, and the points are near,
> And Sleep hath deadened the driver's ear;
> And signals flash through the night in vain.
> Death is in charge of the clattering train!

It is possible that Beaverbrook borrowed this expression from Winston Churchill who also quoted the poem in the first volume of *The Second World War* (1948) saying: 'I had learnt them from a volume of *Punch* cartoons which I used to pore over when I was eight or nine years old at school in Brighton.' That would have been in 1882–3. In fact, the poem did not appear in *Punch* until 4 October 1890. It concerns a railway collision at Eastleigh. Due to fatigue, the driver and stoker failed to keep a proper look-out.

Claus, Santa. See NICHOLAS under SAINTS' NAMES.

Clean. See MR ~.

cleanliness is next to godliness. Although this phrase appears in Sermon 88 'On Dress' by John Wesley within quotation marks, it is without attribution. Brewer claims that it is to be found in the writings of Phinehas ben Yair, a rabbi. Thomas J. Barratt, one of the fathers of modern advertising, seized upon it to promote Pears' Soap, chiefly

in the UK. On a visit to the US in the 1880s, he sought a testimonial from a man of distinction. Shrinking from an approach to President Grant, he ensnared the eminent divine, Henry Ward Beecher. Beecher happily complied with Barratt's request and wrote a short text beginning: 'If cleanliness is next to godliness . . . ' and received no more for his pains than Barratt's 'hearty thanks'.

clerihew. This is a four-line, amusing, biographical poem, named after E. Clerihew Bentley (*d* 1956) who pioneered the genre. E.g., Bentley's own:

> George the Third
> Ought never to have occurred.
> One can only wonder
> At so grotesque a blunder.

According to Anon.:

> When questioned, E. Clerihew Bentley
> Smiled gently.
> Said those who can write a good clerihew
> Are very few.

cleverest young man in England, the. This is an unofficial title bestowed semi-humorously from time to time. In 1976, the recipient was Peter Jay (*b* 1937), then an economics journalist on *The Times*. He was dubbed thus in an article so headed (with the saving grace of a question mark) by the *Sunday Times Magazine* (2 May). Two years earlier he had been included in *Time*'s list of the 150 people 'most likely to achieve leadership in Europe'. He became British Ambassador to Washington at the age of 40, at which point people stopped calling him one of the most promising of his generation.

In September 1938, at the League of Nations, Chips Channon wrote in his diary of: 'John Foster, that dark handsome young intellectual . . . Fellow of All Souls, prospective candidate, and altogether one of the cleverest young men in England'. This was presumably Sir John Foster QC, later a Tory MP. Compare GREATEST LIVING —.

Clio. See GREEK NAMES.

clipper. See YANKEE ~.

Cliveden Set, the. Insofar as it existed, the set was in favour of APPEASEMENT and took its name from the seat of Lord and Lady Astor, who were at the centre of it. The name first appeared in Claud Cockburn's news sheet *The Week* (17 June 1936). Chips Channon wrote in his diary on 4 April 1938 (of a reception given by Lady Astor): 'The function will be criticised, since there is already talk of a so-called "Cliveden" set which is alleged to be pro-Hitler, but which, in reality, is only pro-Chamberlain and pro-sense.' On 8 May 1940, Channon added: 'I think [Lady Astor] is seriously rattled by the "Cliveden Set" allegations which were made against her before the war, and now wants to live them down.'

Clockwork Orange, A. The title of a novel (1962, film UK, 1971) by Anthony Burgess, from the expression, 'queer as a clockwork orange' (i.e. homosexual), and in use since the mid-1950s says Paul Beale in Partridge/*Slang*. The title's relevance to the story – which has no overt homosexual element – is debatable.

clogs, to pop one's. This is a euphemism for 'to die'. Compare the expressions 'to pop off' and 'to die with one's boots on' (see THEY DIED WITH THEIR BOOTS ON), or possibly pop in the sense of 'pawn' (see POP GOES THE WEASEL).

Close Encounters of the Third Kind. This title for the Steven Spielberg science-fiction film (US 1977) is said to be taken from categories used in the US

services to grade observations of Unidentified Flying Objects. A 'close encounter 1' would be a simple UFO sighting; a 'close encounter 2' would be evidence of an alien landing; and a 'close encounter 3' would be actual contact with aliens. The categories were devised by a UFO researcher called J. Allen Hyhek (source: Rick Meyers, *The Great Science Fiction Films*).

The phrase has also been used allusively to describe intimacy: 'For a close encounter of the fourth kind, ring *** ****'; 'Polanski's new movie – Close Encounters with the Third Grade' (graffito, quoted 1982).

close-run. See DAMN ~ THING.

closet. See OUT OF THE ~ ...

close your eyes/lie back and think of England. This advice is given to women when confronted with the inevitability of sexual intercourse, or jocularly to either sex about doing anything unpalatable. The source that Partridge/*Catch Phrases* gives for this saying is the *Journal* (1912) of Alice, Lady Hillingdon: 'I am happy now that Charles calls on my bedchamber less frequently than of old. As it is, I now endure but two calls a week and when I hear his steps outside my door I lie down on my bed, close my eyes, open my legs and think of England.' There *was* an Alice, Lady Hillingdon (*d* 1940) but her *Journals*, if they ever existed, have not been traced. *Salome Dear, Not With a Porcupine* (ed. Arthur Marshall, 1982) has it that the newly-wedded Mrs Stanley Baldwin was supposed to have declared: 'I shut my eyes tight and thought of the Empire.'

Sometimes the phrase occurs in the form 'lie back and think of England' but this probably results from confusion with 'she should lie back and enjoy it'. In 1977, there was a play by John Chapman and Anthony Marriott at the Apollo Theatre, London, with the title

Shut Your Eyes and Think of England. (See also *D P P.*)

clothes. See EMPEROR'S NEW ~.

cloud. See LAND OF THE LONG WHITE ~.

cloud-cuckoo land, to live in. Meaning 'to have impractical ideas', the expression comes from the name *Nephelococcygia*, suggested for the capital city of the birds (in the air), in *The Birds* by Aristophanes (*d c* 380 BC).

cloud nine, on (*or* cloud seven). Meaning 'in a euphoric state', both forms have existed since the 1950s. The derivation appears to be from terminology used by the US Weather Bureau. Cloud nine is the cumulonimbus which may reach 30–40,000 feet. As Morris notes: 'If one is upon cloud nine, one is high indeed.' Morris also records the reason for cloud nine being more memorable than cloud seven: 'The popularity . . . may be credited to the *Johnny Dollar* radio show of the 1950s. There was one recurring episode . . . Every time the hero was knocked unconscious – which was often – he was transported to cloud nine. There Johnny could start talking again.' British playwright Caryl Churchill referred to the phrase in the title of her 1979 play *Cloud Nine*.

cloud no bigger than a man's hand, a. When something is described as such, it is not yet very threatening – as though a man could obliterate a cloud in the sky by holding up his hand in front of his face. The phrase is biblical: 'Behold, there ariseth a little cloud out of the sea, like a man's hand' (1 Kings 18:44). Revd Francis Kilvert, on 9 August 1871, has: 'Not a cloud was in the sky as big as a man's hand.' In a letter to Churchill on 14 December 1952, Bob Boothby MP wrote of a dinner at Chartwell: 'It took me back to the

old carefree days when I was your Parliamentary Private Secretary, and there seemed to be no cloud on the horizon; and on to the fateful days when the cloud was no bigger than a man's hand, and there was still time to save the sum of things.'

Clouds of Witness. The title of a detective novel (1926) by Dorothy L. Sayers: 'Wherefore seeing we also are compassed about with so great a cloud of witnesses' (Hebrews 12:1).

clowns. See SEND IN THE ~.

C M G. See INITIALS.

coach and horses. See DRIVE A ~ THROUGH.

coast. See BOHEMIA ~.

cock-and-bull story. This phrase for a long, rambling, unbelievable tale is used notably in Laurence Sterne's *Tristram Shandy* (1760–7). The last words of the novel are: ' "L—d!" said my mother, "what is all this story about?" – "A cock and a bull," said Yorick, "And one of the best of its kind, I ever heard." ' There are several suggested origins. *O E D2*'s earliest citation in this precise form is from the Philadelphia *Gazette of the United States* (1795): 'a long cock-and-bull story about the Columbianum' (a proposed national college). (See also *D P P.*)

cock a snook, to. A snook is the derisive gesture made with thumb and hand held out from the nose. 'To take a sight' is a variation. Both were known by the mid-nineteenth century, indeed *O E D2* has 'cock snooks' in 1791. The game of **snooker** derives its name not from this, but rather from the military nickname for a raw recruit.

cold. See BLOW HOT AND ~.

cold enough to freeze the balls off a brass monkey. The derivation for this phrase, meaning 'extremely cold', probably has nothing to do with any animal. A brass monkey was the name given to the plate on a warship's deck on which cannon balls (or other ammunition) were stacked. In cold weather the brass would contract, tending to cause the stack to fall down. 'Monkey' appears to have been a common slang word in gunnery days – there was a type of gun or cannon known as a 'monkey' and a 'powder monkey' was the name for a boy who carried powder to the guns.

Cold War. This phrase describes any tension between powers, short of all-out war, but specifically that between the Soviet Union and the West following the Second World War. This latter use was popularized by Bernard Baruch, the US financier and presidential adviser in a speech in South Carolina (16 April 1947): 'Let us not be deceived – we are today in the midst of a cold war.' The phrase was suggested to him by his speechwriter Herbert Bayard Swope who had been using it privately since 1940.

Coliseum. See under ODEON.

collapse of stout party. This catch phrase might be used as the tag-line to a story about the humbling of a pompous person. It has long been associated with *Punch* and was thought to have occurred in the wordy captions given to that magazine's cartoons. But as Ronald Pearsall explains in his book *Collapse of Stout Party* (1975): 'To many people Victorian wit and humour is summed up by *Punch* when every joke is supposed to end with "Collapse of Stout Party", though this phrase tends to be as elusive as "Elementary, my dear Watson" in the Sherlock Holmes sagas.' At least *OED2* manages to find a reference to a 'Stout Party' in the caption to a cartoon in the edition of *Punch* dated 25 August 1855.

'Colonel Bogey'. The title of K.J. Alford's military march (1914) which was famously whistled in the film *The Bridge on the River Kwai* (1957) and to which the words HITLER HAS ONLY GOT ONE BALL had been added during the Second World War. It comes from a golfing term, established by 1893. 'Colonel Bogey' is the lowest number of strokes with which a good player can complete a golf course or an individual hole. The aim is thus to 'beat the Colonel'. The term itself was derived from an earlier song, 'The Bogey Man'.

colour. See ANY ~ SO LONG AS IT'S BLACK.

comb. See FIGHT BETWEEN TWO BALD . . .; FINE-TOOTH ~; KOOKIE KOOKIE LEND ME YOUR ~.

comedy is ended, the. The last words of François Rabelais (who died about 1550) are supposed to have been: '*Tirez le rideau, la farce est jouée*' [Bring down the curtain, the farce is played out]. The attribution is made, hedged about with disclaimers, in Jean Fleury's *Rabelais et ses oeuvres* (1877) (also in the life of Rabelais by Motteux, who died in 1718). In Lermontov's novel *A Hero of Our Time* (1840), a character says: '*Finita la commedia.*' At the end of Ruggiero Leoncavallo's opera *Il Pagliacci* [The Clowns] (1892), Canio exclaims: '*La commedia è finita*' [The comedy is finished/over].

come hell and/or high water. Meaning 'come what may', this phrase is mentioned in Partridge/*Slang* as a cliché but, as phrases go, is curiously lacking in citations. *OED2* finds no examples earlier than this century. *Come Hell or High Water* was used as the title of a book by yachtswoman Clare Francis in

COLLECTIVE NOUNS (or nouns of multitude, nouns of assemblage, company terms, group terms, proper terms, terms of venery).

Those referring to birds and animals probably originated in the hunting field where it was deemed sensible 'not to give the game away' by mentioning its whereabouts explicitly. Sources for what follows include *The Week-End Book* (1924), Eric Partridge's *Usage and Abusage* (1947), and James Lipton's *An Exaltation of Larks, or, The Venereal Game* (1977):

Animals (mammals, fishes, reptiles, insects)

antelopes: a herd
apes: a shrewdness
asses: a pace/herd/drove
baboons: a flange
badgers: a cete
bears: a sloth
bees: a swarm/grist
boars: a singular/sounder
bucks: a herd/brace/leash
buffaloes: a herd
camels: a flock
cats: a clowder/cluster
cats (young): a kindle
cattle: a drove/herd
chamois: a herd
colts: a rag
conies: a bury
cubs: a litter
curs: a cowardice
deer: a herd
dogfish: a troop
dogs: a kennel
eels: a swarm
elephants: a herd
elks: a gang
ferrets: a business (and see *Modern Inventions* p. 76)
fishes: shoal/draught/haul/run/catch/school
flies: a swarm
foxes: a skulk/earth
frogs: an army
giraffes: a herd

gnats: a swarm/cloud
goats: a tribe/herd/flock
gorillas: a whoop
hares: a husk/down/herd/drove/trip
harts: a herd
herrings: a glean/shoal/army
horses: a harras/herd/stable
hounds: a mute/pack
kangaroos: a troop
kine: a drove
kittens: see cats (young)
leopards: a leap
lions: a pride/flock/troop
mares: a stud
martens: a richness
mice: a nest
moles: a labour
monkeys: a troop/tribe/troupe
mules: a barren/rake
oxen: a yoke/drove/team/herd
piglets: a litter
porpoises: a school
pups: a litter
rabbits: a nest
racehorses: a field/string
rhinoceroses: a crash
roe(buck)s: a bevy
salmons: a bind
seals: a herd/pod
sheep: a flock
squirrels: a dray
stoats: a pack
swine (tame): a drift
swine (wild): a sowder/sounder
toads: a knot
trouts: a hover
turtles: a dule/bale
whales: a school/gam/pod
wolves: a rout/pack/herd

Birds

birds: a flock/flight/congregation/volery
bitterns: a sedge/siege
bustards: a flock
capercaillies: a tok
chickens: a brood
choughs: a chattering/clattering
coots: a covert
cranes: a herd/sedge/siege
crows: a murder
curlews: a herd

Collective nouns – cont.

doves: a flight/dule
ducks: a paddling/team (in flight)
eagles: a convocation
finches: a charm
geese: a gaggle/skein (in flight)
goldfinches: a charm
goshawks: a flight
grouse: a covey/pack
guillemots: a bazaar
gulls: a pack
hawks: a cast
hens: a brood
herons: a sedge/siege
humming birds: a charm
jays: a band
lapwings: a desert/deceit
larks: an exaltation
mallards: a sord/sute/flush
martens: a richesse
nightingales: a watch
parrots: a flock
partridges: a covey
peacocks: a muster/ostentation/pride
penguins: a rookery
pheasants: a nye/nide/brood
pigeons: a flight/flock
plovers: a congregation/wing/stand
poultry: a run
quails: a bevy/collection
ravens: an unkindness
rooks: a building/clamour
ruffs: a hill
sheldrakes: a dopping
snipe: a walk/wisp
sparrows: a host
starlings: a mumeration/chattering
storks: a mustering
swallows: a flight
swans: a herd/collection/bevy/wedge
swifts: a flock
teals: a spring
whitings: a pod
widgeon: a company/bunch/knob/flight (in flight)
wildfowl: a plump/trip
woodcocks: a fall
woodpeckers: a descent
wrens: a herd

People
bishops: a bench
boys: a blush/rascal
canons: a dignity
cooks: a hastiness
curates: a charge
gossips: a gaggle
hunters: a blast
ladies: a bevy
magistrates: a bench
monks: an abomination
soldiers: a boast
thieves: a skulk

Modern inventions
accountants: a (double-entry) column
actors: a darling/smirk
aldermen: a guzzle
announcers: a mumble
agitators: a haggle
ballet dancers (male): a mince
bears: a pooh
boxers: a clinch
brassières: a handful
cavers: a grope
clerks: a file
climbers: a summit/peak
colonels: a blimp
commercial travellers: a joke
dentists: a rinse
disc jockeys: a cacophony
dowagers: a frost
ex-Prime Ministers: a lack of principals (suggested by Harold Macmillan)
ferrets: a trouser
footballers: a cuddle
freelances: a wealth/moan
golfers: a drive
homosexuals (male): a charm of fairies/basket of fruit/bundle of faggots/packet of fags/board of trade
Italians: a pinch
librarians: a shush
mayors: a chain gang
nannies: a no-no
pessimists: a grumble
patients (dentist's): a wince
pickpockets: a grab

Collective nouns – cont.

prostitutes: a troop of 'orse/
commentary of 'Arlott's/jam of tarts/
flourish of strumpets/volume of
trollops/anthology of pros/peal of
Jezebels/smelting of ores
pupils: a dilation
puppies: a piddle

schoolgirls: a giggle
steeplejacks: a stack
teachers: a blackboard
tourists: a crush
vicars: a bray
WCs (Wing Commanders): a flush
worms: a diet

1977. She followed it in 1978 with *Come Wind or Weather. Hell and High Water* was the title of a US film in 1954. (See also *DPP*.)

come up and see me sometime.

Mae West had a notable stage hit on Broadway with her play *Diamond Lil* (1928). When she appeared in the 1933 film version SHE DONE HIM WRONG, what she said to a very young Cary Grant (playing a policeman) was: 'You know I always did like a man in uniform. And that one fits you grand. Why don't you come up some time and see me? I'm home every evening.' As a catch phrase, the words have been rearranged to make them easier to say. That is how W.C. Fields says them *to* Mae West in the film *My Little Chickadee* (1939), and she herself took to saying them in the rearranged version.

comforter. See JOB'S ~.

coming. See LIKE ~ HOME.

'Comin' in on a Wing and a Prayer'.

The title of a popular US song of the Second World War (published in 1943) which took its title from an alleged remark by an actual pilot who was coming in to land with a badly-damaged plane. Harold Adamson's lyrics include the lines:

> Tho' there's one motor gone, we can still carry on
> Comin' in on a wing and a pray'r.

A US film about life on an aircraft carrier (1944) was called simply *Wing and a Prayer*.

commanding heights of the economy.

In a speech to the Labour Party conference in November 1959, Aneurin Bevan said: 'Yesterday, Barbara [Castle] quoted from a speech which I made some years ago, and she said that I believed that socialism in the context of modern society meant the conquest of the commanding heights of the economy . . .' Alan Watkins in a throwaway line in his *Observer* column (28 September 1987) said 'the phrase was originally Lenin's'. At the Labour Party Conference in October 1989, Neil Kinnock revived the phrase in saying that education and training were 'the commanding heights of every modern economy'.

commandment. See ELEVENTH ~.

comment. See NO ~.

Common Reader, The. The title of two volumes of Virginia Woolf's collected essays, published in 1925 and 1932, comes from Dr Johnson's life of Gray in *Lives of the English Poets*. Praising the 'Elegy', he writes: 'In the character of his Elegy I rejoice to concur with the common reader . . . The churchyard abounds with images which find a mirror in every mind, and with sentiments to which every bosom returns an echo.'

Communist Party. See ARE YOU NOW OR HAVE YOU EVER BEEN . . .

company terms. See COLLECTIVE NOUNS.

complain. See NEVER ~ . . .

Concordia. See ROMAN NAMES.

condom. This name for a prophylactic sheath does not derive from the town of Condom in south-western France. Indeed, early eighteenth-century use of the term tended to be in the form 'cundum' (*or* 'condon'), suggesting a different source. No 'Dr Condom' who prescribed this method of contraception has been discovered either.

Conduct Unbecoming. The title of a play by Barry England (1969; film UK, 1975), this comes from the same source as the title of the film *An Officer and a Gentleman* (US, 1982). The phrase is 'conduct unbecoming the character of an officer and a gentleman' and seems to have appeared first in the (British) Naval Discipline Act (10 August 1860), Article 24, though the notion has also been included in disciplinary regulations of other services, and in other countries, if not in quite these words.

Confederacy of Dunces, A. The title of this novel by John Kennedy Toole (1980) is after Jonathan Swift's *Thoughts on Various Subjects* (1706): 'Many a true genius appears in the world – you may know him by this sign, that the dunces are all in confederacy against him.'

confutatis (maledictis). See MASS PHRASES.

connect. See ONLY ~.

Contemptibles. See OLD ~.

Cook's tour, to go on a. Thomas Cook was the founder of the world's original travel agency. His first tour was in 1841 when he took a party of fellow teetotallers on a railway trip in the British Midlands. Now the expression 'Cook's tour' suggests one of rather greater extent than originally intended (compare MAGICAL MYSTERY TOUR). Alas, there has always been a certain amount of prejudice against the organized tour. Amelia B. Edwards, the Victorian Egyptologist, is suitably caustic in *A Thousand Miles Up the Nile* (1877): '[The newcomer in Cairo soon] distinguishes at first sight between a Cook's tourist and an independent traveller.'

cool hundred / thousand / million. *OED2* says drily that 'the "cool" gives emphasis to the (large) amount'. Is it because a large amount of money is rather chilling, lacking in warmth, or because of the calm way the money is paid out? Perhaps the word 'cool' in this context anticipates its more modern connection with jazz, as something thrilling, to be admired and approved of. In Henry Fielding's *Tom Jones* (1749) we read: 'Watson rose from the table in some heat and declared he had lost a cool hundred . . .' In Charles Dickens's *Great Expectations* (1861): 'She had wrote a little [codicil] . . . leaving a cool four thousand to Mr Matthew Pocket.' *A Cool Million* is the title of a satire by Nathaniel West (1934), and in Anthony Powell's *Hearing Secret Harmonies* (1975), Lord Widmerpool comments on a smoke-bomb let off at a literary prize-giving: 'I wouldn't have missed that for a cool million.'

coot. See BALD AS A BADGER.

Copia. See ROMAN NAMES.

Copper. See UP TO A POINT LORD ~.

corner. See FOREIGN FIELD.

Cornucopia. See ROMAN NAMES.

Corona. See under ODEON.

corpse, to. When an actor corpses, it means that he has been overtaken by such involuntary laughter that he is unable to go on speaking his lines – or, if he is supposed to be lying dead on the stage, he is unable to stop himself shaking with mirth. Alternatively, the origin of the word lies in the actor being rendered as incapable as a dead body, or, when another actor has made him forget his lines, it is the equivalent of killing him by stopping his performance.

***Corridors of Power*.** This phrase had become established for the machinations of government, especially in Whitehall, by the time C.P. Snow chose it for the title of his novel (1964). Earlier, Snow had written in *Homecomings* (1956): 'The official world, the corridors of power, the dilemmas of conscience and egotism – she disliked them all.'

Cortez. See STOUT ~.

Corydon. See ROMAN NAMES.

***Così fan tutte*.** The title of Mozart's opera (1790), means 'that's what all women do' (*or* 'women are like that'). The phrase had appeared earlier in Da Ponte's text for *Le nozze di Figaro* (1778). In that opera, Don Basilio sings, '*Così fan tutte le belle, non c'è alcuna*

novità' [That's what all beautiful women do, there's nothing new in that'].

couch potato. A US coinage of the 1980s for a person who sits at home watching television. *Sunday Today* explained the word to British readers on 27 July 1986. But why potato? Is it because of the shape of a fat person slouched over a couch? Or does it allude to the consumption of potato crisps or behaving like a 'vegetable'?

couldn't run a whelk-stall. A way of describing incompetence, this appears to have originated with John Burns, the Labour MP: 'From whom am I to take my marching orders? From men who fancy they are ADMIRABLE CRICHTONS ... but who have not got sufficient brains and ability to run a whelk-stall?' (*South-Western Star*, 13 January 1894). Partridge/*Slang* has 'no way to run a whelk-stall' as the UK equivalent of the US '[that's] a hell of a way to run a railroad' (see WHAT A WAY TO RUN A —), and dates it later twentieth century. The phrases **couldn't organize a piss-up in a brewery** and **couldn't fight his/her way out of a paper bag** are more likely to be employed nowadays.

countdown. It is said that the backward countdown to a rocket launch was first thought of by the German film director Fritz Lang. He thought it would make things more suspenseful if the count was reversed – 5-4-3-2-1 – so, in his 1928 film *By Rocket to the Moon* (sometimes known as *Frau im Mond* or *The Woman in the Moon*, from the German title) he established the routine for future real-life space shots.

countries separated by a common language, two. Referring to England and North America, was this said by Shaw or Wilde? Wilde wrote: 'We have really everything in common with America nowadays except, of course, language' (*The Canterville Ghost*, 1887). The 1951 *Treasury of Humorous Quotations* (Esar & Bentley), however, quotes Shaw as saying: 'England and America are two countries separated by the same language', without giving a source. A radio talk prepared by Dylan Thomas shortly before his death (and published after it in the *Listener*, April 1954), contained an observation about European writers and scholars in America 'up against the barrier of a common language'.

country. See ASK NOT WHAT YOUR ~ ...; ~ OF THE BLIND; GOD'S OWN ~.

Country Matters. The title of an ITV drama series (1972) presenting an anthology of stories by H.E. Bates and A.E. Coppard, linked only by their setting in the English countryside. From Shakespeare's *Hamlet* (III.ii.115):

> *Hamlet*: Lady, shall I lie in your lap?
> *Ophelia*: No, my lord.
> *Hamlet:* I mean, my head upon your lap.
> *Ophelia:* Ay, my lord.
> *Hamlet:* Do you think I meant country matters?
> *Ophelia:* I think nothing, my lord.
> *Hamlet:* That's a fair thought to lie between maids' legs.

Shakespeare's bawdy is sometimes obscure, but few can miss that 'country matters' means physical love-making, or fail to note the pun in the first syllable (which also occurs in Wycherley's *The Country Wife*, 1675, and John Donne's poem 'The Good-Morrow', 1635).

country right or wrong, my. ' "My country right or wrong" is a thing that no patriot would think of saying, except in a desperate case. It is like saying, "My mother, drunk or sober".' So wrote G.K. Chesterton in *The Defendant* (1901). He was alluding to the toast given by the US naval hero Stephen Decatur in 1816:

'Our country! In her intercourse with foreign nations may she always be in the right, but our country, right or wrong.' This is sometimes referred to as 'Decatur's Toast'.

court oath, the. See I SWEAR BY ALMIGHTY GOD ...

Coventry, to send someone to. Meaning 'to refuse to speak to a person', this expression may have originated in the old story of soldiers stationed in Coventry who were so unwelcome that the citizens carried on as if they did not exist, alternatively that if women talked to the soldiers, they were ostracized. Another version comes from the Civil War in England in the seventeenth century. When captured Royalists were sent to Coventry, a strongly Roundhead (Parliamentary) town, they were bound to be ignored. This would appear to be supported by a passage in Clarendon's *History of the Rebellion* (VI:83, 1702-4): '[Birmingham] a town so wicked that it had risen upon small parties of the King's [men], and killed or taken them prisoners and sent them to Coventry.'

Cover Her Face. The title of this crime novel (1962) by P.D. James comes from what Ferdinand says to Bosola about the Duchess whom he has just strangled in John Webster's *The Duchess of Malfi*: 'Cover her face; mine eyes dazzle: she died young' (IV.ii.267, 1612/13).

cow. See HOW NOW BROWN ~.

Crackerjack. The title of a BBC TV children's programme (from 1955) which had a noisy studio audience of youngsters who had only to hear the word 'Crackerjack' for them to scream back 'CRACKERJACK!' It was probably not a word known to them before. In the US, it has the meaning 'excellent', and has also been used as the name of a brand of popcorn and syrup.

cradle. See HAND THAT ROCKS THE ~; OUT OF THE ~ . . .

crazy like a fox. The meaning of this expression is 'apparently crazy but with far more method than madness' (Partridge/*Catch Phrases*). Craziness is hardly a quality one associates with foxes, so the expression was perhaps merely formed in parallel with the older 'cunning as a fox'. *Crazy Like a Fox* was the title of a US TV series about a 'sloppy old private eye' and his 'smart lawyer son' (from 1984). Before this, the phrase was used as the title of a book by S.J. Perelman (1945).

crazy man crazy! See GO MAN GO!

creative accountancy/accounting. A term for ingenious manipulation of accounts which may or may not actually be illegal. An early example of the phrase occurs in *The Producers* (film US, 1968): 'It's simply a matter of creative accounting. Let's assume for a moment that you are a dishonest man . . . It's very easy. You simply raise more money than you need.' The film's subject is such accountancy applied in the world of the theatrical ANGEL.

credibility gap. This the difference between what is claimed as fact and what actually is fact. It dates from the time in the Vietnam war when, despite claims to the contrary by the Johnson administration, an escalation in US participation was taking place. 'Dilemma in "Credibility Gap" ' was the headline over a report on the matter in the *Washington Post* (13 May 1965) and may have been the phrase's first outing.

credo (in unum Deum). See MASS PHRASES.

CREEP. See ACRONYMS.

Cressida. See GREEK NAMES.

Crichton. See ADMIRABLE ~.

Cricket on the Hearth, The. This was the title of the Charles Dickens Christmas book for 1846. The cricket, so described, influences the main character to overcome a misunderstanding. Dickens probably took the idea from a ballad in what is known to be one of his favourite books – Goldsmith's *The Vicar of Wakefield* (1766):

> The cricket chirrups on the hearth,
> The crackling faggot flies.

Earlier, in Milton's 'Il Penseroso' (1632) we find:

> Far from all resort of mirth,
> Save the cricket on the hearth.

crime. See MURDERERS RETURN TO THE SCENE OF THEIR ~.

cringe. See CULTURAL ~.

crinklies. See under YUPPIE.

crisis? what crisis? James Callaghan, the British Labour Prime Minister 1976–9, may be said to have been eased out of office by a phrase he did not (precisely) speak. Returning from a sunny summit meeting in Guadaloupe to Britain's WINTER OF DISCONTENT on 10 January 1979, he was asked by a journalist at a London airport press conference: 'What is your general approach and view of the mounting chaos in the country at the moment?' Callaghan replied: 'Well, that's a judgement that you are making. I promise you that if you look at it from the outside (and perhaps you are taking rather a parochial view), I don't think that other people in the world would share the view that there is mounting chaos.' Next day, the *Sun* newspaper carried the headline: 'Crisis? What crisis?' Callaghan lost the May 1979 General Election. The editor of the *Sun* was given a knighthood by the incoming Prime Minister.

crocodile. See HOW DOTH THE LITTLE ~.

Croesus. See GREEK NAMES.

Cromwell: Our Chief of Men. The title of Antonia Fraser's biography (1973) comes from Milton's Sonnet 16, 'To the Lord General Cromwell', which begins:

> Cromwell, our chief of men, who
> through a cloud,
> Not of war only, but detractions rude,
> Guided by faith and matchless fortitude,
> To peace and truth thy glorious way has
> ploughed.

Fraser's book was known, however, as *Cromwell the Lord Protector* in the US.

Cronos. See KRONOS under GREEK NAMES.

crook. See BY HOOK OR BY ~.

cross of gold. One of the most notable examples of US oratory, but little known in Britain, is William Jennings Bryan's speech to the Democratic Convention in July 1896. It contained an impassioned attack on supporters of the gold. 'You shall not press down upon the brow of labour this crown of thorns. You shall not crucify mankind upon a cross of gold.' Bryan had said virtually the same in a speech to the House of Representatives on 22 December 1894. He won the nomination and fought the presidential election against William J. McKinley who supported the gold standard but lost. A 'cross of gold'-type

speech is sometimes called for when a politician (like Edward Kennedy in 1980) is required to sweep a convention with his eloquence.

crossroads. See DIRTY WORK AT THE ~.

crow. See EAT ~.

'Crown Imperial'. The title given to Sir William Walton's march, which was composed for the Coronation of King George VI in 1936; 'Orb and Sceptre' followed for that of Queen Elizabeth II in 1953. In a television interview, Walton said that if he lived to write a march for a third coronation it would be called 'Sword and Mace'. The key to these titles lies in a passage from Shakespeare's *King Henry V* (IV.i.266). The King says:

> 'Tis not the balm, the sceptre and the
> ball,
> The sword, the mace, the crown imperial
> . . . That beats upon the high shore of
> this world.

Oddly enough, the orchestral parts of 'Crown Imperial' bear a different quotation: 'In beauty bearing the crown imperial – William Dunbar'.

crumblies. See under YUPPIE.

cry all the way to the bank, to. Meaning 'to be in a position to ignore criticism', this expression was certainly popularized, if not actually invented, by the flamboyant pianist, Liberace. In his autobiography (1973), Liberace wrote: 'When the reviews are bad I tell my staff that they can join me as I cry all the way to the bank.'

Cry Havoc. See DOGS OF WAR.

cuckoo. See CLOUD ~ LAND.

cud, to chew the. Meaning 'to think deeply about something, especially the past'. This expression refers to the ruminative look cows have when they chew their 'cud' – that is, bring back food from their first stomachs and chew it in their mouths again. 'Cud' comes from Old English *cwidu*, meaning 'what is chewed'.

cultural cringe. Referring to the belief that one's own country's culture is inferior to that of others, this phrase is probably Australian in origin, and is certainly well known in that country. Arthur Angell Phillips wrote in 1950: 'Above our writers – and other artists – looms the intimidating mass of Anglo-Saxon culture. Such a situation almost inevitably produces the characteristic Australian Cultural Cringe – appearing either as the Cringe Direct, or as the Cringe Inverted, in the attitude of the Blatant Blatherskite, the GOD'S-OWN-COUNTRY and I'm-a-better-man-than-you-are Australian bore.'

Cupid. See ROMAN NAMES.

cup runneth over, my. Meaning 'I'm overjoyed; my blessings are numerous', the expression derives from Psalms 23:5: 'Thou preparest a table before me in the presence of mine enemies: thou anointest my head with oil; my cup runneth over.' Shirley Polykoff, the advertising executive, recounts in her book *Does She . . . Or Doesn't She?* (1975) that she once jestingly proposed 'Her cup runneth over' as a slogan for a corset manufacturer. 'It took an hour to unsell him,' she adds.

cup that cheers, the. The reference here is to tea (taken in preference to alcohol). In 'The Winter Evening' from William Cowper's *The Task* (1783), it's in the plural:

Now stir the fire, and close the shutters fast,
Let fall the curtains, wheel the sofa round,
And, while the bubbling and loud-hissing urn
Throws up a steamy column, and the cups,
That cheer but not inebriate, wait on each,
So let us welcome peaceful ev'ning in.

Partridge lists 'cups that cheer but not inebriate' as a cliché in his dictionary, and notes that earlier, in *Siris* (1744), Bishop Berkeley had said of tar water that it had a nature 'so mild and benign and proportioned to the human constitution, as to warm without heating, to cheer but not inebriate'.

curate's egg, like the. Meaning 'patchy, good in parts', the phrase comes from the caption to a *Punch* cartoon (vol.cix, 1895) in which a Bishop is saying: 'I'm afraid you've got a bad egg, Mr Jones'. The nervous young curate, keen not to say anything critical, flannels: 'Oh no, my Lord, I assure you! Parts of it are excellent.'

curtain lecture (*or* Caudle lecture). Meaning 'a private reproof given by a wife to her husband', it refers to the scolding that took place after the curtains round the bed (as on a four-poster) had been closed. The 'Caudle' variation derives from Douglas Jerrold's *Mrs Caudle's Curtain Lectures*, a series published by *Punch* in 1846 in which Mr Caudle suffered the naggings of his wife after they had gone to bed. Lady Diana Cooper in a letter of 12 January 1944 wrote: 'Clemmie has given him [Winston Churchill] a Caudle curtain lecture on the importance of not quarrelling with Wormwood' (quoted in *TRUMPETS IN THE STEEP*).

customer is always right, the. H. Gordon Selfridge (*d* 1947) was an

American who, after a spell with Marshall Field & Co, came to Britain and introduced the idea of the monster department store. It appears that he was the first to say 'the customer is always right' and many other phrases now generally associated with the business of selling through stores.

custom more honour'd in the breach. Usually taken to mean that whatever custom is under consideration has fallen into sad neglect. But in Shakespeare's *Hamlet* (I.iv.16), the Prince tells Horatio that the King's drunken revelry is a custom that would be '*better* honour'd' if it were not followed at all.

customs. See OLD SPANISH ~.

cut and run, to. Meaning 'to escape; run away', the phrase has a nautical origin. In order to make a quick getaway, instead of the lengthy process of hauling up a ship's anchor, the ship's cable was simply cut. This was easy to do when the anchor was attached to a hemp rope rather than a chain.

cut off at the pass, to (*sometimes* **head off . . .).** Meaning 'to intercept; ambush', the phrase derives from Western films, but was made especially famous from its use in the transcripts of the Watergate tapes (published as *The White House Transcripts*, 1974). As spoken by President Nixon it meant simply 'we will use certain tactics to stop them'. The phrase occurred in a crucial exchange in the White House Oval Office on 21 March 1973 between the president and John Dean concerning the Special Counsel's fears that he could be sent to jail for his part in the cover-up of the Watergate robbery:

P: You are a lawyer, you were a counsel . . . What would you go to jail for?
D: The obstruction of justice.
P: The obstruction of justice?
D: That is the only one that bothers me.
P: Well, I don't know. I think that one . . . I feel it could be cut off at the pass, maybe, the obstruction of justice.

cut of someone's jib, not to like the. Meaning 'not to like the look of someone', the expression has a nautical origin – the 'cut' or condition of the 'jib' or foresail signifying the quality of the sailing vessel as a whole.

cuts. See DEATH OF A THOUSAND ~.

Cybele. See GREEK NAMES.

Cyclops. See GREEK NAMES.

Cynthia. See GREEK NAMES.

Daedalus. See GREEK NAMES.

daft as a brush. Meaning 'stupid', the expression was adapted from the northern 'soft as a brush' by the comedian Ken Platt, who said in 1979: 'I started saying daft as a brush when I was doing shows in the Army in the 1940s. People used to write and tell me I'd got it wrong!' (Partridge/*Slang* suggests that 'daft . . .' was in use before this, however.)

dagmars. Motor-car bumpers (fenders in the US) – so dubbed in the US during the 1950s after a well-endowed actress, Virginia Ruth Egnor, known as 'Dagmar', who appeared on a TV show called *Broadway Open House*.

Daleks. This is the name given to the robotic characters in BBC TV's science-fiction series since 1963. They resemble pepper-pots and go around screeching 'Exterminate! Exterminate!' The explanation given by writer Terry Nation in 1971 (and quoted in *OED2*) that he took the name from the spine of an encyclopaedia volume covering DAL-LEK was denied by him in 1973.

damn. See FRANKLY MY DEAR.

damn close-run thing, a. What the 1st Duke of Wellington actually told the memoirist Thomas Creevey about the outcome of the Battle of Waterloo, was: 'It has been a damned serious business. Blucher and I have lost 30,000 men. It has been a damned nice thing – the nearest run thing you ever saw in your life.' (18 June 1915) The *Creevey Papers* in which this account appears were not published until 1903. Somehow out of this description a conflated version arose, with someone else presumably supplying the 'close-run'.

Damia. See GREEK NAMES.

Damocles. See GREEK NAMES.

Damon. See GREEK NAMES.

dance of the seven veils. Salome so beguiled Herod by her seductive dance that he gave her the head of St John the Baptist. In neither Matthew 14:6 nor Mark 6:22 is she called by her name, however, only 'the daughter of Herodias' (the name was supplied by Josephus, the second-century Jewish historian), nor is the nature of her dancing described. By the time of Richard Strauss's opera *Salome* (1905), based on Oscar Wilde's one-act tragedy *Salomé* (1893), the Dance of the Seven Veils is referred to as such. One of Wilde's stage directions is '*Salomé dances the dance of the seven veils*' and one must assume that the idea originated with him.

Dance to the Music of Time, A. The title of Anthony Powell's novel sequence (published 1951–75) giving a panoramic view of postwar Britain. In the first novel, *A Question of Upbringing*, the narrator, Nicholas Jenkins, looking at workmen round a bucket of coke in falling snow, is put in mind of the painting with this title by Nicolas Poussin which hangs in the Wallace Collection, London. Sometimes this painting is called, less interestingly, '*Ballo della vita humana*' [The Dance of Human Life].

dandelion. The plant's name comes from the French *dent de lion* [lion's tooth], from the supposed resemblance of the outline of the widely toothed leaves. The Italians call it, similarly, *dente di leone* and the Spanish, *diente de leon*. The French themselves, however, call it *pissenlit*. Drinks made from dandelion are a powerful diuretic and could make you wet the bed.

dander up, to get one's. Meaning 'to get ruffled or angry', the expression occurs in William Thackeray's *Pendennis*: 'Don't talk to me about daring to do this thing or t'other, or when my dander is up it's the very thing to urge me on' (Chap. 44, 1848–50). In the US, in the nineteenth century, a 'dander' was either a 'calcined cinder' or 'dandruff'. It is hard to see how the expression develops from either of these meanings. The Dutch word *donder* meaning 'thunder', or 'dunder', a Scottish dialect word for 'ferment', may be more relevant.

dangerous age. The title of a 1967 Dudley Moore film comedy was *Thirty Is a Dangerous Age, Cynthia*. This would seem to allude, however distantly and unknowingly, to *Den farlige alder* [The Dangerous Age], a book in Danish by Karin Michaelis (1910), in which the dangerous age was forty.

Daphne. See GREEK NAMES.

Daphnis. See GREEK NAMES.

Darby and Joan. The term is descriptive of an old couple, happy in their long marriage, in modest but contented circumstances. A ballad on this theme was published in 1735, possibly after an actual couple with these names who are said to have lived in either London or West Yorkshire.

Darien. See STOUT CORTEZ.

dark continent/darkest Africa. In 1878, H.M. Stanley, who discovered Dr Livingstone, published *Through the Dark Continent* and followed it, in 1890, with *Through Darkest Africa*. It was from these two titles that we get the expressions 'dark continent' and 'darkest — ' to describe not only Africa but almost anywhere remote and uncivilized. Flexner 2 suggests that 'In darkest Africa' was a screen subtitle in a silent film of the period 1910–14.

dark horse. Figuratively, the phrase refers to a runner about whom everyone is 'in the dark' until he comes from nowhere and wins the race – of whatever kind. It is possible it originated in Benjamin Disraeli's novel *The Young Duke: A Moral Tale Though Gay* (1831) in which 'a dark horse, which had never been thought of . . . rushed past the grandstand in sweeping triumph'. It is used especially in political contexts.

Darkness at Noon. The title of the novel (1940) by Arthur Koestler (originally in German) about the imprisonment, trial, and execution of a Communist who has betrayed the Party. It echoes Milton's *Samson Agonistes* (1671): 'O dark, dark, dark, amid the blaze of noon'. *Darkness at Noon, or the Great Solar Eclipse of the 16th June 1806* was the title of an anonymous booklet published in Boston (1806).

dark night of the soul. Denoting mental and spiritual suffering prior to some big step, the phrase '*La Noche oscura del alma*' was used as the title of a work in Spanish by St John of the Cross. This was a treatise based on his poem 'Songs of the Soul Which Rejoices at Having Reached Union with God by the Road of Spiritual Negation' (*c* 1578). In *The Crack-up* (1936), F. Scott Fitzgerald wrote: 'In a real dark night of the soul it is always three o'clock in the morning, day after day.' Douglas Adams wrote *The Long Dark Tea-time of the Soul* (1988).

Darling Buds of May, The. The title of a novel (1958) by H.E. Bates, and from a popular source – Shakespeare, Sonnet 18:

> Shall I compare thee to a summer's day
> . . . Rough winds do shake the darling
> buds of May
> And summer's lease hath all too short a
> date.

The Darling Buds was the name of a British pop group with a peroxide-haired girl singer (*c* 1989). *Summer's Lease* is the title of a novel by John Mortimer (1988) about goings-on in a villa rented by English visitors to Tuscany.

Darth Vader. Meaning 'dark menacing person', the name derives from a character in the film *Star Wars* (US, 1977). He was a fallen Jedi knight who had turned to evil, appeared totally in shiny black, all skin hidden, and spoke with a distorted voice.

David, St. See SAINTS' NAMES.

day. See EVERY ~ AND IN EVERY WAY . . .; GO AHEAD MAKE MY ~; HAPPY AS THE ~ IS LONG; HAVE A GOOD ~; LITTLE MAN YOU'VE HAD A BUSY ~; OUR ~ WILL COME.

Day for Night. The English title given to François Truffaut's film about film-making (1973). The original French title, *La Nuit Américaine*, was the equivalent film-maker's term for shooting a scene during the day and then tinting it dark to make it look like night.

'Day in the Life, A'. The most-remembered track from the 1967 Beatles album *Sgt Pepper* presumably took its name from that type of magazine article and film documentary which strives to depict twenty-four hours in the life of a particular person or organization. In 1959, Richard Cawston produced a TV documentary which took this form, with the title *This is the BBC*. In 1962, the English title of a novel (film UK 1971) by Alexander Solzhenitsyn was *One Day in the Life of Ivan Denisovich*. John Lennon and Paul McCartney's use of the phrase for the description of incidents in the life of a drug-taker may have had something to do with the *Sunday Times Magazine* feature 'A Life in the Day' (running since the 1960s) and the play *A Day in the Death of Joe Egg* by Peter Nichols (1967, film UK, 1971).

Days of Our Lives. The title of the long-running US TV daytime soap opera (current by 1983) could be alluding to more than one phrase – 'THE HAPPIEST DAYS OF YOUR LIFE', 'the best years of our lives' or 'the best days of our lives'. 'Days of our lives' is not biblical, though there are any number of near-misses, like 'labours all the days of his life' (Ecclesiastes 8:15).

Days of Wine and Roses. This was the title of a film (US, 1962) about an alcoholic (though the phrase is often used to evoke romance). It is taken from Ernest Dowson's poem '*Vitae Summa Brevis*' (1896): 'They are not long, the days of wine and roses.' See also NON SUM QUALIS ERAM.

day war broke out, the. A catch phrase from the radio monologues during the Second World War of Robb

Wilton (d 1957): 'The day war broke out . . . my missus said to me, "It's up to you . . . you've got to stop it." I said, "Stop what?" She said, "The war." ' Later, when circumstances changed, it became 'the day *peace* broke out'.

D-Day. Meaning 'an important day when something is due to begin', the most frequent allusion is to 6 June 1944, the day on which the Allies began their landings in northern France in order to push back German forces. Like H-Hour, D-Day is a military way of detailing elements in an operation. The 'D' just reinforces the 'Day' on which the plan is to be put into effect and enables successive days to be labelled 'D-Day plus one', etc.

dead. See DE MORTUIS . . .; HE BEING ~ . . .; KING IS ~; QUICK AND THE ~.

dead – and never called me mother. This line is recalled as typical of the three-volume sentimental Victorian novel, yet it does not appear in Mrs Henry Wood's *East Lynne* (1861) as is often supposed. Nevertheless, it was inserted in one of the numerous stage versions of the novel (that by T.A. Palmer in 1874) which were made before the end of the century. The line occurs in a scene when an errant but penitent mother who has returned in the guise of a governess to East Lynne, her former home, has to watch the slow death of her eight-year-old son ('Little Willie'), but is unable to reveal her true identity.

dead as a doornail. In the Middle Ages, the doornail was the name given to the knob on which the knocker struck: 'As this is frequently knocked on the head, it cannot be supposed to have much life in it' (Brewer). The phrase occurs as early as 1350, then again in Langland's *Piers Plowman* (1362). Shakespeare uses it a couple of times, in

the usual form and, as in *King Henry I V, Part 2* (V.iii.117):

> *Falstaff:* What, is the old king dead!
> *Pistol:* As nail in door!

Deadlier Than the Male. The title of a film (UK, 1967) and an unrelated novel (1981) by Jessica Mann. It comes from the poem 'The Female of the Species' (1911) by Rudyard KIPLING: 'For the female of the species is more deadly than the male.' A much-quoted line, though sometimes the quoter takes the teeth out of the remark. In 1989, Margaret Thatcher said: 'The female of the species is rather better than the male.' *The Female of the Species* has also been the title of a film – a 1917 silent version of THE ADMIRABLE CRICHTON.

dead ringer. Meaning 'one person closely resembling another', the expression derives from horse-racing in the US, where 'ringer' has been used since the nineteenth century to describe a horse fraudulently substituted for another in a race. 'Dead' here means 'exact', as in 'dead heat'.

deal. See NEW ~.

Dear Brutus. Title of J.M. Barrie's play (1917), comes from Shakespeare's *Julius Caesar* (I.ii.138), where Cassius says: 'The fault, dear Brutus, is not in our stars,/But in ourselves, that we are underlings.'

Dear Lord Rothschild. The title of Miriam Rothschild's biography (1983) of her uncle, the 2nd Lord Rothschild, is taken from the first words of the letter, addressed to him as a leader of British Jewry, on 2 November 1917, and known as the **Balfour Declaration**. In the letter, Arthur Balfour, the Foreign Secretary, wrote that the British government 'looks with favour upon the establishment in Palestine of a national home for the

Jewish people.' This acted as a spur to Zionism and the founding of Israel.

death. See AND ~ SHALL HAVE NO DOMINION; FATE WORSE THAN ~; HIS ~ DIMINISHES US ALL; IN THEIR ~ THEY WERE NOT DIVIDED; KISS OF ~.

death is nothing at all. A popular reading at funerals begins: 'Death is nothing at all. I have only slipped away into the next room.' It ends: 'What is this death but a negligible accident? Why should I be out of mind because I am out of sight? I am but waiting for you, for an interval, somewhere very near, just around the corner. All is well.' The piece comes from a sermon on death written by Henry Scott Holland (*d* 1918) who was an editor of magazines, a canon of St Paul's Cathedral noted for his sermons, and Regius Professor of Divinity at the University of Oxford. Entitled 'The King of Terrors', the sermon was delivered in St Paul's on 15 May 1910, at which time the body of King Edward VII was lying in state in Westminster Hall.

deathless prose. An ironical description of poor writing. From an actor's diary: 'The writer . . . concentrates his most vicious verbal gymnastics [in these scenes]. After we've mangled the deathless prose we have another cup of tea.' (*Independent on Sunday*, 13 May 1990)

death of/by a thousand cuts. Meaning 'the cumulative effect of sniping, rather than of one big blow', the allusion is to the English translation of Chairman Mao's 'LITTLE RED BOOK' (1966): 'He who is not afraid of death by a thousand cuts dares to unhorse the emperor.' In February 1989, Robert Runcie, Archbishop of Canterbury, told the General Synod: 'If the Government does not take the axe to the BBC, there is surely here the shadow of death by a thousand cuts.'

'Death of Nelson, The'. The title of a popular song (1811) (see under *HOME AND BEAUTY*), and also of a painting (1857–63) by Daniel Maclise (now in the Walker Art Gallery, Liverpool).

debate. See GREAT ~.

decisions decisions!. What a harried person might exclaim over however trivial a choice, this is listed among the 'Naff Expressions' in *The Complete Naff Guide* (1983). Partridge/*Catch Phrases* offers '*c* 1955' as a possible starting date. Perhaps an echo of the perpetually-fraught WHITE RABBIT in *ALICE IN WONDERLAND*. Although he doesn't say this, he mutters: 'Oh my ears and whiskers, how late it's getting.'

Decline and Fall. The title of a novel (1928) by Evelyn Waugh, ludicrously extended to *Decline and Fall . . . of a Birdwatcher!* when filmed (UK, 1968). As with all such titles, the origin is *The History of the Decline and Fall of the Roman Empire* (1766–88) by Edward Gibbon. Presumably from a more watery source come the many variations on the 'rise and fall' theme: *The Rise and Fall of Legs Diamond* (film US, 1960); *The Rise and Fall of the Man of Letters* (a book by John Gross, 1969); *The Fall and Rise of Reginald Perrin* (BBC TV comedy series, 1976–80; *The Rise and Rise of Michael Rimmer* (film UK, 1970).

decus et tutamen. The inscription found on the rim of the British pound coin which replaced the banknote in 1983. The same words, suggested by John Evelyn the diarist, had appeared on the rim of a Charles II crown of 1662/3 (its purpose then was as a safeguard against clipping). Translated as 'an ornament and a safeguard' – referring to the inscription rather than the coin – the words come from Virgil's *Aeneid* (Bk.5) '*Decus et tutamen in armis.*' In its full form, this is the motto of the Feltmakers' Company (incorporated 1604).

deep blue sea. See DEVIL AND THE ~.

deep-six, to. Meaning 'to dispose of; destroy', the expression is of nautical origin – from men who took soundings. When they said 'by the deep six', they meant six fathoms (thirty-six feet). In naval circles, 'to deep-six' equally means 'to jettison overboard'. *DOAS* notes an extension to this meaning in jive and jazz use since the 1940s where 'the deep six' means 'the grave'. During Watergate, former presidential counsel John Dean told of a conversation he had had with another Nixon henchman, John Erlichman: 'He told me to shred the documents and "deep-six" the briefcase. I asked him what he meant by "deep-six". He leaned back in his chair and said, "You drive across the river on your way home tonight, don't you? Well, when you cross over bridge . . . just toss the briefcase into the river".' (Erlichman, before going to prison, denied this conversation ever took place.)

deep throat. Meaning 'a person within an organization who supplies information anonymously about wrong-doing by his colleagues', the phrase comes from the nickname given to the source within the Nixon White House who fed *Washington Post* journalists Carl Bernstein and Bob Woodward with information which helped in their Watergate investigations (1972–4). It has been suggested that 'Deep Throat' never existed but was a cover for unjustified suppositions. *Deep Throat*, the most notorious porno movie of the late 1960s, concerned a woman, played by Linda Lovelace, whose clitoris was placed in the back of her throat.

defeat. See WE ARE NOT INTERESTED IN . . .

DEF II. This was the title given to a strand of youth programming on BBC2 TV in 1988. Janet Street-Porter, the executive in charge, said that it was a graffito meaning 'I *defy* you *to* erase this.' On the other hand, the *Guardian*, reporting a young London graffiti artist on 14 October 1987, glossed his use of 'def' as signifying approval of a piece of lettering. Paul Beale in the *Concise Slang* wonders, on this basis, whether it is short for 'definitely'. In Hip-Hop talk of the late 1980s, 'def' was short for 'definitive' (i.e. 'brilliant').

delenda est Carthago. 'Carthage must be destroyed' – the slogan with which Cato the Elder punctuated his speeches to the Roman Senate for eight years *c* 157 BC, realizing the threat which the other state posed.

Delphi. See GREEK NAMES.

déluge. See APRES NOUS LE ~.

Demeter. See GREEK NAMES.

Demi-Paradise, The. See JOHN OF GAUNT SPEECH.

de mortuis nil nisi bonum [Of the dead, speak kindly or not at all]. Sometimes ascribed to Solon (*c* 600 BC), 'Speak not evil of the dead' was also a saying of Chilo(n) of Sparta (one of the Seven Sages (sixth century BC). Later Sextus Propertius (*d* 2 AD) wrote: '*Absenti nemo non nocuisse velit*' [Let no one be willing to speak ill of the absent]. Sometimes simply referred to in the form '*de mortuis . . .*', it is a proverb which appears in some form in most European languages.

denim. Material from which jeans are made, hence 'denims'. The cloth takes its name from Nîmes, the town in southern France where it was originally manufactured, and called *serge de Nîm* or *Nîmes*.

De Profundis. The title of Oscar Wilde's letter of self-justification following his imprisonment (published 1905) comes from the Latin words for 'out of the depths' (Psalm 130).

Derby, The. The original of 'Derbys' run all over the world was started in 1780 by the 12th Earl of Derby who is said to have discussed the idea of a flat race for three-year-old fillies, over dinner with his friend, Sir Charles Bunbury. Tradition has it that they tossed a coin over which of them the race should be named after and Derby won. The idea of a race called the 'Kentucky Bunbury' would have been a little hard to take seriously.

DERV. See ACRONYMS.

desert. See MAKES THE ~ BLOOM.

desperandum. See ILLEGITIMI . . .

desperate diseases require desperate remedies. Commonly ascribed to Guy Fawkes on 6 November 1605 (when he was arrested the day after attempting to blow up the Houses of Parliament): 'A desperate disease requires a dangerous remedy' (the version according to the *DNB*) was apparently said by him to James I, one of his intended victims. The King asked if he did not regret his proposed attack on the Royal Family. Fawkes replied that one of his objects was to blow the Royal Family back to Scotland. He was subsequently tried and put to death. What he said, however, appears to have been a version of an established proverbial saying. In the form: 'Strong disease requireth a strong medicine', *ODP* traces it to 1539. In Shakespeare's *Romeo and Juliet* (IV.i.68, *c* 1595), there is:

I do spy a kind of hope,
Which craves as desperate an execution
As that which we would prevent.

Shakespeare alludes to the saying on two other occasions.

despondency. See SPREAD ALARM AND ~.

despotism tempered by assassination. Lord Reith, the BBC's first Director-General, was asked by Malcolm Muggeridge in the TV programme *Lord Reith Looks Back* (1970) what he considered the best form of government. He replied: 'Despotism tempered by assassination.' The phrase is not exactly original. For example, *Quotations for Speakers and Writers* (1970) quotes the remark of a Russian noble to Count Münster on the assassination of Emperor Paul I in 1800: 'Despotism tempered by assassination, that is our Magna Carta.' *ODQ* prefers a direct quote from Count Münster's *Political Sketches of the State of Europe, 1814–1867* (1868): 'An intelligent Russian once remarked to us, "Every country has its own constitution; ours is absolutism moderated by assassination".' Bartlett attributes the saying direct to the earlier Ernst Friedrich Herbert von Münster (1766–1839). The dates are rather important. How else is one to know whether Thomas Carlyle in his *History of the French Revolution* (1837) was alluding to the saying, when he wrote: 'France was long a despotism tempered by epigrams'? In a speech to the International Socialist Congress (Paris, 17 July 1889), the Austrian, Victor Adler, followed up with: 'The Austrian government . . . is a system of despotism tempered by casualness.'

destiny. See MAN OF ~; RENDEZVOUS WITH ~.

Deucalion. See GREEK NAMES.

Devices and Desires. The title of a novel (1989) by P.D. James alludes to the General Confession in the Prayer Book: 'We have followed too much the devices and desires of our own hearts.'

devil and the deep blue sea, betwixt the. Meaning 'having two courses of action open, both of them dangerous' (as with SCYLLA and CHARYBDIS), the phrase should not be taken too literally. The 'devil' here may refer to the seam of a wooden ship's hull or to a plank fastened to the side of a ship as a support for guns. Either of these was difficult of access, a perilous place to be, but better than in the deep blue sea.

devil can cite scripture for his own purposes, the. Meaning 'an ill-disposed person may turn even good things to his advantage', and in this precise form, this is an allusion to Antonio the Merchant, in Shakespeare's *The Merchant of Venice* (I.iii.93) who says this because Shylock has just been doing so.

devil have all the best tunes?, why must the. According to E.W. Broome's biography of the Revd Rowland Hill (*d* 1833), what he said was: 'I do not see any good reason why the devil should have all the good tunes.' He was referring to Charles Wesley's defence of the practice of setting hymns to the music of popular songs. The phrase is now used generally to rebut the necessity for the virtuous and worthy to be dull and dreary. A perhaps better known – but later – use of the phrase concerns General Booth, the founder of the Salvation Army. It was his practice to use established tunes to accompany religious lyrics. In this way, over eighty music hall songs acquired religious lyrics. 'Champagne Charlie is My Name' for example, became, 'Bless His Name

He Sets Me Free'. When Booth was challenged on the suitability of such a process, he was doubtful at first, but then exclaimed: 'Why should the devil have all the best tunes!'

devil's dozen. See BAKER'S DOZEN.

Diamonds Are Forever. The title of Ian Fleming's James Bond novel (1956, film UK, 1971). In 1939, the South African-based De Beers Consolidated Mines launched a campaign to promote further the tradition of diamond engagement rings. The N.W. Ayer agency of Chicago (copywriter B.J. Kidd) came up with the line 'A diamond is forever'. Having a proverbial ring, the phrase passed easily into the language. Anita Loos in GENTLEMEN PREFER BLONDES (1925) had enshrined something like the idea in: 'Kissing your hand may make you feel very, very good but a diamond and safire bracelet lasts for ever'. The song 'Diamonds Are a Girl's Best Friend' in the stage musical of the book (1949; film US, 1953) was written by Jule Styne and Leo Robin. Technically speaking, however, diamonds do not last forever – being of pure carbon, they *will* burn at a very high temperature.

Diana. See ROMAN NAMES.

Dick Whittington. See STREETS PAVED WITH GOLD.

Dido. See ROMAN NAMES.

did the earth move for you? Jokily addressed to a partner after sexual intercourse, this appears to have originated as 'Did thee feel the earth move?' in Ernest Hemingway's novel *For Whom the Bell Tolls* (1940; not in the 1943 US film, however).

die. See OLD SOLDIERS NEVER ~; EAT DRINK AND BE MERRY . . .; NEVER SAY ~.

dies irae. See MASS PHRASES.

difficulties, little local. This phrase is used to show a dismissive lack of concern. In 1958, as Prime Minister, Harold Macmillan made a characteristically airy reference to the fact that his entire Treasury team, including the Chancellor of the Exchequer, had resigned over disagreement about budget estimates. In a statement at London airport before leaving for a tour of the Commonwealth on 7 January, he said: 'I thought the best thing to do was to settle up these little local difficulties, and then turn to the wider vision of the Commonwealth.'

difficult we do immediately – the impossible takes a little longer, the. Bartlett reports that this motto, now widespread in this form, was used by the US Army Service Forces, and traces the idea back to Charles Alexandre de Calonne (d 1802),who said: '*Madame, si c'est possible, c'est fait; impossible, impossible? cela se fera*' [Madame, if it is possible, it is done; if it is impossible, it will be done]. Henry Kissinger once joked: 'The illegal we do immediately, the unconstitutional takes a little longer' (quoted in William Shawcross, *Sideshow*, 1979).

Diff'rent Strokes. The title of a US TV series (from 1978 onwards) about a widowed millionaire who adopts two black boys. It comes from the street expression 'different strokes for different folks', meaning 'different people have different requirements' (a slight sexual connotation here).

dignity of labour. The phrase refers especially to manual labour. Booker T. Washington, the US Negro writer, alludes to the notion in *Up from Slavery*

(1901): 'No race can prosper till it learns that there is as much dignity in tilling a field as in writing a poem.' Earlier, Thomas Gray in his 'Elegy' (1751) spoke of the '*useful* toil' of the 'rude forefathers' in the countryside. *Useful Toil* was the title of a book comprising 'autobiographies of working people from the 1820s to the 1920s' (published 1974).

dinkies. See YUPPIE.

Diomedes. See GREEK NAMES.

Dionysus. See GREEK NAMES.

dirty work at the crossroads. Meaning 'despicable behaviour; foul play' (in any location), this is a Hollywood idiom, but not quite a cliché. The earliest film citation found is from *Flying Down to Rio* (1933), although P.G. Wodehouse had it in the book *Man Upstairs* in 1914 and Walter Melville, a nineteenth-century melodramatist, had it in *The Girl Who Took the Wrong Turning, or, No Wedding Bells for Him*. Brewer suggests that it might have something to do with the old custom of burying people at crossroads.

disco. Meaning 'a place for dancing to records', the name is a contraction of the French word *discothèque*, which dates from the early 1950s. That in turn was an adaptation of *bibliothèque*, 'a library' (from the Greek word for 'book repository'), conveying the idea of a 'record library' initially, rather than a dancing place.

discuss Ugandan affairs, to. This expression is a euphemism for sexual intercourse. In *Private Eye* No.293 (9 March 1973), there appeared a gossip item: 'I can reveal that the expression "talking about Uganda" has acquired a new meaning. I first heard it myself at a fashionable party given recently by media-people Neal and Corinna Ascherson. As I was sipping my Campari on the ground floor I was informed by my charming hostess that I was missing out on a meaningful confrontation upstairs where a former cabinet colleague of President Obote was "talking about Uganda". Eager, as ever, to learn the latest news from the Dark Continent I rushed upstairs to discover the dusky statesman "talking about Uganda" in a highly compromising manner to vivacious former features editor, Mary Kenny.' Later, references to 'Ugandan practices' or 'Ugandan discussions' came to be used – though whether far beyond the readership of *Private Eye*, is doubtful. In a letter to *The Times* (13 September 1983), Corinna Ascherson (now Corinna Adam) identified the coiner of the phrase as the poet and critic James Fenton. (See also *D P P*.)

diseases. See DESPERATE ~ . . .

disguise. See BLESSING IN ~.

Disgusted, Tunbridge Wells. This is the nickname given to a person of intemperate views. When it was announced in February 1978 that a Radio 4 programme was to be launched with the title *Disgusted, Tunbridge Wells* (providing a platform for listeners' views on broadcasting), there was consternation in the Kent township (properly, Royal Tunbridge Wells). The title was intended to evoke the sort of letter fired off to the press between the wars when the writer did not want to give his/her name – 'Mother of Three', 'Angry Ratepayer', 'Serving Policeman', etc. Tunbridge Wells has long been held as the source of reactionary, blimpish views. (See also *D P P*.)

divided. See HOUSE ~ AGAINST ITSELF . . .; IN THEIR DEATH . . .

do. See I ~.

doctor. See IS THERE A ~ . . .

does she . . . or doesn't she?. This was the slogan for Clairol hair-colouring in 1955, the brainchild of Shirley Polykoff (who entitled her advertising memoirs *Does She . . . or Doesn't She?* in 1975). 'J' saw the suggestive applications of the phrase in *The Sensuous Woman* (1969): 'Our world has changed. It's no longer a question of "Does she or doesn't she?" We all know she wants to, is about to, or does.' (See also *D P P*).

dog. See BLACK ~; IF A ~ BITES A MAN . . .; GIVE A ~ A BAD NAME; LOVE ME LOVE MY ~; PUT ON THE ~; THERE'S LIFE IN THE OLD ~ YET.

Dog Beneath the Skin, The. The title of a play (1935) by W.H. Auden and Christoper Isherwood. According to Humphrey Carpenter's biography of Auden (1981), the title was suggested by Rupert Doone and probably alludes to T.S. Eliot's 'Whispers of Immortality' (compare THE SKULL BENEATH THE SKIN).

Dog It Was That Died, The. The title of a radio play (1983) by Tom Stoppard, it comes from Oliver Goldsmith's 'Elegy on the Death of a Mad Dog':

> But soon a wonder came to light
> That show'd the rogues they lied;
> The man recover'd of the bite
> The dog it was that died.

dogs bark – but the caravan passes by, the. Meaning 'critics make a noise, but it does not last'. Sir Peter Hall, the theatre director, was given to quoting this 'Turkish proverb' during outbursts of public hostility in the mid-1970s. In *Within a Budding Grove* – the 1924 translation of Marcel Proust's *A l'Ombre des Jeunes Filles en Fleurs* (1918) – C.K. Scott Moncrieff has: 'the fine Arab proverb, "The dogs may bark; the caravan goes on!" '

Dogs of War, The. The title of Frederick Forsyth's novel (1974, film UK, 1980), comes from Shakespeare's *Julius Caesar*: 'Cry havoc and let slip the dogs of war' (III.i.273) – as, obviously, is the title of the 1943 US film *Cry Havoc*.

doing. See HOW'M I ~?

Dolce Vita, La. The title of Federico Fellini's 1960 Italian film passed into English as a phrase suggesting a high-society life of luxury, pleasure, and self-indulgence. Meaning simply 'the sweet life', it is not clear how much of a set phrase it was in Italian (compare *dolce far niente* [sweet idleness]) before it was taken up by everybody else.

dollar. See ANOTHER DAY ANOTHER ~.

Dolly Varden. This is the name given to a youthful style of girls' clothing, including slim-waisted, flowered-print dresses and flower-bedecked hats worn coquettishly tilted, with a ribbon under the chin. The name comes from a character in the Charles Dickens novel *Barnaby Rudge* (1841) who was 'the very impersonation of good-humour and blooming beauty'. 'She's a regular Dolly Varden' was an expression, derived from the same character, for any girl like that or who wore similar clothes. Revd Francis Kilvert wrote in his diary: 'Dora looked very pretty in her Dolly Varden dress

with blue scarf and blue veil' (18 September 1871).

DOM. See INTIALS.

Domine Deus. See MASS PHRASES.

dominion. See AND DEATH SHALL HAVE NO ~.

domino theory. The old metaphor of falling over 'like a stack of dominoes' was first used in the context of communist take-overs by the American political commentator, Joseph Alsop. Then President Eisenhower said at a press conference in April 1954: 'You have broader considerations that might follow what you might call the "falling domino" principle. You have a row of dominoes set up. You knock over the first one, and what will happen to the last one is that it will go over very quickly.' In South-East Asia, the theory was proved true to an extent in the 1970s. When South Vietnam collapsed, Cambodia then fell to the Khmer Rouge and Laos was taken over by the Communist-led Pathet Lao. In 1989 when one eastern European country after another *renounced* communism, there was talk of 'reverse domino theory'.

donkeys. See LIONS LED BY ~.

Do Not Fold, Spindle or Mutilate. This was the title of a film (US, 1971). When punched cards and computer cards began to accompany bills and statements in the 1950s, computerization was looked on as a harbinger of the Brave New World (though Bartlett dates the use of this somewhat bossy injunction to the 1930s). By the 1960s, the words evoked a machine age that was taking over. By the 1980s, the cards were no longer necessary. A slogan of the 1960s student revolution was: 'I am a human being – do not fold, spindle or mutilate me.' A graffito (quoted 1974) read: 'I am a masochist – please spindle, fold or mutilate.'

Don't Get Mad Get Even. The title of a book (1983), 'a manual for retaliation' by Alan Abel, it is one of several axioms said to come from the Boston-Irish political jungle or, more precisely, from Joseph P. Kennedy (*d* 1969), father of President Kennedy.

Don't Go Near the Water. The title of a film (US 1957) about sailors stationed on a South Pacific island – based on a William Brinkley novel. The allusion is to the rhyme (best known in the US):

> Mother, may I go out to swim?
> Yes, my darling daughter;
> Hang your clothes on a hickory limb,
> But don't go near the water.

'Yes, My Darling Daughter' was a popular song of 1941 – the Andrews Sisters recorded it – and there was also a play with the title in the late 1930s, subsequently filmed (US, 1939). *No, My Darling Daughter* was the title of a British film comedy (1961).

don't spit – remember the Johnstown flood. This turn-of-the-century Americanism is an admonition against spitting. The Johnstown flood of 31 May 1889 entered US folklore when a dam burst near Johnstown, Pennsylvania, and 2200 died. A silent film, *The Johnstown Flood*, was made in the US in 1926. Partridge/*Catch Phrases* finds that notices bearing this joke were exhibited in bars before Prohibition started in 1919. Safire quotes William Allen White's comment on the defeat of Alfred Landon in the 1936 US presidential election: 'It was not an election the country has just undergone, but a political Johnstown flood.'

don't teach your grandmother to suck eggs. Meaning 'don't try to tell people things which, given their age and experience, they might be expected to know anyway'. According to Partridge/*Slang*, variations of this very old expression include advice against instructing grandmothers to 'grope ducks', 'grope a goose', 'sup sour milk', 'spin', and 'roast eggs'. In 1738, Swift's *Polite Conversation* had 'Go teach your grannam to suck eggs.' (See also *D P P*.)

dooks. See DUKES.

doornail. See DEAD AS A ~.

Doors of Perception, The. This was the title given to Aldous HUXLEY's book (1954) about his experiments with mescalin and LSD. Its source is William Blake's *The Marriage of Heaven and Hell* (*c* 1790): 'If the doors of perception [i.e. the senses] were cleansed, every thing would appear to man as it is, infinite.' This view was seized upon by proponents of drug culture in the 1960s and from it was also derived the name of the US vocal/instrumental group **The Doors.**

Dorian Gray. A hedonistic character in *The Picture of Dorian Gray* (1890, film US, 1945), the novel by Oscar Wilde, who achieves eternal youth by the fact that his portrait ages on his behalf. Hence those references to 'having a portrait in the attic' which tend to be made about people who look unnaturally young and well preserved.

Dorothy. See IS SHE A FRIEND OF ~?

doves. See HAWKS/~.

down. See I MUST ~ TO THE SEAS AGAIN.

down memory lane. This phrase seems to have developed from 'Memory Lane', the title of a popular waltz (1924) written by Buddy De Sylva, Larry Spier, and Con Conrad – not to be confused with 'Down Forget-Me-Not Lane' by Horatio Nicholls, Charlie Chester and Reg Morgan (1941). *Down Memory Lane* was the title of a compilation of Mack Sennett comedy shorts (US 1949). *OED2* gives 'Down Memory Lane' as a 'title by Dannet and Rachel' (1954). Accepting the GOP presidential nomination at Dallas, Texas, on 23 August 1984, Ronald Reagan said: 'Our opponents began this campaign hoping that America has a poor memory. Well, let's take them on a little stroll down memory lane. Let's remind them of how a 4.8 percent inflation in 1976 became . . .' (See also *DPP*.)

do you know the Bishop of Norwich? This question is traditionally addressed to a port drinker who is holding on to the bottle and not passing it round. Partridge/*Slang* lists a 'norwicher' as 'one who drinks too much from a shared jug . . . an unfair drinker'. Perhaps this is a subtle way of calling somebody such? Brewer also has the version: 'Do you know Dr Wright of Norwich?' Had there been a Dr Wright who was Bishop of Norwich? The nearest was Dr White (*d* 1632).

Do You Sincerely Want to Be Rich? The title of a book (1972) by Charles Raw *et al*, it was the question posed to his salesmen, during training, by Bernie Cornfeld (*b* 1928) who made his name and fortune selling investment plans.

Draco. See GREEK NAMES.

Dragon Lady. Nancy Reagan, when US First Lady in the 1980s, attracted criticism for her manipulative and frosty style and was given this nickname. The original 'Dragon Lady' was a beautiful Chinese temptress in the American comic strip 'Terry and the Pirates' (from 1934).

drawing. See BACK TO THE ~ BOARD; ELEPHANT IN YOUR ~ ROOM.

dreams. See SUCH STUFF AS ~ ARE MADE ON.

dream the impossible dream. The expression derives from a line in the song 'The Impossible Dream' in the musical about Don Quixote, *Man of La Mancha* (1965, film US, 1972).

dress. See LITTLE BLACK ~.

dressed. See ALL ~ UP AND NO-WHERE TO GO.

dressed up to the nines. Meaning 'very smartly dressed', this phrase may have come to us via a pronunciation shift. If you were to say dressed up 'to then eyne', that would mean, in Old English, 'dressed up to the eyes' (*eyne* being the old plural of eye). The snag with this is that no examples of the phrase being used occur before the eighteenth century, so the origin remains obscure.

Dreyfus Affair. See under *J'ACCUSE*.

dribble. See WIZARD OF THE ~.

drink. See ANOTHER LITTLE ~ . . .; EAT ~ AND BE MERRY.

drive a coach and horses through something, to. Meaning 'to overturn something wantonly, and to render it useless'. Sir Stephen Rice (*d* 1715), a Roman-Catholic Chief Baron of the Exchequer used the courts in Dublin to get his own back on the Act of Settlement. 'I will drive a coach and six horses through the Act of Settlement,' he is quoted as saying (1672). (See also *DPP*.)

drive/go/ride/sail off into the sunset, to. Meaning 'to end happily, and probably romantically', the expression derives from the visual cliché of the silent film era when a united couple would often do just that at the end of a story. Used inevitably when Ronald Reagan retired from the White House: 'As Reagan rides off into the sunset we offer two opposing verdicts on his eight years in office . . .' (*Observer*, 15 January 1989).

Dr Livingstone, I presume? The famous greeting was put by Sir Henry Morton Stanley, the British explorer and journalist, to the explorer and missionary Dr David Livingstone at Ujiji, Lake Tanganyika on 10 November 1871. Stanley had been sent by the *New York Herald* to look for Livingstone who was missing on a journey in central Africa. In *How I Found Livingstone* (1872), Stanley described the moment: 'I would have run to him, only I was a coward in the presence of such a mob – would have embraced him, only, he being an Englishman, I did not know how he would receive me; so I did what cowardice and false pride suggested was the best thing – walked deliberately to him, took off my hat and said: "Dr Livingstone, I presume?" "Yes," said he, with a kind smile, lifting his cap slightly.'

droit de seigneur. This phrase is used to suggest that a man has exercised some imagined 'right' in order to force a woman to go to bed with him, as perhaps a boss might do with his secretary. The belief is that this 'right' dates from the days when medieval barons would claim first go at the newly wedded daughters of their vassals – the so-called *ius primae noctis* [law of the first night]. In the play *Le Mariage de Figaro* (1784) by Beaumarchais, the Count has just renounced his right and is beginning to regret it. In March 1988, it was reported that Dr Wilhelm Schmidt-Bleibtreu of Bonn had looked into the matter very thoroughly and discovered there was never any such legal right and that reliable records of it ever happening were rare. He concluded that the whole thing was really a male fantasy – and it was exclusively men who had used the phrase – though he didn't rule out the possibility that sex of the kind *had* taken place between lords and brides in one or two cases, legally or otherwise.

drop a clanger, to. The expression means 'to say something socially embarrassing or commit an act of similar kind'. According to a photograph caption in the *Sunday Times Magazine* (30 January 1983): 'the nerveless men who worked on the construction of New York's Woolworth Building in 1912 had nightmares of dropping a girder, or "clanger" in the phrase they gave to the language'. Partridge/*Slang* calls 'clanger' here a synonym for 'testicle', but derives it from the inoffensive 'drop a brick'. *O E D2*'s first citation is from 1958.

'Dropping the Pilot'. Meaning 'to dispense with a valued leader', this phrase comes from the caption to a *Punch* cartoon which appeared on 29 March 1890 and showed Kaiser Wilhelm II leaning over the side of a ship as his recently disposed-of Chancellor, Otto von Bismarck, dressed as a pilot, walked down steps to disembark. Bismarck had been forced to resign following disagreements over home and foreign policy. The phrase was also used as the title of a poem on the same subject. From the *Independent* (12 May 1990): 'Kenneth Baker, the Conservative chairman, yesterday called on Tories to stop idle speculation about the party leadership . . . "We have moved through difficult waters . . . We should not, we must not, we will not drop the pilot".'

drunk/sober comparisons. Said Andrew Bonar Law of Herbert Asquith, the British Liberal Prime Minister: 'Asquith, when drunk, can make a better speech than any of us when sober.' (Asquith was a noted tippler. Compare ANOTHER LITTLE DRINK WOULDN'T DO US ANY HARM.) In a leading article, *The Times* (6 March 1976) said: 'Lord George-Brown drunk is a better man than the Prime Minister [Harold Wilson] sober.'

Dubuque. See LITTLE OLD LADY FROM ~.

duck. See DYING ~ IN A THUNDER STORM; HONEY I FORGOT TO ~; IF IT LOOKS LIKE A ~; LAME ~.

Duck Soup. The title of this Marx Brothers' movie (US, 1933), insofar as it has any relevance to the contents, is a US phrase meaning 'anything simple or easy, a cinch' or 'a gullible person, easily victimized, a pushover'. Groucho Marx admitted that he did not understand the title, but explained it thus: 'Take two turkeys, one goose, four cabbages, but no duck, and mix them together. After one taste, you'll duck soup for the rest of your life.' The film's director Leo McCarey had earlier made a film with Laurel and Hardy with the same title.

dukes/dooks up, to put one's. Describing a summit between Soviet and US leaders, *Time* (20 October 1986) stated: 'Reagan and Gorbachev both came to office not with their hands outstretched but with their dukes up'. If 'dukes' means 'fists', why so? One theory is that because the 1st Duke of Wellington had such a large nose, a 'duke' became a synonym for one. Then, so this theory goes, a man's fist became a 'duke buster'. In time this was shortened, and fists became 'dukes'.

Morris prefers another theory: that the use derives from Cockney rhyming slang, viz. 'Duke of York's' ('forks' meaning 'fingers' – standing for the whole hand or fist). *O E D2* has the expression by 1874. Winston Churchill

neatly played on the phrase in a public speech about House of Lords reform on 4 September 1909: 'In the absence of any commanding voice, the Tory party have had to put up their "dooks".' A report of the speech adds: 'Great laughter and a voice: "What about your grandfather?" ' (Churchill's grandfather was the Duke of Marlborough).

Dunkirk spirit, the. Harold Wilson said in the House of Commons, on 26 July 1961: 'I have always deprecated . . . in crisis after crisis, appeals to the Dunkirk spirit as an answer to our problems.' No sooner had he become the British Prime Minister than he said in a speech to the Labour Party Conference (12 December 1964): 'I believe that the spirit of Dunkirk will once again carry us through to success.'

O E D2 does not find the phrase 'Dunkirk spirit' until 1956, though it does find 'to do a Dunkirk' (meaning 'to extract oneself from disaster') as early as 1944. Both phrases allude to the evacuation from the northern French town of Dunkerque/Dunkirk in May/June 1940. Retreating in the face of the German advance, British and Allied troops had a remarkable escape in an *ad hoc* rescue by small boats. About 338,000 were rescued in this way. It was, in anybody's language a defeat, but almost at once was seen as a triumph. Harold Nicolson wrote to his wife on 31 May: 'It is a magnificent feat once you admit the initial misery of the thing.' Winston Churchill, in his 'We shall never surrender' speech to the House of Commons on 4 June, warned: 'We must be very careful not to assign to this deliverance the attributes of a victory. Wars are not won by evacuations. But there was a victory inside this deliverance which should be noted.'

Dunstan, St. See SAINTS' NAMES.

Duran Duran. The name of a British vocal/instrumental group that flourished in the early 1980s, derives from the name of a character – a lost scientist – in the comic strip BARBARELLA. He also featured in the 1967 film.

dust. See PALM WITHOUT THE ~.

dustbin of history (*sometimes* **dustheap/scrapheap).** This is the fate to which you might wish to convey your opponents or their ideas. The phrase was used by Trotsky, either with reference to the fate of the decrees emanating from Kerensky's provincial government in the Winter Palace in 1917, or to the fate of his opponents generally (as suggested by E.H. Carr in his *Socialism in One Country*, 1958). In a similar coinage, Charles Dickens reflected on Sir Robert Peel's death in 1850: 'He was a man of merit who could ill be spared from the Great Dust Heap down at Westminster.' Augustine Birrell, politician and writer (*d* 1933), wrote of 'that great dust-heap called "history" ' in his essay on Carlyle.

dwarfs. See SEVEN ~.

dying duck in a thunderstorm, like a. As a description of a person's forlorn appearance, *O E D2* finds 'like a duck in thunder' in 1802, and the more familiar form in Sir Walter Scott's *Peveril of the Peak* in 1822. By 1843–4, the phrase was sufficiently well known for Charles Dickens to allude to it in *Martin Chuzzlewit*: 'His eye . . . with something of that expression which the poetry of ages has attributed to a domestic bird, when breathing its last amid the ravages of an electric storm (Chap. 10)'.

E E

Eagle Has Landed, The. The title of a novel (1975, film UK, 1976) by Jack Higgins who suggests in an Author's Note that Heinrich Himmler was informed on 6 November 1943 that, 'The Eagle has landed' – meaning that a small force of German paratroops had safely landed in England in order to kidnap Winston Churchill. The phrase is better known, however, in a very different sphere. In July 1969, when the lunar module bearing Neil Armstrong touched down for the first ever moon visit, he declared: 'Tranquillity Base here – the Eagle has landed' ('Eagle' was the name of the craft, after the US national symbol). A headline from the *Observer Magazine*, 24 June 1990 (on a profile of Robert Maxwell) has: 'The Ego Has Landed'.

ear. See IN YOUR SHELL-LIKE ~.

earner. See NICE LITTLE ~.

earth. See DID THE ~ MOVE FOR YOU?

easier for a camel to go through the eye of a needle, it is. This biblical phrase from Matthew 19:24 and Mark 10:25 continues: '. . . than for a rich man to enter into the kingdom of God'. The Koran contains a similar view and in Rabbinical writings there is the similar expression 'to make an *elephant* pass through the eye of a needle' – which

also appears in an Arab proverb. So why this camel/elephant confusion (see also AN ELEPHANT NEVER FORGETS)? Probably because the word for 'camel' in older Germanic languages, including Old English, was almost like the modern word for 'elephant' (O E *olfend* 'camel'). In this biblical saying, however, it is probable that neither camel nor elephant was intended. The original Greek word should probably have been read as *kamilos* 'a rope', rather than *kamelos*, 'a camel'. The difficulty of threading a rope through the eye of a needle makes a much neater image.

'East Is Red, The'. This was the title of the theme song of the Chinese Cultural Revolution (1966–9). When the first Chinese space satellite was launched in April 1970, it circled the earth, broadcasting the message: *'Tung fang hung – Mao Tse-tung'* ['The east is red – Mao Tse-tung']. The song begins:

> The East turns red, day is breaking,
> Mao Tse-tung arises over Chinese soil
> . . .

East of Suez. In the poem 'Mandalay' (1892), Rudyard KIPLING wrote: 'Ship me somewheres east of Suez', and that would appear to be the origin of this phrase to denote, especially, the British Empire as it was in India and the East, which was usually reached through the Suez Canal (opened in 1869). John

Osborne entitled a play set on a 'sub-tropical island neither Africa nor Europe', *West of Suez* (1971).

easy. See LIFE WASN'T MEANT TO BE ~.

eat crow, to. Meaning 'to have to do something distasteful', it refers to an incident in the British–American war of 1812–14. During a ceasefire, a New England soldier went hunting and crossed over into British lines where, finding no better game, he shot a crow. An unarmed British officer encountered the American and, by way of admiring his gun, took hold of it. He then turned it on him and forced him to eat part of the crow.

eat drink and be merry (for tomorrow we die). This saying derives from Isaiah 22:13: 'Let us eat and drink, for tomorrow we shall die.' Brewer comments: 'A traditional saying of the Egyptians who, at their banquets, exhibited a skeleton to the guests to remind them of the brevity of life.' Ecclesiastes 8:15 has: 'A man hath no better thing under the sun, than to eat, and to drink, and to be merry', and Luke 12:19: 'Take thine ease, eat, drink and be merry.'

eat humble pie, to. Meaning 'to submit to humiliation', the 'humbles' or 'umbles' were those less-appealing parts of a deer (or other animal) which had been killed in a hunt. They would be given to those of lower rank and perhaps served as 'humble pie' or 'umble pie'. A coincidence then that 'humble pie' should have anything to do with being 'humble'. Appropriately it is Uriah Heep in *David Copperfield* (Chap.39, 1849–50) by Charles Dickens, who says: 'I got to know what umbleness did, and I took to it. I ate umble pie with an appetite.'

Eating People Is Wrong. The title of Malcolm Bradbury's novel (1959) comes from the song 'The Reluctant Cannibal' by Michael Flanders and Donald Swann, featured in the revue *At the Drop of a Hat* (1956).

eat your heart out, —! A minor singer having just finished a powerful ballad might exult defiantly: 'Eat your heart out, Frank Sinatra!' Partridge/*Catch Phrases* glosses it as: 'Doesn't *that* make you jealous, fella!' As something said *to* another person, this expression acquired popularity in the mid-twentieth century largely through its American show-business use. As such, it is possibly another of those Jewish expressions popularized by showbiz. 'To eat one's (own) heart out' – simply meaning 'to pine' – was current in English by the sixteenth century, and Leo Rosten in *Hooray for Yiddish* (1983) finds it in the Yiddish *Es dir oys s'harts*.

Ebenezer. See RAISE ONE'S ~.

Echo. See GREEK NAMES.

economical with the truth, being. On 18 November 1986, the British Cabinet Secretary, Sir Robert Armstrong, was being cross-examined in the Supreme Court of New South Wales. The British Government was attempting to prevent publication in Australia of a book about MI5, the British secret service. Defence counsel Malcolm Turnbull asked Sir Robert about the contents of a letter he had written which had been intended to convey a misleading impression. 'What's a "misleading impression"?' enquired Turnbull. 'A sort of bent untruth?' Sir Robert replied: 'It is perhaps being economical with the truth.' This explanation was greeted with derision not only in the court but in the world beyond, and it looked as though a new euphemism for lying had been coined. In fact Sir Robert had prefaced his remark with: 'As one person said . . .' and, when the court apparently found cause for laughter in what he said, added: 'It is not very original, I'm afraid.' Indeed not; earlier users of the idea had included Sir William Strang (1942), Arnold Bennett (1915), Mark Twain (1897), and Samuel Pepys (1669/70). (See also *D P P.*)

economy. See COMMANDING HEIGHTS OF THE ~.

Edge, Celtic. See CELTIC FRINGE.

Edinburgh. See ATHENS OF THE NORTH.

Edna. See AUNT ~.

effluent society. See AFFLUENT SOCIETY.

Egeria. See ROMAN NAMES.

egg(s). See CURATE'S ~; DON'T TEACH YOUR GRANDMOTHER . . .; LAY AN ~.

eggs is eggs, as sure as. Meaning 'absolutely certain', the derivation for this expression is obscure, unless it is a corruption of the mathematician's or logician's '*x* is *x*'. It occurs in *Pickwick Papers* (Chap. 43, 1836–7) by Charles Dickens.

ego. See ARCADIA EGO.

Egypt. See FLESHPOTS OF ~; LITTLE ~.

eight. See ONE OVER THE ~.

Electra. See GREEK NAMES.

elementary my dear Watson! The Sherlock Holmes phrase appears nowhere in the writings of Sir Arthur Conan Doyle, though the great detective does exclaim 'Elementary' to Dr Watson in 'The Crooked Man' in *The Memoirs of Sherlock Holmes* (1894). Conan Doyle brought out his last Holmes book in 1927. His son Adrian (in collaboration with John Dickson Carr) was one of those who used the phrase in follow-up stories – as have adapters of the stories in film and broadcast versions. In the 1929 film *The Return of Sherlock Holmes* – the first of the series with sound – the final lines of dialogue are:

Watson: Amazing, Holmes!
Holmes: Elementary, my dear Watson, elementary.

elephant in your drawing room, the. An Ulster expression, quoted in the *Guardian* (26 June 1988), is that **The Troubles** are 'the elephant in your drawing room' – referring to the debilitating effect of sectarian hostility and violence in the province. Before the present round of civil strife in Northern Ireland started in 1969, 'The Troubles' had been applied specifically to the outburst of Civil War in southern Ireland (1919–23), but was also applied generally to any nationalist unrest – even to events as far back as 1641.

elephant never forgets, an. What one might say of one's self when complimented on remembering a piece of information forgotten by others, it is based on the view that elephants are supposed to remember trainers, keepers, and so on, especially those who have been unkind to them. A song with the title 'The Elephant Never Forgets' was featured in the play *The Golden Toy* by Carl Zuckmayer (London, 1934) and recorded by Lupino Lane. *Stevenson's Book of Proverbs, Maxims and Familiar Phrases* (1949) has that it derives from a

Greek proverb: 'The camel [*sic*] never forgets an injury.'

elephants' graveyard. This expression is applied to any place to which people go to retire, or more loosely, to any place where the formerly important now languish. Partridge/*Slang*, more precisely, prefers 'the elephants' burial ground', referring to Petersfield in Hampshire where 'vast legions of retired admirals' live (an expression dating from the 1940s). The allusion is probably to the known death rituals of elephants, who tend to congregate when one of their number is on the way out – sometimes standing around and providing the pachyderm equivalent of hospital screens.

eleventh commandment. Mencken has that this is 'Mind your own business' as 'borrowed from Cervantes, *Don Quixote*, 1605', but he also records 'The Eleventh Commandment: Thou shalt not be found out – George Whyte-Melville, *Holmby House*, 1860', and that is the much more usual meaning. *O E D2* adds from the *Pall Mall Gazette* (10 September 1884): 'the new and great commandment that nothing succeeds like success' and from *Paston Carew* (1886) by Mrs Lynn Lynton that the eleventh commandment was 'do not tell tales out of school'. In 1850, Charles Kingsley suggested that it was: 'Buy cheap, sell dear'. The 1981 remake of the film *The Postman Always Rings Twice* was promoted with the slogan: 'If there was an 11th Commandment, they would have broken that too.'

eleventh hour, at the. Meaning 'at the last moment', its origin is the parable of the labourers, of whom the last 'were hired at the eleventh hour' (Matthew 20:9). It was used with a different resonance at the end of the First World War. The Armistice was signed at 5 am on 11 November 1918 and came into force at 11 am – 'at the eleventh hour of the eleventh day of the eleventh month'.

Elmo, St. See SAINTS' NAMES.

éminence grise. This nickname is given to any shadowy figure who exercises power or influence. It was first applied to François Leclerc du Tremblay (*d* 1638), known as Père Joseph, private secretary to Cardinal Richelieu. Richelieu, statesman and principal adviser to Louis XIII of France, was something of an '*éminence grise*' himself and virtually ruled France from 1624 till his death. He was known, however, as the **Red Cardinal** or as '*L'Eminence Rouge*'. Du Tremblay, dressed in grey, became known, first of all, as 'the Grey Cardinal' because – although not a cardinal – he exercised the power of one through his influence on Richelieu. Later, the Nazi Martin Bormann was sometimes known as the **Brown Eminence**, perhaps because of his 'Brownshirt' background.

Emma Peel. The name of a self-sufficient female character (played by Diana Rigg) in the British TV series *The Avengers*. The part was introduced in *c* 1965 and the name derives from the producers' desire to give the programme 'M appeal' (or 'Man appeal', as a phrase from Oxo advertising had been putting it since 1958).

emperor's (new) clothes. Describing a person's imaginary qualities whose fictitiousness other people forbear to point out, the origin of this expression lies in a story called 'The Emperor's New Clothes' (1835) by Hans Christian Andersen, in which tailors gull an emperor into wearing a new suit of clothes, supposedly invisible to unworthy people but which do not, in fact, exist at all. None of the emperor's subjects dares point out that this renders him naked – until an innocent boy does just that.

empire. See EVIL ~.

empire upon which the sun never sets. The phrase refers to the British Empire which was so widespread at its apogee, that the sun was always up on some part of it. 'John Wilson' (Christoper North) wrote in *Noctes Ambrosianae*, No.20 (April 1829) of: 'His Majesty's dominions, on which the sun never sets'. Earlier, the idea had been widely applied to the Spanish Empire. In 1641, the English explorer and writer Capt John Smith (of Pocahontas fame) asked in *Advertisements for the Unexperienced* . . .: 'Why should the brave Spanish soldier brag the sun never sets in the Spanish dominions, but ever shineth on one part or other we have conquered for our king?' Ascribed to 'Duncan Spaeth' (is this John Duncan Spaeth, the US educator?) in Nancy McPhee, *The Book of Insults* (1978) is the saying: 'I know why the sun never sets on the British Empire: God wouldn't trust an Englishman in the dark.'

end. See ALL GOOD THINGS COME TO AN ~; BEGINNING OF THE ~; BITTER ~; LIGHT AT THE ~ OF THE TUNNEL.

End Game. The English title of *Fin de Partie*, a play (1957) by Samuel Beckett refers to the expression describing the final stages of a chess game when few pieces remain. Compare *Checkmate*, the title of a ballet by Ninette de Valois and Arthur Bliss (1937), from the term for the actual end of a game of chess, which has been etymologized as from the Arabic *Shah-mat* [the Shah/King is dead].

End of Civilization as We Know It, The. The title of an announced but not released film (US, 1977), it is a Hollywood cliché – the kind of thing said when people are under threat from invaders from Mars, or wherever: 'This could mean the end of civilization as we know it . . .' but it is also applied to other kinds of threat. (See also *DPP*.)

end of history, the. A concept which was promoted by Francis Fukuyama, a US State Department official, in a 1989 article to describe Western democracy's perceived triumph over communism in Eastern Europe: 'What we may be witnessing is not the end of the Cold War but the end of history as such: that is, the end point of man's evolution and the universalization of Western liberal democracy.'

End of the World News, The. The title of Anthony Burgess's novel (1982) derives from what BBC World Service newsreaders have sometimes said at the end of bulletins: 'That is the end of the world news' – leaving open the possibility that it is also the news of the end of the world.

enemies. See WITH FRIENDS LIKE THESE . . .

enemy within. This expression refers to an internal rather than external threat. *ODCIE* suggests that it is a shortened version of 'the enemy/traitor within the gate(s)' – 'one who acts, or is thought to act, against the interests of the family, group, society, etc. of which he is a member'. In 1940, Winston Churchill said of the BBC that it was 'an enemy within the gates, doing more harm than good'. On 22 January 1983, *The Economist* wrote of the industrial relations scene in Britain: 'The government may be trusting that public outrage will increasingly be its ally. Fresh from the Falklands, Mrs Thatcher may even relish a punch-up with the enemy within to enhance her "resolute approach" further.'

Seven months later, Mrs Thatcher was using exactly the same phrase and context regarding the British miners' strike. She 'told Tory MPs that her government had fought the enemy without in the Falklands conflict and now had to face an enemy within . . . she declared that the docks and pit strikers posed as great a threat to democracy as General Galtieri, the deposed Argentine leader.' (*Guardian*, 20 July 1984)

Earlier, in 1980, Julian Mitchell had used the phrase as the title of a play about anorexia. It was also the title of a Tony Garnett BBC TV play in 1974 and of a book (1960) by Robert F. Kennedy about 'organized corruption' in the US labour movement.

England. See CLEVEREST YOUNG MAN IN ~; CLOSE YOUR EYES AND THINK OF ~; THINGS I'VE DONE FOR ~.

England expects. Admiral Horatio Lord Nelson's signal to the English fleet before the Battle of Trafalgar on 21 October 1805 was 'England expects that every man will do his duty.' Mencken found a US saying from 1917 – during the First World War: 'England expects every American to do his duty.' In Britain at about the same time, there was a recruiting slogan: 'England Expects that Every Man Will Do His Duty and Join the Army Today.'

England My England. This was the title of a book of short stories by D.H. Lawrence (1922). Compare A.G. MacDonell's satire on country life, *England, Their England* (1933), and a book of George Orwell's essays, *England, Your England* (1953). The origin is the poem by W.E. Henley called 'For England's Sake' (1892):

> What have I done for you,
> England, my England?

> What is there I would not do,
> England, my own?

English As She Is Spoke. The title of a book of selections (1883) from the notorious French–Portuguese phrasebook *O Novo Guia da Conversacão em frances e portuguez* by José da Fonseca, which had been published in Paris in 1836. The original text was in parallel columns; then, in 1865, a third column, carrying English translations, was added by one Pedro Carolino. Field and Tuer's English book took its title from a phrase in the chapter on 'Familiar Dialogues'. In 1883, Mark Twain also introduced an edition of the complete work in the US. The phrase is now used to describe how the language might be spoken by foreigners or the illiterate.

English had the land and the Africans had the Bible, the. 'Originally, the Africans had the land and the English had the Bible. Then the missionaries came to Africa and got the Africans to close their eyes and fold their hands and pray. And when they opened their eyes, the English had the land and the Africans had the Bible.' This observation was attributed (possibly inaccurately) to Jomo Kenyatta, the one-time Kenyan president, on *Quote . . . Unquote*, BBC Radio (13 October 1984). The *Observer* 'Sayings of the Week' (16 December 1984) had Bishop Desmond Tutu saying it. A version relating to the North American Indians had earlier been said by Chief Dan George (*d* 1982).

Englishman. See GREATEST LIVING ~.

Enola Gay. This was the name of the US aircraft from which the atomic bomb which destroyed Hiroshima was dropped in 1945. From the name of the mother of its pilot, Col Paul W. Tibbets, it was also used as the title of a TV movie (US, 1980) about the plane and its crew.

enough blue to make a pair of sailor's trousers. This saying is listed in *Nanny Says* (1972) as an example of 'nanny philosophy': 'If there's enough blue sky to make a pair of sailor's trousers then you can go out.' Brewer glosses it as 'two patches of blue appearing in a stormy sky giving the promise of better weather' and notes the alternative 'Dutchman's breeches' for 'sailor's trousers'.

enough is enough! A basic expression of exasperation, this is often trotted out in political personality clashes – though usually without result. 'What matters is that Mr Macmillan has let Mr [Selwyn] Lloyd know that at the Foreign Office, in these troubled times, enough is enough' (*The Times*, 1 June 1959). Having fed the story to *The Times*, Macmillan was prevented by the fuss it caused from firing Lloyd and the Foreign Secretary remained in place for a further year. On 10 May 1968, the *Daily Mirror* carried a front page headline: 'Enough Is Enough', referring to the Labour government of Harold Wilson. It was over an article by Cecil H. King, Chairman of the International Publishing Corporation, but it led to *his* fall from power, however, and not the government's.

ENSA. See ACRONYMS.

Eos. See GREEK NAMES.

equal. See ALL ANIMALS ARE ~ . . .

Erato. See GREEK NAMES.

Erebus. See GREEK NAMES.

Erinyes. See GREEK NAMES.

Ernie. See ACRONYMS.

Eros. See GREEK NAMES.

Essoldo. See under ODEON.

Establishment, The. The nickname for a conservative, partly hereditary, secretive, self-perpetuating ruling class. In Britain, it was brought to prominence by Henry Fairlie in a series of articles for the *Spectator* in 1955. On 23 September, he wrote: 'I have several times suggested that what I call the "Establishment" in this country is today more powerful than ever before. By the "Establishment" I do not mean only the centres of official power – though they are certainly part of it – but rather the whole matrix of official and social relations within which power is exercised . . . the "Establishment" can be seen at work in the activities of, not only the Prime Minister, the Archbishop of Canterbury and the Earl Marshal, but of such lesser mortals as the Chairman of the Arts Council, the Director-General of the BBC, and even the editor of the *Times Literary Supplement*, not to mention dignitaries like Lady Violet Bonham-Carter.'

Hugh Thomas, editing a book on the phenomenon called *The Establishment* (1959), stated: 'The word was, however, in use among the thoughtful at least a year previously; I recall myself employing it while passing the Royal Academy in a taxi in company with Mr Paul Johnson of the *New Statesman* in August 1954.' An earlier example of use of the phrase among the 'thoughtful' has, indeed, come to light in A.J.P. Taylor's *Essays in English History*. In one on William Cobbett (originally a review in the *New Statesman* in 1953) he wrote: 'Trotsky tells how, when he first visited England, Lenin took him round London and, pointing out the sights, exclaimed: "That's *their* Westminster Abbey! That's *their* Houses of Parliament!" Lenin was making a class, not a national emphasis. By "them" he meant not the English, but the governing classes, the Establishment so clearly defined and so complacently secure.' *OED2* has other citations of the phrase in its modern sense going back to 1923.

estate. See FOURTH ~.

Eton. See BATTLE OF WATERLOO ...

et tu, Brute? [And you, Brutus?] Julius Caesar's supposed dying words to Brutus, one of his assassins in 44 BC, were made famous through Shakespeare's use of the Latin in *Julius Caesar* in the form: '*Et tu, Brute? –* Then fall, Caesar!' (III.i.77). The Latin words are not to be found in the works of any classical writer but do occur in English drama just before Shakespeare. The anonymous *True Tragedie of Richard Duke of Yorke* (printed in 1595) has the line: 'Et tu, Brute, wilt thou stab Caesar too?' The origin of the phrase probably lies in the account of the assassination by Suetonius, in which Caesar is made to say in *Greek*: 'And thou, my son.' The 'son' has been taken literally – as according to Suetonius, Caesar had had an intrigue with Brutus's mother and looked upon Brutus as his likely son. Chips Channon wrote in his diary (7 April 1939): 'The Italians are occupying Albania ... "Et tu Benito?" – for Mussolini had only recently assured us that he had no territorial claims whatsoever on Albania.'

Eumenides. See GREEK NAMES.

Euro-. A prefix which is used to denote anything of European origin. The form spread like a disease about the time of British entry into the European Common Market (January 1972). *OED2* finds its earliest example (which it compares to Anglo-, Austro- etc.) in 1928. 'Eurocrat', 'Euro-dollar', 'Eurospeak', and 'Eurocommunism' are but some of the scores that have followed. The *Guardian* of 17 December 1973 was already using the

word 'Eurocrap'. However, the first real imposition of this rather medical-sounding (compare neuro-) tag had occurred with the setting up of 'Eurovision' (1951), the television network for the production and exchange of programmes, most notably the 'Eurovision Song Contest' (first shown 1956). The coinage of this word is attributed (in Asa Briggs, *History of Broadcasting in the United Kingdom*, Vol.III) to George Campey, a BBC publicity executive.

Europa. See GREEK NAMES.

Euryalus. See ROMAN NAMES.

Eurydice. See GREEK NAMES.

Euterpe. See GREEK NAMES.

EVA. See INITIALS.

Everest, Mount. See BECAUSE IT IS THERE.

every day and in every way I am getting better and better (*sometimes* **every day in every way ... or** day by day in every way ...**).** The French psychologist Emile Coué was the originator of a system of 'Self-Mastery Through Conscious Auto-Suggestion' which had a brief vogue in the 1920s. His patients had to repeat this phrase over and over and it became a popular catch phrase of the time, though physical improvement did not necessarily follow. The French original was: '*Tous les jours, à tous les points de vue, je vais de mieux en mieux.*' Couéism died with its inventor in 1926, though there have been attempted revivals. John Lennon alludes to the slogan in his song 'Beautiful Boy' (1980).

Every Good Boy Deserves Favour. The title of Tom Stoppard's play for speaker and orchestra (1977), derives from the mnemonic for remembering, in ascending order, the five horizontal black lines of the treble clef – signifying the notes E, G, B, D, and F. The four spaces between the lines are for the notes F, A, C, and E, which hardly need a mnemonic.

Every Home Should Have One. The title of a film (UK, 1970) about an advertising man derives from the all-purpose US advertising slogan of the 1920s/30s.

every man has his price. Mencken says of this proverb: 'Ascribed to Robert Walpole *c* 1740 in William Coxe, *Memoirs of the Life and Administration of Robert Walpole*, 1798'. There the form was: 'All those men have their price'. But *CODP* finds W. Wyndham in *The Bee* (1734) saying: 'It is an old Maxim, that every Man has his Price, if you can but come up to it'.

Every Other Inch a Lady. The title of the autobiography (1973) of Beatrice Lillie, the actress who was Lady Peel in private life. R.E. Drennan in *Wit's End* (1973) quotes Alexander Woollcott (*d* 1943) as having said of Michael Arlen, that: 'for all his reputation [he] is not a bounder. He is every other inch a gentleman.' (The same remark has also been attributed to Rebecca West.) The original expression 'every inch a gentleman' occurs, for example, in William Thackeray, *Pendennis* (Chap. 54, 1848–50).

every picture tells a story. This proverbial expression was originally a slogan used to promote Doan's Backache and Kidney Pills, and was current in 1904. The picture showed a person bent over with pain.

every soldier has the baton of a field-marshal in his knapsack. This is an anglicized form of the saying usually attributed to Napoleon I. The

earliest French version (E. Blaze, *La Vie Militaire sous l'Empire*) has: '*Tout soldat français porte dans sa giberne le bâton de maréchal de France*' which should be more accurately translated as, 'Every French soldier carries in his cartridge-pouch the baton of a marshal of France.' This was how the saying first appeared in English in 1840. The meaning is that even the lowliest soldier may have leadership potential. Mencken ascribes it to Louis XVIII (*d* 1824). Tom Stoppard in EVERY GOOD BOY DESERVES FAVOUR has: 'Every member of the orchestra carries a conductor's baton in his knapsack'.

everything in the garden's lovely. Meaning 'all is well', the saying comes from the title of a song made popular by Marie Lloyd (*d* 1922). *Everything in the Garden* was the title of a stage play (1962) by Giles Cooper, about suburban housewives turning to prostitution.

Everything You Always Wanted to Know About Sex But Were Afraid to Ask. This title of a book (1970) by David Reuben MD, gave to the language a format phrase, compounded by its use as a film title by Woody Allen in 1972 – though, in fact, Allen simply bought the title of the book and none of its contents. Subsequently, almost any subject you could think of was inserted into the sentence. An advertisement for the UK *Video Today* magazine (December 1981) promised: 'All you ever wanted to know about video but were afraid to ask'. In 1984, this short list was drawn up from the scores of books that bore similar titles: *Everything That Linguists Have Always Wanted to Know About Logic but Were Ashamed to Ask*; *Everything You Always Wanted to Know About Drinking Problems and Then a Few Things You Didn't Want to Know*; *Everything You Always Wanted to Know About Elementary Statistics but Were Afraid to Ask*; *Everything You*

Always Wanted to Know About Mergers, Acquisitions and Divestitures but Didn't Know Whom to Ask; *Everything You Wanted to Know About Stars but Didn't Know Where to Ask*; *Everything You Wanted to Know About the Catholic Church but Were Too Pious to Ask*; and *Everything You Wanted to Know About the Catholic Church but Were Too Weak to Ask.*

evidence. See ANYTHING YOU SAY . . .

evil. See BANALITY OF ~; HEAR ALL . . .; MONEY IS THE ROOT OF ALL ~.

evil empire. The Soviet Union was so described by President Reagan in a speech to the National Association of Evangelicals at Orlando, Florida (8 March 1983): 'In your discussions of the nuclear freeze proposals, I urge you to beware the temptation of pride – the temptation blithely to declare yourselves above it all and label both sides equally at fault, to ignore the facts of history and the aggressive impulses of an *evil empire* . . .' The reason for this turn of phrase was made later the same month (23 March) when he first propounded his **Star Wars** proposal as part of a campaign to win support for his defence budget and arms-control project. The proposal, more properly known by its initials SDI (for Strategic Defence Initiative), was to extend the nuclear battleground into space. The president did not use the term 'Star Wars' but it was an inevitable tag to be applied by the media, given his own fondness for adapting lines from the movies. The film *Star Wars* and the sequel *The Empire Strikes Back* had been released in 1977 and 1980, respectively. From the *Independent* (19 May 1990): 'Frank Salmon, an East End protection racketeer who built an "evil empire" on violence and fear, was yesterday jailed for 7$^1/_2$ years at the Old Bailey.'

Evil That Men Do, The. This film title (US, 1984) derives from Mark Antony's speech in Shakespeare's *Julius Caesar* (III.ii.77):

The evil that men do lives after them,
The good is oft interred with their bones.

Evil Under the Sun. The title of Agatha CHRISTIE's thriller about murder in a holiday hotel (1941; film UK, 1982). It is not explained in the text, though Hercule Poirot, the detective, remarks before any evil has been committed: 'The sun shines. The sea is blue . . . but there is evil everywhere under the sun.' Shortly afterwards, another character remarks: 'I was interested, M. Poirot, in something you said just now . . . It was almost a quotation from Ecclesiastes . . . "Yea, also the heart of the sons of men is full of evil, and madness is in their heart while they live".' But Ecclesiastes (which finds everything 'under the sun') gets nearer than that: 'There is a sore evil which I have seen under the sun, namely, riches kept for the owners thereof to their hurt' (5:13) and: 'There is an evil which I have seen under the sun' (6:1, 10:1). Were it not for the clue about Ecclesiastes, one might be tempted to think that Christie had once more turned to an old English rhyme for one of her titles. In this one, the phrase appears exactly:

For every evil under the sun,
There is a remedy or there is none;
If there be one, try and find it;
If there be none, never mind it.

exit pursued by a bear. A famous stage direction, from Shakespeare, *The Winter's Tale* (III.iii.58). It refers to the fate of Antigonus who is on the (in fact, non-existent) sea coast of Bohemia. Most of Shakespeare's stage directions are additions by later editors, but this one may be original. The bear could have been real (as bear-baiting was common in places adjacent to Shakespeare's theatres) or a man in costume.

expects. See ENGLAND ~ . . .

explain. See NEVER ~ . . .

expletive deleted. This is an American way of indicating that an obscenity or blasphemous remark has been omitted from a printed document. It became famous during Watergate on the release of transcripts of conversations between President Nixon and his aides – published as *The White House Transcripts* (1974).

exporting is fun. This was a Harold Macmillan slogan that misfired, though in this instance he never actually 'said' it. The phrase was included in a 1960 address to businessmen, but when he came to the passage he left out what was later considered to be a rather patronizing remark. The press, however, printed what was in the advance text of the speech as though he had actually said it. Compare the earlier 'We must export – or die' which arose out of a severe balance of payments problem under the Labour government in 1945/6.

eye. See ALL MY ~ AND . . .; APPLE OF ONE'S ~; ~ OF A NEEDLE under EASIER FOR A CAMEL . . .

eyeball to eyeball. Meaning 'in close confrontation', this was originally a Black US serviceman's idiom. In the missile crisis of October 1962, the US took a tough line when the Soviet Union placed missiles on Cuban soil. After a tense few days, the Soviets withdrew. Safire records that Secretary of State Dean Rusk was speaking to an ABC news correspondent, John Scali, on 24 October and said: 'Remember, when you report this, that, eyeball to eyeball, they blinked first.' Columnists Charles Bartlett and Stewart Alsop then helped to popularize this as: 'We're eyeball to eyeball and the other fellow just blinked.' (See also *DPP*.)

Eyeless in Gaza. The title of a book (1936) by Aldous HUXLEY, its source is Milton's *Samson Agonistes* (1671): 'Ask for this great deliverer now, and find him/Eyeless in Gaza, at the mill with slaves.'

eyes as windows of the soul. In *Zuleika Dobson* (1911), Max Beerbohm says: 'It needs no dictionary of quotations to remind me that the eyes are the windows of the soul'. Just in case it does, this is a reference to William Blake's 'The Everlasting Gospel' (*c* 1818): 'This life's five windows of the soul/Distort the Heavens from pole to pole,/And leads you to believe a lie/When you see with, not thro', the eye'.

Here, Blake seems to be saying that the five *senses* (or perhaps two eyes, two ears, and a nose?) are the windows to the soul. Compare WINDOWS INTO MEN'S SOULS.

F

F*F*

face. See TOUCH THE ~ OF GOD; UNACCEPTABLE ~ OF CAPITALISM.

Faces in My Time. The title of Vol. III (1980) of Anthony Powell's autobiography *TO KEEP THE BALL ROLLING*, is taken from Shakespeare's *King Lear* (II.ii.90), where Kent says:

I have seen better faces in my time
Than stands on any shoulder that I see
Before me at this instant.

face that launch'd a thousand ships. Referring to Helen of Troy, Christopher Marlowe's mighty line: 'Was this the face that launch'd a thousand ships' occurs in *Dr Faustus* (*c* 1594). Earlier, Marlowe had said something similar in *Tamburlaine the Great* (1587): 'Helen, whose beauty . . . drew a thousand ships to Tenedos.' Shakespeare must have been alluding to Marlowe's line when, in *Troilus and Cressida* (*c* 1601) he said of Helen:

Why she is a pearl
Whose price hath launch'd above a
thousand ships.

He also alludes to it in *All's Well That Ends Well*. The consistent feature of these mentions is the figure of a 'thousand' which was a round number probably derived from the accounts of Ovid and Virgil. Chips Channon records (23 April 1953) in the House of Commons: '[Aneurin] Bevan looked at poor, plain Florence Horsburgh [Independent MP for the Combined English Universities] and hailed her with the words "That's the face that sank a thousand scholarships".' To Jack de Manio, the broadcaster, is attributed a more recent version. Of Glenda Jackson, the actress, he is alleged to have said, in the 1970s: 'Her face could launch a thousand dredgers.'

face the music, to. Meaning 'to face whatever punishment is coming', this saying has two possible origins. (1) An actor or entertainer must not only accept the judgement of the audience but also of the (often hard-to-impress) musicians in the orchestra in front of him – he literally faces the music. (2) More likely is a kinship with the expression 'to be drummed out of' something. At one time, if a soldier was dismissed from the army for dishonourable conduct, he would be drummed out in a ceremony which included having a description of his crime read out and his insignia stripped from his uniform.

facilis descensus Averni [it is easy to go down into Hell]. From Virgil's *Aeneid* (VI.126), this phrase is employed when wanting to suggest that man is readily inclined towards evil deeds. Avernus, a lake in Campania, was a name for the entrance to Hell. The epic poem continues with:

Noctes atque dies patet atri ianua Ditis;

112

Sed revocare gradum superasque evadere
ad auras,
Hoc opus, hic labor est.

[Night and day, the gates of dark Death stand wide; but to climb back again, to retrace one's steps to the upper air – there's the rub, that is the task.]

Fagin. Meaning 'a receiver of stolen goods; a trainer of thieves', the name derives from the character in *Oliver Twist* (1838–41) by Charles Dickens. That he was portrayed as 'a very shrivelled old jew . . . villainous-looking and repulsive' led to allegations of antisemitism. Dickens sought to make amends by introducing a kindly Jew, Mr Riah, in *Our Mutual Friend* (1864–5).

fair day's wages for a fair day's work. T. Attwood in a speech in the House of Commons (14 June 1839) said: 'They only ask for a fair day's wages for a fair day's work.' This is picked up by Charles Dickens in *Our Mutual Friend* (Bk.I, Chap. 13, 1864–5): 'A fair day's wages for a fair day's work is ever my partner's motto.'

Fair Stood the Wind for France. The title of a story (1944) by H.E. Bates, taken from the 'Ballad of Agincourt' (1606) by Michael Drayton: 'Fair stood the wind for France/When we our sails advance.'

Earlier, in Christopher Marlowe's *Edward II*, there was: 'Fair blows the wind for France'.

fais ce que voudras. See FAY . . .

'Faithful Unto Death'. The title of a painting by Sir Edward John Poynter PRA, it shows a centurion staying at his sentry post during the eruption of Vesuvius which destroyed Pompeii in AD 79. In the background, citizens are panicking as molten lava falls upon them. The picture was inspired by the discovery of an actual skeleton of a soldier in full armour excavated at Pompeii in the late eighteenth or early nineteenth century. Many such remains were found of people 'frozen' in the positions they had held as they died. Bulwer-Lytton described what might have happened to the soldier in his *Last Days of Pompeii* (1834). Poynter painted the scene in 1865; it now hangs in the Walker Art Gallery, Liverpool. The phrase occurs earlier in Revelation 2:10: 'Be thou faithful unto death and I will give thee a crown of life.'

fall and rise. See DECLINE AND FALL.

Falstaff. Sir John Falstaff is a fat, jovial, likeable rogue in the first and second parts of Shakespeare's *King Henry IV* and *The Merry Wives of Windsor*, and whose death is referred to in *King Henry V* (see BABBLED OF GREEN FIELDS). Shakespeare's original may have been Sir John Oldcastle (*d* 1417), High Sheriff of Herefordshire. In the history plays, he befriends Prince Hal, plans an abortive robbery at Gad's Hill, but is rejected when the prince becomes king. Tradition has it that Elizabeth I requested Shakespeare to revive him for *The Merry Wives of Windsor*, a light-hearted romantic romp. Hence the term **Falstaffian** to describe any fat, jolly person.

Fame Is the Spur. The title of a novel (1940, film UK 1946) by Howard Spring about an aspiring politician. It is a quotation from Milton's 'Lycidas' (1637):

Fame is the spur that the clear spirit doth
raise
(That last infirmity of noble mind)
To scorn delights, and live laborious
days.

families. See ACCIDENTS WILL OCCUR . . .

family silver. See SELL OFF THE ~.

famous for fifteen minutes, to be. Meaning 'to have transitory fame' of the type prevalent in the twentieth century. It comes from the celebrated saying to be found in a catalogue for an exhibition of Andy Warhol's work in Stockholm (1968). The artist wrote: 'In the future everyone will be world-famous for fifteen minutes.' It is often to be found used allusively, e.g. 'He's had his fifteen minutes', etc. *Famous for Fifteen Minutes* was the title of a series of, naturally, fifteen-minute programmes on BBC Radio 4 in 1990 in which yesterday's headline-makers were recalled from obscurity.

famous last words. This is the kind of response given to someone who has just made a rash statement of the type: 'I always drive better when I've got a few drinks inside me.' There is a book entirely made up of such motorists' boasts called *You Have Been Warned* (1936) with illustrations by Fougasse. This second phrase comes from the 1930s' 'familiar police admonition' (Partridge/*Catch Phrases*).

Fanny Adams. See SWEET ~.

far away is close at hand in images of elsewhere. In the late 1970s, there was this very noticeable piece of graffiti, painted up in large letters, by the side of the track outside Paddington railway station in London. It became quite famous and puzzled many people. No one will ever know who wrote it. ('Peter Simple' in the *Daily Telegraph* attributed it to 'the Master of Paddington'.) Whoever it was may have had in mind the opening lines of the 'Song of Contrariety' by Robert Graves (*Collected Poems*, 1975):

Far away is close at hand
Close joined is far away,
Love shall come at your command
Yet will not stay.

farewell. See AND SO WE SAY ~ . . .

far far better thing I do. See IT IS A FAR FAR . . .

Far From the Madding Crowd. The title of Thomas Hardy's novel (1874; film UK, 1967) comes from Thomas Gray's 'Elegy Written in a Country Church-Yard' (1751):

Far from the madding crowd's ignoble strife
Their sober wishes never learn'd to stray.

'Madding' here means 'frenzied, mad' – not 'maddening'.

fat. See INSIDE EVERY ~ MAN . . .

Fates. See GREEK NAMES.

fate worse than death. Originally referring to rape or loss of virginity, this is an expression dating from the days when such a dishonour in woman would, indeed, have seemed so. It is now used jokingly of any situation one might wish to avoid. *OED2* has the original sense by 1810. In *The Trumpet-Major* (1882), Thomas Hardy reproduces what purports to be a document headed 'Address to All Ranks and Descriptions of Englishmen' dating from the time of Napoleonic invasion scares: 'You will find your best Recompense,' it concludes, '. . . in having protected your Wives and Children from death, or worse than Death, which will follow the Success of such Inveterate Foes.'

father. See AND WHEN DID YOU LAST SEE YOUR ~?

Fat Lady Sings, The. The name of an Irish (popular music) band, *c* 1990, which comes from the modern American

114

proverb: 'The opera isn't over till the fat lady sings' (which means, presumably, that something hasn't ended until an essential, significant part of it has taken place). The *Washington Post* (13 June 1978) attributed this coinage to Dan Cook, a San Antonio sports editor, who was topping another's remark that, 'The rodeo isn't over till the bull riders ride.'

fattening. See ILLEGAL, IMMORAL OR ~.

fat white woman whom nobody loves. Frances Cornford (*d* 1960) wrote a poem called 'To a Fat Lady Seen from a Train' which the *Oxford Companion to English Literature* describes as including the 'curiously memorable though undistinguished lines':

O why do you walk through the fields in gloves
Missing so much and so much
O fat white woman whom nobody loves . . .

Part of the fascination of these lines lies in the fact that we have all wondered about people glimpsed from passing trains. It was Frances Cornford's assumptions about the fat white woman, however, that caused G.K. Chesterton to provide the other part of the story. 'The Fat White Woman Speaks' was published in his *New Poems* (1932):

Why do you flash through the flowery meads,
Fat-head poet that nobody reads;
And why do you know such a frightful lot
About people in gloves as such . . . ?

'Beachcomber' (J.B. Morton) also wrote a riposte, 'The Fat Lady Seen from a Train Replies to the Scornful Poet'.

Faust(us). Meaning 'one who sells his soul to the devil', and so named after Johann Faust(us), a German astrologer and necromancer (*d* 1541) who was reputed to have practised the black arts

and was later celebrated in several plays including Christoper Marlowe's *The Tragical History of Dr Faustus* (*c* 1592) and Goethe's *Faust* (1772–1831). In these plays Faust exchanges his soul for a longer life in which all pleasure and knowledge are his for the asking. Thomas Mann's novel *Dr Faustus* (1947) follows a similar story.

Favourites of the Moon. See MINIONS OF THE MOON.

fay ce que voudras (or fais ce que voudras). Meaning 'do what you will; do as you please', it is an appealing motto and one that has been adopted by more than one free-living soul. It appears first in Bk.I of *Gargantua and Pantagruel* (1532) by Rabelais. Then, in the eighteenth century it was the motto of the Monks of Medmenham, better known as the Hell Fire Club. Sir Francis Dashwood founded a mock Franciscan order at Medmenham Abbey in Buckinghamshire in 1745 and the members of the Club were said to get up to all sorts of disgraceful activities – orgies, black masses, and the like. The politician John Wilkes was of their number. The motto was written up over the ruined door of the abbey.

Aleister Crowley (*d* 1947), the satanist, who experimented in necromancy and the black arts, sex and drugs, also picked up the motto. Newspapers called him the 'Wickedest Man in the World', though he fell short of proving the claim. Of his 'misunderstood commandment', Germaine Greer comments in *The Female Eunuch* (1970): '*Do as thou wilt* is a warning not to delude yourself that you can do otherwise, and to take full responsibility for what you do. When one has genuinely chosen a course for oneself it cannot be possible to hold another responsible for it.'

'Fear, In Place of'. See IN PLACE OF STRIFE.

Fear and Loathing in Las Vegas. The title of a book (1972) by the US writer Hunter S. Thompson, describing a visit to the gambling resort while under the influence of a variety of mind-expanding drugs. Apart from having a much-quoted title, the book is a prime example of what Thompson calls **gonzo** journalism, in which the writer chronicles his own role in the events he is reporting and doesn't worry too much about the facts. The word may be the same as Italian *gonzo* [a fool; foolish].

Feasting with Panthers. The title of a play (1981), devised and directed by Peter Coe, about the trials of Oscar Wilde. The phrase comes from Wilde's DE PROFUNDIS, in a passage about his life before he was sent to Reading gaol for homosexual offences: 'People thought it dreadful of me to have entertained at dinner the evil things of life, and to have found pleasure in their company. But then, from the point of view through which I, as an artist in life, approach them they were delightfully suggestive and stimulating. It was like feasting with panthers; the danger was half the excitement.'

feather in one's cap, to have a. Meaning 'to have an honour or achievement of which one can be proud', the expression dates from 1346, when the Black Prince was awarded the crest of John, King of Bohemia, which showed three ostrich feathers, after he had distinguished himself at the Battle of Crécy. This symbol has since been carried by every Prince of Wales. Later, any knight who had fought well might wear a feather in his helmet.

feeding frenzy. Meaning 'furious media attention', the image here is of fish swimming to retrieve bait thrown to them by a fisherman, or any potential food. An article by Prof Perry W. Gilbert in *Scientific American* (July 1962) has

this: 'As the blood and body juices of the marlin flow from the wound, the other sharks in the pack become more and more agitated and move in rapidly for their share of the meal. Frequently three or four sharks will attack the marlin simultaneously. A wild scene sometimes called a "feeding frenzy" now ensues.' As William Safire observed in the *New York Times Magazine* in (September 1988), packs of journalists in the US had come to be described by that time as 'in a piranha-like feeding frenzy' or behaving like 'sharks in a feeding frenzy'. Alliteration rules once more: '[Hunter S. Thompson's] forthcoming trial has the makings of an international media circus – or "feeding frenzy", as Thompson would put it.' (*Independent*, 14 April 1990)

Female of the Species, The. See DEADLIER THAN THE MALE.

Few, The. This was the name given to fighter pilots of the RAF at the height of the German air attacks on London and the south-east of England in 1940 during what came to be known as the BATTLE OF BRITAIN. Although greatly outnumbered, they wreaked havoc on the Luftwaffe, with heavy losses to themselves. Paying tribute to these airmen, Winston Churchill, Prime Minister, said in the House of Commons on 20 August 1940: 'Never in the field of human conflict was so much owed by so many to so few.' Here we have an echo of Shakespeare's Henry V speaking to his men before the Battle of Agincourt and talking of: 'We few, we happy few, we band of brothers' (*King Henry V*, IV.iii.60). Benham quotes Sir John Moore after the fall of Calpi (where Nelson lost an eye): 'Never was so much work done by so few men.'

Another pre-echo may be found in Vol.2 of Churchill's own *A History of the English-Speaking Peoples* (1956, but largely written pre-war). Describing a

1640 Scottish incursion in the run-up to the English Civil War, he writes: 'All the Scots cannon fired and all the English army fled. A contemporary wrote that "Never so many ran from so few with less ado".' In a speech on the Government of Ireland Bill, in the House of Commons (30 April 1912), Churchill himself had said: 'Never before has so little been asked; and never before have so many people asked for it.' It is interesting to note that Harold Nicolson, noting Churchill's 1940 speech in his diary (20 August), slightly misquotes the passage: '[Winston] says, in referring to the RAF, "Never in the history of human conflict has so much been owed by so many to so few".' By 22 September, Churchill's daughter, Mary, was uttering a *bon mot* in his hearing about the collapse of France through weak leadership: 'Never before has so much been betrayed for so many by so few' (recorded by John Colville, *The Fringes of Power*, Vol.1).

FHB. See INITIALS.

Fiacre, St. See SAINTS' NAMES.

fiddle. See FIT AS A ~.

Fiddler on the Roof. The title of a musical (1964; film US, 1971), from a book by Joseph Stein and with lyrics by Sheldon Harnick. It tells the story of Tevye, a Jewish milkman in pre-Revolutionary Russia, who cheerfully survives family and political problems before emigrating to America. Based on Sholom Aleichem's collected stories *Tevye and His Daughters*, the title is used allusively to describe the easy-going nature of the hero. The title-song merely asks the question, why is the fiddler playing up on the roof all day and in all weathers? It concludes: 'It might not mean a thing/But then again it might!' The expression would seem to signify 'an opportunist, one who takes life easy, one

who does what he pleases, a happy-go-lucky person'.

'Fiddling on the roof' is, however, one of the proverbial expressions portrayed (literally) in the painting known as 'The Proverbs' by David Teniers the Younger (*d* 1690) which hangs in Belvoir Castle. In the key to these Flemish proverbs, 'fiddling on the roof' is compared to 'eat, drink and be merry'. In Marc Chagall's painting 'The Dead Man' (1908), he shows – literally – a fiddler on a roof. Chagall often drew on Russian folktales in his work, and the character also turns up in his painting 'The Fiddler' (1912–13). Werner Haftmann in his book on the artist calls the fiddler on the roof, 'representative of the artist; a solitary individual, isolated by the strangeness and mystery of his art . . . a metaphorical figure who can be identified with . . . Chagall himself'. One source tells me that the writers of the musical were definitely thinking of this second picture when they came to settle on their title. A further attempt at explanation can be found in *Gänzl's Book of the Musical Theatre* (1988) where Tevye is described as: 'the epitome of the Jewish people of Anatevka who each scratch out a living, as the fiddler scratches out his tune, while perilously perched on the edge of existence as represented by the unsafe roof.' Another correspondent is certain that 'fiddler on the roof' is a Jewish euphemism for 'God'.

fiddle while Rome burns, to. Meaning 'to do something irrelevant while there are important matters to be dealt with', for example, in early 1979, the Kuwaiti Ambassador to the UN told the Security Council, referring to Cambodia, 'Rome is burning, children are being orphaned, women widowed, and we haggle.'

The allusion is to the Emperor Nero's behaviour when Rome burned for several days and was two-thirds destroyed in AD 64. It is possible that he knew what he was doing, however. It has been suggested that the fire was started on his orders, as part of what we would now call an 'urban renewal programme'. Nevertheless, being a shrewd politician he blamed the Christians and persecuted them. As to the fiddling: Suetonius states that Nero watched the conflagration, then put on his tragedian's costume and sang the *Fall of Ilium* from beginning to end. The fiddle as we know it had not been invented, so if he played anything it was probably the lyre. Tacitus says, rather, that Nero went on his private stage and 'sang' of the (comparable) destruction of Troy.

The phrase is in English by 1649, when George Daniel wrote in *Trinarchodia*: 'Let Nero fiddle out Rome's obsequies.'

fields. See FRESH ~.

fifteen. See FAMOUS FOR ~ MINUTES.

Fifth Beatle. Referring to someone who has missed out on the success of something he was once a part of, the original 'fifth Beatle' was Brian Epstein, the group's manager. He was so dubbed, much to his annoyance, by Murray the K, a US disc jockey, in 1964. Others could more fittingly have merited the title – Stu Sutcliffe, an early member of the group who was eased out and died before fame struck; Pete Best, who was replaced as drummer by Ringo Starr; Neil Aspinall, road manager, aide and friend; and George Martin, the group's arranger and record producer. When I was discussing this phrase on LBC Radio in 1989, a phone-in listener cleverly suggested that the 'fifth Beatle' was the Volkswagen Beetle which figures on the group's *Abbey Road* album sleeve.

Fifth Column, The. This was the title of Ernest Hemingway's only play (1938). In October 1936, during the Spanish Civil War, the Nationalist General, Emilio Mola, was besieging the Republican-held city of Madrid with four columns. He was asked in a broadcast whether this was sufficient to capture the city and he replied that he was relying on the support of the *quinta columna* [the fifth column], which was already hiding inside the city and which sympathized with his side. Hence the term meaning 'traitors, infiltrators'.

fifty million Frenchmen can't be wrong. As a slightly grudging expression this appears to have originated with US servicemen during the First World War, justifying support for their French allies. The precise number of millions varied. A song with the title (by Billy Rose, Willy Raskin and Fred Fisher) was recorded by Sophie Tucker in 1927. Cole Porter's musical *Fifty Million Frenchmen* opened in New York in 1929.

Where confusion has crept in is that Texas Guinan, the New York nightclub hostess, was refused entry into France with her girls in 1931 and said: 'It goes to show that fifty million Frenchmen *can* be wrong.' She returned to the US and renamed her show *Too Hot for Paris.* George Bernard Shaw also held out against the phrase. He insisted: 'Fifty million Frenchmen can't be right'.

Figaro, Le. The title of the French newspaper (founded 1826) derives from the guileful, amusing character of Figaro in the plays by Beaumarchais, *Le Barbier de Séville* (1775) and *Le Mariage de Figaro* (1784).

fight and fight and fight again. When Austrian armies threatened France, Danton exhorted his fellow countrymen to: 'Dare! and dare! and dare again!' Hugh Gaitskell, leader of the British Labour Party, used a similar construction memorably at the Party Conference on 3 October 1960. When, against the wishes of the Party leadership, the conference looked like taking what Gaitskell called the 'suicidal path' of unilateral disarmament 'which will leave our country defenceless and alone', he was faced with making the most important speech of his life – for his leadership was at issue. 'There are some of us, Mr Chairman,' he said, 'who will fight and fight and fight again to save the Party we love.' Many delegates who were free to do so changed their votes, but the Party executive was still defeated. Nevertheless, Gaitskell reduced his opponents to a paper victory and the phrase is often recalled in tribute to a great personal achievement.

fight between two bald men over a comb, a. This is a proverbial saying, possibly of Russian origin, and meaning 'an unnecessary struggle'. The Argentinian novelist, Jorge Luis Borges, was quoted as saying of the 1982 Falklands War between Britain and Argentina: 'The Falklands thing was a fight between two bald men over a comb.'

fight his/her way out of a paper-bag. See COULDN'T RUN . . .

final solution, the [German, *Endlösung*]. The euphemistic name given to Hitler's plan to exterminate the Jews of Europe was used by Nazi officials from the summer of 1941 onwards to disguise the enormity of what they intended. Gerald Reitlinger in *The Final Solution* (1953) says that the choice of phrase was probably, though not certainly, Hitler's own. Before then it had been used in a non-specific way to cover other possibilities – like emigration for example. It is estimated that the 'final solution' led to the deaths of up to six million Jews. Compare HOLOCAUST.

fine. See HERE'S ANOTHER ~ MESS . . .

Finest Hours, The. The title of a documentary film (UK 1964) about the life of Sir Winston Churchill, which derived from his speech to the House of Commons (18 June 1940): 'Let us therefore brace ourselves to our duties, and so bear ourselves that, if the British Empire and its Commonwealth last for a thousand years, men will say, "This was their finest hour".'

fine-tooth comb, to go through with a. Note, it is 'a fine-tooth comb' rather than 'fine tooth-comb' – the comb has fine teeth (enabling the smallest pieces of dirt to be removed) and isn't necessarily excellent, so the precise meaning of the expression is 'to examine very closely'.

fingerlickin'. See IT'S ~ . . .

Fings Ain't Wot They Used t'Be. This title for the Frank Norman/Lionel Bart musical (1959) came from a catch phrase already used by Mercer Ellington and Ted Persons in their composition 'Things Ain't What They Used to Be' (1939).

Fire Next Time, The. The title of a novel (1963) by James Baldwin, which concludes: 'If we do not now dare everything, the fulfilment of that prophecy, re-created from the Bible in song by a slave, is upon us: *God gave Noah the rainbow sign, No more water, the fire next time!*'

First Among Equals. This was the title of Jeffrey Archer's novel (1984) about the pursuit of the British Prime Ministership. As *primus inter pares* it is an anonymous Latin saying. It has been used about the position of politicians in a number of countries and also of the Pope. *ODCIE* defines it as an idiom meaning 'the one of a group who leads or takes special responsibility but who neither feels himself, nor is held by others, to be their superior'. The Round

Table in Arthurian legend was meant to show not only that there was no precedence among the knights who sat at it but also that King Arthur was no more than first among equals.

Used specifically regarding the British Prime Minister within the Cabinet, the phrase cannot pre-date Sir Robert Walpole (in power 1721–42) who is traditionally the first to have held that position. Lord Morley may have been the first to use the phrase in this context in his life of Walpole (1889) where he says: 'Although in Cabinet all its members stand on an equal footing, speak with equal voice, and, on the rare occasions when a division is taken, are counted on the fraternal principle of one vote, yet the head of the Cabinet is *primus inter pares*, and occupies a position which, so long as it lasts, is one of exceptional and peculiar authority.' In 1988, Julian Critchley M P was quoted as having referred to Margaret Thatcher as '*prima donna inter pares*'.

First Casualty, The. The title of a book (1975) by Phillip Knightley on propaganda in wartime. It comes from a saying of Hiram Johnson, an all-party US senator, in 1917: 'The first casualty when war comes is truth.'

first catch your hare. The meaning of this proverb is that you can't begin to do something until you have acquired a certain necessary element (which may be difficult to acquire). *C O D P* finds the equivalent thought in *c* 1300, translated from the Latin: 'It is commonly said that one must first catch the deer, and afterwards, when he has been caught, skin him.' For a long time, however, the saying was taken to be a piece of practical, blunt good sense to be found in Mrs Beeton's *Book of Household Management* (1851), but it does not appear there. However, in Mrs Hannah Glasse's earlier *The Art of Cookery Made Plain and Easy* (1747), there is the similar:

'Take your hare when it is cased [skinned].' It was known in the familar form by 1855 when it appeared in Thackeray's *The Rose and the Ring*. Similar proverbs include: 'Catch your bear before you sell its skin', 'Never spend your money before you have it' and 'Don't count your chickens before they are hatched.'

firstest with the mostest. To describe anything as 'the mostest' might seem an exclusively US activity. However, *O E D2* finds English dialect use in the 1880s and Partridge/*Slang* recognizes its use as a jocular superlative without restricting it to the US. As such, it is a consciously ungrammatical way of expressing extreme degree. Whether this was consciously the case with the Confederate General, Nathan B. Forrest (*d* 1977) is very much in doubt. He could hardly read or write but he managed to say that the way to win battles was to be 'firstest with the mostest', or that you needed to 'git thar fustest with the mostest'. Bartlett gives this last as the usual rendering of the more formally reported words: 'Get there first with the most men'. In Irving Berlin's musical *Call Me Madam* (1950) there is a song with the title 'The Hostess with the Mostes' on the Ball'. One assumes that Berlin's use, like any evocation of 'the mostest' nowadays, refers back to Forrest's remark.

First Hundred Thousand, The. The title of a war novel (1915) by Ian Hay, which is subtitled 'Adventures of a typical regiment in Kitchener's army'. The book begins with a poem (Hay's own, presumably):

We're off a hundred thousand strong.
And some of us will not come back.

A.J.P. Taylor in his *English History 1914–45*, describing a period of 'patriotic frenzy' in the Great War, says that the 'spirit of 1915 was best expressed by Ian Hay, a writer of light fiction, in *The First*

Hundred Thousand — a book which treated soldiering as joke, reviving "the best days of our lives" at some imaginary public school'.

First World War. Known at first as the 'European War', it became known quite rapidly as the **Great War**. By 10 September 1918, Lt-Col C. à Court Repington, was referring to it in his diary as the 'First World War', thus: 'I saw Major Johnstone, the Harvard Professor who is here to lay the bases of an American History. We discussed the right name of the war. I said that we called it now *The War*, but that this could not last. The Napoleonic War was *The Great War*. To call it *The German War* was too much flattery for the Boche. I suggested *The World War* as a shade better title, and finally we mutually agreed to call it *The First World War* in order to prevent the millennium folk from forgetting that the history of the world was the history of war.' Repington's book entitled *The First World War 1914–18* was published in 1920. Presumably this helped popularize the name for the war, ominously suggesting that it was the first of a series.

fish. See CAN A BLOODY DUCK SWIM; HERE'S A PRETTY KETTLE OF ~; NEITHER ~ FLESH NOR FOWL.

fist. See HAND OVER ~; IRON ~.

fit as a fiddle. A fiddler, when playing quickly, has to be so dextrous with his fingers and bow that he is assumed to be especially lively and awake. Could, then, the phrase that we have be a contraction of 'fit as a fiddler'?

fit to a T, to. This expression means 'to fit perfectly'. A T-square is used by draughtsmen to draw parallel lines and angles, though it seems 'to a T' was in use by the seventeenth century and before the T-square got its name. Perhaps

the original expression was 'fit to a tittle' — a tittle being the dot over the letter *i* — so the phrase meant 'to a dot, fine point'.

five o'clock shadow. This refers to the stubbly growth that some dark-haired men acquire on their faces towards the end of the day, and comes from adverts for Gem Razors and Blades in the US. A 1937 advert added: 'That unsightly beard growth which appears prematurely at about 5 pm looks bad'. The most noted sufferer was Richard Nixon who may have lost the TV debates in his US presidential race against John F. Kennedy in 1960 as a result. In his *Memoirs* (1978) he wrote: 'Kennedy arrived . . . looking tanned rested and fit. My television adviser, Ted Rodgers, recommended that I use television make-up, but unwisely I refused, permitting only a little "beard stick" on my perpetual five o'clock shadow.'

Fixit. See MR ~.

Flanelled Fool. The title of a book (1967), 'a slice of life in the 30s', by the critic, T.C. Worsley. It comes from the poem 'The Islanders' (1902) by Rudyard KIPLING: 'Flannelled fools at the wicket or the muddied oafs at the goals' – where the 'fools' are, of course, cricketers.

Flash Harry. The nickname of Sir Malcolm Sargent (*d* 1967), the orchestral conductor, is said to have originated with a BBC announcer after Sargent had appeared on the radio *Brains Trust* and was also about to be heard in the following programme. Listeners were told that they were to be taken over to a concert conducted by Sargent in Manchester. It sounded as if he had gone there straightaway, in a flash. However, the nickname also encapsulated his extremely debonair looks and manner – smoothed-back hair, buttonhole, gestures and all. When Sir Thomas Beecham heard that Sargent was conducting in

Tokyo, he remarked: 'Ah! Flash in Japan!' In due course, Sir Alexander Gibson (*b* 1926), conductor of the Scottish National Orchestra, was dubbed 'Flash Haggis'.

flavour of the month. Referring to what is currently most popular, this was originally an advertising phrase, principally in the U S, aimed at persuading people to try new varieties of ice cream and not just stick to their customary choice. Latterly, it has become an idiom for any fad, craze, or person that is quickly discarded after a period of being in the news or in demand.

Fleet's Lit Up, The. The title of a 'musical frolic' at the London Hippodrome (1938), originated in the most famous British broadcasting boob, perpetrated by Lt-Cdr Tommy Woodrooffe, a leading B B C Radio commentator of the 1930s. On the night of 20 May 1937 he was due to give a fifteen-minute description of the 'illumination' of the Fleet after the Coronation Naval Review at Spithead. What he said, in a commentary that was faded out after less than four minutes, began: 'At the present moment, the whole Fleet's lit up. When I say "lit up", I mean lit up by fairy lamps. We've forgotten the whole Royal Review. We've forgotten the Royal Review. The whole thing is lit up by fairy lamps. It's fantastic. It isn't the Fleet at all. It's just . . . fairy land. The whole fleet is in fairy land . . .' Naturally, many listeners concluded that Woodrooffe himself had been 'lit up' as the result of enjoying too much hospitality from his former shipmates on board H M S *Nelson* before the broadcast. But he denied this. 'I had a kind of nervous blackout. I had been working too hard and my mind just went blank,' he told the *News Chronicle*. 'I was so overcome by the occasion that I literally burst into tears . . . I found I could say no more.' The B B C took a kindly view and the incident did not put

paid to Woodrooffe's broadcasting career.

A song called 'The Fleet's Lit Up' was written by Vivian Ellis, and the Second World War song 'I'm Going to Get Lit Up When the Lights Go Up in London' by Hubert Gregg (1943) probably owes something to the Woodrooffe affair, though use of 'lit up' to mean 'tipsy' dates back to 1914, at least.

fleshpots of Egypt. Meaning 'any place of comparative luxury', it was originally said by the Israelites (Exodus 16:3): 'Would to God we had died by the hand of the Lord in the land of Egypt, when we sat by the flesh pots, and when we did ate bread to the full.' Clementine Churchill wrote to Winston on 20 December 1910: 'I do so wish I was at Warter with you enjoying the Flesh Pots of Egypt! It sounds a delightful party . . . ' (quoted in *Clementine Churchill* by Mary Soames, 1979).

flick your Bic. Originally a slogan for Bic cigarette lighters, this was coined by U S copywriter Charlie Moss in 1975 and occurred in an ad that showed how smart sophisticated people didn't use lighters – they simply 'flicked their Bics'. The phrase caught on and was picked up by many comedians. During the energy crisis, Bob Hope said: 'Things are getting so bad that the Statue of Liberty doesn't light up any more. She just stands there and flicks her Bic.'

fling. See YOUTH MUST HAVE ITS ~.

Flora. See ROMAN NAMES.

Floreat Etona [May Eton flourish]. This is the motto of Eton College (founded 1440) in Berkshire. It is spoken by the villain 'Captain Hook' (presumably an Old Etonian), just before he is eaten by a crocodile in J.M. Barrie's play *Peter Pan* (1904). (In Barrie's novel, *Peter Pan and Wendy* (1911) he merely cries, 'Bad form'.) It was earlier used as the title of a painting (1882) by Elizabeth, Lady Butler depicting an attack on Laing's Neck (presumably in the Boer War, 1881), after this eye-witness account: 'Poor Elwes fell among the 58th. He shouted to another Eton boy (adjutant of the 58th, whose horse had been shot) "Come along, Monck! Floreat Etona! We must be in the front rank!" and he was shot immediately.'

Flowerpot Men, The. A BBC TV children's puppet series from the 1950s, the title refers to characters who lived in flowerpots in a garden shed, and spoke in a much-imitated meaningless gabble. The Flowerpot Men, a British vocal group who had hit with 'Let's Go to San Francisco' in 1967, adopted the name in order to allude to 'flower' as in F L O W E R P O W E R and 'pot' as another name for then-fashionable marijuana.

Flower Power. A hippy slogan – formed, no doubt, in emulation of 'Black Power', to describe the beliefs of the so-called Flower Children. Flowers were used as a love and peace symbol when the phrase came into use *c* 1967.

flowers. See S A Y I T W I T H ~.

Flynn. See I N L I K E ~.

fog. See N I G H T A N D ~.

fogey. See Y O U N G ~.

Foggy Bottom. The nickname for the US Department of State comes from the name of a marshy part of Washington DC where its offices are located. Compare the similar locational nicknames for: the British Foreign Office, **Whitehall**; the French, *Quai d'Orsay*; and the Russian, **Gorky Street**.

fold one's tents like the Arabs, to. Meaning 'to bring to a conclusion

unostentatiously', the expression comes from Longfellow's 'The Day Is Done':

> And the night shall be filled with music
> And the cares that infest the day
> Shall fold their tents, like the Arabs,
> And as silently steal away.

Alas, at the conclusion of his case for the defence in the Jeremy Thorpe trial (1979), Mr George Carman QC said to the jury: 'I end by saying in the words *of the Bible* [sic]: "Let this prosecution fold up its tent and quietly creep away".'

fools who come to scoff and remain to pray. Referring to people who undergo some kind of conversion or change of heart, the phrase originated in Oliver Goldsmith's *The Deserted Village* (1770):

> At church, with meek and unaffected
>   grace,
> His looks adorn'd the venerable place;
> Truth from his lips prevail'd with double
>   sway,
> And fools who came to scoff, remain'd
>   to pray.

From Clive James, *The Crystal Bucket* (1981): 'I came to mock *Dallas* but I stayed to pray.'

Fool There Was, A. The title of this silent film (US, 1914) came from the opening line of 'The Vampire', a poem (1897) by Rudyard K I P L I N G. It was through this film that Theda Bara popularized the notion of the female V A M P.

foot. See B E S T ~ F O R W A R D; O N E ~ I N T H E G R A V E.

foreign field, some corner of a. See *F O R E V E R E N G L A N D*.

Forests of the Night. The title of a crime novel (1987) by Margaret Moore. Compare *In the Forests of the Night* by James Riddell (1948). Both titles come from 'The Tyger' (*c* 1793) by William Blake:

Tyger! Tyger! burning bright
In the forests of the night.

Forever England. The UK title given to the reissue of the film version of C.S. Forester's novel *Brown on Resolution* (1929; film UK, 1935). In the US, the film was known as *Born for Glory*. For a 1914–18 war film, of the stiff upper lip variety, it was appropriate that the re-issuers should have turned to Rupert Brooke's 1914 poem 'The Soldier':

> If I should die, think only this of me:
> That there's some corner of a foreign
> field
> That is for ever England.

Forget-Me-Not Lane. The title of this Peter Nichols play (1971) comes from the Flanagan and Allen song 'Down Forget-Me-Not Lane' (1941) by Horatio Nicholls, Charlie Chester, and Reg Morgan.

forgets. See AN ELEPHANT NEVER ~.

Forgive Our Foolish Ways. This was the title of a BBC TV drama series (1980) by Reg Gadney about goings-on in a public school after the Second World War. It comes from the hymn 'Dear Lord and Father of Mankind', written by J.G. Whittier, of which this title is the second line.

forgotten. See GONE BUT NOT ~.

Forgotten Army. The nickname given to the British Army in India and South-East Asia, and more precisely, Burma and Malaya during the Second World War. According to John Connell (*Auchinleck*, 1959), it was mentioned in a despatch by Stuart Emeny, a *News Chronicle* war correspondent, in the summer of 1943, but the idea behind it had long been current with the soldiers.

Former Naval Person. In his wartime cables as Prime Minister to President Roosevelt, Winston Churchill used this code name. He had sent his telegrams to the President as 'Naval Person' when First Lord of the Admiralty at the beginning of the Second World War.

fort. See HOLD THE ~.

Forties, Roaring. See ROARING TWENTIES.

Fortuna. See ROMAN NAMES.

Fortune and Men's Eyes. The title of a play (1967) by John Herbert about homosexuals, comes from Shakespeare's Sonnet 29:

> When in disgrace with Fortune and
> men's eyes
> I all alone beweep my outcast state.

forty. See LIFE BEGINS AT ~.

Forty Years On. Alan Bennett's chronicle play of the twentieth century (1968), set in a boys' public school, takes its title from the first line of the Harrow Football Song (which is also the Harrow School Song), written by E.E. Bowen (1872):

> Forty years on, when afar and asunder
> Parted are those who are singing today,
> When you look back, and forgetfully
> wonder
> What you were like in your work and
> your play.

Forum. See under ODEON.

For Whom the Bell Tolls. The title of the novel (1940, film US 1943) by Ernest Hemingway, set in the Spanish Civil War, originates in John Donne's *Meditation XVII*, which begins: 'No man is an Island, entire of it self . . . And therefore never send to know for whom the bell tolls; It tolls for thee.' Hemingway's approach to the matter of choosing the title is described in a letter to Maxwell Perkins (21 April 1940) (included in *Ernest Hemingway Selected Letters 1917–1961*, ed. Carlos Baker, 1981): 'I think it has the magic that a title has to have. Maybe it isn't too easy to say. But maybe the book will make it easy. Anyway I have had thirty some titles and they were all possible but this is the first one that has made the bell toll for me. Or do you suppose that people think only of tolls as long distance charges and of Bell as the Bell of the telephone system? If so it is out. The Tolling of the Bell. No. That's not right.'

four. See GANG OF ~.

Four Horsemen of the Apocalypse, The. The title of this novel (1916, films US, 1921, 1961) by Vicente Blasco Ibánez, refers to the four agents of destruction who appear on different coloured horses in Revelation 6. Compare BEHOLD A PALE HORSE.

Four Hundred, The. The title of a novel (1979) by Stephen Sheppard, it alludes to the term given to the top stratum of society in New York and was originated by Ward McAllister, its leader, in 1888. 'There are only about four hundred people in fashionable New York society,' he told the *Tribune*. 'If you go outside that number you strike people who are either not at ease in a ballroom or else make other people not at ease.' Mrs Ward Astor asked McAllister to help prune her invitation list down to four hundred when giving a ball in a room which could only comfortably hold that number. Earlier, the top level had been called the Upper 10,000 or Upper Ten.

Four Hundred Blows, The. See QUATRE CENTS COUPS.

four more years. In US presidential elections where the incumbent seeks, or is being urged to seek, a further term, this is the standard cry. His supporters chanted it of Richard Nixon in 1972, and look what happened. With it, several times, Ronald Reagan's supporters interrupted his remarks accepting the GOP presidential nomination in Dallas, Texas, on 23 August 1984. Their prayer was answered.

four-square?, are you. Aimée Semple McPherson (*d* 1944), the Canadian-born revivalist, had the Angelus Temple in LA as the centre for her 'Foursquare Gospel'. This phrase was the greeting and slogan of her followers – and was used to mean 'are you solid, resolute?' Being 'square' in this sense, dates from at least 1300. Compare Theodore Roosevelt's campaign promise in 1901: 'We demand that big business give people a **Square Deal** . . . If elected I shall see to it that every man has a Square Deal, no more and no less.' Meaning 'a fair deal', this phrase of US origin was current by 1876.

fourth estate. In 1828, Thomas Macaulay wrote of the House of Commons: 'The gallery in which the reporters sit has become the fourth estate of the realm' – that is, after the Lords Spiritual, the Lords Temporal, and the Commons – and Macaulay has often been credited with coining this expression. But so have a number of others. Edmund Burke, for example, is said to have pointed at the press gallery and remarked: 'And yonder sits the fourth estate, more important than them all.'

The phrase was originally used to describe various forces outside Parliament – such as the Army (as by Falkland in 1638) or the Mob (as by Fielding in 1752). When William Hazlitt used it in 'Table Talk' in 1821, he meant not the Press in general but just William

Cobbett. Two years later, Lord Brougham is said to have used the phrase in the House of Commons to describe the Press in general. So when Macaulay used it in the *Edinburgh Review* in 1828, it was obviously an established usage. Then Carlyle used it several times – in his article on Boswell's *Life of Johnson* in 1832, in his history of *The French Revolution* in 1837, and in his lectures 'On Heroes, Hero-Worship, & the Heroic in History' in 1841. But, just to keep the confusion alive, he attributed the phrase to Burke (who died in 1797). It has been suggested that the BBC (or the broadcast media in general) now constitute a *fifth* estate, as also, at one time, the trades unions.

four thousand holes in Blackburn Lancashire. These odd lines come from the Lennon and McCartney lyrics of 'A DAY IN THE LIFE' on the Beatles' *Sgt Pepper* album (1967):

> I heard the news today oh boy
> four thousand holes in Blackburn,
>   Lancashire
> and though the holes were rather small
> they had to count them all
> now they know how many holes it takes
> to fill the Albert Hall.

The inspiration for them – nothing to do with drug-needle-marks or anything like that – can be traced directly to the *Daily Mail* of 17 January 1967. John Lennon had the newspaper propped up on his piano as he composed. The original brief story, topping the 'Far & Near' column stated: 'There are 4000 holes in the road in Blackburn, Lancashire, or one twenty-sixth of a hole per person, according to a council survey. If Blackburn is typical there are two million holes in Britain's roads and 300,000 in London.'

foxtrot. This dance was supposedly named after the US entertainer Harry Fox whose 1913 *Ziegfeld Follies* contained the steps for it. The word first appears in the 1915 Victor Record catalogue. Before this, a 'foxtrot' was a term in horsemanship for a short-paced step in changing from trotting to walking (presumably because a fox does something similar).

Francis of Assisi, St. See SAINTS' NAMES.

Francis of Assisi, prayer of St. On first becoming British Prime Minister, Margaret Thatcher stood in Downing Street on 4 May 1979 and said: 'I would just like to remember some words of St Francis of Assisi which I think are really just particularly apt at the moment: "Where there is discord, may we bring harmony; where there is error may we bring truth; where there is doubt, may we bring faith; and where there is despair, may we bring hope".' Bartlett has a fuller version and a different translation, saying no more than that the words are 'attributed' to St Francis (*d* 1226). Actually there is some doubt as to whether St Francis had anything to do with the prayer at all. A former Bishop of Ripon writing to the *Church Times* suggested the prayer had only been written in France in 1912 or in the nineteenth century.

Frankie Goes to Hollywood. The name of a British pop vocal group *c* 1983/4, which derived from a newspaper headline referring to Frank Sinatra.

frankly my dear I don't give a damn. In the last scene of the film GONE WITH THE WIND (1939), Scarlett O'Hara is finally abandoned by her husband Rhett Butler. Although she believes she can get him back, there occurs the controversial moment when Rhett replies with these words to her entreaty: 'Where shall I go? What shall I do?' They were only allowed on to the soundtrack after months of negotiation with the Hays Office which controlled film censorship. In those days, the word 'damn' was forbidden in Hollywood under Section V (1) of the Hays Code, even if it was what Margaret Mitchell had written in her novel (though she hadn't included the 'frankly'). Sidney Howard's original draft was accordingly changed to: 'Frankly, my dear, I don't care.' The scene was shot with both versions of the line and the producer, David Selznick, argued at great length with the censors over which was to be used. He did this not least because he thought he would look a fool if the famous line was excluded. He also wanted to show how faithful the film was to the novel. Selznick argued that the *Oxford Dictionary* described 'damn' not as an oath but as a vulgarism, that many women's magazines used the word, and that preview audiences had expressed disappointment when the line was omitted. The censors suggested 'darn' instead. Selznick finally won the day – but because he was technically in breach of the Hays Code he was fined $5000. The line still didn't sound quite right: Clark Gable, as Rhett, had to put the emphasis unnaturally on 'give' rather than on 'damn'.

Fred Karno. An adjective meaning 'inept, disorganized', this was applied humorously to the new British army raised to fight in the First World War. The name comes from the leader (actually, Fred Westcott, *d* 1941) of a music-hall comedy troupe which was popular in the early years of the century. Hence: 'Fred Karno's Army', 'Fred Karno outfit', etc.

free. See NO SUCH THING AS A ~ LUNCH.

free gratis and for nothing. A double tautology, Partridge/*Slang* quotes Thomas Bridges as saying in 1770 that 'the common people' always put 'free' and 'gratis' together; and notes that the longer version occurs in an 1841 book. In fact, a little earlier, Charles Dickens in *The Pickwick Papers* (Chap.26, 1836–7) has Sam Weller's father say 'free gratis for nothin' '. In *Usage and Abusage*, Partridge decides that it is a cliché, only excusable as a jocularity.

freelance. Used to denote a self-employed person, especially a writer or journalist. The word (redolent of the Middle Ages, when an unattached soldier for hire – a mercenary – would have been appropriately called a 'free lance') is in fact a nineteenth-century coinage. Sir Walter Scott in *Ivanhoe* (1820) has: 'I offered Richard the services of my Free Lances.'

Frenchmen. See FIFTY MILLION ~.

frenzy. See FEEDING ~.

fresh fields/woods and pastures new. This should read 'Tomorrow to fresh *woods* and pastures new' whether or not one is aware that Milton's 'Lycidas' (1637) is being quoted. The misquotation probably gained hold because of the alliteration – always a lure in phrase-making.

fretful porpentine. 'His face was flushed, his eyes were bulging, and . . . his hair was standing on end – like quills upon the fretful porpentine, as Jeeves once put it when describing to me the reactions of Barmy Fotheringay-Phipps on seeing a dead snip, on which he had invested largely, come in sixth in the procession at the Newmarket Spring Meeting.' So says Bertie Wooster in *The Code of the Woosters* by P.G. WODE-HOUSE, using one of his favourite Shakespearean images (from *Hamlet*, I.v.20 – though he probably wasn't aware of this). In the original, it is the

Ghost of Hamlet's father who is telling the Prince he 'could a tale unfold' which would make 'each particular hair to stand on end/Like quills upon the fretful porpentine' (i.e. porcupine). In 1986, some of the more literate regulars of the Porcupine pub in Charing Cross Road, London, would talk of repairing to 'the Fretters'.

friend(s). See GUIDE PHILOSOPHER AND ~; IS SHE A ~ OF DOROTHY?; SOME OF MY BEST ~ ARE . . .; WITH ~ LIKE THESE . . .

From a Far Country. The title of a TV film (1981) of dramatized episodes from the early life of Pope John Paul II. Compare *Crowned in a Far Country*, a book (1986) by Princess Michael of Kent about people who had married into the British Royal Family. The source seems to lie in the Old Testament where there are several examples of 'from a far land' and 'from a far country' (Deuteronomy 29:22, 2 Kings 20:14, Isaiah 39:3, etc.) but, perhaps most felicitously, there is 'good news from a far country' (Proverbs 25:25).

from each according to his abilities, to each according to his needs. A saying usually attributed to Karl Marx, but it is not from *Capital* or *The Communist Manifesto*. The slogan appears in his *Critique of the Gotha Programme* (1875), in which he says that after the workers have taken power, capitalist thinking must first disappear. Only then will the day come when society can 'inscribe on its banners: from each according to his ability, to each according to his needs'. John Kenneth Galbraith commented in *The Age of Uncertainty* (1977): 'It is possible that these . . . twelve words enlisted for Marx more followers than all the hundreds of thousands in the three volumes of *Capital* combined.'

There is some doubt as to whether Marx originated the slogan or whether he was quoting either Louis Blanc, Morelly, or M. Bakunin. The latter wrote: 'From each according to his faculties, to each according to his needs' (declaration, 1870, by anarchists on trial after the failure of their uprising in Lyons). Also Saint-Simon, the French reformer, had earlier said: 'The task of each be according to his capacity, the wealth of each be according to his works.' And much earlier, Acts 4:34–35 had: 'Neither was there any among them that lacked: for as many as were possessors of lands or houses sold them, and brought the prices of things that were sold, and laid them down at the apostles' feet: and distribution was made unto every man according as he had need.'

From Here to Eternity. The title of the novel (1951; film US, 1953) by James Jones, comes from Rudyard KIPLING's 'Gentlemen Rankers' (1892):

> Gentlemen-rankers out on the spree,
> Damned from here to Eternity.

From Russia With Love. The obvious derivation of the title of Ian Fleming's James Bond novel (1957, film UK, 1963), is the simple form of wording used to accompany a present, but as a format phrase, it has launched a million allusions of the 'from — with —' variety. Compare *To Paris With Love* (film UK, 1954), *To Sir With Love* (book by E.R. Braithwaite, 1959, film UK, 1967).

from sea to shining sea. A line from the poem 'America the Beautiful' (1893) by Katharine Lee Bates:

> America! America!
> God shed his grace on thee
> And crown thy good with brotherhood
> From sea to shining to shining sea!

These words have also been set to music. The motto of the Dominion of

Canada (adopted 1867) is '*A mari usque ad mare*' [From sea to sea], which came from Psalm 72:8: 'He shall have dominion also from sea to sea.'

frontier. See NEW ~.

frozen mit, to give someone the. Meaning 'to freeze out; give the cold shoulder to someone; exclude' (from 'mit', 'mitten', thence 'hand'). Lady Diana Cooper writing to Duff Cooper on 14 September 1925 (in a letter printed in *A Durable Fire*, 1983) said: 'Duffy, don't be deathly proud, my darling . . . you probably dish out the frozen mit to all, and I want all men to love and admire you.' Partridge/*Slang* finds it in *Punch* in 1915.

fruits ye shall know them, by their. 'By their — ye shall know them' has become almost a format phrase. The original version occurs in Matthew 7:20 in the part of the Sermon on the Mount about bewaring false prophets.

fudge and mudge, to. Meaning 'to produce the appearance of a solution while, in fact, only patching up a compromise', these verbs (and associated nouns) were often wheeled out in discussions of the Social Democratic and the Liberal parties in Britain in the 1980s. One of the SDP's GANG OF FOUR, Dr David Owen, had used it earlier in his previous incarnation, as a member of the Labour Party. He told its Blackpool Conference (2 October 1980): 'We are fed up with fudging and mudging, with mush and slush.'

Full Circle. The title of Sir Anthony Eden's memoirs (1960). See THE WHEEL HAS COME FULL CIRCLE.

full-frontal nudity. Referring to nudity which allows a man or woman's sexual parts to be seen. Before the 1960s, naked people when being photographed had a way of holding large beach balls in front of themselves, but with the advent of naked actors in such shows as *Hair* (1967) and *OH! CALCUTTA!* (1969) a term obviously had to be invented for this great leap forward in civilized behaviour. *OED2* doesn't find the term until 1971, but in my diary for 25 March 1970, I find myself going to see Ken Russell's film *Women in Love* and noting: 'full frontal nudity, too, as they call it, though I don't feel a better man for having seen Oliver Reed's genitals'. The episode of TV's *Monty Python's Flying Circus* broadcast on 7 December 1969 was entitled 'Full Frontal Nudity'.

Fun in a Chinese Laundry. The title of the memoirs (1966) of Josef von Sternberg, the film director, it had been used originally by Thomas Alva Edison, inventor of the cinematograph, as the title of an early short film in the days when titles were literal to the point of ploddingness – like 'A Train Entering a Station'.

Funny Peculiar. The title of a play (1976) by Mike Stott, and also of an (unrelated) series of compilations of newspaper clangers and oddities by Denys Parsons beginning with *Funny Ha Ha and Funny Peculiar* (1965). Both come from the basic distinction made clear by Ian Hay in his play *The Housemaster* (1936):

> That's funny.
> What do you mean, funny? Funny-peculiar, or funny ha-ha?

fury. See HELL HATH NO ~.

future. See I HAVE SEEN THE ~ . . .

fuzz. A popular term for the police, out of the US in the 1960s, though current by the 1920s. Possibly because they are people who make a 'fuss', or a corruption of 'Feds' (federal agents).

G

Gaea. See GREEK NAMES.

gaff. See BLOW THE ~.

gag. See MAN THEY COULDN'T ~.

gaga. Meaning 'senile', this comes from a French word. Also in French, one can use the expression *c'est un vieux gâteux* to describe an old man who is completely gaga. Perhaps 'gaga' developed from '*gâteux*' which as a noun means 'dotard' and as an adjective, 'decrepit' (and has nothing to do with *gâteau*, cake), or it may just be imitative of the way such a person would sound if he tried to speak. Rosie Boycott's suggestion in *Batty, Bloomers and Boycott* (1982), that it has something to do with the Impressionist painter Paul Gauguin (1848–1903) seems unlikely. He may have been mentally disturbed in old age, but the word was known in French by 1875 when he was not.

gaiety of nations. This phrase comes from one of the finest tributes ever penned – Samuel Johnson's lament for his friend, the actor David Garrick (*d* 1779). In his 'Life of Edmund Smith', one of the *Lives of the English Poets* (1779), Johnson wrote: 'At this man's table I enjoyed many cheerful and instructive hours ... with David Garrick, whom I hoped to have gratified with this character of our common friend; but what are the hopes of man! I

am disappointed by that stroke of death, which has eclipsed the gaiety of nations, and impoverished the public stock of harmless pleasure.'

When Charles Dickens died in 1870, Thomas Carlyle wrote: 'It is an event world-wide, a *unique* of talents suddenly extinct, and has 'eclipsed' (we too may say) "the gaiety of nations".'

Galatea. See GREEK NAMES.

Galloping Gourmet. The professional sobriquet of Graham Kerr, a jokey, British-born cookery demonstrator whose TV programmes were made in Canada but seen in many countries during the late 1960s and early 70s. He was billed as such because he did everything very quickly (and was also very popular with the ladies).

Galore. See PUSSY ~.

gamekeeper.
See LADY CHATTERLEY.

game's afoot. Sherlock Holmes, in the stories by Sir Arthur Conan Doyle, had a way of saying: 'Come, Watson, come! The game is afoot' – as in 'The Adventure of the Abbey Grange' (1904). The allusion is to Shakespeare's *King Henry V* (III.i.32):

> I see you stand like greyhounds in the slips,

Straining upon the start . . . The game's
afoot:
Follow your spirit . . .

gammy. Meaning 'lame, crippled' – a form of 'game' which is an eighteenth-century dialect word of unknown origin. Brewer gives it as 'a dialect form of the Celtic *cam* meaning crooked', though *O E D2* disputes this. From 'Focus on Fact' in *Private Eye* (1981) we have: 'The Llewellyns are descended from medieval knight, Sir Dafydd Gam, who got an arrow in his eye at Agincourt . . . hence the expression "gammy" eye, leg etc.' 'Davy Gam, Esquire' is indeed mentioned in Shakespeare's *King Henry V* (IV.viii.106) as having fallen at Agincourt, and it appears that David ap Llewellyn of Brecon was so called because of a squint. So what one can say is, that though the origin of 'gammy' may be from the Celtic fringe, it was probably not derived from Dafydd Gam – merely applied to him.

gamp. A nickname for 'umbrella' which derives from the name of the character 'Sarah Gamp' in *Martin Chuzzlewit* (1843–4) by Charles Dickens. She always carried a large one.

gangbusters, to come on like. Meaning 'to perform in a striking manner', the expression comes from the US radio series *Gangbusters* which ran from *c* 1945–57 and used to begin with the sound of screeching tyres, machine guns, and police sirens, followed by the announcement: '*Gangbusters!* With the co-operation of leading law enforcement officials of the United States, *Gangbusters* presents facts in the relentless war of the police on the underworld, authentic case histories that show the never-ending activity of the police in their work of protecting our citizens.'

gang of four. Now meaning 'any group of four people working in concert', the original 'Gang of Four' was led by Jiang Qing, the unscrupulous wife of Chairman Mao Tse-tung, and so labelled in the mid-1970s when the four were tried and given the death sentence for treason and other crimes (later commuted to life imprisonment). The other three members were Zhang Chunqiao, a political organizer in the Cultural Revolution; Wang Hogwen, a youthful activist; and Yao Wenyuan, a journalist. Chairman Hua Kuo-feng attributed the phrase to his predecessor. Apparently on one occasion, Mao had warned his wife and her colleagues: 'Don't be a gang of four.' The nickname was later applied to the founders of the Social Democratic Party in Britain in 1981 – Roy Jenkins, David Owen, William Rodgers, and Shirley Williams.

Ganymede. See GREEK NAMES.

gap. See CREDIBILITY ~.

garden. See EVERYTHING IN THE ~.

Garnet. See ALL SIR ~.

Gaunt. See JOHN OF ~ 'S SPEECH.

gauntlet. See RUN THE ~.

gay. It was at the end of the 1960s that homosexuals most noticeably hi-jacked the word 'gay'. This was at a time when the US Gay Liberation Front came OUT OF THE CLOSET and used such slogans as 'Say it loud, we're gay and we're proud' and '2-4-6-8, gay is just as good as straight.'

However the word 'gay' had been used in this sense since at least the 1930s and on both sides of the Atlantic. In the last century, 'gay' was used to describe female prostitutes and there is an even earlier use of the word applied to female licentiousness. It may (like CAMP) have gravitated towards its homosexual use from there. Although one regrets the loss of the word to mean 'joyful, light-hearted', perhaps this use goes some way towards making up for the pejorative use of 'bent', 'queer' and 'poof' to describe homosexuals. **Poof** (also **pouf, poove, poofdah** and the Australian **poofter**) dates back at least to the 1850s, and **puff** (pointing to the likely origin) was apparently tramps' slang for homosexual by 1870. *Private Eye* certainly popularized 'poof' in the 1960s but clearly did not invent it, as has been claimed.

Gay Nineties. See NAUGHTY NINE-TIES.

gazump, to. Meaning 'to accept a bid higher than that agreed with an earlier purchaser during house selling', this specific meaning became popular in England and Wales during the early 1970s. The process can only occur in those countries where vendors are allowed to break a verbal agreement to sell if they receive a later, better offer. In Scotland where the 'sealed bid' system operates, gazumping is not possible.

But why the word 'gazump' – alternatively 'gazoomph', 'gasumph', 'gazumph', 'gezumph'? *O E D 2* has citations from English sources from 1928 onwards suggesting that the word has always had something to do with swindling. It occurs to one that it might come from 'goes up!' – meaning the price – along the lines of the term 'gazunder' for 'chamberpot' (because it 'goes under' the bed). Another suggestion is that it is a Yiddish word, *gezumph*.

G C M G. See INITIALS.

general. See CAVIARE TO THE ~.

generation. See LOST ~.

Genghis Khan. See SOMEWHERE TO THE RIGHT OF ~.

gentleman. Whenever the word 'gentleman' is defined, it is often crushingly prescriptive: 'No gentleman goes on a bus' said Henry Cecil Wyld, Merton Professor of English Language and Literature at Oxford (1920–45); 'Gentlemen do not take soup at luncheon' the Bursar of Balliol College, Oxford, was told when he presented Lord Curzon, Chancellor of the University, with a specimen menu for a visit by Queen Mary (1921); 'Gentlemen never wear brown in London' observed Lord Curzon (again) to a fellow member of Cabinet about a colleague's dress; 'No gentleman ever weighs over two hundred pounds' said Thomas B. Reed to David B. Henderson in the (US) House lobby (*c* 1895); 'No gentleman ever has any money', 'No gentleman ever takes exercise', 'A gentleman never looks out of the window' – all said by Oscar Wilde; 'It is almost a definition of a gentleman to say that he is one who never inflicts pain' wrote Cardinal Newman in *The Idea of a University* (1852).

However, 'A gentleman is one who gives up his seat to a lady in a public convenience' is probably just a music-hall joke and appears in *They Died With Their Boots Clean* by Gerald Kersh (1941) where it is part of a homily given by a platoon sergeant to young soldiers before they walk out from barracks on public duties for the first time. (See also LITTLE ~ IN BLACK VELVET; WHAT IS THAT ~ FOR?)

gentleman and a scholar, a. Paul Beale notes in Partridge/*Catch Phrases* that he was familiar with this form of compliment (*c* 1960) with the use of the phrase: 'Sir, you are a Christian, a scholar, and a gentleman' in the British army. It was 'often used as jocular, fulsome, though quite genuine, thanks for services rendered'. Partridge, earlier, had been tracking down a longer version – 'A gentleman, a scholar, and a fine judge of whiskey' – but had only been able to find the 'gentleman and scholar' in Robert Burns (1786):

> His locked, lettered, braw brass collar
> Shew'd him the gentleman an' the scholar.

It looks, however, as though the conjunction goes back even further. *O E D 2* has a citation from 1621: 'As becommed a Gentleman and a Scholer'. The phrase was probably born out of a very real respect for anyone who could claim to have both these highest of attributes. Equally as old is the combination 'a gentleman and a soldier'.

gentleman's agreement. Meaning 'an agreement not enforceable at law and only binding as a matter of honour', this is of U S origin and not known before the 1920s. A.J.P. Taylor in *English History 1914–1945* (1965) says: 'This absurd phrase was taken by [von] Papen from business usage to describe the agreement between Austria and Germany in July 1936. It was much used hereafter for an agreement with anyone who was obviously not a gentleman and who would obviously not keep his agreement.'

gentlemen – be seated! A stock phrase from the days of black minstrels in the U S (1840–1900). 'Mr Interlocutor', the white compère, would say this to the minstrels.

Gentlemen in England. The title of a novel (1985) by A.N. Wilson, it comes from Shakespeare's *King Henry V* (IV.iii.64):

> And gentlemen in England now a-bed
> Shall think themselves accurs'd they were
> not here.

['Here', i.e. at the Battle of Agincourt.]

Gentlemen Prefer Blondes. The title of a novel (1925) by Anita Loos (to which the sequel was *But Gentlemen Marry Brunettes*, 1928). Loos is presumed to have originated the phrase, though a lesser-known Irving Berlin song with this title was being performed in 1926, and in the same year there was another song with the title by B.G. De Sylva and Lewis Gensler.

George, St. See SAINTS' NAMES.

Geronimo! It was during the North African campaign of November 1942 that U S paratroopers are said first to have shouted 'Geronimo!' as they jumped out of planes. It then became customary to do so and turned into a popular exclamation akin to 'Eureka!' A number of American Indians in the paratroop units coined and popularized the expression, recalling the actual Apache Geronimo who died in 1909. It is said that when he was being pursued by the army over some steep hills near Fort Sill, Oklahoma, he made a leap on horseback over a sheer cliff into water. As the troops did not dare follow him, he cried 'Geronimo!' as he leapt. Some of the paratroopers who were trained at Fort Bragg and Fort Campbell adopted this shout, not least because it reminded them to breathe deeply during a jump. In 1939, there had been a film entitled *Geronimo*, which may have reminded them. From Christy Brown, *Down All the Days* (Chap.6, 1970) we have: 'He heard his brothers cry out in unison: "The dirty lousy bastards – hitting a cripple! Geronimo! . . ." And off they flew in maddened pursuit of the ungentlemanly enemy.'

Gesundheit! An exclamation made when someone sneezes, this is German for 'health', but it also has the rhythm of 'God bless you' and of a musical finish (as to a music-hall joke). Sneezing was believed to be the expulsion of an evil spirit, hence the need for such an exclamation. The Romans cried *absit omen!* [flee, omen!]

getaway people, the. Denoting glamorous, dashing folk, akin to the BEAUTIFUL PEOPLE, they were so dubbed in an advertising campaign for National Benzole petrol in the UK, from 1963. Bryan Oakes of the London Press Exchange agency told the authors of *The Persuasion Industry* (1965): 'They were the jet set, clean-limbed beautiful girls, the gods and goddesses who did exotic things. We used expensive cars – E-type Jaguars and Aston Martins – and the promise was that, if you get this petrol, you're aligning yourself with those wonderful people, midnight drives on the beach and so on.'

get away with something scot-free, to. 'If we could do that, she might go scot-free for aught I cared' wrote Charles Dickens in *The Old Curiosity Shop* (1840–1). Not 'scot', as in Scotland, but *sceot*, a medieval municipal tax paid to the local bailiff or sheriff, so it means, in a sense, 'tax-free; without penalty'.

get thee behind me Satan! Nowadays, an exclamation used in answer to the mildest call to temptation. It came originally from St Matthew 16:23, where Jesus Christ rebukes Peter with the phrase for something he has said.

ghost walks, the. Meaning 'it's pay day' (for actors), the expression is said to date from a touring company's production of *Hamlet*. The cast had been unpaid for many weeks and when Hamlet said of his father's ghost: 'Perchance 'twill walk again', the ghost replied: 'Nay, 'twill walk no more until its

salary is paid.' Consequently, a theatrical manager who hands out the pay has sometimes been called a 'ghost'.

G I. See INITIALS.

gibberish. Dr Johnson thought this word for nonsense derived from an Arabian alchemist called *Geber* in the eleventh century who had, in turn, translated into Latin the writings of an eighth-century alchemist called *Jabir* ibn Hayyan. He wrote in a mystical jargon because, if his writings had been discovered, he might have been put to death. The most obvious derivation is from 'gibber' which, like 'jabber', means to speak fast and inarticulately (compare 'gabber' and 'gab'). But the word appears to have an earlier source than this, which might just confirm Dr Johnson's theory. Partridge, meanwhile, thought it had developed from 'Egyptian', like 'gypsy'.

gift horse. See LOOK A ~ IN THE MOUTH.

gifts. See GREEKS BEARING ~.

gild the lily, to. Meaning 'to attempt to improve something that is already attractive and risk spoiling it', the allusion is to Shakespeare's *King John* (IV.ii.11) where, in fact, it is: 'to gild refined gold, to paint the lily'. Arden notes that 'to gild gold' was a common expression by Shakespeare's time.

Giles, St. See SAINTS' NAMES.

'Gioconda Smile, The'. The title of an Aldous HUXLEY short story, it was included in MORTAL COILS (1922) and dramatized in 1948. It refers to Leonardo da Vinci's portrait of a young woman, known as 'Mona Lisa' (c 1503), now in the Louvre, Paris, which has a curious, enigmatic, unsmiling smile, almost a smirk. '*La Gioconda*' and '*La*

Joconde', the titles by which the painting is also known may either be translated as 'the jocund lady', as might be expected, or refer to the sitter's actual surname – she may have been the wife of Francesco del Giocondo (whose name does, however, derive from 'jocund').

The smile was already being mentioned by 1550 in Giorgio Vasari's life of the painter. Vasari probably made up the story that Leonardo employed 'singers and musicians or jesters' to keep the sitter 'full of merriment'. Any number of nineteenth-century writers were fascinated by the smile, some seeing it as disturbing and almost evil. In the twentieth century Laurence Durrell commented: 'She has the smile of a woman who has just dined off her husband', and Cole Porter included 'You're the smile/On the Mona Lisa' in his hit song 'You're the Top!' (1934). Ponchielli's opera *La Gioconda* (1876) – after Victor Hugo's – and D'Annunzio's play (1898) are not connected with da Vinci's portrait (except that they feature jocund girls).

Gipper. See WIN THIS ONE FOR THE ~.

girl. See PAGE THREE ~.

Girl in Every Port, A. This was the title of a film (US, 1928) with Louise Brooks. The more venerable version of the benefit supposedly enjoyed by sailors is a **wife in every port**, which occurs for example in the caption to a *Punch* cartoon (22 May 1907) and as far back as Isaac Bickerstaffe's play *Thomas and Sally* (1761).

give a dog a bad name. Meaning 'say bad things about a person and they'll stick', this possibly comes from the longer 'Give a dog a bad name and hang him', suggesting that if a dog has a reputation for ferocity, it might as well be killed because no one will trust it.

give order! The injunction 'Give order – thank you, please!' became nationally-known when Colin Crompton used it to members of Granada TV's *Wheeltappers and Shunters Social Club*, on ITV 1974–7. 'I had been including the club chairman character in my variety act for some years,' Crompton said in 1979, 'before Johnny Hamp of Granada suggested that we build a sketch round it for inclusion in the stage version of *The Comedians*. This led to *Wheeltappers*. Like most successful catch phrases it was manufactured. It has been used by club concert chairmen for years – and still is.' Crompton also used the version **best of order!** In Christy Brown's novel *Down All the Days* (Chap.15, 1970) we have the cry (at a social gathering): 'Best of order now for the singer!'

give us a child until it is seven and it is ours for life. This saying has been attributed to the Jesuits, founded in 1534 by St Ignatius Loyola, but was possibly wished on to them by their opponents. Another version is: 'Give us the child, and we will give you the man.' Compare what Lenin may have said to the Commissars of Education in Moscow (1923): 'Give us the child for eight years and it will be a Bolshevik for ever.' Muriel Spark in her novel *The Prime of Miss Jean Brodie* (1962) has her heroine, a teacher, say: 'Give me a girl at an impressionable age and she is mine for life.'

Glimmer Twins, the. A nickname for two members of the Rolling Stones pop group. From the *Independent* (26 March 1990): 'There were times when Dr Runcie [Archbishop of Canterbury] and Dr John Habgood, the Archbishop of York, seemed "the glimmer twins" of the Church of England, as the Rolling Stones' foremost members liked to refer to themselves: Runcie up front like Mick

GLADSTONE (W.E.). William Ewart Gladstone (1809–98) was four times British Liberal Prime Minister and dominated the political scene during the second half of the nineteenth century. However, he is often remembered for peripheral things, like the **Gladstone bag**, the type of cheap wine and four-wheeled carriage that are named after him, his penchant for wandering off at night in order to reclaim prostitutes, and his hobby of chopping down harmless trees. Of the latter activity, Lord Randolph Churchill commented: 'The forest laments in order that Mr Gladstone may perspire.' Most famously, he was held up as an example to countless generations of children as the man who **chewed each mouthful of food thirty-two times before swallowing.** In the BBC TV programme *As I Remember* (30 April 1967), Baroness Asquith (Lady Violet Bonham-Carter) recalled having had a meal with Gladstone when she was a little girl, at which he did no such thing. Quite the reverse in fact: he bolted his food. See also GRAND OLD MAN.

Jagger, all lips and charm, while Habgood lurked in the dark, like Keith Richard, ready to kick intruders off the stage'.

glisters. See GLITTERS.

Glittering Prizes, The. The title of the novel and BBC TV drama series (1976) by Frederic Raphael, about a group of Cambridge graduates, came from the Rectorial Address at Glasgow University by F.E. Smith, 1st Earl of Birkenhead (7 November 1923): 'The world continues to offer glittering prizes to those who have stout hearts and sharp swords.'

glitters/glisters is not gold, all that. Meaning 'appearances may be deceptive', the allusion is to Shakespeare's *The Merchant of Venice* (II.vii.65):

All that *glisters* is not gold,
Often have you heard that told.

As indicated, the proverb was common by Shakespeare's time. *CODP* quotes a Latin version – '*Non omne quod nitet aurum est*' [Not all that shines is gold] and also an English one in Chaucer. The now obsolete word 'glisters' rather than 'glitters' or 'glistens' was commonly used in the saying from the seventeenth century onwards, though in poetic use, Thomas Gray, for example, used 'glisters' in his 'Ode on the Death of a Favourite Cat Drowned in a Tub of Gold Fishe' (1748).

Global Village, David Frost's. This was the title of an occasional Yorkshire TV series (from 1979) in which Frost discussed global issues with pundits beamed in by satellite. It comes from Marshall McLuhan's dictum that: 'The new electronic interdependence recreates the world in the image of a global village' (*The Gutenberg Galaxy*, 1962).

gloria (in excelsis Deo). See MASS PHRASES.

Glorious Revolution. When King James II was removed from the English throne in 1688 and replaced by William and Mary of Orange, the process came to be variously described as the 'bloodless' and 'glorious' revolution. But by whom first and when? By 1749, Henry Fielding was writing in *Tom Jones* (Bk. 8, Chap. 14): 'I remained concealed, til the news of the Glorious Revolution put an end to all my apprehensions of danger.' Before that, *OED2* finds only other epithets: 'great revolution' in 1689 and 'prodigious revolution' in 1688 itself. 'That glorious Revolution' was, however, applied in 1725 to the overthrow of the Rump Parliament in 1660. By *c* 1690 a club was founded in Northampton to celebrate the William and Mary 'glorious revolution' and by 1692 'Glorious' had acquired a capital G. If this is true, it would confirm that the phrase arose very early on – but not in a form which can be attributed to any particular person or source.

Glorious Twelfth, the (*or the* Twelfth). This name for 12 August, when grouse-shooting legally begins in Britain, was current by 1895, and was possibly devised in emulation of 'The Glorious First of June', a sea-battle in the French revolutionary war (and known as such since 1794). Compare the Twelfth (of July), celebrated by Protestants in Northern Ireland to commemorate the Battle of the Boyne (1 July 1690, Old Style) at which William III defeated James II.

Gnomes of Zurich. A term which was used to disparage the tight-fisted methods of speculators in the Swiss financial capital who questioned Britain's creditworthiness and who forced austerity measures on the Labour government of Prime Minister Harold Wilson when it came to power in 1964. George Brown, Secretary of State for Economic Affairs, popularized the term in November of that year. Wilson himself had, however, used it long before in a speech to the House of Commons (12 November 1956), referring to 'all the little gnomes in Zurich and other financial centres'. In 1958, Andrew Shonfield wrote in *British Economic Policy Since the War*: 'Hence the tragedy of the autumn of 1957, when the Chancellor of the Exchequer [Peter Thorneycroft] adopted as his guide to action the slogan: I must be hard-faced enough to match the mirror-image of an imaginary hard-faced little man in Zurich. It is tough on the Swiss that William Tell

should be displaced in English folklore by this new image of a gnome in a bank at the end of a telephone line.' ('Lord Gnome', the wealthy and unscrupulous supposed proprietor of *Private Eye* was presumably named after the 1964 use.)

go. See LET MY PEOPLE ~; LET US ~ FORWARD.

go ahead, make my day. In March 1985, President Ronald Reagan told the American Business Conference: 'I have my veto pen drawn and ready for any tax increase that Congress might even think of sending up. And I have only one thing to say to the tax increasers. Go ahead – make my day.' This laconicism was originally spoken by Clint Eastwood, himself brandishing a .44 Magnum, to a gunman he was holding at bay in *Sudden Impact* (1983). At the end of the film he said (to another villain, similarly armed): 'Come on, make my day.' In neither case does he add 'punk', as is sometimes supposed. The phrase may have been eased into Reagan's speech by having appeared in a parody of the New York *Post* put together by editors, many of them anti-Reagan, in the autumn of 1984. Reagan was shown starting a nuclear war by throwing down this dare to the Kremlin.

goal. See OWN ~.

God. See TOUCH THE FACE OF ~.

Goddess. See GREEN ~.

God is an Englishman. The title of this novel (1970) by R.F. Delderfield may derive from an untraced saying of George Bernard Shaw (*d* 1950): 'The ordinary Britisher imagines that God is an Englishman.' Harold Nicolson recorded on 3 June 1942 that three years before, R.S. Hudson, the Minister of Agriculture, was being told by the Yugoslav minister in London of the dangers facing Britain. 'Yes,' replied Hudson, 'you are probably correct and these things may well happen. But you forget that God is English.'

Godiva, Lady. See PEEPING TOM.

godliness. See CLEANLINESS IS NEXT TO ~.

God moves in a mysterious way. A direct quotation from No. 35 of the *Olney Hymns* (1779) by William Cowper, the hymn continues: '. . . His wonders to perform'.

God Protect Me from My Friends. This was the title of a book (1956) by Gavin Maxwell about Salvatore Giuliano, the Sicilian bandit. The full expression is: 'I can look after my enemies, but God protect me from my friends'. CODP traces it to 1477 in the forms 'God keep/save/defend us from our friends' and says it is now often used in the abbreviated form, 'Save us from our friends.' It appears to be common to many languages. The diarist Chips Channon (21 February 1938) has: 'This evening a group of excited Communists even invaded the Lobby, demanding Anthony [Eden]'s reinstatement. God preserve us from our friends, they did him harm.' Morris seems to confuse this saying with the similar WITH FRIENDS LIKE THESE . . ., but finds a quotation from Maréchal Villars who, on leaving Louis XIV, said: 'Defend me from my friends; I can defend myself from my enemies.'

God's Apology. The title of a book (1977) by Richard Ingrams – 'A Chronicle of Three Friends' (Malcolm Muggeridge, Hesketh Pearson and Hugh Kingsmill), derived from Kingsmill's remark that: 'Friends are God's apology for relations.'

God's own country. Referring to one's own country, if one is fond of it, there can be few countries which have not elected to call themselves this.

Of the United States: OED2 provides an example from 1865, and tags the phrase as being of US origin. Flexner says that in the Civil War the shorter 'God's country' was the Union troops' term for the North, 'especially when battling heat, humidity, and mosquitoes in the South. Not until the 1880s did the term mean any section of the country one loved or the open spaces of the West.' A 1937 US film had the title *God's Country and the Woman*.

Of Australia: Dr Richard Arthur, a State politician and President of the Immigration League of Australasia, was quoted in *Australia Today* (1 November 1911) as saying: 'This Australia is "God's Own Country" for the brave.' The *Dictionary of Australian Quotations* (1984) notes that at the time 'Australia was frequently referred to as "God's Own Country", the phrase drawing satirical comments from the foreign unenlightened.'

Of South Africa/Ireland: one has heard both these countries so dubbed informally (in the 1970s), with varying degrees of appropriateness and irony.

Also Yorkshiremen describe their homeland as 'God's own *county*'. 'Yorkshire's natural reluctance to play second fiddle to London has faced some difficulty in the matter of house prices . . . God's own county is at the centre of things yet again' (*Guardian*, 23 January 1989).

God Stand up for Bastards. The title of a book (1973) by David Leitch, which was a study of the author's upbringing and the circumstances of his birth. The title comes from Shakespeare's *King Lear* (I.ii.22) where the Bastard Edmund says of himself:

Edmund the base

Shall top the legitimate: – I grow, I
    prosper;
Now, gods stand up for bastards.

go for gold. As an encouragement to
aim for a gold medal, this was first used
by the US Olympic team at the Lake
Placid Winter Olympics in 1980. (*Going
for Gold* became the title of an Emma
Lathen thriller, 1983, set therein, and of
a TV movie, 1985.) Other teams, including the British, had taken it up by
the time of the 1984 Olympics. A BBC
TV quiz called *Going for Gold* began in
1987. Just to show, as always, that there
is nothing new under the sun: in 1832,
there was a political slogan 'To Stop the
Duke, Go for Gold' which was somehow
intended, through its alliterative force, to
prevent the Duke of Wellington from
forming a government in the run up to
the Reform Bill. The slogan was coined
by a radical politician, Francis Place, for
a poster (12 May 1832), and seems to
have been intended to cause a run on
gold at the Bank of England.

go for it! This may be said as an encouragement to meet any target, especially in
business. In June 1985, President
Reagan's call on tax reform was: 'America, go for it!' Victor Kiam, an American
razor entrepreneur, entitled his 1986
memoirs *Going for it!* and 'Go for it,
America' was the slogan used by British
Airways in the same year to get more US
tourists to ignore the terrorist threat and
travel to Europe. Earlier, Lisa Bernbach
in *The Official Preppie Handbook*
(1980) had pointed to a possible US
campus origin, giving the phrase as a
general exhortation to act crazily. At
about the same time, the phrase was
used in aerobics. Jane Fonda in a work-
out book (1981) and video (*c* 1983),
cried: 'Go for it, go for the burn!' (where
the burn was a painful sensation felt during exercise). There was also a US slogan
(current 1981) for beer: 'Go for it!

Schlitz makes it great.' Partridge/*Slang*
has 'to go for it' as Australian for being
'extremely eager for sexual intercourse'
(*c* 1925).

go forth to war, to. The 1989 BBC
TV comedy series *Black Adder Goes
Forth* was set during the First World
War. The phrase this title embodied was
as used by Bishop Heber in his hymn
(1812) beginning: 'The Son of God goes
forth to war/A kingly crown to gain.'
    Earlier, it was known from the Bible,
occurring in Numbers 1:3 and 2
Chronicles 25:5.

gold. See CROSS OF ~; GO FOR ~;
STREETS PAVED WITH ~; THERE'S ~
IN THEM THAR HILLS.

golden age. The original golden age
was that in which, according to Greek
and Roman poets, men lived in an ideal
state of happiness. It was also applied to
the period of Latin literature from
Cicero to Ovid (which was followed by
the lesser, silver age.) Now the phrase is
widely used in such clichés as 'the
Golden Age of Hollywood' to describe
periods when a country or a creative
field is considered to have been at the
height of its excellence or prosperity.

Golden Ass. See ROMAN NAMES.

golden boy. Meaning 'young person
with talent', it derives chiefly from its use
as the title of a play, *Golden Boy* (1937;
film US, 1939) by Clifford Odets, in
which the violinist hero becomes a successful boxer instead. It was also the title
of a cinema short (*c* 1962) about the
singer, Paul Anka, possibly remembering
the term golden/gilded youth and
Shakespeare's *Cymbeline* (IV.ii.262):

Golden lads and girls all must,
As chimney-sweepers, come to dust.

GOLDWYNISMS. Even as a successful Hollywood producer, Samuel Goldwyn (1882–1974) never quite managed to come to grips with the English language (he was born in Poland). Countless 'Goldwynisms' – apocryphal or not – attest to this. 'If this is the way you do it, gentlemen, include me out!' is genuine (as Goldwyn himself acknowledged when speaking at Balliol College, Oxford, in 1945). 'The trouble with this business is the dearth of bad pictures' and 'They're always biting the hand that lays the golden egg' both have supporters. A too-clever line like 'Anyone who goes to a psychiatrist needs his head examined' is bogus. Hollywood writers vied to manufacture Goldwynisms and pass them off as genuine. George Oppenheimer won a competition to see who could be first to get one of these counterfeits in print with: 'It rolls off my back like a duck.' Samuel Goldwyn Jr has claimed that there are 'twenty-eight' genuine sayings attributed to his father.

go, man, go! This phrase of encouragement was originally shouted at jazz musicians in the 1940s before it took on wider use. At the beginning of the number 'It's Too Darn Hot' in Cole Porter's *Kiss Me Kate* (film version US, 1953) a dancer cried: 'Go, girl, go!' TV newscaster Walter Cronkite reverted famously to 'Go, baby, go!' when describing the launch of Apollo XI in 1969 and this form became a fairly standard cry at rocket and missile departures thereafter. *Time* magazine reported it being shouted at a test firing of a Pershing missile (29 November 1982). **Crazy, man, crazy!** originated at about the same time as 'Go, man, go!' but was, perhaps, better suited to rock'n'roll usage than to the earlier bop.

gone but not forgotten. A sentiment displayed on tombstones, memorial notices and such, and used as the title of a Victorian print showing children at a grave or similar. In the 1950s/60s, there was a Parlophone LP of the BBC Radio *Goon Show* entitled, *Goon . . . But Not Forgotten.*

gone for a burton. Early in the Second World War, an RAF expression arose to describe what had happened to a missing person, presumed dead. He had 'gone for a Burton', meaning that he had gone for a drink (*in* the drink, i.e. the sea) or, as another phrase put it, 'he'd bought it'. Folk memory has it that 'gone for a Burton' had been used in advertisements to promote a Bass beer known in the trade as 'a Burton' (though, in fact, several ales are produced at Burton-on-Trent). More positive proof is lacking. An advert for Carlsberg in Egon Ronay's *Good Food in Pubs and Bars* (1987) described Burton thus: 'A strong ale, dark in colour, made with a proportion of highly dried or roasted malts. It is not necessarily brewed in Burton and a variety of strong or old ales were given the term.'

gone to the big/great — in the sky. This format phrase is used to denote that someone has died. Thus, an actor might go to 'the great Green Room in the sky', a surgeon to 'the great operating theatre in the sky', a boozer to 'the great saloon bar in the sky' etc. From *Joe Bob Goes to the Drive-in* (1987): 'Ever since Bruce Lee went to the big Tai Kwon Do Academy in the sky . . .' Compare HAPPY HUNTING GROUND.

Gone With the Wind. The title of Margaret Mitchell's novel (1936; film US, 1939) comes from Ernest Dowson's poem '*NON SUM QUALIS ERAM*'

(1896): 'I have forgot much, Cynara! Gone with the wind . . .' It refers to the southern United States before the American Civil War, as is made clear by the on-screen prologue to the film: 'There was a land of Cavaliers and Cotton Fields called the Old South. Here in this patrician world the Age of Chivalry took its last bows. Here was the last ever seen of the Knights and their Ladies fair, of Master and Slave. Look for it only in books, for it is no more than a dream remembered, a Civilization gone with the wind . . .'

go now pay later. Daniel Boorstin in *The Image* (1962) makes oblique reference to travel advertisements using the line: 'Go now, pay later'. Was hire purchase ever promoted with 'Buy now, pay later'? It seems likely. These lines – in the US and UK – seem to be the starting point for a construction much used since. *Live Now Pay Later* was the title of Jack Trevor Story's 1962 screenplay based on the novel *All on the Never Never* by Jack Lindsay. As a simple graffito, the same line was recorded in Los Angeles (1970), according to *The Encyclopedia of Graffiti* (1974). The same book records a New York subway graffito on a funeral parlour ad: 'Our layaway plan – die now, pay later.' 'Book now, pay later' was used in an ad in the programme of the Royal Opera House, Covent Garden, in 1977.

gonzo. See FEAR AND LOATHING IN LAS VEGAS.

good. See ALL ~ THINGS MUST COME TO AN END; IF YOU CAN'T BE ~ BE CAREFUL; IT SEEMED LIKE A ~ IDEA.

good and the great, the. This refers to those who are on a British Government list from which are selected members of Royal Commissions and committees of inquiry. In 1983 the list

stood at some 4500 names. In the 1950s, the Treasury division which kept the list was actually known as the 'G and G'.

Goodbye Baby and Amen. The title of a book of photographs (1969) by David Bailey and Peter Evans, subtitled 'A Saraband for the Sixties'. It alludes to Cole Porter's song 'Just One of Those Things' (1935):

> So goodbye, dear, and amen.
> Here's hoping we meet now and then.

Goodbye To All That. The title of the memoirs (1929) of Robert Graves, perhaps its influence can be seen in later titles such as *1066 and All That* (1930) by Sellar and Yeatman.

'Goodbye Yellow Brick Road'. The title of a song (1973) by Elton John and Bernie Taupin. Compare 'Follow the Yellow Brick Road', the song by E.Y. Harburg and Harold Arlen in the film *The Wizard of Oz* (1939). Both titles refer to the road along which 'Dorothy' travels in the original story, THE WONDERFUL WIZARD OF OZ (1900) by L. Frank Baum.

Good — Guide, the. A format for book titles, which is obviously helped by the alliteration. The first in the field was *The Good Food Guide*, edited by Raymond Postgate (1951). Subsequently, there have been Good – Book, Cheese, Hotel, Museums, Pub, Reading, Sex, Skiing, Software, Word – Guides, and many others.

Good the Bad and the Ugly, The. The English title of the Italian 'spaghetti Western' (1966), *Il Buono, il Bruto, il Cattivo*. Colonel Oliver North giving evidence to the Washington hearings on the Irangate scandal in the summer of 1987, said: 'I came here to tell you the truth – the good, the bad, and the ugly'.

Gordon Bennett! Understandably, people shrink from blaspheming: 'Oh Gawd!' is felt to be less offensive than 'Oh God!' At the turn of the century it was natural for people facetiously to water down the exclamation 'God!' by saying 'Gordon!' The name Gordon Bennett was to hand. James Gordon Bennett II (1841–1918) was the colourful editor-in-chief of the *New York Herald* who lived in Europe. The expletive had a revival in the 1980s.

Gorki Street. See FOGGY BOTTOM.

Gotham. (1) A village in Nottinghamshire noted for the (sometimes calculated) folly of its inhabitants. Their reputation was established by the fifteenth century, as in the nursery rhyme:

> Three wise Men of Gotham
> Went to sea in a bowl,
> If the bowl had been stronger,
> My story would have been longer.

(2) New York City, so named by Washington Irving in *Salmagundi* (1807), but with no particular reference to (1). Later 'Gotham City' was the city featured in the Batman cartoon strip.

gotta. See MAN'S ~ DO . . .

gourmet. See GALLOPING ~.

Go West Young Man. The title of a film (1936), which was a vehicle for *Mae West* rather than anything to do with *the* West. *Go West Young Lady* followed in 1940. There have been two films called simply *Go West*, notably the 1940 one, often called *The Marx Brothers Go West*.

To 'go west', meaning 'to die' is a completely separate coinage. It dates back to the sixteenth century and alludes to the setting of the sun.

The saying 'Go west, young man, and grow up with the country', was originated by John Babsone Lane Soule in the

Terre Haute, Indiana, *Express* (1851) when, indeed, the thing to do in the US was to head westwards, where gold and much else lay promised. However, Horace Greeley repeated it in *his* New York newspaper, the *Tribune*, and being rather more famous as he was also a candidate for the presidency, it stuck with him. Greeley reprinted Soule's article to show where he had taken it from, but to no avail.

Graces, The Three. See GREEK NAMES.

grace under pressure. The Latin tag '*Suaviter in modo, fortiter in re*' [Gentle in manner, resolute in action] was reduced to the definition of 'guts' as 'grace under pressure' by Ernest Hemingway in a *New Yorker* article (30 November 1929). It was later invoked by John F. Kennedy in *Profiles in Courage* (1956).

Grande Illusion, La. The title of this film (France, 1937) was taken from *The Great Illusion*, the title of Norman Angell's anti-war book (1910) which had, however, first been published in 1909 as *Europe's Optical Illusion*.

grandmother. See DON'T TEACH YOUR ~ . . .; I WOULD WALK OVER MY ~.

Grand Old Man (or G O M). The nickname of W.E. GLADSTONE was said to have been coined by either Sir William Harcourt or Lord Rosebery or the Earl of Iddesleigh – who said in an 1882 speech (when Gladstone was 73): 'Argue as you please, you are nowhere; that grand old man, the Prime Minister, insists on the other thing.'

Grapes of Wrath, The. The title of the novel (1939; film US, 1940) by John Steinbeck comes from Julia Ward

Howe's 'The Battle Hymn of the Republic' (1862):

> Mine eyes have seen the glory of the
>   coming of the Lord:
> He is trampling out the vintage where
>   the grapes of wrath are stored.

grass widow. This expression is used of a divorced woman or one apart from her husband because his job or some other preoccupation has taken him elsewhere. It originally meant an unmarried woman who had sexual relations with one or more men – perhaps on the grass rather than in the lawful marriage bed – and had had a child out of wedlock. Later it seems to have been applied to women in British India who were sent up to the cool hill country (where grass grows) during the hottest season of the year.

gratias agimus tibi. See MASS PHRASES.

gratis. See FREE ~ AND FOR NOTHING.

grave. See ONE FOOT IN THE ~; TURN OVER IN ONE'S ~.

graveyard. See ELEPHANTS' ~.

Gray, Dorian. See DORIAN ~.

greasy pole, the. Referring to politics, this term comes from the remark made by Benjamin Disraeli to friends when he first became British Prime Minister in 1868: 'Yes, I have climbed to the top of the greasy pole'. The allusion is to the competitive sport, once popular at fairs and games, of climbing up or along a greasy pole without slipping off.

great. See THE GOOD AND THE ~.

Great Balls of Fire. The title of a biographical film (US, 1989) of Jerry Lee Lewis – who popularized the hit song with this title (written by Jack Hammer and Otis Blackwell) in 1957. The exclamation occurs several times in the script of the film Gone With the Wind (1939), confirming its distinctly southern US origins. While OED2 and other dictionaries content themselves with the slang meaning of the phrase 'ball of fire' (glass of brandy/a person of great liveliness of spirit), even Partridge/Slang and American dictionaries avoid recording this phrase.

Great Cham (of Literature), The. The nickname applied to Dr Samuel Johnson by Tobias Smollett in a letter to John Wilkes in 1759. 'Cham' is a form of 'khan' (as in Genghis Khan) meaning 'monarch' or 'prince'.

Great Debate. Politicians like to apply this dignifying label to any period of discussion over policy. 'The Conservative leaders now decided to bring a vote of no confidence against the Government [on its Defence Programme], and on February 15 [1951] the "Great Debate" as it was known in Tory circles was opened, by Churchill himself' (Martin Gilbert, Never Despair, 1988). In a speech at Ruskin College, Oxford, in October 1976, James Callaghan, as Prime Minister, called for a 'national debate' on education policy which also became known as a 'Great Debate'.

greater love hath no man than this. A quotation from St John 15:13, which continues: 'that a man lay down his life for his friends'. In a memorable jibe at Harold Macmillan's NIGHT OF THE LONG KNIVES in 1962, Jeremy Thorpe told the House of Commons: 'Greater love hath no man than this, that he lay down his friends for his life.'

Greatest Living —. David Lloyd George used to annoy C.P. Scott, editor of the Manchester Guardian in the 1910s/20s by always referring to him at

143

public meetings as 'the world's greatest living journalist'. Nigel Dempster, the gossip columnist, who has contributed to *Private Eye* pseudonymously as part of the 'Grovel' column, promoted himself as 'the Greatest Living Englishman' or 'GLE'. The term 'Greatest Englishman of this Age' had been much used of Sir Winston Churchill about the time of his death in 1965 – also ironically of Cyril Connolly, the writer and critic.

greatest show on earth. This slogan was used by P.T. Barnum (*d* 1891) to promote the circus formed by the merger with his rival, Bailey's, in the US, from 1881. It is still the slogan of what is now Ringling Bros and Barnum & Bailey Circus. It was used as the title of a Cecil B. de Mille circus film in 1952.

greatest thing since sliced bread (*sometimes* **best/hottest**). A 1981 ad in the UK declared: 'Sainsbury's bring you the greatest thing since sliced bread. Unsliced bread' – neatly turning an old formula on its head. Quite when the idea that pre-sliced bread was one of the landmark inventions arose is not clear. Sliced bread had first appeared on the market by the 1920s – so a suitable period of time after that.

Great Helmsman. A dignified sobriquet for Chairman Mao Tse-tung during the Cultural Revolution in China of the 1960s, it was applied, jokingly, to Edward Heath, when British Prime Minister (1970–6) because of his enthusiasm for yachting.

Great Leap Forward. Chairman Mao Tse-tung's phrase for the enforced industrialization in China in 1958. It is now used ironically about any supposed move forward.

Great Morning. The title of this volume of memoirs (1947) by Osbert Sitwell is possibly a hunting phrase. It occurs

earlier in Shakespeare's *Troilus and Cressida* and *Cymbeline* (where it means 'broad daylight'). Compare the title *Bright Day*, a novel (1946) by J.B. Priestley.

great Scott! As with GORDON BENNETT!, one is dealing here with a watered-down expletive. 'Great Scott!' clearly sounds like 'Great God!' and yet is not blasphemous. Morris says the expression became popular when US General Winfield Scott was the hero of the Mexican War (1847) and 'probably our most admired general between Washington and Lee'. No rival candidate seems to have been proposed and the origination is almost certainly American. *OED2*'s earliest British English example dates from 1885.

Great Society. This was the name of President Lyndon Johnson's policy platform in the US. In a speech at the University of Michigan (May 1964) he said: 'In your time, we have the opportunity to move not only toward the rich society and the powerful society but upward to the Great Society.'

Great Train Robbery, The. This was the title of a silent film (US, 1903), sometimes considered to be the first 'real' movie. It was applied subsequently to the spectacular hold-up of a Glasgow-to-London train in Buckinghamshire (1963), when £2,500,000 was stolen from a mail van. Those who committed the robbery were consequently dubbed 'the Great Train Robbers'.

Great Unwashed, the. Meaning 'working-class people; the lower orders', this term was originally used by the politician and writer, Edmund Burke (*d* 1797), perhaps echoing Shakespeare's

GREEK NAMES (from myths, legends, literature and history). Many later became part of Roman mythology. Accordingly, some are listed under ROMAN NAMES.

Achilles: the foremost warrior in the Trojan war, who sulked in his tent, and was hero of the *Iliad*. He was vulnerable only at the heel.

Acis: loved GALATEA, was crushed by POLYPHEMUS and turned into a river.

Actaeon: saw ARTEMIS bathing and was turned into a stag, then killed by his own hounds.

Adonis: a beautiful youth, he was loved by APHRODITE and killed by a boar.

Aeolus: the god of winds.

Aeschylus: a dramatist, he was killed by an eagle dropping a tortoise on his bald head.

Aesculapius/Ascelpius: saved by his father APOLLO from the body of his slain mother; the god of healing and medicine.

Aether: the god of atmosphere.

Agamemnon: the leader of the Greeks at the siege of Troy, he sacrificed his daughter Iphigenia at Aulis.

Aglaos: a peasant said by the oracle to be happier than a king.

Aidos: conscience personified.

Ajax the Greater/the Lesser: an irascible/vain warrior in Trojan war.

Alcestis: died in place of her husband Admetus, and returned from the dead.

Alcmena: committed adultery when ZEUS impersonated her husband.

Alethia: truth personified.

Alpheus: the river god who loved ARETHUSA.

Amazons: female warriors.

Ambrosia: the food of the gods, which bestowed immortality.

Amphitrite: the wife of POSEIDON; goddess of the sea.

Amphitryon: the deceived husband of ALCMENA.

Anchises: see main entry.

Andromache: HECTOR's loyal wife.

Andromeda: was saved from sea monster by PERSEUS.

Antigone: killed herself rather than be buried alive.

Aphrodite: female beauty personified.

Apollo: male beauty personified; the god of music, poetry, and the sun.

Arachne: a weaver, she was turned into a spider.

Arcadia: an area of pastoral innocence. See also ARCADIA EGO, ET IN.

Ares: the god of war.

Arethusa: a nymph who was turned into fountain by ARTEMIS.

Argo: the ship of the Argonauts searching for the Golden Fleece.

Argos: ODYSSEUS's unforgetful dog.

Argus: the builder of the ARGO.

Ariadne: gave THESEUS thread to escape from the labyrinth.

Arion: (1) a poet rescued from drowning by a dolphin. (2) winged horse.

Artemis: the goddess of the moon and a virgin huntress. Compare CYNTHIA. See also DIANA under ROMAN NAMES.

Asclepius: See AESCULAPIUS.

Asterius: the Minotaur, born to PASIPHAE and a bull.

Astraea: the goddess of justice.

Atalanta: female endurance personified but she was defeated in a race by a suitor using three golden apples.

Ate: the goddess of wickedness.

Athena/Pallas Athena: the warrior goddess of philosophy. See MINERVA under ROMAN NAMES.

Atlas: the Titan who carried the heavens on his shoulders.

Augeas/Augias: a Peloponnesean king whose stables were cleaned out by HERCULES.

Autolycus: a stealer of sheep.

Bacchus: see DIONYSUS.

Bellerophon: he attempted to fly to heaven on PEGASUS.

Calliope: the muse of lyric poetry.

Callisto: a nymph turned into a bear.

Greek names – cont.

Cassandra: a prophetess, usually of doom.

Cassiop(e)ia: a beauty who became a constellation.

Castor: a twin (and faithful) brother of POLLUX.

Centaurs: half-horses, half-men.

Charon: the ferryman for the dead across the river STYX.

Charybdis: see SCYLLA.

Chloe: the shepherdess loved by DAPHNIS.

Chloris: the goddess of flowers.

Circe: an enchantress, she turned ODYSSEUS's men into swine.

Clio: the muse of history.

Cressida: the unfaithful lover of Troilus.

Croesus: a wealthy king.

Cronos: see KRONOS.

Cybele: the hermaphrodite goddess of fertility and mountains.

Cyclops: a one-eyed giant.

Cynthia: the goddess of the moon. Also called ARTEMIS.

Daedalus: an inventor and builder of the Minoan labyrinth.

Damia: the goddess of health.

Damocles: forced to sit under a sword, for sycophancy.

Damon: made a pact with PYTHIAS to save each other.

Danae: raped by Zeus disguised as a shower of gold.

Daphne: turned into a bay tree to protect her virginity.

Daphnis: an inventor of pastoral poetry; he loved CHLOE.

Delphi: seat of the oracle.

Demeter: the goddess of agriculture.

Deucalion: survived a flood in an ark.

Diomedes: (1) a hero of the Trojan war. (2) a king eaten by horses he had reared to eat human flesh.

Dionysus: the god of fertility and wine. Also called BACCHUS.

Draco: a harsh Athenian law-giver.

Echo: pined away for NARCISSUS till only her voice remained.

Electra: bore great love for AGAMEMNON, her father, and hated her mother, Clytemnestra.

Endymion: kept his youth through eternal sleep; he was loved by SELENE.

Eos: the goddess of dawn. See AURORA under ROMAN NAMES.

Erato: the muse of erotic and lyric poetry.

Erebus: darkness personified.

Erinyes: see EUMENIDES.

Eros: the god of love.

Eumenides: the merciless avengers of crimes.

Europa: seduced by ZEUS as a bull.

Eurydice: returned from the dead but was doomed when ORPHEUS disobeyed.

Euterpe: the muse of Dionysiac music.

Fates: three goddesses who measure out human life.

Gaea/Gaia: the goddess of the earth.

Galatea: (1) a sea nymph. (2) PYGMALION's statue allowed to have life.

Ganymede: a male beauty who was made cupbearer to ZEUS.

Graces: goddesses of charm and beauty (Aglaia, Euphrosyne, and Thalia).

Hebe: the cupbearer to the gods; the goddess of youth.

Hecate: the goddess of witchcraft and magic.

Hector: the bravest of the Trojan warriors.

Hecuba: the wife of PRIAM, mother of HECTOR; she was metamorphosed into a dog.

Helen: a beauty whose abduction by PARIS led to the Trojan war.

Helios: the god of the sun.

Hephaestus: the god of fire and metalworkers.

Hercules: the hero who accomplished twelve difficult tasks.

Hermaphroditus: half-man, half-woman.

Greek names – cont.

Hera: the goddess of childbirth and wife of ZEUS.

Hermes: the messenger of the gods.

Hero: drowned herself when lover LEANDER drowned.

Hesperides: three sisters guarding golden apples.

Himeros: the god of erotic desire.

Hippolyta: the queen of the AMAZONS.

Hydra: a nine-headed serpent destroyed by HERCULES.

Hygeia: the goddess of health.

Hymen(aeus): the god of marriage.

Hyperion: a beautiful Titan.

Icarus: his wings failed because the sun melted the wax on them.

Irene: the goddess of conciliation and peace.

Iris: the messenger of the gods and goddess of the rainbow.

Jason: leader of the Argonauts in pursuit of the Golden Fleece.

Kronos: a Titan who devoured some of his children at birth.

Lamia: a female serpent who swallowed children.

Laocoön: a Trojan priest strangled by sea serpents.

Leander: the lover of HERO; he drowned swimming the Hellespont.

Leda: raped by ZEUS in the form of a swan.

Lycaon: turned into a wolf as a punishment for serving human flesh.

Lysistrata: an Athenian who led women in withdrawal of conjugal rights as a protest.

Medea: a sorceress who married JASON.

Medusa: a hideous, snake-haired Gorgon.

Melpomene: the muse of dramatic tragedy.

Midas: a king whose touch turned everything to gold.

Minotaur: a Cretan monster, half-bull, half-man.

Momus: the god of blame and ridicule.

Muses: nine goddesses of the arts and sciences.

Narcissus: a beautiful youth who fell in love with his own reflection.

Nemesis: the goddess of vengeance.

Nereus: a kindly old sea god, the father of many sea nymphs.

Nestor: a wise old counsellor of the Greeks in the Trojan war.

Nike: the winged goddess of victory.

Odysseus: the hero of the ODYSSEY.

Oedipus: an unfortunate who killed his father and married his mother.

Orestes: killed his mother, CLYTEMNESTRA, to avenge his father, AGAMEMNON.

Orpheus: lost EURYDICE because he looked back as he led her out of Hades.

Pallas Athena: see ATHENA.

Pandora: allowed evils out of her vase (or box), Hope alone remaining in it.

Paris: a Trojan whose abduction of HELEN caused war with the Greeks.

Parthenope: a siren who threw herself in the sea for love of Odysseus.

Pasiphaë: had sex with a bull; the mother of ARIADNE and the MINOTAUR.

Patroclus: wore the armour of Achilles to encourage the Greeks against the Trojans and was slain.

Pegasus: the winged horse of BELLEROPHON.

Pelops: served as a meal to the gods.

Penelope: the faithful wife of itinerant ODYSSEUS.

Persephone: the goddess of fertility, queen of infernal regions.

Perseus: devoted to his wife Andromeda; obtained the head of MEDUSA.

Philoctetes: an archer in the Trojan war who had a foul-smelling wound.

Philomela: turned into a swallow.

Phoebe: (1) a Titan. (2) also called ARTEMIS, the moon, as the sister of PHOEBUS.

Greek names – cont.

Phoebus: the sun. Also called APOLLO.

Pluto(n): the god of the underworld.

Plutus: the god of wealth.

Pollux: twin brother of CASTOR.

Polyphemus: a CYCLOPS blinded by ODYSSEUS.

Poseidon: the god of the sea.

Priam: the king of Troy, father of HECTOR and PARIS, etc.

Priapus: a grotesque god of fertility, with a large phallus.

Procrustes: a robber who 'adapted' the limbs of victims to fit his bed.

Prometheus: a Titan who gave away fire to mortals.

Proteus: an old herdsman who was able to change shape.

Psyche: a maiden loved by CUPID.

Pygmalion: the sculptor who created GALATEA and sought to have her brought to life.

Pythias: made a pact with DAMON.

Rhadamanthus: the impartial judge in the underworld.

Scylla: in the Straits of Messina, rocks opposite the whirlpool of CHARYBDIS – thus, two equally dangerous alternatives.

Selene: the moon as the lover of sleeping shepherd ENDYMION.

Sisyphus: condemned to the everlasting task of rolling a stone up a hill.

Styx: the river to be crossed to reach Hades.

Tantalus: condemned to thirst for water in Hades.

Terpsichore: the muse of dancing.

Thanatos: the god of death; brother of sleep. See also MORS under ROMAN NAMES.

Theseus: the hero of Attica in many exploits.

Thetis: a sea goddess.

Tiresias: blinded by ATHENA when he saw her bathing.

Tithonus: a male beauty who sought immortality but aged and was turned into a grasshopper.

Triton: a sea god, a fish with a human head.

Ulysses: see ODYSSEUS.

Urania: the muse of astrology.

Uranus: heaven personified.

Zephyrus: the west wind.

Zeus: the supreme god. See JUPITER under ROMAN NAMES.

---

reference to 'another lean unwash'd artificer' (*King John*, IV.ii.201). Lytton in *Paul Clifford* (1830) uses the full phrase.

Great War. See FIRST WORLD WAR.

Great Wen. In *Rural Rides* (1830), William Cobbett asked of London: 'But what is to be the fate of the great wen of all? The monster, called . . . "the metropolis of empire"?' A 'wen' is a lump or protuberance on a body; a wart. Compare MONSTROUS CARBUNCLE.

Great White Way. The nickname for Broadway, the main theatre zone of New York City – alluding to the brightness of the illumination, and taken from the title of a novel (1901) by Albert Bigelow Paine. For a while, Broadway was also known as 'the Gay White Way', though for understandable reasons this is no longer so.

Greeks bearing gifts, beware. A warning against trickery, this is an allusion to the most famous Greek gift of all – the large wooden horse which was built as an offering to the gods before the Greeks were about to return home after besieging Troy unsuccessfully for ten years. It was taken within the city walls of Troy, but men leapt out from it, opened the gates and helped destroy the city. Virgil in the *Aeneid* (II.49) has Laocoön (see under GREEK NAMES) warn the Trojans not to admit the horse, saying '*Timeo Danaos et dona ferentes*' [I still fear the Greeks, even when they offer gifts].

Greeks had a word for it, the. An expression used, a trifle archly, when one wishes to express disapproval – as one might say: 'there's a name for that sort of behaviour'. From the title of a US play (1930) by Zoë Akins, although, as she said, the 'phrase is original and grew out of the dialogue', it does not appear anywhere in the text. The 'it' refers to a type of woman. One character thinks that 'tart' is meant, but the other corrects this and says 'free soul' is more to the point.

green-eyed monster, the. From Shakespeare's *Othello* (III.iii.170), where Iago says to Othello:

O, beware jealousy;
It is the green-ey'd monster, which doth mock
That meat it feeds on.

green fields. See BABBLED OF ~.

Green Goddess. An alliterative nickname which has been applied variously to Second World War fire engines (painted green), Liverpool trams, a *crème de menthe* cocktail, a lettuce salad, and a lily. In 1983, Diana Moran, a keep-fit demonstrator on the BBC TV breakfast programme, was so billed. She wore distinctive green exercise clothing. Perhaps all these uses derive from William Archer's play entitled *The Green Goddess* (1923, film US, 1930).

Green Grow the Rushes. The title of a film (UK, 1950), it comes from one of the most-quoted folksongs – also one of the most impenetrable. A pamphlet from the English Folk Dance and Song Society (*c* 1985) remarks: 'This song has

appeared in many forms in ancient and modern languages from Hebrew onwards, and it purports in almost all cases to be theological.' Here, line by line, is what it *may* be about:

I'll sing you one oh,
Green grow the rushes oh,
One is one and all alone and evermore
    shall be so.

[Refers to God Almighty.]

Two, two for the lilywhite boys,
Clothed all in green oh.

[Christ and St John the Baptist as children (though what the green refers to is not clear). Compare the title of Christopher Logue's 1950s' play *The Lily-White Boys*.]

Three, three for the rivals

[The Trinity? The Three Wise Men?]

Four for the Gospel makers

[Matthew, Mark, Luke, and John?]

Five for the symbol at your door

[The Pentagram or five-pointed star inscribed on the threshold to drive away the evil one.]

Six for the six proud walkers

[The six *waterpots* used in the miracle of Cana of Galilee. Compare the title of Donald Wilson's detective series on BBC TV (1954, 1964), *The Six Proud Walkers*.]

Seven for the seven stars in the sky

[The group in Ursa Major called Charley's Wain; or the seven days of the week; or Revelation 1:16: 'And he had in his right hand seven stars and out of his mouth went a two-edged sword'.]

Eight for the eight bold rainers/rangers/archangels

[Bold rainers, i.e. angels? But why eight? There are only four archangels, so why double? A 1625 version refers to the people in Noah's Ark who might well be described as 'bold rangers'.]

149

Nine for the nine bright shiners

[The nine choirs of angels? The nine months before birth?]

Ten for the ten commandments

[Obvious, this one.]

Eleven for the eleven that went up to heaven

[The Apostles without Judas Iscariot.]

Twelve for the twelve apostles.

[Or the tribes of Israel.]

Greening of America, The. The title of a book (1971) by Charles Reich. Here, the 'greening' was not of the environmental kind (that sense was, however, already emerging in Europe in the early 1970s), but rather of the maturing of the US through a new anti-urban counter-culture and consciousness. 'The extraordinary thing about this new consciousness,' Reich concludes, 'is that it has emerged out of the wasteland of the Corporate State. For one who thought the world was irretrievably encased in metal and plastic and sterile stone, it seems a remarkable greening of America.' Oddly, of course, 'to be green' can also mean 'to be immature, inexperienced'.

gremlin. The name for a kind of sprite said to get into machinery and make it malfunction, it was popular in the R A F during the Second World War, although it may have originated during the First World War. The name first appeared in print in 1929, and seems to have been derived from 'goblin', possibly blended with 'Fremlin's' (the name of a Kent beer). Roald Dahl wrote a children's book *The Gremlins* as early as 1943. *Gremlins* was the title of a Steven Spielberg film (U S, 1984).

grind. See AXE TO ~.

grog. Meaning 'rum diluted with water', it was introduced by the British Admiral Edward Vernon in an attempt to prevent scurvy among his crewmen in 1740. It did not work. Vernon's nickname was 'Old Grog' because of his addiction to a cloak made of grogram, a coarse material of silk and wool. The nickname was given by sailors to public houses ashore – hence 'grog shops', places where spirits were sold.

groovy. Meaning 'very good (particularly of music)', the word was especially popular in the 1960s, although *D O A S* traces it back to the mid-1930s and its use among 'swing' musicians and devotees. It comes from 'in the groove', referring to the way a gramophone or phonograph stylus or needle fits neatly into the groove on a record.

grotty. Meaning 'seedy; down-at-heel; crummy; unpleasant; nasty; unattractive,' this was a trendy word in the 1960s (rather like the later NAFF). It is short for 'grotesque' and is very much associated with the Mersey culture that accompanied the Beatles out of Liverpool in 1962–3. Alun Owen put it in his script for the first Beatles film, *A HARD DAY'S NIGHT* (1964) but the word was in general Scouse (Liverpudlian) use before that.

ground. See HIT THE ~ RUNNING.

Group terms. See COLLECTIVE NOUNS.

Grundy. See MRS ~.

guerre. See MAGNIFIQUE MAIS . . .

guide philosopher and friend, my. An ingratiating form of address (compare A GENTLEMAN AND A SCHOLAR), it originally came from Alexander Pope's *An Essay of Man* (1733):

Shall then this verse to future age
    pretend
Thou wert my guide, philosopher and
    friend?

guillotine. Decapitation equipment incorporating a vertically-descending blade, much used during the French Revolution. The French physician Dr Joseph-Ignace Guillotin did not invent it – the device had already been used in Italy and elsewhere and was at first called a *louison* or *louisette* after Dr Antoine Louis who adapted this 'painless' and 'humane' form of execution. What Dr Guillotin did was to push a resolution through the French Constituent Assembly adopting it as the official means of executing criminals in 1792. His family did not take kindly to having their name attached to such a device and, after his death, changed their name rather than put up with it. He narrowly escaped being guillotined himself.

Guilty Men. The title of a tract (July 1940) 'which may rank as literature' (A.J.P. Taylor). It was written by Michael Foot, Frank Owen and Peter Howard using the pseudonym 'Cato' and taunted the appeasers who had brought about the situation where Britain had had to go to war with Germany. (See also *D P P*.)

Gulag Archipelago, The. The title of a novel (1974) by Alexander Solzhenitsyn. See under ACRONYMS.

gun. See SMOKING ~.

gung-ho. Meaning 'enthusiastic, if carelessly so', the word derives from Chinese *kung* plus *ho* meaning 'work together'. Lt Gen Evans F. Carlson of the US Marines borrowed these words to make a slogan during the Second World War. In 1943, a film about the Marines had the title *Gung Ho!*

G W R. See INITIALS.

Hail the Conquering Hero. The title of a film (US, 1944), which probably alludes to Thomas Morell's line 'See, the Conquering Hero Comes!' which occurs in Handel's oratorios *Judas Maccabaeus* (1747) and *Joshua* (1748).

hair of the dog (that bit me). Meaning 'another drink of the same to help cure a hangover', it comes from the old belief that a bite from a mad dog could be cured if you put hair from the same dog's tail on the wound.

half. See HOW THE OTHER ~ LIVES.

halt and the blind, the. From the parable of the great supper in St Luke 14:21: 'Go out quickly into the streets and lanes of the city and bring in hither the poor, and the maimed, and the halt and the blind.' 'Halt' here means 'lame, crippled, limping'.

ham. (1) A bad actor. (2) An amateur radio operator. Various suggestions have been made as to the origin of (1). Possibly it is short for 'hamfatter' – an actor who used fat from ham chops to take off his makeup (US origin, nineteenth century). The radio sense may derive from this in turn, conflated with '(h)amateur'.

Hamlet Revenge! The title of a detective novel (1937) by Michael Innes, it is not from Shakespeare's play but from an earlier one (which is lost to us) on the same theme. Thomas Lodge saw it in 1596 and noted the pale-faced 'ghost which cried so miserably at the theatre, like an oyster-wife, Hamlet, revenge'.

Hamlet without the Prince. Referring to an event without the leading participant. Byron wrote in a letter on 26 August 1818: 'My autobiographical essay would resemble the tragedy of Hamlet . . . recited "with the part of Hamlet left out by particular desire".' This and other early uses of the phrase may possibly hark back to the theatrical anecdote (as told in the *Morning Post*, 21 September 1775): 'Lee Lewes diverts them with the manner of their performing Hamlet in a company that he belonged to, when the hero who was to play the principal character had absconded with an inn-keeper's daughter; and that when he came forward to give out the play, he added, "the part of Hamlet to be left out, for that night".' Compare the title of Philip King's play *Without the Prince* (1946). In 1938, James Agate headed his review of a Ralph Richardson performance: 'Othello without the Moor'.

Hancock. See JOHN ~.

hand. See CLOUD NO BIGGER THAN . . .; IRON ~ under IRON FIST.

Handful of Dust, A. The title of a novel (1934) by Evelyn Waugh, it originates in T.S. Eliot's *The Waste Land* ('The Burial of the Dead') (1922): 'I will show you fear in a handful of dust.' Earlier, a 'handful of earth' was a symbol of mortality.

hand over fist. This is often used in the expression 'to make money hand over fist'. A similar expression, 'pulling it in', provides the origin here. If you are pulling in a rope or hoisting a sail on board ship, you pass it between your two hands and, in so doing, unavoidably put one hand over the fist of the other hand.

hand that rocks the cradle, the. (. . . 'is the hand that rules the world'). This tribute to motherhood comes from 'The Hand that Rules the World' by the US poet William Ross Wallace (d 1881).

hanged drawn and quartered, to be. A form of execution for treason, this was last carried out in the UK in 1867. The order of procedure is actually 'drawn, hanged, and quartered' as is plain from the words of a British judge sentencing Irish rebels in 1775: 'You are to be *drawn* on hurdles to the place of execution, where you are to be *hanged* by the neck but not until you are dead; for, while you are still living, your bodies are to be taken down, your bowels torn out and burned before your faces; your heads then cut off, and your bodies *divided each into four quarters*, and your heads and quarters to be then at the King's disposal; and may the Almighty God have mercy on your souls.'

happening, a. A 1960s' word for an improvised theatrical event or deeply meaningful, possibly provocative act, supposedly of some significance but often disorganized and embarrassing to watch. An early example occurred at the Edinburgh Festival Drama Conference in 1963 when a nude woman was towed across a musicians' gallery.

Happiest Days of Your Life, The. The title of a play (1948; film UK, 1950) by John Dighton, taken from the traditional platitude about schooldays, intoned at school prizegivings. Compare *The Best Years of Our Lives*, the title of an American film (1946) about what happens to a group of ex-servicemen when they return from the war – presumably having 'given the best years of their lives' to their country. In *Monkey Business* (1931), Groucho Marx says, 'Oh, so that's it . . . We don't count, after we've given you the best years of our lives.' 'The best *days* of our lives' is also an expression used in similar contexts. See THE FIRST HUNDRED THOUSAND.

happily. See AND THEY ALL LIVED ~ . . .

happiness is —. This slogan format possibly originated with E.Y. Harburg's lyrics for the song 'Happiness is a Thing Called Joe'(1942). However, it was Charles M. Schultz, creator of the Peanuts comic strip, who really launched the 'Happiness is —' format. In *c* 1957 he had drawn a strip 'centring around some kid hugging Snoopy and saying in the fourth panel that 'Happiness is a warm puppy'.' This became the title of a best-selling book in 1962. (See also *DPP*.)

happy as a sandboy, as. OED2 has 'jolly as a sandboy' as the original nineteenth-century expression, referring to boys who hawked sand from door to door. (See also *DPP*.)

happy as Larry, as. Meaning 'extremely happy', Brewer has this as an Australian expression and referring to the boxer Larry Foley (d 1917). The first

OED2 citation (indeed Australian) is from 1905.

happy as the day is long. This expression, much-used by Dickens who, nevertheless, occasionally varied it. In *David Copperfield* (Chap. 41, 1849–50), he wrote: 'We . . . were happy as the week was long.' In 1820, Lord Norbury joked of Caroline of Brunswick's behaviour with the *dey* (governor) of Algiers: 'She was happy as the dey was long.'

'Happy Birthday to You'. This is the most frequently-sung phrase in English, according to *The Guinness Book of Records 1985* (which also lists 'For He's a Jolly Good Fellow' and 'Auld Lang Syne' as the top songs of all time). It started out as 'Good Morning to All' with words by Patty Smith Hill and music by Mildred J. Hill in *Song Stories for the Kindergarten* (1893). 'Happy Birthday to You' is the first line of the second stanza, but was not promoted to the title-line until 1935. The song has had a chequered legal history, due to the erroneous belief that it is in the public domain and out of copyright.

happy hunting ground. A translation of the North American Indian name for 'heaven, paradise', the phrase is now used of any field that appears fruitful.

Happy Warrior. The nickname of Alfred E. Smith, US Democrat politician, so dubbed by Franklin D. Roosevelt in 1924: 'He is the Happy Warrior of the political battlefield.' It comes from William Wordsworth's 'Character of the Happy Warrior' (1807):

> Who is the happy Warrior? Who is he
> That every man in arms should wish to be?

Hard Day's Night, A. This title for the Beatles' first feature film (UK, 1964) was apparently chosen towards the end of filming when Ringo Starr used the phrase to describe a 'heavy' night (Ray Coleman, *John Lennon*, 1984). What, in fact, Ringo must have done was to use the title of the Lennon and McCartney song (presumably already written if it was towards the end of filming) in a conversational way. Indeed, Hunter Davies in *The Beatles* (1968) noted: 'Ringo Starr came out with the phrase, though John had used it earlier in a poem.' It certainly sounds like a Lennonism and may have had some limited general use subsequently as a catch phrase meaning that one has had 'a very tiring time'.

hard-faced men who had done well out of the war. The members of the House of Commons who had been returned in the 1918 General Election were so described by a 'Conservative politician', according to John Maynard Keynes, the economist, in *The Economic Consequences of Peace* (1919). Stanley Baldwin, a future Conservative Prime Minister, was the one who said it. In the biography of Baldwin by Keith Middlemas, he is also quoted as having noted privately on 12 February 1918: 'We have started with the new House of Commons. They look much as usual – not so young as I had expected. The prevailing type is a rather successful-looking business kind which is not very attractive.'

Hardy. See KISS ME ~.

hare. See FIRST CATCH YOUR ~.

Harmonia. See ROMAN NAMES.

harp. See I TOOK MY ~.

Harry. See FLASH ~; and under LITTLE TOUCH OF SCHMILSSON.

harvest home. This is the name for the bringing in of the last load of corn, accompanied by a special song, or the harvest supper laid on at this time. According to the *DNB*, the church use of 'harvest home' was originated by George Anthony Denison (*d* 1896), Archdeacon of Taunton. According to Brewer, the church 'harvest thanksgiving' (or now more usually, 'harvest festival') originated with the Revd R.S. Hawker, Vicar of Morwenstow, Cornwall, in 1843.

harvest moon. See SHINE ON ~.

Harvey Smith. Meaning 'a V SIGN gesture given as a signal of disapproval', it owes its name to the show-jumping champion, Harvey Smith, who gave it in view of the TV audience at Hickstead in 1971. It looked like contempt of Hickstead's owner, Douglas Bunn, but Smith argued that it was as in V FOR VICTORY.

hatter. See MAD AS A ~.

hat-trick, to perform a. An expression originally used of three wickets taken with successive balls in the game of cricket – which *OED2* finds in 1886. The player so doing is entitled to be awarded a new hat – 'or equivalent' – by the club. The expression went on to mean any three-in-a-row achievement. (See also *DPP*.)

have a good/happy/nice day! William Safire traces the origins of this standard North American parting wish in *On Language* (1980). Beginning with Chaucer's 'The Knight's Tale' ('Fare well, have good day'), he jumps to 1956 and the Carson/Roberts advertising agency in Los Angeles. 'Our phone was answered, "Good morning, Carson/Roberts. Have a happy day",' recalled Ralph Carson. 'We used the salutation on all letters, tie tacks, cuff buttons, beach towels, blazer crests, the works.' Shortly after this, WCBS-TV weathergirl Carol Reed would wave goodbye with 'Have a happy'. In the 1960s 'Have a good day' was still going strong. The early 1970s saw 'Have a nice day' push its insidious way in, although Kirk Douglas had got his tongue round it in the 1948 film *A Letter to Three Wives*. 'Have a nice city' was a slogan in the 1970 Los Angeles mayoral election. 'Have a good day' may also have had some use on the English hunting field.

Have Gun Will Travel. The title of this TV Western series (US, 1957–64) then became a format phrase capable of much variation. Originally it was what might have been on the calling card of a hired gun, e.g. 'Have gun, will travel . . . wire Paladin, San Francisco'. Later, the phrase turned up in many ways – as joke slogans ('Have pill, will'; 'Have wife, must travel') and even as the UK title of another TV series (1981) *Have Girls, Will Travel* (which was known as *The American Girls* in the US).

Have His Carcase. The title of a detective novel (1932) by Dorothy L. Sayers, it is an old joke upon the Latin legal phrase *habeas corpus* [you have the body]. Sam Weller makes the joke in *The Pickwick Papers* (Chap. 40, 1836–7) by Charles Dickens. A habeas corpus is a writ ordering someone who is keeping another in custody to produce him in court. Its aim is to stop people being imprisoned on mere suspicion or kept waiting unduly for trial.

haves and the have-nots, the. The phrase refers to the advantaged and disadvantaged of society. Safire points to Sancho Panza's saying in *Don Quixote*: 'There are only two families in the world, the Haves and the Have-Nots' (Spanish *el tener* and *el no tener*). Edward Bulwer-Lytton in *Athens* (1836) wrote: 'The division . . . of the Rich and the Poor – the havenots and the haves'.

having a wonderful time. See WISH YOU WERE HERE.

hawae the lads! This cry of encouage-ment ('come on!') is from the North-East of England, also in the forms 'Haway' (*or* 'Howay') or 'Away' (*or* 'A-wee'). According to the Frank Graham, *New Geordie Dictionary* (1979), it is a cor-ruption of 'hadaway' as in 'hadaway wi'ye', which means the opposite, 'begone!'

Haw-Haw, Lord. See LORD HAW-HAW.

hawks/doves. These terms are used to denote those for and against tough mili-tary action. The term 'war hawk' was coined by Thomas Jefferson in 1798. A dove traditionally has been a symbol of peace – perhaps since Noah sent one to see if the waters had abated and it returned with an olive leaf (Genesis 8:8–11). The modern division into hawks and doves, much used during the Vietnam War of the 1960s, dates from the Cuban missile crisis of 1962.

hay. See AND THAT AIN'T ~.

head. See HOLE IN THE ~.

head cook and bottle-washer. See CHIEF COOK AND BOTTLE-WASHER

hear all – see all – say nowt. The motto of Yorkshiremen is said to be:

> Hear all, see all, say nowt,
> Aight all, sup all, pay nowt,
> And if ever tha does owt for nowt
> Do it for thisen.

A Noel Gay song written in 1938 for Sandy Powell, the Yorkshire comedian, had the title: 'Hear all, see all, say nowt'. Compare **Hear no evil, see no evil, speak**

no evil which Bartlett describes as a legend related to the Three Wise Monkeys carved over the door of the Sacred Stable, Nikko, Japan in the seventeenth century. The monkeys are represented having their paws over, respectively, ears, eyes, and mouth. 'Hear, see, keep silence' (often accomp-anied by a sketch of the Three Wise Monkeys) is the motto of the United Grand Lodge of Freemasons – in the form *Audi, Vide, Tace.*

heard. See YOU AIN'T ~ NOTHIN' YET.

heart. See CALAIS LYING ON MY ~; EAT YOUR ~ OUT.

heart and stomach of a king, the. What Elizabeth I is supposed to have said in a speech to her 20,000-strong army gathered at Tilbury prior to the Spanish Armada in 1588: 'I know I have the body of a weak and feeble woman, but I have the heart and stomach of a king, and of a king of England too.' The sole source is an undated letter (not pub-lished until 1691) to the Duke of Buckingham from Leonel Sharp, a chap-lain who was at Tilbury but who had a reputation for being 'obsequious and ingratiating' (*DNB*). The only contem-porary account of the speech is by a poet called James Aske but it contains none of the above phrases.

heartbeat away from the presi-dency. The traditional description of the position of the US vice-president and, as Safire puts it: 'a reminder to voters to examine the shortcomings of a vice-presidential candidate'. The earliest use of the phrase Safire finds is Adlai Stevenson beginning an attack on Richard Nixon in 1952 with: 'The Republican vice-presidential candidate, who asks you to place him a heartbeat from the presidency . . .' Jules Witcover entitled a book on vice-president Spiro

Agnew's enforced resignation (1973), *A Heartbeat Away*. The phrase was much in evidence again when George Bush selected Dan Quayle as his running-mate in 1988.

Heart Has Its Reasons, The. The title of the memoirs (1956) of the Duchess of Windsor comes from Pascal's *Pensées*, '*Le coeur a ses raisons que la raison ne connaît point*' [The heart has its reasons which reason knows nothing of].

Heart Is a Lonely Hunter, The. The title of a novel (1940; film US, 1968) by Carson McCullers, it comes from the 'The Lonely Hunter, William Sharp' (Fiona Macleod) (*d* 1905): 'My heart is a lonely hunter that hunts on a lonely hill.'

Heart of Midlothian, The. The title given to the novel (1818) by Sir Walter Scott, referring to the nickname of the Tolbooth or prison which once stood on a site near St Giles' Cathedral in Edinburgh. Heart of Midlothian (or 'Hearts') football team (founded 1873), apparently took its name from a ballroom used by the players in the early days, which in turn had taken its name from the novel.

hearts and minds. These are what has to be won in a war if physical victory is lacking – especially, what had to be won in the Vietnam War by the US Government. John Pilger, writing on 23 August 1967 reports: 'When Sergeant Melvin Murrell and his company of United States Marines drop by helicopter into the village of Tuylon, west of Danang, with orders to sell "the basic liberties as outlined on page 233 of the Pacification Programme Handbook" and at the same time win the hearts and minds of the people (see same handbook, page 86 under WHAM) they see no one: not a child or a chicken' (quoted in *The Faber Book of Reportage*, 1987).

The Blessing in the Holy Communion service of the Prayer Book is: 'The peace of God, which passeth all understanding, keep your *hearts and minds* in the knowledge and love of God, and of his Son Jesus Christ Our Lord.' This is drawn from Philippians 4:7. (See also *DPP*.)

heat. See IF YOU CAN'T STAND THE ~ . . .

Heath Robinson. This phrase, which is applied to complicated, ingenious, and sometimes amateur and makeshift contraptions, is after W. Heath Robinson (*d* 1944) whose drawings of them appeared in *Punch* and elsewhere.

heaven. See ALL THIS AND ~ TOO.

Heaven's Gate. The title of a film (US, 1980), directed by Michael Cimino, in which 'Heaven's Gate' is the name of a roller-skating rink used by settlers and immigrants in Wyoming in 1891. Conceivably, the name is meant to be taken as an ironic one for the rough situation many of the characters find themselves in as they arrive to start a new life. The idea of a 'gate to heaven' goes back to the Bible, e.g. 'This is none other but the house of God, and this is the gate of heaven' (Genesis 28:17) and 'He commanded the clouds from above, and opened the doors of heaven' (Psalm 78:23).

Shakespeare twice uses the phrases. In *Cymbeline* (II.iii.20), there is the song: 'Hark, hark, the lark at heaven's gate sings' and Sonnet 29 has:

Like to the lark at break of day arising

From sullen earth sings hymns at
heaven's gate.

Steven Bach in *Final Cut* (1985), a
book about the making of the film, cites
two more possible sources. William
Blake in *Jerusalem* (1820) wrote:

I give you the end of a golden string;
Only wind it into a ball,
It will lead you in at Heaven's gate,
Built in Jerusalem's wall.

Browning uses the phrase and there is a
poem by Wallace Stevens with the title,
'The Worms at Heaven's Gate'.

Hebe. See GREEK NAMES.

he being dead yet speaketh. Revd
Francis Kilvert (1840–79), the diarist,
was an Anglican curate at Langley
Burrell in Wiltshire, then at Clyro near
the Welsh border. He was then vicar of
Saint Harmon and moved to Bredwardine two years before his early death.
As such he would now be completely
forgotten but for the diary which he kept
from 1870 to his death on 5 August
1879. Having been well pruned first by
his widow (he died a month or so after
their marriage), selections from the diary
were eventually published in 1938–40.
How appropriate therefore that the
inscription on his grave at Bredwardine
(chosen presumably by his widow, not
knowing how apt it was to be for a
posthumously-published diarist) is: 'He
being dead yet speaketh' – from
Hebrews 11:4. In his entry for 16 March
1870, he writes: 'Below Tybella a bird
singing unseen reminded me how the
words of a good man live after he is
silent and out of sight "He being dead
yet speaketh".'

Hebrews 13:8, see. A capsule criticism of the long-running play, *Abie's
Irish Rose* (1922–27) by the American
humorist, Robert Benchley. The text

reads: 'Jesus Christ the same yesterday,
and today, and for ever'.

Hecate. See GREEK NAMES.

Hector. See GREEK NAMES.

Hecuba. See GREEK NAMES.

Heep. See URIAH ~.

heights. See COMMANDING ~.

Helen. See GREEK NAMES.

Helios. See GREEK NAMES.

hell. See ALL ~ BROKE LOOSE; CAT IN
~'S CHANCE; MAD AS ~.

Hell hath no fury. The complete quotation from William Congreve's *The
Mourning Bride* (1697) is:

Heav'n has no rage, like love to hatred
turn'd,
Nor Hell a fury, like a woman scorn'd.

'Hello I Must Be Going!' The title of a
record album (1982) by Phil Collins,
it comes from the song with words by
Harry Ruby and music by Bert Kalmar,
sung by Groucho Marx in *Animal
Crackers* (1930).

**'Hell!' Said the Duchess, or First
Lines.** The title of the book (1985) by
Gemma O'Connor was taken from the
opening lines of Agatha CHRISTIE'S
The Murder on the Links (1923): 'I believe that a well-known anecdote exists
to the effect that a young writer, determined to make the commencement of his
story forcible and original enough to
catch the attention of the most blasé
of editors, penned the first sentence:
" 'Hell!' said the Duchess".' Note also,
Hell! Said the Duchess, 'A Bed-time
Story' by Michael Arlen (1934).
Partridge/*Catch Phrases* dates the longer

phrase: 'Hell! said the Duchess when she caught her teats in the mangle' to *c* 1895. Compare the suggested newspaper headline containing all the ingredients necessary to capture a reader's attention (sex, royalty, religion, etc.): 'Teenage Sex-change Priest in Mercy Dash to Palace' (a joke current by 1976).

helmsman. See GREAT ~.

Hephaestus. See GREEK NAMES.

Hera. See GREEK NAMES.

Hercules. See GREEK NAMES.

here's another fine mess you've gotten me into! This was a catch phrase, subject to variation, of Oliver Hardy after some ineptitude on Stan Laurel's part. One of the comedy duo's thirty-minute features was called *Another Fine Mess* (1930). A graffito from the Falklands war of 1982 declared: 'There's another fine mess you got me into, [Port] Stanley.'

here's a pretty kettle of fish! Meaning 'here's a nice state of affairs, muddle, mess!' In the 1740s, Henry Fielding uses 'pretty kettle of fish' in both *Joseph Andrews* and *Tom Jones,* so it was obviously well established by then. Brewer has a plausible explanation, saying that 'kettle of fish' is an old Border country name for a kind of *fête champêtre* or riverside picnic, where a newly caught salmon is boiled and eaten. 'The discomfort of this sort of party may have led to the phrase.' A 'fish kettle' as the name of a cauldron for cooking fish has been a term in use since the seventeenth century, though it doesn't appear to have anything to do with this expression. Rather preferable is the explanation given in *English Idioms* (published by Nelson *c* 1912) that kettle comes from 'kiddle' [a net]. So all one is saying is: 'here is a nice net of fish', as

one might on drawing it out of the sea, not being totally sure what it contains. (See also *D P P.*)

here's looking at you, kid! From the film *Casablanca* (1942), a line based on an existing drinker's toast and turned into a catch phrase by Humphrey Bogart impersonators. 'Here's Looking at You' had already been the title of one of the first revues transmitted by the BBC from Alexandra Palace in the early days of television (*c* 1936).

here we are again! Perhaps the oldest catch phrase it is possible to attach to a particular performer. Joseph Grimaldi (*d* 1837) used it as Joey the Clown in pantomime and it has subsequently been used by almost all clowns on entering the circus ring or theatre stage.

Here We Go Round the Mulberry Bush. The title of the novel (1965; film UK, 1967) by Hunter Davies derives from the refrain sung in the children's game (first recorded 1897, though undoubtedly earlier) in which the participants hold hands and dance in a ring.

Hermaphroditus. See GREEK NAMES.

Hermes. See GREEK NAMES.

h/Hero. See GREEK NAMES; and under HOME IS THE SAILOR.

Hesperides. See GREEK NAMES.

He That Plays the King. The title of a book of theatre criticism (1950) by Kenneth Tynan is taken from Shakespeare's *Hamlet* (II.ii.318): 'He that plays the king shall be welcome.'

he who is not with us is against us. This view is popularly ascribed to the Russian leader, Joseph Stalin. *Time* (11 August 1986) noted a corollary attributed to the Hungarian Communist

Party leader, Janos Kadar: 'He who is not against us is with us.' In fact Stalin was quoting Jesus Christ who said: 'He that is not with me is against me' (Luke 11:23) and Kadar was also quoting Christ who provided the corollary: 'He that is not against us is for us' (Luke 9:50). It is not surprising that Stalin quoted Scripture. He went from a church school at Guri to the theological seminary at Tiflis to train for the Russian Orthodox priesthood.

Hickory Dickory Dock. The British title of a Hercule Poirot novel (1955) by Agatha CHRISTIE, taken from the nursery rhyme, first recorded *c* 1744. In the US the book is known as *Hickory Dickory Death*.

Hidden Laughter. The title of a play (1990) by Simon Gray taken from T.S. Eliot, *Four Quartets* ('Burnt Norton', V):

> Sudden in a shaft of sunlight
> Even while the dust moves
> There rises the hidden laughter
> Of children in the foliage.

hide. See YOU CAN RUN BUT . . .

Hi-De-Hi! The title of a BBC TV comedy series (from 1980) set in a 1950s' holiday camp. The title probably came to be used in this way from a camper's song special to Butlin's:

> Tramp, tramp, tramp, tramp,
> Here we come, to jolly old Butlin's every year.
> All come down to Butlin's, all by the sea.
> Never mind the weather, we're as happy as can be.
> Hi-de-hi! Ho-de-ho'

(quoted in the *Observer* Magazine, 12 June 1983).

This possibly dates from the late 1930s. The origin of the phrase seems to lie in dance-band vocals of the 1920s/30s – the 'Hi-de-ho, vo-de-o-do' sort of

thing. However, according to Denis Gifford's *The Golden Age of Radio*, 'Hi-de-hi! Ho-de-ho!' was the catch phrase of Christopher Stone, the BBC's first 'disc jockey', when he went off and presented *Post Toasties Radio Corner*, a children's programme for Radio Normandy in 1937. (See also *DPP*.)

hiding to nothing, to be on a. Meaning 'to be in a no-win situation; to be confronted with a thrashing without the chance of avoiding it, to face impossible odds', the origin of this expression is obscure, but possibly comes from horse-racing.

high water. See COME HELL . . .

HILTHYNBIMA. See INITIALS.

Him. See TO KNOW ~ IS TO LOVE ~.

Himeros. See GREEK NAMES.

hinc illae lacrimae [hence all those tears]. Said by way of explanation of the real cause of something, this comes from *Andria* by Terence (*d* 159 BC).

Hippodrome. See under ODEON.

Hippolyta. See GREEK NAMES.

his death diminishes us all. A cliché of obituaries, this possibly derives from John Donne's *Devotions*, XVII (1624): 'Any man's death diminishes me, because I am involved in Mankind: and therefore never send to know for whom the bell tolls; it tolls for thee'.

his master's voice. Referring to the practice of only carrying out what one is instructed to do, or of not revealing one's own thoughts, only those of one's superiors, the phrase comes from the trademark and brand name of the HMV record company. In 1899, the English painter Francis Barraud approached the Gramophone Company in London to borrow one of their machines so that he could paint his dog, Nipper, listening to it. Nipper was accustomed, in fact, to hearing a *phonograph* but his master thought that the larger horn of the gramophone would make a better picture. Subsequently, the Gramophone Company bought the painting and adapted and adopted it as a trademark. In 1901, the Victor Talking Machine Company ('Loud enough for dancing' was its slogan) acquired the US rights. The company later became R C A Victor and took Nipper with them. Nowadays Britain's E M I owns the trademark in most countries, R C A owns it in North and South America, and J V C owns it in Japan. It was used until 1991.

history. See END OF ~.

history is bunk. This is popularly remembered as a saying of Henry Ford I. What he actually said in an interview with the *Chicago Tribune* (25 May 1916) was: 'History is more or less bunk. It's tradition.' In his 1919 libel action against the paper, Ford explained: 'I did not say it was bunk. It was bunk to me . . . but I did not need it very bad.'

History Man, The. Following the B B C T V adaptation in 1981 of the novel of this title by Malcolm Bradbury (1975), the phrase 'history man' was used to describe a particular type of scheming, unidealistic, university lecturer. In fact, the title describes a character who does not appear, but was taken to mean the left-wing sociology don 'hero' – and from that, any similar don at a 'new' university.

'Hitler Has Only Got One Ball'. This was the title of an anonymous song (sung to the tune of COLONEL BOGEY) that was in existence by 1940. As with NOT TONIGHT JOSEPHINE, the basis for this assertion about a political figure

is obscure. The rumour had been widespread in Central Europe in the 1930s and Martin Page in *Kiss Me Goodnight, Sergeant Major* (1973) writes of a Czech refugee who had referred in 1938 to the fact that Hitler had been wounded in the First World War – since when '*ihm fehlt einer*' [he lacks one]. Perhaps it was no more than a generalized slight against the Nazi leader's virility which conveniently fitted the tune and also permitted a 'Goebbels/no balls' rhyme. There had earlier been a nineteenth-century American ballad about a trade union leader which began: 'Arthur Hall/Has only got one ball'.

hit the ground running, to. This expression in business use, meaning 'to get straight on with the business in hand; to deliver the goods without having to get up speed', is probably military in origin – leaping from an assault craft or by parachute may be what is being alluded to. An example of its use comes from the *Independent*: '*The Late Show* has so far generated an overwhelmingly favourable response . . . "To hit the ground running with four shows a week", said Alex Graham, editor of *The Media Show* on Channel 4, "that's really impressive" ' (29 March 1989).

Hobson's Choice. The title of a play (1915; film U K, 1953) by Harold Brighouse comes from the expression meaning 'no choice at all'. Thomas Hobson (*d* 1631) hired horses from a livery stable in Cambridge. His customers were always obliged to take the horse nearest the door. The man's fame was considerable and he was celebrated in two epitaphs by Milton.

hoist with one's own petard, to be. Meaning 'to be caught in one's own trap', its origin has nothing to do with being stabbed by one's own knife, or hung with one's own rope. The context in which Hamlet uses it in Shakespeare's play (III.iv.209) makes the source clear:

> For 'tis the sport to have the engineer
> Hoist with his own petard.

A petard was a newly invented device in Shakespeare's day, used for blowing up walls, etc. with gunpowder. Thus the image is of the operative being blown up into the air by his own device. Compare OWN GOAL.

hokey-pokey. See OKEY-POKEY.

Hold Back the Dawn. The title of a film (US, 1941), this is apparently original, as is also *Hold Back the Night* (US, 1956) and *Hold Back Tomorrow* (US, 1956), and Barbara Taylor Bradford's novel (1985) *Hold the Dream.*

hold the fort. This phrase has two meanings: 'Look after this place while I'm away' and 'Hang on, relief is at hand'. In the second sense, General William T. Sherman signalled to General John M. Corse at the Battle of Allatoona, Georgia (5 October 1864). What he actually semaphored from Keneshaw Mountain was: 'Sherman says hold fast. We are coming' (Mencken) or 'Hold out. Relief is coming' (Bartlett). The phrase became popularized in its present form as the first line of the hymn 'Ho, My Comrades, See the Signal!' by Philip Paul Bliss (in *The Charm, c* 1870):

> 'Hold the fort, for I am coming,'
> Jesus signals still.

(See also *DPP*.)

hole(s). See ACE IN THE ~; BLACK ~; BLACK ~ OF CALCUTTA; FOUR THOUSAND ~ IN BLACKBURN ...; IF YOU KNOW A BETTER ~ ...

hole in the head, to need something like a. Meaning 'not to need something at all', Leo Rosten in *Hooray for Yiddish* (1982) describes this phrase

as 'accepted from Alaska to the Hebrides' and states that it comes directly from the Yiddish *lock in kop*: 'It was propelled into our vernacular by the play *A Hole in the Head* (1957) by Arnold Schulman and more forcibly impressed upon mass consciousness by the Frank Sinatra movie (1959).' *OED2* finds it by 1951.

Holiday Inn. Originally the title of a film (US, 1942), the hotel chain with this name was founded subsequently.

Hollow Crown, The. This was the title of the Royal Shakespeare Company's entertainment (1962) based on Shakespeare's kings and queens. It comes from *King Richard II* (III.ii.160):

> Within the hollow crown
> That rounds the mortal temples of a king
> Keeps death his court.

Holocaust. This is the phrase applied to the mass murder of Jews and the attempted elimination of European Jewry by the German Nazis during the 1939–45 war. A holocaust is an all-consuming conflagration and is not perhaps the most obvious description of what happened to the estimated six million Jews under the Nazis, though many were burned as well as being gassed or killed in some other way (compare FINAL SOLUTION).

The term seems to have arisen because 'genocide' hardly sounded emotive enough. The popular use of 'the Holocaust' for this purpose dates only from 1965 when Alexander Donat published a book on the subject entitled *The Holocaust Kingdom.* However, *OED2* has it in this sense in the *News Chronicle* by 1942, as well as various other 1940s' citations. As early as 1951, the Israeli Knesset had 'The Holocaust and Ghetto Uprising Day' – translated from *Yom ha-Sho'ah.* The use was finally settled when a US TV mini-series called *Holocaust*

(1978) was shown and caused controversy in many countries. Well before *that* happened, Eric Partridge was advising in his *Usage and Abusage* (1947): 'Holocaust is "destruction by fire": do not synonymize it with *disaster*. Moreover, it is properly an ecclesiastical technicality.'

In fact, the word derives from the Greek words *holos* and *kaustos* meaning 'wholly burnt' and was for many years used to describe a sacrifice or offering that was burnt. Some translations of the Bible use it to describe Abraham's preparations to slay his son Isaac. The term has latterly been used to describe what happened to the people of Cambodia at the hands of the Khmer Rouge in the 1970s, and also to the Vietnamese Boat People.

home. See ARE THERE ANY MORE AT ~ LIKE YOU; HARVEST ~; LIKE COMING ~.

Home and Beauty. The title of a play (1919) by Somerset Maugham, concerning the complications surrounding a First World War 'widow' who remarries and then has her original husband turn up (in the US the play was known as *Too Many Husbands*). It comes from the phrase 'England Home and Beauty' which occurs in the notable song 'The DEATH OF NELSON', in the opera *The Americans* (1811) by John Braham and S.J. Arnold.

home is the sailor home from sea. In Robert Louis Stevenson's poem 'Requiem' (1887), it is definitely 'home from sea' – without the definite article, but his grave in Samoa has 'home from the sea'. Compare *Home Is the Hero*, the title of a film (UK, 1959) based on Walter Macken's play.

home is where the heart is. See WHERE THE HEART IS.

Homer nods, even. Meaning 'even the greatest, best and wisest of us can't be perfect all the time, and can make mistakes'. Mencken has 'Even Homer sometimes nods' as an English proverb derived from Horace, *De Arte Poetica* (*c* 8 BC): 'I am indignant when worthy Homer nods', and familiar since the seventeenth century.

honest toil. See DIGNITY OF LABOUR.

honey. See LAND FLOWING WITH MILK AND ~.

honey I forgot to duck. The boxer Jack Dempsey lost his World Heavyweight title to Gene Tunney during a fight in Philadelphia on 23 September 1926. In his *Autobiography* (1977) he recalled: 'Once I got to the hotel, Estelle [his wife] managed to reach me by telephone, saying she'd be with me by morning and that she'd heard the news. I could hardly hear her because of the people crowding the phone. "What happened, Ginsberg?" (That was her pet name for me.) "Honey, I just forgot to duck".' The line was recalled by ex-sports commentator Ronald Reagan when explaining to *his* wife what had happened during an assassination attempt in 1981.

honeymoon. The name for the holiday taken by a bride and groom after their wedding comes from a custom of newly-married couples drinking mead (wine made with honey) for a month after the ceremony. Other languages follow the same pattern: French *lune de miel*, Italian *luna di miele*.

honi soit qui mal y pense [Evil be to him who thinks evil]. This is the motto of the Order of the Garter, founded by Edward III (*c* 1348).

Honour Thy Father. The title of a book (1972; film US, 1973) about the Mafia by Gay Talese comes from Exodus 20. So too does the title of his study of sexual *mores* in the US, *Thy Neighbour's Wife* (1980). His book (1971) about the *New York Times* has the title *The Kingdom and the Power*, which is another of those titles which sounds like a quotation but isn't, although there is perhaps a hint of 'thine is *the kingdom, the power* and the glory' from the LORD'S PRAYER.

Hood, Robin. See ROBIN HOOD.

hook. See BY ~ OR BY CROOK.

hooker. A US term for a prostitute, it probably derives from Corlear's Hook (*or* 'the Hook'), a part of Manhattan where tarts used to ply their trade in the early nineteenth century. General Joseph Hooker may have helped popularize the name during the Civil War when an area of Washington DC became known as 'Hooker's Division' on account of the General's camp-followers. The term was well established by 1845, however, before the Civil War and the General came along.

hooligan. Meaning 'a destructive young ruffian; a vandal', this word derives from the English form of the common Irish name 'Houlihan', or maybe from 'Hooley's Gang', of which there appears to have been one in North London in the late nineteenth century. Which of the various 'Hooligans' is the original is hard to say.

Hooray Henry. Denoting 'a loud-mouthed upper-class twit' (in Britain), the phrase was coined by Jim Godbolt in 1951 to describe the upper-class contingent attracted to the jazz club at 100, Oxford Street, London by the Old Etonian trumpeter, Humphrey Lyttelton. It derives from a character in Damon Runyon's story 'Tight Shoes' who is described as 'strictly a Hurrah Henry'.

hoover, to. Meaning 'to use a vacuum cleaner' the verb is after William H. Hoover who marketed, but did not invent, the original Hoover model. James Murray Spengler invented the 'triple action' machine ('It beats as it sweeps as it cleans') in 1908. Alas for him, we don't say we are going to 'spengler' the carpet.

hope. See ABANDON ~ ALL YE . . .; LAST BEST ~ ON EARTH.

Hope and Glory. The title of a film (UK, 1987), taken from 'Land of Hope and Glory', the title popularly given to the Finale of Sir Edward Elgar's 'Coronation Ode', written for the Coronation of Edward VII in 1902. The words are by A.C. Benson and they were set by Elgar to part of his earlier 'Pomp and Circumstance March' No. 1.

Horatius. See ROMAN NAMES.

horny-handed sons of toil. Denoting labourers bearing the marks of their trade, Denis Kearney used the expression in a speech at San Francisco (*c* 1878). Irish-born Kearney led a 'workingman's protest movement against unemployment, unjust taxes, unfair banking laws, and mainly against Chinese labourers' (Flexner 2). Earlier, J.R. Lowell had written in 'A Glance Behind the Curtain' (1843): 'And blessèd are the horny hands of toil'.

horse(s). See BEHOLD A PALE ~; DARK ~; IF YOU CAN'T RIDE TWO ~ . . .; NEVER CHANGE ~ IN MID STREAM.

Horseman Riding By, A. The title of a novel (1966) by R.F. Delderfield is just possibly an allusion to 'Under Ben Bulben' by W.B. Yeats (1939):

Cast a cold Eye
On Life, on Death.
Horseman, pass by!

horses sweat, men perspire and women merely glow. A saying used to reprove someone who talks of 'sweating'. It is listed as a nanny's reprimand in *Nanny Says* (1972) in the form: 'Horses sweat, gentlemen perspire, but ladies only gently glow.' J.M. Cohen includes it in *Comic and Curious Verse* (1952–9) as merely by Anon, in the form:

Here's a little proverb that you surely
    ought to know:
Horses sweat and men perspire, but
    ladies only glow.

hot. See BLOW ~ AND COLD.

Hot Lips Houlihan. The name of a formidable female character in the film *M*A*S*H* (1970) and the subsequent TV series, she was played by Sally Kellerman in the film and by Loretta Swit on TV. Earlier, in the US radio series *Camel Caravan* (1943–7), there had been a sex-pot character with the name 'Hotbreath Houlihan'.

hottest. See GREATEST THING SINCE . . .

hour. See ELEVENTH ~.

house divided against itself cannot stand, a. Announcing that he would not seek re-election in 1968, President Johnson said: 'It is true that a house divided against itself cannot stand. There is a division in the American house now.' He was alluding to St Mark 3:25, as Abraham Lincoln had done before him in an 1858 speech on the circumstances which led to the Civil War.

House Is Not a Home, A. This was the title of the autobiography (1954) of the New York madam, Polly Adler. 'House' here means 'brothel'. When the book was filmed (US, 1964), there had to be a theme song with this title – which coyly avoided any suggestion as to what sort of 'house' was being talked about.

Houses in Between, The. The title of the novel (1951) by Howard Spring comes from the music-hall song popularized by Gus Elen (*d* 1940), with lyrics by Edgar Bateman and music by George Le Brunn (*c* 1890s):

Oh it really is a wery pretty garden, and
    Chingford to the eastward can be
    seen;
Wiv a ladder and some glasses
You could see to 'Ackney Marshes,
If it wasn't for the 'ouses in between.

how doth the little crocodile. '. . . improve his shining tail?' continues the parody by Lewis Carroll from ALICE IN WONDERLAND. The original is 'Against Idleness and Mischief' (1715) by Isaac Watts: 'How doth the little busy bee/Improve each shining hour . . .' See also 'MY SHINING HOUR'.

how long – O Lord – how long? Now used in mock exasperation, the allusion is to Isaiah 6:11. The prophet has a vision in which God tells him to do various things and he reports: 'Then said I, Lord how long?'

how many beans make five? A catch question or joke riddle, but also uttered as an answer to an impossible question (along the lines of 'how long is a piece of string?' etc.) Miss Alice Lloyd sang a music-hall song in November 1898 which contained the phrase.

how'm I doin'? Ed Koch was Mayor of New York City from 1977–89. He helped balance the books after a period of bankruptcy on the city's part by drastically cutting services. His catch phrase during this period was 'How'm I doing?' He would call it out as he ranged round New York. 'You're doing fine, Ed' the people were supposed to shout back. An old song with the title was disinterred in due course. Unfortunately for him, Koch's achievements in N Y C did not carry him forward to the State governorship as he had hoped and finally everything turned sour on him. A 1979 cartoon in the *New Yorker* showed a woman answering the phone and saying to her husband: 'It's Ed Koch. He wants to know how he's doin'.' A booklet of Koch's wit and wisdom used the phrase as its title.

how now brown cow? This is a phrase used as an elocution exercise, though it was not included along with 'The rain in Spain stays mainly in the plain' and 'In Hertford, Hereford and Hampshire hurricanes hardly ever happen' in the M Y F A I R L A D Y elocution song. However, 'How Now Brown Cow' with words by Rowland Leigh and music by Richard Addinsell was sung by Joyce Barbour in the revue *R S V P* at the Vaudeville theatre in 1926. (See also *D P P*.)

how the other half lives. Meaning 'how people live who belong to different social groups, especially the rich', the expression was used as the title of a book (1890) by Jacob Riis, an American newspaper reporter. He described the conditions in which poor people lived in New York City. The expression seems basically to have referred to the poor but has since been used about any 'other half'. Riis alluded to the core-saying in these words: 'Long ago it was said that "one half of the world does not know how the other half lives".' *O E D 2* finds this proverb in 1607 in English, and in French, in *Pantagruel* by Rabelais

(1532). Alan Ayckbourn entitled a play (1970) *How the Other Half Loves*.

How to Succeed in Business Without Really Trying. The title of a business handbook (1953) by Shepherd Mead, it is more widely known as the title of Frank Loesser's musical (1961; film U S, 1967).

How to Win Friends and Influence People. This was title of a book (1936) by Dale Carnegie. Carnegie's courses incorporating his self-improvement plan had already been aimed at business people for a quarter of a century before the book came out.

Hoyle, according to. Meaning 'exactly; correctly; according to the recognized rules; according to the highest authority', the phrase comes from the name of the one-time standard authority on the game of whist (and other card games). Edmond Hoyle was the author of *A Short Treatise on the Game of Whist* (1742).

Hubert, St. See S A I N T S' N A M E S.

human. See A L L ~ L I F E I S H E R E.

humble pie. See E A T ~.

hundred. See C O O L ~.

hundred days. This phrase is used to refer to a period of intense political action (often immediately upon coming to power). During the 1964 General Election, Harold Wilson said Britain would need a 'programme of a hundred days of dynamic action' such as President Kennedy had promised in 1961. In fact, Kennedy had specifically ruled out a hundred days, saying in his inaugural speech that even 'a thousand days' would be too short (hence the title of Arthur M. Schlesinger's memoir, *A Thousand Days*, 1965). The allusion was to the period during which Napoleon ruled between his escape from Elba and his defeat at the Battle of Waterloo in 1815.

hunting ground. See HAPPY ~.

hush puppies. (1) Deep-fried corn meal batter, often served with fried fish in the southern US. (2) Soft shoes, popular in the 1960s in the US and UK. The food may have got its name from pieces being tossed to hounds with the admonition. 'Hush, puppy!' In 1961, the Wolverine Shoe and Tanning Corp registered 'Hush Puppies' as a trade name in the US. Adrian Room in his *Dictionary of Trade Name Origins* (1982) suggests the name was adopted because it conjures up softness and suppleness. Pictures of beagle-like dogs were shown on the display material. The only connection between the food and the shoe seems to have been a would-be homeliness.

Hyde. See JEKYLL AND ~.

Hydra. See GREEK NAMES.

Hygeia. See GREEK NAMES.

Hymen. See GREEK NAMES.

HUXLEY (Aldous). A British author (1894–1963) who almost invariably used quotations for the titles of his novels and non-fiction books. See AFTER MANY A SUMMER; ANTIC HAY; BEYOND THE MEXIQUE BAY; BRAVE NEW WORLD; BRIEF CANDLES; DOORS OF PERCEPTION; EYELESS IN GAZA; JESTING PILATE; MORTAL COILS; THOSE BARREN LEAVES; TIME MUST HAVE A STOP.

hype. Referring to publicity, particularly in the publishing world, where the promotion is more substantial than the product, the word probably derives from US slang expressions referring to deception, short-changing, and confidence tricks, dating from around the 1920s. Some give the origin of the word as a short form of 'hyperbole', others say it is a short form of 'hypodermic' (something used to give an unnatural boost).

Hyperion. See GREEK NAMES.

I | II

I Am a Camera. The title of a play (1951; film UK, 1955) by John Van Druten, based on the stories of Christopher Isherwood. Later, the play became the basis of the musical *Cabaret*. In 'A Berlin Diary' (included in *Goodbye to Berlin*, 1939) Isherwood wrote: 'I am a camera with its shutter open, quite passive, recording, not thinking.'

I am paying for this broadcast/ microphone. During the New Hampshire primary of 1980, Ronald Reagan won a dispute over who should speak in a debate by declaring: 'I am paying for this microphone, Mr Green!' (the man's name was actually 'Breen'). The line: 'Don't you shut me off, I'm paying for this broadcast' was delivered by Spencer Tracy in the film *State of the Union* (1948).

IBA. See INITIALS.

Icarus. See GREEK NAMES.

Iceland. See SNAKES IN ~.

Iceman Cometh, The. The title of a play (1946) by Eugene O'Neill, about a saloon harbouring alcoholics, it was of endless fascination to the British, to whom the concept of the 'iceman' was all but unknown and the 'cometh' wonderfully affected. In *Salad Days* (1954), there is the line: 'The spaceman cometh!' and there was a song 'The Gas-Man Cometh' by Michael Flanders and Donald Swann (1963). Perhaps the 'cometh' was biblical in origin, as in 'behold this dreamer cometh' (Genesis 37:19).

Ich bin ein Berliner. On 26 June 1963, President John F. Kennedy paid a visit to West Berlin and gave an address to a large and enthusiastic crowd outside the City Hall. He had rejected State Department drafts for his speech and found something better of his own to say: 'Two thousand years ago the proudest boast was "*Civis Romanus sum*" [I am a Roman citizen]. Today, in the world of freedom, the proudest boast is *Ich bin ein Berliner*.' He concluded: 'All free men, wherever they may live, are citizens of Berlin, and therefore, as a free man, I take pride in the words "*Ich bin ein Berliner*".'

Stirring words, and it only detracts from them slightly to know that the President need only have said, '*Ich bin Berliner*' to convey the meaning 'I am a Berliner'. It could be argued that the '*ein*' adds drama because he is saying not 'I was born and bred in Berlin' or 'I live in Berlin', but 'I am one of you'. But by saying what he did, he drew attention to the fact that in Germany '*ein Berliner*' is a doughnut.

I Cover the Waterfront. This was the title of a film (US 1933) about a newspaper reporter, based on a book (1932) by the journalist Max Miller, exposing corruption 'on the waterfront'. Hence 'cover' is in the journalistic sense. The song with this title (by John W. Green and Ed Heyman), sung notably by Billie Holiday, is unconnected with the film and sounds as if it might be about laying paving stones or some other activity. Since the film, 'to cover the waterfront' has meant 'to cover all aspects of a topic'. In *The Wise Wound* (1978) by Penelope Shuttle and Peter Redgrove, 'she's covering the waterfront' is listed among the many slang expressions for menstruation.

I do/I will. When taking marriage vows, which reply is correct? In the Anglican Prayer Book, the response to 'Wilt thou have this man/woman to thy wedded husband/wife . . .?' is obviously, 'I will'. In the Order of Confirmation, to the question: 'Do ye renew the solemn promise and vow that was made . . . at your baptism?' the response is obviously, 'I do'. But in some US marriage services, the question is posed: 'Do you take so-and-so . . .?' to which the response has to be 'I do'. 'Will you' is said to be more popular with American clergy, 'Do you' at civil ceremonies. Jan de Hartog's play *The Four Poster* was turned into a musical with the title *I Do! I Do!* (1966).

I do not choose to run. Having been president since 1923, Calvin Coolidge remarked to newsmen on 2 August 1927: 'I do not choose to run for president in 1928.' Or rather, 'Silent Cal' handed slips of paper with these words on them to waiting journalists. For some reason, the unusual wording of the announcement caught people's fancy and the phrase was remembered. In 1928, there was a silly song recorded in New York about a recalcitrant wristwatch. It was performed by Six Jumping Jacks with Tom Stacks (vocal) and was called 'I Do Not Choose to Run'.

I don't wish to know that – kindly leave the stage. This traditional response to a corny joke is usually said by a person who has been interrupted while engaged in some other activity on stage. It is impossible to say when, and with whom, it started, but in the 1950s the phrase was given a new lease of life by the *Goon Show* on BBC Radio and by other British entertainers who still owe much to the routines and spirit of the music-hall. In the 1930s, the phrase was associated with Murray and Mooney (later, Mooney and King), but may have been used eralier by Dave and Joe O'Gorman.

idiot('s) lantern. See BOX, THE.

if a dog bites a man . . . This definition of news is variously ascribed but chiefly in the form: 'When a dog bites a man, that is not news, because it happens so often. But if a man bites a dog, that is news,' to John B. Bogart, city editor of the New York *Sun* (1873–90). To Charles A. Dana, the editor of the same paper (1868–97), it is ascribed in the form: 'If a dog bites a man, it's a story; if a man bites a dog, it's a good story.'

if anything can go wrong – it will. Most commonly known as **Murphy's Law** (and indistinguishable from **Sod's Law** or **Spode's Law**), this saying dates back to the 1940s. *The Macquarie Dictionary* (1981) suggests that it was named after a character who always made mistakes, in a series of educational cartoons published by the US Navy. *CODP* suggests that it was invented by George Nichols, a project manager for Northrop, the Californian aviation firm, in 1949. He developed the idea from a remark by a colleague, Capt E. Murphy of the Wright Field-Aircraft Laboratory. Film titles have included *Murphy's Law* (US, 1986) and *Murphy's War* (UK, 1971). (See also *DPP*.)

169

if — did not exist it would have to be invented. This format phrase originated in Voltaire's remark: '*Si Dieu n'existait pas, il faudrait l'inventer*' [If God did not exist, it would be necessary to invent him] (*Epîtres*, xcvi, 1770). Other examples include: 'If Austria did not exist it would have to be invented' (Frantisek Palacky, *c* 1845); 'If he [Auberon Waugh, a literary critic] did not exist, it would be un-necessary to invent him' (Desmond Elliott, literary agent, *c* 1977); 'What becomes clear is that Olivier developed his own vivid, earthy classical style as a reaction to Gielgud's more ethereal one . . . So if Gielgud did not exist would Olivier have found it necessary to invent himself?' (review in the *Observer*, 1988); 'If Tony Benn did not exist, the old Right of the Labour Party would have had to invent him' (the *Observer*, 15 October 1989).

if God had intended us to — he wouldn't have given us —. This format phrase is given as a reason for not doing something, e.g. 'If God had intended us to fly, he'd never have given us the railways' (Michael Flanders, *At the Drop of Another Hat*, 1963).

if it ain't broke(n), why fix it? This is a modern proverb, for which the earliest citation is Bert Lance, President Carter's Director of the Office of Management and Budget (1977), speaking on the subject of governmental reorganization. Other examples of its use occur in the *Independent* (3 November 1988), where a TV reviewer asked it of the Government's plans to deregulate broadcasting, and on 12 November, in the same paper, this appeared about changes made in the musical *Chess* once it had opened: 'Tim Rice [the writer, said], "The notices were very good and people liked it, so we could have said, 'If it ain't broken, don't fix it.' But we felt that certain aspects weren't quite right".'

if it looks like a duck, walks like a duck and quacks like a duck, it's a duck. A saying usually ascribed to Walter Reuther, the American labour leader during the McCarthyite witch-hunts of the 1950s, who came up with it as a test of whether someone was a Communist: 'If it walks like a duck, and quacks like a duck, then it just may be a duck.' It has since been applied elsewhere, though usually in politics: 'Mr Richard Darman, the new [US] Budget director, explained the other day what "no new taxes" means. He will apply the **duck test.** "If it looks like a duck, walks like a duck and quacks like a duck, it's a duck" ' (the *Guardian*, 25 January 1989).

If It's Tuesday This Must Be Belgium. This was the title of a film (US 1969) about a group of American tourists rushing around Europe. It popularized a format phrase which people could use when they were in the midst of some hectic activity, whilst also reflecting the confused state of many tourists superficially 'doing' the sights without really knowing where they are. A *Guardian* headline (7 April 1989) on a brief visit to London by Mikhail Gorbachev: 'If It's Thursday, Then It Must Be Thatcherland'.

if you can't beat 'em – join 'em. A modern proverb, probably of US origin, in the alternative form: 'If you can't lick 'em, join 'em'. The earliest citation in the *CODP* is from Quentin Reynolds, the US writer, in 1941. Mencken had it in his dictionary by 1942. Safire calls it 'a frequent bit of advice, origin obscure, given in areas dominated by one (political) party . . . The phrase, akin to the Scottish proverb "Better bend than break", carries no connotation of surrender; it is used to indicate that the way to take over the opposition's strength is to adopt their positions and platform.' (See also *DPP*.)

if you can't be good – be careful!
Mencken calls this an American proverb, though *C O D P*'s pedigree is mostly British, finding its first proper citation here in 1903 (from A.M. Binstead, *Pitcher in Paradise*). But in 1907, there was an American song called 'Be Good! If You Can't Be Good, Be Careful!' It is a nudging farewell, sometimes completed with 'and if you can't be careful, name it after me' or 'buy a pram'.

if you can't ride two horses at once – you shouldn't be in the circus.
Jimmy Maxton was an Independent Labour Party MP when, at a Scottish Conference of the Party in 1931, a motion was moved that the I L P should disaffiliate from the Labour Party. Maxton made a brief statement to the effect that he was against such a move. In the debate, he had been told that he could not be in two parties – or ride two horses – at the same time. 'My reply to that,' he said, 'is . . . that if my friend cannot ride two horses – what's he doing in the bloody circus?'

if you can't stand the heat – get out of the kitchen.
In 1960, former U S President Truman said: 'Some men can make decisions and some cannot. Some men fret and delay under criticism. I used to have a saying that applies here, and I note that some people have picked it up.' When Truman announced that he would not stand again as president, *Time* (28 April 1952) had him give a 'down-to-earth reason for his retirement, quoting a favourite expression of his military jester Maj-Gen Harry Vaughan', namely: 'If you can't stand the heat, get out of the kitchen.' (See also *D P P*.)

if you have to ask the price you can't afford it.
John Pierpoint Morgan Jr (*d* 1943) was head of the U S banking house of Morgan. The story has it that a man was thinking of buying a yacht similar to Morgan's and asked him how much it cost in annual upkeep. Morgan replied with words to the effect: 'If you have to ask, you can't afford it.' Compare the remark of John Paul Getty (*d* 1976): 'If you can actually count your money, you are not really rich.'

if you know a better 'ole – go to it.
This comes from the caption to a cartoon (1915) by the British cartoonist, Bruce Bairnsfather, depicting 'Old Bill', up to his waist in mud on the Somme during the First World War. Two films (U K, 1918; U S, 1926), based on the strip, were called *The Better 'Ole*.

if you want anything – just whistle.
This comes from the film *To Have and Have Not* (1945). What Lauren Bacall actually says to Humphrey Bogart is: 'You know you don't have to act with me, Steve. You don't have to say anything, and you don't have to do anything. Not a thing. Oh, maybe just whistle. You know how to whistle, don't you, Steve? You just put your lips together and blow.'

I Have Been Here Before.
The title of a 'Time' play (1937) by J.B. Priestley. Compare 'I have been here before' in Evelyn Waugh's *Brideshead Revisited* (Chap. 1, 1945) where Charles Ryder says it about Brideshead, hence the 'revisited'.

I have seen the future and it works.
Lincoln Steffens was a U S muck-raking journalist who paid a visit to the newly-formed Soviet Union as part of the William C. Bullitt diplomatic mission of 1919. As did a number of the first visitors to the new Soviet system, he returned with an optimistic view: 'I have seen the future, and it works.' In his *Autobiography* (1931), he phrases it a little differently: '"So you've been over into Russia?" said Bernard Baruch, and I answered very literally, "I have been

over into the future, and it works".'
Bullitt said Steffens had been rehearsing
the formula even before arriving in the
USSR. Later he tended to use the
shorter, more popular form himself. In
1989, an anonymous wit said of politician Kenneth Baker's chances of becoming British Prime Minister: 'I have seen
the future and it smirks.'

I Hear America Talking. The title of a
study of the American language (1976)
by Stuart Berg Flexner, it comes from 'I
Hear America Singing', a poem from
Leaves of Grass (1860) by Walt
Whitman.

IHS. See INITIALS.

Ike. See I LIKE ~.

I Know Where I'm Going. The title of
this film (UK, 1945) set in Scotland,
about a headstrong girl, comes from an
Irish song, also used as the theme song:

> I know where I'm going
> And I know who goes with me
> I know whom I love
> But the dear devil [de'il/Lord]
>   knows whom I'll marry.

I like Ike. This slogan appeared on buttons from 1947 onwards as the Second
World War US general, Dwight David
Eisenhower, began to be spoken of as a
possible presidential nominee (initially
as a Democrat). By 1950, Irving Berlin
was including one of his least memorable
songs, 'They Like Ike', in *Call Me
Madam,* and 15,000 people at a rally in
Madison Square Gardens were urging
Eisenhower to return from a military
posting in Paris and run as a Republican
in 1952, with the chant 'We like Ike'. It
worked. The three sharp monosyllables,
and the effectiveness of the repeated 'i'
sound in 'I like Ike', made it an enduring
slogan throughout the 1950s.

illegal, immoral or fattening.
Alexander Woollcott wrote in *The
Knock at the Stage Door* (1933): 'All the
things I really like to do are either illegal,
immoral, or fattening'. Compare the
song, 'It's Illegal, It's Immoral Or It
Makes You Fat' by Griffin, Hecht, and
Bruce and popularized in the UK by the
Beverley Sisters (1950s).

illegitimi non carborundum. This
cod-Latin phrase – supposed to mean
'don't let the bastards grind you down' –
was used by US general 'Vinegar Joe'
Stilwell as his motto during the Second
World War, though it is not suggested he
devised it. Partridge/*Catch Phrases* gives
it as '*illegitimis*' and its origins in British
army intelligence very early on in the
same war. ('Carborundum' is the trade
name of a very hard substance composed
of silicon carbide, used in grinding.)

The same meaning is also conveyed
by the phrase **nil carborundum . . .** as in
the title of a play by Henry Livings
(1962), a pun upon the genuine Latin **nil
desperandum** meaning 'never despair;
NEVER SAY DIE' from '*Nil desperandum est Teucro duce et auspice Teucro*'
[Nothing is to be despaired of with
Teucer as leader and protector] (Horace,
Odes, I.vii.27). (See also *DPP*.)

Ill Fares the Land. The title of a film
(1982) by Bill Bryden, about people
leaving the island of St Kilda, off the
west coast of Scotland. It comes from
Oliver Goldsmith's *The Deserted Village*
(1770):

> Ill fares the land, to hast'ning ills a prey,
> Where wealth accumulates, and men
>   decay . . .
> A bold peasantry, their country's pride,
> When once destroy'd, can never be
>   supplied.

I'll Go to Bed at Noon. The title of a
book (1944), subtitled 'A Soldier's
Letters to His Sons', by the actor Stephen

Haggard, published posthumously. It is taken from the Fool's last words in Shakespeare's *King Lear* (III.vi.83): 'And I'll go to bed at noon', after Lear has said: 'We'll go to supper i'th'morning.' Haggard had played the Fool in the 1940 Old Vic production with John Gielgud.

Ill Met By Moonlight. The title of a film (UK, 1956) about British agents in Crete during the German occupation, it comes from Oberon's words in Shakespeare's *A Midsummer Night's Dream* (II.i.60): 'Ill met by moonlight, proud Titania'. In the US the film was called *Night Ambush*.

I'll Take Manhattan. The title of a novel (1986) by Judith Krantz, although acknowledging the Rodgers and Hart song 'Manhattan', only alludes to it. The song has 'We'll have Manhattan' rather than 'I'll take Manhattan'.

I Love You Alice B. Toklas. The title of a film comedy (US, 1968) about a lawyer (Peter Sellers) amid the Flower People of San Francisco in the 1960s. Alice B. Toklas (who came, as it happens, from San Francisco) was the secretary and lover of Gertrude Stein – for whom Stein 'ghosted' *The Autobiography of Alice B. Toklas* (1933). The *Alice B. Toklas Cookbook* was the name given to an 'alternative' publication (which had nothing to do with Toklas) in the 1960s and contained recipes for marijuana cookies and such like.

I'm going to make him an offer he can't refuse. In 1969, Mario Puzo published his novel about the Mafia called *The Godfather*. It gave to the language a new expression which, as far as one can tell, was Mr Puzo's invention. Johnny Fontane, a singer, desperately wants a part in a movie and goes to see his godfather, Don Corleone, for help. All the contracts have been signed and there is no chance of the studio chief

changing his mind. Still, the godfather promises Fontane he will get him the part, as he says of the studio chief: 'He's a businessman. I'll make him an offer he can't refuse.' In the film (1971), this became: 'I'm going to make him an offer he can't refuse.' In 1973, Jimmy Helms had a hit with the song 'Gonna Make You an Offer You Can't Refuse'.

I'm just going outside ... When Captain Lawrence Oates (nicknamed 'Titus') walked to his death on Capt R.F. Scott's 1912 polar expedition, in the vain hope of saving his companions, he simply said, with classic stiff-upper-lip understatement: 'I am just going outside, and I may be some time.' As the only record of what Oates said was contained in Scott's diary, it has been suggested that the words were Scott's invention. Even if they were, they provided a joke expression or catch phrase to be used when a person is departing from company for whatever reason. When Trevor Griffiths came to write a TV drama series about Scott's expedition called *The Last Place on Earth* (1985), he accordingly substituted the line: 'Call of nature, Birdie.'

immoral. See ILLEGAL ~ OR FATTENING

important. See — IS TOO ~.

impossible. See DREAM THE ~ DREAM

impossible takes a little longer. See DIFFICULT ...

I must down to the seas again. In John Masefield's poem 'Sea-Fever' (1902), this line – without any 'go' – was apparently as he originally intended it, though the original manuscript is lost. In some editions of his poems (in 1923, 1938 and 1946) 'go down' was printed. No one knows why this divergence occurred, but the pull of Psalm 107 ('They that *go down to the sea* in ships, that do their business in great waters') may have been a factor. John Ireland's musical setting of the poem has the 'go'. Some editions also have a singular 'sea'.

I must follow them for I am their leader. This saying is ascribed to Alexandre Auguste Ledru-Rollin who established France's Second Republic. In the 1848 Paris revolution, he was looking from a window and said: '*Eh, je suis leur chef, il fallait bien les suivre*' [Ah well, I'm their leader, I really ought to follow them].

In a Free State. The title of a novel (1971) by V.S. Naipaul, set in a 'free state' in Africa, this the phrase had earlier been used as the title of a sketch performed on record by Peter Sellers (1959). The latter is a take-off of an interview with a drunken Brendan Behan, the playwright, and thus the title here alludes to the Irish 'Free State'.

In a Glass Darkly. This was the US title given to *Murder Reflected* (1965) by Janet Caird, and of a novel by Sheridan LeFanu (1872). *Through a Glass Darkly* was the English title of an Ingmar Bergman film (1961). Its origin is biblical: 'For now we see through a glass, darkly; but then face to face' (1 Corinthians 13:12).

in bed with my favourite Trollope. An archetypal joke, it is in this case based on a double pun. Kenneth Horne got into trouble on *Beyond Our Ken* (BBC Radio, early 1960s) when he said that there was nothing he liked more of a cold winter's evening than to curl up on the hearth-rug with Enid Blyton. In Chips Channon's diary (4 April 1943) we read: 'At Wells we went over the Cathedral, and then to the Palace where we lunched with the Bishop . . . Much talk of Barchester, "There is nothing I

like better than to lie on my bed for an hour with my favourite Trollope", the Bishop said, to everybody's consternation'. ('Trollop' has meant a 'slut, morally loose woman' since the seventeenth century.)

Incline Our Hearts. The title of this novel (1988) by A.N. Wilson comes from the Prayer Book response to the recital of the Commandments during the service of Holy Communion: 'Incline our hearts to keep this law.'

Independent Television (*or* ITV). A phrase originally coined by Norman Collins to lessen the 'commercial' connotations of the first British television channel ('the other channel'), to be funded by advertising, when it was proposed in the early 1950s. From its inception, therefore, in 1955, the commercial channel was known as ITV and was run under the supervision of the Independent Television Authority (ITA). Of course, it was no more independent of the government than the BBC, and it was also extremely *dependent* on advertisers. But the euphemistic name stuck. ITV, as such, will become 'Channel 3' in 1993, though presumably 'Independent Television' might still be used to describe the system which will continue to supply Channels 3 and 4.

industrial action. This is an odd coinage for a phrase used in British journalism for a strike or stoppage, thus denoting 'inaction', but its use was established by 1971. There even used to be the occasional 'day of action' on which no one did any work.

I Never Promised You a Rose Garden. Originally the title of a novel (1964; film US, 1970) by Joanne Greenberg/Hannah Green, the phrase then became a line in the song 'Rose Garden' (1971), and then a general expression meaning 'it was never going to be roses, roses all the way between us' or 'a bed of roses'. Fernando Collor de Mello, president of Brazil, said in a TV address (reported 26 June 1990) to his shaken countrymen: 'I never promised you a rose garden . . . following the example of developed countries, we are also cutting state spending.'

Infant Phenomenon, the. This was the stage billing of Ninetta Crummles (who has been ten years old for at least five years) in *Nicholas Nickleby* (1838–9) by Charles Dickens. The term also appears earlier in *Pickwick Papers* (Chap. 26, 1836–7) when Sam Weller says to Master Bardwell: 'Tell her I want to speak to her, will you my hinfant fernomenon?' This suggests that the phrase was in general use before or was something Dickens had picked up from an actual case. In 1837, the eight-year-old Jean Davenport was merely billed as 'the most celebrated juvenile actress of the day'. George Parker Bidder (*b* 1806) who possessed extraordinary arithmetical abilities had been exhibited round the country as a child, billed as 'the calculating phenomenon'.

Infants of the Spring. This was the title of Vol. I (1976) of Anthony Powell's autobiography TO KEEP THE BALL ROLLING. He does not indicate a source, but it is probably from Shakespeare's *Love's Labour's Lost* (I.i.101):

> Berowne is like an envious sneaping frost
> That bites the first-born infants of the spring

or *Hamlet* (I.iii.39):

> The canker galls the infants of the spring
> Too oft before their buttons be disclos'd.

in God we trust – all others pay cash. In 1942, Mencken was listing this as an 'American saying'. 'In God we trust' has been the official national motto of the United States since 1956,

when it superseded '*E Pluribus Unum*', but had been known since 1864 when it was first put on a two-cent bronze coin. (See also *D P P*.)

In Good King Charles's Golden Days. The title of a play (1939) by G.B. Shaw, about a visit of Charles II to Isaac Newton in 1680 (and introducing other well-known names from that time). It comes from the first line of the song, 'THE VICAR OF BRAY'.

Inherit the Wind. The title of a film (US, 1960) about the 1925 Scopes 'Monkey Trial'. As is explained in the film, this is from Proverbs 11:29: 'He that troubleth his own house shall inherit the wind.'

in like Flynn. Meaning 'quick in seduction' – at least, according to the Australian use of the phrase, derived from the name of Errol Flynn (*d* 1959), the Australian-born film actor. It alludes to his legendary bedroom prowess, though the phrase can also mean that a person simply seizes an offered opportunity (of any kind). Rather weakly, a US film of 1967 was entitled *In Like Flint*. Partridge/*Catch Phrases* turns up a US version which refers to Ed Flynn, a Democratic machine politician in the Bronx, New York City, in the 1940s. Here the meaning is simply 'to be in automatically' – as his candidates would have been. (See also *D P P*.)

'In Place of Strife'. This was suggested by Ted (later Lord) Castle, a journalist, as the title of the ill-fated government White Paper on industrial relations legislation put forward by his wife, Barbara Castle, in 1969. It was modelled on *In Place of Fear*, the title of a book about disarmament (1952) by Aneurin Bevan.

INRI. See INITIALS.

INITIALS (SETS OF). Sometimes we use sets of initials without really taking in what they stand for. Sometimes also, a joking interpretation of the initials has been supplied (marked here with an *):

AEIOU [the vowel sounds]: *Austria Est Imperare Orbe Universo* [All the earth is subject to Austria]; *Austria's Empire Is Ousted Entirely; etc.

BBC: British Broadcasting Corporation; *Bring Back Comedy; *Boring But Clean.

BLT: Bacon, Lettuce, and Tomato [sandwich].

BOAC: British Overseas Airways Corporation; *Better On A Camel; *Bend Over Again, Christine.

BYOB: Bring Your Own Bottle.

CIBP: Comb In Back Pocket.

CMG: Companion of St Michael and St George; *Call Me God.

DOM: *Deo, optimo, maximo* [To God, most good, most great] (on bottles of Benedictine liqueur since the sixteenth century); *Dirty Old Man.

EVA: Extra-Vehicular Activity.

FHB: Family Hold Back.

GCMG: (Knight or Dame) Grand Cross of the Order of St Michael and St George; *God Calls Me God.

GI: General Issue/Government Issue.

GWR: Great Western Railway; *Great Way Round; *God's Wonderful Railway; *Go When Ready.

HILTHYNBIMA: How I Love To Hold Your Naked Body In My Arms.

IBA: Independent Broadcasting Authority; *Interrupted By Adverts.

IHS: [Roman characters in the form of the Greek spelling of 'Jesus'].

INRI: *Iesus Nazarenus Rex Iudaeorum* [Jesus of Nazareth, King of the Jews].

JAP: Jewish American Princess.

KCMG: Knight Commander of St Michael and St George; *Kindly Call Me God.

LCT: Last Chance Trendy.

LPC: Leather Personnel Carrier [army boot].

MTF: Must Touch Flesh.

NBG: No Bloody Good.

NCD: No Can Do.

N(Q)OCD: Not (Quite) Our Class, Dear.

NQTD: Not Quite Top Drawer.

NST: Not Safe in Taxis.

PAL: Portuguese Air Lines; Pick Another Line.

PLU: People Like Us.

PITP: Pen In Top Pocket.

RAMC: Royal Army Medical Corps; *Rather A Mixed Crowd.

RKO: Radio Keith [impresario's surname] Orpheum [cinema chain].

SAS: Scandinavian Air Services; *Sex and Sandwiches; Special Air Service.

SOB: Son Of a Bitch; Standard Operational Bullshit.

SOS: [does not mean 'Save Our Souls', though the Morse Code dots and dashes do stand for SOS]; *Si Opus Sit* [in medicine, means 'give relief where necessary']; *Slip On Show; *Same Old Slush; *Short Of Sugar.

SPQR: *Senatus Populusque Romanus* [The Senate and People of Rome].

TAP: *Transportes Aèros Portugueses*; *Take Another Plane.

TIR: *Transports Internationaux Routiers.*

TWA: Trans World Airlines; *Try Walking Across; *Travel Without Arrival.

VPL: Visible Panty Line.

W(R)VS: Women's (Royal) Voluntary Service; *Widows, Virgins, and Spinsters.

WHT: Wandering Hand Trouble.

YMCA: Young Men's Christian Association; *Yesterday's Muck Cooked Again.

See also ACRONYMS, BEE GEES.

inside every fat man . . . In *Coming up for Air* (1939), George Orwell wrote: 'I'm fat, but I'm thin inside. Has it ever struck you that there's a thin man inside every fat man, just as they say there's a statue inside every block of stone?' Cyril Connolly wrote in *The Unquiet Grave* (1944): 'Imprisoned in every fat man a thin one is wildly signalling to be let out.' Katharine Whitehorn had written sometime prior to 1985: 'Outside every thin girl there is a fat man trying to get in.'

Instant Sunshine. The name of the British cabaret group (formed 1976) which sings its own humorous songs probably echoes the title of a Cambridge undergraduate revue *Instant Laughter – Just Add Water*, performed not long before. 'Instant Karma' had been the title of a John Lennon song (1970). The group was also 'instant' in that it was formed very quickly when the cabaret booked for a hospital ball failed to materialize. The first of all the many 'instant' things – coffee, soup, tan – was probably Instant Postum, the American breakfast cereal (1912). In February 1980, Margaret Thatcher told TV viewers, 'We didn't promise you instant sunshine.'

interrupted. See AS I WAS SAYING . . .

in their death they were not divided. These are the last words of *The Mill on the Floss* (1860) by George Eliot – the epitaph on the tomb of Tom and Maggie Tulliver. It is a quotation borrowed from the lament of David for Saul and Jonathan (2 Samuel 1:23): 'Saul and Jonathan were lovely and pleasant in their lives, and in their death they were not divided.'

In This Our Life. The title of a film (US, 1942) based on a novel by Ellen Glasgow about a neurotic girl who 'steals her sister's husband, leaves him in the lurch, dominates her hapless family

and is killed while on the run from the police'. The title has a certain ring to it. Is it a phrase from a prayer perhaps? Twice within a scene of Shakespeare's *As You Like It* (II.i.) we find the 'this our life' formula:

> And this our life, exempt from public haunt,
> Finds tongues in trees, books in the running brooks . . .

and:

> Most invectively he pierceth through
> The body of country, city, court,
> Yea, and of this our life.

'Into Each Life Some Rain Must Fall' (. . . 'but too much is falling in mine'). This song title by Allan Roberts and Doris Fisher (1944) comes from Longfellow's 'The Rainy Day' (1842):

> Thy fate is the common fate of all,
> Into each life some rain must fall,
> Some days must be dark and dreary.

In Which We Serve. The title of the film (UK, 1942) comes from the Prayer Book 'Forms of Prayer to Be Used at Sea': 'Be pleased to receive into thy Almighty and most gracious protection the persons of us thy servants, and the Fleet in which we serve.'

in your shell-like (ear). This phrase may be used when asking to have a 'quiet word' with someone: '(let me have a word) in your ear' is all it means, but it makes gentle fun of a poetic simile. Thomas Hood's *Bianca's Dream* (1827) has: 'Her small and shell-like ear'. *The Complete Naff Guide* (1983) has 'a word in your shell-like ear' among 'naff things schoolmasters say'.

Io. See ROMAN NAMES.

Ionic. See ODEON.

Ireland. See SNAKES IN ~.

Ireland: *A Terrible Beauty*. The title of a book (1976) by Jill and Leon Uris, it comes from 'Easter 1916' by W.B. Yeats (1921): 'A terrible beauty is born.'

Irene. See GREEK NAMES.

Iris. See GREEK NAMES.

Irish Question. This was the political/historical term for the issue of whether Ireland should be granted Home Rule by the British in the nineteenth century. W.E.GLADSTONE in the House of Commons (4 April 1893) declared: 'We say that the Irish question is the curse of this House.' Sellar and Yeatman, *1066 and All That* (1930) wrote: '[Gladstone] spent his declining years trying to guess the answer to the Irish question; unfortunately, whenever he was getting warm, the Irish secretly changed the question.'

Iron Curtain. This referred to an imaginary dividing line between East and West blocs in Europe, caused by the hard-line tactics of the Soviet Union after the Second World War. In a speech at Fulton, Missouri (5 March 1946) Winston Churchill said: 'From Stettin in the Baltic to Trieste in the Adriatic, an iron curtain has descended across the Continent.' The phrase in this context dates back to the 1920s, and Churchill had already used it in telegrams to President Truman and in the House of Commons.

iron entered into his soul, the. Meaning 'he has become embittered; anguished', it is what David Lloyd George is supposed to have said of Sir John Simon (who split away from him in the Liberal Party): 'He has sat so long upon the fence that the iron has entered into his soul.' The English title of Jean-Paul Sartre's novel *La Mort dans l'âme* (1949) was *Iron in the Soul*. The allusion is to the Prayer Book version of Psalms 105:18: 'Whose feet they hurt in the stocks: the iron entered into his soul' (which is a mistranslation of the Hebrew).

iron fist/hand in a velvet glove. This expression denotes unbending ruthlessness or firmness covered by a veneer of courtesy and gentle manners. Napoleon I is supposed to have said: 'Men must be led by an iron hand in a velvet glove' but this expression is hard to pin down as a quotation. The Emperor Charles V may have said it earlier.

Iron Lady. The nickname of Margaret Thatcher, British Prime Minister (1979–90). On 19 January 1976, she said in a speech: 'The Russians are bent on world dominance . . . the Russians put guns before butter.' Within a few days, the Soviet Defence Ministry newspaper *Red Star* had accused the 'Iron Lady' of seeking to revive the Cold War. The article wrongly suggested that she was known by this nickname in the UK at that time, although the headline over a profile by Marjorie Proops in the *Daily Mirror* of 5 February 1975 had been 'The IRON MAIDEN'.

Iron Maiden. The name of a British heavy metal group of the 1980s derived from 'The Iron Maiden of Nuremberg', a medieval instrument of torture in the form of a woman-shaped box with spiked doors which closed in on the victims.

I say it's spinach. Meaning 'nonsense', the phrase comes from a caption devised by Elwyn Brooks White for a cartoon by Carl Rose which appeared in the issue of the *New Yorker* of 8 December 1928. It shows a mother at table saying: 'It's broccoli, dear.' Her little child replies: 'I say it's spinach, and I say the hell with it.' Ross, then editor of the magazine, remembered that when

White asked his opinion of the caption the writer was clearly uncertain that he had hit on the right idea. 'I looked at the drawing and the caption and said, "Yeh, it seems okay to me", but neither of us cracked a smile.' The use of the word 'spinach' to mean nonsense stems from this (mostly in the US), as in the title of Irving Berlin's song 'I'll Say It's Spinach' from the revue *Face the Music* (1932) and the book *Fashion Is Spinach* by Elizabeth Dawes (1933).

I shall return. Forced to pull out of the Philippines by the Japanese, US Gen Douglas MacArthur left Corregidor on 11 March 1942. He made his commitment to return not while in the Philippines but during a stop at the railway station in Adelaide, South Australia, on his way to Melbourne. The slogan had been suggested to him by Carlos P. Romulo, a Filipino diplomat who later twice became his country's Foreign Minister. Of the various uses to which the phrase has been put, note that it was the British title of the US film *An American Guerrilla in the Philippines* (1950).

I sing . . . A poet's phrase which is used most notably in the first line of Virgil's *Aeneid*: '*Arma virumque cano*' [I sing of arms and the man]. Robert Herrick in *Hesperides* (1648) begins: 'I sing of brooks, of blossoms, birds, and bowers'. William Cowper begins 'The Sofa' in *The Task* (1785):

> I sing the Sofa. I who lately sang
> Truth, Hope and Charity, and touch'd
>   with awe
> The solemn chords . . .
> Now seek repose upon a humbler theme.

'One's Self I Sing', 'For Him I Sing' and 'I Sing the Body Electric' were the titles of poems by Walt Whitman. Compare also OF THEE I SING.

Island Race, the. Referring to the British, it comes from the title of a poem (1898) by Sir Henry Newbolt.

Is Paris Burning? The title of a film (US, 1965) about the liberation of Paris, it derives from Adolf Hitler's question to Jodl at Oberkommando der Wehrmacht on 25 August 1944: '*Brennt Paris?*', after the recapture of Paris by the Allies. He received no reply.

I spy strangers! This procedural phrase in the House of Commons which draws attention to the presence of outsiders with a view to having them excluded, is a bizarre device used to delay controversial legislation or to embarrass the Government by forcing a division. In this case, the 'strangers' may be members of the public in the galleries, reporters or journalists. The device can be blocked, but succeeded on 18 November 1958.

is she a friend of Dorothy? Meaning 'is he a homosexual?' and probably originating among US gays, this phrase was current by 1984. 'Dorothy' was the put-upon heroine of THE WONDERFUL WIZARD OF OZ and was played in the film by Judy Garland, a much-revered figure in male homosexual circles.

is there a doctor in the house? This is the traditional cry, usually in a theatre or at some other large gathering of people, when a member of the audience is taken ill. One suspects it dates from the nineteenth century, if not before. The *Daily Mirror* (10 October 1984) reports a member of the audience passing out during the film *1984*: 'There was a kerfuffle as people rallied round and an excited rustle as the traditional call went out: "Is there a doctor in the house?" . . . Dr David Owen, a few rows away, continued to be transfixed by the activities on the screen.' (See also *DPP*.)

179

is there life after —? Presumably derived from the question of life after death, there seems no end to the variations on this theme. On 14 October 1984, the *Sunday Times* Magazine had: 'Is there life after redundancy?' and the *Sunday People*: 'Can there be life after Wogan?' An American book with the title *Is There Life After Housework?* (1981) was written by Don A. Aslett and a film (US, 1973) had the title *Is There Sex After Marriage?*

— is too important to be left to the —. This format saying probably began with Georges Clemenceau, the French statesman, saying (possibly as early as 1886): 'War is too serious a business to be left to the generals.' (This has also been attributed to Talleyrand.) De Gaulle followed with: 'Politics is too important to be left to the politicians' (1950s?), and in 1968, Tony Benn, the Labour minister, came up with, 'Broadcasting is too important to be left to the broadcasters.' In 1990, Helmut Sihler, president of a West German chemical company, said, 'The environment is too important to be left to the environmentalists.'

I swear by Almighty God that the evidence . . . There are many versions of the oath sworn by witnesses in courts of law. A composite formed from countless viewings of fictional courts in the UK and the US, might be: 'I swear by Almighty God that the evidence I shall give will be the truth, the whole truth and nothing but the truth. **So help me God.**' The last phrase has never been part of the English court oath, however, but is common in the US. The emphatic repetition of 'the truth' is common to many countries. In Cervantes, *Don Quixote* (1605–15), we find: 'I must speak the truth, and nothing but the truth.'

is your journey really necessary? This slogan was devised in 1939 to discourage evacuated civil servants from going home for Christmas. 'From 1941, the question was constantly addressed to all civilians, for, after considering a scheme for rationing on the "points" principle, or to ban all travel without a permit over more than fifty miles, the government had finally decided to rely on voluntary appeals, and on making travel uncomfortable by reducing the number of trains.' (Norman Longmate, *How We Lived Then*, 1973)

ITALY. See ACRONYMS.

It Girl, The. The nickname of Clara Bow (1905–65), the popular actress of the silent film era who appeared in the film *It* (1928), based on an Elinor Glyn story. 'It' was the word used in billings to describe her vivacious sex appeal. Earlier. 'It' was the title of a song in *The Desert Song* (1926). Elsewhere 'it' has had more basic sexual connotations, such as survive in the expression 'to have it off'.

it is a far, far better thing that I do . . . 'than I have ever done; it is a far, far better rest that I go to, than I have ever known' continue the words at the end of *A Tale of Two Cities* (1859) by Charles Dickens. They are sometimes said to be Sydney Carton's last words as he ascends the scaffold to be guillotined, but he does not actually speak them. They are prefaced with: 'If he had given any utterance to his [last thoughts], and they were prophetic, they would have been these . . .' One editor refers to this as 'a complicated excursus into the pluperfect subjunctive'. In dramatizations, however, Carton has often actually spoken the lines – as did Sir John Martin-Harvey in the play *The Only Way* (1898) by F. Wills. One of the slogans devised by Dorothy L. Sayers in *Murder Must Advertise* (1933) was for margarine: 'It's a far, far butter thing . . .'

it'll be all right on the night. This theatrical saying dates from the late nineteenth century, at least. In the same way, a disastrous dress rehearsal is said to betoken a successful first night. Things quite often *are* better on the subsequent (first) night. It was the title of a song by Alan Melville and Ivor Novello in the musical *Gay's the Word* (1950). I T V hi-jacked the phrase for a long-running series of T V 'blooper' programmes from the 1980s onwards, *It'll Be Alright on the Night.*

it'll play in Peoria. This is a U S political saying. In about 1968, during the Nixon election campaign, John Ehrlichman is credited with having devised a yardstick for judging whether policies would appeal to voters in 'Middle America'. They had to be judged on whether they would 'play in Peoria'. He later told Safire: 'Onomatopoeia was the only reason for Peoria, I suppose. And it . . . exemplified a place, far removed from the media centres of the coasts where the national verdict is cast.' Peoria is in Illinois and was earlier the home-town of one of Sgt Bilko's men in the 1950s T V series – so was picked on humorously even then.

it never rains but it pours. John Arbuthnot, the pamphleteer, entitled a piece thus in 1726, and since then the phrase has gained proverbial status, meaning 'misfortunes never come singly'. A famous U S advertising slogan was **when it rains, it pours**, which was used from 1911 by Morton salt. The logo showed a girl, sheltering the salt under her umbrella, and capitalized on the fact that the Morton grade ran freely from salt cellars even when the atmosphere was damp. The film *Cocktail* (U S 1989), about a barman, was promoted with the line: 'When he pours, he reigns.'

I took my harp to a party '. . . but nobody asked me to play', means 'I went prepared to do something, but wasn't given the opportunity.' It comes from a song by Desmond Carter and Noel Gay, popularized by Gracie Fields and Phyllis Robins in 1933/4.

it pays to advertise. This proverbial saying almost certainly originated in the U S. It was used as the title of a play by Walter Hackett (1914; film U S, 1931) and as the title of a song by Cole Porter, alluding to a number of advertising lines current when he was a student at Yale (*c* 1912). We are probably looking for an origin in the 1870s to 1890s when advertising really took off in the U S (as in the U K). Indeed, *Benham's Book of Quotations* (1960 revision) lists an 'American saying *c* 1870': 'The man who on his trade relies must either bust or advertise', and notes that 'Sir Thomas Lipton [*d* 1931] is said to have derived inspiration and success through seeing this couplet in New York about 1875.'

it seemed like a good idea at the time. Halliwell finds this limp excuse for something that has gone awry in a film called *The Last Flight* (1931), about a group of U S airmen who remain in Europe after the First World War. One of them is gored to death when he leaps into the arena during a bullfight. Journalists outside the hospital ask his friend why the man should have done such a thing. The friend (played by Richard Barthelmess) replies: 'Because it seemed like a good idea at the time.'

it sends me! This was how young people described the effect of popular music on their souls in the 1950s. However, in a letter to *The Times* (18 December 1945), Evelyn Waugh was writing: 'He [Picasso] can only be treated as crooners are treated by their devotees. In the United States the adolescents, speaking of music, do not ask: "What do you think of So-and-so?"

They say: "Does So-and-so *send* you?" '
O E D2 finds this use in the early 1930s.

it's fingerlickin' good! This slogan
for Kentucky Fried Chicken was current
by 1958. Several songs/instrumental
numbers with the title 'Fingerlickin'
Good' appear to have been derived from
this advertising use and in 1968 Lonnie
Smith had a record album called 'Fingerlickin' Good Soul Organ'. 'Licking
good', on its own, was a phrase current
by the 1890s.

it's only rock'n'roll. Meaning 'it
doesn't matter; the importance should
not be exaggerated', the phrase comes
from the title of a Mick Jagger/Keith
Richard composition of 1974. In a 1983
Sunday Express interview, Tim Rice was
quoted as saying: 'It would be nice if [the
musical *Blondel*] is a success but I won't
be upset if it isn't. It is only rock'n'roll
after all and it doesn't really matter a
hoot.'

I T V. See INDEPENDENT TELEVISION.

It Was a Dark and Stormy Night.
The title of a book by Charles M.
Schultz, creator of the Peanuts syndicated cartoon, who gave the line to
Snoopy in his doomed attempts to write
the Great American Novel. As a scene-
setting, opening phrase, this appears to
have been irresistible to more than one
story-teller and has now become a joke.
It was used in all seriousness by the
English novelist Edward Bulwer-Lytton
at the start of *Paul Clifford* (1830). At
some stage, the phrase became part of a
children's joke game 'The tale without
an end'. Iona and Peter Opie in *The Lore
and Language of Schoolchildren* (1959)
describe the workings thus: 'The tale
usually begins: "It was a dark and
stormy night, and the Captain said to the
Bo'sun, 'Bo'sun, tell us a story,' so the
Bo'sun began . . ." And such is any
child's readiness to hear a good story

that the tale may be told three times
round before the listeners appreciate that
they are being diddled.'

I've got his pecker in my pocket.
Meaning 'he is under obligation to me',
this was one of Lyndon Johnson's earthy
phrases from his time as Senate majority
leader in Washington. 'Pecker' means
'penis' in North America (rather less so
in the U K) – though this should not
inhibit people from using the old British
expression **keep your pecker up**, where
the word has been derived from 'peck'
meaning appetite. In other words, this is
merely a way of wishing someone good
health, though *O E D2* has 'pecker'
meaning 'courage, resolution' in 1855.

Ivel, St. See SAINTS' NAMES.

ivory tower, to live in an. Meaning
'to live secluded and protected from the
harsh realities of life', the expression
comes from Sainte-Beuve writing in
1837 about the turret room in which the
Comte de Vigny, the French poet, dramatist, and novelist, worked. He described it as his *tour d'ivoire*, possibly
after the Song of Solomon 7:4: 'Thy
neck is as a tower of ivory; thine eyes
like fishpools . . .'

I was only obeying orders. The
Charter of the International Military
Tribunal at Nuremberg (1945–6)
specifically excluded the traditional
German defence of 'superior orders', but
the plea was, nevertheless, much used
and has been summed up in the catch
phrase: 'I was only obeying orders',
often used grotesquely in parody of such
buck-passing.

I would walk over my grandmother
'. . . to achieve something'. When
Richard Nixon sought re-election as U S
president in 1972, he surrounded himself with an unsavoury crew including
Charles W. Colson, a special counsel and

White House hatchet man. 'I would walk over my grandmother if necessary to get Nixon re-elected!' was his declared point of view. Subsequently convicted of offences connected with Watergate, he described in his book *Born Again* (1977) how a memo to his staff containing the offensive boast had been leaked to the press: 'My mother failed to see the humour in the whole affair, convinced that I was disparaging the memory of my father's mother . . . Even though both of my grandmothers had been dead for more than twenty-five years (I was very fond of both).' Earlier, the editor of the *Pall Mall Gazette*, W.T. Stead, famous for his exposé of the child prostitution racket, once said: 'I would not take libel proceedings if it were stated that I had killed my grandmother and eaten her.' Another earlier image often invoked was of 'selling one's grandmother'.

I Zingari. The name of this itinerant British cricket team (founded 1845) which has no ground of its own, comes from the Italian for 'the gypsies'. It is also the title of a one-act opera by Leoncavallo (1912).

J   JJ

J'accuse. The **Dreyfus Affair** in France arose in 1894 when Capt Alfred Dreyfus, who had Jewish origins, was dismissed from the army on trumped up charges of treason. Condemned to life imprisonment on Devil's Island, he was not reinstated until 1906. In the meantime, the case had divided France. The writer Emile Zola came to the defence of Dreyfus with two open letters addressed to the president of the French Republic and printed in the paper *L'Aurore*. The first, under the banner headline, '*J'accuse*', was published on 13 January 1898.

I Accuse was the title of a film (UK, 1958) about the Dreyfus case. Graham Greene entitled his short book on organized crime in the South of France *J'accuse: the Dark Side of Nice* (1982). *J'Accuse* was also the title of a film (1919) by Abel Gance, in which the dead returned *en masse* from the First World War to accuse the survivors. Another version of this film was made shortly before the outbreak of the Second World War.

Jack. See BEFORE ONE CAN SAY ~ ROBINSON; JOLLY ~; WITH ONE BOUND ~ WAS FREE.

Jackal, the. The nickname of Carlos Martinez (*b* 1949), a Venezuelan-born assassin, who has worked with various terrorist gangs in several countries. A journalistic tag, it derived from the would-be assassin of Charles de Gaulle in Frederick Forsyth's novel *The Day of the Jackal* (1971).

Jackanory. The title of the BBC TV story-telling series for children (from the 1960s onwards) comes from a nursery rhyme first recorded in 1760:

> I'll tell you a story
> About Jack a Nory,
> And now the story's begun;
> I'll tell you another
> Of Jack and his brother,
> And now my story is done.

jack in office, a. Meaning 'a self-important petty official', this term was known by 1700. Sir Edwin Landseer entitled a painting (1833): 'A Jack in Office', which shows a terrier guarding the barrow of a cat-and-dog meat salesman while four mangy, obsequious dogs eye the barrow.

Jack the Ripper. The nickname of the unknown murderer of some eight prostitutes who mutilated his victims in the East of London (1887–9). He may have been a sailor, a butcher, or even a member of the Royal Family, according to various theories. The first time the name was used was in a letter signed by a man claiming to be the killer, which was sent to a London news agency in September 1888. The murders were such a long-lasting sensation that the nickname 'Ripper' has been bestowed on subsequent perpetrators of similar crimes (compare YORKSHIRE RIPPER).

jacuzzi. The name for a type of hot tub or swirling bath used for relaxation, originally in California. In 1968, Roy Jacuzzi saw the commercial possibilities of using a portable pump invented by his relative, Candido Jacuzzi, for the treatment of rheumatoid arthritis, to make a whirlpool bath.

Janus. See ROMAN NAMES.

JAP. See INITIALS.

Jason. See GREEK NAMES.

jaywalking. Describing what a pedestrian does who ignores the rules in a motorized zone, the word is a US coinage from the early twentieth century. 'Jay' was a slang term for a rustic or countrified person, so jaywalking was inappropriate in a city where newfangled automobiles were likely to interrupt the reveries of visitors from quieter parts.

Jazz Age. Another sobriquet for the ROARING TWENTIES, this one comes from the title *Tales of the Jazz Age* (1922) by F. Scott Fitzgerald.

jeans. These hard-wearing trousers get their name from the French '*Genes*' for Genoa, in Italy, where a similar cloth to DENIM, *jene fustian*, was once made. See also LEVIS.

Jekyll and Hyde. A nickname for a person displaying two completely different characters, one respectable, the other not. After the eponymous character in R.L. Stevenson's *The Strange Case of Dr Jekyll and Mr Hyde* (1886) who, by means of a drug, can switch between the good and evil in his own nature. Consequently, a 'Jekyll and Hyde —' is

something that is a mixture of contrasting elements or switches between two such elements.

Jelly Roll Morton. This was the stage name of Ferdinand Le Menthe Morton (*d* 1941), a pianist, and one of the creators of New Orleans jazz. 'Jelly roll' is southern Negro slang for the vagina, for a virile man, and for sundry sexual activities. A jelly roll was an item of food which you would get from a baker's shop (like a Swiss Roll), and the word 'jelly' could refer to the meat of the coconut when it is still white and resembling semen.

Jemmy Twitcher. The nickname of John Montagu, 4th Earl of SANDWICH (*d* 1792) who was an extremely unpopular man, partly because of widespread corruption in the navy when he was First Lord of the Admiralty, partly because he turned against and betrayed his friend, John Wilkes. The nickname was taken from a character in John Gay's *The Beggar's Opera* (1728). He is one of Captain Macheath's associates but betrays him.

Jerome, St. See SAINTS' NAMES.

Jerry. See TOM AND ~.

jerry-built. Meaning 'built badly of poor materials', the word was in use by 1881 (which rules out any connection with buildings put up by German or 'Jerry' prisoners-of-war). There are various suggestions as to its origin: that it has to do with the walls of Jericho which came tumbling down; or that there were two brothers called Jerry who were notoriously bad builders in Liverpool; or that it has something to do with the French *jour* [day] — workers paid on a daily basis were unlikely to make a good job of things. Or that, as with the nautical term 'jury' ('jury-rigging', 'jury mast') it is something temporary.

'Jerusalem'. This is the popular title given to William Blake's preface to his poem 'Milton' (1804–8), especially in the musical setting by Hubert Parry which has, through misinterpretation of the words, acquired the status of an alternative English national anthem or patriotic song. It comes from the lines: 'And was Jerusalem builded here,/ Among these dark Satanic mills?' and 'Till we have built Jerusalem/In England's green and pleasant land'.
See also NEXT YEAR IN ~.

Jerusalem artichoke. An English misnomer, it derived possibly from a mishearing of the Italian *girasole articiocco* [sunflower artichoke].

Jesting Pilate. The title of a travel book (1926) by Aldous HUXLEY, from ' "What is truth?" said jesting Pilate, and would not stay for an answer' (Francis Bacon, 'Of Truth', *Essays*, 1625). Pilate's question to Jesus Christ is reported in John 18:38.

Jesus wept. An expletive, it comes from John 11:35 (the shortest verse in the Bible). It occurs in the story of the raising of Lazarus. Jesus is moved by the plight of Mary and Martha, the sisters of Lazarus, who break down and weep when Lazarus dies. When Jesus sees the dead man he, too, weeps. (See also *DPP*.)

Jethro Tull. This British pop group, successful in the early 1970s, takes is name from the English agriculturalist (*d* 1741) who invented the seed drill.

Jew. See WANDERING ~.

Jewel in the Crown, The. The title of this novel (1966) by Paul Scott was given to the 1984 Granada TV adaptation of the 'Raj Quartet' (of which it is the first volume). In the novel, 'The Jewel in *Her* Crown' [my italics] is the title of a

'semi-historical, semi-allegorical' picture showing Queen Victoria 'surrounded by representative figures of her Indian Empire'. Children at the school where the picture is displayed have to be told that 'the gem was simply representative of tribute, and that the jewel of the title was India herself'. The picture must have been painted *after* 1877, the year in which Victoria became Empress of India. *OED2* refers only to the 'jewels of the crown' as a rhetorical phrase for the colonies of the British Empire, and has a citation from 1901. The phrase was – and is – more generally used to describe 'a bright feature, an outstanding part' of anything. Charles Dickens, *Dombey and Son* (Chap. 39, 1844–6) has: 'Clemency is the brightest jewel in the crown of a Briton's head.' (See also *DPP*.)

jib. See CUT OF SOMEONE'S ~.

Jim. See SUNNY ~.

Jimmy Who? The question was posed when James Earl Carter (*b* 1924) came from nowhere to challenge Gerald Ford, successfully, for the US presidency in 1976. It had almost the force of a slogan. Carter's official slogan, used as the title of a campaign book and song, was **why not the best?** This came from an interview Carter had had with Admiral Hyman Rickover when applying to join the nuclear submarine programme in 1948: 'Did you do your best [at Naval Academy]?' Rickover asked him. 'No, sir, I didn't *always* do my best,' replied Carter. Rickover stared at him for a moment and then asked: 'Why not?'

jingo(ism). See BY ~!

Job's comforter. An expression used to describe one who seeks to give comfort but who, by blaming you for what has happened, makes things worse. It comes from the rebukes Job received from his friends, to whom he says: 'Miserable comforters are ye all.' (Job 16:2)

Joe Bob says check it out. 'Joe Bob Briggs' was the pseudonymous drive-in movie critic of the *Dallas Times Herald* from 1982–5. Written by John Bloom, the reviews represented the views of a self-declared red-neck. They frequently caused offence, not least because they tended to rate movies according to the number of 'garbonzas' (breasts) on display. Joe Bob had a battery of stock phrases, including **no way, José; if you know what I mean, and I think you do;** and the inevitable closing comment: 'Joe Bob says check it out.' The column eventually dropped when Briggs poked fun at efforts to raise money for starving Africans. The columns were published in book form as *Joe Bob Goes to the Drive-in* (1989).

John Birch Society. The name of an extreme right-wing, anti-communist political group in the US (founded 1958). Capt John Birch was a USAF officer who had been killed by Chinese communists in 1945 and is sometimes referred to as 'the first casualty of the Cold War' (Safire).

John Bull. See BULLDOG.

John Hancock. This US nickname for a signature or autograph derives from John Hancock, a Boston merchant, who was one of the first signatories of the Declaration of Independence in 1776. His signature is quite the largest on the document and he is variously reported to have made it that way 'so the King of England could read it without spectacles' and said: 'There! I guess King George [or John Bull] will be able to read that!'

Johnnie, I Hardly Knew You. The title of this novel (1977) by Edna O'Brien comes from the Irish folk song:

With drums and guns, and guns and drums
The enemy nearly slew ye.
My darling dear, you look so queer,
Oh, Johnny, I hardly knew ye.

Johnny, We Hardly Knew Ye was the title given to a volume (1972) by Ken O'Donnell and Dave Powers commemorating the death of President Kennedy (who was of Irish descent). *Daddy, We Hardly Knew You* was the title of a memoir (1989) by Germaine Greer.

John of Gaunt's Speech. In Shakespeare's *King Richard II* (II.i.31), the aged John of Gaunt makes a speech beginning: 'Methinks I am prophet new inspir'd' and including the line 'this royal throne of kings, this scept'red isle', to which allusion is often made. See also THE DEMI-PARADISE; THIS HAPPY BREED; THIS ENGLAND.

Johnstown Flood. See DON'T SPIT . . .

join. See IF YOU CAN'T BEAT . . .

Jolly Jack. The nickname given to the Yorkshire-born writer J.B. Priestley (*d* 1984) was an ironic coinage as he was a champion grumbler. According to his widow, it was first conceived by the staff of the *New Statesman* at a time when he had fallen into a prolonged gloomy mood (quoted in Vincent Brome, *J.B. Priestley*, 1988).

Jones. See KEEP UP WITH THE ~.

Josephine. See NOT TONIGHT ~.

jot and tittle. Meaning 'the least item or detail', the words come from St Matthew 5:18: 'Till heaven and earth pass, one jot or one tittle shall in no wise pass from the law, till all be fulfilled.' 'Jot' is *iota*, the smallest Greek letter (compare 'not one iota') and 'tittle' is the dot over the letter *i* (Latin *titulus*).

Journey's End. The title of a play (1929; film UK/US, 1930) by R.C. Sherriff, this is an old phrase, as used by Shakespeare: 'Journeys end in lovers meeting' (*Twelfth Night*, II.iii.44) or 'Here is my journey's end' (*Othello*, V.ii.268) – and Dryden: 'The world's an inn, and death the journey's end' (*Palamon and Arcite*, *c* 1700). But in his autobiography *No Leading Lady* (1968), Sherriff said: 'One night I was reading a book in bed. I got to a chapter that closed with the words: "It was late in the evening when we came at last to our Journey's End." The last two words sprang out as the ones I was looking for. Next night I typed them on a front page for the play, and the thing was done.' He does not say what the book was.

Jove. See ROMAN NAMES.

Joy in the Morning. The title of this novel (1974) by P.G. WODEHOUSE comes from Psalms 30:4: 'Weeping may endure for a night, but joy cometh in the morning.'

Jude, St. See SAINTS' NAMES.

jumbo. Meaning 'big; elephantine', it comes from the name of a notably large African elephant and the first to be seen in England. Jumbo was exhibited at the London Zoo from 1865 to 1882. It was then sold to Barnum and Bailey's circus in the US where it was killed by a railway engine in 1885.

jump over the broomstick. See BRUSH, TO LIVE OVER THE.

jungle. See BACK TO THE ~.

Juno. See ROMAN NAMES.

Jupiter. See ROMAN NAMES.

justice. See AND ~ FOR ALL.

just one of those things. Meaning 'something inexplicable or inevitable', *OED2* finds this first in John O'Hara's story *Appointment in Samarra* (1934), and in the following year as the title of the Cole Porter song which undoubtedly ensured its place in the language.

kangaroo court. The name applied to a self-appointed court which has no proper legal authority – as in the disciplinary proceedings sometimes to be found among prisoners in gaol. Ironically, *Macquarie*, the Australian dictionary, calls this an American and British colloquialism, but surely it must have something to do with the land of the kangaroo? Perhaps it alludes to the vicious streak that such animals sometimes display?

Karno, Fred. See FRED KARNO.

K C M G. See INITIALS.

keep on truckin'. An expression meaning 'you've got to persevere; keep on keeping on', it was popularized by the US underground cartoonist Robert Crumb in the 1960s. There was a song called simply 'Truckin' ' in 1935 (words by Ted Koehler and music by Rube Bloom) and *OED2* finds that 'the truck' or 'trucking' was a jerky dance that came out of Harlem in the summer of 1934. Partridge/*Catch Phrases* plumps for a suggestion that the phrase, while of Negro dance origin, came out of the great US dance marathons of the 1930s, though one of its contributors hotly disputes this. Stuart Berg Flexner discussing 'hoboes, tramps, and bums' on the US railroad in *Listening to America* (1982) probably gets nearest to the source. He defines 'trucking it' thus:

'riding or clinging to the trucking hardware between the wheels. This may have contributed to the jitterbug's use of *trucking* (also meaning to leave or move on in the 1930s) and to the 1960 students' phrase *keep on trucking*, keep moving, keep trying, keep "doing one's (own) thing" with good cheer.' (See also *DPP.*)

Keep the Ball Rolling, To. See TO KEEP THE BALL ROLLING.

keep up with the Joneses, to. Meaning 'to strive not to be outdone by one's neighbours', the expression comes from a comic strip by Arthur R. 'Pop' Momand entitled 'Keeping up with the Joneses', which appeared in the New York *Globe* from 1913 to 1931. It is said that Momand had at first intended to call his strip 'Keeping up with the Smiths' but refrained because his own neighbours were actually of that name and some of the exploits he wished to report had been acted out by them in real life.

keep your pecker up. See I'VE GOT HIS PECKER . . .

keep your powder dry. Meaning 're-main calm and prepared for immediate action; be prudent, practical, on the alert'. 'Put your trust in God, my boys, and keep your powder dry' Oliver Cromwell is reputed to have said during his Irish campaign in 1649. The remark was ascribed to him about a century after his death by one Valentine Blacker in an Orange ballad. The part about keeping one's powder dry is no more than sensible advice from the days when gunpowder had to be kept dry if it was to be used at all.

Kestrel for a Knave, A. The title of a novel (1968; filmed U K, 1969 as *Kes*) by Barry Hines, concerning a boy misfit who learns about life through training his kestrel hawk. It comes from *The Boke of St Albans* (1486), and a Harleian manuscript: 'An Eagle for an Emperor, a Gyrfalcon for a King; a Peregrine for a Prince, a Saker for a Knight, a Merlin for a Lady; a Goshawk for a Yeoman, a Sparrowhawk for a Priest, a Musket for a Holy water Clerk, a Kestrel for a Knave'.

kettle. See HERE'S A PRETTY ~ OF FISH.

kibosh on something, to put the. Meaning 'to squelch; put an end to; spoil; veto', the expression was current by 1884. It possibly comes from the Irish *cie bais*, meaning 'cap of death', but it is also known in Yiddish.

kick the bucket, to. A euphemism for 'to die', it comes from either the suicide's kicking away the bucket on which he/she is standing, in order to hang him/herself, or from the 'bucket beam' on which pigs were hung *after* being slaughtered. The odd *post mortem* spasm would lead to the 'bucket' being kicked.

Killing Fields, The. The title of a film (U K, 1984) concerning the mass murders carried out by the communist Khmer Rouge, under Pol Pot, in Cambodia between 1975 and 1978, when possibly three million were killed. The mass graves were discovered in April 1979.

In the film, the phrase is seen to refer, literally, to paddy fields where prisoners are first forced to work and where many of them are callously shot. The film was based on the article 'The Death and Life of Dith Pran' by Sydney Schanberg, published in the *New York Times Magazine* (20 January 1980), which tells of the journalist's quest for reunion with his former assistant. The article has the phrase towards the beginning, thus: 'In July of 1975 – two months after Pran and I had been forced apart on April 20 – an American diplomat who had known Pran wrote me a consoling letter. The diplomat, who had served in Phnom Penh, knew the odds of anyone emerging safely from a country that was being transformed into a society of terror and purges and "killing fields".' So it appears that the coinage is due to the unnamed diplomat. Haing S. Ngor, who played Pran in the film, wrote a book called *Surviving the Killing Fields* (1988).

William Shawcross, author of two notable books on Cambodia, says that he had never heard the phrase until the film was in preparation. It is now widely used allusively to describe any place given over to mass executions, sometimes also referred to as 'killing grounds', e.g. 'How Ridley saved his killing fields' [where a British politician went shooting game] (*Observer*, 23 July 1989); and: 'The killing fields revisited' [headline to a travel article about the battlefield of Waterloo] (*Observer*, 25 February 1990).

It is difficult to say whether there is any connection with the U S term 'killing floor', originally referring perhaps to an abattoir but in the 1960s used for a place where sexual intercourse took place.

Kilroy was here. The most widely known of graffiti slogans was brought to Europe by American G Is (*c* 1942). The phrase may have originated with James J. Kilroy (*d* 1962), a shipyard inspector in Quincy, Mass., who would chalk it up to indicate that a check had been made by him. It was also the title of a film (US, 1947).

Kind Hearts and Coronets. The title of a film (UK, 1949), about an aristocratic English family, it derives from Tennyson's 'Lady Clara Vere de Vere':

> Howe'er it be, it seems to me,
> 'Tis only noble to be good.
> Kind hearts are more than coronets,
> And simple faith than Norman blood.

kindly leave the stage. See I DON'T WISH TO KNOW THAT ...

King and Country. The title of this film (UK, 1964) comes from the First World War slogan 'Your King and Country Need You'. 'For King and Country' was the official reply to the question: 'What are we fighting for?' The alliterative linking of the two words was, however, of long standing. Francis Bacon (1625) wrote: 'Be so true to thy-selfe, as thou be not false to others; specially to thy King, and Country.' Earlier, Shakespeare (*King Henry VI, Part 2*, I.iii.157) has:

> But God in mercy so deal with my soul
> As I in duty love my king and country!

king can do no wrong, the. Sir William Blackstone (*d* 1780) in his *Commentaries on the Laws of England* wrote: 'That the king can do no wrong, is a necessary and fundamental principle of the English constitution.' Earlier, Judge Orlando Bridgeman said it in the trial of the regicides after the restoration of the monarchy in 1660. But he went on to say that ministers *could* do wrong *in the king's name* and the fault should therefore be held against the ministers. The saying also occurs in John Selden's *Table-Talk* (1689): 'The King can do no wrong, that is no Process can be granted

against him', and there is a legal maxim to the same effect, expressed in Latin: '*Rex non potest peccare.*' President Nixon tried to assert the same principle on behalf of the US presidency in his TV interviews with David Frost in May 1977: 'When the president does it, that means it is not illegal.'

Kingdom and the Power, The. See *HONOUR THY FATHER.*

king is dead – long live king!, the. This declaration was first used in 1461 upon the death of King Charles VII of France: '*Le roi est mort, vive le roi!*' Julia Pardoe in her *Life of Louis XIV* describes how that king's death was announced by the captain of the body-guard from a window of the state apart-ment: 'Raising his truncheon above his head, he broke it in the centre, and throwing the pieces among the crowd exclaimed in a loud voice, "*Le Roi est mort!*" Then seizing another staff, he flourished it in the air as he shouted, "*Vive le Roi*".' The custom ended with the death of Louis XVIII. The expression is now used allusively to denote a smooth transition of power of any sort, e.g. 'The cry went up: "The Liberal Party is dead. Long live the Liberal Party".' (*Independent*, 25 January 1988)

King of Marvin Gardens, The. This was the title of a film (US, 1972). 'Mar-vin Gardens' is to be found in Atlantic City, New Jersey, but is also one of the places (all taken from that town) fea-tured in the original US version of the Monopoly board game.

'King of the Road'. The title of a song (US, 1965) performed by Roger Miller, by way of allusion to hoboes and tramps, who have more usually been known as 'knights of the road'. The phrase 'King of the Road' had earlier been used (in the UK) as a slogan for Lucas bicycle lamps in the 1920s. In the song 'A Transport of Delight' (1957), Flanders and Swann refer to a London bus as a 'monarch of the road'.

King over the Water!, the. A toast using the name given to the exiled James II after his departure from the English throne in 1688 (also to his son and grandson, the Old Pretender and the Young Pretender). Jacobites would propose the toast while passing the glass over a water decanter.

King's life is moving peacefully towards its close, the. On Monday 20 January 1936, King George V lay dying at Sandringham. At 9.25 pm, Lord Dawson of Penn, the King's doctor, issued a bulletin which he had drafted on a menu-card. It said: 'The King's life is moving peacefully towards its close.' This was taken up by the BBC. All wireless programmes were cancelled and every quarter of an hour the announcer, Stuart Hibberd, repeated the medical bulletin until the King died at 11.55 pm.

kir. A drink made from dry white wine and a drop of *crème de cassis*, known originally as *blanc cassis*, it derives from the name of a notable imbiber rather than its inventor. Canon Felix Kir was a hero of the French Resistance and Mayor of Dijon who died in 1968 aged 92.

Kiss Kiss Bang Bang. The title of a book of film criticism (1968) by Pauline Kael, it comes from the wording on an Italian film poster seen by her: 'perhaps the briefest statement imaginable on the basic appeal of movies'.

kiss me Hardy. These were reputed to be the dying words of Horatio Nelson on HMS *Victory* at the Battle of Trafalgar in 1805, after he had been severely injured by a shot fired from a French ship. Dr Beatty, the ship's surgeon, reported that Nelson's words to Captain

KIPLING (Rudyard). The English poet and novelist (1865–1936) had a curious knack for coining popular phrases: 'white man's burden'; 'he travels fastest who travels alone'; 'the widow at Windsor'; 'palm and pine'; 'flannelled fools'; and 'East is East and West is West, and never the twain shall meet'. George Orwell noted (1942): 'Kipling is the only English writer of our time who has added phrases to the language. The phrases and neologisms which we take over and use without remembering their origin do not always come from writers we admire . . . [but] Kipling deals in thoughts that are both vulgar and permanent.'

See also BRANDY FOR THE PARSON; CAPTAINS AND THE KINGS; CAT THAT WALKS ALONE; DEADLIER THAN THE MALE; EAST OF SUEZ; FEMALE OF THE SPECIES; FLANNELLED FOOL; FOOL THERE WAS; FROM HERE TO ETERNITY; LEST WE FORGET; PREROGATIVE OF THE HARLOT; UNFORGIVING MINUTE.

Hardy were: 'You know what to do. Take care of my dear Lady Hamilton. Kiss me, Hardy.' The captain duly knelt and kissed his cheek. If Hardy did actually kiss him (a gesture that surely couldn't be mistaken), why should Nelson not have asked him to? But it has also been asserted that, according to the Nelson family, he was in the habit of saying 'kismet' (fate) when anything went wrong. It is therefore not too unlikely that he said: 'Kismet, Hardy' to his flag captain, and that witnesses misheard.

Kiss Me Kate. The title of a musical (1948; film US, 1953) by Cole Porter, about a touring company's production of Shakespeare's *Taming of the Shrew*, in which the phrase is spoken to Katherina by Petruchio (V.ii.181).

kiss of death/life. The 'kiss of death' derives from the kiss of betrayal given by Judas to Christ, foreshadowing the latter's death. In the Mafia, too, a kiss from the boss is an indication that your time is up. Compare *Kiss of Death*, the title of a gangster film (US, 1947). Safire defines the political use of the phrase as 'unwelcome support from an unpopular source, occasionally engineered by the opposition'. He suggests that Governor Al Smith popularized the phrase in 1926, when he called William Randolph Hearst's support for Smith's opponent, Ogden Mills, 'the kiss of death'. In Britain, Winston Churchill used the phrase in the House of Commons on 16 November 1948, saying that nationalization and all its methods were a 'murderous theme', and the remarks of a government spokesman about the control of raw materials, 'about as refreshing to the minor firms as the kiss of death'.

The 'kiss of life' as the name of a method of mouth-to-mouth artificial respiration was current by the beginning of the 1960s.

Kiss the Girls and Make Them Cry.
The title of a BBC TV drama series (1979), comes from the nursery rhyme (first recorded 1844):

> Georgie Porgie, pudding and pie,
> Kissed the girls and made them cry;
> When the girls came out to play,
> Georgie Porgie ran away.

kitchen. See IF YOU CAN'T STAND THE HEAT . . .

Kite. See BEING FOR THE BENEFIT OF MR ~.

Klebb, Rosa. See ROSA KLEBB.

knapsack. See EVERY SOLDIER HAS THE BATON . . .

knees. See BEES ~.

knife. See MAC THE ~.

knives. See NIGHT OF THE LONG ~.

knocker. See AS BLACK AS NEWGATE ~.

knocks. See SCHOOL OF HARD ~.

'Know Him Is to Love Him, To'.
In *The Picture of Dorian Gray*, Oscar Wilde has: 'To see him is to worship him, to know him is to trust him.' Blanche Hozier wrote to Mabell, Countess of Airlie, in 1908: 'Clementine is engaged to be married to Winston Churchill. I do not know which of the two is more in love. I think that to know him is to like him.' Thus the format existed, but as 'To Know Him Is to Love Him', it became the title of a song, written by Phil Spector in 1958. The words have a biblical ring to them, but whether Phil Spector was ever aware of the words of No. 3 in *CSSM Choruses* (3rd ed., 1928, by the Children's Special Service Mission, London) we may never know. Written by R. Hudson Pope, it goes:

> All glory be to Jesus
> The sinner's only Saviour . . .
> To know Him is to love Him,
> To trust Him is to prove Him.

Robert Burns came very close to the phrase on a couple of occasions – in 'Bonnie Lesley': 'To see her is to love her/And love but her for ever', and in 'Ae Fond Kiss': 'But to see her was to love her,/Love but her, and love for ever.' In fact, it appears that Phil Spector actually acquired the lines from his father's gravestone.

'Kookie Kookie (Lend Me Your Comb)'.
This was the title of a song

(1960), featuring Ed Byrnes and Connie Stevens. During his time with the TV cop show *77 Sunset Strip* (1958–63), Ed Byrnes played 'Kookie', a teen idol in slick shirts, tight pants, and wearing a 'wet look' hairstyle. He had a habit of constantly combing his hair, and this was celebrated in the hit song.

Krakatoa East of Java. The title of a film (US, 1968) about the volcanic eruption of 1883, which was actually *west* of Java.

Kraken Wakes, The. The title of a science fiction novel (1953) by John Wyndham, which comes from Tennyson's short poem 'The Kraken' about a mythical sea-monster, sleeping in the depths, waiting only to rise and die. The word 'kraken' is of Norwegian origin, and the monster was supposed to be of gigantic size and found off the coast of Norway.

Kronos. See GREEK NAMES.

kyrie eleison. See MASS PHRASES.

L L

labour. See DIGNITY OF ~.

lacrimae. See HINC ILLAE ~.

lacrimosa (dies illa). See MASS PHRASES.

laddie. See ACTOR ~.

lads. See HAWAE THE ~.

lady bountiful. Applied (now only ironically) to a woman who is conspicuously generous to others less fortunate than herself, the expression comes from the name of a character in George Farquhar's play *The Beaux' Stratagem* (1707).

Lady Chatterley. (1) Usually, when this name is invoked, it is not so much the particular character but the whole phenomenon of the book *Lady Chatterley's Lover* by D.H. Lawrence that is being referred to. In October 1960, when Penguin Books Ltd were cleared of publishing an obscene work in the unexpurgated edition of the novel, a landmark in publishing and sexual freedom was established. Philip Larkin, in his poem 'Annus Mirabilis' (1974), said:

> Sexual intercourse began
> In nineteen sixty-three
> . . . Between the end of the *Chatterley*
>   ban
> And the Beatles' first L P.

At the trial, the jury and the public at large were amused by the quaint and patronizing approach of Mervyn Griffith-Jones, the senior prosecuting counsel. He asked: 'Is it a book that you would have lying around in your own house? Is it a book that you would even wish your wife or your servants to read?' (2) In his *Customs and Characters* (1982), Peter Quennell describes the poet Vita Sackville-West's celebrated affair with Virginia Woolf. The former's appearance, he writes, was 'strange almost beyond the reach of adjectives . . . she resembled a puissant blend of both sexes – Lady Chatterley and her lover rolled into one, I recollect a contemporary humorist observing . . . her legs, which reminded Mrs Woolf of stalwart tree trunks, were encased in a gamekeeper's breeches and top-boots laced up to the knee.' Quennell may have been alluding to a rather more pointed remark to the effect that Vita Sackville-West looked **like Lady Chatterley above the waist and the gamekeeper below.** By 'contemporary humorist' he probably meant Cyril Connolly, who went with him on a joint visit to Vita Sackville-West at Sissinghurst in 1936. Certainly, that is the form in which Connolly's remark is more usually remembered.

Lady Godiva. See PEEPING TOM.

Lady in Red. See WOMAN IN RED.

lady preaching – like dog. A saying of Dr Johnson's which is often invoked to describe something about which there is little complimentary to say. From James Boswell's *Life of Johnson* (1791): 'Sir, a woman's preaching is like a dog's walking on his hinder legs. It is not done well; but you are surprized to find it done at all' (remark, 31 July 1763).

Lady's Not for Burning, The. The title of a play (1948) by Christopher Fry. In a speech to the Conservative Party Conference at Brighton in 1980, Mrs Margaret Thatcher came up with what is, in a sense, her most-remembered formally spoken 'line': 'To those waiting with bated breath for that favourite media catch phrase, the U-turn, I have only one thing to say. You turn if you want to. The lady's not for turning.'

Lady with a/the Lamp, The. This was the nickname given to Florence Nightingale, the philanthropist and nursing pioneer, in commemoration of her services to soldiers at Scutari during the Crimean War (1853–6). She inspected hospital wards at night, carrying a lamp – a Turkish lantern consisting of a candle inside a collapsible shade. The phrase 'lady with *a* lamp' appears to have been coined by Longfellow in his poem *Santa Filomena* (1858 – i.e. very shortly after the events described). On her death, Moore Smith & Co. of Moorgate, London, published a ballad with the title 'The Lady with *the* Lamp'. The film biography (1951), with Anna Neagle as Miss Nightingale, was called *The Lady with a Lamp* and was based on a play (1929) by Reginald Berkeley. Very occasionally one finds 'The Lady *of* a Lamp'.

lame duck. Referring to someone or something handicapped by misfortune or by incapacity, this was the name given to a defaulter on the London Stock Exchange in the nineteenth century. In William Thackeray's *Vanity Fair* (Chap. 13, 1847–8), the money-conscious Mr Osborne is suspicious of the financial position of Amelia's father: 'I'll have no lame duck's daughter in my family.' It is said that people who could not pay their debts would 'waddle' out of Exchange Alley in the City of London – hence perhaps, the 'duck'. In the US, the term has come to be applied to a president or other office-holder whose power is diminished because he is about to leave office. In *c* 1970, the term was also applied by British politicians to industries unable to survive without government financial support.

Lamia. See GREEK NAMES.

lamb. See LION SHALL LIE DOWN . . .

lamp. See LADY WITH A ~.

land. See BACK TO THE ~; ENGLISH HAD THE ~.

land flowing with milk and honey. Referring to any idyllic, prosperous situation, the origin of the phrase is to be found in Exodus 3:8: 'And I am come to deliver them out of the hand of the Egyptians . . . unto a land flowing with milk and honey.'

Land Is Bright, The. The title of a play (1941) by George S. Kaufman and Edna Ferber, it comes from 'Say Not the Struggle Naught Availeth' by Arthur Hugh Clough (*d* 1861): 'But westward, look, the land is bright.'

Land of the Long White Cloud. This is an English translation of Aotearoa, the Maori name for New Zealand.

lang may yer lum reek. 'May you have long life', in Scots dialect. A 'lum' is a chimney, 'reek' is smoke – so the phrase literally means: 'long may your chimney smoke'.

language. See COUNTRIES SEPAR-ATED BY A COMMON ~.

Laocoön. See GREEK NAMES.

Larry. See HAPPY AS ~.

Lars Porsena, or the Future of Swearing and Improper Language. The title of a short study (1920) by Robert Graves makes reference to Lord Macaulay's poem 'Horatius' from his *Lays of Ancient Rome* (1842):

> Lars Porsena of Clusium
> By the nine gods he swore . . .

LASER. See ACRONYMS.

last. See FAMOUS – WORDS.

last appeal to reason. On Friday 19 July 1940, Adolf Hitler made a speech to the Reichstag. Following, as it did, the Fall of France and the forced evacuation from Dunkirk, it somewhat surprisingly appeared to contain an offer of peace to the British. Copies of the speech were dropped over England by the Luftwaffe in a leaflet-raid on the night of 1/2 August. It was headed,

> A Last Appeal To Reason
> By
> Adolf Hitler.

last best hope of earth, the. Referring to the act of giving freedom to the slaves by the US, the phrase comes from Abraham Lincoln's Second Annual Message to Congress (1 December 1862): 'We shall nobly save or meanly lose the last, best hope of earth.'

Last Enemy, The. This was the title of a book (1942) by Richard Hillary, about his experiences as an RAF pilot when he was burned in the Battle of Britain. Its origin is Corinthians 15:26: 'The last enemy that shall be destroyed is death.'

Last Hurrah, The. The title of a novel (1956; film US, 1958) by Edwin O'Connor, about an ageing Boston-Irish politician making his last electoral foray, hence the expression 'last hurrah' for a politician's farewell.

Last of the Red-Hot Mamas, The. The stage sobriquet of Sophie Tucker, the singer, taken from the title of a song by Jack Yellen, introduced by her in 1928.

Last of the Summer Wine, The. The title of a BBC TV comedy series (1974 onwards) about a trio of old school friends in a Yorkshire village, finding themselves elderly and unemployed. According to Roy Clarke, the programme's writer (in *Radio Times*, February 1983), it is 'not a quotation, merely a provisional title which seemed to suit the age group and location. I expected it to be changed but no one ever thought of anything better.' The phrase 'last of the wine' had earlier been used to describe things of which there is only a finite amount or of which the best has gone. From a programme note by composer Nicholas Maw for *The Rising of the Moon*, Glyndebourne Festival Opera, 1970: 'In a recent television interview, Noël Coward was asked if he thought it still possible to write comedy for the stage. Did his own generation not have the "last of the wine"?' In the 1950s, Robert Bolt wrote a radio play with the title *The Last of the Wine*.

last supper. The name given to the meal shared by Jesus Christ and his disciples the night before he was crucified and thus, the origin of the Eucharist, Lord's Supper, Holy Communion, and Mass. The phrase does not appear as such in the Bible, but may have become known chiefly through its use as the English title of the painting (1494–7) by Leonardo da Vinci in Milan. This is known in Italian simply as '*La Cena*' [The Supper], though sometimes '*L'Ultima Cena*'.

late. See TOO LITTLE TOO ~.

late unpleasantness. A euphemism for the previous war or recent hostilities, it was introduced by the US humorist David Ross Locke in *Ekkoes from Kentucky* (1868). As 'Petroleum V. Nasby', he referred to the recently ended Civil War as 'the late onpleasantniss' and the coinage spread. It still survives: 'Here, for instance, is Dan Rather, America's father-figure, on the hot-line to Panama during the late unpleasantness [an invasion] . . .' (*Independent*, 20 January 1990).

Latin names. See ROMAN NAMES.

laudamus te. See MASS PHRASES.

laugh and the world laughs with you;/weep and you weep alone. Lines from a poem called 'Solitude' (1883) by Ella Wheeler Wilcox and, as *CODP* points out, an alteration of the sentiment expressed by Horace in his *Ars Poetica*: 'Men's faces laugh on those who laugh, and correspondingly weep on those who weep.' Another alteration is: '. . . weep, and you sleep alone'. In this form it was said to the architectural historian James Lees-Milne and recorded by him in his diary on 6 June 1945 (published in *Prophesying Peace*, 1977).

lay an egg, to. Although *OED2* says the source is American, Morris and other transatlantic sources give the English game of cricket as the origin of this expression meaning 'to fail'. A zero score was called a 'duck's egg' because of the obvious resemblance between the number and object. In the US in baseball, there developed a similar expression, 'goose egg'.

LCT. See INITIALS.

leader. I MUST FOLLOW THEM . . .

lead on Macduff! Meaning 'you lead the way!; let's get started!' the expression is from Shakespeare's *Macbeth* (V.iii.33): 'Lay on, Macduff;/And damn'd be he that first cries, "Hold enough!"'

There has been a change of meaning along the way. Macbeth uses the words 'lay on' defined by *OED2* as: 'to deal blows with vigour, to make vigorous attack, assail'. The shape of the phrase was clearly so appealing that it was adapted to a different purpose.

Leander. See GREEK NAMES.

leap. See GREAT ~ FORWARD; ONE SMALL STEP . . .

leave no stone unturned, to. Meaning 'to search for something with complete thoroughness', the expression was used by President Johnson in 1963 when announcing the terms of the Warren Commission's investigations into the cause of President Kennedy's assassination. Another example of its use is from an anonymously published attack on dice-playing, *c* 1550: 'He will refuse no labour nor leave no stone unturned, to pick up a penny.' Diana Rigg neatly twisted the phrase for her collection of theatrical reviews – *No Turn Unstoned* (1982).

Le Carré, John. This is the pen name of David Cornwell. In an *Observer* interview (3 February 1980), he denied what he had once said, that he took the name from a shoe shop which he saw from a bus on the way to the Foreign Office in

London: 'I couldn't convince anybody it came from nowhere.'

Leda. See GREEK NAMES.

Led Zeppelin. See under ZEPPELIN.

leg. See BREAK A ~.

Legal Decent Honest Truthful. The title of a BBC Radio 4 comedy series about advertising (late 1980s), it comes from a slogan of the Advertising Standards Authority (founded 1962), reflecting the British Code of Advertising Practice view that the essence of good advertising is that 'all advertisements should be legal, decent, honest and truthful'. Originally, this was 'Legal, *Clean*, Honest, Truthful', according to J. Pearson and G. Turner, *The Persuasion Industry* (1965).

Legal Eagles. The title of a film (US, 1986) about lawyers. Obviously the rhyme dictates the 'eagle' bit, though this might be an appropriate epithet for one playing a look-out role. Partridge/*Slang* dates it from 'late 1940s, ex US'. For many years in the 1980s, Jimmy Young on BBC Radio 2 referred to his visiting legal expert as a 'legal eagle' (and also from that, as a 'legal beagle').

legend in one's own lifetime/living legend. Both of these phrases are now clichés of tribute. On 25 August 1984, the *Guardian* reported that Tony Blackburn, a disc jockey, was writing his autobiography: '"It's called *The Living Legend – The Tony Blackburn Story*", he explains more or less tongue-in-cheek. "They call me the Living Legend at Radio One . . . I'm known as the Survivor around there."' Lytton Strachey in *Eminent Victorians* (1918) may have started it all when he wrote of Florence Nightingale: 'She was a legend in her lifetime, and she knew it . . . Once or twice a year, perhaps, but nobody

could be quite certain, in deadly secrecy, she went for a drive in the park. Unrecognised, the living legend flitted for a moment before the common gaze.' (See also *DPP*.)

leotard. The tight, one-piece garment worn by ballet dancers, acrobats, and other performers gets its name from Jules Léotard (*d* 1880), the French trapeze artist and the original of 'The Daring Young Man on the Flying Trapeze' (in the song of this title by George Leybourne, 1860).

less is more. A design statement made by the German-born architect Mies van der Rohe (*d* 1969), meaning that less visual clutter makes for a more satisfying living environment. Robert Browning had used the phrase in a different artistic context in 'Andrea del Sarto' (1855).

Lest We Forget. This was the title of the Fritz Lang film *Hangmen Also Die* (US, 1943) when it was re-issued. It comes from Rudyard KIPLING's 'Recessional' (1897), written as a Jubilee Day warning that while empires pass away, God lives on. Kipling himself, however, may have agreed to the adoption of 'Lest we forget' as an epitaph at the time of his work for the Imperial War Graves Commission after the First World War.

let my people go. The origin of this phrase is Exodus 8:1–2: 'And the Lord spake unto Moses, Go unto Pharaoh, and say unto him, Thus saith the Lord, Let my people go, that they may serve me. And if thou refuse to let them go, behold, I will smite all thy borders with frogs . . .' A soft-porn stage revue (1976) had the title *Let My People Come*.

let's get down to the (real) nitty-gritty. Generally held to be of Negro origin, this phrase meaning 'let's get down to the real basics of the problem or situation', had a particular vogue among

Black Power campaigners *c* 1963. Also in 1963, Shirley Ellis recorded a song 'The Nitty Gritty' to launch a new dance (like 'The Locomotion' before it). The opening line of the record is: 'Now let's get down to the real nitty-gritty'. Flexner 2 comments: 'It may have originally referred to the grit-like nits or small lice that are hard to get out of one's hair or scalp or to a Black English term for the anus.'

Let's Talk of Graves, of Wormsand Epitaphs.
The title of the crime novel (1975) by Robert Player comes from Shakespeare's *King Richard II* (III.ii.145).

let the cat out of the bag, to.
Meaning 'to reveal a secret', this saying derives from the trick played on unsuspecting purchasers of sucking-pigs at old English country fairs. The pig would be shown to the buyer, then put in a sack while the deal was finalized. A substitution of a less valuable *cat* would then be made, and this is what the buyer would take away. When he opened the sack, he would 'let the cat out of the bag'.

let them eat cake.
This remark is commonly ascribed to Marie Antoinette, an Austrian disliked by the French people, after she had arrived in France to marry King Louis XVI in 1770. More specifically she is supposed to have said it during the bread shortage of 1789, though no evidence exists that she did. The saying is to be found earlier in Bk 6 of Rousseau's *Confessions* (published posthumously 1781–8 but written during the 1760s). Rousseau's version, referring to an incident in Grenoble (*c* 1740), goes: 'At length I recollected the thoughtless saying of a great princess who, on being informed that the country people had no bread, replied, "Let them eat cake" [*Qu'ils mangent de la brioche*].' O D Q notes that Louis XVIII in his *Relation d'un Voyage à Bruxelles*

et à Coblentz en 1791 (published 1823) attributes to Marie-Thérèse (*d* 1683), wife of Louis XIV: 'Why don't they eat pastry? [*Que ne mangent-ils de la croûte de pâté?*].' Burnam adds that Alphonse Karr, writing in 1843, recorded that a Duchess of Tuscany had said it in 1760 or before. Later, it was circulated to discredit Marie-Antoinette. Similar remarks are said to date back to the thirteenth century, so if Marie-Antoinette *did* ever say it, she was quoting.

Let the People Sing.
The title of a novel by J.B. Priestley written so that it could first be broadcast by the B B C in (of all months) September 1939. The story, about people fighting to save a village hall from being taken over by commercial interests, was later made into a film (1942). Characters in the story write a song with the title that goes:

> Let the people sing,
> And freedom bring
> An end to a sad old story.
> Where the people sing,
> Their voices ring
> In the dawn of the people's glory.

In December 1939, a song was recorded with this title (music by Noel Gay, lyrics by Ian Grant and Frank Eyton) and featured in the 1940 revue *Lights Up*. Later, E N S A, the forces' entertainment organization, used it as its signature tune. On 1 April 1940, the B B C started a long-running series of programmes with this title – featuring 'songs of the moment, songs of the past, songs of sentiment, songs with a smile, songs with a story, songs of the people'. The phrase almost took on the force of a slogan. Angus Calder in *The People's War* (1969) wrote of Ernest Bevin, the Minister of Labour from October 1940: 'Bevinism in industry was symbolized by the growing understanding of the value of music and entertainment in helping people to work faster . . . There were the

BBC's *Workers' Playtime* and *Music While You Work* which 'progressive' management relayed over loudspeakers several times a day . . . "Let the People Sing", it might be said, was the spiritual essence of Bevinism.' The phrase appears to have originated with Priestley, though one might note the similarity to the hymns: 'Let all on earth their voices raise' and 'Let all the world in every corner sing'.

let us go forward together. A political cliché, it was chiefly made so by Winston Churchill. 'I can only say to you let us go forward together and put these grave matters to the proof' (the conclusion of a speech on Ulster, 14 March 1914); 'Let us go forward together in all parts of the Empire, in all parts of the Island' (speaking on the war, 27 January 1940); and 'I say, "Come then, let us go forward together with our united strength"' (in his BLOOD SWEAT AND TEARS speech, 13 May 1940).

Levis. The name of a specific type of blue denim JEANS originated by Levi Strauss of San Francisco. He turned up during the California Gold Rush in 1850 with a roll of tent canvas under his arm. When he ran out of canvas for making tough trousers, his brothers in New York imported the material from its French source. See also DENIM.

lie. See BR'ER FOX . . .; LION SHALL ~ DOWN . . .

Lies Damned Lies: and Some Exclusives. The title of a book (1984) by Henry Porter, about the British press, it is after the saying: 'There are lies, damn lies — and statistics.' It is often attributed to Mark Twain because it appears in his *Autobiography* (1924), but he was quoting Benjamin Disraeli.

lie travels round the world while truth is putting on her boots, a.

In November 1976, James Callaghan, when British Prime Minister, said in the House of Commons: 'A lie can be half-way round the world before the truth has got its boots on.' Since then, this saying has sometimes been ascribed to him. To Mark Twain has been attributed: 'A lie can travel half way round the world while the truth is putting on its shoes', but the true originator was the Revd C.H. Spurgeon, the nineteenth-century Baptist preacher, who said: 'A lie travels round the world while truth is putting on her boots.'

life. See ALL HUMAN ~ IS THERE; DAY IN THE ~; THERE'S ~ IN THE OLD DOG YET.

Life Begins at Forty. The title of a book (1932) by William B. Pitkin, Professor of Journalism at Columbia University, in which he dealt with 'adult reorientation' at a time when the problems of extended life and leisure were beginning to be recognized. Based on lectures Pitkin had given, the book was full of uplift: 'Every day brings forth some new thing that adds to the joy of life after forty. Work becomes easy and brief. Play grows richer and longer. Leisure lengthens. Life's afternoon is brighter, warmer, fuller of song; and long before shadows stretch, every fruit grows ripe . . . Life begins at forty. This is the revolutionary outcome of our new era . . . today it is half a truth. Tomorrow it will be an axiom.' It is certainly a well-established catch phrase. Helping it along was a song with the title by Jack Yellen and Ted Shapiro (recorded by Sophie Tucker in 1937).

life is what happens to you while you're busy making other plans. In the lyrics of John Lennon's song 'Beautiful Boy' (included on the *Double Fantasy* album, 1980), this is one of two quotations (the other is the slogan of Couéism: 'EVERY DAY AND IN EVERY

W A Y . . .'). In Barbara Rowe's *The Book of Quotes* (1979), she ascribes the saying to Betty Talmadge, divorced wife of Senator Herman Talmadge as: 'Life is what happens to you when you're making other plans.' Dr Laurence Peter in *Quotations for Our Time* (1977) gives the line to Thomas La Mance, who remains untraced.

Life of Riley, The. The title of an American T V sitcom (1949–50) with Jackie Gleason, it comes from an earlier expression meaning 'to have a high old time, wallow in luxury, live it up, without much effort – have an easy life' (with name spelt variously Riley/Reilly/O'Reilly). Partridge/*Catch Phrases* guesses *c* 1935 and suggests an Anglo-Irish origin. In 1939, US adverts for Coronado, 'the air-cooled suit that resists wrinkles', were on the theme 'A Day in the Life of Reilly' (Jim Reilly Jr). In 1919 (also in the US) there was a song by Harry Pease with the title 'My Name is Kelly' which went: 'Faith and my name is Kelly, Michael Kelly,/But I'm living the life of Reilly just the same.'

Bartlett, however, quotes from the chorus of an 1882 song with the title 'Is That Mr Reilly' and adds that this is the 'assumed origin of "the life of Riley"'. Another song sometimes mentioned as a source is from *c* 1900: 'Best of the House Is None Too Good for Reilly'.

Life's Rich Pageant. The title of the autobiography (1984) of writer and broadcaster Arthur Marshall, it is part of a longer expression. Peter Sellers as Inspector Clouseau has just fallen into a fountain in *A Shot in the Dark* (1964) when Elke Sommer commiserates with him: 'You'll catch your death of pneumonia.' Playing it phlegmatically, Clouseau replies: 'It's all part of life's rich pageant.' The origin of this happy phrase – sometimes 'pattern' or 'tapestry' is substituted – may lie in a gramophone record 'The Games Mistress',

written and performed by Arthur Marshall (*c* 1935). The monologue concludes: 'Never mind, dear – laugh it off, laugh it off. It's all part of life's rich pageant.'

Life the Universe and Everything. The title of a novel (1982) by Douglas Adams, this was blended with the title of his first work *The Hitch-Hiker's Guide to the Galaxy* (B B C Radio programme, 1978; novel, 1979) to form an advertising slogan for the *Daily Telegraph* (current 1988): 'The Earth Dweller's Guide to Life the Universe and Everything'. From an untraced source, it is used to signify absolutely everything. Compare the all-embracing title of my own *The Quote . . . Unquote Book of Love, Death and the Universe* (1980).

life wasn't meant to be easy. Malcolm Fraser, Prime Minister of Australia 1975–83, was noted, among other things, for having said: 'Life wasn't meant to be easy.' The phrase was used as the title of a book about him by John Edwards in 1977. Fraser replied to a question from *The Times* (16 March 1981), as to whether he had ever actually said it: 'I said something very like it. It's from *Back to Methuselah* (1918–20) by Bernard Shaw.' 'Life is not meant to be easy, my child; but take courage: it can be delightful.' In a Deakin lecture on 20 July 1971, which seems to have been his first public use of the phrase, Fraser made no mention of Shaw, however. It is not, anyway, a startlingly original view. In one of A.C. Benson's essays in *The Leaves of the Tree* (1912), he quotes Brooke Foss Westcott, Bishop of Durham, as saying: 'The only people with whom I have no sympathy . . . are those who say that things are easy. Life is not easy, nor was it meant to be.'

light. See THOUSAND POINTS OF ~.

light at the end of the tunnel. The phrase used for a glimmer of hope, usually in politics. *OED2*'s earliest citation is from 1922, but in a non-political context. In June 1983, the diarist of *The Times* tried to find the first *Tory* politician to have spotted this phenomenon. Stanley Baldwin in 1929 was the first, it seems, and Neville Chamberlain spotted it again at a Lord Mayor's banquet in 1937. The old expression was later dusted down and invoked with regard to the Vietnam War. (See also *DPP*.)

Light of Common Day, The. See RAINBOW COMES AND GOES.

'Light of the World, The'. The title of a painting (1854) by Holman Hunt, showing Jesus Christ with a lantern, knocking on a door in a tree (to represent the soul). It is also the title of an oratorio (1873) by Sir Arthur Sullivan, and comes from John 8:12: 'Then spake Jesus unto them, saying, I am the light of the world: he that followeth me shall not walk in darkness, but shall have the light of life.'

like a red rag to a bull. Meaning 'obviously provocative'. Christy Brown in *Down All the Days* (Chap. 13, 1970) has: 'Sure they [breasts] only get you into trouble, woman dear . . . Showing them off to a man is like waving a red cloth at a bull.' There is no example of its use before 1873, but John Lyly in *Euphues and His England* (1580) has: 'He that cometh before [a bull] will not wear . . . red', based on the belief that bulls are aggravated by the colour. In fact, they are colour blind. In all probability, if they do react, it is simply the *movement* of material in a bright colour that causes the animal to charge. Charles Dickens in *Bleak House* (Chap. 43, 1853) seems to allude to the saying in: 'You know my old opinion of him . . .

An amiable bull, who is determined to make every colour scarlet.'

like coming home. Meaning 'what is appropriate for one; what one feels completely natural doing'. Winston Churchill said at a Conservative rally in 1924 (having left the Liberal Party): 'It's all very strange for [his wife]. But to me, of course, it's just like coming home.' Other examples are from the *Independent* (31 October 1989): 'For Douglas Hurd, it was just like coming home . . . [he] took his place behind the Foreign Secretary's desk'; and from the *Independent on Sunday* (17 June 1990): [Melvyn Bragg] 'Actually I found arriving at the BBC was like arriving home . . . It was a job I knew I wanted to do.'

like rats deserting/leaving a sinking ship. This comes from the English proverb to the effect that 'rats desert/forsake/leave a falling house/sinking ship'. *ODP* finds an example of the 'house' version in 1579 and of the 'ship' (in Shakespeare) in 1611. Brewer adds: 'It was an old superstition that rats deserted a ship before she set out on a voyage that was to end in her loss.' (See also *DPP*.)

lilacs. See WHEN ~ LAST IN THE DOORYARD . . .

Lilies of the Field. The title of a film (US, 1963) from a novel by William E. Barrett, which alludes to Matthew 6:28: 'Consider the lilies of the field, how they grow; they toil not, neither do they spin.'

lily. See GILD THE ~.

Lily-White Boys, The. See GREEN GROW THE RUSHES.

limey. An old American and then Australian term for 'a Britisher', deriving from the free issue of lime-juice to British sailors to protect them from scurvy, in the eighteenth century. It is short for 'lime-juicer'.

line. See THIN RED ~.

lion. See MARCH COMES IN LIKE A ~.

Lion Is in the Streets, A. The title of a film (US, 1953), based on the Huey Long story, and alluding to Shakespeare's *Julius Caesar*, in which there occur the lines:

> Against the Capitol I met a lion,
> Who glaz'd upon me, and went surly by'
>
> (I.iii.20)

and:

> A lioness hath whelped in the streets,
> And graves have yawn'd and yielded up
> their dead
>
> (II.ii.17).

lion shall lie down with the lamb, the. This is a simplified version of Isaiah 17:6: 'The wolf also shall dwell with the lamb, and the leopard shall lie down with the kid; and the calf and the young lion and the fatling together.'

lions led by donkeys. A German description of British soldiery in the First World War usually ascribed to Erich Ludendorff (d 1937), the German general. Alan Clark in a book called *The Donkeys* (1961) quotes the following exchange which suggests, however, that Ludendorff had only a half-share in the coinage:

> *Ludendorff:* The English soldiers fight like lions.
> *Hoffman:* True. But don't we know that they are lions led by donkeys.

Max Hoffman succeeded Ludendorff as Chief of the General Staff in 1916. Clark gives the source as the memoirs of Field Marshal von Falkenhayn – but the exchange remains untraced.

lips. See READ MY ~.

lips are sealed, my. Meaning 'I am not giving anything away', and deriving originally perhaps, from the expression to seal up *another* person's lips, mouth, to prevent him betraying a secret (*OED2* has this by 1782). 'My lips are not yet unsealed' was said during the Abyssinia Crisis of 1935 by the British Prime Minister, Stanley Baldwin. He was playing for time, with what he subsequently admitted was one of the stupidest things he had ever said. The cartoonist Low portrayed him for weeks afterwards with sticking plaster over his lips.

lit. See FLEET'S ~ UP.

little. See TOO ~ TOO LATE.

little black book. There have been many 'black books' over the centuries containing authoritative records or lists of people in disgrace. The 'little' ones, however, are now more usually those containing lists of girls' telephone numbers such as might be kept by a promiscuous male. 'Guess you got back to my name in your little black book' is a line from the song 'Running Out of Fools' (by K. Rogers and R. Ahlert) recorded by Aretha Franklin in 1964. But note, from the *Independent* (30 June 1990): 'Never the most elegant or fastidious of [football] defenders, Jack [Charlton] kept an infamous little black book for noting opponents he "owed one".'

little black dress. Referring to a simple frock suitable for most social occasions and sometimes abbreviated to 'lbd', it was popular from the 1920s and 30s onwards. The original, a creation of Coco Chanel, was sold at auction for £1500 in 1978. In Britain, the designer Molyneux perfected the dress as the ideal cocktail party wear of the between-the-wars years.

Little Egypt. The stage name of Catherine Devine who made the Coochee-Coochee dance famous at the Chicago Colombian Exposition in 1893. She had a tendency to dance in the nude, and was celebrated in the song 'Little Egypt' (1961) by Lieber and Stoller, sung by The Coasters and Elvis Presley. *Little Egypt* was also the title of a film (US, 1951) about a girl posing as an Egyptian princess at the Chicago World Fair.

Little Foxes, The. The title of the play (1939; film US, 1941) by Lillian Hellman comes from the Song of Solomon 2:10: 'Take us the foxes, the little foxes, that spoil the vines.'

little gentleman in (black) velvet!, the. This was a Jacobite toast (compare KING OVER THE WATER!) to the mole whose hillock caused King William III's horse to stumble in 1702. William died soon afterwards, partly from the injuries sustained.

Little Learning, A. This title for a volume of Evelyn Waugh's autobiography (1964) comes from Alexander Pope's *An Essay on Criticism* (1711):

> A little learning is a dang'rous thing;
> Drink deep, or taste not the Pierian
> Spring

[Pieria, home of the Greek Muses].

'Little Man You've Had a Busy Day'. The title of a song (1934) by Sigler, Hoffman and Wayne has nothing to do with Frances Day, the actress and variety artiste, to whom Bud Flanagan is supposed to have said: 'Little Day, you've had a busy man.'

Little Nell. This was the nickname of Nell Trent, the child heroine of *The Old Curiosity Shop* (1840–1) by Charles Dickens. She attempts to look after her inadequate grandfather and to protect him from various threats, but her

strength gives out. According to one account, 'Does Little Nell die?' was the cry of 6000 book-loving Americans who hurried to the docks in New York to ask this question of sailors arriving from England. Another version is that it was longshoremen demanding 'How is Little Nell?' or 'Is Little Nell dead?' As the novel was serialized, they were waiting for the arrival of the final instalment of the magazine to find out what had happened to the heroine. Little Nell's death came to typify the heights of Victorian sentimental fiction. Oscar Wilde later commented: 'One must have a heart of stone to read the death of Little Nell without laughing.'

little old lady from Dubuque, the. When Harold Ross founded the *New Yorker* in 1925, he said it would 'not be edited for the old lady from Dubuque'. Dubuque, Iowa, thus became involved in another of those yardstick phrases like IT'LL PLAY IN PEORIA on account of it being representative of MIDDLE AMERICA.

Little Orphan Annie. The name of the irrepressible, red-haired waif, succoured by millionaire Daddy Warbucks. She is also the heroine of a comic strip created by Harold Gray (in the US, from 1938).

little red book. This is the name given to the collected thoughts of Chairman Mao Tse-tung which were published in this form (and brandished by Red Guards) during the Chinese Cultural Revolution of the 1960s. An English-language version was published as *Quotations from Mao Tse-tung* by the Foreign Language Press, Peking (1972).

Little Touch of Schmilsson in the Night, A. This was the title of a record album (US, 1973) by the singer Nilsson. Nilsson/Schmilsson is a Yiddish reduplication of no great meaning (as in the joke 'Oedipus, Schmoedipus – what does it matter so long as he loves his mother?'). Nilsson's first name is 'Harry', which takes us back to the Chorus before Act IV of Shakespeare's *King Henry V*. Referring to the king's wandering about, disguised, in the English camp on the eve of the Battle of Agincourt, the Chorus says,

> Behold, as may unworthiness define,
> A little touch of Harry in the night.

living. See GREATEST ~ . . . ; LEGEND IN ONE'S LIFETIME; MACHINE FOR ~.

Livingstone, Dr. See DR ~.

Llareggyb. The name of the Welsh fishing village which is the setting of *Under Milk Wood* (1954) by Dylan Thomas. It was originally 'Llareggub' (and the provisional title of the radio play) until somebody read the name backwards. Subsequently, David Holbrook wrote a study of the poet entitled *Llareggub Revisited* (1962).

Lloyd George Knew My Father. The title of a play (1972) by William Douglas-Home. Even before David Lloyd George's death in 1945, Welsh people liked to claim some affinity with the Great Man. By the 1950s, members of Welsh Rugby Clubs did so by singing the words: 'Lloyd George knew my father, my father knew Lloyd George' to the strains of 'Onward Christian Soldiers', which they neatly fit. In Welsh legal and Liberal circles the credit for this coinage has been given to Tommy Rhys Roberts QC (*d* 1975) whose father did indeed know Lloyd George, having set up a London practice with him in 1897.

Lobby Lud. See YOU ARE MR ~ . . .

local difficulties. See LITTLE ~.

lock stock and barrel. Meaning 'the whole lot', this term comes to us from the armoury where the lock (or firing mechanism), stock and barrel are the principal parts of a gun.

Log Cabin to White House, From. The title of a biography of President James Garfield (1881) by Revd William Thayer. Earlier presidents Henry Harrison and Abraham Lincoln had used the log cabin as a prop in their campaigns. Subsequently all presidential aspirants have sought a humble 'log cabin' substitute to help them on their way.

London. See SWINGING ~; GREAT WEN.

Lonely Are the Brave. The title of a film (US, 1962), based on a novel by Edward Abbey called *Brave Cowboy*. Apparently neither a quotation nor an allusion.

Lonely Sea and the Sky, The. The title given to the memoirs (1964) of Sir Francis Chichester, the solo yachtsman. It comes from 'Sea-Fever' (1902) by John Masefield: 'I MUST DOWN TO THE SEAS AGAIN, the lonely sea and the sky.'

long. See NIGHT OF THE ~ KNIVES.

Long and the Short and the Tall, The. The title of the play (1959; film UK, 1960) by Willis Hall comes from the song 'Bless 'em all' (1940) by Jimmy Hughes and Frank Lake: 'Bless 'em all, bless 'em all,/The long and the short and the tall' (or its parody version 'Sod 'Em All'). The film's US title was *Jungle Fighters*.

Long Arm, The. The title of a film (UK, 1956 – *The Third Key* in the US) about a Scotland Yard superintendent solving a series of robberies. It comes from the idea that the law is an arm and that it is a long one, rooting out the guilty however far away they may hide. Charles Dickens in *The Pickwick Papers* (1836–7) has: 'Here was the strong arm of the law, coming down with twenty gold-beater force', and in *The Mystery of Edwin Drood* (1870): 'The arm of the law is a strong arm, and a long arm.' In Shakespeare's *King Richard II*, Aumerle is quoted as saying (IV.i.11):

> Is not my arm of length,
> That reacheth from the restful English court
> As far as Callice, to mine uncle's head?

It is possibly a development of the proverb 'Kings have long arms/hands/many ears and many eyes', found by *O D P* in Ovid, and in English by 1539.

long chalk, not by a. Meaning 'not by any means', this probably refers to the method of making chalk marks on the floor to show the score of a player or team. A 'long chalk' would mean a lot of points, a great deal.

Longest Pleasure, The. The title of a novel (1986) by Anne Mather, it comes from Byron, *Don Juan* (1819–24):

> Now hatred is by far the longest pleasure:
> Men love in haste, but they detest at leisure.

Long Hot Summer, The. The title of a film (US, 1958) based on the stories of William Faulkner and using a phrase formulated by him in 1928. There was also a spin-off T V series (1965–6). From this we get the cliché of journalism, first aired following the 1967 riots in the Black ghettos of eighteen US cities, notably Detroit and Newark. In June of that year, Revd Dr Martin Luther King Jr warned: 'Everyone is worrying about the long hot summer with its threat of riots. We had a long cold winter when little

was done about the conditions that create riots.' Claud Cockburn's *I, Claud* (1967) has a chapter entitled 'Long Cold Winter'. (See also *D P P*.)

long in the tooth. Older people suffer from receding of the gums and their teeth appear to be longer. The same probably applies to horses, so compare LOOK A GIFT HORSE IN THE MOUTH.

LONG TITLES. See under MARAT/SADE.

loo. A euphemism for lavatory, established in well-to-do British society by the early twentieth century and swept into general middle-class use after the Second World War. Of the several theories, perhaps the most well known is that the word comes from the French *gardez l'eau* [mind the water], dating from the days when chamber-pots were emptied out of the window into the street. Professor A.S.C. Ross, however, who examined the various options in a 1974 edition of *Blackwood's Magazine* favoured a derivation, 'in some way which could not be determined', from *Waterloo*. At one time people probably said: 'I must go the water-closet' and, wishing not be explicit, substituted 'Water-loo' as a weak little joke. The name 'Waterloo' was there, waiting to be used, from 1815 onwards – just as it was in MEET ONE'S WATERLOO.

look a gift horse in the mouth, to. Meaning 'to spoil an offer by enquiring too closely into it', the proverb alludes to the fact that the age of horses is commonly assessed by the length of their teeth. If you are offered the gift of a horse, you would be ill-advised to look in its mouth. You might discover information not to your advantage.

Look Homeward Angel. The title of a novel (1929) by Thomas Wolfe, it comes from 'Lycidas' (1637) by John Milton:

'Look homeward, Angel, now, and melt with ruth.'

looking. See HERE'S ~ AT YOU KID.

Look Stranger. The title of a BBC TV documentary series (1976) derives from W.H. Auden's, 'Look, Stranger' (1936): 'Look, stranger, at this island now.' Another version of the poem has 'on this island'. *Look, Stranger* was the UK title of Auden's second book of poems; the US title was *On This Island*. In 1963, the title of the BBC Radio Reith Lectures by G.M. Carstairs was *This Island Now*.

looney tune. Meaning 'mad person' or, as an adjective, 'mad'. President Reagan commented on the hijacking of a US plane by Shi-ite Muslims: 'We are not going to tolerate these attacks from outlaw states run by the strangest collection of misfits, looney tunes, and squalid criminals since the advent of the Third Reich' (8 July 1985). The reference is to the cinema cartoon comedies called Looney Tunes which have been produced by Warners since the 1940s.

Lord Haw-Haw. The nickname of William Joyce who broadcast Nazi propaganda from Hamburg during the Second World War – speaking in a cultured voice which the *Daily Express* radio correspondent ridiculed with this name. Joyce was found guilty of treason after the war and hanged in 1946. The US equivalents were **Tokyo Rose**, the nickname given to the US-born Iva Ikuko Toguri D'Aquino who broadcast to US servicemen over Japanese radio advising them to give up the unequal struggle; and **Axis Sally**, a US-born Nazi broadcaster who urged US withdrawal from the Second World War. She has been variously identified as Mildred Gillars and Rita Louise Zucca.

Lord of the Flies. The title of the novel (1954; films UK, 1963, US, 1990) by William Golding comes from the literal Hebrew meaning of the word 'Beelzebub', the devil.

lord of words. A complimentary title bestowed upon a 'master of language', it was used to describe the broadcaster, Sir Huw Wheldon, and the playwright, Samuel Beckett, at their deaths in 1986 and 1989, respectively.

Lord's Prayer. The translation, as found in the Prayer Book service of Morning Prayer (which differs slightly from that in Matthew 6: 9–13) has provided the following titles: *Give Us This Day* (film UK 1949), *Our Daily Bread* (film US 1934), THE KINGDOM AND THE POWER, and THE POWER AND THE GLORY. *Deliver Us from Evil* is the title of a book (1953) by Hugh Desmond, and *Thine Is the Kingdom* of unrelated books by Heini Arnold and Paul Marshall.

lose a battle but not the war, to. Charles de Gaulle in his proclamation dated 18 June 1940 and circulated among exiled Frenchmen, said: '*La France a perdu une bataille! Mais la France n'a pas perdu la guerre*' [France has lost a battle, but France has not lost the war!]' Earlier, on 19 May 1940, Winston Churchill, in his first broadcast to the British people as Prime Minister, had said: 'Our task is not only to win the battle – but to win the war' (meaning the battle *for* Britain, which he was later to call the BATTLE OF BRITAIN). In 1962, Harold Macmillan used the formula after a by-election defeat at Orpington: 'We have lost a number of skirmishes, perhaps a battle, but not a campaign.'

lost generation. This phrase refers to the large number of promising young men who lost their lives in the First World War, and also, by extension to those who were not killed in the war but who were part of a generation thought to have lost its values. Gertrude Stein recorded the remark made by a French garage owner in the Midi just after the war. Rebuking an apprentice who had made a shoddy repair to her car, he said: 'All you young people who served in the war [are from] a lost generation' [*une génération perdue*]. Ernest Hemingway used this as the epigraph to his novel THE SUN ALSO RISES (1926) and referred to it again in A MOVEABLE FEAST (1964).

love. See GREATER ~ HATH NO MAN . . .; 'TIS ~ 'TIS ~.

Love among the —. A format used in titles, especially 'among the ruins'. The notion of love among classical ruins seems hauntingly appealing, rather as do the reminders of time and decay in Arcadia (compare 'ET IN ARCADIA EGO'). Evelyn Waugh entitled one of his shorter novels *Love among the Ruins: A Romance of the Near Future* (1953), and Angela Thirkell used the title for a novel about the aristocracy in the post-war period, in 1948 (of which the title only was borrowed in 1974 for a TV movie, with Laurence Olivier and Katharine Hepburn, about an elderly actress who turns to a former lover for legal counsel in a breach of promise case). Earlier than this, there is the painting by Sir Edward Burne-Jones where the lover and his lass embrace among fallen pillars and stones with mysterious inscriptions on them, hemmed in by the briar rose which rambles over all, and search for the way to Cythara where in the end they must separate. The subject comes from the Italian romance *Hypnerotomachia* (1499). The painting dates from 1870–3 and hangs in Wightwick Manor. Earlier still is Robert Browning's poem with the title in *Men and Women* (1855). 'And found young Love among the roses' is a line from an old ballad alluded to by Charles Dickens in *Barnaby Rudge* (1841), and *Love among the Haystacks* is the title of a collection of short stories (1930) by D.H. Lawrence.

loved. See WHOEVER ~ THAT ~ NOT . . .

Love in a —. This format is used in several titles and phrases. William Thackeray refers to 'love in a cottage' in *Pendennis* (1848–50) and Keats has 'love in a hut' in 'Lamia' (1820). Both these deal with the romantic fantasy of love in poverty. *The Comical Revenge, or Love in a Tub* was the title of a play by George Etherege (1664); *Love in a Wood*, a play by William Wycherley (1671); and *Love in a Village*, a comic opera by Isaac Bickerstaffe (1762). *Love in a Cold Climate*, the novel (1949) by Nancy Mitford caused Evelyn Waugh to write to her (10 October): '[It] has become a phrase. I mean when people want to be witty they say I've caught a cold in a cold climate and everyone understands.' Earlier, Robert Southey, the poet, writing to his brother Thomas (28 April 1797) had said: 'She has made me half in love with a cold climate.' *Love in a Mist* (from the popular name for the misty-blue plant *Nigella*) was the title of a silent film (1916) with two popular British stars, Stewart Rome and Alma Taylor, and of several popular songs, especially one in the musical comedy *Dear Love* (London, 1929). It was also the title of a play by Kenneth Horne (the writer not the comedian), presented in London (1942). This last is a light comedy about two couples who find themselves fog-bound in a duck farm on Exmoor. The film *Love in a Goldfish Bowl* followed in the US (1961).

209

Love Is a Many-Splendoured Thing. The title of this novel (1952; film US, 1955) by Han Suyin alludes to Francis Thompson's posthumously published poem, *The Kingdom of God* (1913):

> The angels keep their ancient places;
> Turn but a stone and start a wing!
> 'Tis ye, 'tis your estranged faces,
> That miss the many-splendoured thing.

love means never having to say you're sorry. This saying was used in the film, in the book, and as a promotional tag for the film *Love Story* (1970). Ryan O'Neal says it to Ray Milland, playing his father-in-law. He is quoting his student wife (Ali MacGraw) who has just died young. Eric Segal, who wrote the script, also produced a novelization of the story in which the line appears as the penultimate sentence, in the form 'Love means *not ever* having to say you're sorry.' A graffito (quoted 1974) stated: 'A vasectomy means never having to say you're sorry.' The film *The Abominable Dr Phibes* (UK 1971) was promoted with the slogan: 'Love means never having to say you're ugly.'

love me love my dog. Meaning 'if you are inclined to take my side in matters generally, you must put up with one or two things you don't like at the same time', it comes from one of St Bernard's sermons: '*Qui me amat, amat et canem meum*' [Who loves me, also loves my dog]. Alas, this was a different St Bernard to the one after whom the breed of Alpine dog is named. It was said (or quoted) by St Bernard of Clairvaux (*d* 1153) rather than St Bernard of Menthon (*d* 1008).

Love Pain and the Whole Damn Thing. The English title of a collection (1989) of four short stories by the German writer and film director, Doris Dorrie. Earlier, in 1972, there had been Alan J. Pakula's US film with the title *Love and Pain and the Whole Damn Thing*.

low. See BR'ER FOX HE LAY ~.

L P C. See INITIALS.

Lucky Jim. The title of a comic novel (1953) by Kingsley Amis, about a hapless university lecturer, Jim Dixon, comes from a US song by Frederick Bowers (*d* 1961) and his vaudeville partner Charles Horwitz (though it is usually ascribed to Anon). It tells of a man who has to wait for his childhood friend to die before he can marry the girl they were once both after. Then, married to the woman and not enjoying it, he would rather he was dead like his friend: 'Oh, lucky Jim, how I envy him.'

Lucy, St. See SAINTS' NAMES.

lugger. See ONCE ABOARD THE ~.

Luke, St. See SAINTS' NAMES.

lum. See LANG MAY YER ~ REEK.

lunatic fringe. Referring to a minority group of extremists, usually in politics, the phrase gained currency after Theodore Roosevelt said in 1913: 'There is apt to be a lunatic fringe among the votaries of any forward movement.'

lunch. See NO SUCH THING AS A FREE ~.

lush. Meaning 'a drunk', this term seems to have originated in the US by the beginning of the nineteenth century, building on the English origins of a slang word for 'beer'. In the eighteenth century, there was a London actors' drinking club called 'the City of Lushington'. There may also have been a London brewer called Lushington, and

Dr Thomas Lushington (*d* 1661), chaplain to Bishop Corbet, was a noted tippler.

lux aeterna. See MASS PHRASES.

Lycaon. See GREEK NAMES.

Lyceum. See under ODEON.

lynch, to. Meaning 'to administer summary justice by executing', there are several eponymous candidates for this verb. Most likely is Colonel William Lynch (*d* 1820) of Pittsylvania County, Virginia, who certainly took the law into his own hands, formed a vigilante band and devised what became known as the Lynch Laws. However, as Burnam 2 points out, even he did not really behave in the way 'to lynch' came to mean. There was also an old English word *linch*, meaning punishment by whipping or flogging, and this was sometimes imposed by the 'Lynch' courts of Virginia.

Lyons. See BUTCHER OF ~.

Lysistrata. See GREEK NAMES.

Macbeth. See SCOTTISH PLAY.

McCoy. See REAL ~.

Macduff. See LEAD ON ~.

MacGuffin. This was the name given by the film director Alfred Hitchcock to the distracting device, the red herring, in a thriller upon which the whole plot turns but which, in the end, has no real relevance to the plot or its solution. For example, the uranium in *Notorious* (1946) turns out to be less important than the notorious woman falling for the US agent.

machine for living in. This was Le Corbusier's description of the purpose of a house: '*La maison est une machine à habiter.*' The phrase first appeared in *Vers une Architecture* (1923), but in *Almanach de l'Architecture* (1925), he added that the house is, secondly: 'a place intended for meditation and thirdly a place whose beauty exists and brings to the soul that calm which is indispensable'.

mackintosh. The original waterproof coat is named after Charles Macintosh (*d* 1843). He patented a method of binding together two layers of fabric with indiarubber dissolved in naphtha. Later waterproof garments tended to be treated with silicone which allows air to permeate the fabric, making it more comfortable to wear. The word is now used loosely – with or without the 'k', or as 'mac' – to describe any raincoat.

Mac the Knife. The English name of the character Mackie Messer in *The Threepenny Opera* (1928) by Brecht and Weill, derived from the name MacHeath in Gay's *The Beggar's Opera* (1728). It is now a nickname applied to people with a name beginning Mac/Mc who behave ruthlessly, e.g. Harold Macmillan at the time of the NIGHT OF THE LONG KNIVES, and Ian MacGregor at the National Coal Board when making large-scale redundancies in the 1980s.

mad. See DON'T GET ~ . . .

mad as a hatter. The Hatter in *ALICE IN WONDERLAND* (1865) is not described as the *Mad* Hatter, though he is undoubtedly potty. His behaviour encapsulates a once-popular belief that people working as hat-makers could suffer brain damage by inhaling the nitrate of mercury used to treat felt. In fact, Lewis Carroll may not have been thinking of a hatter at all but rather of a certain Theophilus Carter, a furniture dealer of Oxford, who was notable for the top hat he wore, was also a bit potty and known as the Mad Hatter. And it is the March Hare who is marginally more mad (after the much older expression 'mad as a march hare'). Morris favours a derivation from the Anglo-Saxon word *atter*, meaning poison (and closely related to the adder, the British snake whose bite can cause fever). On the other hand, by 1609, there was a phrase 'mad as a weaver' which takes us back to the peculiarity of specific tradespeople.

mad as hell and I'm not going to take this any more, I'm.

Peter Finch played a TV pundit-cum-evangelist in the film *Network* (1976) who exhorted his viewers to get mad: 'I want you to get up right now and go to the window, open it and stick your head out and yell: I'm as mad as hell, and I'm not going to take this any more!' In 1978, Howard Jarvis, the social activist and author of California's Proposition 13 pegging taxes, campaigned with the slogan: 'I'm mad as hell and I'm not taking any more.' Fifty-seven percent voted to reduce their property taxes. Jarvis entitled his book *I'm Mad as Hell* and credited Paddy Chayevsky, the screenwriter, with the coinage.

madeleine.

A small fancy sponge cake, which in the first volume of *A La Recherche du Temps Perdu* by Marcel Proust triggers off memories of youth. In *Du Côté de Chez Swann* (1913), the author/narrator is reminded of the taste of a little crumb of madeleine which 'on Sunday mornings at Combray' his Aunt Leonie used to give him: 'Dipping it first in her own cup of real or of lime-flower tea'.

Mad Monk.

The nickname of Grigori Efimovich (*d* 1916), otherwise known as Rasputin. Of Siberian peasant origin, he was famous for his debauchery, and the influence he exercised over Tsarina Alexandra. He was murdered by a group of Russian noblemen. *Rasputin the Mad Monk* was the title used in the UK for the 1932 US picture *Rasputin and the Empress*.

Mad Mullah.

This nickname was shared by two Mohammedan leaders of revolt against British rule: one, the 'Mad Mullah of Swat' in the Indian uprisings of 1897–8, the other, the better-known Mohammed bin Abdullah who created terror for tribes friendly to the British in Somaliland (1899–1920). In the plural, the name was reapplied to Iranian religious leaders in the turmoil following the fall of the Shah (1979) and the rise of Ayatollah Khomeini.

Maecenas.

See ROMAN NAMES.

Mae West.

The nickname for an inflatable life-jacket issued to the services in the Second World War, it gets its name from the curvaceous American film star, Mae West. It was in use by May 1940.

'Maggie May'.

This character in a Liverpool song, dating from at least 1830, is a prostitute who steals sailors' trousers, but: 'a policeman came and took that girl away./For she robbed a Yankee whaler,/She won't walk down Lime Street any more.'

A number of groups (including the Beatles) revived the song at the time of Liverpool's resurgence in the early 1960s. Lionel Bart and Alun Owen wrote a musical based on her life and called *Maggie May* in 1964. Margaret Thatcher unwisely alluded to the song in April 1983 when wishing to appear coy about whether she would be calling a general election soon: 'Some say Maggie may, or others say Maggie may not. I can only say that when the time comes, I shall decide.'

Magical Mystery Tour.

This was originally the title of a TV film (UK, 1967) by the Beatles, but has subsequently become the name given to a winding journey, by a driver not knowing where he is going. The simple 'mystery tour' is a journey undertaken in coach or train from a holiday resort when the passengers are not told of the intended destination (and known as such probably since the 1920s). In *Next Horizon* (1973), Chris Bonnington wrote: 'Climbing with Tom Patey was a kind of Magical Mystery Tour, in which no one, except perhaps himself, knew what was coming next.' Another example comes from the *Daily Express* (12 April 1989): 'On and on went the city bus driver's magical mystery tour. Passengers point out their way home – and get a lift to the door.'

magic circle. (sometimes 'of Old Etonians'). In British politics this phrase was introduced by Iain Macleod in an article in the *Spectator* (17 January 1964), on the previous year's struggle for the leadership of the Conservative Party. He was describing the way in which the leader, although supposedly just 'emerging', was in fact the choice of a small group of influential Tory peers and manipulators: 'It is some measure of the tightness of the magic circle on this occasion that neither the Chancellor of the Exchequer nor the Leader of the House of Commons had any inkling of what was happening.' Presumably, Macleod was influenced in his choice of phrase by the magicians' Magic Circle (founded 1905). The phrase has subsequently been applied to other semi-secret cabals to which those who might wish to belong are denied access. A year or two later, and as a result of this experience, the Tory leadership came to be decided instead by a ballot of Conservative M Ps.

magnifique – mais ce n'est pas la guerre, c'est [It is magnificent, but it is not war]. This remark was made by Maréchal Bosquet (1810–61) about the Charge of the Light Brigade at the Battle of Balaclava in 1854. It is the source of several witticisms: *Punch* during the First World War said of margarine: '*C'est magnifique, mais ce n'est pas le beurre* [butter]', and of the façade of Worcester College, Oxford, which has a splendid clock on it, Anon said: '*C'est magnifique, mais ce n'est pas la gare* [station].'

maiden. See IRON ~.

Maine goes so goes Vermont, as. In the 1936 US presidential election, Franklin D. Roosevelt's campaign manager was James Farley. On 4 November, Farley predicted that Roosevelt would carry all but two states – Maine and Vermont. This is how he put it in a statement to the press, alluding to the earlier political maxim: 'As Maine goes, so goes the nation' (which Bartlett dates *c* 1888).

'Mairzy Doats and Dozy Doats'. The title of a song (1943) by Milton Drake, Al Hoffman, and Jerry Livingston, meaning 'Mares eat oats and does eat oats'. 'The joke may be traced back 500 years to a medical manuscript in Henry VI's time,' the Opies point out in the *Oxford Dictionary of Nursery Rhymes*; there is a 'catch' which, when said quickly, appears to be in Latin:

> In fir tar is,
> In oak none is,
> In mud eels are,
> In clay none are.
> Goat eat ivy
> Mare eat oats.

make a beeline for, to. Meaning 'to go directly', from the supposition that bees fly in a straight line back to the hive.

make-do and mend. Popularized during the Second World War, when there were Make-do-and-Mend departments in some stores, this phrase was designed to encourage thrift and the repairing of old garments, furniture, etc., rather than expenditure of scarce resources on making new. It was possibly derived from 'make and mend' which was a Royal

Navy term for an afternoon free from work and devoted to mending clothes.

make 'em laugh make 'em cry make 'em wait. This was a suggested recipe for writing novels to be published in serial form (as done by Charles Dickens and many others in the nineteenth century). Charles Reade who wrote *The Cloister and the Hearth* (1863) came up with it.

make love not war. A 'peacenik' and FLOWER POWER sentiment from the mid-1960s onwards. It was not just applied to the Vietnam War but used to express the attitude of a whole generation of protest. Coinage of the slogan has been attributed to G. Legman, a sexologist with the Kinsey Institute.

make no bones about, to. Meaning 'to get straight to the point; not to conceal anything', the expression refers either to drinking a bowl of soup in which there are no bones, which is easy to swallow and there is nothing to complain about; or, from 'bone' meaning 'dice'. Here 'making no bones' means not making much of, and not attempting to coax the dice in order to show favour.

make the desert bloom. The modern state of Israel has made this injunction come true, but it 'dates from Bible times', according to Daniel J. Boorstin in *The Image* (1960). Adlai Stevenson also alluded to the phrase in a speech at Hartford, Connecticut (18 September 1952): 'Man has wrested from nature the power to make the world a desert or to make the deserts bloom.' The exact phrase does not appear in the Bible, though Isaiah 35:1 has: 'The desert shall rejoice, and blossom as the rose', and 51:3 has: 'For the Lord shall comfort Zion . . . and he will make . . . her desert like the garden of the Lord.' Cruden's *Concordance* points out: 'In the Bible this word [desert] means a deserted place, wilderness, not desert in the modern usage of the term.'

Malaprop. See MRS ~.

Malice Aforethought. The title of a crime novel (1931) by Francis Iles, it comes from the English legal term (current by 1670) for a wrongful act carried out against another person *intentionally*, without just cause or excuse (originally Old French *malice prepense*).

Malice in Wonderland. The title of a novel (1940) by 'Nicholas Blake' (C. Day Lewis), and also of an unrelated T V movie (U S, 1985) about Hollywood gossip columnists. It was also a record album by the U K group Nazareth (1980) – all obviously playing upon ALICE IN WONDERLAND.

man. See EVERY ~ HAS HIS PRICE; GRAND OLD ~; OLD ~ OF THE SEA.

Man for All Seasons, A. The title of a play (1960; film U K, 1966) by Robert Bolt about Sir Thomas More. It derives from a description by a contemporary, Robert Whittington: 'More is a man of angel's wit and singular learning; I know not his fellow. For where is the man of that gentleness, lowliness and affability? And as time requireth, a man of marvellous mirth and pastimes; and sometimes of as sad a gravity: as who say a man for all seasons.' Whittington wrote the passage for schoolboys to put into Latin, in his book *Vulgaria* (c 1521). It translates a comment by Erasmus – who wrote in his preface to *In Praise of Folly* (1509) that More was '*omnium horarum hominem*'. It is now a popular phrase for an accomplished, adaptable person. (See also *D P P*.)

Man from —, the. There has been an intermittent tendency to describe U S presidents as if they were tall-walking characters from Westerns. Thus Harry

Truman was dubbed 'The Man from Missouri', Dwight Eisenhower 'The Man from Abilene', and Jimmy Carter 'The Man from Plains'. None of this was very convincing and the craze is best left to the cinema whence we have had *The Man from Bitter Ridge/Colorado/ Dakota/Del Rio/Laramie/the Alamo/ Wyoming*, not to mention, any number of 'The Man Who —s and 'A Man Called —s.

See also next entry.

Man from UNCLE, The. The title of a US TV series (1964–7) about an international spy organization. The letters stood for 'United Network Command for Law and Enforcement'. Any number of BBC stars have been dubbed 'the Man from AUNTIE' in consequence.

Manhattan Transfer, The. The name of the US vocal group (*c* 1977), was taken from the novel *Manhattan Transfer* (1925) by John Dos Passos, depicting the 'shifting and variegated life of New York City' which was in turn named after the station on the Pennsylvania Railroad in New Jersey which enabled passengers between NYC and points south and west to change trains.

man in the street, the. A cliché of journalism, as in: 'Let's find out what the man in the street wants to know/really thinks.' Greville was using the phrase in his memoirs by 1831. Compare MAN ON THE CLAPHAM OMNIBUS.

Man of Destiny, The. The nickname for Napoleon Bonaparte was used as the title of a play about him (1895) by George Bernard Shaw. Sir Walter Scott had earlier used the phrase in his *Life of Napoleon Bonaparte* (1827).

man on the Clapham omnibus, the. Referring to the ordinary or average person, the MAN IN THE STREET, particularly when his/her point of view is

instanced by the courts, newspaper editorials, etc., the phrase was first invoked (1903) by Lord Bowen when hearing a case of negligence: 'We must ask ourselves what the man on the Clapham omnibus would think.' (See also *DPP*.)

'Man Proposes God Disposes'. The title of a painting (1864) by Sir Edwin Landseer, showing two polar bears amid the wreckage of a ship caught in Arctic ice. It comes from an old proverb found in Greek, Hebrew, and Latin. Thomas à Kempis, *De Imitatione Christi* (1427) has it in the form: '*Homo proposit, sed Deus disponit.*' Proverbs 16:9 has: 'A man's heart deviseth his way; but the Lord directeth his steps.'

man's gotta do what a man's gotta do, a. A statement of obligation, as in film Westerns. Partridge/*Catch Phrases* dates this from *c* 1945, but its origin remains untraced, although an early example occurs in John Steinbeck's novel *The Grapes of Wrath* (Chap. 18, 1939): 'I know this – a man got to do what he got to do.' The film *Shane* (US 1953), based on a novel by Jack Shaeffer, is sometimes said to contain the line, but does not (nor does the book). By the 1970s, several songs had been recorded with the title.

Man They Couldn't Gag, The. This was the nickname/by-line of Peter Wilson (*d* 1981), a sports journalist on the *Daily Mirror* who was famous for his hard-hitting style and outspoken opinions.

Man Who —, The. This was a format title for a cartoon series of the 1920s/30s by H.M. Bateman, which showed people who had committed some solecism or other. Among them: 'The Man Who Missed the Ball on the First Tee at St Andrews', 'The Man Who Lit His Cigar Before the Royal Toast', 'The Girl Who

Marat/Sade, The. This is the short version of one of the longest-ever play titles: *The Persecution and Assassination of Jean-Paul Marat, as Peformed by the Inmates of the Asylum of Charenton under the Direction of the Marquis de Sade* by Peter Weiss (first performed with the title in German, Berlin, 1964; film UK, 1966). The world record for a long title is held by a sixteenth-century play whose title goes on for about a page recounting the plot in such detail it is unnecessary to see the play. In films, theatre, and TV there was a particular vogue for long titles in the 1960s. Among them: *Dr Strangelove, or How I Learned to Stop Worrying and Love the Bomb*; *It's a Mad, Mad, Mad, Mad World*; HOW TO SUCCEED IN BUSINESS WITHOUT REALLY TRYING; *A Funny Thing Happened on the Way to the Forum*; *That Was The Week That Was*; *Not So Much a Programme, More a Way of Life*; *Oh Dad, Poor Dad, Mama's Hung You in the Closet and I'm Feeling So Sad*; STOP THE WORLD I WANT TO GET OFF; *The Roar of the Greasepaint, the Smell of the Crowd*; *Who Is Harry Kellerman and Why Is He Saying Those Terrible Things about Me?*; *Can Hieronymus Merkin Ever Forget Mercy Humppe (and Find True Happiness)?*

More recent entrants to the long-title stakes include the novel *On Grand Central Station I Sat Down and Wept* and the play/film *Come Back to the Five & Dime, Jimmy Dean, Jimmy Dean*.

Ordered a Glass of Milk at the Café Royal', and, 'The Man Who Asked for "A Double Scotch" in the Grand Pump Room at Bath'.

Man You Love To Hate, The. This was the title of a film (US, 1979), made as a tribute to the Hollywood director Erich Von Stroheim (*d* 1957). It came from a billing phrase applied to Von Stroheim when he appeared as an actor in the 1918 propaganda film *The Heart of Humanity*. In it, he played an obnoxious German officer who not only attempted to violate the leading lady but nonchalantly tossed a baby out of the window. It is now a phrase generally applied to 'hate figures'.

Mappa Mundi. This is the name given specifically to the primitive world map, dating from *c* 1300, which is to be found in Hereford Cathedral, but a 'mappamonde' was a normal medieval term for one of these (it occurs in Chaucer *c* 1380). The Latin means 'map of the world', although '*mappa*' also means 'napkin, cloth' (upon which the map was drawn). Compare the modern '*mappamondo*', the modern Italian word for 'globe'.

March comes in like a lion. On 1 March 1876, Revd Francis Kilvert wrote in his diary: 'March came in like a lion with wild wind and rain and hail.' It is from the saying: 'March comes in like a lion and goes out like a lamb', proverbial by 1625.

Maria. See BLACK ~.

marmalade. In Europe, this is still a word used for jams in general, though in Britain it has for a long time been applied to a preserve made of orange, lemon or grapefruit. *Marmelo* is the Portuguese word for quince: quince jam is '*marmelada*', '*marmelade*' is the French form. As the word has been known since at least 1480, the theory that it derives from the favourite food of Mary Queen of Scots (*b* 1542) when she was ill – '*Marie Malade*' – is clearly mistaken.

Mark Twain. See TWAIN.

Mars. See ROMAN NAMES.

Mars Bar. The chocolate-coated soft-toffee bar, manufactured in the UK from 1932, was named after Forrest Mars, an American, who founded the company which makes it. In the 1960s, it became unforgettably associated with Marianne Faithfull, the singer, who was the girlfriend of Mick Jagger 1967–70. See Philip Norman, *The Rolling Stones* (Chap. 9, 1984).

Martha. The nickname given to a house-wifely woman, derives from the biblical Martha, sister of Lazarus and Mary. While Mary sat listening to Jesus, her sister got on with the housework – 'distracted with much serving' – and Martha complained to Jesus, who nevertheless supported Mary (Luke 10:38–42). A modern example of the word's use occurs in *One of Us* by Hugo Young (1989): 'There was an almost obsessive reluctance to refer to [Margaret Thatcher's mother] ... If she was alluded to at all, it was under the patronizing designation of "rather a Martha".'

Martin, Betty. See ALL MY EYE ...

martini. There has been a firm, Martini and Rossi, makers of Italian vermouth since 1894, but the origin of the term 'dry martini' may have nothing to do the firm (even though it can, of course, be made with Martini). The 'dry martini' is said to have been invented by Martini di Armi di Taggia, head bartender at the Knickerbocker Hotel, New York City *c* 1910. He stipulated one third vermouth, two thirds dry gin. However, Flexner 2 finds that people were drinking something called a *martinez* in the US in the 1860s (half gin, half dry vermouth).

Martin of Tours, St. See SAINTS' NAMES.

Marx Brothers. Each member of the famous US family of comedians who appeared on stage and in films used a name other than the one he was born with. The nicknames were acquired at a poker game (*c* 1918): Leonard became Chico; Adolph became Harpo (he played the harp); Julius became Groucho; Milton became Gummo (though he left the act early on); and Herbert became Zeppo (though he also left in due course). On the record album *An Evening with Groucho Marx* (1972), Groucho attempted to explain the nicknames. Chico was a 'chicken-chaser'; Zeppo was 'after the ZEPPELIN which arrived in Lakehurst, New Jersey, at the time he was born' (1901); and Gummo 'wore gumshoes'. As for Groucho, 'I never did understand ...'

Mary Magdalene, St. See SAINTS' NAMES.

MASH. See ACRONYMS.

masochism. Sexual activity in which gratification is derived from humiliation and pain inflicted by oneself or by other people. The term takes its name from Leopold von Sacher-Masoch (*d* 1895), an Austrian novelist, who submitted to various women who gratified his wishes in this way, and ended up in an asylum. The German psychiatrist Krafft-Ebing coined the word to describe the condition. More recently, the meaning of the word has been broadened beyond the primarily sexual to include more general forms of enjoying humiliation.

MASS (PHRASES FROM THE).

These names are commonly given to parts of the Mass, especially to their musical settings, and are all Latin with the exception of *kyrie eleison*, which is Greek. Some of the phrases only occur in requiem masses. They are listed here in alphabetical sequence, not the order in which they are sung.

agnus dei: lamb of God.
benedictus: blessed (is He).
confutatis (maledictis): (when the damned) are cast away.
credo (in unum Deum): I believe (in one God).
dies irae: day of wrath.
Domine Deus: O Lord God.
et incarnatus est: and was incarnate.
gloria (in excelsis Deo): glory (be to God on high).
gratias agimus tibi: we give thanks to Thee.
kyrie eleison: Lord, have mercy.
lacrimosa (dies illa): (this day full of) tears.
laudamus te: we praise Thee.
lux aeterna: eternal light.
pie Jesu: gentle Jesus.
qui tollis peccata mundi: (Thou) that takest away the sins of the world.
quoniam tu solus Sanctus: for Thou only art holy.
recordare: remember.
rex tremendae (majestatis): king of awful majesty.
Sanctus: Holy.
tuba mirum (spargens sonum): the trumpet, scattering its awful sound.

Master, The. The nickname of Sir Noël Coward (*d* 1973), actor and writer, who was known thus throughout the theatrical profession from the 1940s, but not by those close to him. He professed to dislike the name (perhaps because it had already been applied to D.W. Griffith, the film pioneer, and W. Somerset Maugham, the writer) and, when asked to explain it, replied: 'Oh, you know, jack of all trades, master of none . . .'

masters. See WE ARE THE ~ NOW.

Matilda. See WALTZING ~.

maverick. Meaning 'an individualist, an unorthodox independent-minded person', the word derives from Samuel A. Maverick (*d* 1870), a Texas cattle-owner who left the calves of his herd unbranded because he said the practice was cruel. It also enabled him to claim any unbranded calves he found on the range. In time, the word came to be used in politics and more generally, describing someone who would not affiliate with a particular party or cause.

Mean Streets. The title of a film (US, 1973) about an Italian ghetto in New York, it probably alludes to a noted sentence by Raymond Chandler in 'The Simple Art of Murder' (1950): 'Down these mean streets a man must go who is not himself mean; who is neither tarnished nor afraid' (referring to the heroic qualities a detective should have). However, in 1894, Arthur Morrison had written *Tales of Mean Streets* about impoverished life in the East End of London.

meanwhile back at the ranch . . .
One of the captions/subtitles from the days of the silent cinema which still has some currency as a sign-posting phrase in story-telling. It may also have been used in US radio 'horse operas', when recapping the story after a commercial break.

Medea. See GREEK NAMES.

Medusa. See GREEK NAMES.

megaphone diplomacy. Referring to political 'dialogue' which consists of shouted sloganeering rather than a genuine meeting of minds, the phrase was used (by 1985) in particular to describe the abusive tone of relations between the US and the USSR, prior to the *rapprochement* of the late 1980s.

Melba. See PEACH ~.

Melpomene. See GREEK NAMES.

memory. See DOWN ~ LANE.

mend. See MAKE-DO AND ~.

Mercury. See ROMAN NAMES.

Meredith we're in! This shout of triumph originated in a music-hall sketch called 'The Bailiff' (*or* 'Moses and Son'), performed by Fred Kitchen, the leading comedian with FRED KARNO's company. The sketch was first seen in 1907 and the phrase was uttered each time a bailiff and his assistant looked like gaining entrance to the house. Kitchen even had it put on his gravestone.

mesmerize, to. Meaning 'to fascinate; act in a spell-binding way', the verb derives from Dr Franz or Friedrich Anton Mesmer (*d* 1815), a German physician who practised a form of hypnotism in Vienna as a way of treating ailments. His theory of 'animal magnetism' was discredited in his lifetime but his reputation was rescued by a pupil who identified what Mesmer had done and gave it the name 'mesmerism'.

mess. See HERE'S ANOTHER FINE ~.

Messengers of Day. The title of Vol.II (1978) of Anthony Powell's autobiography *TO KEEP THE BALL ROLLING*, comes from Shakespeare's *Julius Caesar* (II.i.104): 'Yon grey lines/That fret the clouds are messengers of day.'

mess of potage. 'To sell one's birthright for a mess of potage', meaning 'to sacrifice something for material comfort', has biblical origins but is not a direct quotation from the Bible. 'Esau selleth his birthright for a mess of potage' appears as a chapter heading for Genesis 25 in one or two early translations of the Bible, though not in the Authorized Version of 1611. The word 'mess' is used in its sense of 'a portion of liquid or pulpy food'. 'Potage' is thick soup (compare French *potage*).

Me Tarzan – you Jane. In the first sound Tarzan film – *Tarzan the Ape Man* (1932), the ape-man hero whisks Jane away to his tree-top abode and indulges in some elementary conversation with her. Thumping his chest, he says: 'Tarzan!'; pointing at her, he says: 'Jane!' So he does not say the catch phrase commonly associated with him. The dialogue appears to have been 'written' by the British playwright and actor Ivor Novello. In the original novel, *Tarzan of the Apes* (1914), by Edgar Rice Burroughs, the line does not occur – not least because, in the jungle, Tarzan and Jane are only able to communicate by writing notes to each other.

methinks she doth protest too much. Gertrude's line from Shakespeare's *Hamlet* (III.ii.225) is often evoked to mean 'there's something suspicious about the way that person is complaining – it's not natural'. However, what Hamlet's mother is actually doing is giving her opinion of 'The MOUSETRAP', the play-within-a-play. What she means to say is that the Player Queen is overdoing her protestations, and uses the word 'protest' in the sense of 'state formally', not 'complain'.

Metro. See ODEON.

Micawber. Meaning 'an incurable optimist', the word comes from the character Wilkins Micawber, in Charles Dickens, *David Copperfield* (1849) who lives a hand-to-mouth existence with his family but is always hoping that something will 'turn up'.

mickey. See TAKE THE ~.

mickey finn. Anything slipped into people's drinks in order to knock them out. *D O A S* claims that to begin with the term meant a laxative for horses. The original Mickey Finn may have been a notorious bartender in Chicago (d 1906) who proceeded to rob his unconscious victims.

microphone. See I AM PAYING FOR THIS ~.

Midas. See GREEK NAMES.

Middle America. Originally a geographical expression, this phrase was applied to the US conservative middle class in 1968 during Richard Nixon's campaign for the presidency. It corresponded to what he was later to call the SILENT MAJORITY and was alluded to in the expression IT'LL PLAY IN PEORIA. The expression is said to have been coined by the journalist Joseph Kraft.

Middle Way, The. The title of a book (1938) by Harold Macmillan, setting out the arguments for a middle course in politics, occupying 'the middle ground' between extremes. Winston Churchill had earlier ended an election address on 11 November 1922 by saying: 'What we require now is not a period of turmoil, but a period of stability and recuperation. Let us stand together and tread a sober middle way.'

midstream. See NEVER CHANGE HORSES IN ~.

milk. See LAND FLOWING WITH ~ AND HONEY.

Million. See COOL HUNDRED.

mills of God grind slowly ('. . . yet they grind exceeding small'). The meaning of this saying is that the ways in which reforms are brought about, crime is punished, etc., are often slow, but the end result may be perfectly achieved. The saying comes from Longfellow's translation of Friedrich von Logau, a German seventeenth-century poet.

minds. See HEARTS AND ~.

Mine Own Executioner. The title of this novel (1945; film UK, 1947) by Nigel Balchin comes from John Donne's *Devotions upon Emergent Occasions* (Meditation XII): 'But I do nothing upon myself, and yet I am mine own executioner.'

Minerva. See ROMAN NAMES.

minions of the moon. Meaning 'night-time robbers'. In 1984, a French film was released in the English-language market with the title *Favourites of the Moon*. It was a quirky piece about various Parisian crooks, petty and otherwise, whose activities overlapped in one way or another, and the English title hardly seemed relevant to the subject. Indeed, the original French title was *Les Favoris de la Lune* and, as a caption made clear, this was a French translation of a Shakespeare quotation: in *King Henry IV, Part 1* (I.ii.25), Falstaff says to Prince Hal: 'Let not us that are squires of the night's body be called thieves of the day's beauty: let us be Diana's foresters, gentlemen of the shade, minions of the moon.'

Ministry of Fear. The title of this novel (1943; film US, 1944) by Graham Greene, about a spy hunt in wartime

London, is said to be derived from Wordsworth, but his only relevant line is 'ministry of pain and evil' from 'The Borderers' (1842).

Minnie. See MOANING ~.

Minotaur. See GREEK NAMES.

minutes. See FAMOUS FOR FIFTEEN ~.

Mirror Crack'd from Side to Side, The. The title of this Miss Marple novel (1962) by Agatha CHRISTIE comes from Tennyson's 'The Lady of Shalott' (1833).

Mission Impossible. The title of this TV series (US, 1966–72) about government agents/investigators in the Impossible Missions Force has now become a catch phrase: 'When Kissinger took the commission post, his associates warned that it was mission impossible' (the *Washington Post*, 3 January 1984), and: 'Hostage rescue is mission impossible' (headline in the *Observer*, 19 August 1990).

misspent youth. See SIGN OF A ~.

mit. See FROZEN ~.

Mitty. See WALTER.

Moaning Minnie. Anyone who complains is a 'moaner' and a 'minnie' can mean a lost lamb which finds itself an adoptive mother. The *Observer* (20 May 1989) had: 'Broadcasters are right to complain about the restrictions placed on them for the broadcasting of the House of Commons . . . But the Moaning Minnies have only themselves to blame.' The phrase is also descriptive of someone singing the blues – there was a song in the 1930s with the title.

The original 'Moaning Minnie' was, however, something quite different. In

the First World War, a 'Minnie' was the slang name for a German *Minenwerfer*, a trench mortar or the shell that came from it, making a distinctive moaning noise. In the Second World War, the name was also applied to air-raid sirens which also made the noise. (See also *DPP*.)

mole. The name is applied to one who infiltrates a large organization, but particularly a spy who is placed in another country's intelligence network often years before being needed. The CIA term for this process is 'penetration' and former CIA chief Richard Helms told Safire he had never encountered this use of the word 'mole'. Although flirted with by other writers (as early as Francis Bacon), the term was introduced by John Le Carré in his novel *TINKER, TAILOR, SOLDIER, SPY* (1974). In a BBC TV interview in 1976, he said he *thought* it was a genuine KGB term which he had picked up.

Molotov cocktail. The incendiary device, similar to a petrol bomb, acquired its name in Finland during the early days of the Second World War. V.M. Molotov had become Soviet Minister for Foreign Affairs in 1939. The Russians invaded Finland and these home-made grenades proved an effective way for the Finns to oppose their tanks.

Moltke. A name given to a taciturn, unsmiling person. Michael Wharton ('Peter Simple' columnist in the *Daily Telegraph*) was so nicknamed by his German grandfather after the famous general, Helmuth Graf von Moltke (*d* 1891): 'who seldom spoke and was said to have smiled only twice in his life'. Walter Bagehot quotes a remark that Moltke was 'silent in seven languages'.

moment of truth. Meaning 'a decisive turning point; a significant moment', the phrase comes from '*el momento de la* *verdad*' in Spanish bullfighting – the final sword-thrust that kills the animal. *Il Momento della Verità* was the title of an Italian/Spanish film (1964) on a bullfighting theme. In *I, Claud* (1967), Claud Cockburn said of European intellectuals who had fought in the Spanish Civil War: 'They proclaimed, however briefly, that a moment comes when your actions have to bear some kind of relation to your words. This is what is called the Moment of Truth.'

Momus. See GREEK NAMES.

monarch of all I survey. This lighthearted proprietorial boast comes from William Cowper's 'Verses Supposed to be Written by Alexander Selkirk' (the original of 'Robinson Crusoe'), *c* 1779:

> I am monarch of all I survey,
> My right there is none to dispute;
> From the centre all round to the sea
> I am lord of the fowl and the brute.

Kenneth Tynan, writing about Noël Coward (in *Panorama*, Spring 1952) said: 'He is, if I may test the trope, monocle of all he surveys.'

'Monarch of the Glen, The'. The title of a much-reproduced painting (1851) by Sir Edwin Landseer, showing a stag rampant on a small rock (and now in the possession of John Dewar & Sons Ltd, the whisky firm). When the painting was first exhibited at the Royal Academy, the catalogue entry contained a poem only identified as 'Legends of Glenorchay', which ends:

> Uprose the Monarch of the Glen
> Majestic from his lair,
> Surveyed the scene with piercing ken,
> And snuffed the fragrant air.

Monday. See BLACK ~.

money. See TAKE THE ~ AND RUN.

money is the root of all evil. Strictly speaking this should be: 'the *love* of money is the root of all evil' (1 Timothy 6:10).

monk. See MAD ~.

monkey. See COLD ENOUGH TO FREEZE . . .

monkey's uncle, I'm a/I'll be a. This expression of surprise was current by 1926. One derivation is that it has something to do with the Scopes 'Monkey Trial' of 1925 when a young teacher in Tennessee was accused of illegally teaching the Darwinian theory of evolution. Another explanation is that a 'monkey' in London East End parlance is £500 and an 'uncle' is a pawnbroker, but that isn't very helpful.

monster. See GREEN-EYED ~.

monstrous carbuncle. In June 1984, Prince Charles described a proposed design for a new wing of the National Gallery in London as: 'a kind of vast municipal fire station . . . I would understand better this type of high-tech approach if you demolished the whole of Trafalgar Square, but what is proposed is like a monstrous carbuncle on the face of a much-loved and elegant friend.' (In the same speech he called a planned Mies van der Rohe office building in London a 'glass stump', and opening a factory in May 1987 he likened the new building to a 'Victorian prison'.)

The Prince of Wales's ventures into architectural criticism have not gone unnoticed and the image of a 'monstrous carbuncle' ('a red spot or pimple on the nose or face caused by habits of intemperance' *O E D2*) has become part of the critical vocabulary. A report in the *Independent* (1 March 1988) about plans for a new lifeboat station dominating the harbour at Lyme Regis concluded by quoting a local objector: 'They've called this building a design of the age. What we've got here is a Prince Charles Carbuncle, and we don't like carbuncles down on Lyme harbourside.' The Prince's stepmother-in-law, the Countess Spencer, had earlier written in a book called *The Spencers on Spas* (1983) of how 'monstrous carbuncles of concrete have erupted in Gentle Georgian squares'. Even longer before, in 1821, William Cobbett had characterized the whole of London as 'the GREAT WEN of all' – a 'wen' being a lump or protuberance on a body, a wart.

month. See FLAVOUR OF THE ~.

moon. See ONCE IN A BLUE ~; OVER THE ~.

Moon and Sixpence, The. The title of a novel (1919) by W. Somerset Maugham, which came from a review of his earlier book OF HUMAN BONDAGE in the *Times Literary Supplement* which had said that the main character was: 'like so many young men . . . so busy yearning for the moon that he never saw the sixpence at his feet'.

Moon's a Balloon, The. The title of the first volume (1971) of David Niven's autobiography comes from an e.e.cummings poem called '& N &' (1925):

> Who knows if the moon's
> a balloon, coming out of a keen city in
>   the sky
> – filled with pretty people?

moonshine. Meaning 'illicit liquor', the word is of US origin where it was used to describe whisky illegally *made* at night. Even before this, however, the word had been used in England to denote brandy illegally *smuggled* in by moonlight.

more. See LESS IS ~.

more efficient conduct of the war (*sometimes* **energetic . . .).** This almost became a slogan of the First World War for what was required of the British Government (*c* 1916) prior to the replacement of Prime Minister Asquith by Lloyd George. However, the coalition government announced by Asquith on 26 May 1915 had claimed that this was what it was promoting.

morituri te salutant [those who are about to die salute you]. These words were addressed to the emperor by gladiators in ancient Rome on entering the arena. The practice seems to have been first mentioned in *Claudius* by Suetonius. In time, the phrase was extended to anyone facing difficulty, and then ironically so.

morning. See NEVER GLAD CONFIDENT ~.

Morpheus. See ROMAN NAMES.

Mors. See ROMAN NAMES.

Mortal Coils. The title of a collection of short stories (1922) by Aldous HUXLEY comes from Shakespeare's *Hamlet*, in the TO BE OR NOT TO BE soliloquy: '. . . when we have shuffled off this mortal coil'.

mortuis. See DE MORTUIS.

mostest. See FIRSTEST WITH THE ~.

Mother. See DEAD AND NEVER CALLED ME ~.

Mother Shipton. The prophecies attributed to 'Mother Shipton' are suspect, yet she herself appears to have existed. Ursula Southeil was born in a cave in Knaresborough, Yorkshire in 1488. She married Toby Shipton in 1512 and gained a reputation as a fortune-teller, if not as the witch she physically resembled. She was said to have predicted both the Civil War and the Great Fire of London, so much so that when Prince Rupert heard of the fire he said: 'Now Shipton's prophecy is out!' However, her alleged anticipation of railway trains and the telegraph appears to have been the work of Charles Hindley, a London bookseller, who brought out *The Prophecies of Mother Shipton* (1862–71).

Mother Teresa. Mother Teresa (*b* Agnes Gonxha Bojaxhiu, 1910, in Skopje, Yugoslavia) received the Nobel Peace Prize (1979) for her charitable works, notably running a mission among the starving in Calcutta, and her name has now become a byword for goodness. For example, the *Independent* (6 June 1990), quoting a lawyer for arrested Panamanian defendants in the US: 'If you had Mother Theresa sitting at the table next to [General] Noriega, she'd have trouble getting past the jury.'

motley. See ON WITH THE ~.

mould. See BREAK THE ~.

mountain top, to be at the. On the night before he was assassinated, Revd Dr Martin Luther King Jr said in a speech at Memphis (3 April 1968): 'I've been to the mountain top . . . I've looked over and I've seen the promised land.' The 'promised land' (not called as such in the Bible, and referring to Canaan, Western Palestine, and by association, Heaven) was promised to the descendants of Abraham, Isaac and Jacob. In Numbers 14:39–40: 'Moses told these sayings unto all the children of Israel . . . And they rose up early in the morning and gat them up into the top of the mountain, saying, Lo, we be here, and will go up unto the place which the lord hath promised.'

Mounties always get their man. The unofficial motto of the Royal Canadian Mounted Police. John J. Healy, editor of the Fort Benton (Montana) *Record*, wrote on 13 April 1877 that the Mounties 'fetch their man every time'. The official motto since 1873 has been 'Maintain the right' [*Maintiens le droit*].

mousetrap. See BEAT A PATH . . .

Mousetrap, The. The play (1952) by Agatha CHRISTIE, which has become the longest continuous-running show in the world, takes its name from the play-within-a-play of Shakespeare's *Hamlet* (II.ii.40–43).

mouth. See LOOK A GIFT HORSE IN THE ~.

move/shift the goalposts, to. Meaning 'to change the rules or conditions after something has started, in order to upset the "players"'. The *Guardian* (1 March 1989) said: 'The people of Kent vote solidly for the Conservative Party . . . Why are these people, therefore, trying to attempt to move the goalposts after the football match has started [by imposing a new rail line through the county]?'

Moveable Feast, A. The title of a book (1964) by Ernest Hemingway. The epigraph explains: 'If you are lucky enough to have lived in Paris as a young man, then wherever you go for the rest of your life, it stays with you, for Paris is a moveable feast.' In the ecclesiastical world, a moveable feast is one which does not fall on a fixed date but – like Easter – occurs according to certain rules.

moved. See WE SHALL NOT BE ~.

moves. See GOD ~ IN A MYSTERIOUS WAY.

Moving Finger, The. The title of a 'Miss Marple' novel (1943) by Agatha CHRISTIE, it alludes to THE WRITING ON THE WALL. Later the US title became *Murder in Our Midst*. Could this be because four other writers (including E. Phillips Oppenheim) had used *The Moving Finger?*

Mr Big. This nickname is given to the supposed mastermind behind substantial crimes (e.g. the GREAT TRAIN ROBBERY of 1963). *OED2* finds the expression not only in a Groucho Marx letter of 1940 but more significantly in Raymond Chandler's *The Long Goodbye* (1953). *Mister Big* was the title of a 1943 B-movie starring Donald O'Connor. (See also *DPP*.)

Mr Chad. See CHAD.

Mr Chips. A name applied to an elderly schoolmaster, once feared but now revered, it derives from the character in the novel *Goodbye, Mr Chips* (1934) by James Hilton.

Mr Clean. The nickname for one who makes a point of being honest and upright, it was originally the name of a US household cleaner. 'The Secretary of State, James Baker, always regarded as Mr Clean among several highly placed roguish officials in Ronald Reagan's administration . . .' (*Independent*, 15 February 1989). Others to whom it has been applied are: Pat Boone (*b* 1934), the US pop singer and actor noted for his clean image and habits (he would never agree to kiss in films); John Lindsay (*b* 1921), Mayor of New York (1965–73); and Elliot Richardson (*b* 1920), US Attorney-General who resigned in 1973 rather than agree to the restrictions President Nixon was then placing on investigations into the Watergate affair.

Mr Fixit. A nickname for one who has a reputation for solving problems. Chips Channon wrote in his diary (30 November 1936) of the Abdication: 'Beaverbrook, while enjoying his role of Mr Fixit, and the power he now holds in his horny hands, is now nearly distraught.' *OED2* finds 'Mr and Mrs Fix-It' as the title of a Ring Lardner story in 1925.

Mr Nice Guy, no more. 'Mr Nice Guy' is a nickname applied to 'straight' figures (especially politicians) who may possibly be following someone who is palpably not 'nice' (Gerald Ford after Richard Nixon, for example). They then sometimes feel the need to throw off some of their virtuous image, as presidential challenger Senator Ed Muskie did in 1972 – and his aides declared: 'No more Mr Nice Guy'. In April 1973, Alice Cooper had a song entitled 'No More Mr Nice Guy' in the British charts. Safire dates to the mid-1950s the joke about Hitler agreeing to make a comeback with the words: 'But this time – no more Mr Nice Guy'.

Mrs Grundy. Meaning 'a censorious person; an upholder of conventional morality', the name comes from Thomas Morton's play *Speed the Plough* (1798) in which a character frequently asks: 'What will Mrs Grundy say?' Compare the later names of **Mrs Ormiston Chaunt**, an actual woman who campaigned in the late nineteenth century against immorality in the music-hall, and **Mrs** (**Mary**) **Whitehouse** who attempted to 'clean up' British TV from 1965 onwards.

Mrs Malaprop. The name of a character in *The Rivals* (1775) by Richard Brinsley Sheridan after whom 'malapropisms' are called. 'Her select words [are] so ingeniously *misapplied*, without being *mispronounced*' (II.ii.). Among her misapplied but inspired words are: '*pineapple* of politeness', 'a nice *derangement* of epitaphs' and 'as headstrong as an *allegory* on the banks of the Nile'. She was not the first character to have such an entertaining affliction: Shakespeare's Dogberry and Mistress Quickly are similarly troubled. After the French phrase *mal à propos* ('awkward, inopportune').

Mrs Mouse Are You Within? The title of a play (1968) by Frank Marcus, its origin is the nursery rhyme 'A Frog He Would A-wooing Go' (first recorded 1611):

> Pray, Mrs Mouse, are you within?
> Heigh ho! says Rowley.

Private Eye (No. 299, June 1973) quoted what the elderly 10th Duke of Marlborough had said on returning from one of his honeymoons: 'I'm afraid Mr Mouse didn't come out to play.'

Mrs Sarah Gamp. See GAMP.

Mrs Worthington. The name for the archetypal aspiring actress's mother comes from Noël Coward's song 'Mrs Worthington' (1935) which contains the refrain: 'Don't put your daughter on the stage, Mrs Worthington'.

M T F. See INITIALS.

muddling through. This is supposedly what the British have a great talent for. Mencken has 'The English always manage to muddle through . . . author unidentified; first heard *c* 1885'. Ira Gershwin celebrated the trait in the song 'Stiff Upper Lip' from *A Damsel in Distress* (1937). He remembered the phrase 'Keep muddling through' from its use at the time of the First World War, but knew that it had first been noted in a speech by John Bright MP, *c* 1864 (though, ironically, Bright was talking about the Northern States in the US Civil War).

mudge. See FUDGE AND ∼.

mufti. This word is used for plain clothes or 'civvies' – as when a military person is not wearing uniform. A 'mufti' is a doctor in Muslim law. Perhaps an English officer put on the robes as disguise, for some reason, and the word stuck as a way of describing the 'clothes that you don't usually wear'.

mullah. See MAD ∼.

multitude, nouns of. See COLLECTIVE NOUNS.

mum's the word. Meaning 'we are keeping silent on this matter', no mother is invoked here: 'mum' is just a representation of 'Mmmm', the noise made when LIPS ARE SEALED. The word 'mumble' obviously derives from the same source. Shakespeare has the idea in *King Henry VI, Part 2* (I.ii.89): 'Seal up your lips and give no words but mum.'

Murder Most Foul. The title of a film (UK, 1964) based on the Agatha CHRISTIE novel *Mrs McGinty's Dead* (1952), with Miss Marple substituted for Hercule Poirot. It comes from Shakespeare's *Hamlet* (I.v.27):

> *Ghost:* Murder most foul, as in the best it is,
> But this most foul, strange and unnatural.

murderers return to the scene of the crime. There is no obvious source for this proverbial saying. A French propaganda poster from the First World War has the slogan: '*Les assassins reviennent toujours . . . sur les lieux de leur crime.*'

Murder She Wrote. The title of a US TV series (1984 onwards), with Angela Lansbury as Jessica Fletcher, a widowed best-selling crime writer who becomes involved in solving actual murder cases. Modelled on Miss Marple perhaps, there was another nod in the direction of Agatha CHRISTIE in the title. *Murder She Said* was the title given to a film version (UK, 1961) of the Miss Marple story *4.50 from Paddington*. In turn, that echoed *Murder He Says* (film US, 1945) and 'Murder, He Says', the curious Frank Loesser lyric to music by Jimmy McHugh which was sung by Betty Hutton in the film *Happy Go Lucky* (1942).

Murphy's Law. See IF ANYTHING . . .

Muses. See GREEK NAMES.

music. See FACE THE ~.

Mussolini made the trains run on time. Efficiency may be the saving grace of a fascist dictatorship, but did Mussolini ever boast: 'I will make the trains run on time and create order out of chaos'? Or did he ever claim afterwards that this is what he had done? One of his biographers says he did eventually boast of the efficiency of Italian railways, though quite how efficient they were is open to doubt. Perhaps they just ran *relatively* more on time than they had done before. But they had managed all right for the famous 'March on Rome' (October 1922) which – despite its name – was largely accomplished by train.

My Fat Friend. The title of a play (1972) by Charles Laurence, about a fat girl's changed fortunes when she loses weight. It was originally going to be called *The Fat Dress*. An allusion is possible to Beau Brummell's famous question to Lord Alvanley about the Prince Regent. Brummell, a dandy almost by profession, had fallen out with the Prince of Wales and when they met in London in July 1813, the Prince cut him and greeted his companion. As the Prince walked off, Brummell asked in ringing tones: 'Tell me, Alvanley, who is your fat friend?'

My Fair Lady. The title of Lerner and Loewe's musical (1956; film US, 1964), based on George Bernard Shaw's play *Pygmalion*. It comes from the refrain of the nursery rhyme (first recorded in the eighteenth century):

> London Bridge is broken down,
> Broken down, broken down,
> London Bridge is broken down,
> My fair lady.

It has also been suggested that they were drawn to the title because 'my fair lady' is how a cockney flower-seller would pronounce the phrase 'Mayfair lady'. Either way, it was not the first choice of title for the musical. Rex Harrison said that when he first heard of the project it was called 'Lady Liza'.

My Husband and I. The title of an ITV comedy series (1988) with Mollie Sugden, taken from the stock phrase of Queen Elizabeth II. Her father, George VI (*d* 1952) had quite naturally spoken the words 'The Queen and I'. The musical *The King and I* was first performed in 1951 (film US, 1956). But something in the Queen's drawling delivery turned her version into a joke. It first appeared during her second Christmas broadcast (made from New Zealand) in 1953 – 'My husband and I left London a month ago' – and still survived in 1962: 'My husband and I are greatly looking forward to visiting New Zealand and Australia in the New Year.' By 1967, the phrase had become 'Prince Philip and I', and at a Silver Wedding banquet in 1972, the Queen allowed herself a little joke: 'I think on this occasion I may be forgiven for saying "My husband and I".'

My Mother Said I Never Should. The title of a play (1989) by Charlotte

Keatley comes from the nursery rhyme (not recorded in print before 1922):

> My mother said I never should
> Play with the gypsies in the wood.

my name is mud. This exclamation might be uttered as an acknowledgement that one has made a mistake and is held in low esteem. When John Wilkes Booth was escaping from the theatre in which he had just assassinated President Lincoln in 1865, he fell and broke his leg. A country doctor called Dr Samuel Mudd tended Booth's wound without realizing the circumstances under which it had been received. When he did realize, he informed the authorities, was charged with being a co-conspirator, and sentenced to life imprisonment.

As Morris points out, however, 'mud' in the sense of scandalous and defamatory charges, goes back to a time well before the Civil War. There had been an expression 'the mud press' to describe mud-slinging newspapers in the US before 1846, so it seems most likely that the expression was well established before Dr Mudd met his unhappy fate. Indeed, *OED2* has an 1823 citation from 'Jon Bee' in *Slang* for 'And his name is mud!' as an ejaculation at the end of a silly oration and also by then from *A Dictionary of the Turf* as a name for a stupid fellow.

'My Shining Hour'. The title of a song (first sung in the film *The Sky's the Limit*, 1943) by Johnny Mercer and Harold Arlen, which comes from the Isaac Watts poem 'Against Idleness and Mischief' (1715):

> How doth the little busy bee
> Improve each shining hour,
> And gather honey all the day
> From every opening flower!

Compare HOW DOTH THE LITTLE CROCODILE.

mysterious way. See GOD MOVES IN A ~.

my word is my bond. This is the motto of the London Stock Exchange (since 1801), where bargains are made 'on the nod', with no written pledges being given and no documents being signed. Its Latin form is: *'Dictum meum pactum.'*

NN

NAAFI. See ACRONYMS.

naff. Meaning 'in poor taste; unfashionable; bad' and largely restricted to British use, this word had a sudden vogue in 1982. Keith Waterhouse had used the participle 'naffing' in his novel *Billy Liar* (1959), remembering it from his service in the RAF (*c* 1950). Attempts have been made to derive the adjective 'naff' from 'fanny' in back-slang, from NAAFI, and from the French '*rien à faire*', none very convincingly.

Naked Truth, The. This was the title of a film (UK, 1957) and as a phrase for 'the absolute truth', it comes from an old fable which tells how Truth and Falsehood went swimming and Falsehood stole the clothes that Truth had left upon the river bank. Truth declined to wear Falsehood's clothes and went naked. In Latin, as in the works of Horace, the phrase is '*nudas veritas*'.

namby-pamby. Meaning 'insipid; wishy-washy; soft', the word derives from Ambrose Philips (*d* 1749), a writer and politician whom the dramatist Henry Carey ridiculed with this nickname after Philips had written some insipid verses for children.

name. See GIVE A DOG A BAD ~.

name liveth for evermore, their. This is a frequent inscription over lists of the dead in First World War cemeteries, echoing Ecclesiasticus 44:14: 'Their bodies are buried in peace; but their name liveth for evermore.' Kilvert writes (31 January 1875): 'So Charles Kingsley is dead. "His body is buried in peace, but his name liveth for evermore." We could ill spare him.'

Name of the Game, The. The title of a US TV series (1968–71), following a US TV movie (1966) *Fame Is the Name of the Game*. It comes from the phrase '– is the name of the game' meaning '– is what it's really about'. Partridge/*Catch Phrases* finds an example in 1961. US National Security Adviser McGeorge Bundy talking about foreign policy goals in Europe in 1966 said: 'Settlement is the name of the game.'

Naples. See SEE ~ AND DIE.

Narcissus. See GREEK NAMES.

nasty brutish and short. This description of life was given by Thomas Hobbes in *Leviathan, or the Matter, Form, and Power of a Commonwealth, Ecclesiastical and Civil* (Chap. 13, 1651). In this treatise of political philosophy, Hobbes sees man not as a social being but as a selfish creature. The state of nature in which he resides is one in which there are: 'No arts; no letters; no society; and which is worst of all, continual fear and danger of violent death; and the life of man, solitary, poor, nasty, brutish, and short.'

nations. See GAIETY OF ~.

nation shall speak to nation. The motto of the BBC (1927) echoes Micah 4:3: 'Nation shall not lift up a sword against nation.' In 1932, however, it was decided that the BBC's primary mission was to serve the home audience and not that overseas. Hence, '**Quaecunque**' [whatsoever] was introduced as an alternative reflecting the Latin inscription (composed by Dr Montague Rendall) in the entrance hall of Broadcasting House, London, and based on Philippians 4:8: 'Whatsoever things are beautiful and honest and of good report . . .' In 1948, the original motto was reintroduced. '*Quaecunque*' was also taken as the motto of Lord Reith, the BBC's first Director-General.

NATSOPA. See ACRONYMS.

nature abhors a vacuum/a straight line. Rabelais quotes the first maxim in its original Latin form '*natura abhorret vacuum*' in *Gargantua* (1535) and Galileo (*d* 1642) asserted it as the reason why mercury rises in a barometer. 'Nature abhors a straight line' was a saying of CAPABILITY BROWN (*d* 1783). (Clare Boothe Luce (*d* 1987) said: 'Nature abhors a virgin.')

Naughty but Nice. The title of a film (US, 1939) and also of various songs, notably one by Johnny Mercer and Harry Warren in *The Belle of New York* (film, 1952). Compare also: 'It's Foolish but It's Fun' (Gus Kahn/Robert Stolz) sung by Deanna Durbin in *Spring Parade* (1940). The catch phrase in full is: 'It's naughty but it's nice.' Partridge/*Slang* glosses it as 'a reference to copulation since *c* 1900 ex a song that Minnie

Schulte sang and popularized in the USA, 1890s'.

The phrase was also used in a series of advertisements for cream, run in the late 1980s by the National Dairy Council. (See also *DPP*.)

Naughty Nineties (*also* Gay Nineties). Referring to the 1890s in England, when VICTORIAN VALUES softened somewhat in the face of hedonism in certain circles. The most characteristic figure was that of Oscar Wilde. *OED2* does not find the sobriquet in use until 1925.

Naval Person. See FORMER ~.

NBG. See INITIALS.

NCD. See INITIALS.

'Nearer My God to Thee'. The title of a hymn by J.B. Dykes (*d* 1876), which the ship's band was rumoured to have been playing when the *Titanic* sank in 1912. According to Burnam 2, however, the band played ragtime until the ship's bridge dipped underwater, then the bandmaster led his men in the Episcopal hymn, 'Autumn'.

nectar. See AMBER ~.

needle, eye of a. See EASIER FOR A CAMEL . . .

needs. See FROM EACH ACCORDING TO HIS ABILITIES . . .

neither fish flesh nor good red herring. Meaning 'neither one thing nor another; suitable to no class of people', the phrase sometimes occurs in the form: 'neither fish, flesh, nor fowl', where the origin of the expression (which dates from the Middle Ages) is that whatever is under discussion is unsuitable food for a monk (fish), for people generally (flesh), or for the poor (red, smoked, herring).

A 'red herring' in the sense of a distraction, diversion or false clue, derives from the practice of drawing the strongly smelling fish across the path of foxhounds to put them off the scent.

Nell. See LITTLE ~.

Nellie. See NOT ON YOUR ~.

Nelson. See DEATH OF ~.

Nelson touch, the. Denoting any action bearing the hall-mark of Horatio Nelson, his quality of leadership and seamanship, this term was coined by Nelson himself before the Battle of Trafalgar (1805): 'I am anxious to join the fleet, for it would add to my grief if any other man was to give them the Nelson touch.' The *Oxford Companion to Ships and the Sea* describes various manoeuvres to which the term could be applied, but adds, also: 'It could have meant the magic of his name among officers and seamen of his fleet, which was always enough to inspire them to great deeds of heroism and endurance.' The British title of the film *Corvette K-225* (US, 1943) was *The Nelson Touch*.

Nemesis. See GREEK NAMES.

ne plus ultra [not further beyond] was the supposed inscription on the Pillars of Hercules in the Strait of Gibraltar preventing ships from going further. It subsequently came to mean 'the furthest attainable point; the acme of something'.

Neptune. See ROMAN NAMES.

Nerd, The. The title of a play (1986) by Larry Shue and similarly, a US 'college hi-jinks' film, *The Revenge of the Nerds* (1984), this US slang expression for a boring, stupid person (sometimes **nurd**,

perhaps alluding to 'turd') became popular in the 1970s but has been around since the 1950s.

Nereus. See GREEK NAMES.

Nestor. See GREEK NAMES.

never again! was a slogan used during and after the First World War. Winston Churchill in his *The Second World War* (Vol.1) says of the French: 'with one passionate spasm [they cried] never again'. Later, in the mid-1960s, it became the slogan of the militant Jewish Defence League – referring to the HOLOCAUST. A stone monument erected near the birthplace of Adolf Hitler at Branau, Austria, in 1989 (the centenary of his birth) bore the lines: 'For Peace, Freedom and Democracy – Never Again Fascism [*Nie wieder Faschismus*] – Millions of Dead Are a Warning.'

never change/swap horses in mid-stream. Meaning 'don't alter course in the middle of doing something', Mencken has 'Never swap horses crossing a stream' as an 'American proverb, traced to *c* 1840'. CODP's earliest citation is Abraham Lincoln saying in 1864: 'I am reminded . . . of a story of an old Dutch farmer, who remarked to a companion once that "it was best not to swap horses when crossing streams".' This would seem to confirm the likely US origin. 'Don't change barrels going over Niagara' was a slogan attributed (satirically) to the Republicans during the presidential campaign of 1932, and is clearly derived from the foregoing.

never complain and never explain. Stanley Baldwin said to Harold Nicolson (21 July 1943): 'You will find in politics that you are much exposed to the attribution of false motive. Never complain and never explain.' Earlier, to Admiral Lord Fisher (*d* 1920) is attributed:

'Never complain and never apologise.' Each must, however, have been referring back to Benjamin Disraeli who was quoted as having said this in John Morley's *Life of Gladstone* (1903).

never glad confident morning again. A much-quoted phrase of disappointment with respect to a person's performance, its origin is in Robert Browning's poem 'The Lost Leader' (1845) in which he regretfully portrayed William Wordsworth as a man who had lost his revolutionary zeal. A correct – and devastating – use of the phrase came on 17 June 1963 when the British Government under its Prime Minister Harold Macmillan was rocking over the Profumo scandal. In the House of Commons, Tory M P Nigel Birch quoted the lines at Macmillan:

> Let him never come back to us!
> There would be doubt, hesitation and pain.
> Forced praise on our part – the glimmer of twilight,
> Never glad confident morning again!

In November 1983, on the twentieth anniversary of President Kennedy's assassination, Lord Harlech, former British Ambassador in Washington, paid tribute thus in the *Observer Magazine*: 'Since 1963 the world has seemed a bleaker place, and for me and I suspect millions of my contemporaries he remains the lost leader – "Never glad confident morning again".' Harlech may have wanted to evoke a leader who had been lost to the world, but surely it was a mistake to quote what is a criticism of one? Also in November 1983, in the *Observer*, Paul Johnson wrote an attack (which he later appeared to regret) on Margaret Thatcher: 'Her courage and sound instincts made her formidable. But if her judgement can no longer be trusted, what is left? A very ordinary woman, occupying a position where ordinary virtues are not enough. For me,

I fear it can never be "glad confident morning again".'

Never Mind the Quality Feel the Width. The title of a multi-ethnic I T V comedy series (1967–9) about 'Manny Cohen' and 'Patrick Kelly' running a tailoring business in the East End of London. It comes from what a street-tradesman (or Jewish tailor) might say. Paul Beale in Partridge/*Catch Phrases* suggests that this 'mid-twentieth-century' saying had, by the later twentieth century come to be used in more serious contexts: 'e.g. the necessity of eking out meagre resources of government aid to cover an impossibly large and neglected field'. A headline from an *Observer* editorial (29 January 1989) on a National Health Service where 'the pressure will be on to cut overheads and generally sacrifice quality for price' read: 'Never Mind the Quality', and the *Independent* (1 March 1989) had: 'England's senior chief inspector of schools warned ... "Nor must there be attempts, in trying to reduce shortages, to dilute standards by taking a 'never mind the quality, feel the width' approach".'

Never Never. (1) The land where the Lost Boys live in J.M. Barrie's *Peter Pan* (1904), though it may not be an original coinage. Winston Churchill said in the House of Commons (5 April 1906): 'That constitution now passes away into the never never land, into a sort of chilly limbo . . .' 'Never Never Land' was the English title of a song *Naar de Specituin* (1954) by Beryenberg and Froboess. (2) The Australian outback, as in *We of the Never Never* by Mrs Aeneas Gunn in 1908, though known as such by 1882. (3) Alternative name for hire purchase, as 'the never-never' (by 1926).

never say die! This exclamation, meaning 'never give in', was used by

Charles Dickens in several of his novels, starting with *The Pickwick Papers* (1836–7), though it is presumably not original to him. It is notably the catch phrase of Grip, the raven, in *Barnaby Rudge* (1841).

never work with children or animals. This piece of show-business lore probably originated in US vaudeville, and is occasionally adapted: '"Never work with children, dogs, or Denholm Elliott," British actors are said to advise one another' (*Guardian*, 29 April 1989). Phyllis Hartnoll in *Plays and Players* (1985) has: 'W.C. Fields is quoted as saying, "Never act with animals or children".' Although this line reflects his known views, the attribution may result from confusion with the saying more usually (though mistakenly) attributed to him: 'Any man who hates dogs and babies can't be all bad.' (See also *D P P*.)

new. See BRAND ~.

New Deal. The slogan of Franklin D. Roosevelt (though Abraham Lincoln had used it on occasions). To the 1932 Democratic Convention which had just nominated him, Roosevelt said: 'I pledge you, I pledge myself to a New Deal for the American people . . . a new order of competence and courage . . . to restore America to its own people.'

New Frontier. A slogan of John F. Kennedy which he first used on accepting the Democratic nomination in 1960: 'We stand today on the edge of a New Frontier. The frontier of the 1960s . . . is not a set of promises – it is a set of challenges. It sums up not what I intend to offer the American people, but what I intend to ask of them.' In 1964, Harold Wilson said in a speech in Birmingham:

'We want the youth of Britain to storm the new frontiers of knowledge.'

Newgate. See BLACK AS ~ KNOCKER.

Newman. See ALFRED E. ~.

news. The word meaning 'tidings' is the plural of 'new', and not an acronym of the four main points of the compass. Nowadays, the word is singular, but Shakespeare's *King Henry VI, Part 2* (III.ii.378) has: 'Ay me! What is this world! What news are these!' Queen Victoria, in an 1865 letter reacting to the assassination of President Lincoln, wrote: 'These American news are most dreadful and awful! One never heard of such a thing! I only hope it will not be catching elsewhere.' (See also ALL THE ~ THAT'S FIT TO PRINT.)

next year in Jerusalem! A familiar Jewish toast. In the Diaspora, it was the eternal hope – expressed particularly at the Feast of the Passover – that all Jews would be reunited . . . 'next year in Jerusalem'. Passover originally celebrated the exodus of the Jews from Egypt and their deliverance from enslavement some 3200 years ago. In the centuries of the Diaspora, the central Jewish dream was of being reunited in the land of Israel. In June 1967, following the Six Day War, when the modern state of Israel encompassed once more the old city of Jerusalem all Jews could, if they were able, end their exile and make this dream more of a reality.

NIBMAR. See ACRONYMS.

nice. See HAVE A GOOD DAY; MR ~ GUY.

Nice Guys Finish Last. The title of a book (1974) by Paul Gardner, subtitled 'Sport and American Life'. During his time as manager of the Brooklyn Dodgers baseball team (1951–4), Leo

Durocher became known for this view – also in the form: 'Nice guys don't finish first' or '. . . don't play ball games'. Partridge/*Catch Phrases* dates the popular use of the phrase from July 1946.

nice little earner. This stock phrase was used by George Cole in the character of 'Arthur Daley' in the I T V series *Minder* (from the late 1970s onwards) about petty criminals in the south of London. 'Earner' on its own, for 'money earned' (often shadily), may go back to the 1930s. From the *Independent* (27 April 1989) came: '[A large number of claims for tripping over broken paving stones in Northern Ireland], said Michael Latham, Tory M P for Rutland, meant that either the state of local pavements was "exceptionally disgraceful . . .", or the locals saw a "nice little earner there and are trying it on".'

Nicholas, St. See SAINTS' NAMES.

night. See DARK ~ OF THE SOUL.

Night and Fog. *Nacht und Nebel* was the name of a 1941 decree issued under Hitler's signature. It described a simple process: anyone suspected of a crime against occupying German forces was to disappear into 'night and fog'. Such people were thrown into the concentration camp system, in most cases never to be heard of again. Alain Resnais, the French film director, made a cinema short about a concentration camp called *Nuit et Brouillard* (1955). The phrase comes from Wagner's opera *Das Rheingold* (1869): '*Nacht und Nebel niemand gleich*' is the spell that Alberich puts on the magic Tarnhelm which renders him invisible and omnipresent. It means approximately, 'In night and fog no one is seen.'

Night Has a Thousand Eyes, The. The title of a story (1945) by Cornell Woolrich (about a vaudeville entertainer

who can predict the future), which was adapted as a film (US, 1948), and gave rise to several songs. It comes from the poem by Francis William Bourdillon in *Among the Flowers* (1878):

> The night has a thousand eyes,
> And yet the day but one;
> Yet the light of the bright world dies
> With the dying sun.

'Nightingale Sang in Berkeley Square, A'. The title of a song (1940) by Eric Maschwitz and Manning Sherwin. Earlier, 'When the Nightingale Sang in Berkeley Square' was the title of a short story by Michael Arlen, included in *These Charming People* (1923).

Night of Broken Glass [*Kristallnacht*]. A euphemism attributed to Walther Funk to describe the Nazi pogrom against Jews in Germany on the night of 9/10 November 1938.

Night of the Long Knives. During the weekend of 29 June/2 July 1934, there occurred in Nazi Germany '*Die Nacht der langen Messer*'. Hitler, aided by Himmler's black-shirted S S, liquidated the leadership of the brown-shirted S A. These latter undisciplined storm-troopers had helped Hitler gain power but were now getting in the way of his dealings with the German army. Some eighty-three were murdered on the pretext that they were plotting another revolution.

The phrase has passed into common use for any kind of surprise purge. It was applied, for example, to Harold Macmillan's wholesale reorganization of his Cabinet in 1962. When Norman St John Stevas was dropped from his Cabinet post in a 1981 re-shuffle, one wit described the changes as Mrs Thatcher's 'night of the long hatpin'. (See also D P P.)

Nike. See GREEK NAMES.

NICKNAMES. A nickname is simply an added or alternative name. It may endure for a lifetime, providing miniature character assessment, or it may be the creation of a moment and soon discarded. In some cases, it becomes an honorific that one can hardly imagine anybody using. In other cases, the nickname can be used to characterize a whole nation (LIMEY, UNCLE SAM).

Art and Literature

Bainbridge, Beryl: Basher
Beardsley, Aubrey: Awfully Weirdly; Daubaway Weirdsley
Beauvoir, Simone de: Notre Dame de Sartre
Boswell, James: Bozzy
Bunyan, John: the Immortal Tinker
Burns, Robert: the Ayrshire Poet
Carlyle, Thomas: the Sage of Chelsea
Cartland, Barbara: the Animated Meringue
Chatterton, Thomas: the Bristol Boy; the Marvellous Boy
Christie, Agatha: the Queen of Crime
Clark, Kenneth (Lord): 'K'; Lord Clark of Civilization
Douglas, Lord Alfred: BOSIE
Eliot, T.S.: Possum
Johnson, Dr Samuel: Dictionary Johnson; the Great Moralist; the English Socrates; Ursa Major; the GREAT CHAM OF LITERATURE
Leverson, Ada: the Sphinx
Philips, Ambrose: NAMBY-PAMBY
Shakespeare, William: BARD OF AVON; Sweet Swan of Avon; Avonian Willy

Film

Andrews, Julie: the Hockey Stick
Arbuckle, Roscoe: Fatty
Arliss, George: the First Gentleman of the Screen
Bardot, Brigitte: the Sex Kitten
Barrymore, John: the World's Greatest Actor
Beatty, Warren: the Kid

Bogart, Humphrey: Bogey
Bow, Clara: the IT GIRL.
Brando, Marlon: the Fat One
Bushman, Francis X.: the Handsomest Man in the World
Chaney Sr, Lon: the Man of a Thousand Faces
Crabbe, Clarence L.: Buster; the King of the Serials
Crawford, Joan: the Clothes Horse
Keaton, Buster: Stoneface
Marx Bros.: see MARX BROTHERS
Miranda, Carmen: the Brazilian Bombshell
Stroheim, Eric von: the MAN YOU LOVE TO HATE

History

Adams, John: the Colossus of (American) Independence/of Debate; the Machiavelli of Massachusetts
Adams, John Quincy: the Accidental President; Old Man Eloquent
Anglesey, 1st Marquess of: One-Leg Paget
Arthur, Chester: the Dude President; America's First Gentleman; the First Gentleman of This Land; His Accidency
Baden-Powell, 1st Baron: 'B P'; Bathing Towel
Barbie, Klaus: the BUTCHER OF LYONS
Bismarck, Prince Otto: the Iron Chancellor
Bormann, Martin: the BROWN EMINENCE
Brummell, George Bryan: Beau
Bryan, William Jennings: the Boy Orator of the Platte; the Great Commoner
Buchanan, James: the Bachelor President; Old Public Functionary
Buren, Martin van: the Little Magician; the Wizard of Kinderhook; Old Kinderhook
Burgoyne, Gen. John: Gentleman Johnny
Canary, Martha Jane: CALAMITY JANE

Nicknames – cont.

Capone, Al: Scarface
Channon, Sir Henry: Chips
Churchill, Sir Winston: FORMER NAVAL PERSON; the GREATEST LIVING —; Winnie
Clemenceau, Georges: the Tiger
Cleveland, Stephen Grover: the Man of Destiny; His Accidency; the Perpetual Candidate; the Stuffed/Dumb Prophet; Old Veto; Sir Veto
Cody, William F.: BUFFALO BILL.
Coolidge, Calvin: Silent Cal
Cromwell, Oliver: Almighty Nose; the Brewer; Copper Nose; Crum-Hell; Nosey; Ruby Nose; King Oliver
Cromwell Richard: Queen Dick; King Dick; Tumbledown
Crowley, Aleister: the Beast 666; the Great Beast; the Wickedest Man in the World
Dilke, Sir Charles: Three-in-a-Bed
Durham, Lord: King Jog
Garrick, David: the English Roscius
George, David Lloyd: the Goat; the Welsh Wizard
Gladstone, W.E.: the GRAND OLD MAN; the Great Commoner; Old Glad Eye(s); the Woodcutter of Hawarden
Goebbels, Josef: the POISON(ED) DWARF.
Grant, Ulysses S.: the Butcher; Old Three Stars; the American Sphinx; Unconditional Surrender; American Caesar
Hamilton, William Gerard: Single Speech
Hickock, J.B.: WILD BILL
Ismay, Gen Sir H.: Pug
Johnson, Dr Hewlett: the Red Dean
Kennedy, Revd G.S.: Woodbine Willy
Koch, Ilse: the Bitch of Buchenwald
Kramer, Josef: the BEAST OF BELSEN
Langtry, Lily: Jersey Lily

Lincoln, Abraham: the (Great) Emancipator; Honest Abe; the Rail Splitter; Old Abe; Ape; the Illinois Baboon; the Tycoon; Father Abraham; Fox Populi (see under VOX POPULI)
Louis XIV, King: the Sun King
Louis XVI, King: the BAKER
Marie Antoinette: the BAKER'S WIFE
Mengele, Josef: the ANGEL OF DEATH
Napoleon I: Boney; the Little Corporal; the Violet Corporal; the MAN OF DESTINY
Napoleon III: the Man of Sedan; the Prisoner of Ham
Nelson, Lord: the Magnet
Nightingale, Florence: the LADY WITH A/THE LAMP
Palmerston, Lord: Lord Cupid; Pam
Patton, George S.: Old Blood 'n' Guts
Peel, Sir Robert: Orange Peel; the Runaway Spartan
Pitt the Elder, William: the Great Commoner
Pitt the Younger, William: the BOTTOMLESS PITT
Robespierre, M.: the SEA-GREEN INCORRUPTIBLE
Russell, Lord John: the Widow's Mite
Sandwich, 4th Earl of: JEMMY TWITCHER; Twitch
Scott, Capt R.F.: Birdie
Smith, W.H.: Old Morality
Stalin, Joseph: the Man of Steel; Uncle Joe
Stilwell, General Joseph: Vinegar Joe
Walters, Catherine: Skittles
Warwick, Frances Countess of: Darling Daisy; the Red Countess
Wellington, 1st Duke of: the Iron Duke; Conkey; (Old) Nosey; the Great Captain; Beau
Wilberforce, Samuel: Slippery/Soapy Sam
Wilhelm II, Kaiser: Kaiser Bill

Nicknames – cont.

Music

Anka, Paul: GOLDEN BOY
Armstrong, Louis: Satchmo; Pops
Avalon, Frankie: GOLDEN BOY; the Young Sinatra
Basie, William: Count
Boone, Pat: MR CLEAN; Mr Toothpaste
Callas, Maria: the Divine Callas
Calvert, Eddie: the Man with the Golden Trumpet
Caruso, Enrico: the Man with the Orchid-Lined Voice
Clapton, Eric: Old Slow Hand
Crosby, Harry L.: Bing; the Old Groaner; One-Take
Domino, Antoine: Fats
Gillespie, J.B.: Dizzy
Haitink, Sir Bernard: Clogs
Holiday, Billie: Lady Day
Jagger, Mick: Biglips
Jones, Oran: Juice
Lind, Jenny: the Swedish Nightingale
Lloyd, Marie: Our Marie; the Queen of the Halls/Music-Hall
Lynn, Vera: the Forces' Sweetheart
Morton, F.J.Le M.: JELLY ROLL
Norman, Jessye: Jessyenormous
Parker, Charlie: Bird
Piaf, Edith: the Little Sparrow
Presley, Elvis: the Pelvis; the King (of Rock'n'Roll)
Rossini, G.A.: the Swan of Pesaro
Sinatra, Frank: Bones; the Gov'nor; the Voice; the Chairman of the Board; Ol' Blue Eyes
Springsteen, Bruce: the Boss
Vivaldi, Antonio: the Red Priest

Nationalities

American (USA): Doughboy/GI (services); Yankee; Uncle Sam (US personified)
Australian: Aussie; Digger
Canadian: Canuck; Jean Baptiste (French Canadian)
Dutchman: Mynheer

Englishman: LIMEY; POM; Tommy (military); John Bull (country personified)
Frenchman: Frog; Johnny
German: Bosch; Fritz; Heinz; Jerry; Kraut
Irishman: Mick; Paddy; Pat
Italian: Itie
New Zealander: Kiwi
Pole: Polack (mostly US)
Russian: Russki; Ivan
Scot: Jock; Mac; Sandy
Spaniard: SPIC; Dago
Welshman: Taffy

Politics, Modern

Adenauer, Konrad: *der Alte* [the Old Man]
Amin, Idi: Big Daddy
Asquith, H.H.: Squiff; PJ [Perrier-Jouët]
Baldwin, Stanley: Bonzo; God; Tiger
Balfour, Arthur J.: Pretty Fanny
Banda, Dr Hastings: Little Black Banda
Beaverbrook, 1st Lord: the Beaver; Robin Badfellow
Benn, Tony: Wedgie
Bevan, Aneurin: Nye
Bevin, Ernest: the Dockers' KC
Botha, P.W.: the (Big) Crocodile
Bush, Barbara: the First Granny
Bush, George: Poppy
Callaghan, James (Lord): SUNNY JIM
Carter, Jimmy: President Peanut; Jiminy Peanuts; Peanut; JIMMY WHO?
Carter, Lillian: Miss/Miz Lillian
Carter, Rosalynn: see under STEEL MAGNOLIAS
Cohn-Bendit, Daniel: Danny the Red/ Le Rouge
Currie, Edwina: Cruella De Ville
Dewey, Thomas E.: the MAN ON THE WEDDING CAKE
Dukakis, Mike: the Duke
Duvalier, Jean-Claude: Baby Doc
Duvalier, François: Papa Doc
Eisenhower, Dwight D.: IKE

Nicknames – cont.

Gromyko, A.A.: Grim Grom; Mr Nyet
Heseltine, Michael: Tarzan
Howe, Sir Geoffrey: Sir Geoffrey Who
Ibarruri, Dolores: LA PASIONARIA
[Passion flower]
Kinnock, Neil: the Ginger Whinger; the
Welsh Windbag
Macmillan, Harold: MAC THE KNIFE;
Macwonder; Supermac
Mandela, Winnie: the Mother of the
Nation
Molotov, V.M.: Iron Pants; Old Stone
Bottom
Mondale, Walter: Fritz; Norwegian
Wood
Nixon, Richard M.: Tricky Dicky
Reagan, Ronald: Dutch; the Gipper;
the Great Communicator; Old
Hopalong
Roosevelt, F.D.: Sphinx; the Squire of
Hyde Park; Houdini in the White
House
Roosevelt, Theodore: the Bull
Moose; Rough Rider; the Man on
Horseback
Shawcross, Sir Hartley: Sir Shortly
Floorcross
Staller, Ilona: *La Cicciolina* [the Little
Fleshy One]
Thatcher, Margaret: Attila the Hen;
the Blessed Margaret; Hilda; the
Leaderene; Milk Snatcher; SHE
WHO MUST BE OBEYED; TINA;
the IRON LADY; TBW [That Bloody
Woman]
Truman, Harry S: Give 'Em Hell
Harry; THE MAN FROM Missouri
Wilson, Harold (Lord): Wislon; the
Houdini of Politics

Royalty, British
Andrew, Prince: Randy Andy
Anne, Queen: Brandy Nan; Mrs Bull
Anne of Cleves: the Flanders Mare
Charles I, King: the Last Man
Charles II, King: the Merry Monarch;
Old Rowley
Charles, Prince: ACTION MAN

Edward VII, King: Tum-Tum; Bertie;
Teddy; Old Peacock; Edward the
Caresser
Elizabeth I, Queen: Gloriana; Good
Queen Bess; the Virgin Queen
Elizabeth II, Queen: Lillibet; Brenda
George III, King: Farmer George
George IV, King: Prinny; Fum the
Fourth
George V, King: Sprat; the Sailor
Prince/King; Grandpapa England
Henry II, King: Curtmantle
Margaret, Princess: Yvonne
Mary I, Queen: Bloody Mary
William II, King: William Rufus
William IV, King: the Sailor King

Show Business
Askey, Arthur: Big-Hearted Arthur
Beaumont, Hugh: BINKIE
Berle, Milton: Mr Television
Bernhardt, Sarah: the Divine Sarah
Connolly, Billy: the Big Yin
Coward, Noël: the MASTER
Devine, Catherine: LITTLE EGYPT
Durante, Jimmy: Schnozzle
Elliott, G.H.: the Chocolate-Coloured
Coon
Fields, Gracie: Our Gracie
Jolson, Al: the World's Greatest
Entertainer
Merman, Ethel: the Golden Foghorn
Mirvish, Ed: Honest Ed
Murdoch, Richard: Stinker
Sykes, Norma: Sabrina; the
Hunchfront of Lime Grove; (see also
under *SABRINA FAIR*)
Woodward, Edward: Fart in the Bath

Sport
Ali, Muhammad: the Louisville Lip; the
Mouth
Borg, Björn: the Iceberg
Botham, Ian: Guy the Gorilla
Bradman, Sir Don: the Don
Connolly, Maureen: Little Mo
Dempsey, Jack: the Manassa Mauler
Di Maggio, Joe: the YANKEE CLIPPER

Nicknames – cont.

Edwards, Eddie: the Eagle
Farr, Tommy: the Tonypandy Terror
Frazier, Joe: Smokin' Joe
Grace, W.G.: the Grand Old Man of English Cricket
Louis, Joe: the BROWN BOMBER
Matthews, Sir Stanley: the King of World Soccer; WIZARD OF THE DRIBBLE

McEnroe, John: Superbrat
Perry, William: the Refrigerator
Piggot, Lester: the Long Fellow
Ruth, G.H.: the BABE

See also BEAST OF JERSEY; BUNGALOW BILL; CAPABILITY BROWN; GREEN GODDESS; JOLLY JACK; MAN THEY COULDN'T GAG.

---

nil carborundum. See ILLEGITIMI . . .

nilometer. See SWINGOMETER.

NIMBY. See ACRONYMS.

nine days' wonder. Referring to something of short-lived appeal and soon forgotten, the expression comes from an old proverb: 'A wonder lasts nine days, and then the puppy's eyes are open' – alluding to the fact that dogs (like cats) are born blind. After nine days, in other words, their eyes are open to see clearly. (See also *DPP*.)

nines. See DRESSED UP TO THE ~.

Nine Tailors, The. The title of a novel (1934) by Dorothy L. Sayers. In bell-ringing it was possible to indicate the gender of a dead person for whom the bells were being tolled. 'Nine tailors' or 'nine tellers' (strokes) meant a man. But the phrase also appears to be a proverb in contempt of tailors: 'It takes nine tailors to make a man', which apparently came from the French *c* 1600. The meaning of this seems to be that a man should buy his clothes from various sources. Apperson shows that, until the end of the seventeenth century, there was some uncertainty about the number of tailors mentioned. In *Westward Ho* by John Webster and Thomas Dekker (1605) it appears as three.

Nineteen Eighty-Four. The title of a novel (1949) by George Orwell which was a warning of a totalitarian future. It is said that Orwell originally wished to call it '1948' to show that it was a contemporary warning rather than a prophecy. Like the adjective **Orwellian**, the title came to stand for a bleak, soulless world.

See also BIG BROTHER IS WATCHING YOU.

nineties. See NAUGHTY ~.

Nisus. See ROMAN NAMES.

nitty-gritty. See LET'S GET DOWN TO THE ~.

No Blade of Grass. The title of a film (UK, 1970) about worldwide food shortages brought about by industrial pollution, and based on a book by John Christopher called *The Death of Grass* (1956). It is a turn of phrase with no precise origin. The nearest the Bible gets is Isaiah 15:6: 'The grass faileth, there is no green thing.' Amelia B. Edwards in *A Thousand Miles up the Nile* (1877) writes: 'The barren desert hems us in to right and left, with never a blade of green between the rock and the river.' A 1902 citation of an old Turkish proverb in *ODP* is: 'Where the hoof of the Turkish horse treads, no blade of grass ever grows.' Other examples are found in Agatha Christie's *Autobiography* (1977): 'There was no scrap of garden anywhere. All was asphalt. No blade of grass showed green.' And from *The Life of Kenneth Tynan* by Kathleen Tynan (1987): 'I felt there was nothing about the country in Ken at all. Not a blade of grass . . .'

no comment. This is a consciously inadequate form of evasion, used to enquiring journalists. Winston Churchill appears not to have known it until 1946, so perhaps it was not generally known until then, at least not outside the US. After a meeting with President Truman, Churchill said: 'I think "No Comment" is a splendid expression. I got it from Sumner Welles [US diplomat and presidential adviser].' (See also *DPP*.)

nods. See EVEN HOMER ~.

noise and the people!, the. This was the reaction of a certain Capt Strahan to being in a battle. According to *ODQ*, quoting the *Hudson Review*, Winter 1951, he said it after the Battle of Bastogne in 1944. However, various correspondents suggest it was earlier in the Second World War. Roy T. Kendall writes: 'I heard this phrase used, in a humorous manner, during the early part of 1942. It was related to me as having been said by a young Guards officer, newly returned from Dunkirk, who, on being asked what it was like, used the expression: the inference being, a blasé attitude to the dangers and a disdain of the common soldiery he was forced to mix with.' Tony Bagnall Smith adds that the Guards officer was still properly dressed and equipped when he said it, and that his reply was: 'My dear, the noise and the people – how they smelt!'

No Man's Land. The title of a play (1974) by Harold Pinter, and an unrelated film (US, 1987), it comes from the old expression (current by 1320) for

unowned, waste land. The expression is also used to describe the space between entrenched armies (as in the First World War).

No My Darling Daughter. See DON'T GO NEAR THE WATER.

None But the Brave. This film title (US, 1965) about the Second World War, comes from Dryden's *Alexander's Feast* (1697): 'None but the brave deserves the fair.' Sir Edwin Landseer's painting 'None But the Brave Deserve the Fair' (1838) shows two stags fighting while anxious hinds look on.

None But the Lonely Heart. The title of this novel (1943; film US, 1944) by Richard Llewellyn is apparently an original coinage. But compare, 'None But the Weary Heart', the title often given to a song by Tchaikovsky (Op.6, No.6). This originated as 'Mignon's Song' in the novel *Wilhelm Meister* by Goethe – '*Nur wer die Sehnsucht kennt*' [Only those who know what longing is] – which was translated into Russian by Mey. The lyrics of Tchaikovsky's song have been translated into English as, 'None but the weary heart can understand how I have suffered and how I am tormented.'

'Non Sum Qualis Eram' [I am not what I was]. The title of a poem (1896), also known as 'Cynara', by Ernest Dowson, from which come the titles 'ALWAYS TRUE TO YOU IN MY FASHION', DAYS OF WINE AND ROSES and GONE WITH THE WIND. 'Cynara' is a woman to whom the poet professes faithfulness even when consorting with others.

N or M? The title of the spy story (1941) by Agatha CHRISTIE comes from the guide answer to the first question in the Catechism in the Prayer Book: 'What is your Name?' (referring only to the answerer's Christian name or names). 'N' is the first letter of the Latin *nomen* [name]; 'M' is a contraction of NN standing for the plural *nomina* [names].

normalcy. See BACK TO ~.

Nor the Moon by Night. The title of a film (UK, 1958) about a game warden in Africa, it comes from Psalm 121:5–6: 'The Lord is thy shade upon thy right hand. The sun shall not smite thee by day, nor the moon by night.' In the US, the film was called *Elephant Gun*.

North by North West. The title of this film (US, 1959) is taken from Shakespeare's *Hamlet* (II.ii.374): 'I am but mad north-north-west. When the wind is southerly, I know a hawk from a handsaw.'

North-South divide. This is a political phrase for (1) the perceived difference in living standards between the developed nations (mostly to be found in the northern hemisphere) and the underdeveloped nations in the southern hemisphere; (2) the division between the prosperous south of England and the rest of the country. In a speech on 4 February 1927, Winston Churchill said: 'I saw a comparison made in the "Nation" newspaper of the conditions prevailing north and south of a line which the writer had drawn across the country from Cardiff to Hull.'

Norwich/NORWICH. See DO YOU KNOW THE BISHOP OF ~?; and under ACRONYMS.

nose. See PAY THROUGH THE ~.

No Sex Please We're British. The title of the long-running farce (1971; film UK, 1973) by Anthony Marriott and Alastair Foot is much-alluded to by headline writers and such.

nosey parker. Meaning 'an interfering, inquisitive person', from the fact that the nose has long been associated with an inquisitive nature. Traditionally, a link has been suggested with Matthew Parker, Elizabeth I's Archbishop of Canterbury. Partridge/*Slang* wonders whether the 'parker', meaning 'park-keeper', wasn't rather someone who enjoyed spying on love-making couples in London's Hyde Park.

Nostalgia Isn't What It Used To Be. The title of the autobiography (1978) of Simone Signoret came from a graffito chalked up on a wall in New York City. As 'Nostalgia ain't what it used to be' the remark has been attributed to the US novelist Peter de Vries.

no such thing as a free lunch. Meaning 'there's no getting something for nothing', this US saying dates back to the mid-nineteenth century. Flexner puts an 1840s date on the supply of 'free lunch' – even if this amounted to no more than thirst-arousing snacks like pretzels – in saloon bars. This was not strictly speaking 'free' because you had to buy beer to obtain it. The notion was given a new lease of life in the 1970s by the economist Milton Friedman. Indeed, the saying was sometimes ascribed to him by virtue of the fact that he published a book with the title, and wrote articles and gave lectures incorporating the phrase. (See also DPP.)

no surrender! In 1689, the year after the Catholic King James II was replaced with the Protestant William of Orange on the British throne, forces still loyal to James maintained a siege against the citizens of Derry in Ulster. The siege was raised after a month or two. 'No surrender!' was the Protestant slogan and 'Long Live Ulster. No surrender' is still a Loyalist slogan. Another version is: 'No Popery, no surrender'. *No Surrender* was the title of a 1985 film written by Alan

Bleasdale about warring Protestant and Roman Catholic factions in Liverpool.

Nothing But the Truth. The title of three films (US 1920, 1929, 1941) based on James Montgomery's play (pre-1920). *The Whole Truth* was also the title of a film (UK 1958). See I SWEAR . . .

Nothing Like the Sun. The title of a novel (1964) by Anthony Burgess, about the life of Shakespeare, and of a record album by Sting (1987), its origin is Shakespeare's Sonnet 130: 'My mistress' eyes are nothing like the sun.'

nothing venture nothing win. The first recorded use of the proverb in this precise form is in Sir Charles Sedley's comedy *The Mulberry Garden* (1668). However, the variants 'nothing venture, nothing gain' and 'nothing venture, nothing have' go back further, and may derive from a Latin original. W.S. Gilbert used this form in the 'proverb' song in Act II of *Iolanthe* (1882) and Sir Edmund Hillary, the mountaineer, used it as the title of his autobiography (1975).

not on your Nellie! Meaning 'not likely; not on your life!' this is probably rhyming slang from Nellie Duff (puff, meaning 'breath' i.e. life).

Not Prince Hamlet. The title of the autobiography (1989) by the critic and translator of plays, Michael Meyer, comes from T.S. Eliot's 'The Love Song of J. Alfred Prufrock' (1917):

> No! I am not Prince Hamlet, nor was
> meant to be;
> Am an attendant lord, one that will do
> To swell a progress, start a scene or two.

not tonight Josephine. This catch phrase is now used when declining to participate in any activity. Napoleon Bonaparte did not, as far as we know, ever say the words which have become popularly linked with him. The idea that he had better things to do than satisfy the Empress Josephine's famous appetite, or was not inclined or able to, must have grown up during the nineteenth century. The phrase was popularized by the film *I COVER THE WATERFRONT* (1933).

not with a bang but a whimper. This phrase, used to express an anti-climax, alludes to T.S. Eliot, *The Hollow Men* (1925): 'This is the way the world ends/Not with a bang but a whimper'.

Not With a Bang was the title of an ITV series (1990), and the *Observer* (8 July 1990) reported: 'After some 70 hours Ernest Saunders finally left the Southwark witness box on Thursday afternoon not with a bang or whimper but more with a chorus of the familiar refrains which had echoed . . .'

Now Barabbas . . . This was the title of a film (UK, 1949) about prisoners, based on a play by William Douglas-Home, but also known as *Now Barabbas Was a Robber*. Its origin is John 18:40: 'Now Barabbas was a robber.'

now Barabbas was a publisher . . . The story has it that when John Murray, Byron's publisher, sent the poet a copy of the Bible in return for a favour, Byron sent it back with the words 'Now Barabbas was a robber' (see previous entry) altered to: 'Now Barabbas was a publisher . . .' This story was included in Kazlitt Arvine's *Cyclopedia of Anecdotes of Literature and the Fine Arts* published in Boston, Mass. in 1851. The present head of the firm, John G. Murray, stated in 1981 that those involved were in fact the poet Coleridge and *his* publishers, Longmans. Mencken, on the other hand, gives Thomas

Campbell (*d* 1844) as the probable perpetrator, and so does Benham.

Now Barabbas Was a Rotter. The title of a biography of Marie Correlli (1978) by Brian Masters, alluding to the novel *Barabbas*, which was Corelli's first success. See NOW BARABBAS . . .

now is the time for all good men to come to the aid of the party. This typewriter exercise was originated by Charles E. Weller, a court reporter in Milwaukee (1867) to test the efficiency of the first practical typewriter, which his friend, Christopher L. Scholes, had made. Unfortunately, he did not do a very good job because the phrase only contains eighteen letters of the alphabet. **The quick brown fox jumps over the lazy dog**, on the other hand, has all twenty-six. This was once thought to be the shortest sentence in English containing all the letters of the alphabet but it was superseded by: 'Pack my box with five dozen liquor jugs' (which has three fewer letters overall).

Now Voyager. The title of this novel (1941; film US, 1942) by Olive Higgins Prouty comes from a favourite phrase of Walt Whitman in *Leaves of Grass* (1871 version). 'Now Finalé to the Shore' has: 'Now Voyager depart (much, much for thee is yet in store') while 'The Untold Want' has: 'Now voyager sail thou forth to seek and find'.

Nox. See ROMAN NAMES.

N(Q)OCD. See INITIALS.

NQTD. See INITIALS.

NST. See INITIALS.

nudity. See FULL-FRONTAL ~.

number one son. This nickname for an eldest son, in imitation of Chinese speech, was popularized in the many 'Charlie Chan' films of the 1930s which featured an oriental detective (who had a large family).

OO

O

Oates, 'Titus'. See I'M JUST GOING OUTSIDE . . .

oath, court. See I SWEAR . . .

obeying. See I WAS ONLY ~ ORDERS.

Odysseus. See GREEK NAMES.

Oedipus. See GREEK NAMES.

offensive. See CHARM ~.

offer. See I'M GOING TO MAKE HIM AN ~ . . .

office. See JACK IN ~.

Officer and a Gentlemen, An. See CONDUCT UNBECOMING.

off one's trolley, to be. Meaning 'to be mad', *DOAS* finds this (in the US) by 1909 and calls it 'probably the oldest of the "off [one's] —" = crazy terms',

---

Odeon. Now the name of any typical British cinema, it originally referred to those in a chain built by Oscar Deutsch and company in the 1930s. He had come across the word *odeion*, for amphitheatre, on a visit to Greece. It had already been taken up by the French as a word for 'concert hall' and thence into American English as part of 'nickelodeon' (first as a word for a coin-operated player piano, then for cinemas which charged a nickel). Later, someone suggested it could also be an acronym for 'Oscar Deutsch Entertains Our Nation'.

As for other common names for places of entertainment, a character in Nancy Mitford's novel *Pigeon Pie* (1940) joked that: 'All the sights in Rome are called after London cinemas . . .' Latin is certainly the source of **Coliseum**, **Forum** and (via Greek) **Hippodrome**. **Palladium** is from the Greek *palladion* (an image of Pallas Athene); **Lyceum** is the Greek name of the garden where Aristotle taught philosophy; **Metro** presumably is an abbreviation of 'metropolitan', as in Metro-Goldwyn-Mayer; **Astoria** is after the district in New York where Paramount had sound studios in the 1920s, which in turn probably derived from the port in Oregon, founded by John Jacob *Astor*; **Corona** like **Stella** has 'star' connotations, appropriate for a cinema; **Ionic** continues the Greek architectural theme; **Plaza** is Spanish for 'place' and **Scala** presumably refers to La Scala opera house in Milan (in Italian, *scala* is a ladder or musical scale). As for **Essoldo**, it seems to have emerged from the name of Sol Sheckman, the company founder.

---

but 'off one's head' and 'rocker' are a little older. (See also *D P P.*)

Of Human Bondage. The title of the novel (1915) by W. Somerset Maugham is from the title of one of the books in Spinoza's *Ethics* (1677).

Of Mice and Men. The title of the novel (1937; film US, 1939) by John Steinbeck comes from Robert Burns, 'To a Mouse' (1785):

> The best laid plans o' mice and men
> Gang aft a-gley.

often a bridesmaid but never a bride. The phrase applied to someone who never takes the principal part in anything, comes from the slogan for Listerine mouthwash in the US (*c* 1923), though there is also an echo of the British music-hall song: 'Why Am I Always a Bridesmaid?' made famous by Lily Morris (1917).

Of Thee I Sing. This was the title of a musical (1931) by Gershwin/Gershwin/Kaufman/Ryskind, about the US presidency (title song: 'Of Thee I Sing, Baby'). Its origin is 'America' (1831) by Samuel Francis Smith (which is sung to the tune of the British National Anthem): 'My country 'tis of thee, sweet land of liberty, of thee I sing'.

Oh! Calcutta! The title of Kenneth Tynan's sexually explicit stage revue (1969) derives from a curious piece of word play, being the equivalent of the French '*Oh, quel cul t'as*' [Oh, what a lovely bum you've got]. French *cul* is derived from the Latin *culus* 'buttocks' but, according to the context, may be applied to the female vagina or male anus. In her *Life of Kenneth Tynan* (1987), Kathleen Tynan states that she was writing an article on the surrealist painter Clovis Trouille, one of whose works was a naked odalisque lying on her side to reveal a spherical backside. The title was 'Oh! Calcutta! Calcutta!': 'I suggested to Ken that he call his erotic revue *Oh! Calcutta!* . . . I did not know at the time that it had the further advantage of being a French pun.'

OK! The origin of this expression has occasioned more debate than any other in this dictionary. Here are some of the suggested origins, though one probably need go no further than explanations (1) and (2).

(1) President Andrew Jackson (*d* 1837), when a court clerk in Tennessee, would mark ' O K' on legal documents as an abbreviation for the illiterate 'Oll Korrect'. The first recorded use in the US of this jocular form is in the Boston *Morning Post* (23 March 1839).

(2) It was used by President Martin van Buren as an election slogan in 1840. The initials stood for 'Old Kinderhook', his nickname, which derived from his birthplace in New York State.

(3) Inspectors who weighed and graded bales of cotton as they were delivered to Mississippi river ports for shipment would write *aux quais* on any found faulty (i.e. 'not O K'). This meant they had to be sent back to the jetty.

(4) It comes from Aux Cayes, a port in Haiti famous for its rum.

(5) It is an anglicization of the word for 'good' in Ewe or Wolof, the West African language spoken by many of the slaves taken to the southern US.

(6) It derives from the Greek words *ola kala* meaning 'all is fine; everything is good'.

(7) In the First World War, soldiers would report each night the number of deaths in their group. ' O K' stood for '0 killed'.

(8) A railroad freight agent, Obadiah Kelly, used his initials on bills of lading.

(9) An Indian chief, Old Keokuk, used his initials on treaties.

(10) It stood for 'outer keel' when shipbuilders chalked it on timbers.

(11)   Teachers used it instead of *omnes korrectes* on perfect exam papers.

(12)   From boxes of Orrins-Kendall crackers, popular with Union troops in the Civil War.

(13)   From an English word 'hoacky', meaning 'the last load of a harvest'.

(14)   From a Finnish word *oikea* meaning 'correct'.

(15)   From a Choctaw word *okeh* [it is] or *hoke*.

See also RULES OK.

okey-pokey/hokey-pokey. The name of imitation ice cream made from shaved ice mixed with syrup was current by 1900. Perhaps it was thought that the imitation was a form of hocus-pocus or trickery, or else it could have been a corruption of '*ecce, ecce!*', the cry with which Italian street vendors would call attention to their wares. Iona and Peter Opie in *The Lore and Language of Schoolchildren* (1959) wonder whether it could derive from Italian '*O che poco!*' [O how little!] though why anyone should say that they do not explain.

old as my tongue and a little older than my teeth, as. This is what nannies (and other older folk) traditionally reply when asked how old they are by young NOSEY PARKERS. Swift has it in *Polite Conversation* (1738).

Old Bill. A nickname for the police (and in particular, the Metropolitan Police of London). So many policemen wore walrus moustaches after the First World War that they reminded people of Bruce Bairnsfather's cartoon character 'Old Bill'. He was the one who said: 'IF YOU KNOW A BETTER 'OLE, GO TO IT'. Partridge/*Slang*, which provides this explanation, also wonders whether there might be some connection with the US song 'Won't You Come Home, Bill Bailey' (*c* 1902) or with the Old Bailey courts. 'The Bill' is an abbreviation of the name and was used as the title of a ITV cops series (*c* 1990).

Old Contemptibles. This nickname was gladly taken unto themselves by First World War veterans of the British Expeditionary Force who crossed the English Channel in 1914 to join the French and Belgians against the German advance. It was alleged that Kaiser Wilhelm II had described the army as 'a contemptibly little army' (referring to its size rather than its quality). The British press was then said to have mistranslated this so that it made him appear to have called them a 'contemptible little army'. The truth is that the whole episode was a propaganda ploy masterminded by the British.

Old Grey Whistle Test, The. The title of this BBC TV pop music series (from the 1970s) came from the alleged practice in TIN PAN ALLEY of trying new pop songs out on the elderly grey-haired doormen. If they could pick up the tune to the extent of being able to whistle it, the song stood a chance.

Old Man of the Sea, The. The name of a troublesome character in *The Arabian Nights* who climbed on the back of Sinbad the Sailor and was hard to dislodge, hence, the phrase for 'a burden'. The title of Ernest Hemingway's novel *The Old Man and the Sea* (1952; film US, 1958) presumably alludes lightly to him.

Old Men Forget. The title of the memoirs (1953) of Duff Cooper, 1st Viscount Norwich, comes from Shakespeare's *King Henry V* (IV.iii.49):

> Old men forget; yet all shall be forgot,
> But he'll remember with advantages
> What feats he did that day.

old soldiers never die, they simply fade away. Following his dismissal by

President Truman, Gen Douglas MacArthur was allowed to address Congress on 19 April 1951. He ended: 'I still remember the refrain of one of the most popular barrack ballads of that day [turn of the century], which proclaimed, most proudly, that "Old soldiers never die. They just fade away." And like the old soldier of that ballad. I now close my military career and just fade away . . .' He was quoting a British army parody of the gospel hymn 'Kind Words Can Never Die' which (in spite of MacArthur's dating) came out of the First World War. J. Foley copyrighted a version of the parody in 1920. (See also *DPP*.)

old Spanish customs. The phrase refers to practices which are of long standing but are unauthorized. Although current by the 1930s, the term came to prominence in the mid-1980s to describe the irregular behaviour of newspaper production workers in Fleet Street (cheating over pay-packets, especially). Why the Spanish are blamed is not clear, except that Spaniards tend to attract pejoratives (see SPIC) – not least with regard to working practices (the *mañana* attitude). In Elizabethan times, William Cecil is quoted as saying of Sir Thomas Tresham, architect of Rushton Triangular Lodge, that he was not given to 'Spanish practices' (i.e. Roman Catholic ones). These, being irregular at the time, could provide us with an origin for the phrase.

omnibus. See MAN ON THE CLAPHAM ~.

once aboard the lugger and the girl is mine! 'A male catch phrase either joyously or derisively jocular' notes Partridge/*Catch Phrases*. It came originally from a late Victorian melodrama – either *My Jack and Dorothy* by Ben Landeck (*c* 1890) or from a passage in *The Gypsy Farmer* by John Benn

Johnstone (*d* 1891). In 1908, A.S.M. Hutchinson called a novel *Once Aboard the Lugger – the History of George and Mary*. The phrase occurs in the music-hall song 'On the Good Ship Yacki-Hicki-Doo-La', written and composed by Billy Merson in 1918. Benham has a different version, as often. According to him: 'Once aboard the lugger and all is well' was said to have been an actor's gag in *Black Eyed Susan*, a pantomime (*c* 1830).

Once and Future King, The. The title of T.H. White's Arthurian romance (1958) derives from the epitaph '*Hic jacet Arthurus, rex quondam rexque futurus*' [Here lies Arthur, the once and future king]. This is what Sir Thomas Malory in *Morte d'Arthur* (1469–70) says was written on the tombstone of the legendary king.

once in a blue moon. Meaning 'very rarely, if ever', the notion of a 'blue moon' being something you *never* saw and could not believe in, was current by 1528. However, given that in some circumstances the moon can appear blue, this less stringent expression had established itself by 1821.

once upon a time . . . The traditional start to 'fairy' stories. George Peele has the line in his play *The Old Wives' Tale* (1595). The Old Woman begins a story she is telling with: 'Once upon a time there was a King, or a Lord, or a Duke . . .' which suggests that it was a format phrase even then. Thirteen of the twenty-four *Classic Fairy Tales* collected in their earliest English versions by Iona and Peter Opie (1974) begin with the words. Mostly the versions are translations from the French of Charles Perrault's collected *Histories, or Tales of Past Times* (1697). The ready-made English phrase is used to translate his almost invariable: '*Il estoit une fois*'. (See also *DPP*.)

one. See ALL FOR ~ . . .

One Brief Shining Moment. The title
of a book (1983) by William Manchester, on the twentieth anniversary of President Kennedy's assassination. It comes from a favourite lyric of the late president in the Lerner and Loewe musical *Camelot*:

> Don't let it be forgot
> That once there was a spot
> For one brief shining moment
> That was known as Camelot.

One Flew Over the Cuckoo's Nest.
The title of a novel (1962; film US, 1975) by Ken Kesey, which comes from the rhyme (chiefly known in this version in the US):

> One flew east, one flew west,
> One flew over the cuckoo's nest.

one foot in the grave, to have.
Meaning 'to be near death', the earliest citation in the *OED2* is from Burton's *Anatomy of Melancholy* (1621): 'An old acherontic dizzard that hath one foot in his grave'. Swift in *Gulliver's Travels* (1726) uses the phrase in connection with the immortal Struldbruggs of Laputa. There is also a punning inscription upon the grave of the actor and dramatist, Samuel Foote (*d* 1777), in Westminster Abbey:

> Here lies one Foote, whose death may
>   thousands save,
> For death has now one foot within the
>   grave.

One Is One. The title of a novel (1989)
by Lucy Irvine, about being single. See under *GREEN GROW THE RUSHES*.

One More River. The title of the film
(US, 1934) based on John Galsworthy's 1933 novel *Over the River* (which was how the film was known in the UK). The altering of the title for the US market would suggest an allusion to the traditional song 'One More River to Cross' (also known as 'Noah's Ark') which refers to the Jordan:

> Old Noah once he built the Ark
> There's one more river to cross.
> And patched it up with hick'ry bark
> There's one more river to cross.
> One more river, and that's the river of
>   Jordan,
> One more river
> There's one more river to cross.

One of Our Aircraft Is Missing. The
title of a film (UK, 1941). In *A Life in Movies* (1986), Michael Powell writes of a moment in the Second World War: 'After I returned from Canada and I had time to listen to the nine o'clock news on the BBC, I had become fascinated by a phrase which occurred only too often: "One of our aircraft failed to return".' He determined to make a film about such a failed bombing mission. 'Our screenplay, which was half-finished, was entitled *One of Our Aircraft Is Missing*. We were never too proud to take a tip from distributors, and we saw that the original title, *One of Our Aircraft Failed to Return*, although evocative and euphonious, was downbeat'. In 1975, Walt Disney came up with a film called *One of Our Dinosaurs Is Missing*.

one over the eight. This expression
for 'drunk' is services' slang, but not before the twentieth century. For some reason, eight beers was considered to be a reasonable and safe amount for an average man to drink. One more and you were incapable.

one small step for (a) man, one
giant leap for mankind. What Neil Armstrong claimed he said when stepping on to the moon's surface for the

first time on 20 July 1969 was: 'That's one small step for a man, one giant leap for mankind.' The indefinite article before 'man' was, however, completely inaudible, thus ruining the sense. (See also *D P P*.)

one step forward two steps back. In 1904, Lenin wrote a book about 'the crisis within our party' under this title. A more recent example of the phrase comes from *Cosmopolitan*: 'Alternatively, try retro-dressing. It's here again. One step forward, thirty years back. The Fifties look is determined to make a comeback . . .' (February 1987). (See also *D P P*.)

One Two Buckle My Shoe. The title of this Agatha CHRISTIE novel (1940), comes from the children's counting rhyme first recorded in 1805.

only connect. This is the epigraph to *Howard's End* (1910), the novel by E.M. Forster. Goronwy Rees wrote in A CHAPTER OF ACCIDENTS (1972): 'It could be said that those two words, so misleading in their ambiguity, had more influence in shaping the emotional attitudes of the English governing class between the two world wars than any other single phrase in the English language.' The words also occur in the body of Forster's book: 'Only connect! That was the whole of her sermon. Only connect the prose and the passion, and both will be exalted, and human love will be seen at its height. Live in fragments no longer. Only connect, and the beast and the monk, robbed of the isolation that is life to either, will die.' Forster's message was that barriers of all kinds must be dismantled if the harmony lacking in modern life is to be discovered.

Only Fools and Horses. The title of a BBC TV comedy series (from 1981) by John Sullivan, about a pair of wide-boy brothers in London, comes from what is said to be an old Cockney expression: 'Only fools and horses work.'

Only in America. The title of an ITV series (1980) which derives from the catch phrase meaning 'only in America is this possible'. Leo Rosten in *Hooray for Yiddish!* (1982) writes: 'Not a week passed during my boyhood (or two weeks, since then) without my hearing this exclamation. It is the immigrants' testament, an affirmation of the opportunities imbedded in that Promised Land . . . America. Scarcely a new shop, new product, a new journal or school or fad could appear without ecstatic *Only in America*!s.'

Only When I Larf. This was the title of a novel (1968; film UK, 1968) by Len Deighton. *Only When I Laugh* was the title of an ITV comedy series (1979–84) set in a hospital, and of a film (US, 1981) which was released in the UK as *It Hurts Only When I Laugh* – which points to its origin. There is an old joke about an English soldier in Africa who gets pinned to a tree by an assegai. When asked if it hurts, he replies with this stiff-upper-lip statement.

on one's tod. Meaning 'on one's own', this expression derives from rhyming slang: Tod Sloan was a noted US jockey (*d* 1933).

onwards and upwards! Perhaps this humorously uplifting phrase designed to encourage, derives from a religious notion of striving onwards and upwards through the everlasting night? In James Russell Lowell's *The Present Crisis* (1844) we find: 'They must upward still, and onward, who would keep abreast of truth.' The first lines of the nineteenth-century hymn 'Onward! Upward!' (words by F.J. Crosby, music by Ira D. Sankey) are:

Onward! upward! Christian soldier.
Turn not back nor sheath thy sword;
Let its blade be sharp for conquest
In the battle for the Lord.

Sankey also set the words of Albert Midlane in 'Onward, Upward, Homeward!', of which the refrain is:

Onward to the glory!
Upward to the prize!
Homeward to the mansions
Far above the skies!

Or could the words be from a motto? The Davies-Colley family of Newfold, Cheshire, have them as such in the form 'Upwards and Onwards'. 'Nicholas Craig' in I, An Actor (1988) asks of young actors: 'Will you be able to learn the language of the profession and say things like "onwards and upwards", "Oh well, we survive" and "Never stops, love, he *never stops*".'

on with the motley! Partridge/*Catch Phrases* suggests that this is what one says to start a party or trip to the theatre. It may also mean 'on with the show, in spite of what has happened'. Either way, the allusion is to the Clown's cry – '*vesti la giubba*' – in Leoncavallo's opera I Pagliacci (1892). The Clown has to 'carry on with the show' despite having a broken heart. So it might be said jokingly nowadays by anyone who is having to proceed with something in spite of difficulties. Laurence Olivier used the phrase in something like its original context when describing a sudden return dash home from Ceylon during a crisis in his marriage to Vivien Leigh: 'I got myself on to a plane . . . and was in Paris on the Saturday afternoon. I went straight on home the next day as I had music sessions for The Beggar's Opera from the Monday; and so, on with the motley.' (Confessions of an Actor, 1982)

'*Giubba*' in Italian, means simply 'jacket' (in the sense of costume), and 'the motley' is the old English word for an actor's or clown's clothes, originally the many-coloured coat worn by a jester or fool (as mentioned several times in Shakespeare's As You Like It).

on your bike! This expression meaning 'go away; be off with you!' Partridge/ *Slang* dates from c 1960. It is often confused with what the newly appointed employment secretary, Norman Tebbit told the Conservative Party conference on 15 October 1981. He related how he had grown up in the 1930s when unemployment was widespread: '[My father] did not riot. He got on his bike and looked for work. And he kept on looking till he found it.'

open sesame! Meaning 'open up (the door)!' or as a mock password, the phrase comes from the tale of 'The Forty Thieves' in the ancient Oriental Tales of the Arabian Nights.

opera. See FAT LADY SINGS.

orange. It is sometimes asserted that there is no rhyme for this word. Irving Berlin (d 1989) almost rose to the challenge when he suggested to Walter Winchell, the US columnist, that 'door-hinge' spoken with a Bronx accent might do. Others have suggested rhymes involving 'sporange' (case holding spores), 'porringer', and the mountain called 'Blorenge' in South Wales.

Orcus. See ROMAN NAMES.

orders. See I WAS ONLY OBEYING ~.

Orestes. See GREEK NAMES.

orphan. See LITTLE ~ ANNIE.

Orpheus. See GREEK NAMES.

Oscar. An Academy Award, one of a number of statuettes presented each year since 1928 by the American Academy of Motion Picture Arts and Sciences. The nickname originated in a comment made by Margaret Herrick, a secretary at the Academy (c 1931): 'Why, it looks just like my Uncle Oscar' (who was Oscar Pierce, a wheat and fruit grower).

our day will come. This is an English translation of the Provisional I R A slogan, which is in Gaelic *'Tiocfaidh Ar La'*. Relatives of those accused of trying to blow up the British Prime Minister at Brighton in 1984 shouted it out as the defendants were being sentenced in court on 23 June 1986. It was also the title of a song performed by the American vocal group Ruby and the Romantics (1963).

Our Mutual Friend. The title of the novel (1864) by Charles Dickens refers to its hero, John Harmon, who feigns death and whose identity is one of the mysteries of the plot. This is a rare example of Dickens using an established phrase for a title (he usually chooses the invented name of a character). 'Our mutual friend' was an expression established by the seventeenth century but undoubtedly Dickens encouraged its use. Some would object that 'mutual friend' is a solecism, arguing that it is impossible for the reciprocity of friendship to be shared with a third party.

où sont les neiges d'antan?, mais [but where are the snows of yesteryear?] A line, now used only in mock yearning, which occurs as a refrain in the 'Ballade des Dames du Temps Jadis' from *Le Grand Testament* (1461) by the French poet François Villon.

Out of Africa. The title of a film (U S/ U K, 1985) based on Isak Dinesen's book (1938) – originally in Danish, *Den Afrikanske Farm*. It possibly alludes to Pliny's version of a Greek proverb, '*Ex Africa semper aliquid novi*' [there is always something new/some novelty coming out of Africa]. (See also *D P P*.)

out of the Ark. Meaning 'something that is very old indeed', alluding to the antiquity of Noah's Ark. Thackeray in *Roundabout Papers* (1860–3) has: 'We who lived before railways, and survive out of the ancient world, are like Father Noah and his family out of the Ark.'

out of the closet (and into the street). This was the slogan of the U S homosexual rights organization known as the Gay Liberation Front (c 1969). The starting point was the term 'closet homosexual' or 'closet queen' for one who hid his inclinations away in a closet ('cupboard' in U S usage rather than 'lavatory' or 'small room' as in British English).

out of the cradle endlessly rocking. A silent film subtitle occurring in D.W. Griffith's epic *Intolerance* (1916), 'out of the cradle, endlessly rocking' accompanies a shot of Lillian Gish rocking a cradle, and is repeated many times during the course of the long film. It comes from the title of a poem (1859) by Walt Whitman.

outside. See I'M JUST GOING ~.

Outrageous Fortune. The title of this film (U S, 1987), about rival actresses aspiring to be in a production of *Hamlet*, comes from TO BE OR NOT TO BE in Shakespeare's *Hamlet*.

overcome. See WE SHALL ~.

over the moon. In the diaries of May, Lady Cavendish (published 1927) there is an entry for 7 February 1857 saying how she broke the news of her youngest brother's birth to the rest of her siblings: 'I had told the little ones who were first utterly incredulous and then over the moon.' The family of Catherine Gladstone (*née* Gwynne), wife of the Prime Minister, is said to have had its own idiomatic language and originated the phrase. However, the nursery rhyme:

Hey diddle
The cat and the fiddle,
The cow jumped over the moon

dates back to 1765 at least and surely conveys the same meaning. The specific application to football was already in evidence in 1962, when Alf Ramsey (a team manager) was quoted as saying, on one occasion: 'I feel like jumping over the moon.' Compare SICK AS A PARROT. (See also *DPP*.)

over the top. Meaning 'exaggerated in manner of performance; too much'. The earlier expression 'to go over the top' originated in the trenches of the First World War. It was used to describe the method of charging over the parapet and out of the trenches on the attack. The phrase was later adopted for use by show-business people when describing a performance that had gone beyond the bounds of restraint. In 1982, a near-the-bone TV series reflected this by calling itself *OTT*, after which one heard people saying that something was 'a bit *OTT*' instead of the full expression.

own goal, to score an. Originally meaning (in football) 'to score a goal against one's own side', this expression has acquired the meaning 'to bring harm upon oneself'. The phrase was adapted by members of the security forces in Northern Ireland in the 1980s and was used to describe what happened when terrorists were blown up by their own bombs. It is a very similar coinage to 'shooting oneself in the foot' or being HOIST WITH ONE'S OWN PETARD. The *Guardian*, 20 March 1989 has: 'Ozal risks own goal in move to kick life into slack election' [by attending a Turkish football team's foray into European soccer – when it might have lost the game].

P P

Page Three girl. Meaning 'a topless photographic model', the allusion is specifically to the kind regularly featured on page three of the *Sun* newspaper, but can be broadly applied to any nude model. Larry Lamb, the editor, introduced the feature within a year of the paper's relaunch on 17 November 1969, following its acquisition by Rupert Murdoch, the Australian-born newspaper proprietor.

painting in the attic. See PICTURE OF DORIAN GRAY.

PAL. See INITIALS.

pale. See BEYOND THE ~.

Pale Horse, The. See BEHOLD A PALE HORSE.

Palinurus. See ROMAN NAMES.

Palladium. See under ODEON.

Pallas Athene. See ATHENA under GREEK NAMES.

palm without the dust. It was said of Lord Rosebery, the British Liberal Prime Minister in the 1890s, that 'he wanted the palm without the dust', an allusion to Horace, the Roman author, who talked of 'the happy state of getting the victor's palm without the dust of racing'.

'*Palma non sine pulvere*' [no palm without labour] is a motto of the Earls of Liverpool, among others.

Pancras, St. See SAINTS' NAMES.

Pandora. See GREEK NAMES.

Pangloss. 'An imperturbably optimistic person', so named after the philosophical tutor in Voltaire's *Candide* (1759) who believes that: 'All is for the best in the best of all possible worlds'. Hence, the adjective **panglossian**.

paper bag. See COULDN'T FIGHT . . .

Paper Moon. The title of this film (US, 1973) comes from the song 'It's Only a Paper Moon' (1932) by E.Y. Harburg, Billy Rose and Harold Arlen.

Paper Tiger. The title of a film (UK, 1975) about a coward who pretends to be otherwise, the phrase is usually applied to a person who appears outwardly strong but is, in fact, weak. It was popularized by the Chinese leader, Mao Tse-tung, who told a US interviewer in 1946: 'All reactionaries are paper tigers. In appearance, the reactionaries are terrifying, but in reality they are not so powerful.'

Parcae. See ROMAN NAMES.

Paris. See GREEK NAMES.

Paris by Night. The title of a film (UK, 1989) by David Hare, it has been a promotional tag for tourism in the French capital, in use since the 1950s at least. A London West End revue used the somewhat nudging phrase as its title in 1955. From the 1930s there had been a cheap perfume, available from Woolworth and manufactured by Bourjois, called 'Evening in Paris' – which also traded on the city's reputation for sophisticated pleasures.

parish. See WHOLE WORLD AS ONE'S ~.

parker. See NOSEY ~.

Parker, Dorothy. See AS ~ ONCE SAID.

Parkinson's Law. The observation that 'work expands so as to fill the time available for its completion' was first promulgated by Professor C. Northcote Parkinson in the *Economist* magazine (1955).

parrot. See SICK AS A ~.

Parthenope. See GREEK NAMES.

party. See COLLAPSE OF STOUT ~; I TOOK MY HARP TO A ~.

party's over, the. This cliché phrase is used to describe the end of anything, but is inevitably used in political contexts. On 4 June 1990, the *Daily Express*, *Sun*, and *Daily Mirror* all used it in headlines regarding the collapse of the British Social Democratic Party. In 1975, Anthony Crosland, the Labour minister, said that local government was 'coming to realize that, for the time being at least, the party is over'. The allusion could be to either of two songs: Noël Coward's 'The Party's Over Now' from *Words and Music* (1932) or 'The Party's Over' from *Bells Are Ringing*

(1956) by Comden and Green, and Jules Styne.

Pasionaria, La [Passion flower]. This was the nickname of Dolores Ibarruri (*d* 1990), the Spanish Communist leader at the time of the Civil War. Margaret Thatcher was dubbed 'La Pasionaria of Privilege' in 1975 by Denis Healey, the Labour minister.

Pasiphaë. See GREEK NAMES.

pass. See AND THIS TOO SHALL ~; CUT OFF AT THE ~.

Passage to India, A. The title of a novel (1924) by E.M. Forster, who recalled the title of a poem 'Passage to India' (1871) in Walt Whitman's *Leaves of Grass*.

pass the buck, to. Meaning 'to shift responsibility on to someone else', the phrase derives from some card games, where a marker called a 'buck' is put in front of the dealer to remind players who the dealer is. When it is someone else's turn, the 'buck' is 'passed'. The original marker may have been a buckthorn knife or, in the Old West, a silver dollar – hence the modern use of the word 'buck' for a dollar.

pastures. See FRESH FIELDS AND ~ NEW.

Paths of Glory. The title of the novel (1935; film US, 1957) by Humphrey Cobb comes from Thomas Gray's *Elegy in a Country Churchyard* (1742–50): 'The paths of glory lead but to the grave'.

Patrick, St. See SAINTS' NAMES.

Patriot for Me, A. The title of a play (1965) by John Osborne. A distinguished servant of the Austrian Empire was being recommended to

Franz II as a sterling patriot, so the Emperor actually asked: 'But is he a patriot for me?'

Patroclus. See GREEK NAMES.

pavlova. This dessert, consisting of meringue, whipped cream, and fruit (often strawberry), was created in the Antipodes (places and dates vary, but it was current in New Zealand by 1927) as a sort of compliment to Anna Pavlova, the Russian-born ballerina (*d* 1931). The concoction may resemble the spread-out skirts on a ballerina's tutu.

paw. See CAT'S ~.

Pax. See ROMAN NAMES.

pay. See GO NOW ~ LATER.

paying. See I AM ~ FOR THIS BROAD-CAST.

pay through the nose, to. Meaning 'to pay heavily', one possible explanation for the origin of the phrase lies in the 'nose' tax levied upon the Irish by the Danes in the ninth century. Those who did not pay had their noses slit.

peace at any price. 'Peace at any price; peace and union' was the slogan of the American (Know-Nothing) Party in the 1856 US presidential election. The party supported ex-President Fillmore and the slogan meant that it was willing to accept slavery for blacks in order to avoid a civil war. Fillmore lost to James Buchanan.

It has been suggested that the phrase had been coined earlier (in 1848 or 1820) by Alphonse de Lamartine, the French foreign affairs minister in his *Méditations Poétiques* in the form: '*La paix à tout prix*'. However, the Earl of Clarendon quoted an 'unreasonable calumny' concerning Lord Falkland in his *History of the Rebellion* (written in 1647): 'that he was so enamoured on peace, that he would have been glad the king should have bought it at any price'. When Neville CHAMBERLAIN signed his pact with Hitler in 1938, many praised him for trying to obtain 'peace at any price'.

peace for/in our time. On his return from signing the Munich agreement with Hitler in September 1938, Neville CHAMBERLAIN spoke from a window at 10 Downing Street ('not of design but for the purpose of dispersing the huge multitude below' [according to his biographer Keith Feiling]). He said: 'My good friends, this is the second time in our history that there has come back from Germany to Downing Street PEACE WITH HONOUR. I believe it is peace for [*sic*] our time. Go home and get a nice quiet sleep.' His phrase 'peace for our time' is often misquoted as 'peace *in* our time' – as by Noël Coward in the title of his 1947 play set in an England after the Germans have conquered. Perhaps Coward, and others, were influenced by the words from the Book of Common Prayer: 'Give Peace in our time, O Lord.'

peace is our profession. Motto (by 1962) of the US Strategic Air Command. In 1972, there was a US film called *Lassie: Peace Is Our Profession*.

peace with honour. When Benjamin Disraeli returned from the Congress of Berlin (1878), called to settle the 'Balkan question', this was what he claimed to have achieved. Two days before Neville CHAMBERLAIN returned from signing the Munich agreement with Hitler, someone had suggested that he might like to use the Disraeli phrase. He impatiently rejected it, but then, according to John Colville in *Footprints in Time* (1976), he used the phrase at the urging of his wife (see PEACE FOR/IN OUR TIME).

Peach Melba. This dessert consists of peaches in vanilla-flavoured syrup on top of ice cream and coated with raspberry sauce. It was named after Dame Nellie Melba, the Australian opera singer, who was staying at the Savoy Hotel in London in 1892 when the chef, Auguste Escoffier, created this dessert for her. It was served as though between the wings of a swan – alluding to *Lohengrin*, in which she was appearing at Covent Garden. In 1897, Escoffier also invented **Melba toast** (made with extremely thin bread), though the name was applied by M.L. Ritz. (Melba was born Helen Mitchell. For her stage name she adapted a portion of 'Melbourne', her home town.)

pearls before swine. Referring to things of quality put before the unappreciative, the source is Matthew 7:6: 'Give not that which is holy unto the dogs, neither cast ye pearls before swine.'

peccavi [I have sinned]. *O E D2* sees it as part of the expression 'to cry *peccavi*', an acknowledgement or confession of guilt. The earliest citation given is Bishop John Fisher's Funeral Sermon at St Paul's for Henry VII (1509): 'King David that wrote this psalm, with one word speaking his heart was changed saying *peccavi*.' This refers to Psalm 41:4: 'I said, Lord, be merciful unto me: heal my soul, for I have sinned against thee.' The phrase occurs in a number of other places in the Bible, mostly in the Old Testament – e.g. 'And Saul said unto Samuel, I have sinned' (1 Samuel 15:24).

The word is often, mistakenly, thought to have furnished a famous pun. Here is Charles Berlitz's version in *Native Tongues*: 'Sir Charles Napier, a British officer in India, was given command of an expedition to annex the

kingdom of Sind in (1843) . . . To announce the success of his mission, he dispatched to the headquarters of the British East India Company a one-word message, the Latin word *peccavi*, which means "I have *sinned*".' Alas, Napier did no such thing. It was *Punch* (18 May 1844) which suggested that Caesar's *'Veni, vidi, vici'* was beaten for brevity by 'Napier's dispatch to Lord Ellenborough . . . *Peccavi*'. *O D Q* credits the joke to a young girl, Catherine Winkworth. It seems, however, that the joke was soon taken as genuine, even at *Punch* itself. On 22 March 1856, the magazine (confusing sender and receiver in the original) included the couplet:

> '*Peccavi* – I've Scinde,' wrote Lord Ellen, so proud.
> More briefly Dalhousie wrote – '*Vovi* – I've Oude'.

Pecksniff, Seth. The hypocritical character in *Martin Chuzzlewit* (1843–4) by Charles Dickens, is an oily man, 'fuller of virtuous precepts than a copybook', who behaves in a manner contrary to a 'moral man'. Hence the word **Pecksniffian** and other derivatives.

Peeping Tom. The title of a film (U K, 1959), about a man who films his victims while murdering them, it comes from the name given to voyeurs of any kind. That, in turn, derives from the name of Tom the Tailor who was struck blind because he peeped when **Lady Godiva** rode by. In the legend, Lady Godiva's husband, the Lord of Coventry, only agreed to abolish some harsh taxes if she would ride naked through the town. The townspeople responded to her request that they should stay behind closed doors – all except Peeping Tom. This element of the story was probably grafted on to the record of an actual happening of the eleventh century.

peg. See SQUARE ~ IN A . . .; TAKE SOMEONE DOWN A ~.

Pegasus. See GREEK NAMES.

peel. See BEULAH ~ A GRAPE.

Pelops. See GREEK NAMES.

pencil. See BLUE ~.

Pendennis. The name of the 'diary' column in the *Observer* since 1957, it is after the hero of the novel *The History of Pendennis* (1848–50) by William Thackeray, presumably because he flirts with literary journalism at one stage. Arthur Pendennis is a young man who goes through various flirtations and entanglements on the way to the getting of wisdom. He is also the narrator of Thackeray's *The Newcomes* and *The Adventures of Philip*. His uncle, Maj Arthur Pendennis, might seem an even better role model for a newspaper diarist: 'If there were any question about . . . society, who was married to whom . . . Pendennis was the man to whom every one applied . . . And every other man he met was a lord.' Thackeray probably took the name from Pendennis Castle and Point near Falmouth, Cornwall.

Penelope. See GREEK NAMES.

pen is mightier than the sword, the. In Edward Bulwer-Lytton's play *Richelieu* (II.ii., 1839), the Cardinal says:

> Beneath the rule of men entirely great,
> The pen is mightier than the sword.

CDP finds several earlier attempts at expressing the idea, to which one might add this corollary from Shakespeare's *Hamlet* (II.ii.344): 'Many wearing rapiers are afraid of goose-quills.'

'Penny Plain and Twopence Coloured, A'. This was the title of a noted essay (in *The Magazine of Art*, 1884) by Robert Louis Stevenson on the toy theatres or 'juvenile drama' of his youth. *Tuppence Coloured* was the title of a theatrical novel by Patrick Hamilton (1927) and of a revue (with Joyce Grenfell and others) in 1947. As a phrase, *ODCIE* has that it means 'in cheap or more expensive (attractive or merely showy) form (from, formerly, paper cut-outs of characters and scenery for toy theatres)'. On the other hand, the *Longman Dictionary of English Idioms* (1979) takes things a little further: '*rather old-fash.*: although one of two similar things may be more attractive or bright in appearance than the other, they both basically have the same use or value'. There is no question that, meaning 'plain or fancy', the saying was principally connected with toy theatres of the last century and referred to the prices of characters and scenery you could buy already coloured or in black and white to colour yourself.

people. See BEAUTIFUL ~; GETAWAY ~; NOISE AND THE ~; WE THE ~.

Peoria. See IT'LL PLAY IN ~.

Perchance to Dream. The title of this musical (1945) by Ivor Novello, comes from the TO BE OR NOT TO BE speech in Shakespeare's *Hamlet*.

Persephone. See GREEK NAMES.

Perseus. See GREEK NAMES.

petard. See HOIST WITH ONE'S OWN ~.

Peter Principle. The observation that 'in a hierarchy every employee tends to rise to his level of incompetence' was first promulgated by Dr Laurence J.

Peter in *The Peter Principle – Why Things Go Wrong* (with R. Hull) (1969).

phenomenon. See INFANT ~.

Philemon. See ROMAN NAMES.

Philoctetes. See GREEK NAMES.

Philomela. See GREEK NAMES.

philosopher. See GUIDE ~ AND FRIEND.

Phoebe. See GREEK NAMES.

Phoebus. See GREEK NAMES.

Pickwick, Samuel. The founder of the Pickwick Club in *The Pickwick Papers* (1836–7) by Charles Dickens, and the very type of genial, honourable bachelor, bald and bespectacled. Dickens took the name from Moses Pickwick who operated coaches between London and Bath – who, in turn, may have taken his name from the hamlet of Pickwick, near Bath. Hence **Pickwickian** to describe humorous or idiosyncratic language – also meaning 'obese' after the 'Fat Boy' in the same novel.

picture. See EVERY ~ TELLS A STORY.

picture is worth a thousand words, a. This saying – alluded to, for example, in the David Gates song 'If' (1975) – is sometimes said to be a Chinese proverb. Bartlett lists it as such in the form: 'One picture is worth more than ten thousand words' and compares what Turgenev says in *Fathers and Sons* (1862): 'A picture shows me at a glance what it takes dozens of pages of a book to expound.' But CODP points out that it originated in a US paper *Printers' Ink* (8 December 1921) in the form: 'One look is worth a thousand words' and was there ascribed by its actual

author, Frederick R. Barnard, to a Chinese source (to give it instant proverbial status, one supposes).

pidgin. Jargon made up of mainly English words but arranged according to Chinese methods and pronounced in a Chinese way. It arose to facilitate communication between Chinese and Europeans at seaports and has nothing to do with 'pigeon'. Rather, it is the Chinese pronunciation of 'business', although now 'pidgin' can be formed from any two languages and is not restricted to Chinese and English.

pie. See EAT HUMBLE ~.

pie Jesu. See MASS PHRASES.

pig. See MALE CHAUVINIST ~.

Pillars of Society. The English title of Henrik Ibsen's play *Samfundets Stotter* (1877), in the translation by William Archer. When the play was first produced in London in 1880 it was, however, called *Quicksands*. In the play, the 'pillars of society' are described as being 'the spirit of truth and the spirit of freedom'. The phrase has now come to mean people who are the main supporters of church, state, institutions or principles (compare 'pillars of state', 'pillar of faith').

pilot. See DROPPING THE ~.

Piltdown Man. See SELSDON MAN.

Pincher Martin. The title of a novel (1956) by William Golding, about a drowning sailor. 'Pincher' has become an inseparable nickname for anyone surnamed 'Martin' ever since the days of Adm Sir William F. Martin (*c* 1860). He was a strict disciplinarian who insisted on ratings being put under arrest ('pinched') for even minor offences.

Piper at the Gates of Dawn, The. The title of the first record album recorded by Pink Floyd in 1967 comes from the title of Chapter 7 of Kenneth Grahame's *The Wind in the Willows* (1908). 'The Piper at the Gates of Dawn' describes a lyrical, not to say mystical experience, that Mole and Ratty have when they hear the god Pan piping at dawn.

pissed/tight as a newt. Partridge/*Slang* gives various metaphors for drunkenness from the animal kingdom – 'pissed as a coot/rat/parrot' among them. None seems particularly apposite. And why 'newt'? Could it be that the newt, being an amphibious reptile, can submerge itself in liquid as a drunk might do? Or is it because its tight-fitting skin reflects the state of being 'tight'? (See also *DPP*.)

piss up in a brewery. See COULD RUN A . . .

pit/Pitt. See BOTTOMLESS ∼.

PITP. See INITIALS.

Place in the Sun, A. The title given to the 1951 film of Theodore Dreiser's *An American Tragedy*, echoes the phrase for German colonial ambitions in East Asia, which had been coined by Bernard von Bülow, the German Chancellor, in a speech to the Reichstag in 1897: 'In a word, we desire to throw no one into the shade, but we also demand our own place in the sun [*Platz an der Sonne*].' In 1901, Kaiser Wilhelm II took up the theme in a speech at Elbe: 'We have fought for our place in the sun and won it. Our future is on the water.' The notion was much referred to in the run-up to the First World War. An early appearance occurs in the *Pensées* of Blaise Pascal (Walker's translation, 1688): 'This Dog is mine, said those poor Children; That's my place in the

Sun. This is the beginning and Image of the Usurpation of all the Earth.' The phrase is now hardly ever used in this precise sense, but simply to indicate a rightful piece of good fortune, a desirable situation, e.g.: 'Mr Frisk could bring Aintree punters their place in the sun' (headline from the *Independent on Sunday*, 1 April 1990).

Places Where They Sing. The title of a novel (1970) by Simon Raven in his ALMS FOR OBLIVION sequence. It comes from the Rubric after the Third Collect in Morning and Evening Prayer in the Prayer Book: 'In Quires and Places where they sing, here followeth the Anthem.'

plans. See LIFE IS WHAT HAPPENS WHILE . . .

playing fields of Eton. See BATTLE OF WATERLOO . . .

Play It Again Sam. The title of a play (1969; film US, 1972) by Woody Allen, about a film critic who is abandoned by his wife and obtains the help of Humphrey Bogart's 'shade'. AS EVERY SCHOOLBOY KNOWS by now, neither Humphrey Bogart nor Ingrid Bergman uses this wording precisely in the film *Casablanca* (1942).

Plaza. See under ODEON.

pleasure dome. See XANADU.

Plinge. See WALTER ∼.

plonk. A word for 'cheap wine' probably first used in Australia (by 1919). It may reflect the sound of a cork being drawn out of a bottle or come from '*vin blanc*', the French for white wine.

Ploughman's Lunch, The. The title of a film (UK, 1983), about how history gets rewritten. The use of the term for a meal of bread, cheese, and pickle, though redolent of olden days, was in fact a marketing ploy of the English Country Cheese Council in the early 1970s.

P L U. See INITIALS.

plume de ma tante, la. As 'the cat sat on the mat' is to learning the English language, so *'je n'ai pas la plume de ma tante'* is to learning French. It must have occurred in some widely used French grammar in British schools – possibly just prior to the First World War. In Terence Rattigan's play *French Without Tears* (1936) a character says: 'If a Frenchman asked me where the pen of his aunt was, the chances are I could give him a pretty sharp comeback and tell him it was in the pocket of the gardener.' A revue with the title played at the Garrick Theatre in 1955.

Pluto. See GREEK NAMES.

Plutus. See GREEK NAMES.

Pocket Full of Rye, A. The title of this 'Miss Marple' novel (1953) by Agatha CHRISTIE comes from the nursery rhyme 'Sing a Song of Sixpence', first recorded *c* 1744. Christie also used 'Sing a Song of Sixpence' (1934) and 'Four and Twenty Blackbirds' (1960) from the same source for the titles of short stories.

Pogues, The. The name of an Irish pop group (*fl.* 1989), originally called 'Pogue Mahone', from the Gaelic for 'kiss my arse'.

point(s). See THOUSAND ~ OF LIGHT; UP TO A ~ LORD COPPER.

poison(ed) dwarf. A name given to any unpleasant person of small stature. According to episode one of the I T V series *The World at War* (1975), this was a popular German nickname in the late

1930s for Hitler's diminutive propaganda chief, Joseph Goebbels. The literal German *Giftzwerg* is defined by the Collins German dictionary as 'poisonous individual; spiteful little devil'. In Wagner's *Das Rheingold* (1869), however, Wellgunde calls Alberich *'Schwefelgezwerg'* (literally 'sulphurous dwarf'). Knowing how a Wagnerian phrase like NIGHT AND FOG was adapted in the Nazi era, this seems a likely source for the phrase.

pole. See GREASY ~.

police caution, the. See ANYTHING YOU SAY . . .

politics. See ART OF THE POSSIBLE.

Pollux. See GREEK NAMES.

Pollyana. The name for an (excessively) optimistic person comes from the heroine of *Pollyanna*, a novel (1913) by Eleanor Porter.

Polyphemus. See GREEK NAMES.

pom(my). Meaning 'an Englishman' in Australian usage ('pommy bastard', 'whingeing poms'), this was established by 1912. It is possibly from a melding of 'pomegranate' and 'immigrant'; or from the French *pomme* ('apple') – compare LIMEY; or from an acronym stamped on the shirts of convict settlers, P O H M S ('Prisoners Of Her Majesty').

Pomona. See ROMAN NAMES.

'Pomp and Circumstance'. The title of five marches by Sir Edward Elgar (Nos. 1–4 composed 1901–7, and No. 5 in 1930, comes from Shakespeare's *Othello* (III.iii.360):

O farewell . . .
Pride, pomp, and circumstance of
glorious war!

poodle. See BALFOUR'S ~.

poodlefaker. Denoting a man who
cultivates the society of women, this is
an Anglo-Indian services term describing
a type of man to be found in the hill
stations and alluding to lap-dogs.

poof(dah)/poofter/poove. See GAY.

poor are always with you. This biblical phrase is to be found in Matthew
26:11, Mark 14:7, and John 12:8: 'For
the poor always ye have with you.' *The
Rich Are Always With Us* was the title of
a film (US, 1932) and *The Rich Are
With You Always*, the title of a novel
(1976) by Malcolm Macdonald.

'Poor Little Rich Girl'. The title of a
film (1917) starring Mary Pickford and
of a song (1925) by Noël Coward, this
phrase is now used for a woman whose
wealth has not brought her happiness.

poor thing but mine own. In 1985, a
painter called Howard Hodgkin won the
£10,000 Turner prize for a work (of art)
called 'A Small Thing but My Own'. It
was notable that he used the word
'small' rather than 'poor'. Nevertheless,
he was presumably alluding to Touchstone's line in Shakespeare's *As You Like
It* (V.iv.57): 'A poor virgin, sir, an ill-
favoured thing, sir, but mine own'. Here
Touchstone is not talking of art but of
Audrey, the country wench he woos. The
line is nowadays more likely to be used
(in mock-modesty) about a thing rather
than a person.

Pop Art. Lawrence Alloway invented
this designation for art that refers to
popular culture (comic-strip images,
etc.), in the mid-1950s, although originally he used it as a synonym for 'popular culture'. The first recorded use of the
word 'Pop' *in* art is in Eduardo
Paolozzi's picture 'I Was a Rich Man's
Plaything' (*c* 1947) which is a modest
collage of advertisements and the cover
of *Intimate Confessions*. A pistol,
pointed at a pin-up, is going 'Pop!'

Popeye. The one-eyed, pipe-smoking,
spinach-eating sailor originally appeared
in strip cartoons but is best known
through the many short animated films
made for cinema and TV. Created by
Elzie Crisler Sefar, Popeye first appeared
in a syndicated strip 'Thimble Theatre'
in the 1930s. His personal philosophy is
summed up by his refrain: 'I yam what I
yam and that's all that I yam.' His slen-
der, shrewish girlfriend is Olive Oyl.

pop goes the weasel. At some time in
the nineteenth century, possibly in 1853,
W.R. Mandale may have written the
celebrated words:

Up and down the City Road,
In and out of the Eagle,
That's the way the money goes –
Pop goes the weasel!

He may have put these words to a tune
for a country dance which already
existed, but what did he mean by them?
What is plain is that 'the Eagle' refers to
the Eagle Tavern, then a theatre and pub
in the City Road, London (the present
tavern was built at the turn of the century). Those who went 'in and out' spent
plenty of money and were forced to
'pop', or pawn, something. But what
was the 'weasel' they pawned? A kind of
tool used by a carpenter or a hatter, a
tailor's flat iron, a coat (from rhyming
slang 'weasel and stoat'), have all been
suggested. (See also *DPP*.)

pop one's clogs. See CLOGS.

porpentine. See FRETFUL ~.

POP GROUP NAMES. From the 1960s onwards, pop groups took on increasingly bizarre names. The **Beatles** were originally the 'Silver Beatles' (no such insect, a simple 'beat/beetle' pun – though echoing 'Bootle', the district of Merseyside). The **Rolling Stones** came not directly from the proverb ('a rolling stone gathers no moss') but via the title of the Muddy Waters song 'Rolling Stone'. The obscurer reaches of pop nomenclature like Velvet Underground, The The and Prefab Sprout must perforce remain unexplored.

See ABBA; AMEN CORNER; BEE GEES; BOOKER T AND THE MGS; DARLING BUDS; DOORS (under *DOORS OF PERCEPTION*); DURAN DURAN; FAT LADY SINGS; FRANKIE GOES TO HOLLYWOOD; INSTANT SUNSHINE; JETHRO TULL; LED ZEPPELIN (under ZEPPELIN); MANHATTAN TRANSFER; POGUES; PROCUL HARUM; SEARCHERS; SOFT MACHINE; THEY MIGHT BE GIANTS; UB40.

Porridge. The title of a BBC TV comedy series (1974–7) about prison life. The term 'porridge' for 'time spent in prison' has been current since the 1950s at least. It is supposedly from rhyming slang 'borage and thyme' (time). The porridge-stirring connection with the (more American) expressions 'stir' (meaning 'prison'), 'in stir' (in prison) and 'stir crazy' (insane as a result of long imprisonment) may just be coincidental. These terms are said to derive from the Anglo-Saxon word *styr*, meaning 'punishment', reinforced by the Romany *steripen*, meaning 'prison' (*DOAS*). On the other hand, if porridge was once the prisoner's basic food – and it was known as 'stirabout' – it may be more than coincidence that we have here.

port. See WIFE IN EVERY ~.

Portrait of the Artist as a Young Dog, A. The title of a book of mostly autobiographical short stories (1940) by Dylan Thomas, probably derives from *Portrait of the Artist as a Young Man*, the novel (1914–15) by James Joyce, also largely autobiographical. It alludes to the customary way of describing self-portraits in art, e.g. 'Portrait of the Artist with Severed Ear' (van Gogh).

Poseidon. See GREEK NAMES.

posh. The mythical etymology for this word meaning 'smart; grand' is that it is an acronym for 'Port Out Starboard Home', as the requirement for the most desirable staterooms on ships travelling to and from British India. The P&O Line, which was the principal carrier, has no evidence of a single POSH booking, nor would it have made much difference to the heat of the cabin which side you were on. *OED2* has no citations before the twentieth century. However, meaning 'dandy' or 'money' the word was nineteenth-century thieves' and especially Romany slang. It is not hard to see either of these meanings, or both combined, contributing to what we now mean by 'posh'.

possible. See ART OF THE ~.

Postillion Struck by Lightning, A. The title of the first volume of Dirk Bogarde's autobiography (1977). Describing a holiday in early childhood (1920s presumably), he mentions an old phrase book (seemingly dated 1898) which contains lines like: 'This muslin is too thin, have you something thicker?'; 'My leg, arm, foot, elbow, nose, finger is broken'; and 'The postillion has been struck by lightning.' Which phrase book was this? Not ENGLISH AS SHE IS SPOKE, in which the 'postillion' line does not occur. A writer in *The Times* (30 July 1983) noted: '"Look, the front postillion has been struck by lightning" . . . supposed to feature in a Scandinavian phrase book: but it may well be apocryphal.' In the third volume of Bogarde's autobiography, *An Orderly Man* (1983), describing the writing of the first, he says: 'My sister-in-law, Cilla, on a wet camping holiday somewhere in northern France . . . once sent me a postcard on which she said . . . she had been forced to learn a little more French than the phrase "Help! My postillion has been struck by lightning!" I took the old phrase for the title of my book . . .'

post-war bulge. See BABY BOOMER.

potato. See COUCH ~.

potage. See MESS OF ~.

pouf. See GAY.

pours. See IT NEVER RAINS BUT IT ~.

power. See BLACK ~; FLOWER ~.

power to the people. A slogan shouted with clenched fist raised by the Black Panther movement and publicized as such by its leader Bobby Seale, in Oakland, California, in July 1969. It was also used by other dissident groups, as illustrated by Eldridge Cleaver: 'We say "All power to the people" – Black Power for Black People, White Power for White People, Brown Power for Brown People, Red Power for Red People, and X Power for any group we've left out.' It was this somewhat generalized view of 'People Power' that John Lennon appeared to promote in the 1971 song 'Power to the

People (Right On!)' 'All Power to the Soviets' was a cry of the Bolsheviks during the Russian Revolution of 1917.

'Praise the Lord and Pass the Ammunition'. The title of the song (1943) by Frank Loesser came from the remark supposedly made by a US naval chaplain during the Japanese attack on Pearl Harbor (1941). Howell M. Forgy (*d* 1983) and W.H. Maguire (*d* 1953) are possible perpetrators, though the phrase dates from the American Civil War.

pray. See FOOLS WHO COME TO SCOFF . . .

prayer. See COMIN' IN ON A WING AND A ~; FRANCIS OF ASSISI; LORD'S ~; TORY PARTY AT ~.

preaching. See LADY ~ . . .

Precious Bane. The title of the novel (1924) by Mary Webb is taken from Milton's *Paradise Lost* (1667):

> Let none admire
> That riches grow in hell; that soil may best
> Deserve the precious bane.

prepared. See BE ~.

Prerogative of the Harlot, The. The title of a book (1980) by Hugh (Lord) Cudlipp, about Fleet Street, alludes to Stanley Baldwin's attack on the press lords (18 March 1931): 'What the proprietorship of these papers is aiming at is power, and power without responsibility – the prerogative of the harlot throughout the ages.' Baldwin's cousin, Rudyard KIPLING was the originator of the remark.

Present at the Creation. The title of the book (1969) by Dean Acheson, a former US Secretary of State, comes from Alfonso the Wise, King of Castille (on studying the Ptolemaic system): 'Had I been present at the Creation, I would have given some useful hints for the better ordering of the universe.'

Present Laughter. The title of a play (1942) by Noël Coward is a quotation from Shakespeare's *Twelfth Night* (II.iii.48): 'What is love? 'Tis not hereafter,/Present mirth hath present laughter'.

presidency. See HEARTBEAT AWAY FROM THE ~.

pressure. See GRACE UNDER ~.

prestigious. Now meaning 'having prestige', originally this word meant quite the opposite: 'cheating, deceptive, illusory'. Compare 'prestidigitation' ('juggling, trickery'). But that meaning slips easily into the idea of 'dazzling', and has done so.

pretty. See HERE'S A ~ KETTLE OF FISH.

Priam. See GREEK NAMES.

Priapus. See GREEK NAMES.

price. See EVERY MAN HAS HIS ~; IF YOU HAVE TO ASK THE ~.

Prick Up Your Ears. The title of a film (UK, 1987) about the life and murder of Joe Orton, the playwright. In his diary for 18 February 1967, Orton wrote: 'Started typing up my final version [of the first draft] of *Up Against It*. Kenneth suggested that I call it *Prick Up Your Ears*. But this is much too good a title to waste on a film.' The 'Kenneth' was Kenneth Halliwell, Orton's flat-mate who murdered him later that year. It was indeed too good a title to waste on the abortive *Up Against It*, Orton's planned film for The Beatles. In 1978, John Lahr

used the phrase as the title of his biography of Orton. In his edition of *The Orton Diaries* (1986), Lahr noted: 'The title is a triple-pun, "ears" being an anagram of "arse". Orton intended using it as the title for a farce about the backstage goings-on prior to a coronation.' When the film *Prick Up Your Ears* came out, there were reports of enthusiastic punsters in London climbing up to re-arrange the lettering over cinema doors. In c 1974, a *Financial Times* crossword clue was: 'Listen carefully, or a sexual perversion (5,2,4,4)'.

Pride and Prejudice. The title of the novel (written as *First Impressions*, 1797, published 1813) by Jane Austen, has been said to derive from the second chapter of Edward Gibbon's *The Decline and Fall of the Roman Empire* (published 1776). Writing of the enfranchisement of the slaves, Gibbon says: 'Without destroying the distinction of ranks a distant prospect of freedom and honours was presented, even to those whom pride and prejudice almost disdained to number among the human species.' More to the point, the phrase occurs no less than three times, in bold print, towards the end of Fanny Burney's *Cecilia* (1787): ' "The whole of this unfortunate business," said Dr Lyster, "has been the result of Pride and Prejudice . . . Yet this, however, remember; if to Pride and Prejudice you owe your miseries, so wonderfully is good and evil balanced, that to Pride and Prejudice you will also owe their termination".' This seems the most likely cue to Jane Austen. On the other hand, *O E D 2* provides six citations of the phrase 'pride and prejudice' before Burney, one of which has capital Ps.

pride goeth before a fall. This might seem to be a telescoped version of 'Pride goeth before destruction and an haughty spirit before a fall' (Proverbs 16:18) but the proverb seems to have developed independently. *C O D P* cites Alexander Barclay's *The Ship of Fools* (1509): 'First or last foul pride will have a fall', and Samuel Johnson wrote in a letter (2 August 1784): 'Pride must have a fall.' The wording from an early translation of the Bible was presumably grafted on to the original proverb at some stage. One of Swift's clichés in *Polite Conversation* (1738) is: 'You were afraid that Pride should have a Fall.'

Prime Minister. See BEST ~ . . .

prince. See HAMLET WITHOUT THE ~.

private eye. Although it is true that a private investigator's job consists of keeping an eye on people, there may be more to it than that. The term could derive from 'private *in*vestigator' or from the wide-open 'eye' symbol of the Pinkerton detective agency, founded in Chicago (1850). It went with the slogan 'We never sleep' and was referred to as the 'Eye' by criminals and others. The full phrase seems to have emerged in the 1930s and 40s, particularly through the fiction of Raymond Chandler and others.

Procrustes. See GREEK NAMES.

Procul Harum (also known as **Procol Harum**). The name of a British pop group (*fl.* 1967) which had a hit with 'A WHITER SHADE OF PALE' came from the Latin for 'beyond these things'.

Prometheus. See GREEK NAMES.

prominent in his field. This phrase was possibly first used in hunting. As for 'prominent, mainly because of the flatness of the surrounding countryside', it seems to be a rare joke by Karl Marx. In Vol.1, Chap 16 of *Capital* (1867), he writes: 'On a level plain, simple mounds look like hills; and the insipid flatness of our present bourgeoisie is to be measured by the altitude of its "great intellects".' Marx comments thus after having demolished one of John Stuart Mill's arguments.

Promises to Keep. The title of a memoir (1971) by Chester Knowles, and of an unrelated film (US, 1985), and of a novel (1988) by George Bernau. It is taken from Robert Frost's poem 'Stopping by Woods on a Snowy Evening' (1923):

> The woods are lovely, dark and deep
> But I have promises to keep,
> And miles to go before I sleep.

pro patria mori. This epitaph, frequently put on the graves of those killed on active service, is also a family motto. The full saying is '*Dulce et decorum est pro patria mori*' [It is sweet and honorable to die for one's country] (Horace, *Odes*, III.ii.13). The poet Wilfred Owen (1893–1918) used the saying with an ironic sense in his 1917 poem 'Dulce et Decorum Est'.

proper Charlie. The phrase **right Charlie**, meaning the same, i.e. a fool or simpleton, probably grew out of rhyming slang 'Charlie Hunt' (during the Second World War?). 'Proper Charlie' presumably developed from the same source. It was commandeered by the comedian Charlie Chester on radio immediately after the war and later used by him as the title of a radio show. A recent example of its use comes from the *Guardian* (1 December 1988) concerning a judge, Sir Harold Cassel QC: 'He once gave a robber an hour's bail, warning: "If you do not turn up you will make me look a proper Charlie." The man never returned.' (See also *DPP*.)

prose. See DEATHLESS ~.

Proserpina/e. See ROMAN NAMES.

protest. See METHINKS SHE DOTH ~ . . .

Protestant work ethic. An attitude towards business, based on the teachings of Calvin and the analysis of Max Weber (1904), which suggests that it is one's duty to be successful through hard work.

Proteus. See GREEK NAMES.

proud as Punch. See PLEASED AS PUNCH.

ps and qs, to mind one's. Meaning 'to be careful', the phrase has several explanations for its origin: (1) the letters 'p' and 'q' look so alike, a child might well be admonished to be careful writing them; (2) because you have to be careful to remember your 'pleases and than-kyous'; (3) because in a public house 'pints' and 'quarts' would be chalked up on a blackboard for future payment; (4) in the days of wigs, Frenchmen had to be warned not to get their *pieds* (feet) mixed up with their *queues* (wig-tails) when bowing and scraping.

pseud. Referring to a pseudo-intellectual person, this word is some-times thought to have been a *Private Eye* coinage because of the 'Pseud's Corner' feature (from 1968 onwards). But the prefix 'pseudo-' for 'counterfeit; spuri-ous' is very old, and Daniel J. Boorstin in *The Image* (1960) had recently used the term **pseudo-event** for an occasion laid on solely for the purpose of attracting news coverage.

PS I Love You. The title of a memoir (1981) of his father, Peter by Michael

Sellers, comes from the title of a Lennon and McCartney song (1963), also from one by Johnny Mercer and Gordon Jenkin (1934).

Psyche. See GREEK NAMES.

public enemy No. 1. John Dillinger was the first officially designated 'Public Enemy No. 1'. He robbed banks and killed people in Illinois, Indiana and Ohio (1933–4) to such an extent that the Attorney General, Homer Cummings, called him this. In fact, he was the only person ever so-named. The FBI's 'Ten Most Wanted Men' list did not give a ranking. Dillinger's exploits and his escape from captivity aroused great public interest. He was eventually shot dead by FBI agents outside a cinema in Chicago. See *THE WOMAN IN RED*.

The coinage of the term 'Public Enemy' in this context has been attribu-ted to Frank Loesch, president of the Chicago Crime Commission, who had to try to deal with Al Capone's hold over the city in 1923. The idea was to try and dispel the romantic aura such gangsters had been invested with by the popular press. The phrase soon passed into gen-eral usage.

In June 1934, P.G. Wodehouse, refer-ring in a letter to difficulties with US income-tax officials, said: 'I got an offer from Paramount to go to Hollywood at $1500 a week and had to refuse as I am Public Enemy No. 1 in America, and can't go there.' James Cagney starred in a gangster film called *The Public Enemy* in 1931. Other US film titles were: *Public Hero Number One* (1935), *Public Menace* (1935), and *Public Enemy's Wife* (1936). There was a British musical called *Public Nuisance No. 1* and in the musical comedy *Seeing Stars* at the Gaiety Theatre, London (1935), Flo-rence Desmond had a hit with the song 'Public Sweetheart Number One'. In *Anything Goes* (1934), Cole Porter had a song 'Public Enemy Number One', and

PSEUDONYMS. Here is a selection of name changes, stage-names, *noms de plume*. The new names are in alphabetical order and are preceded by the original names:

Allen Stewart Konigsberg → Woody Allen
Angelo Siciliano → Charles Atlas
Betty Joan Perske → Lauren Bacall
Anne Italiano → Anne Bancroft
Theodosia Goodman → Theda Bara
John Blythe → John Barrymore
François Silly → Gilbert Becaud
David Green → David Ben-Gurion
William Berkeley Enos → Busby Berkeley
Israel Baline → Irving Berlin
Priscilla White → Cilla Black
Borge Rosenbaum → Victor Borge
David Jones → David Bowie
Charles Buchinski → Charles Bronson
Acton/Currer/Ellis Bell → Anne/ Charlotte/Emily Brontë
Elaine Bookbinder → Elkie Brooks
Dora Broadbent → Dora Bryan
Taidje Khan Jr → Yul Brynner
Nathan Birnbaum → George Burns
Richard Jenkins → Richard Burton
Lynda Denise Crapper → Marti Caine
Maurice Micklethwaite → Michael Caine
Samile Diane Friesen → Dyan Cannon
Truman Persons → Truman Capote
Joyce Botterill → Judy Carne
Charles Lutwidge Dodgson → Lewis Carroll
Bob Davies → Jasper Carrott
Jean Shufflebottom → Jeannie Carson
Barbara McCorquodale → Barbara Cartland
Tula Finklea → Cyd Charisse
Leslie Charles Yin → Leslie Charteris
Ernest Evans → Chubby Checker
Thomas Conner → Sean Connery
Trevor Stanford → Russ Conway
Vince Furnier → Alice Cooper
Lucille Le Sueur → Joan Crawford
Michael Dumble-Smith → Michael Crawford

Bernie Schwarz → Tony Curtis
Durante Aligheri → Dante
Doris Kappelhoff → Doris Day
Peggy Middleton → Yvonne de Carlo
Pauline Matthews → Kiki Dee
Alexandra Zuck → Sandra Dee
Carl Henty-Dodd → Simon Dee
Bernard Winogradsky → Bernard (Lord) Delfont
Victoria Gamez → Victoria de los Angeles
Sidney B. de Millstein → Cecil B. de Mille
Edris Stannus → Ninette de Valois
Nigel Davies → Justin de Villenueve
Diana Fluck → Diana Dors
Issur Danielovitch Demsky → Kirk Douglas
Robert Zimmerman → Bob Dylan
Mary Ann Evans → George Eliot
Maurice Cole → Kenny Everett
Douglas Ulman → Douglas Fairbanks Sr
Terence Neilhams → Adam Faith
Clive Powell → Georgie Fame
Grace Stansfield → Gracie Fields
William Claude Dukinfield → W.C. Fields
Chaim Ruben Weintrop → Bud Flanagan
Joan de Havilland → Joan Fontaine
Margaret Hookham → Margot Fonteyn
Leslie L. King → Gerald R. Ford
Ronald Wycherley → Billy Fury
Greta Gustafson → Greta Garbo
Frances Ethel Gumm → Judy Garland
Paul Gadd → Gary Glitter
Samuel Gelbfisch → Samuel Goldfish → Sam Goldwyn
Lewis Winogradsky → Lew (Lord) Grade
James Stewart → Stewart Grainger
Archibald Leach → Cary Grant
Harlean Carpentier → Jean Harlow
Larushka Mischa Skikne → Laurence Harvey
James Alfred Wight → James Herriot
Judith Tovim → Judy Holliday
Peggy Askins → Evelyn Home
Erich Weiss → Harry Houdini

Pseudonyms – cont.

Roy Scherer → Rock Hudson
Arnold/Gerry Dorsey → Englebert Humperdinck
Reginald Dwight → Elton John
Thomas Jones Woodward → Tom Jones
Vernon Watson → Nosmo King
Sandor Kellner → Sir Alexander Korda
Constance Ockleman → Veronica Lake
Alfredo Cocozza → Mario Lanza
Daniel Carroll → Danny La Rue
Pal → Lassie
Arthur Stanley → Jefferson Stan Laurel
David Cornwell → John LE CARRE
Norma Egstrom → Peggy Lee
Vivian Hartley → Vivien Leigh
Vladimir Ilyich Ulyanov → V.I. Lenin
Lazlo Loewenstein → Peter Lorre
Marie Lawrie → Lulu
Pat Welch → Vera Lynn
Shirley Beaty → Shirley Maclaine
Alfred Willmore → Michael MacLiammoir
Malcolm Little → Malcolm X
Vera Jane Palmer → Jayne Mansfield
Lilian Marks → Alicia Markova
Dino Crocetti → Dean Martin
Walter Matuschanskayasky → Walter Matthau
Helen Mitchell → Dame Nellie MELBA
Ada Thompson → Vivien Merchant
Ethel Zimmerman → Ethel Merman
Reginald Truscott-Jones → Ray Milland
Thomas Sargent → Max Miller
Jean-Baptiste Poquelin → Molière
Terry Parsons → Matt Monro
Norma Jean Baker → Marilyn Monroe
Eric Bartholomew → Eric Morecambe
Marjorie Robertson → Anna Neagle
Ivor Davies → Ivor Novello

Estelle O'Brien Merle → Merle Oberon
Victor von Samek → Vic Oliver
Raymond Sullivan → Gilbert O'Sullivan
John Ravenscroft → John Peel
James Smith → P.J. Proby
John Pompeo → Johnny Ray
Charles Alden/Olden → Ted Ray
Harry Webb → Cliff Richard
Harold Rubin → Harold Robbins
Emanuel Goldenberg → Edward G. Robinson
Walker Smith → Sugar Ray Robinson
Leonard Slye → Roy Rogers
Michael Shalhouz → Omar Sharif
Sandra Goodrich → Sandi Shaw
Frank Morrison → Mickey Spillane
Mary O'Brien → Dusty Springfield
Bernard Jewry → Shane Fenton → Alvin Stardust
Richard Starkey → Ringo Starr
Thomas Hicks → Tommy Steele
Edward Mainwaring → Ed Stewart
Thomas Straussler → Tom Stoppard
Norma Sykes → Sabrina
Spangler Arlington Brough → Robert Taylor
Thomas Terry Hoar-Stevens → Terry-Thomas
Charles Sherwood Stratton → Tom Thumb
Herbert Khaury → Tiny Tim
Samuel Langhorne Clemens → Mark TWAIN
Lesley Hornby → Twiggy
Harold Jenkins → Conway Twitty
Frank Abelson → Frankie Vaughan
Marion Morrison → John Wayne
Reg Smith → Marty Wilde
Barbara Deeks → Barbara Windsor
Steveland Judkins Hardaway → Stevie Wonder
Georgette Withers → Googie Withers

so did Harold Rome for the 1937 *Pins and Needles*.

The words have since been applied to any form of supposed undesirable, while Raymond Postgate, founder of the *Good Food Guide*, was dubbed 'Public Stomach No. 1', and Beverley Nichols, the author and journalist, called himself 'Public Anemone No. 1'.

Public Faces. The title of this book (1932) by Harold Nicolson comes from W.H. Auden's 'Marginalia' (1932):

> Private faces in public places
> Are wiser and nicer
> Than public faces in private places.

Publish and Be Damned! The title of a book (1955) by Hugh Cudlipp, it derives from the 1st Duke of Wellington's comment to a blackmailer who offered not to publish anecdotes of the Duke and his mistress, Harriet Wilson, in return for payment. Richard Ingrams declared on several occasions (*c* 1977) that a suitable motto for *Private Eye*, of which he was editor, would be: 'Publish and Be Sued'.

publisher. See NOW BARABBAS.

Publish It Not . . . The title of a book (1975) by Christopher Mayhew and Michael Adams, which was subtitled 'the Middle East cover-up'. The origin is biblical: 'Tell it not in Gath, publish it not in the streets of Askelon' (Samuel 1:19).

puff. See GAY.

pull the wool over someone's eyes, to. When wigs were commonly worn, they were sometimes referred to as wool (because of the resemblance, particularly of the curls). Thus to pull the wool over people's eyes was to pull wigs

over their eyes and render them incapable of seeing. Hence the modern meaning 'to hoodwink'.

Punch. See AS PLEASED AS ~.

pun would pick a pocket, he who would make a. An almost proverbial saying, this was originally a remark made by the critic John Dennis to Henry Purcell, the composer (*c* 1779).

puppies. See HUSH ~.

Pussy Galore. One of the most intriguingly named of all James Bond's women in the novels of Ian Fleming was the heroine of *Goldfinger* (1959; film UK, 1964). Other Bond women included 'Honeychile Rider', 'Kissy Suzuki', 'Giovanna Goodthighs', and not forgetting 'Miss Moneypenny' and ROSA KLEBB.

put a sock in it! Meaning 'shut up!', this is the sort of expression that might be addressed to a noisy person. Neil Ewart in *Everyday Phrases* (1983) confidently asserts that this dates from the days of wind-up, 'acoustic' gramophones where the sound emerged from a horn. With no electronic controls to raise or lower the volume, the only way to regulate the sound was to put in or take out an article of clothing, which deadened it. *O E D2* has a citation from 1919 – an explanation of the term from the *Athenaeum* journal – which suggests the phrase was not widely known even then. (See also *D P P*.)

put a spoke in someone's wheel, to. Meaning 'to prevent someone from doing something', this is an odd expression if one knows that bicycle wheels already have spokes in them. Here, however, what is evoked is the days when carts had solid wheels and no spokes in the modern sense. The spoke then was a pin which could be inserted into a hole on the wheel to act as a brake.

put on (the) dog, to. Meaning 'to put on airs, fine clothes', this is a US expression dating from the 1870s, probably from among college students (especially at Yale) who had to wear stiff, high collars (jokily known as 'dog-collars') on formal occasions.

put one's best foot forward, to. See BEST FOOT FORWARD.

Put Out More Flags. The title of a novel (1942) by Evelyn Waugh. According to the author, it comes from a Chinese saying: 'A drunk military man should order gallons and put out more flags in order to increase his military splendour.'

put the screws on, to. Meaning 'to apply pressure on someone to do something', 'screws' here is short for 'thumb-screws', the medieval method of torturing prisoners. This could be why prison guards have been nicknamed 'screws', although another explanation is from screw meaning 'key'. Gaolers were sometimes known as 'turnkeys', as this would be their most significant function.

Pygmalion. Before George Bernard Shaw's play with this title, there had been a play called *Pygmalion and Galatea* (1871) by W.S. Gilbert – which Revd Francis Kilvert in his diary (27 May 1872) refers to as *Pygmalion and the Statue*. See also under GREEK NAMES.

Pythias. See GREEK NAMES.

Q

QQ

QANTAS. See ACRONYMS.

QE2. This is the popular name for the Cunard Liner which made its maiden voyage in May 1969. It was the successor to the liner known as *Queen Elizabeth* named after the wife of King George VI and launched by her in 1938. The idea seems to have been *not* to call the ship *Queen Elizabeth II* or *Queen Elizabeth the Second* (after HM Queen Elizabeth II), but to evoke a second *Queen Elizabeth* liner like the first. During building, it was known as 'Q3' – the third of the queens, the other having been the *Queen Mary*. Nevertheless, when the reigning Queen launched the ship in 1967, she distinctly named her the 'Queen Elizabeth the Second', as though after herself. On the bow and stern of the vessel is written '*Queen Elizabeth II*'.

Quai d'Orsay. See FOGGY BOTTOM.

quango. The name of a type of statutory body set up outside the Civil Service but appointed by and financed by central government, it seems to have originated in the US in the 1960s. It became popular in the UK in the 1970s, standing for 'QUasi - Autonomous - Non - Governmental-Organization', though sometimes 'National' has been substituted for 'Non-Governmental'.

Quatre Cents Coups, Les [The Four Hundred Blows]. The title of a film (France, 1958) by François Truffaut, it comes from the French slang expression '*faire les quatre cents coups*' (meaning 'to paint the town red' or 'to be up to all sorts of tricks').

Queen Anne's dead. This phrase might be used to put down someone who has just told you some very old news or what you know already. Mencken glosses it slightly differently: 'Reply to an enquiry for news, signifying that there is none not stale'. He also supplies the alternative 'Queen Elizabeth is dead' and says that both forms appear to date from *c* 1720.

In George Colman the Younger's play *The Heir-at-Law* (1797), there occurs the line: 'Tell 'em Queen Anne's dead.' She actually died in 1714. Partridge/*Slang* dates 'Queen Anne is dead' to 1722, in a ballad cited by Apperson: 'He's as dead as Queen Anne the day after she dy'd' (which doesn't seem to convey the modern meaning of the expression); and 'Queen Elizabeth is dead' to 1738 in Swift's *Polite Conversation*:

What news, Mr Neverout?
Why, Madam, Queen Elizabeth's dead.

'My Lord Baldwin is dead' is dated *c* 1670–1710. A US equivalent is, 'Bryan has carried Texas' – presumably referring to William Jennings Bryan (*d* 1925) who stood three times unsuccessfully for the US presidency.

queen for a day. Referring to a woman who is given a special treat, the phrase comes from the title of a US radio programme which ran for ten years in the 1940s. According to an informant: 'Being a queen for a day didn't mean they gave you a country; you only got your wish, that's what. No one complained.' Adapted as a daytime TV show, it was a big hit from 1955–64, though *Halliwell's Television Companion* calls it 'the nadir of American TV'. When Radio Luxembourg adopted the format (from 1955, introduced by Richard Attenborough, sponsored by Phensic) they changed the title to *Princess for a Day*. Was this because the wishes fulfilled were more modest, the participants younger, or had the word 'queen' become too tainted by that time? There had been a 1951 film called *Queen for a Day*.

Queer Street, to be in. Meaning 'to be in debt'. Possibly from the tradesmen's habit of putting a 'query' next to the names of people whose creditworthiness was dubious. The expression has also been used (since 1811) to describe being in any kind of difficulty.

quick and the dead. 'Quick' here has the old sense of 'the living', as on several occasions in the Bible, e.g. 'judge of the quick and the dead' (Acts 10:42).

quick brown fox . . . See NOW IS THE TIME . . .

quiet calm deliberation disentangles every knot. When Harold Macmillan was Prime Minister (1957–63) he wrote out in longhand a motto for his Private Office and the Cabinet Room when at 10 Downing Street. It came from W.S. Gilbert's lyrics for *The Gondoliers* (1889):

In a contemplative fashion
And a tranquil frame of mind,
Free from every kind of passion,
Some solution let us find.
Let us grasp the situation,
Solve the complicated plot –
Quiet, calm deliberation
Disentangles every knot.

quisling. Meaning 'a traitor' – from the name of Vidkun Quisling, former Minister of Defence in Norway who supported the invasion of his country by the Germans in 1940. He headed a puppet government under the Nazi occupation. After the German defeat he was tried and executed in 1945. Chips Channon wrote in his diary (8 May 1940): 'We watched the insurgents file out of the Opposition [in the House of Commons lobby] . . . "Quislings," we shouted at them, "Rats." "Yes-men," they replied.'

qui tollis peccata mundi. See MASS PHRASES.

quiz. It is said this word came into use in the 1780s when Mr Daly, a Dublin theatre manager, had a bet that he could introduce a new word into the language within twenty-four hours. Somehow he came up with this word and had it chalked all over Dublin. *OED2* dates the word at 1782 with the now rare meaning 'an odd or eccentric person, in character or appearance', but it is not far from the Latin interrogative pronoun *quiz* ('who?' or 'what?') and also resembles the second syllable of the word 'inquisitive' (from the Latin *inquisitere*, to acquire) which was current by the sixteenth century.

quoniam tu solus Sanctus. See MASS PHRASES.

Quo Vadis? The title of a film (US 1951, and two previous Italian ones) and an opera (1909) by Jean Nouguès, all based on the novel (1896) by a Pole,

Henryk Sienkiewicz. The words '*Quo vadis?*' (Whither goest thou?) come from the Latin translation (the Vulgate) of John 13:36: 'Simon Peter said unto him, Lord, whither goest thou? Jesus answered him, Whither I go, thou canst not follow me now'; and from John 16:5 in which Christ comforts his disciples before the Crucifixion. The words also occur in Genesis 32:17 and in the Acts of St Peter among the New Testament Apocrypha in which, after the Crucifixion, Peter, fleeing Rome, encounters Christ on the Appian Way. He asks Him, '*Domine, quo vadis?*' ('Lord, whither goest thou?') and Christ replies, '*Venio Romam, iterum crucifigi*' ('I am coming to Rome to be crucified again').

race to the sea. This phrase dates from the Autumn of 1914, during the early months of the First World War. In his *English History 1914–45*, A.J.P. Taylor writes: 'Both combatant lines hung in the air. Some 200 miles of open country separated the German and French armies from the sea. Each side tried to repeat the original German strategy of turning the enemy line. This was not so much a "race to the sea", its usual name, as a race to outflank the other side before the sea reached. Both sides failed.' Martin Gilbert uses the phrase evocatively of a phase of the Second World War in the official biography of Winston Churchill (Vol. 6, Chap. 21): 'As dawn broke on May 26 [1940], the news from France dominated Churchill's thoughts, and those of his advisers and staff. The road to Dunkirk was open. The race to the sea was about to begin.' (In his own *The Second World War*, Vol. 2, Churchill entitled the chapter dealing with Dunkirk, 'The March to the Sea'.)

Racing Demon. The title of a play (1990) by David Hare, about the Church of England, comes from the name of a 'patience' card game played by several players, each with his own pack of cards.

radar. See ACRONYMS.

Radical Chic & Mau-Mauing the Flak Catchers. This was the title of a book (1970) by Tom Wolfe. His phrase 'radical chic', first coined in a 1970 article, refers to the fashionable espousal of left-wing, radical causes, clothes and lifestyle.

radio. See STEAM ~.

rag. See CHEW THE ~.

rags-to-riches. This is the name given to a certain type of fiction, often in publishers' BLURBS, or to the actual stories of people who have risen from poverty to wealth. It comes from the story of CINDERELLA, of course. It was also the title of a popular song (1953) by Adler and Ross. *O E D2*'s earliest citation is from 1947.

railroad. See WHAT A WAY TO RUN A ~.

rain. See INTO EACH LIFE . . .

Rainbow Comes and Goes, The. The title of the first volume of the auto-biography (1958) by Lady Diana Cooper. The sequels were *The Light of Common Day* (1959) and *Trumpets from the Steep* (1960). All come from William Wordsworth's 'Ode. Intimations of Immortality' (1807):

> The Rainbow comes and goes,
> And lovely is the rose;
> At length the Man perceives it die away,
> And fade into the light of common day;

The Cataracts blow their trumpets from
the steep,
No more shall grief of mine the season
wrong.

rain cats and dogs, to. Meaning 'to
rain extremely heavily', there is no very
convincing explanation for this phrase.
According to Morris, it comes from the
days when street drainage was so poor
that a heavy rain storm could easily
drown cats and dogs. After the storm
people would see the number of dead
cats and dogs and assume they had fallen
out of the sky. Brewer suggests, on the
other hand, that in northern mythology
cats were supposed to have great influence on the weather and dogs were a
signal of wind, 'thus cat may be taken as
a symbol of the downpouring rain, and
the dog of the strong gusts of wind
accompanying a rain-storm'.

rain-check. See TAKE A ~.

rains. See IT NEVER ~ BUT . . .

raise Cain, to. Meaning 'to make trouble, a fuss, a disturbance', the allusion
here is to the biblical Cain ('the first
murderer') who killed his brother Abel
(Genesis 4:2–8). A person who makes
trouble 'raises the spirit' of Cain by
doing so.

**raise one's Ebenezer, to (*some-
times* to get one's Ebenezer up).**
Meaning 'to be angry', this expression
was in US use by the mid-1830s,
Ebenezer being a nickname for the devil.
It is not to be confused with what is
referred to in the hymn: 'Come Thou
Fount' (R.Robinson, 1758) – 'Here I
raise my Ebenezer', where Ebenezer is
the Hebrew 'stone of help', as in the
name of a type of chapel. Samuel raised a
thanksgiving stone at Ebenezer after the
defeat of the Philistines. Plenty of scope

for double-entendres, of course – especially, if the hymn is sung at weddings, as
has been known.

'Raleigh, The Boyhood of'. The title
of a painting by Sir John Everett Millais
(1870) showing the young Sir Walter
Raleigh with a friend being told stories
by an old sea-going man. The man gestures towards the sea as he talks. The
picture is now in the Tate Gallery,
London.

Rambo: First Blood Part Two. The
title of a film (US, 1985), a sequel to
First Blood (1982). In it, John Rambo, a
Vietnam veteran, goes back to
South-East Asia to free POWs in best
comic-book mode. The terms **Ramboesque**, 'Rambo-like' and 'Ramboism'
were rapidly adopted for mindless,
forceful heroics.

RAMC. See INITIALS.

ranch. See MEANWHILE BACK AT
THE ~.

Random Harvest. The title of this
novel (1941; film US, 1942) by James
Hilton took its name from an error in
wartime propaganda when the Germans
claimed to have attacked the town of
'Random'. They did so on the basis of a
British communiqué which had said that
'bombs were dropped at random'.

raspberry. See under BRONX CHEER.

rats. See LIKE ~ DESERTING . . .

Razor's Edge, The. The title of a novel
(1944; film US, 1946) by W. Somerset
Maugham, it comes from the Katha-
Upanishad: 'The sharp edge of a razor is
difficult to pass over; thus the wise say
the path to Salvation is hard.'

read my lips. Meaning 'listen hard because I want you to hear what I've got to

say', this phrase was popularized by George Bush in his speech accepting the Republican nomination on 19 August 1988. Wanting to emphasize his pledge not to raise taxes, whatever pressure Congress applied, he said: 'I'll say no, and they'll push, and I'll say no, and they'll push again, and I'll say to them, "Read my lips, no new taxes".' According to William Safire in an article in the *New York Times Magazine* (September 1988), the phrase is rooted in 1970s rock music (although a song with the title copyrighted by Joe Greene in 1957 shows the phrase had been around for some time before then). (See also *D P P*.)

read the riot act, to. The meaning of this phrase is 'to make strong representations about something; express forcibly that something must cease'. The actual Riot Act that was passed by the British Parliament in 1714 (and finally repealed in 1973), provided for the dispersal of crowds (defined as being of more than twelve persons) by those in authority. The method used was for someone to stand up and, literally, read out the terms of the Act so that the rioters knew what law they were breaking.

real McCoy, the. Meaning 'the real thing'; the genuine article', the phrase probably derived from 'Kid' McCoy, a US welterweight boxing champion in the late 1890s. When challenged by a man in a bar to prove he was who he said he was, McCoy flattened him. When the man came round, he declared that this was indeed the 'real' McCoy. As Burnam 2 notes, 'Kid' McCoy promoted this story about himself. However, Messrs G. Mackay, the Scottish whisky distillers, were apparently promoting their product as 'the real *Mackay*' in 1870, as though alluding to an established expression. This could have derived from the Mackays of Reay in

Sutherland claiming to be the principal branch of the Mackay clan. Robert Louis Stevenson used this version in an 1883 letter. (See also *D P P*.)

Real Men Don't Eat Quiche. The title of a book (1983) by Bruce Feirstein, following the title of an article by him in *Playboy* (1982). It became a jokey yardstick of manliness in popular sociological discussions.

reappraisal. See AGONIZING ~.

Reap the Wild Wind. The title of a film (U S 1942), presumably alluding to Hosea 8:7: 'They have sown the wind, and they shall reap the whirlwind.'

reason. See LAST APPEAL TO ~.

recordare. See MASS PHRASES.

Recording Angel. Referring to an angel who keeps a record of every person's good and bad deeds, this was a concept known by 1761 (in Sterne's *Tristram Shandy*), but not mentioned as such in the Bible.

red. See BETTER ~ THAN DEAD; LIKE A ~ RAG TO A BULL; LITTLE ~ BOOK; THIN ~ LINE; WOMAN IN ~.

Red Baron was the nickname of Manfred Freiherr von Richthofen (*d* 1918), the German fighter ace of the First World War. He flew a red Fokker plane and was credited with having destroyed eighty Allied planes. The Red Baron also features in Charles M. Schulz's 'Peanuts' cartoon strip.

Red Cardinal. See under EMINENCE GRISE.

red herring. See NEITHER FISH ...

red-hot mamas. See LAST OF THE ~.

red-letter day. Denoting a special day, because in almanacs and old calendars, feast days and saints' days were often printed in red rather than black ink.

reds under the bed. This became a watchword of anti-Bolshevik scares, and was current within a few years of the 1917 October Revolution in Russia. A red flag was used in the 1789 French Revolution and the colour had come to be associated with revolutionary movements during the nineteenth century before being adopted by communists and their sympathizers. It was said that originally the flag had been dipped in the blood of victims of oppression.

red tape. Referring to delay caused by bureaucrats, the allusion, dating from the eighteenth century, is to the ribbons that lawyers and other public officials still use to bind up their papers (although they look more pink than red).

refuse. See I'M GOING TO MAKE HIM AN OFFER . . .

reine le veult, la. In Britain, the Royal Assent to Parliamentary bills is still given in Norman French (written, never spoken). So, it is either '*Le Roy*' or '*La Reine le veult*' [the King/Queen allows it]. The negative form would be '*Le roi/ la reine s'avisera*' [will consider it], though this veto has not been used since Queen Anne opposed a Scottish Militia Bill in 1707.

Rejoice! Rejoice! Margaret Thatcher is sometimes reported as having said this to newsmen outside 10 Downing Street on 25 April 1982 following the recapture of South Georgia by British forces during the Falklands War. What she actually said was: 'Just rejoice at that news and congratulate our forces and the Marines. Goodnight. Rejoice!' Either way, can one detect signs of her Methodist upbringing? Although

'Rejoice, rejoice!' is quite a common expression, each verse of Charles Wesley's hymn 'Rejoice! the Lord is King' ends: 'Rejoice, again I say, rejoice'. There was also a nineteenth-century hymn (words by Grace J. Frances), 'Rejoice, Rejoice, Believer!'.

relationship. See SPECIAL ~.

remember the — ! This is a common theme of sloganeering, particularly as a way of starting conflicts or keeping them alive, especially in the US. Probably the first was **remember the River Raisin!** – a war cry of Kentucky soldiers dating from the War of 1812. In the Raisin River massacre, 700 Kentuckians, badly wounded trying to capture Detroit, were scalped and butchered by Indians who were allies of the British. Then came **remember the Alamo!** after the siege of 1836, and **remember Goliad!** from the same Texan conflict. **Remember the *Maine*!** helped turn the sinking of the battleship *Maine* in Havana harbour (1898) into an excuse for the Spanish–American War (as well as for the contemporary graffito: 'Remember the Maine/To hell with Spain/Don't forget to pull the chain'). **Remember the *Lusitania*!** followed the sinking of another ship (in 1915). **Remember Belgium!** was originally a recruiting slogan of the First World War. It eventually emerged with ironic emphasis amid the mud of Ypres, encouraging the rejoinder: 'As if I'm ever likely to forget the bloody place!' **Remember Pearl Harbor!** followed from the 1941 incident and **remember the *Pueblo*!** commemorated the capture of the USS *Pueblo* by North Korea in 1968.

rendezvous with destiny. In a TV address on behalf of Senator Barry Goldwater (27 October 1964), Ronald Reagan told viewers: 'You and I have a rendezvous with destiny. We will preserve for our children this, the LAST

BEST HOPE OF man on EARTH.'
Earlier, in a speech to the Democratic
Convention in 1936, President Franklin
D. Roosevelt had said: 'This generation
of Americans has a rendezvous with
destiny.'

— revisited. A frequently used title
format. In January 1989, Channel 4
showed a programme marking the
fiftieth anniversary of the publication of
a John Steinbeck novel, with the title
'*The Grapes of Wrath*' *Revisited*. In
1989, the South Bank Centre ran a commemoration of the 200th anniversary of
the French Revolution under the blanket
title 'Revolution Revisited'.

All such uses now owe something to
the title of Evelyn Waugh's novel
Brideshead Revisited (1945), and especially to the TV adaptation in 1981,
though the format was well established
before Waugh got hold of it. A book by
E.V. Lucas (1916) has the title *London
Revisited*. William Wordsworth wrote
poems entitled 'Yarrow Unvisited'
(1803), 'Yarrow Visited' (1814), and
'Yarrow Revisited' (1831).

revolution. See GLORIOUS ~.

rex tremendae (majestatis). See
MASS PHRASES.

Rhadamanthus. See GREEK NAMES.

rhubarb, rhubarb! Actors mumble this
in crowd scenes to give the impression of
speech, as a background noise, without
actually producing coherent sentences.
Some may think they could actually get
away with saying 'rhubarb', but the idea
is to repeat a word, which uttered by
various voices, adds together to sound
like the noise a crowd makes. This may
not date from much before this century
but it is a well-known concept now, as
demonstrated by the use of 'to rhubarb',
meaning 'to talk nonsense'. (See also
DPP.)

rich. See under POOR ARE ALWAYS
WITH YOU.

Rich and Famous. The title of a film
(US, 1981), this is now very much a
cliché phrase – on the basis that the
words are always and inevitably put
together. An example occurs in the film
Breakfast at Tiffany's (1961). A US TV
series *Lifestyles of the Rich and Famous*
was established by 1986, and the
Independent (4 April 1989) reported:
'The [Press] Council's assistant director,
said yesterday that lawyers acting for the
rich and famous were becoming aware
of the fast track system for getting
speedy corrections of untruths.'

Rich and Strange. The title of a film
(UK 1932), directed by Alfred
Hitchcock, it comes from Shakespeare,
The Tempest (I.ii.402):

> Nothing of him that doth fade,
> But doth suffer a sea-change
> Into something rich and strange.

Rich Are Different, The. This was the
title of a novel (1977) by Susan
Howatch. As discussed in Burnam 2,
Ernest Hemingway is popularly supposed to have replied to F. Scott
Fitzgerald's remark 'The very rich are
different from you and me' with: 'Yes,
they have more money' – indeed, the
'exchange' was put by Hemingway into
the original magazine version of 'The
Snows of Kilimanjaro' (1936). In fact,
what Fitzgerald had written in his short
story 'The Rich Boy' (1926) was: 'Let me
tell you about the very rich. They are
different from you and me.' On another
occasion (in 1936), the critic Mary
Colum had told Hemingway: 'The only
difference between the rich and other
people is that the rich have more money.'
Hemingway conflated these two sources.

rich man in his castle. The popular
hymn 'ALL THINGS BRIGHT AND

BEAUTIFUL' (1848) by Mrs Cecil Frances Alexander is in danger of being known as the hymn from which a verse had to be dropped. Causing all the trouble is the third verse with its apparent acceptance of, to modern ears, an unacceptable status quo:

> The rich man in his castle, the poor man
>   at his gate,
> God made them, high or lowly, and
>   ordered their estate.

Mrs Alexander was the wife of a Bishop of Derry and Archbishop of Armagh. Most modern hymnbook compilers omit the words. *Songs of Praise Discussed* (1933) calls it an 'appalling verse . . . She must have forgotten Dives, and how Lazarus lay "at his gate"; but then she had been brought up in the atmosphere of a land-agent on an Irish estate. The *English Hymnal* led the way in obliterating this verse from the Anglican mind.' The verse remains in *Hymns Ancient and Modern* (Standard Edition, reprinted 1986), but it has disappeared from the *Irish Hymnal*.

riddle of the Sphinx, the. The riddle is: 'What animal walks on four feet in the morning, two feet at noon, and on three feet in the evening – but has only one voice; its feet vary, and when it has most it is weakest.' The answer is: Man – because he crawls on all fours as an infant, walks on two feet when full grown, but in old age moves upon his feet and a staff. As mentioned in *Oedipus Rex* by Sophocles, Oedipus answered the riddle correctly when he encountered the Sphinx on the road to Thebes. The Sphinx killed herself in despair, and the Thebans made Oedipus their king out of gratitude. If he had not answered correctly, the Sphinx would have killed him.

ride. See IF YOU CAN'T ~ . . .

ridiculous. See SUBLIME TO THE ~.

right(s). See BANG TO ~; ~ CHARLIE see under PROPER CHARLIE; COUNTRY ~ OR WRONG

Right Stuff, The. The title of a book (1979; film US, 1983) by Tom Wolfe, referring to the qualities needed by test pilots and would-be astronauts in the early years of the US space programme. 'The right (sort of) stuff' had, however, been applied much earlier to qualities of manly virtue, of good officer material, and of good cannon fodder. Partridge/ *Slang* has an example from the 1880s. In this sense, the phrase was used by Ian Hay as the title of a novel – 'some episodes in the career of a North Briton' – in 1908. It has also been used as an expression for alcohol (like 'the hard stuff'). (See also *DPP*.)

ringer. See DEAD ~.

Rings on Their Fingers. The title of a BBC TV comedy series (from 1979) about live-in lovers who decide to get married. It comes from the nursery rhyme (first recorded 1784) 'Ride a Cock-horse to Banbury Cross' which contains the line: 'Rings on her fingers and bells on her toes'.

riot. See READ THE ~ ACT.

Ripper. See JACK THE ~; YORKSHIRE ~.

rise and fall. See DECLINE AND FALL.

Rising of the Moon, The. The title of an opera (Glyndebourne, 1970) with libretto by Beverley Cross and music by Nicholas Maw, also of a short play by Lady Gregory (d 1932) and of a film (Ireland, 1957). All these works (with Irish themes) borrow the title of an Irish patriotic song. The phrase came to be synonymous with the rising of the Irish themselves.

ritzy. (1) Smart, glamorous, ostentatiously rich. (2) Flashy, pretentious. The adjective derives from the surname of César Ritz, the Swiss-born hotelier (*d* 1918) who established luxury hotels in Paris, London, New York, and elsewhere at the turn of the century.

river. See SOLD DOWN THE ~.

rivers of blood. On 20 April 1968, Enoch Powell, the Conservative opposition spokesman for Defence, made a speech in Birmingham on the subject of immigration. He concluded with the words: 'As I look ahead, I am filled with foreboding. Like the Roman, I seem to see "the River Tiber foaming with much blood".' The next day, Powell was dismissed from the Shadow Cabinet for a speech 'racialist in tone and liable to exacerbate racial tensions'.

What became known as the 'Rivers of Blood' speech certainly produced an astonishing reaction in the public, unleashing anti-immigrant feeling that had largely been pent up until this point. Later, Powell said that he should have quoted the remark in Latin to emphasize that he was only evoking a classical prophecy of doom and not actually predicting a bloodbath. In Virgil's *Aeneid* (VI:87), the Sibyl of Cumae prophesies: '*Et Thybrim multo spumantem sanguine cerno.*' 'Rivers of blood' was thus quite a common turn of phrase before Powell made it notorious. Speaking on European unity (14 February 1948), Winston Churchill said: 'We are asking the nations of Europe between whom rivers of blood have flowed, to forget the feuds of a thousand years.'

R K O. See INITIALS.

road. See KING OF THE ~.

Roaring 20s. The decade label for the 1920s had established itself by 1939, reflecting the heady, buoyant atmosphere in certain sections of society following the horrors of the First World War. The adjective 'roaring', meaning 'boisterous, riotous, noisy', had previously been applied to the 1850s and, in Australia, to the 'roaring days' of the gold rush. The same meaning occurs in the expression 'roaring drunk'. The 1940s do not appear to have been given a label, least of all **Roaring Forties** – that term had already been applied to parts of the oceans between 40 degrees and 50 degrees south where strong westerly winds blow.

roast. See RULE THE ROOST.

Robin Hood. The name for one who robs the rich to benefit the poor comes from the English outlaw, celebrated since the fourteenth century, who may or may not have actually existed. Early versions of the tales about him were set in either Yorkshire or Nottinghamshire (particularly in Sherwood Forest, with the villainous Sheriff of Nottingham always in hot pursuit). The cast of characters surrounding Robin Hood included his love, Maid Marian, and fellow outlaws Little John, Allen-a-dale, Friar Tuck and Will Scarlet.

Robinson. See BEFORE ANYONE CAN SAY JACK ~; HEATH ~.

rock'n'roll. This name for a type of popular music was first popularized by Alan Freed, a US disc jockey, who is generally credited with first discovering and promoting it. In 1951, he was hosting *Moondog's Rock'n'Roll Party* on a radio station in Cleveland, Ohio. It was not until he moved to New York City in 1954, however, that the term took hold. Earlier, in 1934, there had been a song by Sidney Clare and Richard Whiting with the title 'Rock and Roll' in the film *Transatlantic Merry-Go-Round*, referring to a ship's movements. The phrase may also have been Black English slang for the sexual act. (See also IT'S ONLY ~.)

Roland. See CHILDE ~.

roll. See TURN OVER IN ONE'S GRAVE.

Rolling Stones. See POP GROUP NAMES.

Rolls-Royce. This description of anything of the highest quality ('the Rolls-Royce of bicycles', 'a Rolls-Royce speaking voice') comes from the name of the motor car or the aero engine, after the founders of the manufacturing company, the Hon Charles Stewart Rolls and Frederick Henry Royce (who met for the first time in the Midland Hotel, Manchester, in 1904).

Rome. See FIDDLE WHILE ~ BURNS; WHEN IN ~.

Romulus and Remus. See ROMAN NAMES.

Room at the Top. The title of a novel (1957; film UK, 1958) by John Braine, it is from what *CODP* lists as a proverb 'commonly used to encourage competition', but doesn't record the occasion when Daniel Webster (*d* 1852), the US politician, said it. Responding to a suggestion that he shouldn't become a lawyer because the profession was overcrowded, he said: 'There is always room at the top.' At one point in Braine's novel, the hero, Joe Lampton, is told: 'You're the sort of young man we want. There's always room at the top.'

Room of One's Own, A. The title of a feminist essay (1929) by Virginia Woolf, arguing that women will not be able to succeed in writing fiction until they have the independence signified by a room of their own to write in.

Room With a View, A. The title of a novel (1908; film UK, 1985) by E.M. Forster. Noël Coward's song with this title did not appear until *This Year of Grace* (1928).

root. See MONEY IS THE ~ OF ALL EVIL.

Rosa Klebb. An unlovely Russian-born villainess, with sadistic and lesbian tendencies, in Ian Fleming's novel *FROM RUSSIA WITH LOVE* (1957; film UK, 1963).

Rosebud. This was the mystifying last word spoken by the eponymous hero of *Citizen Kane* (US film 1941). Finding out what it meant to him is a theme of the picture. It is finally glimpsed written on the side of a snow-sledge and presumably was a powerful talisman of childhood innocence, or a 'symbol of maternal affection, the loss of which deprives him irrecoverably of the power to love or be loved' (Kenneth Tynan).

rose is a rose is a rose. The poem 'Sacred Emily' by Gertrude Stein (*d* 1946) does not include the line 'a rose is a rose is a rose', but: 'Rose is a rose is a rose is a rose' (i.e. upper case 'R', no indefinite article at the start, and three not two repetitions). The Rose in question was not a flower but an allusion to the English painter Sir Francis Rose 'whom she and I regarded', wrote Constantine Fitzgibbon, 'as the peer of Matisse and Picasso, and whose paintings – or at least painting – hung in her Paris drawing-room while a Gauguin was relegated to the lavatory' (letter to the *Sunday Telegraph*, 7 July 1978). Stein also refers to a 'Jack Rose' (not a 'Jack' rose) earlier in the poem.

The format is now a commonplace: 'Bad reviews are bad reviews are bad reviews are bad reviews' ('Nicholas Craig', *I, An Actor*, 1989); 'A Tory is a

ROMAN NAMES (*or* **Latin names) (from Myths, Legends, Literature, and History).** Some of these names are of Greek origin, or are part of Greek mythology, and could as well appear under GREEK NAMES.

Achates: the Trojan companion of AENEAS, noted for his faithfulness.

Aeneas: of Greek origin, the legendary founder of the Roman race; a warrior in the Trojan war and hero of the *Aeneid*.

Amaryllis: a rustic beauty.

Androcles: was spared by a lion in the arena because he had once extracted a thorn from its paw.

Atticus: a scholar and patron of the arts.

Aurae: nymphs of the breezes.

Aurora: the goddess of the dawn (see EOS under GREEK NAMES).

Avernus: see *FACILIS DESCENSUS AVERNI*.

Bona Dea: the chaste goddess of the earth.

Cerberus: a three-headed dog guarding the gates of hell.

Ceres: the goddess of agriculture; mother earth.

Cincinnatus: a farmer-soldier who returned to his plough having defeated Rome's enemies.

Concordia: the goddess of harmony, peace and unity.

Copia: the goddess of abundance.

Cornucopia: a conical receptacle representing abundance.

Corydon: a lovesick rustic shepherd.

Cupid: the god of love.

Diana: the goddess of fertility, the moon and hunting (see ARTEMIS under GREEK NAMES).

Dido: the queen and founder of Carthage, who kills herself when abandoned by AENEAS.

Egeria: the goddess of childbirth; a wise counsellor.

Euryalus: a warrior companion of NISUS.

Flora: the goddess of flowers, presiding over whatever blooms.

Fortuna: the goddess of chance.

Golden Ass: Lucius, as a donkey, observes mankind.

Harmonia: the child of the union of opposites (MARS and VENUS).

Horatius: held the Etruscans at bay while the Romans burnt a bridge.

Io: a priestess seduced by JUPITER disguised as a cloud; she was briefly a heifer.

Janus: the two-faced keeper of the gate of heaven.

Jove: another name for JUPITER.

Juno: the air personified; the queen of heaven, and protectress of women in marriage (see HERA under GREEK NAMES).

Jupiter: the supreme god (see ZEUS under GREEK NAMES).

Maecenas: the patron of poets.

Mars: the god of war (see ARES under GREEK NAMES).

Mercury: the winged messenger god (see HERMES under GREEK NAMES).

Minerva: the goddess of wisdom (see ATHENA under GREEK NAMES).

Morpheus: the god of dreams.

Mors: death personified (see THANATOS under GREEK NAMES).

Neptune: the god of the sea (see POSEIDON under GREEK NAMES).

Nisus: a warrior who died rescuing his companion EURYALUS.

Nox: the goddess of night.

Orcus: a spirit presiding over the dead, and thus a name given to hell itself.

Palinurus: AENEAS's helmsman, who falls asleep and then overboard.

Parcae: the Fates (as under GREEK NAMES) who measure out human life.

Pax: the goddess of peace.

Philemon: with Baucis, a hospitable old couple.

Pomona: the goddess of gardens and fruit trees.

Roman names – cont.

Proserpina/e: the queen of the underworld.
Romulus and Remus: suckled by she-wolf; the founders of Rome.
Saturn: the god of time (see CRONUS under GREEK NAMES).
Silenus: a fat, drunk follower of BACCHUS (see GREEK NAMES).
Silvanus: the god of woods and agriculture.

Somnus: the god of sleep.
Sors: the god of chance.
Venus: the goddess of love and beauty (see APHRODITE under GREEK NAMES).
Vesta: the virgin goddess of the hearth.
Vulcan: the god of destruction, fire, and metalworkers (see HEPHAESTUS under GREEK NAMES).

Tory is a Tory, whatever he might think' (Hugo Young, *One of Us*, 1990).

Rosencrantz and Guildenstern Are Dead. The title of a play (1966) by Tom Stoppard, concerning two of the minor characters in Shakespeare's *Hamlet*. The line is spoken (V.ii.376) by one of the English ambassadors after Hamlet has arranged for the killing of his two old student friends (who had been set up by his uncle Claudius to kill *him*). The two characters are also referred to in a play by W.S. Gilbert, *Rosencrantz and Guildenstern* (1891).

Ruffian on the Stair, The. The title of a radio play (1964) by Joe Orton comes from the poem 'To WR' in *Echoes* (1888) by W.E. Henley:

Madame Life's a piece in bloom,
Death goes dogging everywhere:
She's the tenant of the room,
He's the ruffian on the stair.

'Rule Britannia'. The words for the song now known as this were written by James Thomson in *Alfred: a Masque* (1740). The music was by Dr Thomas Arne. Thomson's words, in their original form, are these (my italics):

When Britain first, at Heaven's command,
Arose from out the azure main,
This was the charter of the land,

And guardian angels sung this strain:
'Rule, Britannia, *rule* the waves;
Britons never *will* be slaves.

Many now prefer to sing 'rules' and 'shall'. There is a difference, however, between a poetic exhortation – 'rule' – and a boastful assertion in – 'rules'. As for the difference between will/shall, it has been argued that Thomson, a Scot following Scottish usage could have put 'shall' anyway.

— rules OK. An affirmative phrase, said to have originated in gang-speak of the late 1960s in Scotland and Northern Ireland, though some would say it dates back to the 1930s. A gang, a football team, or the Provisional IRA would be said to 'rule OK'. Later this was turned into a joke with numerous variations – 'Queen Elizabeth rules UK', 'Rodgers and Hammerstein rule OK, lahoma', and so on. It soon became an all but unstoppable cliché. 'Vulgarity rules OK' wrote Peregrine Worsthorne in the *Sunday Telegraph*, 7 June 1987. (See also *DPP*.)

rule the roost, to. Meaning 'to lord it over others', this possibly derives from the image of a cock's behaviour towards hens on the roosting-perch. The existence of the (probably) earlier expression 'to **rule the roast**' – presiding as the head of the dinner table (as in Shakespeare,

King Henry VI, Part 2 (I.i.108) – may point to a more likely source (though just possibly the two phrases developed side by side).

Rum Bum and Concertina. The title of a volume of George Melly's autobiography (1977) alludes to the old naval saying: 'Ashore it's wine, women and song, aboard it's rum, bum and concertina.' Winston Churchill's version in response to a remark about naval tradition (recounted in Harold Nicolson's diary, 17 August 1950) was: 'Naval tradition? Monstrous. Nothing but rum, sodomy, prayers and the lash.'

run. See I DO NOT CHOOSE TO ~; YOU CAN ~ BUT YOU CAN'T HIDE.

runneth. See CUP ~ OVER.

running. See HIT THE GROUND ~.

running dogs. A phrase meaning 'lackeys' and popularized by Chairman Mao Tse-tung. In a 'Statement Supporting the People of the Congo Against US Aggression' (28 November 1964), he said: 'People of the world, unite and defeat the US aggressors and all their running dogs!' This provided a vivid weapon for use against the 'lackeys' of the US during the Vietnam War. Edgar

Snow had earlier recorded him using the term in 1937.

run the gauntlet, to. An expression meaning 'to endure something of a prolonged, testing nature, to be attacked on all sides', this has nothing to do with the type of glove but is from the Swedish *gatlop* or *gatloppe* which means 'lane run'. It carries the idea of someone having to run as a punishment (in the military) between two lines of tormentors.

Russians Are Coming, The Russians Are Coming, The. The title of a film (US, 1966) which took its inspiration from: 'The British are coming! The British are coming!' – Paul Revere's reputed cry to warn people of approaching British troops during the American War of Independence. However, on his night ride of 18 April 1775, from Boston to Lexington, it is more likely that he cried 'The regulars are out.'

Russians with snow on their boots. In September 1914, there was an unfounded rumour that a million Russian troops had landed at Aberdeen in Scotland and passed through England on their way to the Western Front. The detail that they were seen to have had 'snow on their boots' was supposed to add credence to the report. It had to be officially denied by the War Office.

S

S*S*

SABENA. See ACRONYMS.

Sabrina Fair. The title in the UK of Billy Wilder's 1954 film (US, *Sabrina*), based on a play by Samuel Taylor, about the daughter of a chauffeur who gets wooed by the two brothers who employ her father. Did the British distributors think it would be more appropriate to have an allusion to the poetic name for the River Severn, as applied to the nymph in Milton's masque 'Comus' (1634)?:

> Sabrina fair,
> Listen where thou art sitting
> Under the glassy, cool, translucent wave,
> In twisted braids of lilies knitting
> The loose train of thy amber-dropping
>   hair.

On the other hand, the British distributors might have been sending cinemagoers a message that the film had nothing at all to do with Sabrina, a busty model, who was at that time featured on TV shows with Arthur Askey, the comedian. Alas, this second theory does not fit, as Norma Sykes (her real name) did not appear until 1956 and, in fact, she took her stage name from the title of the film.

sack, to give someone the. The suggestion is that this expression dates from the days when workers would carry the tools of their trade around with them, from job to job, in a bag which they would leave with their employer. When their services were no longer required, they would be given the bag back.

Sad Cypress. The title of this Hercule Poirot novel (1940) by Agatha CHRISTIE comes from the Clown's Song in Shakespeare's *Twelfth Night* (II.iv.51):

> Come away, come away death,
> And in sad cypress let me be laid

(probably a coffin made of cypress wood, or a shroud of Cyprus lawn, i.e. linen).

safety first. A slogan that was first used in the US in connection with railroad safety. In the UK of the 1890s, this was also the original use of the slogan when a railway notice declared: 'The Safety of the Passengers is our First Concern'. In 1915, it became the motto of the National Council for Industrial Safety in the US. In 1916, the London General Bus Company formed a London 'Safety First Council'. The 1922 British general election saw the phrase in use as a political slogan for the Conservatives. Again, in 1929, it was the Tory slogan under which Stanley Baldwin fought for re-election, but it proved a loser. In 1934, the National Safety First Association was formed, concerned with road and industrial safety, and it is in this connection that the slogan has endured.

SAINTS' NAMES. The following are the names of prominent saints and what they are patrons of or are noted for:

Agatha: her breasts were cut off for resisting advances; the patroness of bell-founders.

Agnes: a virgin and martyr; the patroness of young virgins.

Alexis: lived by begging and sharing the proceeds with the poor; the patron saint of beggars and hermits.

Andrew: a fisherman, apostle and missionary, he was crucified; the patron saint of Scotland.

Ant(h)ony (the Great): the founder of monasticism; the patron of herdsmen.

Audrey: see under TAWDRY.

Augustine of Canterbury: a missionary bishop, he brought Christianity to England.

Barbara: a virgin and martyr; her name is invoked against lightning; the patroness of gunners, artillery companies and miners.

Bernadette (Soubirous): had a vision of the Virgin Mary at Lourdes.

Bernard of Menthon/Montjoux: gave his name to a breed of dog (see LOVE ME LOVE MY DOG), and to two Alpine passes.

Bride/Brigid: the second patron saint of Ireland.

Bruno: always pictured with his head bent as a sign of humility; the founder of the Carthusian order; the brand of tobacco with this name may be linked to the growing of tobacco by monks at Valdemosa, Spain.

Catherine of Alexandria: a martyr, who first managed to resist death on a spiked wheel.

Cecilia: a martyr; the patroness of music and the blind.

Christopher: a martyr; the patron of wayfarers and motorists.

Clare of Assisi: the first abbess of the 'Poor Clares' religious order.

Claus: see NICHOLAS.

David: the patron saint of Wales.

Dunstan: the patron saint of goldsmiths.

Elmo/Erasmus: the patron saint of sailors.

Fiacre: prayed to by the sick (especially those with piles); the patron saint of gardeners.

Francis of Assisi: the founder of the Franciscan order; noted for his love of animals.

George: the patron saint of England; the legendary slayer of a dragon.

Giles: the patron of cripples and the impoverished.

Hubert: the patron saint of hunting.

Ivel: he never existed – the brand name for dairy products is an invention.

Jerome: a hermit and scholar; compiler of the Vulgate; usually pictured with a lion.

Jude: an apostle (not Judas Iscariot).

Lucy: her vision was restored after her eyes were gouged out; the patron saint of those with eye troubles.

Luke: a physician evangelist; the patron saint of physicians and painters of pictures.

Martha: the patron saint of housewives (see also MARTHA).

Martin of Tours: the patron saint of innkeepers and former drunks (see also ALL MY EYE AND BETTY MARTIN).

Mary Magdalen(e): a weeping repentant prostitute; the patron saint of penitents.

Nicholas: as Santa Claus, the bringer of presents to children at Christmas; the patron saint of children of Russia, and of pawnbrokers, etc.

Pancras: martyred at the age of fourteen; the patron saint of young boys.

Patrick: a missionary; the patron saint of Ireland.

Saints' names – cont.

Sebastian: a Roman soldier, sentenced to be shot at with arrows.
Simeon Stylites: spent thirty years on a pillar.
Thomas: the doubting apostle; the patron saint of architects.

Veronica: offered a cloth to Christ on His way to Calvary.
Vitus: a martyr; dancing before his statue was said to secure good health.
Winifred: the patron saint of North Wales.

Salad Days. The title of a musical (1954) by Julian Slade and Dorothy Reynolds, it comes from Shakespeare, *Antony and Cleopatra* (I.v.73):

> My salad days,
> When I was green in judgement, cold in blood.

Sally Lunn. A tea-cake named after a pastry-cook who sold them in Bath during the eighteenth century, or from the French *soleil lune* ('sun and moon' cake).

Salome. See DANCE OF THE SEVEN VEILS.

saloon-bar Tory. 'There is in Britain a political animal known as a "saloon-bar Tory". He sits in the most comfortable bar of his local pub, sipping gin and tonic, bemoaning the state of the nation and saying how much better everything would be if only managements and everyone else would stand up to the dreadful unions.' (Michael Leapman, *Barefaced Cheek*, 1983)

S A L T. See ACRONYMS.

salt of the earth. Meaning 'the best of mankind', this expression comes from Jesus Christ's description of his disciples in Matthew 5:13: 'Ye are the salt of the earth: but if the salt have lost his savour, wherewith shall it be salted?' Which suggests, rather, that they should give the world an interesting flavour, be a ginger group, and not that they were simply jolly good chaps. The New English Bible conveys this meaning better as 'you are salt to the world'.

Samson Agonistes. See AGONISTES.

Sam Weller. The cheerful, devoted, Cockney character who becomes man-servant to Samuel PICKWICK in *The Pickwick Papers* (1836–7) by Charles Dickens. He was noted for his 'Wellerisms' – folksy proverbs and sayings ('Be wery careful of widders'), often bizarrely expressed.

Sanctus. See MASS PHRASES.

sandboy. See HAPPY AS A ~.

sandwich. This snack, originally of beef between two slices of bread, was invented by John Montagu, 4th Earl of Sandwich (*d* 1792) who, being a committed gambler, disliked having to stray from the table for such small matters as eating. He once played for twenty-four hours non-stop. The Sandwich Islands in the Pacific (now part of Hawaii) were named by Capt Cook after him rather than the food.

san fairy ann. This expression meaning 'it doesn't matter; why worry?' dates from the First World War and is a corruption of the French *ça ne fait rien* [that's nothing, makes no odds].

sans peur et sans reproche [without fear and without reproach]. The Chevalier de Bayard (*d* 1524), a French knight, was known as *le chevalier sans peur et sans reproche*. Mark Twain once proposed '*sans peur et sans culottes*' [knee britches] as the motto of a gentlemen's dining club and Harry Graham of *Punch* proposed '*sans beurre et sans brioche*' [butter/brioches].

Sarah Gamp. See GAMP.

S A S. See INITIALS.

Satan. See GET THEE BEHIND ME ~.

Satchmo. The nickname of Louis Armstrong (*d* 1971), the jazz trumpeter and singer, is a contraction of 'satchelmouth'. It was consquently given to a type of fungus which appears to exhibit a very large mouth.

Saturn. See ROMAN NAMES.

say. See ANYTHING YOU ~ . . .

say it with flowers. This slogan was originally devised for the Society of American Florists, and invented in 1917 by its chairman, Henry Penn of Boston, Massachusetts, with Maj Patrick O'Keefe, head of an advertising agency. O'Keefe suggested: 'Flowers are words that even a babe can understand' – a line he had found in a poetry book. Penn considered that too long. O'Keefe, agreeing, rejoined: 'Why, you can say it with flowers in so many words.' Later came several songs with the title.

Scala. See under ODEON.

Schmilsson. See LITTLE TOUCH OF ~.

scholar. See GENTLEMAN AND A ~.

schoolboy. See AS EVERY ~ KNOWS.

school of hard knocks. Referring to experience and hardship, considered as an educative force, *O E D2* calls this 'US Slang' and finds it in 1912. *The Complete Naff Guide* (1983) has as a 'naff boast': 'But then, of course, I left university without a degree. I like to think I have a First from the School of Hard Knocks.' Receiving an honorary doctorate in the humanities from the University of Nevada in May 1976, Frank Sinatra said: 'I am a graduate of the school of hard knocks', and on losing his job as chairman of Mecca in October 1978, Eric Morley said: 'I went to the College of Hard Knocks, and last week I got my doctorate.' At least he didn't say he had attended **the university of life**. (Partridge/*Slang* prefers 'the university of hard knocks' and dates it *c* 1910.) Lord Baden-Powell wrote a book called *Lessons from the 'Varsity' of Life* (1933).

scoff. See FOOLS WHO COME TO ~ . . .

scot-free. See GET AWAY WITH . . .

'Scots wha hae'. It sounds like an exclamation – 'wu-hey!' or 'HAWAE THE LADS!' – but it is the title of a battle song by Robert Burns (also known as 'Robert Bruce's March to Bannockburn'). The poem begins:

> Scots, wha hae [lit. 'who have] wi'
>   Wallace bled,
> Scots, wham Bruce has often led,
> Welcome to your gory bed,
> Or to victorie.

Scott. See GREAT ~.

Scottish play. Theatrical superstition is understandable in a profession so dependent on luck. However, the euphemism 'Scottish play', invariably used for Shakespeare's *Macbeth*, is based on a well-documented history of bad luck associated with productions of the play. Merely to utter the name of the play would be enough to invoke misfortune.

scrapheap. See DUSTBIN.

Scratch an Actor. The title of the book (1969) by Sheilah Graham, the Hollywood gossip-columnist, comes from Dorothy Parker's remark: 'Scratch an actor and you'll find an actress.'

scratch 'n' sniff. This was a gimmick used originally in the cinema whereby audience members scratched cards to release smells appropriate for the scene they were watching. The first 'scratch 'n' sniff' opera production may have been *The Love for Three Oranges* at the English National Opera in 1989.

screws. See PUT THE ~ ON.

scripture. See DEVIL CAN CITE ~ . . .

SCUBA. See ACRONYMS.

Scylla. See GREEK NAMES.

sea. See DEVIL AND THE DEEP BLUE ~; FROM ~ TO SHINING ~; OLD MAN AND THE ~; WORSE THINGS HAPPEN AT ~.

Seagreen Incorruptible. This was the nickname of Robespierre, the French revolutionary leader. He established the Reign of Terror (1793–4) but was executed in it himself. The name comes from Thomas Carlyle's *History of the French Revolution*. There was no connection between Robespierre's greenness and his incorruptibility. He was green because of poor digestion, and he was incorruptible because he was a fanatic.

sealed. See LIPS ARE ~.

Seamless Robe, A. The title of a book, subtitled 'Broadcasting Philosophy and Practice' (1979) by Sir Charles Curran, a former Director-General of the BBC. The phrase was meant to describe 'the impossibility of separating out any one strand of the job from another . . . It was impossible to disentangle, in the whole pattern, one thread from another.' It is from John 19:23: 'The soldiers, when they had crucified Jesus, took . . . his coat: now the coat was without seam, woven from the top throughout.'

Searchers, The. The name of the Liverpool pop group (*fl.* 1963–6) derived from the title of the John Wayne film (US, 1956).

seas. See I MUST DOWN TO THE ~ AGAIN.

Sea Shall Not Have Them, The. The title of a film (UK, 1954) and of a novel (1953) by John Harris. Presented in the film as the motto of an air-sea rescue unit in the Second World War.

seated. See GENTLEMEN BE ~.

Sea The Sea, The. The title of a novel (1978) by Iris Murdoch, is taken from Xenophon's story (in *Anabasis*, IV.vii. 24) of how his Greek mercenaries retreated to the Black Sea following their defeat in battle (401 BC). When they reached it, the soldiers cried: '*Thalatta, thalatta!*' The Chevalier Sigmund Neukomm (*d* 1858) also wrote a song with this title, which was parodied in H.J. Byron's version of *Aladdin* with reference to tea-clippers in 1861:

The Tea! The Tea!
Refreshing Tea.
The green, the fresh, the ever free
From all impurity.

Sebastian, St. See SAINTS' NAMES.

Second Time As Farce, The. The title of a book on the theatre (1988), by the playwright David Edgar, is an allusion to Karl Marx, *The Eighteenth Brumaire of Louis Napoleon* (1852): 'Hegel says somewhere that all great events and personalities in world history reappear in one fashion or another. He forgot to add: the first time as tragedy, the second as farce.'

Second World War. See WORLD WAR TWO.

Seems Like Old Times. The title of a film (US, 1980) and of a book (1989) by Alan Coren (made up of his old pieces from *The Times*). It comes from the title of the song (c 1946) by John Jacob Loeb and Carmen Lombardo, which had been preceded by 'It Seems Like Old Times' (1939) by Sammy Stept and Charles Tobias.

seen. See CHILDREN SHOULD BE ~ AND NOT HEARD; YOU AIN'T ~ NOTHIN' YET.

see Naples and die. This old Italian saying either suggests that once you have been to Naples there is nothing more beautiful to be seen on earth or, more ominously, dates from the time when the city was a notorious centre for typhoid, cholera and other diseases. This extract dated 3 March 1787 from Goethe's *Italian Journey* would seem to support the first origin: 'I won't say another word about the beauties of the city and its situation, which have been described and praised so often. As they say here, "*Vedi Napoli e poi muori!*" See Naples and die!'

seigneur. See DROIT DE ~.

Selene. See GREEK NAMES.

sell down the river, to. See SOLD DOWN THE RIVER.

sell off the family silver, to. Meaning 'to dispose of valuable assets which, once gone, cannot be retrieved', this allusion was memorably used in a speech to the Tory Reform Group by the 1st Earl of Stockton (Harold Macmillan) on 8 November 1985. Questioning the government's policy of privatizing profitable nationalized industries, he said: 'First of all the Georgian silver goes, and then all that nice furniture that used to be in the saloon. Then the Canalettos go.' This was summarized as 'selling off the family silver'.

Selsdon Man. This name, for a mythical primitive beast destroying the benefits of socialism in postwar Britain, was coined in Labour Party circles (possibly by Harold Wilson) in 1970. It was applied to the Conservative Party, following a much-publicized policy-making session by Edward Heath's Shadow Cabinet, held at the Selsdon Park Hotel near Croydon. The allusion is to the **Piltdown Man**, the name given to the celebrated forgery of a prehistoric skull.

send in/on the clowns. The tradition that the **show must go on** grew out of the circus. Whatever mishap occurred, the band was told to go on playing and the cry went up 'send in/on the clowns' – for the simple reason that panic had to be avoided, the audience's attention had to be diverted, and the livelihood of everybody in the circus depended on not having to give the audience its money back. However, no one seems able to turn up a written reference much before 1930. In 1950, 'the show must go on' is spoken in the film *All About Eve* and, in the same decade, Noël Coward wrote a song which posed the question '*Why* Must the Show Go On?' Stephen Sondheim chose the 'Send *in* . . .' form as the title of a song in *A Little Night Music* (1974).

Perhaps 'send in' was right for the circus, 'send on' for the stage?

sends. See IT ~ ME.

sera. See CHE ~.

Serious Money. The title of a play (1987) by Caryl Churchill, about greed in the City of London financial world. It comes from the phrase meaning 'money in excessive amounts' which the *Longman Register of New Words* (1989) surmises 'seems to have started life among the fast-burning earners of the post-BIG BANG, pre-Bust city of London, who, when speaking of salaries in the six-figure bracket, would concede that this was "serious money".' The *Register* also notes that the usage 'serious —' might spread to other areas: 'Annie's – a bar favoured by serious drinkers' (*Sunday Times*, 28 August 1988).

servants. See LADY CHATTERLEY.

Sesame. See OPEN ~.

sets. See EMPIRE UPON WHICH . . .

set the Thames on fire, to. This expression is often used in the negative: 'Well, he didn't exactly set the Thames on fire' – meaning 'he failed to make an impression'. W.S. Gilbert in *Princess Ida* (1884) has:

> They intend to send a wire?
> To the moon – to the moon
> And they'll set the Thames on fire
> Very soon – very soon.

Versions of this saying date back to the eighteenth century, and similar things have been said about the Rhine, Seine and Liffey in the appropriate languages. The Romans had the expression: '*Tiberium accendere nequaquam potest*' [It isn't at all possible to set the Tiber on fire]. The Thames, famously, once used

to freeze over, which would only serve to increase the achievement should anyone manage to set it on fire.

seven. See GIVE US A CHILD UNTIL IT IS ~ . . .

Seven Deadly Sins, the. These are pride, wrath, envy, lust, gluttony, avarice and sloth – 'mortal' sins (as opposed to 'venial', i.e. pardonable sins) which entail spiritual death. They are not listed in the Bible, and may have grown out of medieval morality plays and were known as such by the early fourteenth century.

Seven Dwarfs, the. The story of 'Snow White and the Seven Dwarfs' was one of the old fairy tales collected by the Brothers Grimm in 1823. In the Walt Disney film version (US, 1937), the dwarfs were named: Bashful, Doc, Dopey, Grumpy, Happy, Sleepy and Sneezy.

Seven Per Cent Solution, The. The title of a novel (1974; film US, 1976) by Nicholas Meyer, about Sherlock Holmes being treated by Sigmund Freud for a persecution complex and cocaine addiction. Its origin is Sir Arthur Conan Doyle's *The Sign of Four* (1889), where Holmes says to Dr Watson: 'It is cocaine . . . a seven per cent solution. Would you care to try it?'

Seven Pillars of Wisdom. The title of a military chronicle (1926) by T.E. Lawrence derives from Proverbs 9:1: 'Wisdom hath builded her house, she hath hewn out her seven pillars.'

Seven Year Itch, The. The title of a play (1952; film US, 1955) by George Axelrod, this phrase now means the urge to be unfaithful to a spouse after a certain period of matrimony. *OED2* provides various examples of the phrase going back from the mid-twentieth to the mid-nineteenth centuries, but without the specific matrimonial context. For example, the 'seven year itch' describes a rash from poison ivy which was believed to recur every year for a seven-year period. Then one has to recall that since biblical days seven-year periods (of lean or fat) have had special significance, and there has also been the army saying: 'Cheer up – the first seven years are the worst!' 'Itch' had long been used for the sexual urge but, as Axelrod commented on *Quote . . . Unquote* (BBC Radio 4, 1979): 'There was a phrase which referred to a somewhat unpleasant disease but nobody had used it in a sexual [he probably meant 'matrimonial'] context before. I do believe I invented it in that sense.' Oddly, 'itch' doesn't appear to have been used in connection with venereal diseases. Nonetheless, in *W.C. Fields: His Follies and Fortunes* (1950), Robert Lewis Taylor writes: 'Bill exchanged women every seven years, as some people get rid of the itch.'

'Sexy Sadie'. The title of a Lennon and McCartney song (1968), which was originally called 'Maharishi' after the Maharishi Mahesh Yogi whom John Lennon considered a 'randy old goat'. But Lennon was dissuaded from naming him in the song.

shadow. See FIVE O'CLOCK ~.

shakes. See TWO ~ OF A LAMB'S TAIL.

shake/show a leg, to. 'Shake a leg' means no more than to dance, but 'show a leg' (meaning 'to get up out of bed in the morning or get a move on') dates from the days when women were allowed to spend the night on board when ships of the Navy were in port. Next morning at the cry: 'Show a leg!', if a woman's leg was stuck out of a hammock, she was allowed to sleep on. If it

was a man's, he had to get up and on with his duties.

Shangri-La. This name for an earthly paradise comes from the name of the hidden Tibetan lamasery in James Hilton's novel, *Lost Horizon* (1933). All who remain there enjoy long life.

She Done Him Wrong. The title of a film (US, 1933) based on Mae West's play *Diamond Lil*, it alludes to the refrain of the anonymous US ballad 'Frankie and Johnny' which Mencken dates *c* 1875 and which is sung in the film. There are numerous versions (200 is one estimate) and it may be of Negro origin. 'Frankie and Johnnie were lovers' [or husband and wife] but he [Johnnie] does her wrong by going off with other women – 'He was her man, but he done her wrong.' So, to equal the score, Frankie shoots him, and has to be punished for it (in some versions in the electric chair):

Frankie walked up to the scaffold, as calm as a girl could be,
She turned her eyes to Heaven and said 'Good Lord, I'm coming to Thee;
He was my man, but I done him wrong.'

shell-like. See IN YOUR ~ EAR.

she who must be obeyed. The original 'she' in the novel *She* (1887) by H. Rider Haggard was the all-powerful Ayesha: 'who from century to century sat alone, clothed with unchanging loveliness, waiting till her lost love is born again'. But also: 'She was obeyed throughout the length and breadth of the land, and to question her command was certain death.' From the second of these two quotations we get the use of the phrase by barrister Horace Rumpole regarding his formidable wife in the 'Rumpole of the Bailey' stories by John Mortimer (in TV plays from 1978, and novelizations therefrom). Hence, too,

SHAKESPEARE (William).
The most quoted and alluded to of all authors. Because the references to his works in this dictionary are so numerous, they are not dated. However, here is a note of the approximate date of composition of his works:

1590–1	*King Henry VI, Parts 2 & 3*
1591	*King Henry VI, Part 1*
	Titus Andronicus
1592	*The Comedy of Errors*
1592–3	Start of Sonnets
	The Taming of the Shrew
	Love's Labour's Lost
	The Two Gentlemen of Verona
	King Richard III
	Venus and Adonis
1594	*A Midsummer Night's Dream*
	Lucrece
	Romeo and Juliet
1595	End of Sonnets
	King Richard II
1596	*King John*
	The Merchant of Venice
1597	*King Henry IV, Parts 1 & 2*
1598	*As You Like It*
	Much Ado About Nothing
1599	*The Passionate Pilgrim*
	King Henry V
	Julius Caesar
1600	*Twelfth Night*
1600–1	*Hamlet*
1601	*The Merry Wives of Windsor*
	The Phoenix and the Turtle
1601–2	*Troilus and Cressida*
1603	*All's Well That Ends Well*
1604	*Measure for Measure*
	Othello
1605	*King Lear*
1606	*Macbeth*
1607	*Antony and Cleopatra*
1608	*Coriolanus*
	Timon of Athens
1609	*Pericles*
1609–10	*Cymbeline*
1611	*The Winter's Tale*
1612	*The Tempest*
	King Henry VIII

For titles of adaptations of Shakespeare's works, see under CATCH MY SOUL. For other phrases with Shakespearean connections, see also 'ALL OUR YESTERDAYS' SPEECH; BABBLED OF GREEN FIELDS; BARD (OF AVON); FALSTAFF; HAMLET WITHOUT THE PRINCE; JOHN OF GAUNT'S SPEECH; 'TO BE OR NOT TO BE' SPEECH; etc.

one of the many nicknames applied to Margaret Thatcher – 'She-Who-Must-Be-Obeyed'.

'Shine on Harvest Moon'. This was the title of a song (1908) by Nora Bayes and Jack Norworth. The harvest moon seems particularly bright between 15 and 20 September, thus enabling farmers to bring in their crops by moonlight, should they need to. An ITV series was subsequently (1982–5) entitled *Shine on, Harvey Moon*.

shining. See FROM SEA TO ~ SEA.

shining city on a hill, a. In a speech on 14 October 1969, Ronald Reagan quoted Governor Winthrop of the Massachussetts Bay Colony who told new settlers in 1630: 'We shall be as a city upon a hill, the eyes of all people are upon us.' It was meant as a warning as much as a promise. Winthrop didn't use the word 'shining'. Later he was often to use the image of a shining city on a hill to describe the US as a land of security and success. He used the phrase particularly during his bid for re-election as president in 1984. At the Democratic Convention, New York Governor Mario Cuomo remarked that a shining city might be what Reagan saw 'from the veranda of his ranch' but he failed to see despair in the slums. 'There is despair, Mr President, in the faces that you don't see, in the places that you don't visit in your shining city . . . This nation is more a tale of two cities than it is just a shining city on a hill.'

If anything, the image is biblical. Matthew 5:14 has: 'A city that is set on a hill cannot be hid . . . Let your light so shine before men that they may see your good works'; the 'holy hill' of Zion is a 'sunny mountain' according to one etymology; the New Jerusalem is the jewelled city lit by the glory of God, in Revelation.

Shipton. See MOTHER ~.

shift the goalposts. See MOVE ~.

ship(s). See FACE THAT LAUNCH'D A THOUSAND ~; LIKE RATS DESERTING . . .

Shock of the New, The. The title of a TV series and a book (1980) by the art critic, Robert Hughes, it came from Ian Dunlop's study of seven modernist exhibitions (pub. 1972), as acknowledged.

Shoot the Moon. The title of a film (US, 1981) which alludes to the US expression for 'to do a moonlight flit', meaning 'to remove one's goods at night in order to cheat the bailiff'. 'To shoot the moon' can also mean 'to go for broke' in card playing.

Shoot the Pianist/Piano-Player. The English title given to the film *Tirez sur le pianiste* (France, 1960), echoes the notice once reported by Oscar Wilde from a bar in the US Rocky Mountains: 'Please do not shoot the pianist. He is doing is his best.' In 1972, an Elton John record album was entitled *Don't Shoot Me, I'm Only the Piano-Player*.

Short Sharp Shock, A. The title of this play (1980) by Howard Brenton and Tony Howard (originally *Ditch the Bitch*, referring to Margaret Thatcher)

came from a phrase used by William Whitelaw, Home Secretary, in a speech to the Conservative Party Conference (10 October 1979) describing a new method of hard treatment for young offenders. The expression had been used by other Home Secretaries before him and is a quotation (referring to execution) from W.S. Gilbert's lyrics for *The Mikado* (1885).

shoulder. See CHIP ON ONE'S ~.

show a leg. See SHAKE ~.

showbiz. See THAT'S ~.

show must go on. See SEND IN THE CLOWNS.

sic transit gloria mundi. The phrase meaning 'so passes away the glory of the world' – perhaps now mostly used ironically when something has failed – is an allusion to *Of the Imitation of Christ* (c 1420) by Thomas à Kempis ('O quam cito transit gloria mundi' [O, how quickly the world's glory passes away']). It is used at the coronation ceremony of Popes when a reed surmounted with flax is burned and a chaplain intones: '*Pater sancte, sic transit gloria mundi*' to remind the new 'Holy Father' of the transitory nature of human vanity. ODQ, however, says it was used at the crowning of Alexander V at Pisa in July 1409, and is of earlier origin, which, if so, would mean that it was à Kempis who was doing the quoting.

sick as a parrot. Meaning 'heartbroken; very disappointed', a likely origin for the expression is in connection with psittacosis or parrot disease/fever. In about 1973, there were several cases of people dying of this in West Africa. It is basically a viral disease of parrots (and other birds) but can be transmitted to humans. Even so, there may be an older source. In the seventeenth and eighteenth centuries, there was an expression 'melancholy as a (sick) parrot' (in the plays of Aphra Behn, for example), and Desmond Morris in *Catwatching* (1986) claims that the original expression was 'as sick as a parrot with a rubber beak', meaning that the animal was incapacitated without a sharp weapon, as in the expression: 'no more chance than a cat in hell with no claws'. (See also *D P P*.)

sideburns (*or* sideboards). Denoting strips of hair in front of the ears, the word was originally **burnsides** after General Ambrose E. Burnside (*d* 1881) who fought in the American Civil War and was noted for having a generous pair himself (joined to his moustache but with his chin clean-shaven). The syllables had been transposed by 1887, probably because 'sideburns' was a fraction easier to say than 'burnsides' and echoic of the older term 'sidewhiskers'.

sighed as a lover obeyed as a son. In Edward Gibbon's *Autobiography* (1796), he recounts how he forbore to marry a certain Swiss woman on account of his father's objections: 'After a powerful struggle, I yielded to my fate. I sighed as a lover. I obeyed as a son.' In Thomas Hardy's *The Trumpet-Major* (1880) this is apparently alluded to in the sentence: 'Having spoken as a mother, she sighed as a woman.'

sign of a misspent youth. Under Herbert Spencer (*d* 1903), the *O D Q* has: 'It was remarked to me by the late Mr Charles Roupell . . . that to play billiards was the sign of an ill-spent youth.' On the other hand, in the archives of the Savile Club in London it is recorded that Robert Louis Stevenson, who was a member (1874–94), propounded to Herbert Spencer that 'proficiency in this game [note: probably billiards – because it was said in the Savile billiards room] is a sign of a misspent youth'. Other clubs also claim the

honour and other people would supply the word 'snooker' or 'bridge' instead of 'billiards'. Though a keen billiards player, Herbert Spencer was displeased when the saying kept being ascribed to him and dictated a denial to Dr David Duncan, who edited his *Life and Letters* (1908). Benham notes that a similar expression had earlier appeared in *Noctes Ambrosianae* in March 1827.

silence is golden. This encouragement to silence is from a Swiss inscription written in German and best known in the English translation by Thomas Carlyle: '*Sprechen ist silbern, Schweigen ist golden*' [Speech is silver(n), silence is golden].

silent majority. On 3 November 1969, President Richard Nixon gave a T V address on Vietnam and called for the support of a particular section of U S opinion – 'the great silent majority of my fellow Americans', by which he meant MIDDLE AMERICA or at least, that part of the U S not involved in the vociferous anti-war protest movement. Earlier, the phrase had been used in the nineteenth century to describe the dead. The dying words of Lord Houghton in 1884 were: 'Yes, I am going to join the Majority and you know I have always preferred Minorities.'

silent upon a peak in Darien. See STOUT CORTEZ.

Silenus. See ROMAN NAMES.

Silly Billy. The most notable person to be given this nickname for a fool was William Frederick, 2nd Duke of Gloucester (*d* 1834), uncle of William IV – though it was also applied to the king himself. In the wrangles between Whigs and Tories, when the king supported the former, Gloucester is reported to have asked: 'Who's Silly Billy now?' Partridge/*Slang* has Henry Mayhew in

1851 finding 'Silly Billy . . . very popular with the audience at the fairs' (as a name used by a clown for his stooge). (See also *DPP*.)

silly season. This phrase refers to the period of time around August/September when, for lack of hard news, newspapers traditionally fill their pages with frivolities. Although Parliament and the law courts are in recess, and Britain (like France) increasingly seems to stop work for the month of August, the fact is that important news does *not* cease happening. The Soviet invasion of Czechoslovakia took place then, as did the resignation of President Nixon, and the 1990 Gulf Crisis, not to mention the start of two world wars.

Silvanus. See ROMAN NAMES.

silver. See SELL OFF THE FAMILY ∼.

Simeon Stylites, St. See SAINTS' NAMES.

sinews of peace/war. Winston Churchill's speech at Fulton, Missouri, on 5 March 1946, which introduced the old phrase IRON CURTAIN to a wider audience, was entitled 'The Sinews of Peace'. This was an allusion to the phrase *'nervi belli pecunia'* from Cicero's *Philippics* where the 'sinews of war' means 'money'. The 'sinews of peace' recommended by Churchill in dealing with the Soviet Union amounted to recourse to the newly formed United Nations Organization.

sing. See I ∼.

Singer Not the Song, The. The title of a film (UK, 1960) based on a novel (1959) by Audrey Erskine Lindop, who in turn took her title from a West Indian calypso.

sinking. See LIKE RATS DESERTING . . .

sins. See SEVEN DEADLY ∼.

Sisyphus. See GREEK NAMES.

sitcoms. See under YUPPIE.

sitting. See ARE YOU ∼ COMFORTABLY?

Situation Hopeless but Not Serious. The film (US 1965) with this title probably derived it from an Austrian saying: 'The situation in Germany is serious but not hopeless; the situation in Austria is hopeless but not serious.' Conan Doyle in 'The Second Stain' (*The Return of Sherlock Holmes*, 1905) has the basic, 'The situation is desperate, but not hopeless.'

sixes and sevens, to be at. Meaning 'to be confused; in an unresolved situation', the usual origin given for this expression is that in the days when the medieval guilds of London took pride in their order of precedence, the Merchant Taylors and the Skinners could not agree who should be sixth, and who seventh. After an intervention by the Lord Mayor, they agreed to take it in turns – as they do to this day. Morris, on the other hand, supports the theory that it dates from a dice game (as mentioned by Chaucer in one of his poems) in which the dice bore marks up to seven, if not further: 'Only a confused or disorganized person would roll for this point' (i.e. a 'six and seven'). This is the origin favoured by OED2.

Shakespeare's only use of the phrase occurs in *King Richard II* (II.ii.122):

> All is uneven,
> And everything is left at six and seven.

In *Pericles* (IV.vi.74) he may be making a punning allusion to it when (in a sexual context) Lysimachus says: 'Did you go to't [copulate] young? Were you a gamester at five or at seven?'

six of one and half a dozen of the other. This phrase is used to describe a situation where there is no difference. Revd Francis Kilvert writes in his diary (6 September 1878): 'There was a great deal of talk at that time in London about the quarrel between the King [George IV] and the Queen [Caroline]. There was about six for one and half a dozen for the other.'

sixpence. See BANG GOES ~.

Six Proud Walkers, The. See GREEN GROW THE RUSHES

sixties, swinging. See SWINGING LONDON.

sixty-four (thousand) dollar question. This is the question which would solve all our problems if only we knew the answer to it. *Webster's Dictionary* says that $64 *was* the highest award in a CBS radio quiz called *Take It or Leave It* which ran from 1941–8 and in which the value of the prize doubled every time the contestant got a right answer (in the progression $1 - 2 - 4 - 8 - 16 - 32 - 64$ – hence the title *Double Your Money* given to the first of the UK TV versions). An example of the original use in the 1950s is contained in a *Daily Express* article about P.G. Wodehouse written by Rene McColl (undated): '"Wodehouse, Esq.," I observed, "Could I, to use the vernacular of this our host nation, pop the jolly old 64-dollar question? If you were back in Germany, a prisoner, and you had it all to do again – would you do it?"' Subsequently, in the US TV version of the show (1955–7), the top prize did go up to $64,000 – though, cunningly, when ITV imported the show for British viewers shortly afterwards, the title was simply *The 64,000 Question* or

Challenge, making no mention of the denomination of currency involved. (See also *DPP*.)

Skin of Our Teeth, The. The title of a play (1942) by Thornton Wilder, 'to escape by the skin of one's teeth' means to do so by a very narrow margin indeed. The origin is Job 19:20: 'My bone cleaveth to my skin, and to my flesh, and I am escaped with the skin of my teeth.'

Skull Beneath the Skin, The. The title of a crime novel (1982) by P.D. James, taken from T.S. Eliot's 'Whispers of Immortality' (1920): 'Webster was much possessed by death/And saw the skull beneath the skin'.

sky. See GONE TO THE BIG — IN THE ~.

sliced. See GREATEST THING SINCE . . .

slippers. See WHERE THE DEVIL ARE MY ~?

Sloane Ranger. Denoting a posh, upper-class woman of good family, (originally) living in the Sloane Square area of London, the joke allusion is to the Western character, the Lone Ranger. The term was invented in 1975 by the magazine *Harpers and Queen*, and when the Princess of Wales ('Supersloane') entered public life in 1981, the term became much more widely understood.

Small Earthquake in Chile. The title of a book (1972) by Alastair Horne about the Allende affair (in Chile). It comes from the famously mousy headline with which Claud Cockburn claimed to have won a competition for dullness among subeditors on *The Times* during the 1930s which went: 'Small Earthquake in Chile. Not Many Dead.' The original has proved impossible to trace and may just have been a smoking-room story. However, the idea lives on: the journalist Michael Green called a volume of memoirs, *Nobody Hurt in Small Earthquake* (1990), and the cartoonist Nicholas Garland called his 'journal of a year in Fleet Street', *Not Many Dead* (1990).

Small Is Beautiful. The title of a book (1973) by Professor E.F. Schumacher, on the expansionist trend in business and organizations that was very apparent in the 1960s and 70s. It was popular with those who wanted 'economics on a human scale', and probably echoed BLACK IS BEAUTIFUL.

SMERSH. See ACRONYMS.

Smike. This is the title of a stage musical (published 1976) by R. Holmes and Simon May. There is an unwritten rule that when the novels of Charles Dickens are adapted for stage and screen, and particularly as musicals, they are named after (possibly) the most interesting character – so *Oliver Twist* becomes *Oliver!* (1960, film UK, 1968) (note the significant exclamation mark), *A Christmas Carol* becomes *Scrooge* (film UK, 1970), *Nicholas Nickleby* becomes *Smike* (or the Brahms-Sherrin-Grainer *Nickleby and Me*, Stratford East, 1975–6), though retaining the original title in the Royal Shakespeare Company adaptation; and *The Old Curiosity Shop* becomes *Mister Quilp* (film UK, 1974). There has also been a stage version of *David Copperfield* (with Jess Conrad) called *Pip*.

Smith. See HARVEY ~.

smoke-filled room. Suite 408–409–410 (previously rooms 804–5) of the Blackstone Hotel in Chicago was the original 'smoke-filled room' in which Warren Harding was selected as the Republican presidential candidate in June 1920. The image conjured up by this phrase is of cigar-smoking political bosses coming to a decision after much horse-trading. Although he denied saying it, the phrase seems to have come out of a prediction by Harding's chief supporter, Harry Daugherty (*d* 1941). He foresaw that the convention would not be able to decide between the two obvious candidates and that a group of senators 'bleary-eyed for lack of sleep' would have to 'sit down about two o'clock in the morning around a table in a smoke-filled room in some hotel and decide the nomination'. This was precisely what happened and Harding duly emerged as the candidate.

smoking gun/pistol. Meaning 'incriminating evidence', as though a person holding a smoking gun could be assumed to have committed an offence with it – as in Conan Doyle's Sherlock Holmes story 'The "Gloria Scott"' (1894): 'Then we rushed on into the captain's cabin . . . and there he lay . . . while the chaplain stood, with a smoking pistol in his hand.' The term was popularized during Watergate. For example, Representative Barber Conable said of a tape of President Nixon's conversation with H.R. Haldeman, his chief of staff, on 23 June 1972, containing discussion of how the FBI's investigation of the Watergate burglary could be limited, 'I guess we have found the smoking pistol, haven't we?'

SNAFU. See ACRONYMS.

snakes in Iceland/Ireland. 'There are no snakes to be met with throughout the whole island' – those words are the entire contents of Chapter 72 of *The Natural History of Iceland* by a Dane called Horrebow (1758). Dr Samuel Johnson used to boast of being able to repeat the whole chapter (Boswell's *Life*, 13 April 1778). Sometimes Ireland rather than Iceland is mentioned in telling the 'joke', presumably on the grounds that ST PATRICK drove out all the snakes from that country by ringing a bell.

Snobbery With Violence. The title of a book (1971) by Colin Watson, surveying the modern crime story. Earlier, in Alan Bennett's play *Forty Years On* (1969) a character had talked of: 'Sapper, Buchan, Dornford Yates, practitioners in that school of Snobbery with Violence that runs like a thread of good-class tweed through twentieth-century literature'.

snook. See COCK A ~.

snow. See RUSSIANS WITH ~ . . .

snowman. See ABOMINABLE ~.

S O B. See INITIALS.

sober. See DRUNK/ ~.

socialists. See WE ARE ALL ~ NOW.

society. See AFFLUENT ~; GREAT ~.

sock. See PUT A ~ IN IT.

'So Deep Is the Night'. The title of a song (1939) by Sonny Miller, first featured in the 1940 film *Hear My Song*, though originally Mario Melfi's setting of Chopin's Etude in E Major, Op. 10, No. 3, appears to have had French words under the title '*Tristesse*'. Compare the film title (US, 1946) *So Dark the Night*.

Sod's Law. See IF ANYTHING CAN GO WRONG . . .

Softly Softly. The title of a BBC TV police drama series (1966–76), which comes from the 'Negro proverb' 'Softly, softly, catchee monkee' – more particularly, in this case, from the saying's use as the motto of the Lancashire Constabulary Training School which inspired the series.

Soft Machine. The name of the UK vocal/instrumental group (*fl.* 1970), taken from *The Soft Machine*, the title of a novel (1961) by William Burroughs.

soft underbelly. This phrase is used when referring to a vulnerable part. Speaking to the House of Commons on 11 November 1942, Winston Churchill said: 'We make this wide encircling movement in the Mediterranean . . . having for its object the exposure of the under-belly of the Axis, especially Italy, to heavy attack.' In *The Second World War* (Vol.4), Churchill describes a meeting with Stalin before this, in August 1942, at which he had outlined the same plan: 'To illustrate my point I had meanwhile drawn a picture of a crocodile, and explained to Stalin with the help of this picture how it was our intention to attack the soft belly of the crocodile as we attacked his hard snout.' Somewhere subsequently, the 'soft' and the 'under-belly' must have joined together to produce the phrase in the form in which it is now used.

sold down the river, to be. Meaning 'to be betrayed', this expression is of US origin. In the South, after 1808, it was illegal to import slaves, so they were brought down the Mississippi to the slave markets of Natchez and New Orleans. Hence, if a slave was 'sold down the river', he lost his home and family. The saying particularly relates to the practice of selling troublesome slaves to the owners of plantations on the lower Mississippi where conditions were harsher than in the northern slave states. Mark Twain's novel *Pudd'nhead Wilson* (1894) is dominated by this theme and the expression occurs in it some fifteen times, e.g. ' "Very good," said the master, putting up his watch, "I will sell you *here*, though you don't deserve it. You ought to be sold down the river".'

soldier(s). See EVERY ∼ HAS THE BATON ... ; OLD ∼ NEVER DIE; UNKNOWN ∼.

so little done – so much to do. The gist of what the colonial financier and statesman Cecil Rhodes said before he breathed his last on 26 March 1902 is: 'So little done, so much to do'. It was a theme that had obviously preoccupied him towards the end of his life. He had said to Lord Rosebery: 'Everything in the world is too short. Life and fame and achievement, everything is too short.' Earlier, Tennyson wrote these lines in *In Memoriam* (lxxiii, 1850):

> So many worlds, so much to do,
> So little done, such things to be.

The actual last words of Rhodes were much more prosaic: 'Turn me over, Jack.'

solution. See FINAL ∼.

Somebody up There Likes Me. The title of the autobiography (1955, film US 1956) of Rocky Graziano, World Middleweight Boxing Champion of 1947–8. There was a title song from the film; also a song called 'Somebody up There Digs Me' (1957).

Some Like It Hot. The title of a film (US, 1959) about two unemployed musicians who are accidental witnesses of the St Valentine's Day Massacre and flee to Miami disguised as members of an all-girls jazz band. So the 'hotness' may come from the jazz or the position they find themselves in. There had, however, been an unrelated US film with the same title in 1939 (starring Bob Hope). The source is apparently the nursery rhyme 'Pease porridge hot' (first recorded about 1750), of which the second verse goes:

> Some like it hot
> Some like it cold
> Some like it in the pot
> Nine days old.

This is such nonsense that it is sometimes ended with a riddle: 'Spell me that without a P' ('that' being quite easy to spell without a P). Ring Lardner's story 'Some Like Them Cold' (*c* 1926, collected 1935) contains a song, referring to women: 'Some like them hot, some like them cold/Some like them fat, some like them lean' (etc.)

some of my best friends are — (*usually* **Jewish**). The phrase is a self-conscious (and now jokey) disclaimer of prejudice. In a May 1946 letter, Somerset Maugham replied to charges that he was anti-semitic and said: 'God knows I have never been that; some of my best friends in England and America are Jews . . .' So clearly, at that date the phrase could be used without irony. However, the line may – according to one source – have been rejected as a cartoon caption by the *New Yorker* prior to the Second World War, and presumably dates, in any case, from the Nazi persecution of the Jews from the 1930s onwards. In the (Jewish) Marx Brothers film *Monkey Business* (1931), there is the line: 'Some of my best friends are *housewives.*' The Russian Prime Minister, Alexei Kosygin, was apparently unaware of the phrase's near-cliché status in 1971 when he said: 'There is no anti-semitism in Russia. Some of my best friends are Jews.'

someone had blundered. The Charge of the Light Brigade at Balaclava, near Sebastopol, took place on 25 October 1854, during the Crimean War. Owing to a misunderstood order, 247 officers and men out of 637 were killed or wounded. Tennyson's famous poem about it was published in the *Examiner* newspaper on 9 December that same year. The second stanza ran:

'Forward the Light Brigade!'
Was there a man dismay'd?
Not tho' the soldier knew
Someone had blundered.
Their's not to make reply,
Their's not to reason why,
Their's but to do and die:
Into the valley of Death
Rode the six hundred.

According to Christopher Ricks's edition of the poems, Tennyson wrote this one on 2 December 'in a few minutes, after reading . . . *The Times* in which occurred the phrase *someone had blundered*, and this was the origin of the metre of his poem'.

In fact, *The Times* had spoken rather (in a leader on 13 November) of 'some hideous blunder'. Advised to be careful because controversy would offend the War Office, Tennyson allowed the 'someone had blundered' line to be deleted when his next collection of poems was published (*Maud, and Other Poems*, 1855). When he heard that the Society for the Propagation of the Gospel intended to circulate this *revised* poem to the troops, he had copies of the uncut version printed and sent to the Crimea.

Someone to Watch Over Me. The title of this film (US, 1987) about a bodyguard who falls for the woman he is minding, comes from the title of the George and Ira Gershwin song (1926) in *Oh! Kay.*

Something Wicked This Way Comes. The title of a novel (1962; film US, 1983) by Ray Bradbury. See *BY THE PRICKING OF MY THUMBS.*

somewhere in England. On 24 August 1941, Winston Churchill broadcast a report on his meeting with President Roosevelt: 'Exactly where we met is secret, but I don't think I shall be indiscreet if I go so far as to say that it was "somewhere in the Atlantic".' The previous year there had been a film *Somewhere in England* (UK 1940) which begot a series of British regional comedies (Halliwell lists *Somewhere in Camp/on Leave/in Civvies* and *in Politics*). This construction originated in the First World War, for security reasons (e.g. 'somewhere in France . . .'), and its use came to be broadened to anywhere one cannot, or does not want to be too precise about.

somewhere to the right of Genghis Khan. A description of someone's politics, if they are of the extreme right. Arthur Scargill, president of the National Union of Mineworkers, told John Mortimer in the *Sunday Times* (10 January 1982): 'Of course, in those days, the union leaders were well to the right of Genghis Khan.' An allusion from the *Independent* (28 January 1989): 'Close friends say he [Kenneth Clarke] has been an emollient force behind the doors of the Department of Health, but Genghis Khan would have looked like a calming influence alongside his ebullient ministers David Mellor and Edwina Currie.' Genghis Khan (*d* 1227) was a Mongol ruler who conquered large parts of Asia.

Somnus. See ROMAN NAMES.

son. See NUMBER ONE ~.

son and heir, the. This phrase is now used only jokingly to describe an eldest son. Charles Dickens has 'together with the information that the Son and Heir would sail in a fortnight' in *Dombey and Son* (Chap. 17, 1846–8). Shakespeare has 'the son and heir to that same Faulconbridge' (*King John*, I.i.56) but here the quotation marks are not yet quite around the phrase.

song and story, in. A would-be poetic phrase, the earliest example to hand is from W.S. Gilbert, *The Pirates of Penzance* (Act II, 1879):

> Go ye heroes, go to glory,
> Though you die in combat glory,
> Ye shall live in song and story.

son of a gun. Nowadays, this is an inoffensively jocular way of addressing someone. However, in sea-faring days, if a pregnant woman somehow found herself upon a warship and was ready to go into labour, the place traditionally made available to her was between two guns. If the father was unknown, the child could be described as a 'son of a gun'. Partridge/*Slang*, however, quoting an 1823 source, defines the term as meaning a '*soldier*'s bastard', so perhaps there was an army equivalent of the space made available.

sorry. See LOVE MEANS NEVER HAVING TO SAY . . .

Sors. See ROMAN NAMES.

SOS. See INITIALS.

soufflé rise twice, you can't make a. The meaning of this expression is that it is pointless to try and make something happen again if it is unrepeatable. Alice Roosevelt Longworth is supposed to have said it of Thomas E. Dewey's nomination as the Republican challenger in 1948 (Dewey had previously stood against F.D. Roosevelt in 1944). Paul McCartney has more than once used the phrase to discount the possibility of a Beatles reunion. Some say that it is not an impossible feat.

soul(s). See DARK NIGHT OF THE ~; EYES AS WINDOWS OF THE ~; IRON ENTERED HIS ~; WINDOWS INTO MEN'S ~.

Sound of Two Hands Clapping, The. The title of this book (1975) of Kenneth Tynan's critical writings comes from a Zen koan ('a riddle used in Zen to teach the inadequacy of logical reasoning'): 'We know the sound of two hands clapping. But what is the sound of one hand clapping?' This koan also appears as the epigraph to J.D. Salinger's *Nine Stories* (1953).

sour grapes. This is the explanation given for the behaviour of someone who affects to despise something because he knows he cannot have it. The source is Aesop's fable of 'The Fox and the Grapes' in which a fox tries very hard to reach some grapes but, when he is unable to do so, says they looked sour anyway.

Spanish. See OLD ~ CUSTOMS.

Spare Rib. The title of a British feminist magazine (founded 1972), is a punning reference to the cuts of meat known as 'spare ribs'. See also ADAM'S RIB.

Sparks Fly Upward. This is the title of the autobiography (1981) of the actor, Stewart Grainger. Frank (Lord) Chapple, the former trade union leader, called his autobiography (1984) *Sparks Fly*. Chapple had been leader of the Electricians' Union and 'sparks' has been the nickname given to members of that trade since the First World War at least. Both authors drew on Job 5:7: 'Man is born unto trouble, as the sparks fly upward.'

speaketh. See HE BEING DEAD YET ~.

Speak for England. This is the title of a book (1976) of oral history, edited by Melvyn Bragg. It comes from what L.S. Amery is supposed to have cried out in the House of Commons on 2 September 1939. Neville Chamberlain was holding out the prospect of a further Munich-type peace conference, when Arthur Greenwood, the acting Labour leader, rose to speak. Amery called out: 'Speak for England, Arthur' (though, in his own account, he omits the 'Arthur' and the interjection was not recorded in *Hansard*).

speak softly and carry a big stick. Speaking at the Minnesota State Fair in September 1901, President Theodore Roosevelt gave strength to the idea of backing negotiations with threats of military force when he said: 'There is a homely adage which runs, "Speak softly and carry a big stick; you will go far." If the American nation will speak softly and yet build up and keep at a pitch of the highest training a thoroughly efficient navy, the Monroe Doctrine will go far.' The 'homely adage' is said to have started life as a West African proverb.

special relationship. This is the term used to describe affiliations between countries (the earliest *O E D2* citation is for one between Britain and Galicia in 1929) but particularly referring to that supposed to exist between Britain and the U S on the basis of historical ties and a common language. The notion was principally promoted by Winston Churchill in his attempts to draw the US into the 1939–45 war, though whether he used the phrase prior to 1941 is not clear. In the House of Commons on 7 November 1945, Churchill said: 'We should not abandon our special relationship with the United States and Canada about the atomic bomb.' In his 1946 'IRON CURTAIN' speech at Fulton, Missouri, he asked: 'Would a special relationship between the United States and the British Commonwealth be inconsistent with our over-riding loyalties to the World Organization? [the U N].'

Speed-the-Plow. The title of a play (1988) by David Mamet, about two Hollywood producers trying to get a project off the ground. It comes from a very old phrase indeed: in the form 'God speed the plough', it was what one would say when wishing someone luck in any venture (and not just an agricultural one). The phrase was in use by 1500 at least and is also the title of a traditional song and dance. *Speed the Plough* was the title of a novel (1798) by Thomas Morton which introduced the unseen character of MRS GRUNDY.

spend a penny, to. A euphemism for 'to go to the lavatory'. The first public convenience to charge one penny opened in London in 1855, but *O E D2* does not find the phrase before 1945.

Sphinx. See RIDDLE OF THE ~.

spic. This pejorative term for Spanish-speaking people sounds like a contraction of 'Spanish-speaking' or 'Hispanic'. The journal *American English* suggests rather that the word comes from 'spiggoty', an abusive term for Spanish-speakers in Central and South America (*c* 1900). When the Panama Canal was being constructed (1901–4), Panamanians would say: 'No spikee de English' and 'spikee de' became 'spiggoty'. *D O A S* adds that in the U S 'spic' has also been applied to Italians or Italian-Americans and derives from 'spaghetti . . . reinforced by the traditional expression "No spika da English".' Rodgers and Hart had a song (1939) called 'Spick and Spanish'.

spinach. See I SAY IT'S ~.

spit. See DON'T ~ . . .

Spitting Image. The title of an I T V comedy series (from 1984) using puppets to satirize current events. Given the venom involved, it might be thought that any spitting had to do with saliva. The theories are, however, that the phrase is a corruption of 'speaking image' or 'splitting image' (two split halves of the same tree which provide an exact likeness), or a black southern US pronunciation of 'spirit and image' (which a true likeness might have).

Splendour in the Grass. The title of this film (US, 1961) comes from William Wordsworth's 'Ode (Intimations of Immortality)' (1807):

> Though nothing can bring back the hour
> Of splendour in the grass, of glory in the flower.

splice the main brace, to. Meaning 'to have a drink', the expression comes from a comparison between the reviving effect of alcoholic drink and repairing or strengthening the mainbrace on board ship, where the mainbrace is the rope for holding or turning one of the sails. As used in the navy itself, the expression refers to the rare occurrence of an extra tot of GROG all round.

Spode's Law. See IF ANYTHING CAN GO WRONG . . .

spoke. See PUT A ~ IN.

SPQR. See INITIALS.

spread alarm and despondency, to. The meaning is 'to have a de-stabilizing effect, purposely or not'. During the Second World War, Lt-Col Vladimir Peniakoff ran a small raiding and reconnaissance force on the British side which became known as 'Popski's Private Army'. In his book *Private Army* (1950), he wrote: 'A message came on the wireless for me. It said "Spread alarm and despondency . . . The date was, I think, May 18th, 1942".'

When a German invasion was thought to be imminent at the beginning of July 1940, Winston Churchill had issued an 'admonition' to 'His Majesty's servants

---

SPOONERISMS. The accidental transposing of the beginnings of words is named after Revd William Spooner (*d* 1930), Warden of New College, Oxford. The word had been coined by 1900 and many of his reported efforts must be apocryphal. 'In a dark glassly' and 'a half-warmed fish' are two of the more likely ones. 'Kinquering Congs Their Titles Take' – announcing the hymn in New College Chapel (1879) – sounds reasonable, but 'Sir, you have tasted two whole worms; you have hissed all my mystery lectures and been caught fighting a liar in the quad; you will leave Oxford by the next town drain', seems utterly contrived (compare most GOLDWYNISMS). Had he been an ornithologist, Spooner might well have described himself as a word-botcher.

---

in high places . . . to report, or if necessary remove, any officers or officials who are found to be consciously exercising a disturbing or depressing influence, and whose talk is calculated to spread alarm and despondency'. Prosecutions for doing this did indeed follow. The phrase goes back to the Army Act of 1879: 'Every person subject to military law who . . . spreads reports calculated to create unnecessary alarm or despondency . . . shall . . . be liable to suffer penal servitude.'

spring. See WITH ONE BOUND . . .

Spy Who Came in from the Cold, The. The title of a novel (1963; film UK, 1966) by John LE CARRE, after which, anyone coming in from any kind of exposed position, or returning to favour, might find themselves described as 'coming in from the cold'. On 22 June 1990, Douglas Hurd, British Foreign Secretary, speaking in Berlin, said: 'We should not forget the reason for which Checkpoint Charlie stood here for so many years but no one can be sorry that it is going. At long last we, we are bringing "Charlie" in from the cold.'

squad. See AWKWARD ∼.

square deal. See FOUR-SQUARE.

square one. See BACK TO ∼.

square peg in a round hole, a. Meaning 'someone badly suited to his job or position', the expression is mostly in twentieth-century use. However, Sydney Smith's *Lectures on Moral Philosophy* (1804): 'If you choose to represent the various parts in life by holes upon a table, of different shapes, – some circular, some triangular, some square, some oblong, – and the persons acting these parts by bits of wood of similar shapes, we shall generally find that the triangular person has got into the square hole, and a square person has squeezed himself into the round hole.'

stage. See I DON'T WISH TO KNOW THAT ...

Star Danced, A. The title of Gertrude Lawrence's autobiography (1945) comes from Shakespeare, *Much Ado About Nothing* (II.i.316):

> You were born in a merry hour
> ... A star danced, and under that I was born.

Stars and Bars. The title of this novel (1984; film US, 1988) by William Boyd, came from the name for the flag of the Confederate States of the US (1861), which differed from the 'Stars and Stripes'.

Stars Look Down, The. The title of this novel (1935; film UK, 1939) by A.J. Cronin, alludes to the situation of the controllers of earthly destiny looking down on human behaviour. The situation also occurs in a song of the 1940s called 'Tonight' (also known as 'Perfidia'), written by Milton Leeds to music by Alberto Dominguez: 'While the Gods of love look down and laugh at what romantic fools we mortals be'. There is a more obvious allusion to the situation in Shakespeare's *A Midsummer Night's Dream* (III.ii.115) when the sprite Puck says to Oberon, King of the Fairies: 'Lord, what fools these mortals be!' In *Coriolanus* (V.iii.184), we find: 'The gods look down, and this unnatural scene/They laugh at.'

'Stately Homes of England, The'. Although this phrase is best known as the title of Noël Coward's song from the show *Operette* (1938), it began life in a ballad 'The Homes of England' (1827) by Mrs Hemans:

> The stately homes of England,
> How beautiful they stand!
> Amidst their tall, ancestral trees,
> O'er all the pleasant land.

State of the Nation, The. The title of ITV current affairs specials (from 1966), this phrase might seem to have been devised in emulation of the US president's 'State of the Union' message, his annual address to Congress, which is required of him by the 1787 Constitution. However, in John Aubrey's plans for a 'Register Generall of People' which he devised *c* 1684, he writes: 'The design is to have Abstracts of all the above particulars ... so as to give the King a true State of the Nation at all times' – which may suggest that the concept was known in the seventeenth century.

states. See WAR BETWEEN THE STATES.

steam radio. This pejorative term for sound broadcasting is said to have been coined by Norman Collins in the early

1950s when he transferred his attentions as a broadcasting executive to television. The comparison alluded to is that between steam and electric trains. See also INDEPENDENT TELEVISION.

Steel Magnolias. The title of a film (1990) based on Robert Harling's off-Broadway stage play, revolving round a beauty parlour and the friendship of six women who form the backbone of society in a small Louisiana town. The women share their secrets and, presumably, the title was chosen to suggest their underlying strengths. Earlier, Rosalynn Carter, wife of President Jimmy Carter, had been nicknamed 'the Steel Magnolia'. This First Lady's role apparently went further than holding hands with her husband in public. He consulted her on policy matters and she seems to have had some influence over his decisions. The magnolia is a flower particularly associated with southern US areas.

Compare IRON HAND IN A VELVET GLOVE.

Stella. See ODEON.

step. See ONE ~ FORWARD; ONE SMALL ~ FOR MAN . . .

stock. See LOCK ~ AND BARREL.

stolen kisses. See *BAISERS VOLES*.

stomach. See HEART AND ~ OF A KING.

stone. See LEAVE NO ~ UNTURNED.

stop – look – listen. This is said to have been devised in 1912 by Ralph R. Upton for use on notices at railway crossings in the US. Certainly, on 27 December 1915 there opened a show (with music by Cole Porter) at the Globe Theater, New York, called *Stop! Look! Listen!* A George Robey song from *The Bing Boys Are Here* (1916) was entitled,

'I Stopped, I Looked, I Listened', and by 1936, an advertisement for H.H. Sullivan Inc 'Technical merchandise' (Rochester, New York) was playing with the phrase to the extent of 'Stop, look and kiss 'em' to accompany the picture of a leggy girl in cheesecake pose.

Stop the World I Want to Get off. The title of this musical (1961; film UK, 1966) is said to have been found as a graffito.

stout. See COLLAPSE OF ~ PARTY.

stout Cortez. There are two minor errors of fact in the poem 'On First Looking into Chapman's Homer' (1817) by John Keats:

> . . . Or like stout Cortez when with eagle eyes
> He star'd at the Pacific – and all his men
> Look'd at each other with a wild surmise –
> Silent, upon a peak in Darien.

In fact, it was Balboa, a companion of Cortez, who became the first European to set eyes on the Pacific Ocean at Darien on the Isthmus of Panama in 1513. Nor was he silent: he exclaimed, '*Hombre!*'

Straight on Till Morning. The title of this film (UK, 1972) comes from J.M. Barrie's *Peter Pan* (1904): 'Second star to the right, and straight on till morning'.

strangers. See I SPY ~.

Strangers All Are Gone, The. The title of Vol. IV (1982) of Anthony Powell's autobiographical sequence *TO KEEP THE BALL ROLLING*, comes from a line spoken by the Nurse in Shakespeare's *Romeo and Juliet* (I.v.143).

Straw Dogs. The title of this film (UK, 1971) came from a saying of Lao-tzu

307

(*d c* 531 BC): 'Heaven and Earth are not humane. They regard all things as straw dogs [used in sacrifices].'

street. See MAN IN THE ~; QUEER ~.

streets paved with gold, to find the. In the story of Dick Whittington, he makes his way to London from Gloucestershire because he hears the streets are paved with gold and silver. The actual Dick Whittington was thrice Lord Mayor of London in the late fourteenth and early fifteenth centuries. The popular legend does not appear to have been told before 1605. The streets of heaven are also sometimes said to be paved with gold – referred to in Revelation 21:21: 'and the street of the city was pure gold'. There is, however, a Negro spiritual where the 'streets in heaven am paved with gold', and the Percy French song 'The Mountains of Mourne' (1896) mentions 'diggin' for gold in the streets [of London]'. (See also *D P P*.)

strictly for the birds. Meaning 'of no consequence', this is a US expression (by 1951), alluding to horse manure which is only good for picking over by small birds. It was the title of a Dudley Moore instrumental number (1961), and also, rather oddly, given the origin, was used in a Rexona soap advertisement (1968).

strife. See IN PLACE OF ~.

stuff. See SUCH ~ AS DREAMS ARE MADE ON.

Styx. See GREEK NAMES.

sublime to the ridiculous, from the. This is usually quoted now without the final qualifying phrase: '. . . there is but one step'. The proverb most probably came to us from the French. After the retreat from Moscow in 1812, Napoleon is said to have uttered: '*Du* *sublime au ridicule il n'y a qu'un pas.*' However, Thomas Paine had already written in *The Age of Reason* (1795): 'The sublime and the ridiculous are often so nearly related, that it is difficult to class them separately. One step above the sublime, makes the ridiculous; and one step above the ridiculous, makes the sublime again.'

substances. See CERTAIN ~.

such stuff as dreams are made on. If one is quoting Prospero's words from Shakespeare, *The Tempest* (IV.i.156): 'We are such stuff/As dreams are made on' – it is definitely 'on' not 'of' (though Shakespeare did use the 'of' form elsewhere). Humphrey Bogart as Sam Spade in *The Maltese Falcon* (1941) is asked: 'What is it?' before speaking the last line of the picture, and replies: 'The stuff that dreams are made of.' The title of the 1964 Cambridge Footlights revue was *Stuff What Dreams Are Made Of.*

Suez. See EAST OF ~.

Sultan of Swat. See BABE.

Summer's Lease. See DARLING BUDS OF MAY.

sun. See EMPIRE UPON WHICH . . .

Sun Also Rises, The. The title of a novel (1926; film US, 1957)(also known as *Fiesta* in the UK) by Ernest Hemingway, about US expatriates in Europe. The source is Ecclesiastes 1:5: 'The sun also riseth, and the sun goeth down, and hasteth to his place where he arose.' It gave rise to the Hollywood joke, 'The son-in-law also rises', when Louis B. Mayer promoted his daughter's husband (David O. Selznick) in *c* 1933. More recently, there has been a book about the Japanese economy called *The Sun Also Sets* by Bill Emmott (1990).

Sunday Bloody Sunday. See
BLOODY SUNDAY.

Sunday Too Far Away. The title of
this film (Australia, 1977) comes from
the lament of an anonymous sheep-
shearer's wife: 'Friday night too tired,
Saturday night too drunk, Sunday night
too far away'.

sunlit. see BROAD ~.

Sunny Jim. One might say: 'Ah, there
you are . . . I've been looking for you,
Sunny Jim' – even if the person isn't
called Jim. It is a name applied to a
cheerful person but can also be used
slightly patronizingly. It originated with
a character who appeared in adverts for
Force breakfast cereal (from *c* 1903). He
was the invention of two young
American women, a Miss Ficken and
Minnie Maud Hanff (the latter usually
credited with the phrase), who came up
with a jingle and rough sketch of the
character for the Force Food Company.

sunset. See DRIVE.

superstar. This suffix became fashionable following the success of the musical
Jesus Christ Superstar (1970). Tim Rice,
its lyricist, says that he and the composer, Andrew Lloyd Webber, settled on
the title after seeing a 1960s Las Vegas
billing for 'Tom Jones – Superstar'. The
showbiz use of the term 'superstar'
although very much a 1960s thing (it
was also used by Andy Warhol) has been
traced back to 1925 by the *O E D 2*
which finds in that year talk of 'cinema
super-stars'.

supper. See LAST ~.

sure. See EGGS IS EGGS.

surrender. See NO ~; UNCONDI-
TIONAL ~.

survey. See MONARCH OF ALL I ~.

suspicion. See CAESAR'S WIFE.

S W A L K. See ACRONYMS.

swap. See NEVER CHANGE HORSES.

sweat. See BLOOD ~ AND TEARS;
HORSES ~ . . .

Sweeney, The. The title of an I T V
drama series (1974–8) about Scotland
Yard's Flying Squad comes from rhyming slang: Sweeney Todd (Flying Squad).
Sweeney Todd, 'the demon barber of
Fleet Street', murdered his customers in
the play sometimes called *A String of
Pearls, or, The Fiend of Fleet Street*
(1847) by George Dibden-Pitt, though
the title *Sweeney Todd, the Barber of
Fleet Street* seems to have originated
with a play (on the same theme) by F.
Hazelton in 1865.

Sweeney Agonistes. See AGON-
ISTES.

**sweet Fanny Adams/sweet FA/
sweet fuck-all.** There actually was a
person called Fanny Adams from Alton
in Hampshire, who was murdered, aged
eight, in 1867. At about the same time,
tinned meat was introduced to the Royal
Navy, and sailors – unimpressed – said it
was probably made up from the remains
of the murdered girl. 'Fanny Adams'
became the naval nickname for mutton
or stew, and then the meaning was extended to cover anything that was
worthless. The abbreviation 'Sweet FA'
being re-translated as 'Sweet Fuck-All' is
a more recent coinage.

Sweet Smell of Success. This film
title (U S, 1957) by Ernest Lehman,
based on a short story, is apparently an

309

original coinage. Subsequently, Laurence Olivier was quoted as saying that 'Success smells like Brighton'.

swim. See CAN A BLOODY DUCK ~?

swinging London/the Swinging Sixties. 'Swinging' had been a musician's commendation for many years before it was adopted to describe the free-wheeling uninhibited atmosphere associated with the 1960s. By extension, 'swinging' came to denote sexual promiscuity. 'A swinger' was one who indulged in such activity. Before this, in the early 1960s, the comedian Norman Vaughan would say 'swinging!' as a catch phrase, but Frank Sinatra had had an album entitled *Songs for Swinging Lovers* (1958), Peter Sellers, *Songs for Swinging Sellers* (1959), and Diana Dors, *Swinging Dors* (1960).

The coming together of 'swinging' and 'London' may first have occurred in an edition of the *Weekend Telegraph* magazine on 30 April 1965 in which the words of the US fashion journalist Diana Vreeland were quoted: 'I love London. It is the most swinging city in the world at the moment.' In addition, a picture caption declared: 'London is a swinging city.' Almost exactly one year later, *Time* magazine picked up the angle and devoted a cover story to the concept of 'London: The Swinging City' (15 April 1966).

swingometer. This is a device for demonstrating the swing (transfer of votes from one party to another) in British general elections, as used by Robert McKenzie in BBC election night broadcasts (from 1959). The suffix '-ometer', for a measuring device (as in 'barometer') was not new. Egyptologists of the eighteenth century were using the name **Nilometer** for a device found in ancient temples and used to measure the height of the Nile. In the 1960s, the ITV talent show *Opportunity Knocks* had a **clapometer** which gave a visual indication of the loudness of applause given to individual acts. Hence, from the *Evening Standard* (12 October 1989): 'Nigel Lawson's speech registered well on the clapometer', and other variations of the same: 'Even recent [architecture], like a sheltered housing scheme, would score highly on the Prince Charles-ometer.' (*Independent*, 20 January 1990)

sword. See PEN IS MIGHTIER THAN THE ~.

T*T*

T. See FIT TO A ~.

tabloid. This word for a newspaper with smaller pages than a 'broadsheet' and written in a downmarket, popular style, was coined by the chemist Sir Henry Wellcome in the 1880s to describe a small new tablet he had invented. 'Tabloid' was registered as a trademark, but in a short space of time came to be applied to anything that was miniature. Newspaper magnates Alfred Harmsworth and Lord Northcliffe both used the word to describe the new, small, popular papers at the start of the twentieth century, and the name stuck.

tacks. See BRASS ~.

tail. See CAT HOUSE.

take a rain-check, to. Originally, in the US, a rain-check (*or* -cheque) was a ticket for re-admission to a sporting event when the event had had to be postponed because of rain. The person to whom it was given would be able to produce it at a later date and claim free admission. Now broadened, the expression is used to mean 'let's put this "on hold", let's not make any arrangements about this until the time is more opportune'. Obviously, the phrase can be used as a polite way of postponing something indefinitely, but basically

there is some kind of commitment to 'renegotiate' at a later date.

Taken at the Flood. This title of a 'Hercule Poirot' novel (1948) by Agatha CHRISTIE was re-titled *There Is a Tide* in the US. Both from the same source – Shakespeare's *Julius Caesar* (IV.iii.217):

> There is a tide in the affairs of men,
> Which, taken at the flood, leads on to
> fortune.

take someone down a peg, to. Meaning 'to humble; reduce in self-esteem', the expression derives from nautical use, in connection with flags which were raised and lowered with pegs. A flag flying high would carry more honour than one lower down.

take the mickey, to. Meaning 'to send up; tease', this expression dates from the 1950s, from rhyming slang: Mickey Bliss (piss). Later, 'are you by any chance extracting the Michael?' became quite common. An alternative derivation of 'mickey' for 'piss' is from the word 'micturition' (urination/overwhelming desire to urinate frequently).

take the money and run. Meaning 'settle for what you've got and don't hang about', this advice might also be given to people worried about the worth of the job they are doing. It was the title of a Woody Allen film (1968).

tale. See AND THEREBY HANGS A ~.

Talent to Amuse, A. The title of Sheridan Morley's biography (1969) of Noël Coward comes from Coward's song 'If Love Were All' from *Bitter Sweet* (1929):

> I believe that since my life began
> The most I've had is just
> A talent to amuse.

A collection of Nancy Mitford's writings, edited by Charlotte Mosley, was published as *A Talent to Annoy* in 1986.

talent will out. This is a modern proverbial saying, meaning that if a person has talent, a way of expressing it will be found. An advertisement for Lloyds Bank Young Theatre Challenge (June 1988) had: 'Talent will out, they say. But only under the right conditions.' The young Beatrix Potter in her diary for 5 June 1891 mentions: 'A theory I have seen – that genius – like murder – will out – its bent being simply a matter of circumstance.' The proverb 'murder will out' (i.e. will be found out, will reveal itself) goes back at least to 1325, and 'truth will out' to 1439. Hannah Cowley in *The Belle's Stratagem* (1782) has: 'Vanity, like murder, will out.'

tall dark and handsome. This description of a romantic hero's attributes (as found especially in romantic fiction) seems to have surfaced in the early 1900s. Flexner puts it in the late 1920s as a Hollywood term referring to Rudolph Valentino (though, in fact, he was not particularly tall). Cesar Romero played the lead in the 1941 film *Tall Dark and Handsome* which no doubt helped fix the phrase in popular use. However, in a piece called 'Loverboy of the Bourgeoisie' (collected in 1965), Tom Wolfe writes: 'It was Cary Grant

that Mae West was talking about when she launched the phrase 'tall, dark and handsome' in *She Done Him Wrong* (1933).'

tanker. See TURNING A ~.

Tantalus. See GREEK NAMES.

TAP. See INITIALS.

TARDIS. See ACRONYMS.

Tarzan. See ME ~.

Taste for Death, A. The title of this crime novel (1986) by P.D. James comes from A.E. Housman's *Additional Poems* (No. XVI, 1937):

> Some can gaze and not be sick,
> But I could never learn the trick.
> There's this to say for blood and breath,
> They give a man a taste for death.

tawdry. The word meaning 'cheap; trashy' comes from 'St Audrey' (otherwise Etheldreda, Abbess of Ely in the seventh century AD). She developed a breast tumour which she blamed on wearing rich necklaces of jewels as a child, and she died of it in 679. Much later, in the sixteenth and early seventeenth century, women wore necklaces of *silk* which they called 'St Audrey's lace'. Alas, poor imitations of the lace drove out the good and, by an unfortunate process, her name came to be given to something of a gaudy nature.

teach. See DON'T ~ YOUR . . .

tears. See BLOOD SWEAT AND ~.

Teenage Mutant Ninja Turtles. This is the title of a film (US, 1990) about the adventures of four turtles (named Leonardo, Donatello, Raphael and Michelangelo) who gain incredible strength when they fall into toxic waste. It began (*c* 1982) as a spoof cartoon strip. A less energetic cartoon version for children was produced for T V and shown in the U K as *Teenage Mutant Hero Turtles*. A ninja is a type of feudal Japanese-trained assassin, skilled in the martial art of *ninjutsu*, and already familiar from such films as *Enter the Ninja* (U S, 1981).

teeth. See OLD AS MY TONGUE . . .

teetotal. Someone who is teetotal (i.e. abstains from alcohol) may drink a lot of 'tea', but the word probably comes from a simple emphasis on the initial 't' of 'total'. The totality of abstaining became important when the American Temperance Union extended its ban beyond hard liquor to include beer, wine and cider in 1836. However, three years before, the word 'teetotal' had been used in this context by Richard Turner of Preston, England (and, indeed, credit for the coinage is on his gravestone). Probably the U K and U S uses arose independently. Flexner says the word 'teetotally' had been used in the U S as early as 1807 by Parson Mason Locke Weems in the 'T – totally' rather than abstinence sense.

Tell England. The title of a novel by Ernest Raymond (1922; film U K, 1931 – though the film was known in the U S as *The Battle of Gallipoli*). Twice in the novel, Raymond quotes this epitaph:

> Tell England, ye who pass this
>   monument,
> We died for her, and here we rest
>   content

but does not indicate the source. However, it does echo the epitaph by the ancient Greek poet Simonides on the Spartans who died at Thermopylae (delaying the vastly greater Persian army at the cost of their own lives): 'Tell the Spartans, stranger, that here we lie, obeying their orders.'

Tell-Tale Tits. This was the title of the autobiography (1987) of the actress Fiona Richmond. As Iona and Peter Opie record in *The Lore and Language of Schoolchildren*, the rhyme:

> Tell tale tit
> Your tongue shall be slit,
> And all the dogs in the town
> Shall have a little bit

has been 'stinging in the ears of blabbers for more than two hundred years' (or since 1780, at least).

Ten Days That Shook the World. The title of a book (1919) by John Reed, about the Russian Revolution, it was also used as the alternative, English, title of Sergei Eisenstein's 1927 film *October*.

Tender Is the Night. The title of this novel (1934; film U S, 1961) by F. Scott Fitzgerald, comes from the 'Ode to a Nightingale' (1819) by John Keats: 'Already with thee! tender is the night'.

tender loving care. This is the phrase used for ministry to the sick taking the form of warmth and affection rather than medicine. Although Shakespeare uses the phrase in another context, its earliest use, in this sense, occurs in the final chapter, 'T L C Treatment', of Ian Fleming's *Goldfinger* (1959). James Bond says to Pussy Galore: 'All you need is a course of T L C.' 'What's T L C?' she asks. 'Short for Tender Loving Care Treatment,' Bond replies. 'It's what they write on most papers when a waif gets brought in to a children's clinic.' (See also *D P P*.)

Ten Little Niggers. The title of a novel (1939) by Agatha CHRISTIE, which has been dramatized and thrice filmed. Understandably, the U S title of the book became *Ten Little Indians*, and the U K 1966 film also had this title. *And Then There Were None* was the title of the U S 1945 film (U K, *Ten Little Niggers*)

313

and also of the UK 1974 film. Actually 'Ten Little Injuns' was the title of the *original* song, written by the US songwriter Septimus Winner (*c* 1868). Frank Green's British version, 'Ten Little Niggers' was published in 1869, and begins:

> Ten little nigger boys went out to dine;
> One choked his little self, and then there
> were nine.

tennis. See ANYONE FOR ~?

tents. See FOLD ONE'S ~ LIKE THE ARABS.

Teresa. See MOTHER ~.

Terpsichore. See GREEK NAMES.

Thames. See SET THE ~ ON FIRE.

Thanatos. See GREEK NAMES.

that's showbiz/show business! This exclamation used to cover disappointment at bad luck or the failure of anything, and is as such no longer limited to the world of entertainment. At the end of an article on auditions: 'That, as they say, is show business' (*Independent*, 23 May 1990). Certainly in use by the early 1960s, the expression is akin to 'that's life!' The similar-sounding 'That's Entertainment' was used by Howard Dietz and Arthur Schwarz as the title of a song in the film *Band Wagon* (1953) and as the title of two films (US, 1974; 1976).

there ain't gonna be no war. As Foreign Secretary to Anthony Eden, Harold Macmillan attended a four-power summit conference at Geneva where the chief topic for discussion was German reunification. Nothing much was achieved but the 'Geneva spirit' was optimistic and on his return to London he breezily told a press conference on 24 July 1955: 'There ain't gonna be no war.' He was quoting from the (*c* 1910) music-hall song which was sung in a raucous Cockney accent by a certain Mr Pélissier who had a show called 'Pélissier's Follies' during the reign of King Edward VII:

> There ain't going to be no war
> So long as we've a king like Good King
> Edward.
> 'E won't 'ave it, 'cos 'e 'ates that sort of
> fing.
> Muvvers, don't worry,
> Not wiv a king like Good King Edward.
> Peace wiv honour is 'is motter [*snort*] –
> Gawd save the King!

Some time before December 1941, an American called Frankl wrote a song with the title 'There Ain't Gonna Be No War', but Sir David Hunt has confirmed that it was the Pélissier song that Macmillan had in mind. In fact, Hunt sang it to him on one occasion.

thereby. See AND ~ HANGS A TALE.

There Is a Happy Land. The title of the novel (1957) by Keith Waterhouse comes from the hymn by C.H. Bateman.

There Is a Tide. See TAKEN AT THE FLOOD.

there is no alternative. When asked for the origin of Margaret Thatcher's famously nannyish statement in 1984, her political secretary replied: 'I am not sure that the Prime Minister ever actually used the phrase ... and my suspicion, shared by others, is that TINA was coined by those who were pressing for a change of policy.' But in a speech Mrs Thatcher made to the Conservative Women's Conference on 21 May 1980, marking the end of her first year in office, she had said: 'There is no easy popularity in [harsh economic measures], but I believe people accept *there is no alternative*.' The acronym TINA, said to have been coined by Young Conservatives, was flourishing by the time of the Party Conference in September 1981. (See also *DPP*.)

there's gold in them thar hills.

Meaning 'there are opportunities in the way indicated', this phrase was presumably established in US gold-mining by the end of the nineteenth century. It seems to have had a resurgence in the 1930s/40s, probably through its use in Western films. Frank Marvin wrote and performed a song with the title in the 1930s; a Laurel and Hardy short called *Them Thar Hills* appeared in 1934; the melodrama *Gold in the Hills* by J. Frank Davis has been performed every season since 1936 by the Vicksburg Theatre Guild in Mississippi. *OED2*'s earliest citation is from 1941.

there's life in the old dog yet. This

expression of wonder may be uttered at the unexpected possession of some power by someone or some thing thought to be 'past it' (especially when referring to a person's love life). It was used as the title of a painting (1838) – also called 'The Life's in the Old Dog Yet' – by Sir Edwin Landseer, which shows a Scottish ghillie rescuing a deerhound which, unlike a stag and two other hunting dogs, has not just plunged over a precipice.

There's No Business Like Show Business. The title of a musical (film

US, 1954), which earlier had been the title of a song in *Annie Get Your Gun* (1946) by Irving Berlin.

there you go again! In a TV debate

with President Carter in 1980, the Republican challenger, Ronald Reagan, laughed off Carter's charge that he would dismantle federal health support for the elderly, saying: 'There you go

again!' The phrase stuck with the voters and became a campaign refrain.

Theseus. See GREEK NAMES.

These You Have Loved. The title of a

BBC Radio record programme which has a history going back to 1938 when Doris Arnold introduced favourite middle-of-the-road music. The title was still being used forty years later. Originally it was chosen by way of allusion to the line 'These I have loved' in the poem 'The Great Lover' (1914) by Rupert Brooke. This is a 'list' poem in which Brooke mentions some of his favourite things (rather as the song with that title does in the much later musical *The Sound of Music*). Brooke's 'loves' include 'white plates and cups' and 'the rough male kiss of blankets'.

Thetis. See GREEK NAMES.

They Died with Their Boots on. The

title of an Errol Flynn film (1941) about General Custer and his death at Little Big Horn. 'To die with one's boots on' means to die violently or be hanged summarily (sometimes 'to die in one's boots/ shoes'). *OED2* finds this by the eighteenth century, and in the American West in 1873. In one sense, it can suggest an ignominious death (say, by hanging) but in a general way it can refer to someone who dies 'in harness', going about his work, like a soldier in the course of duty. 'To die with one's boots *off*' suggests, of course, that one dies in bed.

They Might Be Giants. The title of a

film (US, 1972), from a play by James Goldman about a man who thinks he is Sherlock Holmes. He recruits a female Dr Watson who says (in the film): 'You're just like Don Quixote, you think that everything is always something else.' Holmes replies: 'He had a point – of course, he carried it a bit too far, that's all. He thought that every wind-mill was a giant . . . If we never looked at things and thought what they *might* be we'd still all be in the tall grass with the apes.' A US band took the name 'They Might Be Giants' *c* 1989. See also TILT AT WINDMILLS.

They Shoot Horses Don't They?
The title of a novel (1935; film US, 1969) by Horace McCoy is apparently the source of this quasi-proverbial expression.

thin. See INSIDE EVERY FAT MAN . . .

things. See JUST ONE OF THOSE ~.

things fall apart the centre cannot hold. Of all the quotations used by and about politicians, the most commonly used by far in recent years in Britain has been the lines from 'The Second Coming' (1921) by W.B. Yeats:

> Things fall apart; the centre cannot hold;
> Mere anarchy is loosed upon the
>   world . . .
> The best lack all conviction, while the
>   worst
> Are full of passionate intensity.

The trend was probably started by Roy Jenkins in his Dimbleby Lecture of 23 November 1979 (which pointed to-wards the setting up of the centrist Social Democratic Party).

Chinua Achebe drew the title of his novel *Things Fall Apart* (1958) from Yeats's poem.

things I've done for England, the.
In Sir Alexander Korda's film *The Private Life of Henry VIII* (1933), Charles Laughton as the King is just about to get into bed with one of his many wives when, alluding to her ugli-ness, he sighs: 'The things I've done for England'. This became a catch phrase, to be used ironically when confronted with any unpleasant task. In 1979, Prince

Charles on a visit to Hong Kong sampled curried snake meat and, with a polite nod towards his forebear, exclaimed: 'Boy, the things I do for England . . .'

thin red line. A report by William Howard Russell in *The Times* (25 October 1854) described the first stage of the Battle of Balaclava in the Crimean War (the Charge of the Light Brigade followed a few hours later). Russell wrote of the Russian charge repulsed by the British 93rd Highlanders: 'The ground lies beneath their horses' feet; gathering speed at every stride, they dash on towards that thin red streak topped with a line of steel.' By the time he was writing *The British Expedition to the Crimea* (1877), Russell put: 'The Russians dashed on towards *that thin red line tipped with steel* [his italics].' Thus was created the jingoistic Victorian phrase 'the thin red line', standing for the supposed invincibility of British infantry tactics.

Compare Kipling's poem 'Tommy' from *Departmental Ditties* (1890) which goes: 'But it's "Thin red line of 'eroes" when the drums begin to roll'.

Third Man, The. The title of a film (UK, 1949) about the black market in postwar Vienna. The 'third man' is a fielding position in cricket, but in the film he is supposed to be one of three witnesses to a traffic accident which has taken the life of 'Harry Lime', a 'pusher', played by Orson Welles. It turns out that Lime himself is the Third Man and that he is very much alive. The film probably led to the use of 'Third Man', 'Fourth Man' and even 'Fifth Man' to describe those who were suspected of having tipped off the spies Burgess and Maclean to defect to Moscow in 1954. The 'Third Man' was later identified as Kim Philby, the 'Fourth Man' as Anthony Blunt.

thirtysomething. This was the title of a US TV drama series (from 1987). There was nothing new about giving someone's age as 'twenty something' or 'thirty something', when you didn't know the exact figure, but the TV series about couples around that age helped popularize the usage. 'Eighties pop for the thirty-somethings' said an ad in *Barclaycard Magazine* (1989); 'Judy is a successful and attractive businesswoman toward the far end of her thirtysomething decade. Yet she feels frustrated, alone and angry about her failed relationships with men.' (*Washington Post*, 13 March 1990)

This Above All. The title of this film (UK, 1942) based on the novel by Eric Knight, comes from Shakespeare's *Hamlet* (I.iii.78):

> Polonius: This above all: to thine own self be true.

This England. The title of a film (UK, 1941) – known in Scotland as *Our Heritage* [*sic*]. It comes from JOHN OF GAUNT'S SPEECH.

This Happy Breed. The title of this play (1943; film UK, 1944) by Noël Coward is taken from JOHN OF GAUNT'S SPEECH.

Thomas, St. See SAINTS' NAMES.

Those Barren Leaves. The title of this novel (1925) by Aldous HUXLEY, is taken from William Wordsworth's 'The Tables Turned' (1798):

> Enough of science and of art;
> Close up these barren leaves . . .

those whom the Gods love die young. So said Lord Byron in *Don Juan* (1819), adding that it was 'said of yore'. Indeed, Menander the Greek and Plautus said it in times BC. *Whom the Gods Love* was the title of a film (UK,

1936) about Mozart. Related to this saying is what Euripides and other classical authors put in the form: '**whom the Gods wish to destroy, they first make mad**'. Sophocles in *Antigone* (*c* 450 BC) quotes as a proverb: 'Whom Jupiter would destroy, he first makes mad.' Cyril Connolly in *The Unquiet Grave* (1944) added: '. . . they first call promising'.

thousand. See COOL HUNDRED; DEATH OF A ~ CUTS; FACE THAT LAUNCH'D A ~ SHIPS.

thousand points of light, a. A political catch phrase used by George Bush in the 1988 presidential election campaign and in his acceptance speech for the Republican nomination: 'I will keep America moving forward, always forward – for a better America, for an endless enduring dream and a thousand points of light.' It was said to symbolize individual endeavour, voluntary charity efforts, across the country. Perhaps it was supposed to echo Shakespeare's *The Merchant of Venice* (V.i.90):

> How far that little candle throws his
>   beams!
> So shines a good deed in a naughty
>   world.

Light often comes in thousands: 'It was but for an instant that I seemed to struggle with a thousand mill-weirs and a thousand flashes of light' (Charles Dickens, *Great Expectations*, Chap. 54, 1860–1). (See also *DPP*.)

Thou Swell Thou Witty. The title of the collected lyrics (1976) of Lorenz Hart (edited by Dorothy Hart), which came from his song 'Thou Swell' from *A Connecticut Yankee* (1927) with music by Richard Rodgers: 'Thou swell, thou witty, thou sweet, thou grand'.

Three Faces of Eve, The. The title of a film (US, 1957) about a woman with three distinct personalities. It gave rise to the format '— faces of —', as in BBC2 TV's 'seven faces of the week' programming policy in 1964.

throat. See DEEP ~.

throw in one's chips. See CASH ...

thunder, to steal another's. Meaning 'to get in first and do whatever the other wanted to make a big impression with', the expression is said to derive from an incident involving the dramatist John Dennis (*d* 1734). He had invented a device for making the sound of thunder in plays and had used it in an unsuccessful one of his own at the Drury Lane Theatre, London. Subsequently, at the same theatre, he saw a performance of *Macbeth* and noted that the thunder was being produced in his special way. He remarked: 'That is *my* thunder, by God; the villains will play my thunder, but not my play.'

Thunderer, The. The nickname of *The Times* newspaper of London. It was known as such from the 1830s onwards, because of its magisterial leading articles. The assistant editor, Edward Sterling (*d* 1847) said on one occasion: 'We thundered forth the other day in an article on the subject of social and political reform.'

thunderstorm. See DYING DUCK IN A ~.

thus far shalt thou go and no further. Charles Stewart Parnell, the champion of Irish Home Rule, said in Cork in 1885: 'No man has a right to fix the boundary of the march of a nation; no man has a right to say to his country, Thus far shalt thou go and no further.' On the other hand, George Farquhar, the (Irish-born) playwright has this in *The Beaux' Stratagem* (1707): 'And thus far I am a captain, and no farther' (III.ii.)

And then again, the Book of Job 38:11 has: 'Hitherto shalt thou come, but no further: and here shall thy proud waves be stayed.'

Thy Neighbour's Wife. See HONOUR THY FATHER.

tight. See PISSED AS A NEWT.

Tight Little Island. The US title of the film (UK, 1948) from Compton Mackenzie's novel *Whisky Galore*. The new title is from Thomas Dibdin's song 'The Snug Little Island' (written in the late 1700s when Britain was threatened by Napoleonic invasion):

> Oh, it's a snug little island!
> A right little, tight little island.

Till Death Us Do Part. The title of a BBC TV comedy series (1964–74), a sequel to which (1985) was called *In Sickness and In Health*. Both phrases come from the marriage service in the Prayer Book (originally, the first was 'till death us depart' i.e. 'separate completely'). *Till Death* was re-made in the US as *All in the Family*. Films with titles from the marriage service include *For Better for Worse* (UK, 1954) and *To Have and to Hold* (UK, 1963).

tilt at windmills, to. Meaning 'to try and overcome imaginary obstacles', from Don Quixote's belief in the novel (1605–15) by Cervantes that windmills were giants and needed to be fought. Compare THEY MIGHT BE GIANTS.

Time and Chance. The title of autobiographies by Group Capt Peter Townsend (1978) and James (Lord) Callaghan, the former British Prime Minister (1987). The origin of the phrase is Ecclesiastes 9:11: 'The race is not to the swift, nor the battle to the strong ... but time and chance happeneth to them all.'

Time Must Have a Stop. The title of this novel (1944) by Aldous HUXLEY, comes from Shakespeare's *King Henry IV, Part 1* (V.iv.80):

> Life, time's fool,
> And time, that takes survey of all the
>   world,
> Must have a stop.

Time . . . the Place . . . , The. The title of an itinerant ITV audience debate programme (from 1987), which probably originated in the staccato narratives of US (crime) fiction: 'The year, 1934; the place, Fresno, California . . .' By *c* 1966, a British TV ad for Players Weights Tipped cigarettes was saying: 'The time . . . the pace [*sic*] . . . the cigarette'.

Time to Love and a Time to Die, A. The title of a film (US, 1958), from a novel by Erich Maria Remarque (*Zeit zu leben und Zeit zu sterben*, 1954). It is a blending of 'a time to love, and a time to hate' from Ecclesiastes 3:8 and 'a time to be born, and a time to die' (3:2). *A Time to Dance*, from the same source, was the title of a novel (1990) by Melvyn Bragg.

TINA. See THERE IS NO ALTERNATIVE.

Tinker Tailor Soldier Spy. The title of the spy novel (1974) by John LE CARRE comes from the children's fortune-telling rhyme: 'Tinker, tailor, soldier, sailor, rich man, poor man, beggar man, thief' (first recorded in something like this form, 1883). *Rich Man, Poor Man* is the title of a novel (1970) by Irwin Shaw, of which the sequel was *Beggarman, Thief* (1977).

Tin Pan Alley. This was the name given, by 1908, to the area in Manhattan where music publishers work – because the noise of countless pianos being tinkled must have sounded like tin pans being bashed. A 'tin pan' was also (*c* 1900) the name given to a cheap, tinny piano. In London, the equivalent area around Denmark Street, off the Charing Cross Road, was so known by 1934.

TIR. See INITIALS.

Tiresias. See GREEK NAMES.

'tis love 'tis love that makes the world go round. This is the proverb the Duchess speaks in *ALICE IN WONDERLAND* (1865). W.S. Gilbert in *Iolanthe* (1882) has a song made up of proverbial sayings, including:

> In for a penny, in for a pound –
> It's love that makes the world go round.

Ian Bradley in his *Annotated Gilbert and Sullivan* (Vol.1) notes how a previous commentator wondered if this had to do with the old saying: 'It's drink that makes the world go round', and also finds it in *Our Mutual Friend* by Charles Dickens [published in the same year as ALICE IN WONDERLAND]. But earlier than these was a French song (published 1851, but recorded as early as 1700):

> *C'est l'amour, l'amour*
> *Qui fait le monde*
> *À la ronde.*

There is an English song, 'Love Makes the World Go Round' by Noel Gay (written *c* 1936).

tiswas, all of a. Meaning 'confused, in a state', this might be from an elaboration of 'tizz' or 'tizzy', with a hint of 'dizziness' thrown in for good measure, but no one really knows. The acronym 'Today Is Saturday, Wear A Smile' seems not to have anything to do with the meaning of the word and to have been imposed later. The acronym-slogan was the apparent reason for the title *Tiswas* being given to a children's ITV show of the 1970s, famous for its bucket-of-water-throwing and general air of mayhem. Broadcast on Saturday mornings, its atmosphere was certainly noisy and confused.

Titanic. The name of the ship which famously sank when it hit an iceberg on its maiden voyage in 1912. The name comes from the Titans, twelve giants of classical mythology, but the word has long been used to describe anything massive. In a speech on 22 May 1909, Winston Churchill said: 'We have arrived at a new time . . . and with this new time strange methods, huge forces and combinations – a Titanic world – have spread all around us.'

Tithonus. See GREEK NAMES.

tittle. See JOT AND ~.

toads unknown in Ireland. See SNAKES IN ICELAND.

To Catch a Thief. The title of a film (US, 1955) which comes from 'set a

'To Be or Not To Be' Speech. The first line of Hamlet's famous soliloquy in Shakespeare's play (III.i.56) was used as the title of a film comedy (US 1942, 1983) about Polish actors under the Nazis. *Slings and Arrows* was a post-Second World War revue in London, with Hermione Gingold. There is also a book by John Hay called *The Undiscovered Country* and that title was also used for Tom Stoppard's 1980 adaptation of a play by Arthur Schnitzler. A thriller by Cyril Hare is entitled *With a Bare Bodkin* and Graham Greene has a novel, *The Name of Action* (1930).

See also OUTRAGEOUS FORTUNE; PERCHANCE TO DREAM; MORTAL COILS.

thief to catch a thief', quoted as an old saying in Richard Howard's *The Committee* (1665).

tod. See ON ONE'S ~.

toil. See HORNY-HANDED SONS OF ~.

To Keep the Ball Rolling. This was the overall title given to Anthony Powell's autobiographical sequence (1976–82). He says it comes from Joseph Conrad's *Chance* (1913): 'To keep the ball rolling I asked Marlow if this Powell was remarkable in any way. "He was not exactly remarkable," Marlow answered with his usual nonchalance. "In a general way it's very difficult to become remarkable. People won't take sufficient notice of one, don't you know".'

See also FACES IN MY TIME; INFANTS OF THE SPRING; MESSENGERS OF DAY; THE STRANGERS ALL ARE GONE.

Toklas. See I LOVE YOU ALICE B. ~.

Tokyo Rose. See LORD HAW-HAW.

Tom and Jerry. (1) Characters in Pierce Egan, *Life in London; or, The Day and Night Scenes of Jerry Hawthorn, Esq., and his Elegant Friend Corinthian Tom* (1821) – riotous young men about town. (2) The cat (Tom) and mouse (Jerry) featuring in many short cartoon films (US, from 1937).

tomorrow is another day. The last words of the film GONE WITH THE WIND (1939), spoken by Vivien Leigh as Scarlett O'Hara, are: 'Tara! Home! I'll go home, and I'll think of some way to get him back. After all, tomorrow is another day!' The last sentence is as it appears in Margaret Mitchell's novel, but the idea behind it is proverbial. In

Rastell's *Calisto & Melebea* (*c* 1527) there occurs the line: 'Well, mother, to morrow is a new day.'

tongue. See OLD AS MY ~ ...

too clever by half. Meaning 'more clever than wise; overreaching', the most notable political use of this phrase was by the 5th Marquess of Salisbury, a prominent Conservative, about another such, Iain Macleod. In a speech to the House of Lords in 1961, he said: 'The present Colonial Secretary has been too clever by half. I believe he is a very fine bridge player. It is not considered immoral, or even bad form to outwit one's opponents at bridge. It almost seems to me as if the Colonial Secretary, when he abandoned the sphere of bridge for the sphere of politics, brought his bridge technique with him.' The remark seems to run in the family. The 3rd Marquess had anticipated him in a debate on the Irish Church Resolutions in the House of Commons on 30 March 1868, when he said of an amendment moved by Disraeli: 'I know that with a certain number of Gentlemen on this side of the House this Amendment is popular. I have heard it spoken of as being very clever. It is clever, Sir; it is too clever by half.'

too little too late. The US professor Allan Nevins wrote in an article in *Current History* (May 1935): 'The former allies had blundered in the past by offering Germany too little and offering even that too late, until finally Nazi Germany had become a menace to all mankind.' That was where the phrase began. On 13 March 1940, the former Prime Minister David Lloyd George said in the House of Commons: 'It is the old trouble – too late. Too late with Czechoslovakia, too late with Poland, certainly too late with Finland. It is always too late, or too little, or both.' From these, the phrase passed into more

general use, though often political. From the *Guardian* (30 January 1989) came: 'The Home Office is preparing a video to warn prisoners of the dangers [of AIDs] – but is it too little, too late?'

tooth. See FINE- ~ COMB; LONG IN THE ~.

top. See OVER THE ~.

Tora! Tora! Tora! The title of a film (US, 1970) about the Japanese raid on Pearl Harbor in 1941, '*Tora-tora-tora*' (meaning 'tiger') was the signal to confirm that the US fleet was being taken by surprise and was given by pilot Mitsuo Fuchida who was leading the Japanese attack.

Tory. See SALOON-BAR ~.

Tory Party at prayer, the. This description of the Church of England is often attributed to Benjamin Disraeli. However, Robert Blake, the historian and author of *Disraeli* (1966) told the *Observer* (14 April 1985) that he could not say who had said it first, and that a correspondence in *The Times* some years before had failed to find an answer. According to Robert Stewart's *Dictionary of Political Quotations*, Agnes Maude Royden, the social reformer and preacher, said in an address at the City Temple, London (1917): 'The Church should no longer be satisfied to represent only the Conservative Party at prayer' – but this sounds rather as though it is alluding to an already established saying.

To Serve Them All My Days. The title of a novel (1972) by R.F. Delderfield, which contains echoes of several religious lines: 'And to serve him truly all the days of my life' from the

Catechism in the Prayer Book; 'To serve thee all my happy days', from the hymn 'Gentle Jesus, Meek and Mild' in the Methodist Hymnal; the Devon carol, 'We'll bring him hearts that love him/To serve him all our days'; and the Sunday school hymn:

> I must like a Christian
> Shun all evil ways,
> Keep the faith of Jesus,
> And serve him all my days.

To the Manor Born. The title of a TV comedy series (1979–81), created by Peter Spence about a lady of the manor, plays upon Shakespeare, *Hamlet* (I.iv.14): 'Though I am native here/And to the manner born'. Shakespeare may have intended a play on the word 'manor' too.

touch. See NELSON ~.

touch the face of God, to. In his TV broadcast after the space shuttle *Challenger* disaster (28 January 1986), President Reagan said: 'We will never forget them nor the last time we saw them this morning as they prepared for their journey and waved goodbye and slipped the surly bonds of earth to touch the face of God.' He was alluding to 'High Flight' (1943), a sonnet written by John Gillespie Magee who was a US-born pilot with the Royal Canadian Air Force in World War Two. In his lyrics for the musical *Les Misérables*, Herbert Kretzmer blended these words with something from Evelyn Waugh's *Brideshead Revisited* ('to know and love another human being is the root of all wisdom') to produce the line: 'To love another person is to see the face of God'. Magee's original words are curiously reminiscent of Oscar Wilde's lines prefixed to his *Poems* (Paris edition, 1903):

> Surely there was a time I might have trod
> The sunlit heights, and from life's
>   dissonance
> Struck one clear chord to reach the ears
>   of God.

tour. See COOK'S ~.

train(s). See CLATTERING ~; MUSSOLINI MADE THE ~ . . .

transfer. See MANHATTAN ~.

Tread Softly for You Tread on My Jokes. The title given by Malcolm Muggeridge to a collection of his articles (1966), alludes to 'Tread softly because you tread on my dreams', from the poem 'He Wishes for the Cloths of Heaven' (1899) by W.B. Yeats.

tree. See BARK UP THE WRONG ~.

tree-felling. See GLADSTONE.

Trelawny. See AND SHALL ~ DIE?

trick. See HAT- ~.

trick or treat. This phrase derives from the Hallowe'en custom of children, suitably dressed up, knocking on the doors of complete strangers and demanding a 'trick or treat' – i.e. that the house owners should hand over some small present (sweets, money) or have a trick played on them (a message written on the front door in shaving foam, for example). The US origins of the custom seem somewhat obscure (*OED2* does not find the phrase before 1947). In 1989, *Trick or Treat* was the title of an ITV game show which aimed to do one or the other to its contestants.

trillion. See BILLION.

Triton. See GREEK NAMES.

Trivial Pursuit. There had been a quiz game called 'Trivia' in the 1960s, but this was the title under which a hugely successful board game, using trivia questions, was launched from Canada in 1979. It reached its worldwide peak *c* 1985. Quite why it was given this name is a mystery, as describing something as a 'trivial pursuit' was not a very established figure of speech, but it became a phrase which was then used in other spheres.

Trolley. See OFF ONE'S ~.

Trollope. See IN BED WITH ONE'S FAVOURITE ~.

truckin'. See KEEP ON ~.

true. See ALWAYS ~ TO YOU IN MY FASHION.

True Glory, The. The title of this documentary film (UK/US 1945) about the end of the Second World War, was taken from the dispatch from Sir Francis Drake to Sir Francis Walsingham before the Battle of Cadiz (1587): 'There must be a beginning of any great matter, but the continuing unto the end until it be thoroughly finished yields the true glory.' In a speech on 15 August 1945 about the surrender of Japan, Winston Churchill said: 'This is the true glory, and long will it gleam upon our forward path.' It was also a favourite phrase of Margaret Thatcher.

trumpet. See BLOW ONE'S OWN ~.

Trumpets from the Steep. See *RAINBOW COMES AND GOES.*

trust. See IN GOD WE ~.

truth. See ECONOMICAL WITH THE ~; LIE TRAVELS ROUND THE WORLD . . .; MOMENT OF ~.

tuba mirum (spargens sonum). See MASS PHRASES.

Tuesday. See BLACK FRIDAY.

Tull. See JETHRO ~.

Tunbridge Wells. See DISGUSTED ~.

tunes. See DEVIL HAVE ALL THE BEST ~.

tunnel. See LIGHT AT THE END OF THE ~.

turn. See BUGGINS'S ~.

turning a tanker round, like. This phrase may be used to describe any slow, difficult task. 'Clive Leach, managing director, said that reversing the trend on [TV] advertising was rather like "turning a tanker round".' (*Independent*, 24 May 1990) Similarly, in 1988, Dr Billy Graham was quoted as saying of the difficulty of converting China to Christianity: 'I think what Winston Churchill or somebody like that said is true: "You can't turn the Queen Mary on a dime".'

Turning Point, The. The title of two unrelated films (US 1952, 1977) though the latter is about ballet (so a pun of sorts). The phrase meaning 'a key moment in a person's career, a crisis' seems to have arisen in religious writings. *OED2*'s earliest citation is from John Keble in 1836. On the other hand, Revd Francis Kilvert (diary, 19 May 1873) found it as the title of a painting which impressed him at a Royal Academy exhibition: 'The beautiful face and eyes of the wife looking up to her husband's stern sullen countenance as she leans on his breast, beseeching him, pleading with him, oh so earnestly and imploringly, to give up drinking'.

turn/roll over in one's grave, to.
Meaning 'for a dead person to demon-strate horror at what has just happened or been proposed by someone living', Mencken has: 'It is enough to make — turn over in his grave' as an 'English saying, not recorded before the nine-teenth century'. William Thackeray has: ' "Enough to make poor Mr Pendennis turn in his grave," said Mrs Wapshot' (*Pendennis*, Chap. 16, 1848). In about 1976, one of the idiocies attributed to President Gerald Ford was: 'If Abraham Lincoln was alive today, he'd be turning in his grave.'

tutti-frutti.
Meaning 'all the fruits' in Italian, this phrase was first applied early in the nineteenth century in the US to ice cream containing pieces of various chopped-up fruits. Then it became the name of a proprietary brand of fruit-flavoured chewing gum. More recently, it has been used as the title of a B B C television series (1987), and immorta-lized as the title of a rock'n'roll number written and sung by Little Richard (from 1957). Alas, the lyrics are impenetrable and almost certainly have nothing to do with ice cream or chewing gum.

T W A. See INITIALS.

Twain, Mark.
The pen-name of Samuel Langhorne Clemens (*d* 1910), which comes from the cry 'mark twain' mean-ing 'two fathoms deep' used when taking soundings on the Mississippi steam-boats.

Twelfth. See GLORIOUS ~.

twelve good men and true.
'It is a maxim of English law that legal memory begins with the accession of Richard I in 1189 . . . with the establishment of royal courts, giving the same justice all over the country, the old diversity of local law was rapidly broken down, and a law common to the whole land and to all men soon took its place . . . The truth of [witnesses'] testimony [was] weighed not by the judge but by twelve "good men and true".' (Winston Churchill, *A His-tory of the English-Speaking Peoples*, Vol. 1) Probably there were twelve mem-bers of a jury because that was the num-ber of Christ's disciples (or the tribes of Israel, or the signs of the zodiac). The overall phrase seems to have been estab-lished by the sixteenth century. 'Are you good men and true' occurs on its own in Shakespeare's *Much Ado About Noth-ing* (III.iii.1). Dogberry puts the ques-tion, and being a constable would naturally use legal terminology.

twilight. See CELTIC ~.

twilight of empire.
This phrase refers to Britain at any time after the death of Queen Victoria in 1901, but particularly when the colonies started moving towards independence. In Malcolm Muggeridge's diary (21 December 1947) he calls it a 'phrase which occurred to me long ago'. One suspects it is after 'twilight of the gods' (German '*Götter-dämerung*').

Twilight's Last Gleaming.
The title of this film (U S/West Germany, 1977) is from 'The Star-Spangled Banner', with words by Francis Scott Key (1814):

> O, say, can you see, by the dawn's early
> light,
> What so proudly we hailed at the
> twilight's last gleaming.

Twilight Zone.
The title of a US T V series (1959–65) about the supernatural. The phrase had existed in the early 1900s for an 'indistinct boundary area' (like NO MAN'S LAND) but undoubt-edly the T V use reinforced it, e.g. 'Several key officials charged with form-ulating foreign policy remain in a

bureaucratic twilight zone one HUN-DRED DAYS after Reagan's inaugu-ration.' (*Washington Post*, 26 April 1981)

twinkle twinkle little bat. The Hatter's song in ALICE IN WONDER-LAND (which goes on 'How I wonder what you're at!/Up above the world you fly,/Like a tea-tray in the sky') is a par-ody of Jane Taylor's poem 'The Star' (1806):

Twinkle, twinkle, little star.
How I wonder what you are!
Up above the world so high,
Like a diamond in the sky.

Diamonds in the Sky was the title of a BBC TV documentary series (1980) about civil aviation.

Twitcher. See JEMMY ~.

UU

U

UB40. The name of this British pop group (*fl.* 1980) derives from the number of the government form to be filled in by persons seeking *U*nemployment *B*enefit.

Ugandan. See DISCUSS ~ AFFAIRS.

ultra. See *NE PLUS* ~.

Ulysses. See GREEK NAMES.

umbrella, Chamberlain's. Of Prime Ministerial props in the twentieth century, one thinks of Churchill's cigars, Baldwin's and Wilson's pipes, and Chamberlain's umbrella. At the time of the Munich Agreement, Chips Channon noted in his diary (28 September 1938): 'The Saviour of Peace got quietly into his car, umbrella and all', and later referred to Chamberlain as 'Old Brolly'.

unacceptable face of capitalism, the. In 1973, it was revealed that a former Tory Cabinet minister, Duncan Sandys, had been paid £130,000 in compensation for giving up his £50,000 a year consultancy with the Lonrho company. The money was to be paid, quite legally, into an account in the Cayman Islands to avoid British tax. This kind of activity did not seem appropriate when the Government was promoting a counter-inflation policy. Replying to a question from Jo Grimond MP in the House of Commons on 15 May, Edward Heath, the Prime Minister, created a format phrase which has since been used to describe almost anything. He said: 'It is the unpleasant and unacceptable face of capitalism, but one should not suggest that the whole of British industry consists of practices of this kind.' (In the text from which he spoke, it apparently had 'facet'.)

Uncertain Glory. The title of this film (US, 1944) is probably from Shakespeare's *Two Gentlemen of Verona* (I.iii.85):

> O, how this spring of love resembleth
> The uncertain glory of an April day.

uncle/UNCLE. See BOB'S YOUR ~; MAN FROM ~; MONKEY'S ~.

unconditional surrender. In almost every conflict a time arrives when one of the combatants decides that it will not be enough for the other side to stop fighting, there will have to be 'unconditional surrender':

(1) In the American Civil War, Gen Ulysses S. Grant sent a message to Gen Simon B. Buckner at Fort Donelson on 16 February 1862: 'No terms except an unconditional and immediate surrender can be accepted. I propose to move immediately upon your works.' (The capture of Fort Donelson was the first major Union victory.) One of Grant's

nicknames became 'Unconditional Surrender', matching his initials, U.S.

(2) Prior to the Armistice in the First World War, the US Gen Pershing, in defiance of President Wilson, proposed to fight on until the Germans agreed to 'unconditional surrender'.

(3) In the 1926 General Strike, Winston Churchill, as Chancellor of the Exchequer, brought out an official government newspaper, the *British Gazette*, in which he denounced British working men as 'the enemy' and demanded 'unconditional surrender'.

(4) At the Casablanca conference of January 1943, President F.D. Roosevelt produced his terms for ending the Second World War, including the 'unconditional surrender' of Germany and Italy, a phrase he had used to his military advisers before leaving Washington and which was endorsed by Churchill (though the British would have preferred to exclude Italy). It was a controversial policy and later blamed for prolonging the war. According to Churchill's own account in Vol. 4 of *The Second World War*, Roosevelt admitted he had consciously been echoing U.S. Grant, though the phrase had been used even before Grant in both the US and UK.

underbelly. See SOFT ~.

Under the Greenwood Tree. The title of the novel (1872) by Thomas Hardy, is taken from Shakespeare's *As You Like It* (II.v.1):

> Under the greenwood tree,
> Who loves to lie with me . . .

Uneasy Lies the Head. The title of the autobiography (1962) of King Hussein of Jordan, comes from Shakespeare's *King Henry IV, Part 2* (III.i.31): 'Uneasy lies the head that wears a crown.'

Unforgiving Minute, The. The title of the autobiography (1978) of Beverley Nichols, is taken from Rudyard KIPLING's poem 'If' (1910):

> If you can fill the unforgiving minute
> With sixty seconds' worth of distance
> run . . .

university of life. See SCHOOL OF HARD KNOCKS.

Unknown Prime Minister, The. The title of the biography (1955) of Andrew Bonar Law by Robert Blake, comes from H.H. Asquith's remark at Bonar Law's funeral (1923): 'It is fitting that we should have buried the Unknown Prime Minister by the side of the Unknown Soldier.'

Unknown Soldier/Warrior. The 'Unknown Warrior' was buried in Westminster Abbey on Armistice Day 1920. On the tombstone, set into the floor of the Nave, is an inscription, written by Dean Ryle, concluding with the words: 'They buried him among the kings because he had done good toward God and toward his house.' This is based on 2 Chronicles 24:16 (concerning Jehoiada, a 130-year-old man): 'And they buried him in the city of David among the kings, because he had done good in Israel, both toward God, and toward his house.'

The idea of such a burial first came to a chaplain at the Front in 1916 after he had seen a grave in a back garden in Armentières, at the head of which was a rough wooden cross and the pencilled words: 'An unknown British Soldier'. The US 'Unknown Soldier' was buried on 11 November 1921 at Arlington National Cemetery and lies under the inscription: 'Here Rests in Honored Glory an American Soldier Known But to God'. Over the graves of most of the unknown dead, in Europe, had been put the simple inscription: 'A Soldier of the Great War Known unto God'.

Unofficial Rose, An. The title of the novel (1962) by Iris Murdoch is taken from Rupert Brooke's 'The Old Vicarage, Grantchester' (1912):

> Unkempt about these hedges blows
> An unofficial English rose.

unpleasantness. See LATE ~.

unplumb'd salt estranging sea. The last sentence of *The French Lieutenant's Woman* (1969) by John Fowles is: 'And out again, upon the unplumb'd, salt, estranging sea'. It comes from Matthew Arnold's 'To Marguerite – Continued' (1852):

> A God, a God their severance ruled!
> And bade betwixt their shores to be
> The unplumb'd, salt, estranging sea.

unwashed. See GREAT ~.

uplands. See BROAD SUNLIT ~.

up to a point Lord Copper. This phrase may be used by way of disagreeing with someone it is prudent not to differ with, or simply of disagreeing without being objectionable about it. It comes from Evelyn Waugh's novel about journalists, *Scoop* (1938): 'Mr Salter's side of the conversation was limited to expressions of assent. When Lord Copper [a newspaper proprietor] was right he said, "Definitely, Lord Copper"; when he was wrong, "Up to a point".'

An example from the *Independent* (4 April 1990): 'We are told that [Norman Tebbit] was only trying to help . . . he was out to "stop Heseltine". Well, up to a point, Lord Whitelaw.'

upwards. See ONWARDS AND ~.

Urania. See GREEK NAMES.

Uranus. See GREEK NAMES.

Uriah Heep. The unctuous, fawning, hypocritical clerk who makes much of his humility – 'I'm a very umble person' – in *David Copperfield* (1849–50) by Charles Dickens. (See also EAT HUMBLE PIE.)

used. See WOULD YOU BUY A ~ CAR . . .

u-turn, to make a. The word 'u-turn' was probably first used in the US (by 1937) to describe the turn a motor car makes when the driver wishes to proceed in the opposite direction to the one he has been travelling in. The political use of the term to denote a reversal of policy was established in the US by 1961. In British politics, it was in use at the time of the Heath government (1970–4). For Margaret Thatcher's attitude to the term, see THE LADY'S NOT FOR BURNING.

VV

vacuum. See NATURE ABHORS A ~.

vamp. The name for a flirtatious, predatory woman, much in vogue in early silent films, the 'vamp ' character reached her final form in the performances of Theda Bara. In *A FOOL THERE WAS* (US, 1914), she played a *femme fatale* who lures a European financier. He forsakes all for her and dies in her arms.

However, the idea of a woman who behaves towards men as a vampire behaves towards its victims predates the coining of 'vamp'.

Vanity Fair. The title of the novel (1847–8) by William Thackeray, alludes to John Bunyan's *Pilgrim's Progress* (1678–84): 'It beareth the name of Vanity-Fair, because the town where 'tis kept, is lighter than vanity.' The title has also been used for magazines, notably the one published in New York from 1914–36.

velvet. See BLACK ~; BLUE ~; IRON FIST IN A ~ GLOVE; LITTLE GENTLEMAN IN BLACK ~.

venery, terms of. See COLLECTIVE NOUNS.

vengeance is mine saith the Lord. Paul the Apostle in his epistle to the Romans (12:19) actually has: 'Dearly beloved, avenge not yourselves, but rather give place unto wrath: for it is written, Vengeance is mine; I will repay, saith the Lord.' Paul is quoting 'To me belongeth vengeance, and recompence', which occurs in Deuteronomy 32:35 and is also alluded to in Psalms 94:1 and Hebrews 10:30.

veni vidi vici. According to Suetonius: 'I came, I saw, I conquered' was an inscription displayed in Latin in Julius Caesar's Pontic triumph of 47 BC. According to Plutarch, it was written in a letter by Caesar, announcing the victory of Zela (in Asia Minor) which concluded the Pontic (Black Sea) campaign. In North's 1570 translation of Plutarch, it states: 'Julius Caesar fought a great battle with King Pharnaces and because he would advertise one of his friends of the suddenness of this victory, he only wrote three words unto Anicius at Rome: *Veni, Vidi, Vici*: to wit, I came, saw, and overcame. These three words ending all with like sound and letters in the Latin, have a certain short grace, more pleasant to the ear, than can well be expressed in any other tongue.' Shakespeare alludes to Caesar's 'thrasonical brag' in four plays, including *Love's Labour's Lost* (IV.i.68) and *As You Like It* (V.ii.30).

venture. See NOTHING ~ NOTHING WIN.

Venus. See ROMAN NAMES.

VERDI. See ACRONYMS.

Vermont. See AS MAINE GOES SO GOES ~.

Veronica, St. See SAINTS' NAMES.

Vestal Virgins. Members of the cult of the chaste Roman goddess Vesta (see under GREEK NAMES), who presided over the fire in the domestic hearth. There were six of them. If they ceased to be virgins, they were buried alive, and if they managed to serve thirty years, they were allowed to marry. The term 'vestal virgin' may now be applied to anyone of innocent, totally spotless behaviour.

V for victory. The 'V for Victory' slogan of the Second World War started as a piece of officially encouraged graffiti inscribed on walls in occupied Belgium by members of the anti-German 'freedom movement'. The Flemish word for freedom begins with a V – *Vrijheid* – and the French word for victory is, of course, *Victoire*. The idea came from Victor de Laveleye, the BBC's Belgian Programme Organizer, who, in a broadcast on 14 January 1941, suggested that listeners should adopt the letter 'V' as 'a symbol of their belief in the ultimate victory of the allies'. They were to go out and chalk it up wherever they could. From Belgium, the idea spread into the Netherlands and France and 'multitudes' of little Vs started appearing on walls in those countries. Winston Churchill spoke of the 'V' sign as a symbol of the 'the unconquerable will of the people of the occupied territories'.

The symbol was expressed in other ways, too. The opening three notes of Beethoven's Fifth Symphony corresponded to the (. . . -) of the 'V' in Morse Code and, accordingly, the music was used in BBC broadcasts to occupied Europe. People gave the 'V for Victory' salute with parted middle index fingers – though Winston Churchill confused matters by presenting his fingers the wrong way round in a manner akin to the traditionally obscene gesture. His Private Secretary, John Colville, noted in his diary on 26 September 1941: 'The PM *will* give the V SIGN with two fingers in spite of the representations repeatedly made to him that this gesture has quite another significance.'

Vicar of Bray. Meaning 'a person who changes allegiance according to the way the wind blows; a turncoat', after a vicar of Bray, Berkshire, in the sixteenth century who is supposed to have changed his religious affiliation from Roman Catholic to Protestant more than once during the reigns of Henry VIII to Elizabeth I. However, there was more than one vicar in this period. Whatever the case, by the time of Thomas Fuller's *Worthies* (1662) there was a proverb: 'The Vicar of Bray will be Vicar of Bray still.'

As for the song beginning 'IN GOOD KING CHARLES'S GOLDEN DAYS . . .', it was probably written at the beginning of the eighteenth century and describes a different (perhaps completely fictional) vicar of Bray who changed his religion to suit the different faiths of monarchs from Charles II to George I. Can there have been two such turncoat vicars – or was the song merely an updating of the circumstances of the actual first vicar?

vices. See ANCESTRAL ~.

Victorian values. In the General Election of 1983 and thereafter, Margaret Thatcher and other Cabinet Ministers frequently commended the virtue of a return to Victorian values. The phrase appears to have been coined by Brian Walden in a TV interview with Mrs Thatcher on ITV's *Weekend World* on 17 January 1983. He suggested that she was trying to restore 'Victorian values'. She replied: 'Very much so. Those were the values when our country became great. But not only did our country become great internationally, also much advance was made in this country – through voluntary rather than state action.' Mrs Thatcher also said in an L B C radio interview on 15 April: 'I was brought up by a Victorian grandmother. We were taught to work jolly hard. We were taught to prove ourselves; we were taught self-reliance; we were taught to live within our income . . . You were taught that cleanliness is next to godliness. You were taught self-respect. You were taught always to give a hand to your neighbour. You were taught tremendous pride in your country. All of these things are Victorian values. They are also perennial values.' On 23 April, the *Daily Telegraph* quoted Dr Rhodes Boyson, the Minister for Schools, as saying: 'Good old-fashioned order, even Victorian order, is far superior to illiterate disorder and innumerate chaos in the classroom', and Neil Kinnock, then Chief Opposition spokesman on education, as saying: 'Victorian Britain was a place where a few got rich and most got hell. The "Victorian values" that ruled were cruelty, misery, drudgery, squalor and ignorance'.

View to a Kill, A. This was the title of a James Bond film (U K, 1985). The original title of the short story by Ian Fleming (published in 1960 in *For Your Eyes Only*) is '*From* a View to a Kill'. As such it is very close to the title of Anthony Powell's 1933 novel *From a View to a Death* which is a direct quotation from the song 'D'ye Ken John Peel', written in 1832 by John Woodcock Graves:

> Yes, I ken John Peel, and Ruby too,
> Ranter and Ringwood, BELLMAN AND
>   TRUE,
> From a find to a check, from a check to
>   a view,
> From a view to a death in the morning.

In foxhunting terminology, a 'check' is a loss of scent, a 'view (halloo)' is the huntsman's shout when a fox breaks cover, and a 'kill' or a 'death' is what it says.

Vile Bodies. The title of the novel (1930) by Evelyn Waugh, comes from Paul's Epistle to the Philippians 3:21: 'Who shall change our vile body, that it may be fashioned like unto His glorious body [referring to Christ's resurrection]' – which is also part of the interment service in the Prayer Book.

Vitus, St. See SAINTS' NAMES.

voice(s). See ANCESTRAL ~; HIS MASTER'S ~.

vox populi. In British broadcasting of the 1950s/60s there was a vogue for what was known in the business as 'vox pops' – namely, street interviews with passers-by presenting views on issues of the day which, with luck, were amusingly expressed and – for reasons of balance – effectively cancelled each other out. '*Vox populi*' [voice of the people] is naturally of venerable origin. Alcuin wrote in a letter to the Emperor Charlemagne in A D 800: '*Nec audiendi sunt qui solent dicere, "Vox populi, vox Dei"; cum tumultuositas vulgi semper insaniae proxima sit*' [Nor should we listen to those who say, 'The voice of the people is the voice of God', for the turbulence of the mob is always close to insanity]. So, clearly, even though he didn't like it, the phrase was not of his making.

'Fox populi' was a nickname given to Abraham Lincoln (presumably on account of his looks or his populism) by *Vanity Fair* magazine, London, in 1863. The same year, the US Gen W.T. Sherman in a letter to his wife on 2 June wrote: 'Vox populi, vox humbug' – by which he meant 'the voice of the people is humbug'.

VPL. See INITIALS.

V sign. The obscene gesture (easily confused with Churchill's V FOR VICTORY sign) may have come about as described by Anthony Sher in *Year of the King* (1985): 'The two-fingered sod-off sign comes from Agincourt. The French, certain of victory, had threatened to cut off the bow-fingers of all the English archers [this is attested to in a contemporary French account of the battle]. When the English were victorious, the archers held up their fingers in defiance.'

Vulcan. See ROMAN NAMES.

W W

wage. See FAIR DAY'S ~.

Wages of Fear, The. The English title of the film *Le Salaire de la Peur* (France/Italy, 1953) may possibly allude to: 'The wages of sin is death' (Romans 6:23).

wait. See MAKE 'EM LAUGH . . .

walks. See GHOST ~.

wall. See BACKS TO THE ~.

walls have ears. This was a security slogan in the Second World War. The idea of inanimate objects being able to hear is a very old one – even beyond 1727, when Jonathan Swift wrote: 'Walls have tongues, and hedges ears.' In Vitzentzos Kornaros's epic poem *Erotokritos* (*c* 1645) there is the following couplet (here translated from the Greek):

> For the halls of our masters have ears
> and hear,
> And the walls of the palace have eyes
> and watch.

wally. Meaning 'a foolish, inept or ineffectual person', this was a vogue word in Britain *c* 1983, and many origins have been put forward for it. It may be Scottish and possibly derives from the name 'Walter'. An opera by Catalani called *La Wally* was first performed in 1892. Toscanini so esteemed it that he named his daughter 'Wally' after the heroine.

Walter Mitty. The name of a fantasist who daydreams of achievements which are beyond him in real life (compare the character 'Billy Liar' in the 1959 novel of that name by Keith Waterhouse). It comes from the short story 'The Secret Life of Walter Mitty' (1939; film US, 1947) by James Thurber.

Walter Plinge. In British theatre, when an actor plays two parts, he traditionally uses this name rather than his own in one of them. It is said that Mr Plinge was a stage-struck pub landlord from near the Theatre Royal, Drury Lane, in the nineteenth century. Having his name so used was the nearest he ever came to being on the stage. The US equivalent is 'George Spelvin'.

'Waltzing Matilda'. The title of a song (1894, not published till 1903) by A.B. 'Banjo' Paterson, which has acquired the status of an Australian national anthem in all but name. It comes from the Australian phrase for carrying your 'Matilda' or back-pack, as a tramp does. Hence the first verse goes:

> Oh! there once was a swagman
> [itinerant labourer carrying his swag, or
> bundle]
> camped in a Billabong [dead water,
> backwater]

Under the shade of a Coolabah tree;
And he sang as he looked at his old billy
  [cooking-pot] boiling,
'Who'll come a-waltzing Matilda with
  me?'

The *Macquarie Dictionary* suggests a derivation from the German *walzen*, to move in a circular fashion 'as of apprentices travelling from master to master', and German *Mathilde*, a female travelling companion or bed-roll (from the girl's name).

Wandering Jew, The. A legendary character, dating from medieval times, who was condemned to wander about the earth until Christ's second coming because he had urged Christ to move faster as he carried the cross to Calvary.

war. See COLD ~; DAY ~ BROKE OUT; FIRST WORLD ~; GO FORTH TO ~; HARD-FACED MEN WHO . . .; LOSE A BATTLE BUT NOT THE ~; MAKE LOVE NOT ~; MORE EFFICIENT CONDUCT OF THE ~; WORLD ~ TWO.

War and Peace. The English title of Leo Tolstoy's epic novel (1865–8). According to Henry Troyat's biography, Tolstoy did not decide on a title until very late. '*The Year 1805* would not do for a book that ended in 1812. He had chosen ALL'S WELL THAT ENDS WELL, thinking that would give the book the casual, romantic tone of a long English novel.' Finally, the title was 'borrowed from Proudhon' – *La Guerre et la Paix* (1862).

war between the states, the. This term for the US Civil War (1861–5), like 'the War Between the North and the South', did not catch on until the conflict was well over (Flexner suggests the 1890s for both.) 'The Civil War' was an earlier Northern name for it (1861).

Southerners had called it 'the Revolution', 'the War of Independence', 'the Second War of Independence', or 'the War of Secession'.

Hence, however, the punning title of the novel (1974) by Alison Lurie: *The War Between the Tates.*

warned, you have been. See under FAMOUS LAST WORDS.

warrior. See HAPPY ~; UNKNOWN ~.

War That Will End War, The. The title of a book (1914) by H.G. Wells, that gave rise to the slogan: 'The war to end wars'.

warts and all. This phrase, meaning 'including all the details that someone might prefer to have left out', is from Oliver Cromwell's instruction to Lely who was painting his portrait: 'Remark all these roughnesses, pimples, warts, and everything as you see, otherwise I will never pay a farthing for it.'

WASHINGTON (George).
George Washington (1732–99), the first US president (1789–97) is, like GLADSTONE, famous for many things but one in particular. Apart from giving his name to the city, the state, a lily and a pie, he featured in a tale possibly invented by his first popular biographer, Mason Locke Weems (1800). In it, Washington, as a small boy, is asked by his father if he has chopped down a **cherry tree** in the garden. Replies he: 'I cannot tell a lie. I did cut it with my hatchet.'

WASP. An acronym for 'White Anglo-Saxon Protestant', denoting the dominant middle- and upper-class ruling clique in the US which is descended from early European immigrants. The coinage has variously been ascribed to E.B. Palmore (1962) and E. Digby Baltzell.

Watch on the Rhine, The. The title of a play (1941; film US, 1943) by Lillian Hellman, it comes from the poem '*Die Wacht am Rhein*' by Max Schnekenburger (1840), set to music by Karl Wilhelm (1854), which became a German national song. There was a British parody in the First World War: 'When We've Wound up the Watch on the Rhine'.

watch the skies. The last words of the film *The Thing* (US, 1951) were: 'Watch everywhere, keep looking, watch the skies!' This phrase was subsequently used to promote the film *Close Encounters of the Third Kind* (1977) and, indeed, was its original title.

watchtower. See ALL ALONG THE ~.

water. See KING OVER THE ~.

waterfront. See I COVER THE ~.

Waterloo. See BATTLE OF ~.

water water everywhere but not a drop to drink. What Samuel Taylor Coleridge wrote in his poem 'The Rime of the Ancient Mariner' (1798) was:

> Water, water everywhere,
> And all the boards did shrink;
> Water, water, everywhere
> *Nor any* drop to drink.

Watson. See ELEMENTARY MY DEAR ~.

Waverley. The title of the first novel (1814) by Sir Walter Scott, which was then given to the whole series of his novels set in Scotland. The name of the hero of the novel was taken from

Watergate. The name for the scandal in US politics which led to the resignation of President Richard Nixon in 1974. It came from the Watergate apartment block in Washington DC where a bungled burglary by those seeking to re-elect the president led to a cover-up and then the scandal. Consequently, it has become standard practice to apply the suffix '—gate' to any political scandal: Koreagate, Lancegate, Billygate, Liffeygate, Westlandgate, Contragate, Irangate, Thatchergate and so on. (See also DPP.) For other Watergate phrases see: ALL THE PRESIDENT'S MEN; CUT OFF AT THE PASS; DEEP-SIX; DEEP THROAT; EXPLETIVE DELETED; I WOULD WALK OVER MY GRANDMOTHER; SMOKING GUN.

Waverley Abbey, near Farnham, in Surrey. From the Scott association, the main railway station in Edinburgh was named Waverley Station. There is an Overture, 'Waverley' (1828) to an uncompleted opera by Hector Berlioz.

waves. See WHAT ARE THE WILD ~ SAYING?

way. See GREAT WHITE ~.

Way of All Flesh, The. The title of the novel (1903) by Samuel Butler, comes from the expression 'to go the way of all flesh', meaning 'to die' (alternatively, 'to experience life'). The 1609 Douai Bible translates I Kings 2:2 as: 'I enter into the way of all flesh', repeating an old mistranslation of 'the way of all the earth'.

Way to the Stars, The. The title of a film (UK, 1945), set near an RAF airfield during the Second World War, and based on Terence Rattigan's stage play *Flare Path*. It presumably alludes to the RAF motto '*Per ardua ad astra*' [Through striving, to the stars].

However, in Bartlett, '*Sic itur ad astra*' from Virgil's *Aeneid* (IX.641) is translated as: 'That's the way to the stars.' In the US, perhaps to avoid any such questions, the film was called *Johnny in the Clouds* (after the line 'Johnny head-in-air' from the poem 'For Johnny' by John Pudney, which is recited in the film).

Weaker Vessel, The. The title of a book (1984) by Antonia Fraser about 'woman's lot in seventeenth-century England'. Its origin is 1 Peter 3:7: 'Wives, be in subjection to your husbands . . . husbands, giving honour unto the wife, as unto the weaker vessel.'

we are all Socialists now. King Edward VII is supposed to have said this when Prince of Wales, in a speech at the Mansion House, London, on 5 November 1895. ODQ dropped the entry after pointing out in the Corrigenda to the 1941 edition that the saying should more correctly be ascribed to Sir William Harcourt. He is quoted as saying it in *Fabian Essays* (1889, edited by Bernard Shaw). Harcourt was Lord Rosebery's (Liberal) Chancellor of the Exchequer and an impassioned enemy of the House of Lords. He introduced estate duty tax in his Budget of 1894.

Whoever said it first, the foundation was laid for a much later remark by Jeremy Thorpe, the Liberal politician, in a speech in the House of Commons on 6 March 1974. After a General Election which resulted in no party having a clear majority – a Liberal coalition with the Conservatives had been mooted but rejected – he observed: 'Looking around the House, one realizes that we are all minorities now.' John Biffen MP, on the fringe of the 1981 Tory Party Conference, said: 'We are all Social Democrats now.'

we are not amused. The subject of whether Queen Victoria ever uttered this famous put-down was raised in the

Notebooks of a Spinster Lady (1919) by Miss Caroline Holland: '[The Queen's] remarks can freeze as well as crystallize . . . there is a tale of the unfortunate equerry who ventured during dinner at Windsor to tell a story with a spice of scandal or impropriety in it. "We are not amused," said the Queen when he had finished.' Interviewed in 1978, Princess Alice, Countess of Athlone, said she had once asked her grandmother about the phrase and she had denied ever having said it.

we are not interested in the possibilities of defeat. During one week of the South African War in December 1899 – 'Black Week' as it came to be called – British forces suffered a series of setbacks in their fight against the Boers. Queen Victoria 'braced the nation in words which have become justly famous' (W.S. Churchill, *A History of the English-Speaking Peoples*, Vol. 4): 'Please understand,' she told A.J. Balfour, who was in charge of the Foreign Office, 'that there is no one depressed in *this* house. We are not interested in the possibilities of defeat. They do not exist.' Margaret Thatcher quoted the words during the Falklands War (1982), having seen them as a motto on Winston Churchill's desk in his Second World War bunker beneath Whitehall.

we are the masters now. The boast of Sir Hartley Shawcross (later Lord Shawcross), Attorney-General in Britain's first postwar Labour Government, in the House of Commons on 2 April 1946. What he actually said was: 'We are the masters at the moment.' Winding up for the Government in the third reading of the Trade Disputes and Trade Unions Bill, he drew attention to what he saw as the Conservative Opposition's lack of support for a measure it had promised to introduce itself if it had won the 1945 election: '[We made this an issue at the election] when [Churchill] invited us to submit this matter to the verdict of the people . . . I realize that [Churchill] is such a master of the English language that he has put himself very much in the position of Humpty-Dumpty in ALICE . . . "When I use a word," said Humpty-Dumpty, "it means just what I intend it to mean, and neither more nor less." "But," said Alice, "the question is whether you can make a word mean different things." "Not so," said Humpty-Dumpty, "the question is which is to be the master. That's all." We are the masters at the moment, and not only at the moment, but for a very long time to come. As hon. Members opposite are not prepared to implement the pledge which was given by their leader in regard to this matter at the General Election, we are going to implement it for them.'

weasel. See POP GOES THE ~.

Weathermen. The original name of a violent radical group in the US (*fl.* 1969), which then became the Weather Underground. It derived from the lyrics of 'Subterranean Homesick Blues' (1965) by Bob Dylan:

> Keep a clean nose
> Watch the plain clothes
> You don't need a weather man
> To know which way the wind blows.

wedding cake. See BRIDEGROOM ON THE ~.

Wednesday. See BLACK FRIDAY.

Week In Politics, A. The title of Channel 4's TV political review programme (by 1985), after Harold Wilson's much-quoted dictum: 'A week is a long time in politics' – probably first uttered at a meeting with the Parliamentary lobby correspondents in the wake of the sterling crisis shortly after he first took office as Prime Minister in 1964. When he took his peerage twenty years later, his motto was: '*Tempus Rerum Imperator*' [Timing is everything]. (See also *DPP*.)

weeks rather than months. Meaning 'sooner rather than later', e.g. 'Sir Simon Gourlay, president of the NFU, said the Government had to restore market confidence in "weeks rather than months", or farmers would go "needlessly out of business".' (*Independent*, 21 May 1990) This echoes Harold Wilson's use of the phrase at the Commonwealth Prime Ministers' Conference (January 1966): 'The cumulative effect of . . . sanctions [against Rhodesia] might well bring the rebellion to an end within a matter of weeks rather than months.'

Weeping and the Laughter, The. The title of a novel (1988) by Noel Barber, and of autobiographies by Viva King (1976) and J. Maclaren-Ross (1953). Their origin is Ernest Dowson's poem '*Vitae Summa Brevis*' (1896): 'They are not long, the weeping and the laughter.'

Weller. See SAM WELLER.

well he would wouldn't he? 'Oscar Wilde said the Alps were objects of appallingly bad taste. He would, wouldn't he?' wrote Russell Harty (*Mr Harty's Grand Tour*, 1988). This has become a popular catch phrase since Mandy Rice-Davies used it during the Profumo political scandal of 1963. In a magistrates' court, she was questioned about the men she had had sex with. When told by Ward's defence counsel that Lord Astor – one of the names on the list – had categorically denied any involvement with her, she replied chirpily: 'Well, he would, wouldn't he?' The court burst into laughter, the expression passed into the language, and is still resorted to because – as a good catch phrase ought to be – it is bright, useful in various circumstances, and tinged with innuendo.

Wellington (Duke of). The 1st Duke of Wellington (1769–1852) most famously gave his name (by 1817) to Wellington boots, now waterproof rubber boots but originally military boots that came over the knee or short boots worn under the trousers. His name has also been bestowed upon: a coat, a hat, trousers, a cooking apple, a bomber, a chest of drawers, a term in card-playing, a public school, and, as 'Wellingtonia', to a type of coniferous tree. See also BATTLE OF WATERLOO . . .

Wench Is Dead, The. The title of a crime novel (1989) by Colin Dexter, this was also used as the epigraph of T.S. Eliot's poem 'Portrait of a Lady' (1917). It is from Christopher Marlowe's *The Jew of Malta* (*c* 1592):

> But that was in another country;
> And besides the wench is dead.

we never sleep. This was the slogan of Pinkerton's national detective agency which opened its first office in Chicago, 1850 (and which – through its open eye symbol – *may* have given us the term PRIVATE EYE). Was there an echo of this in the line chosen to promote Citibank's new 24-hour service in 1977: 'The Citi Never Sleeps' – apart, that is, from an allusion to the 1953 film title *The City That Never Sleeps*?

Went the Day Well? The title of a film (UK, 1942) based on a short story by Graham Greene entitled 'The Lieutenant Died Last' about a typical English village repelling Nazi invaders in its midst. (In the US, the film was re-titled *48 Hours.*) At the start, there appears on screen the anonymous epigraph:

> Went the day well?
> We died and never knew.
> But, well or ill,
> Freedom, we died for you.

The question, 'Went the day well?' sounds as if it ought to come from Shakespeare's *Henry V*, though it does not. However, in the battle in *King John*, the king has the understandable query: 'How goes the day with us?' (V.iii.1)

wept. See JESUS ~.

we shall not be moved. This shout or chant of defiance is, according to Bartlett, originally from a Negro spiritual (echoing more than one psalm): 'Just like a tree that's standing by the water/We shall not be moved'. It was widely taken up as a song of the civil rights and labour movements from the 1960s.

we shall not see his like again. This cliché of obituaries alludes to Shakespeare's *Hamlet* (I.ii.187), where the Prince says of his late father: 'A was a man, take him for all in all;/I shall not look upon his like again'. In *Joyce Grenfell Requests the Pleasure* (1976), the actress recalls being rung by the United Press for a comment on the death of Ruth Draper, the monologist: 'My diary records: "I said we should not see her like again. She was a genius." Without time to think, clichés take over and often, because that is why they have become clichés, they tell the truth.'

we shall overcome. This is the phrase from the song that became a civil rights anthem of the early 1960s. It originated in pre-Civil War times, was adapted as a Baptist hymn called 'I'll Overcome Some Day' (*c* 1900) by C. Albert Hindley, and first became famous when sung by black workers on a picket line in Charleston, South Carolina (1946). In the Spanish Civil War, there was a Republican chant '*venceremos!*' which means the same. Pete Seeger and others added verses including: 'Oh, deep in my heart, I know that I do believe/We shall overcome some day'.

Westward Ho! The title of a novel (1855) by Charles Kingsley, from which comes the name of the Devon seaside resort Westward Ho! Earlier, there had been a play *Westward Ho!* by Webster and Dekker (*c* 1600). *Westward Ha! or Around the World in 80 Clichés* was the title of a book (1948) by S.J. Perelman.

we the people. These are the opening words of the Preamble to the 1787 Constitution of the United States: 'We the people of the United States . . . do ordain and establish this Constitution for the United States of America.'

wets. (1) States opposed to Prohibition in the US. Those who were in favour were 'drys'. (2) Margaret Thatcher's word for Conservative politicians who took a cautious middle-of-the-road line (by 1980, although privately as early as 1976).

we who are about to die . . . See *MORITURI*.

what about the workers? Usually written, 'Wot abaht . . .', this is traditionally a proletarian heckler's cry during a political speech. It is almost a slogan in its own right, but is now only used satirically. It occurs along with other rhetorical clichés in the 'Party Political Speech' (written by Max Schreiner) on the Peter Sellers comedy album *The Best of Sellers* (1958). (See also *DPP*.)

'What Are the Wild Waves Saying?' The title of a Victorian song with words by J.E. Carpenter and music by Stephen Glover:

> What are the wild waves saying,
> Sister, the whole day long:
> That ever amid our playing,
> I hear but their low, lone song?

The song is a duet between Paul and Florence Dombey and based on an incident in *Dombey and Son* (1848) by Charles Dickens. Nowhere in the novel does Dickens use the words, 'What are the *wild* waves saying?' though the book is fairly awash with the idea of a 'dark and unknown sea that rolls round all the world' (Chap. 1). The title of Chapter 16 is 'What the Waves Were Always Saying'.

What Are You Doing After the Show? The title of a long-forgotten ITV comedy show (1971), comes from a pick-up line, presumably of show-business origin. The previous year's Swedish film *Rötmånad* had been given the English title *What Are You Doing After the Orgy?*

what a way to run a —! A format phrase which probably originated in a cartoon in the US *Collier's* magazine (though *Ballyhoo* in 1932 has also been suggested) which showed two trains about to collide. A signalman is looking out of his box and the caption is: 'Tch-tch – what a way to run a railroad!' The Boston and Maine railroad picked up this line when it sought 'a statement which would explain some of the problems of the railroad in times of inclement weather'. It took the 'stock railroad phrase', derived from the cartoon, and put it between each paragraph of the advertisement in the form: 'That's a H—l of a Way to Run a Railroad!' Thus the phrase came into the language as an exclamation concerning mismanagement or chaos of any kind, in the form: 'What a way (*or* hell of a way) to run a railroad/railway'. (See also *DPP*.)

What Did You Do in the War Daddy? The title of this film (US, 1966) derives from the First World War recruiting slogan: 'Daddy, what did *you* do in the Great War?' The accompanying picture showed an understandably appalled family man puzzling over what to reply to the daughter on his knee. It became a catch phrase in the form, 'What did you do in the Great War, Daddy?' and gave rise to such responses as 'Shut up, you little bastard. Get the Bluebell and go and clean my medals' (Partridge/*Catch Phrases*).

what is that (gentle)man *for*? This innocent but pertinent question from a young person has variously been aimed at Charles James Fox, Benjamin Disraeli and Randolph Churchill. The original may have been as recorded by G.W.E. Russell in *Collections and Reminiscences* (1898): 'What is that fat gentleman in such a passion about?' – said about Charles James Fox by Charles Shaw-Lefevre, Viscount Eversley (1794–1888) when a child. Another example comes from Michael Billington: 'I am reminded of the small boy who once pointed at Hermione Gingold and asked, "Mummy, what's that lady for?" ' (*Guardian*, 21 July 1988).

What Makes Sammy Run? The title of a novel (1941) by Budd Schulberg about how 'a dynamic but vicious opportunist achieves success' (Halliwell). It provided an alternative phrase to 'what makes so-and-so tick?'.

What's Bred in the Bone. Meaning 'what's part of one's nature can't be repressed', this was the title of a novel (1985) by Robertson Davies, who cites 'What's bred in the bone will not out of the flesh' as an 'English proverb from the Latin, 1290'.

What's Up Doc? The title of this film (US, 1972) comes from the characteristic enquiry of Bugs Bunny, the cartoon character, in the film series which ran from 1937–63. It was addressed to Elmer Fudd, the doctor who devoted his life to attempting to destroy the rabbit. Bugs made his official debut in 1940. In full the phrase, was: 'Er, what's up, Doc?' – followed by a carrot crunch. Its origins may lie in an old Texan expression, introduced to the films by one of the animators, Tex Avery.

What the Butler Saw. The title of a play (1969) by Joe Orton, set in a psychiatric clinic, where characters tend to lose items of clothing, and also of a comedy first performed at Wyndham's Theatre on 2 August 1905. It comes from the name given to a type of penny-in-the-slot machine introduced in the UK *c* 1880. It was a frisky development of the very old peep show. The female so observed was probably doing something mild in corsets. Florrie Forde, the music-hall star, recorded a song called 'What the Curate Saw' (*c* 1920), which is clearly an allusion. (See also *DPP*.)

wheel has come/turned full circle, the. This cliché is after Edmund the Bastard who says: 'The wheel is come full circle' in Shakespeare's *King Lear* (V.iii.173). He is referring to the wheel of fortune, being at that moment back down at the bottom where he was before it began to revolve. Chips Channon writes in his diary (13 October 1943): 'I turned on the wireless and heard the official announcement of Italy's declaration of war on Germany. So now the wheel has turned full circle.'

whelk-stall. See COULDN'T RUN A ~.

when did you last see your father? See AND WHEN . . .

when did you stop beating your wife? This is an almost proverbial example of a leading question (because by attempting to answer it you admit that you *did* once beat your wife).

when in Rome – do as the Romans do. This maxim suggests that one should adapt to prevalent customs. Its probable source is St Ambrose (*d* 397): '*Si fueris Romae, Romano vivito more;/ Si fueris alibi, vivito sicut ibi*' [If you are at Rome, live in the Roman style; if you live elsewhere, live as they live elsewhere].

'When Lilacs Last in the Dooryard Bloom'd'. The title of the poem by Walt Whitman, written a few weeks after the April 1865 assassination of President Lincoln which it commemorates. Whitman also wrote a prose description of the assassination in which he said: 'I find myself always reminded of the great tragedy of that day by the sight and odour of these blossoms.'

When the Boat Comes In. The title of the BBC TV drama series (1975–7) comes from the nursery rhyme (first recorded *c* 1806):

> Dance to your daddy.
> My little babby . . .
> In a little dishy,
> You shall have a fishy when the boat comes in.

When the Kissing Had to Stop. The title of a novel (1960) by Constantine Fitzgibbon about a Russian takeover of Britain, it derives from Robert Browning's poem 'A Toccata of Galuppi's' (1855): 'What of soul was left, I wonder,/When the kissing had to stop?'

'When the World Was Young'. The English title of a song (1952) by Johnny Mercer, based on the French song '*Le Chevalier de Paris*' or '*Ah! Les Pommiers Doux*' (1950). It is a wistful expression about 'long ago' and a time more innocent than the present. It may derive ultimately from a verse in the Apocrypha: 'For the world has lost his youth, and the times begin to wax old' (2 Esdras 14:10). Precisely as 'When the World Was Young', it is the title of a painting (1891) by Sir E.J. Poynter PRA, which shows three young girls in a classical setting, relaxing by a pool. Compare the lines from 'Young and Old' in *The Water Babies* (1863) by Charles Kingsley:

> When all the world is young, lad,
> And all the trees are green
> . . . Young blood must have its course, lad,
> And every dog his day.

Where Angels Fear to Tread. The title of a novel (1906) by E.M. Forster, from Alexander Pope's *An Essay on Criticism* (1711): 'For fools rush in where angels fear to tread'. *Fools Rush In* was the title of a play (1947; film UK, 1949) by Kenneth Horne.

where do we find such men? In 1984, on the fortieth anniversary of the D-Day landings, President Reagan visited Europe and made a speech in which he eulogized those who had taken part in the event. 'Where do we find such men?' he asked. On a previous occasion he had said: 'Many years ago in one of the four wars in my lifetime, an admiral stood on the bridge of a carrier watching the planes take off and out into the darkness bent on a night combat mission and then found himself asking, with no one there to answer – just himself to hear his own voice – "Where do we find such men?".' But the very first time he had used the line he had made it clear where it came from. The story comes from James Michener's novel *Bridges at Toko-Ri*, later filmed (1954) with

William Holden who asks: 'Where do we get such men?'

where's the beef? This was an advertising slogan that turned into a political catch phrase. The Wendy International hamburger chain promoted its wares in the US (from 1984), with TV commercials, one of which showed elderly women eyeing a small hamburger on a huge bun – a competitor's product. 'It certainly is a big bun,' asserted one. 'It's a very big fluffy bun,' the second agreed. But the third asked: 'Where's the beef?' Walter Mondale, running for the Democratic nomination, used it to question the substance of his rival Gary Hart's policies.

Where's the Rest of Me? The title of an early autobiography (1965) by Ronald Reagan comes from the line spoken by him in the film *King's Row* (1941) when he wakes to find his legs have been amputated by a sadistic doctor.

where the devil are my slippers? The last line of the film version (UK 1938) of Shaw's *Pygmalion* has Professor Higgins exclaiming: 'Where the devil are my slippers, Eliza?' Similarly, the last line of the film (US, 1965) of MY FAIR LADY is: 'Eliza, where the devil are my slippers?' In both cases, the intention appears to be to hint at some romantic interest in Eliza Doolittle. Shaw always opposed this. Even his published text of the film script (1941) shuns the line. Although Higgins says it during the course of the play, it is not addressed to Eliza.

Where the Heart Is. The title of this film (US, 1990) by John Boorman, comes from the proverb: 'Home is where the heart is', not recorded before 1870. Mencken claims it as an 'American saying, author unidentified'.

Where Were You When the Lights Went Out? The title of a film (US, 1968), inspired by the great New York blackout of 1965 when the electricity supply failed and, it was popularly believed, the birthrate shot up nine months later. The question echoes an old music-hall song and perhaps also the American nonsense rhyme:

> Where was Moses when the light went
> out?
> Down in the cellar eating sauerkraut.

This last appears to have developed from the 'almost proverbial' riddle (in *The Riddler's Oracle*, c 1821) as cited by the Opies in *The Lore and Language of Schoolchildren*, 1959):

> Q. Where was Moses when the light went
> out?
> A. In the dark.

whimper. See NOT WITH A BANG BUT A ~.

whispers. See CHINESE ~.

whistle. See BLOW THE ~ ON; IF YOU WANT ANYTHING . . .

'Whistle and I'll Come to You My Lad, Oh'. The title of a short story in *Ghost Stories of an Antiquary* (1904) by M.R. James, in which the wind is 'whistled up'. It comes from the poem (c 1788) by Robert Burns, 'O, Whistle, and I'll Come to You, My Lad'.

Compare 'Whistle and she'll come to you' from *Wit Without Money* (IV.iv.,1639) by Francis Beaumont and/or John Fletcher.

Whistle Down the Wind. The title of this novel (1958; film UK, 1961) by Mary Hayley Bell, comes from the expression meaning: (1) To abandon, to cast off lightly (from the releasing of a hawk down wind, from the fist, by whistling), as in Shakespeare's *Othello* (III.iii.266): 'I'ld whistle her off, and let her down the wind.' This is what you do in falconry when you are turning a hawk loose. You send it into or against the wind when it is pursuing prey. (2) To talk or argue purposelessly. Noël Coward was quoted in *Panorama* magazine, spring 1952, as saying: 'I marched down to the footlights and screamed: "I gave you my youth! Where is it now? Whistling down the wind! *OU SONT LES NEIGES D'ANTAN?*" ... And I went madly on in French and Italian.' (3) Something to be avoided on board ship. The superstition is that whistling, because it sounds like the wind, can raise the wind, as if by magic – though this may more properly be 'whistle up the wind', as in 'to whistle for something'. (Whistling backstage at the theatre is also said to bring bad luck.)

whistle-stop. This was originally the name given to a place in the US too small to have scheduled train calling at it. If a passenger did want to alight, the conductor would signal to the engineer/driver and he would respond by pulling the whistle. As a political term for a short train visit to a place by a campaigning politician, it was introduced by Robert Taft (1948) in remarks about President Truman who had been criticizing Congress from the platform of a train in journeys about the country. A 'whistle-stop tour' might now be used of any series of quick visits, not necessarily by a politician or by train.

white. See FAT ~ WOMAN; GREAT ~ WAY.

White Goddess, The. The title of a book (1948) by Robert Graves, who claims that worship of the ancient goddess of fertility and the moon was the origin of poetry.

Whitehall. See FOGGY BOTTOM.

White House. See LOG CABIN TO ~.

white man's burden. See KIPLING.

White Rabbit. The name of a character in Lewis Carroll's ALICE IN WONDERLAND who is anxious because he fears he will be late for something, and thus applied to anyone similarly disposed. Compare DECISIONS DECISIONS!

The White Rabbit is the title of a book (1952) by Bruce Marshall about the exploits of Wing-Commander F.F.E. Yeo-Thomas, a British secret agent in the Second World War. The phrase was his nickname.

'Whiter Shade of Pale, A'. The title of a song (1967) written by Garry Brooker and Keith Reid and performed by PROCUL HARUM, which appears to contain several allusions. 'We skipped the light fandango' echoes the expression 'to trip the light fantastic', for 'to dance', which in turn echoes Milton's 'L'Allegro' ('Come, and trip it as ye go/On the light fantastic toe') or 'Comus' ('Come, knit hands, and beat the ground/In a light fantastic round'). 'As the miller told his tale' presumably refers to the Miller's Tale in Chaucer's *Canterbury Tales*, and 'One of sixteen VESTAL VIRGINS/Were leaving for the coast' presumably refers to 'The Coast', i.e. the eastern/western seaboard of the US.

Whittington, Dick. See STREETS PAVED WITH GOLD.

who breaks a butterfly upon a wheel? Meaning 'to go to great lengths to accomplish something trifling', the expression comes from the 'Epistle to Dr

Arbuthnot' (1735) by Alexander Pope. As 'Who Breaks a Butterfly on a Wheel', it was used as the headline to a leader in *The Times* (1 July 1967) when Mick Jagger was given a three-month gaol term on drugs charges.

whoever lov'd that lov'd not at first sight? A 'saw' (saying) from Christopher Marlowe's poem 'Hero and Leander' which was published in 1598, though probably written in 1593, the year of his death. Phebe, the shepherdess in Shakespeare's *As You Like It* (probably written in 1598), quotes the line (II.v.82). For another Shakespearean allusion to Marlowe, see FACE THAT LAUNCH'D A THOUSAND SHIPS.

who goes home? This is the cry that goes up in the House of Commons, echoed by policemen, when the House has finished a sitting and is about to close its doors. It stems from the days when, to protect themselves against robbers, M Ps would form small groups for mutual protection on the way home. Chips Channon wrote in his diary (17 March 1937) on Stanley Baldwin's tribute to the late Austen Chamberlain: 'His closing sentence "Austen has at last gone home" made us all think of the attendant's call "Who goes home?" ' On the same day, Harold Nicolson wrote: 'The Prime Minister makes an adequate oration but rather spoils it by introducing at the end a somewhat unsuccessful play on the phrase "Who Goes Home?".'

who he? This is a mock editorial interjection made after a little-known person's name has been mentioned, and popularized by *Private Eye* in the 1980s. 'This month, for instance, has been the time for remembering the 110th anniversary of the birth of Grigori Petrovsky. Who he?' (*New Statesman*, 26 February 1988). It came from the actual interjection of Harold Ross (*d* 1951), editor of

the *New Yorker*. James Thurber in *The Years with Ross* (1959), describes how Ross would customarily add this query to manuscripts (though not for publication) on finding a name he did not know in an article (sometimes betraying his ignorance). He said the only two names everyone knew were Houdini and Sherlock Holmes. A book with the title *Who He? Goodman's Dictionary of the Unknown Famous* was published in 1984. The phrase echoes the Duke of Wellington's peremptory 'Who? Who?' on hearing the names of ministers in Lord Derby's new administration (1852).

whole world as one's parish, to look upon the. Meaning 'to be knowledgeable about many peoples and places; to look upon the world as one's oyster', from the saying of John Wesley (*d* 1791), the founder of Methodism, who included in his diary for 11 June 1739 a letter to Revd James Hervey in which he defended himself against charges that he had invaded the parishes of other clergymen. 'You . . . ask, "How is it that I assemble Christians, who are none of my charge, to sing psalms and pray and hear the Scriptures expounded? and think it hard to justify doing this in other men's parishes, upon catholic principles . . . Seeing I have now no parish of my own, nor probably ever shall . . . Suffer me now to tell you my principles in this matter. I look upon all the world as my parish . . . This far I mean, that, in whatever part of it I am, I judge it meet, right, and my bounden duty to declare unto all that are willing to hear the glad tidings of salvation".'

whom the Gods wish to destroy . . . See THOSE WHOM . . .

Who Pays the Ferryman? The title of the BBC TV drama series (1977) by Michael J. Bird, about a former Greek Resistance fighter in Crete, alludes to

Charon (see GREEK NAMES) demanding a fee to ferry the dead across the River Styx, in Greek legend.

Who's Afraid of Virginia Woolf?
The title of a play (1962; film US, 1966) by Edward Albee, derived from a piece of graffiti, and after the song 'Who's Afraid of the Big Bad Wolf' by Churchill/Ronell in the Walt Disney film *Three Little Pigs* (1933).

Whose Life Is It Anyway?
This was the title of a play (1978; film US, 1981) by Brian Clark. Later a BBC Radio/Channel 4 TV improvisatory game was given the title *Whose Line Is It Anyway?* (by 1989).

who's for tennis? See ANYONE FOR TENNIS?

WHT. See INITIALS.

why not the best? See JIMMY WHO?

Wicked Witch of the West, the.
This was the name of a character in *The Wonderful Wizard of Oz* (1900) by L. Frank Baum. Allan Massie, writing on Margaret Thatcher (quoted in Michael Cockerell, *Live From Number 10*, 1989): 'It would not convert those for whom she is SHE WHO MUST BE OBEYED and the Wicked Witch of the West rolled into one.'

Wide Sargasso Sea.
The title of a novel (1966) by Jean Rhys. The Sargasso Sea in the North Atlantic is made up of masses of floating seaweed, creating sluggish waters.

widow. See GRASS ~.

wife. See ALL THE WORLD AND HIS ~; CAESAR'S ~; WHEN DID YOU STOP BEATING YOUR ~?; ~ IN EVERY PORT under GIRL IN EVERY PORT.

Wigan Pier. An imaginary focus of jokes (compare the Swiss Navy), in this case, the creation of the music-hall comedian George Formby Sr (*d* 1921). Wigan, an industrial town in Lancashire, is not a seaside resort, but is one of those places dear to the British, the mention of whose name is sufficient to provoke laughter (compare BASINGSTOKE, Scunthorpe, Chipping Sodbury, Neasden).

In 1937 George Orwell investigated living and working conditions in the north of England in *The Road to Wigan Pier*, and in the 1980s, a derelict warehouse alongside a basin of the Leeds–Liverpool canal, at Wigan, was renovated and given the name.

Wild Bill. The nickname of James Butler Hickock (*d* 1876), US frontiersman and marshal. His nickname probably arose during his wilder days when – in 1861 – he challenged a whole crowd to a fight. All the people scattered.

will, I. See I DO.

William, Father. See ARE YOU OLD . . .

willies, the. Meaning 'the effect of being frightened; nerves' – as in 'that gave me the willies'. *OED2* suggests a US nineteenth-century origin. Another possible source is 'wiffle woffle' meaning stomach-ache. Note also that in the ballet *Giselle* (Paris, 1841) there are things called *Wilis* – spirits of maidens who die before marriage.

Wilson Keppel and Betty.
The name of a British music-hall act whose three members performed a comic Egyptian sand dance 'Cleopatra's Nightmare', the two men wearing fezzes and moustaches. Jack Wilson and Joe Keppel teamed up in the US and made their first British appearance at the London Palladium in

1932. Several 'Bettys' followed the original, Betty Fox.

wimp. Meaning 'a weak, ineffectual man', the word is probably a shortened form of 'whimperer'. 'The Wymps' were characters in children's books written by Evelyn Sharp in the 1890s. They were fond of playing jokes but apt to cry when jokes were played on them. The US author George Ade wrote in his *Handmade Fables* (1920): 'Next day he sought out the dejected Wimp.' In *Arrowsmith* (1925) by Sinclair Lewis, we find: 'Wimpish young men with spectacles, men whose collars do not meet'. Then came J. Wellington Wimpy, a character in the POPEYE comic strip. He was very corpulent, but sloppily dressed and always forgot to pay for his hamburgers. (He gave his name *to* **Wimpy** hamburgers in Chicago in 1935.) The word 'wimp' resurfaced in the 1980s, for some reason, and George Bush, before he became US president, was said to worry about suffering from the Wimp Factor.

windmills. See TILT AT ~.

wind of change. Speaking to both houses of the South African parliament on 3 February 1960, Prime Minister Harold Macmillan gave his hosts a message they cannot have wanted to hear: 'The most striking of all the impressions I have formed since I left London a month ago is of the strength of this African national consciousness. In different places it may take different forms, but it is happening everywhere. The wind of change is blowing through this continent. Whether we like it or not, this growth of national consciousness is a political fact.' The phrase was not original but O E D2 acknowledges that the use of the phrase 'wind(s) of change' increased markedly after the speech. When Macmillan sought a title for one of his volumes of memoirs he plumped

for the more common plural – *Winds of Change*. In a similar windy metaphor Stanley Baldwin had said in 1934: 'There is a wind of nationalism and freedom round the world, and blowing as strongly in Asia as elsewhere.' President George Bush made 'a new breeze is blowing' the theme of his inauguration speech on 20 January 1989.

windows into men's souls, not liking to make. Elizabeth I is often cited as saying this, when in fact the phrase is Francis Bacon's rationalization of her religious intolerance. He was attempting to say that the Queen, while not liking to do so, was forced into it by the people she had to deal with. Compare EYES AS WINDOWS OF THE SOUL.

Winds of War, The. The title of a US TV series (1983) by Herman Wouk, from his novel (1971). Compare Winston Churchill's speech to the House of Commons, 3 September 1939: 'Outside, the storms of war may blow and the lands may be lashed with the fury of its gales, but in our own hearts this Sunday morning there is peace.'

wing. See COMIN' IN ON A ~ AND A PRAYER.

Winifred, St. See SAINTS' NAMES.

winter of discontent. This political cliché is after Shakespeare's *Richard III* (I.i.1):

> Now is the winter of our discontent
> Made glorious summer by this son of York;
> And all the clouds that lour'd upon our House
> In the deep bosom of the ocean buried.

The British winter of 1978–9 was so dubbed after life had been disrupted by all kinds of industrial protests against the Labour government's attempts to keep down pay rises. Rubbish remained uncollected and began to pile up in the streets and a grave-diggers' strike in one area reputedly left bodies unburied. It was apparently a coinage of the *Sun*. On 30 April 1979, as part of a series on the issues of the General Election in the week before polling, the paper splashed across two pages the words: 'WINTER OF DISCONTENT. Lest we forget . . . the *Sun* recalls the long, cold months of industrial chaos that brought Britain to its knees.'

win this one for the Gipper. A slogan of Ronald Reagan, referring to George Gipp, a character he had played in *Knute Rockne – All-American* (1940). Gipp was a real-life football star who died young. At half-time in a 1928 army game, Rockne, the team coach, recalled something Gipp had said to him: 'Rock, someday when things look real tough for Notre Dame, ask the boys to go out there and win one for me.' Reagan used the slogan countless times. One of the last was at a campaign rally for Vice-President George Bush in San Diego, California, on 7 November 1988. His peroration included these words: 'So, now we come to the end of this last campaign . . . And I hope that someday your children and grandchildren will tell of the time that a certain president came to town at the end of a long journey and asked their parents and grandparents to join him in setting America on the course to the new millenium . . . So, if I could ask you just one last time. Tomorrow, when mountains greet the dawn, would you go out there and win one for the Gipper? Thank you, and God bless you all.'

Wish You Were Here! The title of an ITV travel programme (from 1973), taken from the cliché of holiday correspondence. Also the title of at least two songs (reaching the UK charts in 1953 and 1984). In the full form: '**Having a wonderful time**, wish you were here,'

Partridge/*Catch Phrases* suggests a beginning in Edwardian times. But why not earlier, at any time since the introduction of the postcard in Britain, which was in 1870? To be sure, cards on which you wrote your own message did not come on the scene until 1894 and the heyday of the picture postcard was in Edwardian times. Perhaps in the early days the message was already printed on the card by the manufacturer? Nowadays the wording is only used in jest or ironically. *Having a Wonderful Time*, a play about a holiday hotel in the Catskills, by Arthur Kober (1937) became, in an exchange of phrases, the musical *Wish You Were Here* in 1952. *Wish You Were Here* was also used in 1987 as the title of a British film about sexual awakenings in a seaside resort.

witch. See WICKED ~ OF THE WEST.

With an Independent Air. The title of the autobiography (1977) of Howard Thomas, the British broadcasting executive and early participant in INDEPENDENT TELEVISION. It is taken from 'As I walk along the Bois de Boulogne with an independent air' from the song 'The Man Who Broke the Bank in Monte Carlo' (1900) by Fred Gilbert.

with friends like these who needs enemies? A phrase which may be used in desperation after one has been betrayed by a supporter – the earliest example to hand is of something Richard Crossman said of certain Labour MPs in 1969 – or ironically of others in difficulty. The *Daily Telegraph* used it as the headline over a picture spread of Richard Nixon's henchmen on 9 August 1974, but it is of much older provenance. Charlotte Brontë said it, in a letter, concerning the patronizing reviewer of one of her books. Partridge/*Slang* compares it to the proverb: 'With a Hungarian for a friend, who needs an enemy.' George Canning, the nineteenth-century politician, wrote a verse ending: 'Save, save, Oh, save me from the candid friend.'

within. See ENEMY ~.

With Malice Towards Some. The title of a book (1938) about the British by an American, Margaret Halsey, taken from Abraham Lincoln's Second Inaugural (1865), after the Civil War: 'With malice toward none; with charity for all; with firmness in the right . . . let us strive on to finish the work we are in'.

with one bound/spring he/Jack was free. This may be said of anyone who escapes from a tricky situation or tight corner. The origin of the expression lies in cartoon strips, subtitles to silent films, or *Boy's Own Paper*-type serials of the early twentieth century. The hero would frequently escape from seemingly impossible situations, most usually after he had been condemned to them in a 'cliff-hanger' situation. The phrase underlines the preposterousness of the adventures in which such lines can be 'spoken'. Author Barbara Newman, writing from Washington DC to the *Observer* (29 October 1989), says of TV correspondent and former Beirut hostage Charles Glass: 'His motivation is to keep alive the fiction that he miraculously escaped from his Hizbollah capturers, offering a RAMBOesque picture of himself amounting to "and with one spring Jack was free".'

Wizard of the Dribble. A soubriquet applied to footballers who excel at this activity (kicking the ball forward very softly, so that it stays close to the boot). Hunter Davies commented in the *Independent* (10 April 1990): 'Anyone who's a regular follower of football will have noticed that dribbling has almost gone out of the game. The word itself sounds positively archaic. Yet, at one time, every team had at least one Wizard

of the Dribble who would mesmerise the opposition. Where are they now?' According to *The Times* (31 January 1985), footballer Sir Stanley Matthews bore the title 'The "Wizard of Dribble" ' for years.

woman. See BEHIND EVERY MAN STANDS . . .; FAT WHITE ~.

Woman in Red, The. The title of two unrelated films (US 1935, and 1984). Compare the 'woman/lady in red' used to describe the mysterious girlfriend of the criminal John Dillinger ('PUBLIC ENEMY NO. 1'), who alerted the FBI to his whereabouts and was herself the subject of a film (US 1979) called *The Lady in Red*. The day after Dillinger was shot by the FBI in 1934, this graffito verse appeared on a wall nearby:

> Stranger, stop and wish me well,
> Just say a prayer for my soul in Hell.
> I was a good fellow, most people said,
> Betrayed by a woman all dressed in red.

women and children first! This catch phrase is used jokingly in a situation where people might appear to be behaving as though caught in a shipwreck (in a crowded bus or train perhaps). It originated in the incident involving HMS *Birkenhead*, one of the first ships to have a hull of iron, in 1852. She was taking 476 British soldiers to the eighth 'Kaffir War' in the Eastern Cape of South Africa when she ran aground fifty miles off the Cape of Good Hope. It was clear that the ship would go under but only three of the eight lifeboats could be used and these were rapidly filled with the twenty women and children on board. According to tradition, soldiers remained calm and did not even break ranks when the funnel and mast crashed down on to the deck, with the loss of 445 lives. Thus was born the tradition of 'women and children' first. In naval

WODEHOUSE (P.G.)

Few writers have employed literary allusions to the same extent as P.G. Wodehouse (1881–1975) in his novels and short stories featuring Bertie Wooster and Jeeves, his gentleman's gentleman. 'Hullo, fathead . . . what news on the Rialto?' – unusually, this is Bertie's Aunt Dahlia plucking a line from *The Merchant of Venice* in *Aunts Aren't Gentlemen*. Usually, it is Bertie who is fumbling for the apt quotation and, more often than not, believing that Jeeves invented all the best lines. When Jeeves quotes 'IT IS A FAR, FAR BETTER THING', Bertie comments: 'As I said before, there is nobody who puts these things more neatly than he does.' A quotation from Shakespeare is frequently accompanied by, 'As I have heard Jeeves put it' or 'To quote one of Jeeves's gags'. For example: 'Leaving not a wrack behind, as I remember Jeeves saying once'. Although we all know that Jeeves is quite capable of reading Spinoza's *Ethics*, such faith in his ability to coin a neat phrase is strange in a Wooster educated at Eton and Oxford and winner of the Scripture Knowledge prize. But as Richard Usborne has pointed out, Bertie's frame of reference is no more than one would expect of an educated man in the early twentieth century. There are lapses, though: 'The next moment I was dropping like the gentle dew upon the place beneath. Or is it rain? Jeeves would know.' Occasionally Bertie resorts – as so many of us do – to 'as the fellow said'. In one book, he refers to the 'works of somebody called Wordsworth'. Some quotations recur throughout the Jeeves canon. 'With a wild surmise' probably crops up most often. Bertie worries obsessively and understandably over 'the cat i' the adage' and 'FRETFUL PORPENTINE'. What is more, Wodehouse larded the novels with more and more literary allusions as he grew older. *Jeeves in the Offing* (1960) contains some forty-eight.

It is a delight when Bertie alludes to 'Shakespeare and those poet Johnnies' by way of attribution or when he scrambles his allusions, as in 'One man's caviare is another man's major-general, as the old saw has it'. He would have found this dictionary invaluable.

circles, this is still known as the Birkenhead Drill.

wonder. See NINE DAYS' ~.

Wonderful Wizard of Oz, The. The title of the children's novel (1900; film US, 1939) by L. Frank Baum. The book was first of all turned into a musical (1901), and the title was shortened to *The Wizard of Oz* for the first film version and to *The Wiz* for the second (1978). See also GOODBYE YELLOW BRICK ROAD; IS SHE A FRIEND OF DOROTHY?; WICKED WITCH OF THE WEST.

Wonderland. See ALICE IN ~.

wool. See PULL THE ~ OVER . . .

woopies. See under YUPPIE.

word(s). See FAMOUS LAST ~; GREEKS HAD A ~ FOR IT; LORD OF ~; MY ~ IS MY BOND.

work. See DIRTY ~ AT THE CROSSROADS; FAIR DAY'S WAGES . . .; PROTESTANT ~ ETHIC.

workers. See BLACK-COATED ~; WHAT ABOUT THE ~?

world. See ALL THE ~ OWES . . .; FIRST ~ WAR; LIGHT OF THE ~; ~ WAR TWO; WHOLE ~ AS ONE'S PARISH.

World Owes Me a Living, The. The title of a novel (1939; film U K, 1944) by John Llewellyn Rhys, and also the title of a song (by Larry Morey and Leigh Harline) in one of the first of Walt Disney's 'Silly Symphonies' (1934) based on Aesop's fable 'Of the Ant and the Grasshopper' (as it is called in Caxton's first English translation, 1484). The fable tells of a grasshopper asking an ant for corn to eat in winter. The ant asks: 'What have you done all the summer past?' and the grasshopper can only answer: 'I have sung.' The moral is that you should provide yourself in the summer with what you need in winter. The earliest found use of this expression is in the U S author W.G. Sumner's *Earth Hunger* (1896). He writes: 'The men who start out with the notion that the world owes them a living generally find that the world pays its debt in the penitentiary or the poorhouse.' (See also *DPP*.)

World the Flesh and the Devil, The. The title of this film (U S 1959) comes from the Litany in the Prayer Book: 'From fornication, and all other deadly sins; and from all the deceits of the world, the flesh, and the devil, Good Lord, deliver us'. Compare *Flesh and the Devil* (film U S 1927).

world turned upside down, the. (1) A popular name for an inn. (2) The title of a U S tune played when the English surrendered at Yorktown (1781). (3) A figure of speech, as in Robert Burton's *The Anatomy of Melancholy* (1621–51): 'Women wear the breeches . . . in a word, the world turned upside-ward' (4) Title of a well-known tract dating from the English Civil War concerning 'ridiculous fashions' (1646). The origin for all these is possibly biblical: 'Those that have turned the world upside down are come hither also' (Acts 17:6). Compare the French expression *la vie à l'envers* [life upside down/the wrong way round], used as the title of a film (1964).

World War II/Two. After the FIRST WORLD WAR, what could be more natural than to have the **Second World War**? But, of course, it was not immediately recognized as such. At first, some tried to refer to it as 'the war in Europe', but *Time* magazine was quick off the mark: 'World War II began last week at 5:20 am (Polish time) Friday, September 1, when a German bombing plane dropped a projectile on Puck, fishing village and air base in the armpit of the Hel Peninsula . . .' Soon after this, Duff Cooper published a book of his collected newspaper articles entitled *The Second World War*. When it quite clearly *was* a world war, in 1942, President Roosevelt tried to find an alternative appellation. After rejecting 'Teutonic Plague' and 'Tyrants' War', he settled for 'The War of Survival'. But this did not catch on. Finally, in 1945, the U S *Federal Register* announced that, with the approval of President Truman, the LATE UNPLEAS- ANTNESS was to be known as 'World War II'. (In other less global conflicts, the name of a war depends on which side you are on: the Vietnam War is known to the Vietnamese as 'the American War'.)

World Without End. The title of this film (U S, 1956) comes from the LORD'S PRAYER.

worse. See FATE ~ THAN DEATH.

worse things happen at sea. This consolatory phrase was first recorded in

1829 (Pierce Egan, *Boxiana*) in the form 'Worse accidents occur at sea!'

Worthington. See MRS ~.

would, wouldn't he? See WELL HE ~.

would you buy a used car from this man? Although attributed by some to Mort Sahl and by others to Lenny Bruce, and though the cartoonist Herblock denied that he was responsible (*Guardian*, 24 December 1975), this is just a joke and one is no more going to find an origin for it than for most such. The line accompanies a shifty looking picture of Richard Nixon and dates from 1952 at least (before any of the above-named humorists really got going). Hugh Brogan wrote in *New Society* (4 November 1982): 'Nixon is a double-barrelled, treble-shotted twister, as my old history master would have remarked; and the fact has been a matter of universal knowledge since at least 1952, when, if I remember aright the joke, "Would you buy a second-hand car from this man?" began to circulate.' In the 1964 British General Election, Anthony Barber, a Tory minister, asked: 'Would you buy a used car from Harold Wilson?' (See also *DPP*.)

wrinklies. See under YUPPIE.

writing on the wall. Referring to an event presaging disaster, the idea – though not the precise phrase – comes from the Bible (Daniel 5) where King Belshazzar is informed of the forthcoming destruction of the Babylonian Empire through the appearance of a man's hand writing on a wall. (See also *DPP*.)

wrong. See COUNTRY RIGHT OR ~; KING CAN DO NO ~.

W R V S. See INITIALS.

XX

Xanadu. The title of a film musical (US, 1980), about a disco so-named. It comes from the poem 'Kubla Khan' (1798) by S.T. Coleridge:

> In Xanadu did Kubla Khan
> A stately pleasure-dome decree . . .

It is a name and a concept which appeals to pop musicians. For example, in 1984, Frankie Goes to Hollywood had a single and an album with the title *Welcome to the Pleasure Dome*. Graham Greene's collected film criticism 1935–40 was published as *The Pleasure-Dome* (1972). See also ANCESTRAL VOICES/ VICES.

Yankee Clipper. The nickname of Joe DiMaggio, the leading US baseball player of the 1940s, after the type of US merchant ship built in the 1840s/50s (from *clip* meaning 'trim, shipshape', then 'fast-moving'). Earlier there had been a Baltimore Clipper.

years. See FOUR MORE ~.

Years Between, The. The title of a film (UK, 1946) and a song published after the film came out, possibly comes from the earlier song 'I'm Gonna Love That Guy (Like He's Never Been Loved Before)' (1945) by Frances Ashe, which includes the lines:

> And the years between
> Might never have been.
> We'll be starting our life anew.

Year Zero. This was the term used *c* 1975 by the Khmer Rouge during their takeover of Cambodia – meaning that the past had been obliterated, nothing had come before. *Cambodia: Year Zero* is the title of a relevant book (1978) by François Ponchaud. The phrase has also been applied to other 'starting from scratch' situations: an Italian/West German film (1947) set in postwar Berlin was entitled *Germania, Anno Zero* [*Germany, Year Zero*]; a film (US, 1962) set in Los Angeles after a nuclear attack was called *Panic in Year Zero*.

Yellow Brick Road. See GOODBYE ~.

yellow peril. The phrase, first recorded in 1900, denotes the supposed threat to white people or the world generally from the Asiatic peoples. On 4 September 1909, Winston Churchill said in a speech: 'It [the worst threat to Britain] is not in the Yellow Peril, or the Black Peril, or any danger in the wide circuit of colonial and foreign affairs. It is here in our midst.'

ye olde tea shoppe. The form 'ye olde' (pronounced 'yee oldee') has become the conventional way of evoking and reproducing the speech and writing of English earlier than, say, 1600. It is, however, based on a misconception that the letter 'þ' appearing on old manuscripts is the equivalent of the modern 'y'. In fact 'þ' – known to Old English and Icelandic philologists as the letter 'thorn' – is pronounced with a 'th' sound. Thus, even in Anglo-Saxon times, however peculiar some pronunciations might have been, 'þe' would have been pronounced like modern 'the'. 'Ye' did, of course, exist as the second person pronoun.

Yes Minister. The title of a BBC TV comedy series (1980–5) about the relationship between British government

353

ministers and the Civil Service in Britain. It comes from a description by Richard Crossman, a minister in Labour governments of the 1960s and 70s, of his first day in office as a Cabinet Minister, in October 1964: 'Already I realize the tremendous effort it requires not to be taken over by the Civil Service. My Minister's room is like a padded cell, and in certain ways I am like a person who is suddenly certified a lunatic and put safely into this great vast room, cut off from real life . . . Of course, they don't behave *quite* like nurses because the Civil Service is profoundly deferential – 'Yes, Minister! No, Minister! If you wish it, Minister!' (*The Diaries of a Cabinet Minister*, Vol.1, 1975)

yesterdays. See 'ALL OUR ~' SPEECH.

Yesterday's Men. The title of a BBC TV programme (1971) about how Labour leaders defeated in the previous year's General Election were faring in Opposition (and which soured relations between the BBC and the Labour Party for a long while afterwards). The phrase 'Yesterday's Man' was an established idiom applied to any 'has been' – a song with that title had been a hit for Chris Andrews in the British charts (1965) – and 'Yesterday's Men' had been used as a Labour slogan in the 1970 election. The Party issued a poster showing crudely coloured models of Conservative politicians (Edward Heath, Iain Macleod, Lord Hailsham and others) and the additional line: 'They failed before'. In fact, Labour lost the election to the men it had ridiculed as 'yesterday's' but the phrase continued to cause trouble.

Yield to the Night. The title of a film (UK, 1956), from a novel by Joan Henry about a convicted murderess. The source is untraced – except that it occurs in a translation of a passage in Bk.VII of

Homer's *Iliad*: 'But night is already at hand; it is well to yield to the night.'

YMCA. See INITIALS.

Yorkies. The name applied to long-distance lorry drivers, after the chocolate bars introduced in the early 1980s. Originally these were promoted with commercials showing lorry drivers eating them. The *Independent on Sunday* (13 May 1990) had: 'Every lorry driver in Britain was supposed to sound his horn at noon . . . The *Sun* even devoted its Friday front page to a large picture of a clock so that Yorkies would recognise noon.' Earlier, a 'Yorkie' was a nickname for a Yorkshireman or the Yorkshire terrier.

Yorkshire Ripper, the. The nickname (after JACK THE RIPPER) applied to this murderer by a Yorkshire newspaper during the course of a prolonged police pursuit. As was eventually revealed, Peter Sutcliffe (*b* 1946) had murdered some thirteen women in the north of England during the period 1975–80.

you ain't heard/seen nothin' yet! Partridge/*Catch Phrases* has a combined entry for 'you ain't seen nothin' yet' and 'you ain't heard nothin' yet', in which 'seen' is described as the commoner of the two versions. Both date from the 1920s. Bachman-Turner Overdrive, the Canadian pop group, had a hit with a song called 'You Ain't Seen Nothin' Yet' in 1974. President Ronald Reagan also appropriated this catch phrase as a kind of slogan in his successful 1984 bid for re-election. He used it repeatedly during the campaign and, on 7 November, in his victory speech. As for 'heard', it seems that when Al Jolson exclaimed 'You ain't heard nothin' yet!' in the first full-length talking picture *The Jazz Singer* (1927), he wasn't just ad-libbing as is usually supposed. He was promoting the title of one of his songs! He had recorded 'You Ain't Heard Nothing Yet', written by Gus Kahn and Buddy de Sylva, in 1919.

you are Mr Lobby Lud ... A circulation-raising stunt for newspapers in the 1920s took the form of a challenge readers were encouraged to put to a man they were told would be in a certain place (usually a seaside resort) on a particular day. His description and a photograph were given in the paper and 'You are so-and-so and I claim my £10' (or whatever the prize was) became the formula. The reader had, of course, to be carrying a copy of that day's paper. The first in the field was the *Westminster Gazette* in August 1927 and the correct challenge was: 'You are Mr Lobby Lud – I claim the *Westminster Gazette* prize' (which was initially £50, though if it was unclaimed it increased weekly). The name 'Lobby Lud' came from the *Gazette*'s telegraphic address – 'Lobby' because of the Westminster connection and 'Lud' from Ludgate Circus off Fleet Street. The stunt did nothing for the paper which closed the following year, but the idea was taken up by the *Daily News* and the *News Chronicle* and ran on for several years.

You Are What You Eat. This neat encapsulation of a sensible attitude to diet was used as the title of an 'alternative' film (US, 1969), of which, *Films and Filming* (April 1969) noted: '"You are what you eat," says an old hermit in a fairy-tale-painted wood; a band of blissfully beautiful people hopefully munch flowers in the park.' The BFI's *Monthly Film Bulletin* described the film as: 'A disjointed psychedelic picture of America's hippy revolution ... The moralising note struck by the title is echoed nowhere else in the film.' The idea behind the phrase has been around for many a year. Compare Brillat-Savarin in *La Physiologie du goût*: 'Tell me what you eat and I will tell you what you are'

and L.A. Feuerbach: 'Man is what he eats [*Der Mensch ist, was er ißt*]' – in a review of Moleschott's *Lehre der Nahrungsmittel für das Volk* (1850). The German film chronicle *Heimat* (1984) included the version: '*Wie der Mensch ißt, so ist er*' [As a man eats, so he is].

you can run but you can't hide. In the wake of the hijacking of a TWA airliner to Beirut in the summer of 1985, President Reagan issued a number of warnings to international terrorists. In October, he said that the US had 'sent a message to terrorists everywhere. The message: "You can run, but you can't hide".' He was alluding to an utterance of the boxer Joe Louis who said of an opponent in a World Heavyweight Championship fight in June 1946: 'He can run, but he can't hide.' The opponent was Billy Conn, who was a fast mover, and Louis won the fight on a knock-out.

You Can't Take It With You. The title of a play (1936; film US, 1938) by George S. Kaufman and Moss Hart, which comes from the (nineteenth-century?) saying which suggests that there is no point in holding on to money as it will be no good to you when you are dead. 'You can always take one with you' was a slogan suggested by Winston Churchill when invasion by the Germans threatened in 1940.

You Don't Have to Be Jewish ... Title of a show of Jewish humour which was running on Broadway in 1965. Later 'You don't have to be Jewish to love Levy's Real Jewish Rye' was a slogan current in the US in 1967. The point was reinforced by the words being set next to pictures of patently non-Jewish people (Indians, Chinese, Eskimos).

you have been warned. See under FAMOUS LAST WORDS.

You Might As Well Live. The title of the biography (1970) of Dorothy Parker by John Keats, taken from Parker's poem 'Resumé' in *Enough Rope* (1927):

> Guns aren't lawful;
> Nooses give;
> Gas smells awful;
> You might as well live.

You Must Remember This. The title of a novel (1987) by Joyce Carol Oates, which comes from the song 'As Time Goes By' (1932) by Herman Hupfeld:

> You must remember this, a kiss is still a kiss
> . . . as time goes by.

young fogey. This phrase refers to a man below the age of forty who dresses and behaves as if he were prematurely middle-aged. The species was fashionable from 1984 onwards although observed and commented on as early as 1909 (by the philosopher C.S. Peirce). Obviously, a play upon the phrase 'old fogey' (a Scots word from the 1780s) applied to a person displaying all the attitudes of old age.

Young Gifted and Broke. The title of an ITV comedy (1989) about five young lads working on a Youth Training Scheme. It alludes to the title of a hit song 'Young, Gifted and Black', recorded by the Jamaican duo Bob and Marcia in 1970. The *Observer* (16 April 1989) had: 'They're young, gifted, and the hippest fun things since . . . CFC-free aerosols.'

Your Mother Wouldn't Like It. An ironic warning, used as the title of a rock-music programme on Capital Radio presented by Nicky Horne from 1973. It was possibly inspired by the slogan 'Mother wouldn't like it' used in MG motor advertisements (by April 1972), though an older phrase. Suzi

Quatro recorded a song with the title 'Your Mama Won't Like Me' in 1975.

youth must have its fling. Meaning 'let the young enjoy themselves while they can', this proverbial saying appears in W.S. Gilbert's lyrics for *The Pirates of Penzance* (1879):

> I pray you, pardon me, ex-Pirate King,
> Peers will be peers, and youth must have its fling

and *The Mikado* (1885): 'But youth, of course, must have its fling.' Gilbert greatly enjoyed proverbs and, indeed, wrote two songs completely made up of them. In this instance, he appears to have created a more memorable version of the older proverbs 'Youth will have his course' (known from the sixteenth century) and 'Youth will be served' (though this latter did not appear until the early nineteenth century). In *The Water Babies* (1863), Charles Kingsley has:

> When all the world is young lad
> And all the trees are green:
> . . . Young blood must have its course, lad
> And every dog his day.

yumpie. See under YUPPIE.

yuppie. Meaning 'Young Urban Professional People/Person', this was one of a stream of ACRONYMS created in the late 1970s and 1980s designed to identify select groups. This one lasted longest in the UK because it answered a need for a (eventually pejorative) term describing young, brash money-makers of the period. The term originated in the US, as in Piesman and Hartley's *The Yuppie Handbook* (1983). It featured prominently in reports of Senator Gary Hart's bid for the Democratic nomination in the 1984 presidential race. He and his supporters appeared to belong to the Yuppie tendency. The launch of the word was slightly confused by the similar-sounding **yumpie** ('Young Upwardly-Mobile People'). Other similar coinages of the period, but less used, included: **dinkies** ('Dual Income No Kids'), **sitcoms** ('Single Income, Two Children, Outrageous Mortgage'), **woopies** ('Well Off Older People'), and the non-acronyms **wrinklies** (middle-aged person, aged 40–50) and **crinklies** (older person, 50–70), sometimes **crumblies**.

ZZ

Zephyrus. See GREEK NAMES.

Zeppelin. A type of airship, named after Count Ferdinand von Zeppelin (*d* 1917), the German aeronautical pioneer who designed and built them (*c* 1900). The name of the British rock group **Led Zeppelin** (*c* 1968) presumably alludes to this by playing upon the expression 'to go down like a lead balloon', meaning 'to flop'. The spelling of 'led' was designed to reduce the likelihood of mispronunciation, especially in the US.

Zero. See YEAR ~.

Zeus. See GREEK NAMES.

Zingari. See I ~.

ZIP. See ACRONYMS.

Zurich. See GNOMES OF ~.